TORT LAW FOR LEGAL ASSISTANTS

Second Edition

Linda L. Edwards and J. Stanley Edwards

The West Legal Studies Series

Your options keep growing with West Legal Studies

Each year our list continues to offer you more options for every area of the law to meet your course or on-the-job reference requirements. We now have over 140 titles from which to choose in the following areas:

Administrative Law	Family Law
Alternative Dispute Resolution	Federal Taxation
Bankruptcy	Intellectual Property
Business Organizations/Corporations	Introduction to Law
Civil Litigation and Procedure	Introduction to Paralegalism
CLA Exam Preparation	Law Office Management
Client Accounting	Law Office Procedures
Computer in the Law Office	Legal Research, Writing, and Analysis
Constitutional Law	Legal Terminology
Contract Law	Paralegal Employment
Criminal Law and Procedure	Real Estate Law
Document Preparation	Reference Materials
Environmental Law	Torts and Personal Injury Law
Ethics	Will, Trusts, and Estate Administration

You will find unparalleled, practical support

Each book is augmented by instructor and student supplements to ensure the best learning experience possible. We also offer custom publishing and other benefits such as West's Student Achievement Award. In addition, our sales representatives are ready to provide you with dependable service.

We want to hear from you

Our best contributions for improving the quality of our books and instructional materials is feedback from the people who use them. If you have a question, concern, or observation about any of our materials, or you have a product proposal or manuscript, we want to hear from you. Please contact your local representative or write us at the following address:

West Legal Studies, 3 Columbia Circle, P.O. Box 15015, Albany, NY 12212-5015

For additional information point your browser at
www.westlegalstudies.com

West Legal Studies
an imprint of Delmar Publishers

an International Thomson Publishing company I(T)P®

TORT LAW FOR LEGAL ASSISTANTS

Second Edition

Linda L. Edwards, J.D. *Phoenix College*
J. Stanley Edwards, J.D.

WEST LEGAL STUDIES

an International Thomson Publishing company I(T)P®

Albany • Bonn • Boston • Cincinnati • Detroit • London • Madrid
Melbourne • Mexico City • Minneapolis/St. Paul • New York • Pacific Grove
Paris • San Francisco • Singapore • Tokyo • Toronto • Washington

NOTICE TO THE READER

Cover Design: Susan Mathews, Stillwater Studio
Cover Image: David Chalk, Chalkmark Graphics

Delmar Staff

Publisher: Susan Simpfenderfer
Acquisitions Editor: Joan Gill
Developmental Editor: Rhonda Dearborn

Production Manager: Wendy Troeger
Production Editor: Laurie A. Boyce
Marketing Manager: Katherine M.S. Hans

Printed in the United States of America
6 7 8 9 10 XXX 03 02 01

For more information, contact Delmar, 3 Columbia Circle, PO Box 15015, Albany, NY 12212-0515;
or find us on the World Wide Web at http://www.westlegalstudies.com

International Division List

Japan:
Thomson Learning
Palaceside Building 5F
1-1-1 Hitotsubashi, Chiyoda-ku
Tokyo 100 0003 Japan
Tel: 813 5218 6544
Fax: 813 5218 6551

Australia/New Zealand
Nelson/Thomson Learning
102 Dodds Street
South Melbourne, Victoria 3205
Australia
Tel: 61 39 685 4111
Fax: 61 39 685 4199

UK/Europe/Middle East:
Thomson Learning
Berkshire House
168-173 High Holborn
London
WC1V 7AA United Kingdom
Tel: 44 171 497 1422
Fax: 44 171 497 1426

Latin America:
Thomson Learning
Seneca, 53
Colonia Polanco
11560 Mexico D.F. Mexico
Tel: 525-281-2906
Fax: 525-281-2656

Canada:
Nelson/Thomson Learning
1120 Birchmount Road
Scarborough, Ontario
Canada M1K 5G4
Tel: 416-752-9100
Fax: 416-752-8102

Asia:
Thomson Learning
60 Albert Street, #15-01
Albert Complex
Singapore 189969
Tel: 65 336 6411
Fax: 65 336 7411

Spain:
Thomson Learning
Calle Magallanes, 25
28015-MADRID
ESPANA
Tel: 34 91 446 33 50
Fax: 34 91 445 62 18

Library of Congress Cataloging-in-Publication Data
Edwards, Linda L.
    Tort law for legal assistants / Linda L. Edwards, J. Stanley
Edwards. — 2nd ed.
      p. cm.
    Includes bibliographical references and index.
    ISBN 0-314-12635-X
    1. Torts—United States. 2. Legal assistants—United States—
Handbooks, manuals, etc. I. Edwards, J. Stanley. II. Title.
KF1250.Z9E38 1998
3346.7303—dc21
                         98-8349
                          CIP

DEDICATION

To our parents, whose continued support and encouragement gave us the strength to persevere; and to our friends, Cristina, Me-sah, Jack, and Harry, whose inspiration and guidance helped keep us on the path.

CONTENTS

PREFACE

Readability and accessibility continue to be the hallmarks of this text. We have sought to make each student's journey through the "land" of torts as enjoyable and meaningful as possible. Toward that end we have added cases that both enlighten and entertain. These cases bring the real matter of the law to the student first-hand, illustrating and amplifying the textual discussions. Students should note, however, that these are heavily edited excerpts; in most instances, citations and footnotes have been omitted for improved utility and comprehensibility. Full citations to the cases from which the excerpts were drawn are given for those wishing to pursue further research.

While continuing the same basic format that made the first edition so successful, we have added "Putting It Into Practice" exercises throughout the text to allow students to determine how well they understand the material they have just read. The courts' or Restatement's responses can be found in Appendix A, thereby giving students an opportunity for immediate feedback.

The Practice Pointers continue to introduce practical procedural skills, such as drafting pleadings, locating records, identifying witnesses, documenting damages, and preparing trial exhibits. They have been modified, however, to ensure that they relate directly to the concepts in the chapter in which they appear. Although some revisions have been made in the overall organization of the text, each chapter still begins with a hypothetical situation designed to stimulate reader curiosity, includes a summary that encapsulates the key concepts, and concludes with Tort Teasers that require application and integration of the concepts presented in the chapter.

An Instructor's Manual is available that provides questions suggested for classroom discussion, exam questions, edited versions of the cases cited in the Tort Teasers, and suggested answers to the questions posed in the Tort Teasers. A supplementary student study guide tracks the material in the text, helping students focus on major concepts and helping them become actively involved in the learning process. Sample forms are also provided in the study guides so that students can see the documents mentioned in the text.

Revising a text is a team effort and we wish to thank all those at Delmar who helped make it as smooth a process as possible. We offer special thanks to Elizabeth Hannan and Rhonda Dearborn, our two developmental editors, whose gentle guidance and subtle prodding made this second edition possible. We would also like to thank Joan Gill, Acquisitions Editor; Kathy Hans, Marketing Manager; and Wendy Troeger, Production Manager.

A new edition is only as good as the suggestions given for change. We were most fortunate to have a dedicated team of reviewers who took their task to heart and most generously devoted their time and thought to creating a text that was more useful and usable than the first edition. We thank them sincerely for their wonderful ideas and we hope this edition is everything they envisioned.

Melody K. Brown
College of Great Falls

Angela Carson
Cleveland State Community College

Paula D. Emmons
Watterson College Pacific

Mary D. Fawcett
North Harris College

Wendy Geertz
Kirkwood Community College

Jane S. Johnson
May Technical College

Gail M. Krebs
Commonwealth College

Mary Pavlovich
Duff's Business Institute

Best of luck to all who embark on the journey laid out in this text. May you find tort law as captivating a subject as we do!

LINDA L. EDWARDS
J. STANLEY EDWARDS

ACKNOWLEDGMENTS AND CREDITS

Various: Reprinted from *Handbook of the Law on Torts* 202, by William Prosser (1941), with permission of the West Publishing Company.

Chapter 17:

p. 404, quotation from *USA Today:* Copyright 1986, USA TODAY. Reprinted with permission.

p. 404, quotation from Dan Quayle: *Standing Firm* 312, by Dan Quayle (1994). HarperCollins Publishers.

pp. 426–427: "What's Wrong with a Little Tort Reform?," 32 *Idaho Law Review* 557 (1996). Excerpted by permission of John Hasnas, Assistant General Counsel, Kock Industries, Inc.

Appendix C:

p. 511, list: Reprinted from W. Freedmans, *Richardson on the Law of Insurance* (6th ed., Lawyers Cooperative Publishing, 1991).

TABLE OF CASES

Part One

INTRODUCTION

CHAPTER

1

Introduction

CHAPTER OBJECTIVES

In this chapter you will learn to:
• Define a tort and distinguish between a tort and a crime, as well as between a tort and a contract
• Trace the evolution of tort law
• Recognize the philosophical principles and arguments underpinning tort law

You come home one evening to find that one of your children has been bitten by your next-door neighbor's dog, who was safely secured behind the fence when your child, contrary to your instruction, entered the yard to retrieve a wayward ball. Your neighbor took every precaution of isolating the dog, short of locking the fence. Should the neighbor be held liable?

Someone in your family contracts a deadly disease whose cause can be traced to chemical contaminants found in toxic wastes dumped by the city in which you live. The city dumped the wastes several decades before the area became residential and, at the time, was totally ignorant of the long-term effects. Should the city be held liable?

You allow your grandfather, whom you know has imbibed more than his usual two shots, to drive and he injures someone. Should you be held responsible?

Someone trespasses and falls into a hole on your property. Should you be held liable?

Your daughter finally succeeds in becoming a famous actress. Without her permission, a magazine publishes nude photographs of her. Should she be able to sue for invasion of privacy?

Your son is wrongfully detained because a storekeeper suspects him of shoplifting. Should he be able to sue the store for the emotional distress he endures?

Should the attorney for whom you work be held liable for your negligent acts?

Should you be held liable for the intentional torts of your children?

Your home has been burglarized on several occasions and, in a desperate attempt to protect your property, you set up a mechanical protective device. Should you be held liable if a would-be burglar is seriously injured by the device?

These questions, which illustrate the broad scope of human concerns that fall under tort law, will be examined in this text. Tort law is an intriguing area of the law that covers virtually every aspect of human endeavor. It not only governs the conduct of many in our society but also reflects our attitudes toward living itself. Within the parameters of tort law can be discovered many of the philosophical underpinnings of our society.

BACKGROUND

It has been said that tort liability is like a tax that makes products and services more costly to all and ultimately unaffordable to some. This "tax," it is argued, has put some gynecologists out of business, prohibited the sale of certain drugs, and severely hampered municipalities and other governmental bodies in their delivery of services. (See P. Huber, Liability (1988) for a discussion of this issue.)

Advocates of expanded tort liability see tort law as the knight in shining armor, duly anointed to protect the interests of the consumer. In their perception, manufacturers and those who deliver services are better able than consumers to predict and prevent potential accidents. The burden of injury, they reason, should be borne by those who create risks rather than by those who fall prey to them. The philosophical and political debates on the issue of risk allocation have gained new significance in one of the most recent developments in tort law—product liability.

WHAT IS A TORT?

But what is this thing we call a "tort"? Although the term has evaded concrete definition, it has been described as a civil wrong for which the victim receives a remedy in the form of damages (Figure 1-1). Included under this heading are intentional torts (assault, battery, and false imprisonment are some examples), negligence (acts committed without intent but in violation of a reasonable person standard), and strict liability (acts committed with no intent at all).

REASONABLENESS OF CONDUCT

The common thread interweaving most torts is the notion that socially unreasonable conduct should be penalized and those who are its victims should be compensated. Of course, determining what is unreasonable

FIGURE 1-1 Definition of a Tort

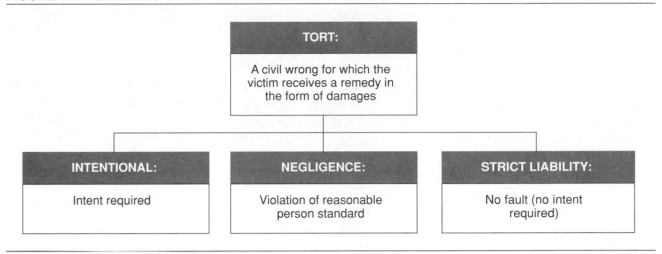

is a formidable task, because reasonableness, like beauty, is in the eye of the beholder. The overall goal in defining reasonableness is to balance the plaintiff's need for protection against the defendant's claim of freedom to pursue his own ends. But how does one determine reasonableness of conduct? Should one take into consideration, for example, the parties' religious beliefs, their physical disabilities, or their emotional idiosyncrasies?

To get a feeling for where you stand on this issue of reasonableness, consider the following. You are sitting as a juror on a case in which the plaintiff, a devoutly religious Catholic woman, was severely injured by the negligent driving of the defendant. The plaintiff was pregnant at the time of her injury and was told that because of the serious pelvic injury she had sustained she would be in grave danger if she carried her baby to term. Because of her intense aversion to abortion, she chose to deliver the baby and died in the process.

Do you think the defendant should be required to compensate the plaintiff's family for her death? How would you determine the reasonableness of the plaintiff's conduct? Would you require her to conform to the conduct of the "average" person, or would you compare her conduct to that of a reasonable person holding her beliefs? These are just some examples of the types of questions with which jurors and courts must grapple in their struggle to assign fault and apportion damages equitably.

Sometimes the reasonableness of the defendant's conduct is not at issue because of the far-reaching social consequences of his or her actions. In the area of product liability, for example, even those manufacturers and sellers who act reasonably are held liable to plaintiffs injured by their products. This is done in the name of protecting society. By holding manufacturers and sellers responsible for all such losses, the argument is made, consumers will be better protected and sellers and manufacturers will be more conscientious in the delivery of their services and products. Similarly, one who innocently defames another will be held liable despite his benign intent. The victim's reputation is irreparably tarnished no matter how reasonable the defamer's conduct, goes the rationale, and so compensation is required.

PUBLIC POLICY

Tort law often goes beyond recompensing individuals and considers, more broadly, the interests of society. These interests are often referred to by the courts as **public policy** concerns. The ideals of justice, fairness, and equality dominate discussions regarding public policy.

Why, you might ask, must the needs of society be considered when dealing with a dispute between two individuals? Because our common law system is based on case precedent; every decision rendered by a court has the potential of establishing a rule that must be followed by other courts. All members of society, therefore, have an interest in seeing that disputes between litigants are resolved in such a manner that the principles set forth in that process of resolution are fair and just for all concerned. The very principles set forth today will be those that govern the cases of tomorrow.

Others argue that we have become too paternalistic in our efforts to protect individuals and that we should allow people to bear the consequences of their decisions. After all, they point out, the process of living comes with no guarantees and the assurance of safety is too high a price to pay for freedom.

In addition to this philosophical concern, there is reluctance to burden a defendant, particularly an industry, with all losses, for fear of financial ruin. As a result, new technological developments may be inhibited or become financially prohibitive.

This problem of distribution of losses continues to haunt those who seek an equitable balance between the needs of plaintiffs and defendants. Judges must decide the proper solution to this controversy. Suffice it to say that whichever philosophical trail they choose to follow predetermines their resolution of many cases.

MORALITY OF CONDUCT

Is the morality of a defendant's conduct relevant in tort law? Although personal morality may be subject to variation, tort law borrows heavily from a sense of public morality. It can be said that, at least in certain cases, we all have a sense of what is universally regarded as right and wrong. Tort law generally reflects that sense.

There are circumstances, however, in which a defendant can be held liable even though he or she has violated no moral code. One who, for example, trespasses on the land of another in the reasonable belief that it is his own land is still liable for trespass. With the increasing popularity of no-fault torts, such as strict liability, we appear to be moving away from a need to cast moral judgment on a defendant's conduct. In contrast, tort law does not deal with all blatantly immoral acts. Although it may be morally reprehensible, for example, to allow a stranger to die when you could save her, in most circumstances you will have committed no tort.

"SLIPPERY SLOPE" ARGUMENTS

Another concern that has affected the development of tort law is the consideration of the effect of a ruling on future case law. Courts are often hesitant to crack open a legal door in a particular case for fear of creating a "flood of litigation," an occurrence they are ever on the alert to avoid. For that reason, some types of flagrant misdeeds go unavenged in tort law. Relatively trivial concerns must also go by the wayside in an effort to protect the courts. Many of our most grievous hurts are inflicted in the context of interpersonal relationships and yet most of these must go without redress. Lovers are jilted, children are verbally belittled by parents, friends are "used," and so on. Yet the law cannot become enmeshed in these psychically damaging events if the legal system is to avoid an administrative nightmare created by an onslaught of cases. Clearly, not all human wrong can be remedied. It is the province of the courts to decide which shall and shall not be eligible for litigation.

Perhaps you have heard of the **"slippery slope" argument,** which means, essentially, that allowance of an argument in one case will allow application of that same argument in innumerable other cases. The metaphor is used to show that once you take the first step, it is too easy to fall down the slippery slope to the bottom of the hill, presumably into a morass of undesirable outcomes. The slippery slope argument is, in essence, an administrative concern. A court fears that if it finds negligence on behalf of the sympathetic plaintiff before it, hundreds of thousands of similarly situated individuals or those whose situations are analogous to the case will also seek redress.

Keep in mind that although courts are to focus on the long term in making their decisions, they sometimes are understandably sympathetic to the plight of the individuals before them. In such cases they often render decisions that meet the short-term goals of justice but that prove untenable over the long run. Justice, you will soon discover, is an illusory goal that often eludes capture by even the most conscientious judge.

CREATION OF CASE LAW

Tort law is largely a product of case law, which involves case-by-case decision making by the state courts. This decision-making process is affected, to some degree, by statutes, which the courts are mandated to follow unless statutory gaps exist that leave a court with unanswered questions. Some statutes, such as the wrongful death and survival acts, directly address issues that arise in the context of tort law. Others, such as certain criminal statutes, serve as guidelines to the courts in establishing policy. A statute, for example, that makes it a misdemeanor to drive while under the influence of alcohol sets forth the standard of care expected of drivers. A driver having a blood alcohol level in excess of the statutory limit would be considered to have breached the duty of care he owed to those around him.

Another guideline that courts use in formulating their holdings is the *Restatement of the Law of Torts.* The Restatement was compiled by eminent legal scholars and practitioners in an attempt to provide lawyers and judges with black-letter principles (legal principles generally accepted by the legal community) of tort law. Adopted in many jurisdictions, the Restatement is frequently cited in court opinions.

Although criticized for creating the impression of uniformity in the law where there is none, the Restatement is, nevertheless, a frequently used guide through the maze of tort law decisions. For this reason, the Restatement is often cited throughout this text. Keep in mind, however, that your state may not have adopted the Restatement position. Consult the case law in your state when dealing with a specific case.

RELATIONSHIP BETWEEN TORT LAW AND OTHER AREAS OF THE LAW

Torts versus Crimes

How does a tort differ from a crime? Although the two share several similarities, they differ in terms of the interests affected, the remedy granted, and some of the procedural mechanisms used (see Figure 1-2). A crime is considered an offense against society, whereas a tort is an offense against another individual or group of individuals. The purpose of prosecuting someone who has committed a crime is to vindicate the interests of society by punishing the offender. The purpose of suing in tort, in contrast, is to compensate the victim.

Although the primary purpose of criminal law is punishment and the primary purpose of tort law

FIGURE 1-2 Torts versus Crimes

	TORTS	CRIMES
PURPOSE	Compensation	Punishment
STANDARD OF PROOF	Preponderance of Evidence	Beyond a Reasonable Doubt
INTERESTS VIOLATED	Individual's Interest	Society's Interest
PROCEDURAL RULES	Civil Rules	Criminal Rules

is compensation, there is some overlap between the two. Compensation of a crime victim (known as *restitution*) is frequently used by the courts as part of an offender's sentence. By the same token, punitive damages, which are intended to punish the tortfeasor (one who has committed a tort), are used in certain circumstances in tort law. Despite this overlap, the primary functions of criminal law and tort law remain distinct.

Moreover, the rules of civil procedure are used in tort cases, whereas the rules of criminal procedure are used in criminal cases. Also, the plaintiff's burden of proof in a tort case is by a preponderance of the evidence; the state's burden of proof in a criminal case is beyond a reasonable doubt. The rules of evidence applicable in criminal cases vary, to some degree, from those applicable in civil cases.

Many acts may be both a crime against the state and a tort against the individual. If a drunk driver, for example, is involved in a vehicular accident, she may be charged with a criminal offense as well as sued by the injured parties for negligence. For this reason (among others) those charged with criminal offenses often plead nolo contendere (no contest). If they were to plead guilty, their admission of guilt could be used against them in a subsequent civil trial, whereas a plea of nolo contendere could not. This is true, however, only if the issue tried in the criminal case is also relevant to some aspect of the tort action. Because of the lower standard of proof in a civil case, the plaintiff in a tort case will have an easier time establishing liability than the state will have proving guilt.

Torts versus Contracts

Tort law differs from contract law in terms of the voluntariness of entering into an agreement. When two or more parties create a contract, they each agree to give up something in return for receiving some benefit. In a contract action the parties have voluntarily and knowingly assumed duties or obligations to others. In tort law, by contrast, duties are imposed by the law without the express consent or awareness of those

involved (Figure 1-3). If a guest is injured on a landowner's premises, the landowner is liable, not because he expressly contracted to prevent injury to the guest, but because the law imposes certain obligations on him by virtue of being a landowner.

Just as with criminal law, however, there is an overlap between tort law and contract law. Certain tort duties may coincide with those duties set forth in a contract, for example, so that if a party fails to live up to its obligations, an action may lie in either tort or contract. Additionally, some quasi-contractual obligations (such as the obligation to act in good faith) are imposed by law without the consent of the parties, just as in tort law.

One other distinction between contract and tort law is that in contract law obligations are made to specific individuals, whereas in tort law duties are owed to people in general. In tort law one is bound to act as a reasonable person toward all other persons, but in contract law one is bound in contract only to certain chosen individuals. This distinction is not completely valid, however, in that tort law principles impose special duties in some cases because of the relationship one has with another. An employer, for example, owes duties of care to her employees that she does not owe to other persons.

You will find as you pursue your study of torts that this area of law overlaps with most other areas of law.

FIGURE 1-3   Torts versus Contracts

	TORTS	CONTRACTS
DUTIES ASSIGNED	Imposed by Law	By Parties' Consent
OBLIGATIONS MADE TO	Society in General	Specific Individuals

Therefore, you will frequently find yourself referring to knowledge that you have gained from the study of property law, constitutional law, criminal law, contract law, corporate law, and so on.

BRIEF HISTORY OF TORT LAW

If this is the point in most textbooks where you skip ahead, try to persevere. You might be surprised at how interesting the evolution of tort law really is (Figure 1-4).

In barbaric societies the only "law" that seemed to control group behavior had its roots in the blood feud. The protocol of the blood feud required that the clan go to war against any outsider who inflicted harm on a clan member, thereby dishonoring the clan as a whole. Atonement for the humiliation suffered by the victim's kin seemed the primary goal.

Despite the obvious deterrence this system of justice provided, its inherent violence and its toll on those who were obligated to protect family and clan members prompted reform. Ultimately a negotiation process was developed in which the victim summoned the perpetrator to the "moot"—a forum in which the victim pleaded his case to the community and asked for a redress of his grievance. Community members offered advice about how best to resolve the dispute. When a solution acceptable to both victim and perpetrator was found, the parties dispersed and the blood feud was averted.

FIGURE 1-4 Evolution of Tort Law

Blood feud (no fault)

Action in trespass (no fault)
(*Vi et armis*)
(Direct use of force)

Trespass on the case (wrongful intent or negligence)
(No force or indirect injury)

Negligence (fault required)

Strict liability (no fault)

When the law first assumed a more civilized veneer, the remedies created served as substitutes for the feuding process, and thus emerged the concept of monetary compensation. Early in Anglo-Saxon history, individuals were assigned a monetary value based principally on their rank. Money instead of blood was offered as a salve for injured clan pride. Compensation was directed toward the clan rather than the individual and awards were distributed proportionately among the injured person's relatives. There was no distinction between crimes and torts. Furthermore, there seemed to be no concern regarding issues of fault or blameworthiness. Even the most remote causal connection was sufficient to justify the imposition of punishment.

Interestingly enough, during this same time period vengeance was exacted on whatever was determined to be the immediate cause of death, even if it were an animal or inanimate object. The offending object, be it a horse or a sword, might be turned over to the victim or the victim's family to be used as they saw fit, or delivered to the king.

Action in Trespass

Over time the moot process of dispute resolution led to the establishment of certain fundamental rules. Communities discovered, through trial and error, those decisions that led to the greatest peace and harmony. Following the Norman Conquest, the dispute resolution process fell to the royal justices of the king's courts. They soon discovered that following the already established local rules provided optimal efficiency in resolving conflict. As a result, the local rules eventually evolved into what is now known as the common law.

The **action in trespass,** which emerged sometime in the middle of the thirteenth century, was one of the products of the common law evolution. This action, which was basically of a criminal nature, dealt with serious and forcible breaches of peace. One of its requirements was the showing of force and arms, referred to as *vi et armis.*

The plaintiff had to allege that the defendant had used force directly on the plaintiff's person or property; thus, the term *vi et armis* appeared in every writ of trespass as a matter of course. No further showing of blameworthiness or fault on the part of the defendant was necessary. As time went on, however, even mild, innocuous physical contact was sufficient for the plaintiff to prevail in a trespass action and the pleading of *vi et armis* became a mere technical device.

CASE

Case & Davis v. Mark
2 Ohio 169 (1825)

Distinction between case and trespass: Whenever the injury is direct and immediate, trespass is the proper action.

Where trespass is the proper action, plaintiff can not at his election bring case.

THIS cause came before the court upon a writ of error to the common pleas of Hamilton county, and was reserved for decision here by the Supreme Court of that county.

It was an action on the case, and the declaration contained a single count, in which it was charged, that the defendant "so carelessly and negligently navigated his steamboat upon the Ohio river, that he run foul of, and struck the flat-boat of the plaintiffs, by means whereof it immediately sunk, and was lost to the plaintiffs."

A verdict was rendered for plaintiffs upon trial; the defendant moved in arrest of judgment, upon the ground that the facts stated in the declaration constituted a direct trespass, for which an action on the case would not lie. The court of common pleas arrested the judgment, to reverse which, error was brought, and the general error assigned.

* * *

Opinion of the court by Judge BURNET:

The error assigned in this case is, that the court of common pleas arrested the judgment, on the ground that the facts amounted to a trespass vi et armis, and that this action could not be sustained. It became necessary, therefore, to ascertain the distinction between trespass and case, and apply it to the facts and circumstances set out in the declaration.

The plaintiffs charge that the defendant was the owner and commander of a certain steamboat, called the *Congress,* navigating the Ohio river—that he so carelessly navigated, managed, and steered the said steam-boat, that he run her foul of, struck, and broke a certain coal-boat, owned and navigated by the plaintiffs, by means of which the said coal-boat immediately sunk, and was lost.

The plaintiffs contend that the injury here described was consequential and not direct; but if direct, that it was the result of negligence, and that in either event, the action ought to be case.

The first part of this proposition certainly can not be sustained. The terms consequential and immediate are well understood. That is immediate which is produced by the act to which it is ascribed, without the intervention or agency of any distinct, immediate cause, but the effect of an intermediate cause is sometimes considered as a trespass, produced by a preceding cause, when the former is the immediate effect of the latter. Thus, the effect of pulling the trigger of a loaded gun is the production of fire, which causes the powder to burn, which gives motion to the ball, by which the injury is produced; here the whole transaction is considered as one act, and the trespass is ascribed to the pulling of the trigger, though the injury is the immediate effect of an intervening cause, which gave motion and force to the ball. . . . In this case the defendant was at the helm, directing the course of his boat—the steam which gave it motion was under his control; the boat therefore received its motion and course from the defendant, by which it was made to strike the plaintiffs' boat, so that it was broken, and immediately sunk. Here there was no distinct intermediate agency. The injury was the breaking and sinking of the coal-boat—the cause of that injury was the act of the defendant, in running the steamboat against her. The injury, therefore, can not be considered as consequential—it was direct and immediate.

The second part of the proposition is equally untenable. The defendant could not shelter himself under the plea of negligence, and the plaintiffs are not at liberty to force on him an apology of which he could not avail himself. The character of the transaction, in reference to the form of the suit can not be affected by the presence or absence of negligence. That circumstance may, in some cases, have an impression on the amount of damages recovered, by varying the degree of malice, but it can not change the nature of the act. If it has the ingredient that stamps it with the character of a trespass, it must be treated as such. If a man shooting at game, does it so carelessly and negligently as to wound a person happening to be in the vicinity, the fact that it was done carelessly, and without design, will not protect him from an action of trespass. So if a man in self-defense, aims a blow at another, and by negligence or want of care strikes a third person, it is a trespass.

The proposition set up by the plaintiffs that where there is negligence, although the injury be immediate, the party may waive the immediate injury, and claim the damages only which is the consequence of the injury, amounts to this, that he may take up an entire, connected transaction by parts, and rely on as much of it as will answer his purpose, to the exclusion of the residue. This would be a convenient privilege, as it would often save a plaintiff from the unpleasant consequences of a nonsuit; but it would destroy established distinctions, and introduce an uncertainty in judicial proceedings which would be inconvenient and injurious. One of the reasons given for not sustaining actions on the case, where the circumstances amount to a clear trespass, and vice versa, is the necessity of preserving the boundary of actions, by which I understand the rules that prescribe what particular action or form of suit, shall be brought for each particular injury. These rules can not be uniform, if plaintiffs are permitted to garble their cases, so as to convert an unequivocal trespass, into trespass on the case. Were this permitted, I can not conceive of any trespass that may not be sued for in the form of case. What are the ordinary concomitants of a severe battery? They are plain, bodily and mental—incapacity for business—the expense of medical aid, and disgrace in the public estimation. If under the pretense of waiving the immediate injury, which is pain, the party may go for the consequential damage, which is the incapacity for business, expense, etc., it will be a matter of but little moment whether he sue in trespass or in case, as the only difference in the result would be the portion of damage that might be allowed for the pain inflicted. If this be conceded, the boundary between trespass and case is at once broken down—courts have

no control over it—it is in the power of every plaintiff, and may be varied as the convenience of the moment may require. Should a party mistake his remedy, and sue in case for an undoubted trespass, he has only to turn on his opponent, and say, I waive the immediate injury, and he is perfectly safe.

* * *

Something may . . . be ascribed to the reluctance with which courts yield to the necessity of deciding against a just claim, on a technical objection, or of turning a party round, because he has mistaken his remedy. In some instance this feeling has induced judges to avail themselves of circumstances in support of a case, having justice and equity on its side, that do not form a legal distinction, or bring it within any established rule. The same circumstances are relied on in other cases, which tends to render the law apparently doubtful. For example, in some cases we find the lawfulness or unlawfulness of the act much insisted on, from which an inattentive reader might conclude that that circumstance formed the rule of distinction between trespass and case; but it is well known that acts strictly lawful frequently amount to trespass, while those that are not unlawful are attended with injuries, for which trespass can not be sustained. Thus, if a man shooting at a target, which is lawful, miss his aim and wound another, trespass will lie; but if he dig a pit in the highway, into which a traveler falls, trespass will not lie, although the act was unlawful.

In some cases, great stress is laid on the force that accompanies the act, by which an injury is done, but this is not a distinguishing fact—it forms no criterion by which to decide the character of the injury, or of the remedy. This will appear from the very familiar case of the log: if it be thrown into the highway with great force and violence, and afterward a traveler falls over it, he can not have trespass; but it if be laid very gently on his foot, by which he is injured, trespass will lie. So if if a man quietly enters the inclosure of his neighbor and picks up an apple, trespass will lie; but if he should, by forcible and violent effort, obstruct a watercourse, whereby the water is caused to flow back on his neighbor's land, it would not be a trespass—he would be liable only in an action on the case.

It has also been contended, as it is in this case, that when the act from which the injury proceeds, was done willfully, trespass is the proper remedy; but not so when it is the effect of carelessness, or negligence. But this distinction can not be sustained, as will be evident from a little reflection. In the cases before mentioned, the log was thrown into the highway, and the water-course was obstructed intentionally, and it might be, to produce the very injury that ensued, but trespass could not be maintained. On the other hand, if, while a person is carelessly handling a loaded gun, he should unintentionally cause it to go off and wound another, trespass would lie, although the act was not willful, and the injury was the effect of negligence. So if a man should carelessly throw a brickbat from the scaffold and unintentionally wound another, trespass would lie. . . .

The true distinction unquestionably is, whether the injury be immediate, or consequential . . . .

* * *

[W]e are well satisfied that whatever may be the apparent discrepancy between the cases, the rule is clearly and judiciously settled, that where the injury is direct and immediate, the action must be trespass, whether the act were done willfully or by negligence and want of care; and as the facts set out in the declaration show that such was the character of the injury complained of in this case, the judgment of the common pleas must be affirmed.

Trespass on the Case

The action in trespass was highly restrictive, in that it precluded recovery by those who could show no use or only indirect use of force by the defendant. A companion form of action known as **trespass on the case** arose to allow recovery in the absence of force or in cases where an injury was inflicted indirectly. A plaintiff who was injured when the defendant wielded a plank of wood against him could pursue an action in trespass to redress his injuries, whereas a plaintiff who tripped over that same piece of wood left carelessly in her path by the defendant had to resort to an action on the case.

Although damage to the plaintiff was implied in an action in trespass, the plaintiff in a trespass on the case was required to show injury and damage. Trespass on the case actions demanded proof of the defendant's wrongful intent or negligence, whereas an action in trespass required no showing of fault. Trespass on the case was frequently used as a means of recovering for breach of a legal duty grounded on custom. Those who served the public, such as innkeepers, were frequently the defendants in such cases. Read *Case & Davis v. Mark* for a better understanding of the distinction between an action in trespass and trespass on the case.

Negligence

The development of public transportation seems to have had a profound influence on the evolution of tort law. As the courts were faced with more traffic-related cases, they came to the realization that decisions mechanically rendered in favor of victims under the trespass theory (which merely required the showing of direct force) would have a prohibitive effect on the use of highways. Under this approach, few could afford to risk traveling on the highways and losing their fortunes as a result of accident. Thus, the idea of negligence emerged as a compromise. Travelers were granted some measure of protection from liability as long as they drove in such a manner that they reduced the risk of accidents.

The rise of negligence as a cause of action coincided with the disintegration of actions in trespass and trespass on the case, although negligence ultimately assumed many of the characteristics of a trespass on the case action. The distinction between trespass and trespass on the case has basically disappeared except in a few states where some trace of the distinction has been retained through common law pleadings. One vestige of the distinction that continues to hang on, however, is the necessity of proving damages. Torts that trace their ancestry back to trespass require no proof of actual damages; those that trace back to trespass on the case do require such proof. Although reminders of these dinosaurs of tort law emerge occasionally, they have for the most part been replaced by the modern torts that are the subject of this text.

COMING FULL CIRCLE

This brief overview of the development of tort law demonstrates the cyclical evolution of our attitude toward the notion of fault. Strict liability (no fault) reigned supreme during early Anglo-Saxon law and was evident in the action in trespass. Only in actions on the case did the notion of duty and neglect arise. Now, as we near the beginning of the twenty-first century, strict liability has once again assumed importance in our legal system. More and more modern courts are assigning liability even where there is no showing of fault.

How did this notion of no fault assume such importance in tort law? To understand, we must look back to the scientific revolution that followed the Civil War. Influenced by the technological wonders of the Industrial Revolution, intellectuals embraced the supremacy of scientific thought. Legal scholars, led by Oliver Wendell Holmes (an influential Supreme Court Justice), also adopted the scientific paradigm as they sought to create common principles that specified when individuals were entitled to compensation for the wrongs they had suffered. In so doing, these "scientific" scholars created a general duty of care that resulted in a fault theory of tort law.

At the beginning of the twentieth century, problems of poverty and social disadvantage began to be seen as societal rather than individual problems. Increasingly the government was called upon to intervene and redress the wrongs visited upon individuals. The tort "scientists," who had been content to systematically catalog the rules of tort law, gave way to the legal "realists," who saw themselves more as revolutionaries than as mere observers. No longer content with rules that created fair results between parties, these scholars strove for rules that equitably distributed losses. In other words, tort law came to be viewed more as a means of creating a just society than as simply a peaceful resolution of interpersonal disputes. The fault theory of tort law was abandoned in favor of a system that provided social justice. William Prosser, one of the most noted tort scholars and author of one of the most influential treatises on tort law, advocated that the purpose of tort law was to provide justice rather than to simply punish and deter inappropriate conduct. He

forcefully and successfully lobbied for the adoption of strict liability in reference to defective products on the premise that liability should be borne by those best able to bear it (the manufacturer).

For what reason have we taken this brief excursion through the historical roots of tort law? Learning tort law is not just about memorizing case law and legal principles. A true understanding of tort law requires a knowledge of the purposes it serves and its relationship to societal goals and needs.

Much ado is being made today about the reform of tort law, but these reforms have essentially arisen as members of society wrestle with certain basic issues. Should society bear the cost of losses suffered by individuals, or should that responsibility be shifted to the individual? What role should fault play in tort law? Is the purpose of tort law merely to resolve disputes, or is it to see that justice is done?

Looking into the mirror of the past often helps us better understand where we are going in the future. Knowing the historical derivation of tort law will give you some insights about the tort reforms advocated today. Knowing how those who have come before us have answered the questions raised above helps us as today's legislators, voters, jurors, and judges struggle to answer these same questions. In Chapter 17 we examine tort reform issues. Those issues cannot be adequately addressed without considering the philosophical implications they raise. Our brief interaction with tort law of the past shows that these philosophical questions are neither new nor easily resolved.

CLASSIFICATION OF TORTS

Today torts are divided into three categories, depending on the nature of the defendant's conduct: intentional torts, negligence, and strict liability. By far the most common is negligence. The bulk of personal injury practice centers around automobile accident cases, "slip and fall" cases, and other types of cases in which someone failed to use reasonable care. Strict liability is found to a lesser degree, usually in the context of product liability. Intentional torts are rarely encountered in practice.

The organization of this text reflects the relative importance of each of these tort classifications. Although considerable coverage is devoted to negligence and related topics, relatively little consideration is given to intentional torts. Although intentional torts are conceptually easier to comprehend than negligence, negligence is addressed in depth because paralegals must have a solid foundation in negligence when they begin practicing, even if their understanding of intention is a bit superficial.

We divide our discussion into three separate areas, but you should be aware that many torts may be based on any one of the three types of conduct. Misrepresentation, for example, can be committed intentionally, negligently, or with no fault (strict liability), as can defamation. Malpractice is a tort based on negligence. Bad faith is primarily an intentional tort. But many other causes of action are hybrids that defy precise classification. Rather than trying to pigeonhole all torts into neat categories, recognize that some distinctions are blurred.

SUMMARY

A tort can be defined as a civil wrong for which the victim receives compensation in the form of damages. The feeling that socially unreasonable conduct should be penalized underlies tort law and much of the case law is focused on determining what constitutes unreasonable conduct. In some cases, however, reasonableness is not an issue because the goal is to protect society no matter how reasonable the conduct.

Public policy concerns prevail throughout tort law. These concerns center primarily around the ideals of justice, fairness, and equality. One of the philosophical dilemmas that permeates tort law is how much weight should be placed on the needs of society when resolving disputes between individuals. In balancing these needs, courts frequently resort to slippery slope arguments to justify their refusal to grant relief to sympathetic plaintiffs.

Tort law is largely a product of common law although statutes are, in some instances, relied on. The courts frequently look to the *Restatement of the Law of Torts* in formulating the law.

Although similar in some ways to crimes, torts differ in terms of purpose, burden of proof, and procedural rules. Many acts are considered both a crime and a tort. Torts differ from contracts in that the duties assigned according to tort law are those imposed by law, whereas those assigned in the context of contracts are by virtue of the party's consent. Furthermore, in contract law obligations are assumed toward specific individuals, whereas tort law assumes that obligations are owed to society as a whole.

The origin of tort law can be traced back to the blood feud, which evolved into the "moot" process of dispute resolution and ultimately developed into the common law. When the concept of monetary compensation emerged, it was directed toward the clan rather than the individual. The action in trespass, which evolved in the thirteenth century, required proof that the defendant used force directly on the plaintiff or his property. The plaintiff did not, however, have to prove fault on the part of the defendant. In contrast, trespass on the case allowed recovery even when the defendant did not use force or inflicted injury indirectly. Proof of damages and the defendant's wrongful intent or negligence were, however, required in a trespass on the case action. The concept of negligence developed along with the evolution of public transportation. At the same time, actions in trespass and trespass on the case fell into disfavor and ultimately disappeared. Strict liability has now assumed an important role in tort law and is evidence of its cyclical evolution, in that the law began with no fault (action in trespass) and has now culminated in no fault. Tort law bears the imprint of the "scientific" scholars and legal realists who sought its reform.

TORT TEASERS

As indicated in this chapter, the issue of risk allocation is a troublesome matter that the courts and legal scholars have grappled with over the years. To help clarify the questions relating to risk allocation, consider the following hypothetical situation. After unsuccessfully administering Ritalin and several other drugs, as well as using counseling and behavior modification techniques, a psychologist resorts to giving lithium to Lisa, a hyperactive five-year-old, who is violent toward others and self-destructive. Lisa's behavior becomes manageable once the dosage is adjusted; she is kept on the lithium for five years. As an adult, she is diagnosed as having severe, life-threatening liver damage that requires a liver transplant. The doctor traces the liver condition back to Lisa's ongoing lithium usage. Long-term studies indicate that lithium can cause liver damage, especially in children who have had protracted exposure to the drug. These studies were not available when Lisa was given the medication.

Write out all the reasons supporting your belief that the psychologist should or should not be held liable for Lisa's damages. Be sure to include in your discussion public policy arguments you think are relevant.

KEY TERMS

Action in trespass (*vi et armis*)
Early cause of action involving serious, forcible breaches of peace that evolved to encompass even minor physical contact; no showing of fault was required.

Public policy
Consideration by judges of the effects of a proposed legal principle on society as a whole.

Slippery slope argument
Argument that once you take a first step in allowing something in one instance, you are in danger of sliding the "slippery slope" into a bottomless pit of circumstances requiring comparable treatment.

Trespass on the case
Early cause of action involving injuries inflicted indirectly and requiring some showing of fault.

CHAPTER

2

Overview of a Tort Case

CHAPTER TOPICS

CHAPTER OBJECTIVES

In this chapter you will be given a procedural overview of a tort case and will learn the terminology associated with:

- The initiation of a complaint and a response to that complaint
- The conduct of the discovery process
- The preparation for trial
- The conduct of a trial
- The implementation of posttrial procedures

HYPOTHETICAL TORT CASE

After leaving work on Friday afternoon, Hanna drove to Happy Valley Bank to cash her paycheck. Leaving the bank, as she prepared to enter Sunshine Avenue, the street on which the bank was located, she came to a complete stop and looked into the mirror provided by the bank to see if there was any oncoming traffic. The bank had found it necessary to install this mirror because customers experienced so much difficulty in seeing any oncoming cars. The curved shape of the street obstructed their view. (See Figure 2-1.) As fate would have it, rain from earlier that afternoon had caused the mirror to fog over. Consequently, Hanna did not see the car being driven by Fred and pulled out directly in front of his car. Fred, being unable to stop in time, rammed into Hanna's car, causing it to spin around and collide with the car being driven by Sunny, who was proceeding in the opposite direction. Fred and Sunny sustained only minor injuries in the accident but Hanna received a broken leg and a concussion. As a result, Hanna was out of work for a month.

Hanna relates these events to an attorney and then tells the attorney that she wants to sue the bank, who Hanna believes was the ultimate cause of her accident. Hanna is aware that Fred and Sunny may sue her for the property damage and physical injuries they incurred. Let us walk through the likely chain of events that will occur as Hanna enters the legal world (see Figure 2-2).

FIGURE 2-1 Bank Parking Lot

FIGURE 2-2 Overview of a Case

INITIATING A COMPLAINT	• Interview • Investigation • Filing of complaint
DEFENDANT'S RESPONSE	• Answer • File counterclaim or cross-claim • File motions • Default
DISCOVERY	• Interrogatories • Depositions • Requests for admissions • Requests for production of documents • Requests for medical or psychological exam • Motions to compel and for protective order • Motions for summary judgment
PRETRIAL PROCEDURES	• Pretrial conference • Motions in limine • Opening statements • Direct and cross-examination
TRIAL	• Voir dire (challanges for cause and peremptory challenges) • Opening statements • Direct and cross-examination • Motion for directed verdict • Closing arguments • General or special verdict
POSTTRIAL PROCEDURES	• Motion for new trial • JNOV • Appeal and cross-appeal

INITIATING A COMPLAINT

First, the attorney must ascertain whether the legal elements of a negligence claim have been met. Did the bank have a duty to maintain the mirror in a safe condition and, if so, did the bank breach that duty by allowing the mirror to fog over? The attorney must also determine whether the mirror was, in fact, the cause of the accident and whether Hanna sustained monetary and other damages as a result of the accident.

To address these questions the attorney will need to find out several things. Who owns the mirror? Who is responsible for maintenance of the mirror? Who owns the bank? Does the bank have any agreements with the city regarding maintenance of the mirror? Is the design of the street itself defective? Was Hanna negligent in her use of the mirror? Were there any witnesses to the accident? Does the extent of Hanna's money damages warrant a lawsuit?

After conducting her investigation, if the attorney concludes that Hanna does have a viable claim, she will send a **demand letter** to Happy Valley Bank. In this letter she will explain why she believes the bank is liable, she will detail the extent of her client's damages, and she will put forth a demand for settlement of the case. If she cannot negotiate a settlement she will initiate the case by filing a **complaint** (FRCP 8(a)).[1]

A complaint has four basic elements (see Figure 2-3). First, a complaint must state that the court has jurisdiction, i.e., the authority to hear the case. The attorney must show, for example, that she has met any residence or amount-in-controversy requirements of the court. The plaintiff has the right to choose the court within which to file her complaint so long as she meets the jurisdictional requirements of that court.

Second, the complaint must list the parties to the action. In this case Hanna would be the plaintiff and Happy Valley Bank the defendant.

Third, the complaint must provide a brief summary of each of the elements of the case along with the basic facts that will be used to prove each element. Hanna's

---

1. The Federal Rules of Civil Procedure are cited throughout this text as FRCP.

FIGURE 2-3 Elements of a Complaint

attorney must allege that Happy Valley Bank had a duty to maintain the mirror in a safe condition, that it breached that duty, that as a result of the breach Hanna was injured, and that she sustained monetary damages. The degree of factual detail required in this part of the complaint is dictated by the procedural rules of the particular state in which the complaint is being filed (check the Rules of Civil Procedure in your state).

Finally, the complaint must specify the relief being sought by the plaintiff. In Hanna's case she will be asking for compensation for her hospital and medical bills and her lost salary, as well as additional monies for the pain and suffering she endured. In some states a verification must be submitted along with the complaint. The **verification** is an affidavit indicating that the plaintiff has read the complaint and that, to the best of his or her knowledge, it is true. The Rules of Civil Procedure in Hanna's state will determine how defendant Happy Valley Bank should be served with the complaint, where the complaint should be filed, and who may serve it.

DEFENDANT'S RESPONSE

Once Happy Valley Bank has been served, it has several options. If the bank does nothing, Hanna can get a **default judgment** in which the court would resolve the case in Hanna's favor because of Happy Valley Bank's lack of opposition (FRCP 55). Such a default judgment would normally be set aside if the defendant could show it had a good reason for failing to act.

Defendant Happy Valley Bank could choose to file an **answer** (FRCP 8(b)). In so doing it would admit those allegations in Hanna's complaint it thought to be true, deny those with which it disagreed, and indicate lack of sufficient knowledge for those allegations requiring further investigation. At the same time the defendant could raise any affirmative defenses it might have, such as contributory negligence. An **affirmative defense** is any defense that the party asserting it must affirmatively prove or, in other words, for which it bears the burden of proof (FRCP 8(d)). So if Happy Valley Bank asserted that Hanna's negligence was the cause of her damages (thus using contributory negligence as an affirmative defense), it would have the burden of proving that negligence.

The defendant may at this time also raise any counterclaims or crossclaims. A **counterclaim** is a claim raised by the defendant against the plaintiff; a **crossclaim** is a claim raised against a co-party. For example, if Fred sued Hanna and Happy Valley Bank to recover for his injuries and property damage, Hanna could raise a counterclaim against Fred alleging that he was contributorily negligent and a crossclaim against Happy Valley Bank alleging negligence.

At the same time Happy Valley Bank answers Hanna's complaint, it could file a *motion* (FRCP 12). Motions can be filed alleging, among other things, a lack of jurisdiction over the person or subject matter, improper venue, insufficiency of process, or failure to state a claim upon which relief can be granted. The most important of these is a motion for failure to state a claim upon which relief can be granted, which is referred to in some states as a motion for dismissal or a **demurrer**. By filing such a motion the defendant, in essence, is asserting that the plaintiff has failed to state a legally necessary element of the cause of action. If, for example, Happy Valley Bank did not own the mirror and had no legally recognizable duty to maintain it, the element of duty would be unfulfilled. If that were the case, Happy Valley Bank could file a motion alleging that Hanna had failed to state a claim upon which relief could be granted. By granting the motion, the court would dismiss the case.

DISCOVERY

If the case were not dismissed in these early stages of the process, it would move into the **discovery** phase (FRCP 26). The theory underlying discovery is that the more each side finds out about the other side's case, the more likely it is that the parties will be able to settle the case and the final outcome will be an equitable one. Discovery can be compared to a game of poker. In this game each party tries to gain as much information as possible about the opposing side's position while revealing as little information as possible about its own position. Admittedly the stakes in litigation are often higher than those in poker, but the strategies employed are remarkably similar. It is fair to say that most cases today are won or lost in the discovery process. Because legal assistants play a major role in this process, you must become adept at creating and manipulating the tools of discovery.

There are five basic types of discovery: (1) interrogatories, (2) depositions, (3) requests for admission, (4) requests for production of documents, and (5) requests for medical and psychological examinations.

Interrogatories are written questions submitted to the opposing party which that party must answer in writing and under oath (FRCP 33). Interrogatories are a relatively inexpensive way of soliciting basic objective information. Hanna's counsel, for example, will want to use interrogatories to find out the names, addresses, and duties of the employees of Happy Valley Bank who maintain the mirror, as well as information regarding Happy Valley Bank's relationship to the owner of the property on which the bank is located. Interrogatories are limited in usefulness because they are usually answered by or with the assistance of opposing counsel, whose aim is typically to provide as little information as possible.

A **deposition**, however, is an oral examination of a witness (or a party to the suit) under oath (FRCP 27–32). Because depositions are considerably more time-consuming and more expensive than interrogatories, attorneys carefully select those whom they want to depose. At a deposition, deposing counsel not only will

be able to pursue lines of questioning more thoroughly than by using interrogatories, but also will be able to assess how a jury might respond to the deponent. A court reporter, present during the deposition, prepares a transcript of everything that is said. The transcript can then be introduced at trial. For that reason an attorney may opt to depose a witness whose testimony she wants to use at trial if she believes that witness will not appear for the trial. Counsel can also use the witness's statements made during the deposition to impeach (discredit) his testimony at trial.

Happy Valley Bank's counsel would most likely want to depose Hanna to elicit detailed information from her about what she did before the accident, as well as to assess her probable demeanor before a jury. This kind of information would be pertinent to counsel not only in mapping a trial strategy but also in considering the advisability of settlement.

Requests for admissions are simply requests by one party asking that the other party admit certain facts (FRCP 36). If Hanna's attorney, for example, ascertained that the bank did in fact own, install, and maintain the mirror, she would want the bank to admit those facts. Once a party admits a fact, that matter is conclusively established and cannot be argued at trial. Under the Federal Rules and the rules in many states, if a party fails to respond to requests for admissions, those matters are deemed admitted.

Documents vital to a case that are in the possession of the opposing party can be obtained via a **request for production of documents** (FRCP 34). Hanna's attorney will want to review any maintenance records pertaining to the maintenance of the mirror and defense counsel will want to examine Hanna's hospital and medical records. Both can do so by filing a request for production of documents. Because Hanna has put her medical condition at issue in this case, Happy Valley Bank's counsel will also want to select a physician to examine Hanna in order to get a second opinion about the seriousness of her injuries. This can be done through a **request for medical examination** (FRCP 35).

During the pretrial discovery process both parties can make discovery-related motions as well as motions for summary judgment. Discovery-related motions include motions to compel and motions for protective orders. A **motion to compel** is appropriate when the opposing party refuses to reveal discoverable material (FRCP 37). **A motion for a protective order**, in contrast, prevents discovery of information that is privileged and, therefore, not discoverable (FRCP 26(c)).

During the discovery process a party may glean sufficient information to determine that there is no material fact at issue and that a court could render a decision as a matter of law without having to go to trial. In this event the party will file a **motion for summary judgment**, requesting that the court enter a judgment on its behalf, thus dispensing with the need for a trial (FRCP 56). A party can also request a partial summary judgment which, in effect, eliminates particular issues. If Hanna's attorney filed a motion for a partial summary judgment and the court determined, as a matter of law, that Happy Valley Bank had a duty to maintain the mirror in a safe condition and that it breached that duty, then the only remaining issue to resolve would be the extent of Hanna's injuries and whether Happy Valley Bank was the proximate and actual cause of Hanna's injuries.

To rebut a motion for summary judgment the opponent must show that a genuine factual dispute exists and that a trial will be necessary to resolve that dispute. The mere allegation that a factual dispute exists is, however, insufficient. Using answers from interrogatories, deposition answers, and affidavits, the opposing party must show that it can controvert the facts alleged by the other side.

PRETRIAL PROCEDURES

If the parties cannot resolve the dispute during the discovery process, the case will proceed toward trial. Most courts require a **pretrial conference** to clarify the issues and defenses for trial, to establish the witnesses and exhibits that will be used at trial, and to promote settlement (FRCP 16). How vehemently the judge pushes for settlement depends on his or her philosophical bent. Statistics tell us, however, that most cases settle at or before the pretrial conference.

Before trial the parties will once again have an opportunity to move for dismissal as well as to make motions in limine. The purpose of a **motion in limine** is to resolve evidentiary questions so that they need not be brought up before the jury. In that way only evidence that is relevant and not unduly prejudicial will be presented. For example, if Hanna's attorney wanted to introduce testimony that Happy Valley Bank had instituted a new procedure for maintenance of the mirror subsequent to Hanna's accident, Happy Valley Bank's attorney would want to make a motion in limine to prevent that testimony. The generally prevailing argument, by the way, is that a motion such as this should be granted, as admission of this type of evidence would inhibit defendants from taking measures to remove or correct dangerous conditions.

TRIAL

If Hanna's case goes to trial, she will have the opportunity to decide between a **bench trial** (trial before a judge) and a jury trial (FRCP 39). In a jury trial all factual issues are resolved by the jury while all legal issues are resolved by the judge. In a bench trial the judge decides both factual and legal issues. Whether to opt for a jury trial or a bench trial is a strategic decision, although case law does limit the right to a jury in certain types of cases.

Jury selection is conducted through a process known as **voir dire**, which consists of a series of questions asked of potential jurors by the trial judge or the attorneys, depending on local practice (FRCP 47). A party who wants to excuse a particular juror, and can show that the juror has already formed a judgment as to how the case should be decided or for some reason is unable to decide the case impartially, may use a **challenge for cause** (FRCP 47 (c)). The party who wants to dismiss a particular juror but cannot allege bias may remove the juror using a **peremptory challenge** (FRCP 47(e)). No reason need be given for a peremptory challenge.

Although an attorney has an unlimited number of challenges for cause, he or she has a limited number of peremptory challenges (the specific number depends on local practice). Hanna's attorney might want to use her peremptory challenges to eliminate jurors engaged in a particular occupation if research has shown that members of that profession are generally reluctant to compensate plaintiffs generously. She will also want to excuse persons that instinct or observation tell her will be unsympathetic to her client's plight.

When the trial begins Hanna's counsel will be given an opportunity to make *opening statements*. She will probably give an overview of the basic elements of her case, introduce the parties and witnesses that will be involved in the trial, and in general set the tone and theme of her case. Opening statements are not considered part of the evidence, but they are extremely important, especially in light of research showing that the majority of jurors decide the outcome of the case during opening statements and do not change their minds after hearing the testimony. Because Hanna has the burden of proving each element of her case by a *preponderance of the evidence* (that each element is more likely than not), she will be given the opportunity not only to begin the trial with opening statements but also to end the trial by making the final statement in closing arguments.

The evidence in any civil case consists of witness testimony and exhibits. On *direct examination* questions are posed by the counsel calling the witness; *cross-examination* is conducted by opposing counsel. The function of cross-examination is to impeach (discredit) testimony given by the witness during direct examination. This process continues through redirect and recross-examination and so on until counsel exhaust all their questions.

During the course of the trial counsel may object to questions being asked or evidence being presented. The trial court will rule on the admissibility of evidence using the Rules of Evidence appropriate for that court. If the court sustains (grants) an objection to a question, that question cannot be asked but if the court overrules (denies) an objection, that question can be asked.

After Hanna's counsel rests, counsel for Happy Valley Bank will probably move for a **directed verdict**, arguing that Hanna failed to meet the requisite burden of proof on all the elements of her case (FRCP 50). Such motions, though frequently made, are commonly denied, but if a motion for a directed verdict is granted, the case, in essence, is dismissed. Hanna's counsel will make a similar motion if Happy Valley Bank presents evidence regarding an affirmative defense. At the close of Happy Valley Bank's case, Hanna will be given an opportunity to present rebuttal evidence, which is used to refute evidence presented by the defendant.

Because Hanna has the burden of proof, her counsel will be given the opportunity to present the first *closing argument*. In this argument Hanna's attorney will summarize the facts of the case, showing how the evidence established each of the legal elements. Using the theme established in her opening statements, she will use her most persuasive rhetoric to convince the jury that Hanna should prevail and that generous damages should be awarded. Counsel for Happy Valley Bank will do likewise in his closing arguments and then Hanna's attorney will close with a rebuttal argument.

Finally, in a process known as **charging the jury**, the judge will instruct the jury on the rules of law to be applied (FRCP 50). In some states standard jury instructions are used. In others attorneys draft proposed instructions for the judge's consideration and, in a conference conducted outside the earshot of the jury, argue which instructions should be adopted. Much attention is given to the adoption of jury instructions and counsel are given an opportunity to object to any instructions the judge gives or fails to give. Jury instructions are important because objections to these instructions are typically the fundamental components of an appeal.

The jury will then be asked to render either a general or special verdict (FRCP 49). In Hanna's case a **general verdict** would require the jury to decide if Happy

Valley Bank was liable for Hanna's injuries and to determine what damages should be awarded. If a **special verdict** were requested, the jury would be required to answer special interrogatories and the judge would have to determine the prevailing party after reviewing the jury's answers. In a case tried before a judge alone, the attorneys may be required to submit trial briefs in which they present the applicable law and show how it would apply to the facts of the particular case.

POSTTRIAL

If Hanna loses she can make a *motion for a new trial*, arguing that errors were committed during the trial (FRCP 59). Or she can move for a **judgment notwithstanding the verdict (JNOV)**, arguing that the verdict reached was contrary to the evidence and law (FRCP 50(b)). Such motions are generally contingent on counsel making appropriate objections during the trial; if counsel fails to do so, these procedural remedies will be denied. Hanna could also *appeal* (see Federal Rules of Appellate Procedure) the decision to a higher court and if Happy Valley Bank were unhappy with part of the outcome at the trial level, it could file a *cross-appeal*. Once a final judgment was entered, however, and all appeals were completed, the issues litigated would be **res judicata**, in that they could not be relitigated at a later time. The philosophy underlying this rule is that litigation must ultimately come to an end and cannot be allowed to go on forever.

EMPHASIS ON DISCOVERY THROUGHOUT THIS TEXT

Although this overview of a civil case is certainly not exhaustive, lacking many of the subroutes parties can pursue in litigation, it does give you a framework within which to analyze tort problems. Examples will be provided throughout the text of typical discovery tools and you will be encouraged to consider the information presented in each chapter in the context of how it could be applied in discovery. Keep the importance of discovery foremost in your mind as you work through

this book. Remember that a key contribution paralegals can make to the litigation team lies in their ability to create, manipulate, and organize discovery tools.

SUMMARY

To initiate a tort claim, the plaintiff must file a complaint. This complaint must state the basis for the court's jurisdiction, the parties to the action, the elements of the case, and the relief being sought. The defendant may then file an answer admitting or denying allegations in the plaintiff's complaint and raising any affirmative defenses. The defendant may also bring a counterclaim against the plaintiff or a crossclaim against a co-party. Additionally, he or she may file a motion alleging, for example, that the plaintiff failed to state a claim upon which relief can be granted.

In the discovery phase both parties try to find out as much as possible about the other side's case while revealing as little as possible about their own. Interrogatories, depositions, requests for admission, request for production of documents, and requests for medical and psychological examinations are the most frequently used tools of discovery. A party may also file a motion for summary judgment if no material fact is arguably at issue.

A case that cannot be resolved during the discovery process moves on to trial. Before trial, most courts require the parties to attend a pretrial conference and to resolve evidentiary questions by making motions in limine. At the trial the parties are allowed to select jurors through a process of voir dire, dismissing jurors on the basis of either a challenge for cause or peremptory challenge. At trial the plaintiff has the burden of proving each element of his or her case by a preponderance of the evidence. Both counsel are given the opportunity to introduce their cases by making opening statements, to elicit testimony through direct examination, and to impeach witnesses through cross-examination. Motions for directed verdict are generally made after opposing counsel has presented his or her case. After both counsel have given closing arguments, the judge charges the jury. The jury is then asked to render either a general or special verdict, the latter of which requires the answering of special interrogatories.

Subsequent to trial, a party can move for a new trial or a judgment notwithstanding the verdict. Appeals and cross-appeals can also be filed, but once a final judgment is entered and all appeals are completed, the issues litigated are considered res judicata.

■ TORT TEASERS □

Make a flowchart of the events and activities leading up to trial, those events that occur at trial, and those events that occur after trial. Which of these events do you think you will be most involved in as a legal assistant?

KEY TERMS

Affirmative defense
Any defense that a party asserts for which it bears the burden of proof.

Answer
A pleading in which the defendant responds to the plaintiff's complaint.

Bench trial
Trial before a judge.

Challenge for cause
Request to remove a potential juror because of his or her alleged inability to decide the case impartially.

Charging the jury
Process in which the judge instructs the jurors in rules of law they are to apply.

Complaint
An initial pleading filed on behalf of the plaintiff the purpose of which is to provide the defendant with the material elements of the plaintiff's demand.

Counterclaim
A claim presented by a defendant in opposition to the plaintiff's claim.

Crossclaim
A claim brought by a defendant against a co-defendant in the same action.

Default judgment
Judgment entered due to lack of opposition on behalf of the opposing party.

Demand letter
A letter detailing a client's damages and setting forth the reasons for her demand.

Demurrer
Motion for dismissal based on a defect in the form or content of a complaint.

Deposition
Oral examination of a witness under oath.

Directed verdict
Dismissal of a case because of the opposing party's failure to meet the requisite burden of proof.

Discovery
Process through which parties try find out as much as possible about the other side's case.

General verdict
Verdict in which a jury decides issues of liability and damages.

Interrogatories
Written questions submitted to the opposing party which that party must answer in writing and under oath.

JNOV (Judgment notwithstanding the verdict)
A decision that the verdict reached was contrary to the evidence and the law.

Motion for protective order
Motion that protects a party from having to disclose privileged information.

Motion for summary judgment
Motion requesting that the court enter a judgment on the party's behalf because there is no material fact at issue.

Motion in limine
Motion to prevent evidence from being presented to the jury.

Motion to compel
Motion to force the opposing party to comply with a request for discovery.

Peremptory challenge
Request to remove a potential juror for no articulated reason.

Pretrial conference
Conference involving the judge and parties at which issues and procedures for the trial are clarified and efforts are made at settlement.

Res judicata
Legal principle stating that issues litigated cannot be relitigated at a later time.

Request for admissions
Request by one party asking the other party to admit certain facts.

Request for medical examination
Request that the opposing party be examined by a physician chosen by the party making the request.

Request for production of documents
Request for document in possession of the opposing party.

Special verdict
Verdict in which the jury is required to answer special interrogatories, which the judge must review to determine who the prevailing party is.

Verification
Affidavit indicating that the plaintiff has read the complaint and to the best of his or her knowledge believes it to be true.

Voir dire
Process of jury selection involving the use of challenges for cause and peremptory challenges.

CHAPTER

3

Intentional Torts

CHAPTER TOPICS

What Is an Intentional Tort?
Intentional Torts Against Persons
Intentional Torts Against Property
Defenses

CHAPTER OBJECTIVES

In this chapter you will learn to:
- Identify the elements of assault, battery, false imprisonment, and infliction of mental distress
- Identify the elements of trespass to land, trespass to chattels, and conversion
- Recognize circumstances in which it is appropriate to raise the defenses of consent or necessity
- Recognize when force can be used to defend self, others, property, to regain possession of chattels, or to reenter land

Suppose you come home one evening to discover that your teenage son "borrowed" your car and went on the following spree. First, he dropped by his girlfriend's house to pick her up but once there met with considerable resistance from her parents. Not to be intimidated by her father, who stood menacingly in front of the car as he started the engine, your son yelled out the window that he would run over her father if he did not get out of the way. The father, who doggedly stood his ground until the last possible moment, barely escaped injury when he finally jumped aside.

Unbeknownst to either your son or his girlfriend, her younger brother had crawled into the back of the car during the fracas with the father. Once under way, the little boy screamed to be released from the car. Your son, who harbored some latent hostility toward the little brother, took great delight in holding him captive for several miles before letting him out of the car to walk home.

Next the twosome headed to a remote place in the country to enjoy a little privacy. Deeply involved in professing their love for each other, neither noticed the approach of a man brandishing a gun. The man punctuated each demand to get off his land by firing a shot in the air. Thoroughly frightened, the two lovers beat a hasty retreat but, with one last act of bravado, your son took aim at a sign on the man's property and obliterated it with the car. Later your son, as an afterthought, casually mentioned to you that before leaving the property he took the opportunity to fire a few shots in the man's direction with a gun that he had "borrowed" from you.

Ultimately, he arrived safely at home with a car that was only slightly scratched from its close encounter with a sign. In the course of his escapade, what intentional torts did your son commit and what defenses might he raise to justify his conduct? To answer these questions let us first consider the nature of an intentional tort.

WHAT IS AN INTENTIONAL TORT?

The state of the tortfeasor's mind separates an intentional tort from a negligent one. Although negligent torts can be committed unintentionally, **intentional torts,** as the name implies, require that the tortfeasor intend or have a desire to bring about a particular consequence. The tortfeasor need not desire to harm a person, but he or she must be aware that certain consequences are substantially certain to result from his or her acts. If, for example, the defendant intends to do nothing more than play a practical joke on the plaintiff and has absolutely no desire to injure him, he may still be liable if he harms the plaintiff. The intent to bring about a particular result is what is important. The fact that he wishes no harm to the plaintiff has no bearing on his intent.

If a defendant knows with substantial certainty that a result will occur, he or she will be liable for the consequences. An individual who throws a firecracker into the middle of a dense crowd, for example, may not actually want to hit anyone but if she knows with substantial certainty that someone will get hit, she has acted intentionally. If the consequences are merely highly likely but not substantially certain, the defendant will be considered negligent but will not be deemed to have acted intentionally. Note that intent can be distinguished from motive. Intent is the desire to bring about a consequence; motive is connected to the reason for desiring such a consequence.

You will recall that intentional torts can also be crimes. An assault is both a tort and a crime, as are trespass and false imprisonment. A police officer who deliberately and unlawfully detains an individual can be sued for the damages sustained by the detainee (false imprisonment) and can be punished criminally as well (although the crime is often referred to as unlawful imprisonment). Be cautious, however, in drawing too many analogies between tort law and criminal law. The purposes and historical derivations of criminal and tort law are different, so the terms and concepts used in the criminal area do not necessarily correspond to those used in tort law.

Transferred Intent Doctrine

If a tortfeasor intends to punch A but A ducks and the tortfeasor inadvertently strikes B, the intent to strike A will be transferred from A to B. Under the **transferred intent doctrine,** the intent with respect to one person is transferred to the person who is actually injured. Therefore, in such cases the tortfeasor is deemed to have committed an intentional tort. This same rule is applicable if the tortfeasor intends to commit one kind of tort and in fact commits another. If the tortfeasor uses his dog to terrorize A (an assault) and the dog escapes and bites B (a battery), the tortfeasor will be liable for the battery even though he intended an assault.

Categorization of Intentional Torts

Intentional torts are generally divided into two categories: intentional torts against persons and intentional torts against property. The torts against persons that are discussed in this chapter are battery, assault, false imprisonment, and infliction of mental distress (see Figure 3-1). The torts against property that are discussed are trespass to land, trespass to chattels, and conversion.

FIGURE 3-1 Intentional Torts Against Persons

BATTERY	ASSAULT
Intentional infliction of harmful or offensive contact.	Intentional causing of apprehension of harmful or offensive contact.

FALSE IMPRISONMENT	INFLICTION OF MENTAL DISTRESS
Intentional confinement of another.	Intentional infliction of severe emotional or mental distress as a result of extreme and outrageous conduct (can also be committed recklessly).

INTENTIONAL TORTS AGAINST PERSONS
Battery

If two people become engaged in a heated argument and one pushes the other to the ground, the person who does the shoving commits a battery. **Battery** is defined as the intentional infliction of a harmful or offensive contact upon a person. If the tortfeasor intends only to frighten the victim and accidentally makes "harmful or offensive contact," he or she has still committed a battery. As indicated earlier, whether the tortfeasor intends to actually injure the plaintiff is irrelevant. To satisfy the elements of battery the tortfeasor must only intend to make contact and the contact must actually be made.

What Is Considered Contact?

The function of the law concerning battery is to protect individuals from undesired and unpermitted contacts. This tort extends to contact with any part of a person's body or anything attached to or identified with the body. Contact with a purse, with an object in the plaintiff's hand, or with the car in which the plaintiff is riding all constitute contact for the purposes of battery. In one case the plaintiff, a black man, was attending a luncheon at the defendant's hotel. One of the defendant's employees grabbed the plate from the plaintiff's hand while he was waiting to be served and shouted that the plaintiff could not be served in the club because he was black. Although the plaintiff was never actually touched or frightened by the defendant's employee, he did suffer a battery because the intentional snatching of the plate from his hand constituted an offensive invasion of his person (*Fisher v. Carrousel Motor Hotel, Inc.,* 424 S.W.2d 627 (Tex. 1967)).

The defendant need not actually touch the plaintiff with his body. A person who orders his dog to attack or who throws water on someone has committed a battery (Restatement (Second) of Torts § 18, cmt. c).

Neither must the plaintiff suffer pain or bodily damage to recover for battery. The contact need only be "offensive." In determining whether a contact is offensive, the question is whether a person with a reasonable sense of dignity would be offended. If a woman gently taps her boyfriend on the shoulder to get his attention, she has not committed a battery. Touching by a friend is not offensive to an ordinary person and therefore is not actionable.

Awareness of Contact

The plaintiff is not required to have any awareness of the contact at the time it occurs. If the plaintiff gives consent for a biopsy to be done and the doctor decides while the patient is under anesthetic to go ahead and perform surgery, the doctor has committed battery. Even though she obtained consent for the biopsy, she lacks the plaintiff's consent to perform the surgery. The fact that the plaintiff is unaware of the doctor's actions at the time of the surgery is irrelevant.

Extent of Liability

The defendant who commits battery is liable for any consequences regardless of how unforeseen they may be. Suppose the defendant grabs the plaintiff around the waist and playfully squeezes her in a manner that would normally cause no bodily harm. Because the plaintiff is suffering from osteoporosis, however, she sustains extensive damage to her ribs, resulting in long suffering. The defendant is liable for the full extent of the plaintiff's bodily harm even though he could not have reasonably anticipated that harm.

Assault

Assault is defined as the intentional causing of an apprehension of harmful or offensive contact. Apprehension does not mean fear but does require the plaintiff to be aware of the impending contact. A woman who shakes her broom at someone to frighten or chase him away has committed assault if the object of her threats believes she is trying to strike him. A defendant can commit assault by either intending to commit a battery or merely intending to frighten the plaintiff, with no intent of actual contact. A defendant, for example, who attempts to strike the plaintiff but misses commits an assault, but so does the defendant who makes a fist at the plaintiff with no intent of actually hitting him.

The doctrine of transferred intent is as applicable to assault as it is to battery. Therefore, if a defendant throws a stone at A and B fears being hit, the defendant will be liable to B for assault even though he never intended to hit or frighten B.

Plaintiff's Attitude

Unlike battery, a plaintiff alleging assault must be aware of the threatened contact. So if A intends to frighten B by discharging a pistol behind him but B, who is stone deaf, does not hear the pistol, A will not be liable to B for assault (Restatement (Second) of Torts § 22, illus. 1).

An individual will not be able to recover for assault if his apprehension is that someone else will be touched and not himself. If a husband, for example, disarms a robber just before he shoots the husband's wife, the husband cannot recover for assault, because the attack was directed at his wife and not himself (Restatement (Second) of Torts § 26).

A plaintiff need not be fearful that he will be harmed. A plaintiff confident in his ability to protect himself can still be the victim of assault. His awareness that he could be harmed if he failed to take defensive action is sufficient.

Defendant's Ability to Carry Out Threat

A defendant must appear to the plaintiff to have the present ability to carry out the threatened contact. In one case the defendant repeatedly threatened to kill the plaintiff if she sued him. After the plaintiff filed suit, the defendant came to her home, beat on the door, tried to pry it open, and repeated his threats to kill her. The defendant argued that no assault had been committed because he had made no overt action toward the plaintiff. The court concluded that the evidence supported a finding that the defendant had the apparent ability to carry out the threatened act. *Holcombe v. Whitaker*, 318 So. 2d 289 (Ala. 1975). If a plaintiff believes the defendant has the ability to carry out his threatened contact even though he actually does not, the elements of assault are met.

What Constitutes a Threat?

Any threats of harm must be imminent to constitute an assault. Threats of future harm are not sufficient, although they may satisfy the criteria for the tort of intentional infliction of mental distress. If A threatens to shoot B, for example, but must go to her car to get her revolver, A has not committed assault (Restatement (Second) of Torts § 29, illus. 4).

The courts are in some disagreement as to whether words alone constitute an assault. Some courts require that words be accompanied by some overt act that tends to enhance the threatening character of the words; other courts, in accordance with the Restatement (Second), require no accompanying overt act. If a member of a juvenile gang, holding a knife in his hand, approaches a member of another gang and, without movement, says, "You die," many courts would conclude that an assault had been committed.

Note that the tort of assault is complete as soon as the plaintiff apprehends the contact. If, after the plaintiff's apprehension, the defendant suddenly abandons his plan, he will still be liable for assault.

PUTTING IT INTO PRACTICE 3.1

When Mike Tyson steps out of his limousine, he is confronted by a fan who jumps in front of him, assumes a boxing stance, and jabs at him. Tyson laughs at the fan. Has the fan committed a tort?

False Imprisonment

The tort of **false imprisonment** is committed when a person intentionally confines another. Originally confinement was restricted to actual incarceration, but today confinement includes restraint in an open street or in a moving vehicle. The restraint must be more than a mere obstruction of the plaintiff's right to go wherever she pleases. Blocking the plaintiff's path in one direction only does not constitute confinement as long as alternative routes are available. The doctrine of transferred intent is applicable to this tort. If the defendant, in his intent to confine one person, inadvertently confines another as well, he will be liable to both for false imprisonment.

What Constitutes Confinement?

The plaintiff is not required to subject herself or her property to any risk of harm in an effort to extricate herself from her confinement. Suppose a defendant closes off every exit except one. If the plaintiff can escape only by exposing herself to the possibility of substantial bodily harm, the defendant has confined her. Similarly, if the defendant blocks all doors except one and steals the plaintiff's clothing, leaving the plaintiff naked, and the plaintiff can leave only by walking through a room filled with persons of both sexes, the defendant has confined the plaintiff (Restatement (Second) of Torts § 36, illus. 3 and 5).

Confinement can be achieved by something less than physical force. If a defendant threatens by his body language alone to harm the plaintiff if the plaintiff tries to escape, he has still confined the plaintiff. Threats need not be aimed directly at the plaintiff, either. If the defendant threatens to harm another if the plaintiff leaves the confinement area, the defendant has committed false imprisonment. Any threats, however, must be of imminent harm. Threats of future harm are not sufficient. Finally, the plaintiff must be aware of her confinement at the time it occurs. If a person does not discover until after her release that she was confined, she cannot claim she was falsely imprisoned.

False Imprisonment in Law Enforcement

False imprisonment most often occurs in the context of law enforcement. A valid defense to the allegation of false imprisonment is the police officer's assertion of the legal right to make an arrest. An officer can claim such a defense even if the arrest or detention later turns out to be unlawful. He or she is required only to act reasonably and in good faith in carrying out the arrest. An officer who serves the plaintiff with an invalid arrest warrant but who reasonably believes the warrant to be valid has not committed false imprisonment.

Shoplifting

In most states today a merchant who reasonably believes that a customer has stolen property has a right to detain the suspected individual for a short period of time for the purpose of investigation. The right to detain is very restricted, however, and will be lost if the detention is unreasonably long, if the plaintiff is bullied or insulted, if the plaintiff is publicly accused of shoplifting, or if the detention is used to coerce payment or the signing of a confession. In most states the right to detain is limited to detention on the defendant's premises and is lost when the plaintiff leaves the premises. The pivotal question is whether the merchant had reasonable grounds for the detention. Consult the statutes and common law in your state to ascertain more specifically the rights of merchants in your jurisdiction.

PUTTING IT INTO PRACTICE 3.2

A man and his wife go to a "Private After-Hours Sale" at a department store. The man, who is recovering from a recent kidney transplant, is still partially paralyzed, has bloodshot eyes and visible needle marks, and walks with a faltering gait. He is given a shopping bag by one of the store's employees and believes that he is to use this bag for shopping. He goes to the men's department and selects ties, shirts, and cuff links, which he puts in his bag. When he leaves the men's department and moves toward the escalator, he is apprehended by a store security guard who has been observing his actions. The man is searched and then interrogated for a considerable length of time before he is released. Has this man been falsely imprisoned?

Infliction of Mental Distress

A relative newcomer to tort law is the claim of infliction of mental distress. This tort can be committed either intentionally or recklessly. If committed intentionally, the tortfeasor must want to bring about a particular consequence or must know with substantial certainty that a specific result is likely to occur. If the tort is committed recklessly, the defendant must act in deliberate disregard of the emotional distress that he knows he is very likely to cause the plaintiff. Such recklessness rises above negligence.

What Is "Extreme and Outrageous" Conduct?

It is not enough for this tort that the defendant act unreasonably; the conduct must be "extreme and outrageous." *Outrageous conduct* is any conduct considered intolerable in any civilized society and is characterized as exceeding all possible bounds of decency. For example, if the defendant tells the plaintiff that her husband has been critically injured in an accident, when in fact no such accident has occurred, the defendant is liable for any emotional distress the plaintiff suffers (Restatement (Second) of Torts § 46, illus. 1).

Mere insults and petty manipulation of others are not sufficient for this tort. However, a defendant who uses his or her position abusively may be liable for any emotional distress this causes. A high school principal, for example, who browbeats a student, threatening her with public disgrace and even prison unless she confesses to immoral conduct with certain men, will probably be liable for any emotional distress suffered by the student (Restatement (Second) of Torts § 46, illus. 6).

The peculiar characteristics of the plaintiff may be taken into consideration in evaluating the defendant's conduct. A defendant who takes advantage of a plaintiff of below-average intelligence may be liable for any distress she causes the plaintiff even though that same conduct would not be deemed outrageous if the plaintiff were an adult of average intelligence.

Considerable differences exist among the courts as to what does and does not constitute "extreme and outrageous" conduct. To illustrate, consider two cases from different jurisdictions. In the first case (*Kentucky Fried Chicken National Management Co. v. Weathersby*, 607 A.2d 8 (Md. 1992)), the employee's supervisor accused her of stealing money from the store safe, ordered her to take polygraph test, and, in front of customers and other employees, took away her store keys and suspended her for ten days "pending an investigation." Because of personality traits of the employee, of which the employer was unaware, the employer's actions resulted in the employee's hospitalization for depression and severe suicidal and homicidal tendencies. The court held that because the employer had no knowledge of the employee's peculiar sensitivities, no cause of action may have existed. Barring that knowledge, however, the court concluded that the employer's conduct, however unlaudable it may have been, did not rise to the level of intentional infliction of emotional distress. The court also opined that a "certain amount of arbitrary nastiness" in the workplace is a "fact of life we must accept" and that "[t]he workplace is not always a tranquil world where civility reigns."

In the second case (*Doe v. Mills*, 536 N.W.2d 824 (Mich. 1995)), members of a religious order protested outside an abortion clinic, holding up large signs displaying the real names of the plaintiffs and begging them not to "kill their babies." The trial court granted the defendants' motion for summary judgment, but the appellate court reversed on the ground that reasonable persons could conclude that the defendants' conduct was sufficiently outrageous and extreme as to warrant liability. The court observed that the defendants' actions were "more than mere insults, indignities, threats, annoyances, or petty oppressions." Do you believe the outcomes in these two cases are consistent, or do you think each court has a different sense of what constitutes "extreme and outrageous" conduct?

Transferred Intent Doctrine

The doctrine of transferred intent is generally not applicable in cases of intentional infliction of mental distress. To apply this doctrine would be to open the courthouse doors to all those who suffered emotional distress as a result of viewing tortious acts being intentionally committed against others. An exception to this general prohibition occurs when the defendant directs his or her conduct against a member of the plaintiff's immediate family and is aware that the plaintiff is present at the time. For example, if a man severely beats a child's father and is aware at the time of the beating that the child is watching, he will be liable for the emotional distress suffered by that child.

The transferred intent doctrine also is not applicable if the defendant fails to commit the tort he intended to commit and succeeds only in causing the plaintiff emotional distress. A defendant who is weary of the incessant barking of his neighbor's dog, and who shoots at the dog with the intent to kill it but misses, will not be liable for the emotional distress suffered by the dog's owner. His intent to commit conversion, in other words, is not transferred to the emotional distress he actually causes (Restatement (Second) of Torts § 47, illus. 2).

Type of Harm Suffered

A plaintiff must prove that he or she actually suffered severe emotional distress and must, at the very least, have sought medical attention. Some courts require that the plaintiff suffer some kind of physical harm, although most modern courts have no such requirement. A plaintiff who suffers harm only because of a peculiar vulnerability or sensitivity will not be allowed to recover if the defendant is not aware of these vulnerabilities or sensitivities.

Higher Standard for Those in Public Service

Common carriers and public utilities are held to a higher standard of conduct than the rest of the popu-

lace and can be held liable, for example, for highly insulting language. Although an insult to an ordinary person would almost never be considered actionable, an insult to a customer by an employee of a utility or carrier would be considered cause for an infliction of mental distress claim. This rule apparently stems from a concern that those who provide such services not be rude to their customers.

PUTTING IT INTO PRACTICE 3.3

The manager of a Radio Shack outlet is told on two occasions about unsatisfactory practices in his store. His supervisor and two security people come to his store to investigate. He is questioned at thirty-minute intervals throughout the day during which he claims he is cursed at, threatened, and denied his medication. Later that afternoon he is asked to submit to a polygraph test, which he agrees to, but he is not allowed to take his medication, Valium, because it may interfere with the test. He is brought to the testing place but hyperventilates and must be taken home. He returns to work the next day but cannot remain on the job, and eventually is hospitalized by a psychiatrist. Does he have a viable claim for intentional infliction of emotional distress?

INTENTIONAL TORTS AGAINST PROPERTY

Trespass to Land

A person who enters or wrongfully remains on another's land has committed the tort of trespass (see Figure 3-2). By the same token, trespass occurs if an individual fails to remove an object from another's land if she is under a duty to remove it. Historically, trespass was a strict liability tort, allowing liability even if the defendant's contact with the land was unintentional. Today, almost all courts have rejected strict liability except when the defendant is engaging in an abnormally dangerous activity, such as blasting.

Defendant's Intent

The defendant's only intent must be to make physical contact with the plaintiff's land. He or she need not intend any harm to the plaintiff's property nor even be aware that any harm might occur. A defendant is still liable for trespass even if his or her contact with the plaintiff's land is the result of a reasonable mistake. An intentional trespass is committed, for example, if a defendant walks on another's land thinking it to be his own or believing he is entitled to enter the land.

Type of Contact Required

The defendant need not enter or make contact with the land himself; an indirect invasion is sufficient. If a

FIGURE 3-2 Intentional Torts Against Property

TRESPASS TO LAND	TRESPASS TO CHATTELS	CONVERSION
Intentionally entering or wrongfully remaining on another's land	Intentional interference with another's use or possession of chattel (personal property)	Intentional interference with another's use or possession of chattel to the extent fairness requires that the defendant pay the full value of the chattel

child fires his BB gun at the plaintiff's barn, for example, he is liable for trespass even if he never sets foot on the plaintiff's property. Furthermore, a defendant who does not intend to enter the plaintiff's land but who knows that such an entry is reasonably certain to happen is liable for trespass. If a person builds up an embankment next to his adjoining neighbor's land and during an ordinary rain the dirt washes from his land to the other's land, he is liable for trespass. Even a defendant who allows gases or particles to enter the plaintiff's property will, according to most modern courts, be liable for trespass. Similarly, most courts today hold that a trespass is committed when the defendant sets off a blast that causes concussions or vibrations on the plaintiff's property.

Because landowners, under the common law, are considered to own the airspace above their property and the surface below their property, those who violate such space can be sued for trespass. Someone who fires a gun over the plaintiff's property may be liable for trespass even though no bullet lands on the property. In this day of general aviation, however, landowners cannot be allowed to sue for any invasion of their airspace. The airspace above certain minimum flight altitudes, as established by federal statutes and administrative regulations, is considered public domain. Therefore, damages cannot be awarded for any flights occurring above these altitudes. A landowner who can show that he has suffered actual harm resulting from the flight of aircraft over his property at permissible altitudes may, however, be able to sue on the basis of a nuisance theory. This theory of recovery is discussed in more detail in Chapter 11.

Revocation of Permission to Enter

Trespass is also committed if a defendant who has permission to enter the plaintiff's land refuses to leave when the permission is revoked. Similarly, if the defendant refuses or neglects to remove something when she is supposed to, she may be liable for trespass. For example, a person who is given permission to park his car on the plaintiff's land for a month and who at the end of the month removes the car but forgets to remove the gas can that he put beside the car has committed a trespass.

Extent of Liability

A defendant is liable for almost all consequences of the trespass, no matter how unpredictable those consequences might be. Even if a defendant has no reason to believe that the plaintiff or others will be injured as a result of his trespass, he will be liable. In some courts he will be liable as well for any emotional distress suffered as a result of the trespass, even if the plaintiff suffers no physical harm.

A veterinarian receives the permission of the Copelands to allow a student interested in a career in veterinary medicine to accompany him as he cares for their cat in their home. The student does not tell the veterinarian or the Copelands that in addition to being a student she is an employee of a local television station. She videotapes the veterinarian's session with the cat and parts of that videotape are aired when an investigative report on the veterinarian is broadcast. Do the Copelands have grounds for a trespass claim against the television station?

Trespass to Chattels

Trespass to chattels is committed by the intentional interference with the plaintiff's use or possession of **chattel** (personal property). A defendant who damages the plaintiff's china or who deliberately hides the plaintiff's bicycle so as to deprive him of its use has committed trespass to chattels. The length of the deprivation is irrelevant. Recovery will be allowed even if the loss of possession is only temporary. The owner of the chattel need not be in possession of the chattel at the time the trespass occurs. Both the owner and possessor of a chattel are entitled to sue.

The only intent required for this tort is the intent to interfere in some way with the plaintiff's chattel. The defendant need not intend to cause harm to the property. Neither is the defendant's mistaken belief that the property is his own a defense.

Unlike the plaintiff who sues for trespass, however, the plaintiff who sues for trespass to chattels must prove actual harm. A child who climbs on the back of a dog and pulls on its ears has not committed trespass to chattels as long as the dog is not harmed in any way (Restatement (Second) of Torts § 218 illus. 2).

Conversion

If the defendant's interference with the plaintiff's property is so substantial that justice demands that he or she pay the plaintiff the full value of the property, the defendant has committed the tort of **conversion.** As with trespass to land and trespass to chattels, no intent to harm the plaintiff's property or possessory rights is required. An innocent mistake by the defendant is sufficient. The plaintiff must show only that the defendant intended to interfere with his or her possessory rights. As with trespass to chattels, the plaintiff in a conversion action need not be the owner but can be the person in possession of the property at the time of the conversion.

Distinction Between Conversion and Trespass to Chattels

From the defendant's standpoint the distinction between trespass to chattels and conversion is an important one. A defendant who is in possession of the chattel at the time suit is brought has the right to return the goods in the case of trespass to chattels. Returning the goods is an effort to mitigate the plaintiff's damages. In the case of conversion, however, title is deemed to have transferred from the plaintiff to the defendant because of the defendant's interference. As a result the defendant is required to pay the full value of the property. In a sense, conversion may be looked on as a "forced sale" because the defendant pays for the full value of the property rather than for just the damage done.

Indicia of Conversion

Six factors are taken into consideration in determining whether a defendant's interference with the plaintiff's property rises to the level of conversion (Restatement (Second) of Torts § 222A). These factors are:

• The extent and duration of the defendant's exercise of control over the property.

• The extent and duration of the resulting interference with the plaintiff's right to control.

• The defendant's intent to assert a right inconsistent with the plaintiff's right of control.

• The defendant's good faith.

• The harm done to the chattel.

• The inconvenience and expense caused to the plaintiff.

To illustrate how these factors are weighed, consider a defendant who, upon leaving a restaurant, mistakenly picks up the plaintiff's hat, believing it to be his own. When he reaches the sidewalk he discovers his mistake and promptly reenters the restaurant and returns the hat. Because no harm was done, the defendant acted in good faith, and his interference with the plaintiff's right of control was limited, no conversion would be committed (Restatement (Second) of Torts § 222A, illus. 1).

Suppose that the defendant keeps that hat for three months before discovering his mistake and returning the hat. Such a lengthy confiscation of the hat would be considered a conversion because of the defendant's substantial interference with the plaintiff's use of his property. The defendant's acting in good faith would not make it any less a conversion (Restatement (Second) of Torts § 222A, illus. 2).

When the defendant gets to the sidewalk, if a sudden gust of wind blows the hat into an open manhole, he will be liable for conversion because the plaintiff's property interest is completely destroyed. Again, the defendant's good faith would not change the outcome (Restatement (Second) of Torts § 222A, illus. 3).

Suppose the defendant knowingly takes the plaintiff's hat but returns it to the restaurant because he sees a police officer coming toward him. He has committed a conversion because of his bad faith even though the duration of his control over the hat is relatively short (Restatement (Second) of Torts § 222A, illus. 4). Although the distinction between trespass to chattels and conversion is a blurred one, these guidelines will assist you in making reasonable distinctions.

Removal and Transfer of Goods

Conversion can be committed by ways other than taking possession of the plaintiff's property. A defendant may also be liable for conversion by the removal of goods. The removal must create a relatively serious interference with the plaintiff's right to possession and control of his or her property. Suppose, for example, the defendant takes possession of a house of which the plaintiff and defendant are co-owners. If the defendant removes the plaintiff's furniture when they become engaged in a dispute about ownership, he will be liable for conversion if he refuses to make the furniture available when the plaintiff demands it back. However, if the defendant complies with the plaintiff's request, the defendant's interference will constitute trespass to chattels but not conversion. In the latter case the defendant's interference is not so severe as to constitute conversion but is considered intermeddling with the plaintiff's goods, which is the essence of trespass to chattels.

Conversion also occurs when the defendant transfers chattel to someone who is not entitled to it. A parking lot attendant, for example, who gives a car to the wrong person commits conversion if he creates an interference with the car owner's rights that is sufficiently severe. By the same token, a parking lot attendant who intentionally refuses to return the plaintiff's car to him is liable for conversion if the refusal is done in bad faith and the resultant interference with the plaintiff's right to possession is substantial.

Conversion of Intangibles

In recent years a number of courts have allowed conversion suits for intangibles, such as stock certificates, promissory notes, insurance policies, and savings bank books. Generally, however, these intangible rights must be linked to some kind of document to support a conversion action. A defendant who steals a plaintiff's customer, for example, is not liable for conversion although he or she may be liable for some other tort, such as interference with contractual relations (discussed in Chapter 11).

■ PUTTING IT INTO PRACTICE 3.5 ☐

When Matthew moves into a home he has recently rented, he discovers that the former tenant (John) has still not removed his furniture. Matthew wants to bring in his own furniture, so he makes arrangements to have John's furniture stored in a warehouse in John's name. He calls John immediately to let him know of these arrangements but is unable to get in touch with John for a week. Has Matthew committed a conversion?

What if Matthew moved the furniture to a warehouse that was so distant that John was greatly inconvenienced and forced to go to great expense to recover his furniture?

Suppose that instead of moving the furniture, Matthew changed the locks. When John, after being notified of the change, came to the house to retrieve his furniture, Matthew was not home. Has Matthew committed a conversion if John is able to return the next day and pick up his furniture?

Suppose Matthew loans John his truck to drive to the warehouse to pick up the furniture but John makes a ten-mile detour to pick up his girlfriend. Has John committed a conversion? Would your answer change if on the way to his girlfriend's house, John is involved in an accident that causes significant damage to Matthew's truck?

DEFENSES

Mistake

Mistake in and of itself is not a defense to an intentional tort. A defendant who intentionally enters the land of another, acting in the honest and reasonable belief that the land is her own, is still liable for the tort of trespass. Mistake is, however, an element of consideration in some of the other defenses discussed in this chapter. A defendant who reasonably but mistakenly believes that he must defend himself or another can still claim self-defense even though his acts are premised on an erroneous belief. The effect of mistake is considered throughout the remaining sections of this chapter.

Consent

In general, a defendant is not liable for an intentional tort if the plaintiff consents to the defendant's intentional interference (see Figure 3-3). In most cases the plaintiff does not explicitly consent, but the consent may be implied from the plaintiff's conduct or from any customs surrounding such conduct. Because defendants are not expected to be mind readers, the issue of whether a plaintiff has consented is determined by objective manifestations and not by the plaintiff's subjective mental state. Simply put, the question is whether a reasonable person in the defendant's shoes would have believed that the plaintiff has consented to an invasion of his interest. Suppose a man announces

FIGURE 3-3 Defenses to Intentional Torts

CONSENT	If a plaintiff who has the capacity to consent to interference with his person or property voluntarily does so, either explicitly or implicitly, the defendant will not be liable for such interference.
SELF-DEFENSE	A defendant is entitled to (privileged) to use reasonable force to protect himself or another against imminent harm if he reasonably believes it is necessary to do so (most courts require that any person being aided must be privileged to act in self-defense).
DEFENSE OF PROPERTY	A defendant is entitled to use reasonable (not deadly) force to protect his property against imminent harm if he reasonably believes it is necessary to do so and he verbally demands that the intruder stop first (if circumstances permit).
REGAINING POSSESSION OF CHATTELS	A property owner is entitled to use reasonable force to regain possession of chattel if the chattel was wrongfully taken and the owner is in fresh pursuit.
REENTRY ON LAND	In some states a land owner may use reasonable force to reenter his land, although the majority of courts deny that right to landlords attempting to evict tenants.
NECESSITY	
PUBLIC NECESSITY	A defendant may harm the property interest of another when necessary to prevent a disaster to the community or a substantial number of people. No reimbursement of the plaintiff is required.
PRIVATE NECESSITY	A defendant may harm the property interest of another if necessary to protect his own interests or those of a few private citizens because no less damaging way to prevent the harm exists. Reimbursement of the plaintiff is required if there is substantial harm to the plaintiff's property.

to his date while they are standing at her front door that he is going to kiss her goodnight. If she says or does nothing to indicate her displeasure, it can be inferred from her conduct that she has given consent.

Consent or lack of consent can also be inferred from custom. One court, for example, allowed a professional football player to bring a tort action against another football player who intentionally struck him on the back of his head and neck. The court concluded that the customs of football do not encompass intentional punching or striking of others from the rear (*Hackbart v. Cincinnati Bengals, Inc.*, 601 F.2d 516 (10th Cir. 1979)).

Capacity to Consent

Consent is not a defense if the plaintiff is incapable of or incompetent to give consent. Someone who is unconscious or obviously intoxicated, for example, is incapable of giving consent. Consent will be implied, however, if emergency action is immediately necessary to save an incapacitated person's life, if no indication exists that he would have refused to give consent, and if a reasonable person would have consented under like circumstances. A patient's consent is implied, for example, when a doctor performs emergency surgery that is immediately necessary to save the patient.

Generally, if a plaintiff consents only because she is mistaken about some material fact, her consent will still be considered effective. If, however, the defendant either knows of or induces the plaintiff's mistake, the plaintiff's consent will be deemed ineffective. If the defendant, for example, induces the plaintiff to engage in sexual intercourse with him by staging what he knows to be a fake wedding ceremony, he will be liable for battery because her consent will be considered ineffective.

The question of mistaken consent most often arises in the context of medical cases in which the plaintiff alleges that the doctor did not adequately inform her about the risks involved in the proposed treatment. Generally, the courts consider consent to be ineffective if the doctor fails to disclose the consequences of a procedure that he or she knows will definitely follow from the treatment. If, however, the doctor simply fails to mention a minor risk that may or may not be a consequence of the treatment, most courts will consider the plaintiff's consent to be effective.

The courts are split in reference to the effectiveness of a plaintiff's consent to a criminal act. The majority of courts find such consent ineffective. A minority of courts and the Restatement (Second) consider the consent effective unless the crime is intended to protect a class of persons against their own poor judgment and the plaintiff is a member of that protected class. A defendant who commits statutory rape, for example, is liable regardless of the plaintiff's consent. Because the plaintiff is a member of the class the statute is intended to protect, she cannot give her consent.

Voluntariness of Consent

If a plaintiff consents only because she is under duress and that duress creates an immediate and serious threat to herself or another, her consent will be deemed involuntary. Threats of future harm and threats involving economic duress are generally not sufficient to render a plaintiff's consent involuntary. A plaintiff who agrees to have sex with the defendant because of his threat to blackmail her in the future cannot claim duress because the threat pertains to future action.

Scope of Consent

A defendant must not exceed the scope of the plaintiff's consent. A defendant who invades a plaintiff's interest in a way that substantially deviates from that consented to will be liable for his or her act. Suppose a plaintiff consents to gallbladder surgery but the surgeon decides to remove her appendix as well. Because the plaintiff's consent did not extend to her appendix, the doctor will be liable for battery. However, if the condition of the patient's appendix justified an emergency removal, the patient will be deemed to have implicitly consented to that operation. The issue of consent in the area of medical practice is largely academic today because most hospitals require patients to fill out extremely general consent forms, which, unless unduly vague, protect hospitals from liability.

■   PUTTING IT INTO PRACTICE 3.6   ☐

A patient who has had his larynx removed because of cancer allows the surgeon who removed the larynx to take photographs of him to record the progression of his tumor. The patient gives no written consent but implies through his actions that he is willing to comply with the surgeon's request. On the surgeon's last visit, he once again proceeds to take the patient's photograph, but the patient raises his fist and tries to move his head out of range of the camera. Does the patient's consent to the previous photographs entitle the surgeon to take the last photograph despite the patient's apparent resistance?

Self-Defense

In the area of self-defense two questions are generally raised. Was the defendant privileged to use force to defend herself and was the degree of force that she used reasonable? (The answers to these two questions will differ somewhat in the civil arena as compared to the criminal arena.) A person may defend herself against any threatened harmful or offensive bodily contact as well as any threatened confinement. Whether the threat posed is intentional or negligent does not matter. The defendant need not even actually be harmed to invoke this defense.

Defendant's Belief

The defendant must reasonably believe that a threat exists, even if he or she is wrong. This result is probably based on the idea that "self-preservation is the first law of nature." Suppose a police officer apprehends a suspect known to her to be armed and dangerous. If the suspect reaches into his pocket for what the officer mistakenly believes to be a gun and the officer shoots him, the officer will be deemed to have acted in self-defense so long as her mistaken belief is a reasonable one. If the officer were exceptionally timid or paranoid, unreasonably believed that the suspect was about to shoot her, and no objective facts supported her perception, she could not claim self-defense.

What Constitutes Reasonable Force?

A defendant may use only that force that is reasonably necessary to protect herself against a threatened harm. She cannot use force to defend herself against words alone unless those words are accompanied by some type of hostile act. Nor can she use force to protect herself against future harm. Any threat of harm must appear to the defendant to be imminent. Furthermore, she must reasonably believe that she has no reasonable alternative to the use of force to protect herself from the impending danger.

For obvious reasons a defendant may not claim self-defense if he uses force against someone who is helpless. If A takes a swing at B and in the process slips and falls flat on his back, rendering him incapacitated, B cannot take that opportunity to avenge himself. Nor can self-defense be used to justify any retaliation for a previously committed tort. If a small child throws a snowball at the defendant, hitting her in the eye, the defendant is not justified in using force to punish the child (Restatement (Second) of Torts § 63, illus. 4). In summary, the use of force is not considered reasonable if it is used against someone who is helpless, in response to a threat of future harm, in retaliation for a previously committed tort, or in response to words unaccompanied by a hostile act.

How much force a defendant may use depends on the degree of force necessary to prevent the impending harm. Suppose A threatens B with clenched fists. B cannot claim self-defense if she responds using a knife, because her response exceeds the amount of force necessary to protect herself. Furthermore, a defendant may not use deadly force (defined as that force likely to cause death or serious bodily injury) unless she is in danger of death or serious bodily harm herself (Restatement (Second) of Torts §§ 65–66). Consequently, someone threatened with rape or some other type of serious bodily harm may defend herself using deadly force, whereas someone threatened with trespass to chattels may not. This rule is based on an objective standard in that the conduct of the defendant is compared to that of a reasonable person under similar circumstances.

Defense of Home

A common question that arises in the area of self-defense pertains to the use of force when someone invades another's home. The oft-quoted advice that if someone shoots a person who is outside her house, she must drag the body inside in order to claim self-defense, is erroneous. All one need show is that she reasonably believed she was in imminent danger of death or serious bodily harm and that no lesser degree of force was sufficient to prevent the harm.

The courts are split, however, on whether a defendant has a duty to retreat. Some courts, giving homage to individual honor and dignity, allow a defendant to use deadly force even if she can safely retreat. Other courts, attaching more importance to the sanctity of human life, require a defendant to retreat if she can do so safely. Even the latter courts, however, do not require someone who is attacked in her own home to retreat. This result is apparently based on the precept that "one's home is one's castle."

Prevention of Felonies

According to the Restatement, deadly force may also be used to prevent certain types of felonies, such as robbery, kidnapping, and rape. The defendant must believe that the felony cannot otherwise be prevented and the type of harm threatened must involve death or serious bodily injury (Restatement (Second) of Torts § 143). Notice that the defendant in this case is entitled to use force even though he or she is not personally endangered.

Defense of Others

Reasonable force may be used to protect others, including complete strangers. To claim the privilege of defense of another, the defendant must reasonably believe that the circumstances would support a claim of self-defense and that his or her intervention is immediately necessary for the protection of the other person.

Problems arise when the defendant intervenes on behalf of another, mistakenly believing assistance is necessary. Suppose A sees B being tackled and injured by C and he intervenes on B's behalf. If it turns out that C is an undercover police officer attempting to arrest B, should A be able to claim the privilege of defense of another as long as he reasonably believed that B was in imminent danger? Most courts reason that the intervenor (A) "steps into the shoes of the person he has sought to champion (B)." If it turns out that the person being rescued is not privileged to act in self-defense, the intervenor is precluded from claiming such a privilege. A minority of courts, including the Restatement (Second), however, allow the intervenor to claim the privilege as long as he reasonably believes the person he is aiding would have been privileged to use self-defense.

PUTTING IT INTO PRACTICE 3.7

George is walking his date, Sandy, to the theater when a man suddenly lunges before them, wielding a knife, which he slashes menacingly at them. George grabs the gun that he carries in his belt holster and points it at the man. Can he lawfully shoot the man?

Suppose the attacker is mentally ill and likes to scare people but is actually quite harmless. If the "knife" is actually a plastic toy knife and incapable of causing harm, is George still justified in using deadly force to protect himself and Sandy?

Defense of Property

The same rationale used in defense of persons applies to defense of property. A property owner may use only that degree of force that is reasonably necessary to protect the property (some states, such as Texas, allow deadly force to be used to protect property). Furthermore, the owner must verbally insist that an intruder stop before he or she is justified in using force. An exception to this general rule is allowed if the defendant reasonably perceives that the request to stop will be useless or that the harm will occur immediately (Restatement (Second) of Torts § 77(c)). Beyond this an owner may not use deadly force to protect property unless she believes such force is immediately necessary to prevent death or serious bodily harm to herself or another or to prevent certain types of felonies.

Mechanical Devices

Property owners frustrated by frequent burglaries that the local police appear impotent to prevent sometimes turn to mechanical devices for protection. These devices can range from strings of barbed wire to spring guns, which are mechanically rigged guns designed to go off automatically when someone enters the premises. As a general rule, a property owner is entitled to use such a device only if she could use a similar degree of force if she herself were present when the intruder entered. Because such devices are usually considered deadly force, they may be used only to prevent death or serious bodily harm or the commission of certain felonies. A homeowner will be liable, therefore, if a trespasser is seriously injured by an electric fence erected by the homeowner. Because the owner would not be justified in using deadly force against the trespasser if she confronted the trespasser in person, she would not be justified in using a mechanical device that constituted deadly force.

The classic case of *Katko v. Briney,* 183 N.W.2d 657 (Iowa 1971), which you can read below, aptly illustrates the principle regarding the use of mechanical devices. In *Katko* the defendants owned an unoccupied, boarded-up farmhouse that had been broken into many times. To prevent further burglaries the defendants constructed a spring gun that was designed to discharge if a person entered the bedroom. The plaintiff, who broke into the house in an effort to steal bottles and jars that he believed to be antique, was severely injured when the gun went off. The court held that a property owner may not use deadly force against a trespasser unless that trespasser is endangering human life or committing some violent felony.

CASE

Katko v. Briney
183 N.W. 2d 657 (Iowa 1971)

MOORE, Chief Justice

The primary issue presented here is whether an owner may protect personal property in an unoccupied boarded-up farm house against trespassers and thieves by a spring gun capable of inflicting death or serious injury.

We are not here concerned with a man's right to protect his home and members of his family. Defendants' home was several miles from the scene of the incident to which we refer infra.

Plaintiff's action is for damages resulting from serious injury caused by a shot from a 20–gauge spring shotgun set by defendants in a bedroom of an old farm house which had been uninhabited for several years. Plaintiff and his companion, Marvin McDonough, had broken and entered the house to find and steal old bottles and dated fruit jars which they considered antiques.

At defendants' request plaintiff's action was tried to a jury consisting of residents of the community where defendants' property was located. The jury returned a verdict for plaintiff and against defendants for $20,000 actual and $10,000 punitive damages.

After careful consideration of defendants' motions for judgment notwithstanding the verdict and for new trial, the experienced and capable trial judge overruled them and entered judgment on the verdict. Thus we have this appeal by defendants.

I. In this action our review of the record as made by the parties in the lower court is for the correction of errors at law. We do not review actions at law de novo. Rule 334, Rules of Civil Procedure. Findings of fact by the jury are binding upon this court if supported by substantial evidence. Rule 344 (f), par. 1, R.C.P.

II. Most of the facts are not disputed. In 1957 defendant Bertha L. Briney inherited her parents' farm land in Mahaska and Monroe Counties. Included was an 80-acre tract in southwest Mahaska County where her grandparents and parents had lived. No one occupied the house thereafter. Her husband, Edward, attempted to care for the land. He kept no farm machinery thereon. The outbuildings became dilapidated.

For about 10 years, 1957 to 1967, there occurred a series of trespassing and housebreaking events with loss of some household items, the breaking of windows and 'messing up of the property in general'. The latest occurred June 8, 1967, prior to the event on July 16, 1967 herein involved.

Defendants through the years boarded up the windows and doors in an attempt to stop the intrusions. They had posted 'no trespass' signs on the land several years before 1967. The nearest one was 35 feet from the house. On June 11, 1967 defendants set 'a shotgun trap' in the north bedroom. After Mr. Briney cleaned and oiled his 20-gauge shotgun, the power of which he was well aware, defendants took it to the old house where they secured it to an iron bed with the barrel pointed at the bedroom door. It was rigged with wire from the doorknob to the gun's trigger so it would fire when the door was opened. Briney first pointed the gun so an intruder would be hit in the stomach but at Mrs. Briney's suggestion it was lowered to hit the legs. He admitted he did so 'because I was mad and tired of being tormented' but 'he did not intend to injure anyone'. He gave no explanation of why he used a loaded shell and set it to hit a person already in the house. Tin was nailed over the bedroom window. The spring gun could not be seen from the outside. No warning of its presence was posted.

Plaintiff lived with his wife and worked regularly as a gasoline station attendant in Eddyville, seven miles from the old house. He had observed it for several years while hunting in the area and considered it as being abandoned. He knew it had long been uninhabited. In 1967 the area around the house was covered with high weeds. Prior to July 16, 1967 plaintiff and McDonough had been to the premises and found several old bottles and fruit jars which they took and added to their collection of antiques. On the latter date about 9:30 p.m. they made a second trip to the Briney property. They entered the old house by removing a board from a porch window which was without glass. While McDonough was looking around the kitchen area plaintiff went to another part of the house. As he started to open the north bedroom door the shotgun went off striking him in the right leg above the ankle bone. Much of his leg, including part of the tibia, was blown away. Only by McDonough's assistance was plaintiff able to get out of the house and after crawling some distance was put in his vehicle and rushed to a

doctor and then to a hospital. He remained in the hospital 40 days.

Plaintiff's doctor testified he seriously considered amputation but eventually the healing process was successful. Some weeks after his release from the hospital plaintiff returned to work on crutches. He was required to keep the injured leg in a cast for approximately a year and wear a special brace for another year. He continued to suffer pain during this period.

There was undenied medical testimony plaintiff had a permanent deformity, a loss of tissue, and a shortening of the leg.

The record discloses plaintiff to trial time had incurred $710 medical expense, $2056.85 for hospital service, $61.80 for orthopedic service and $750 as loss of earnings. In addition thereto the trial court submitted to the jury the question of damages for pain and suffering and for future disability.

III. Plaintiff testified he knew he had no right to break and enter the house with intent to steal bottles and fruit jars therefrom. He further testified he had entered a plea of guilty to larceny in the nighttime of property of less than $20 value from a private building. He stated he had been fined $50 and costs and paroled during good behavior from a 60-day jail sentence. Other than minor traffic charges this was plaintiff's first brush with the law. On this civil case appeal it is not our prerogative to review the disposition made of the criminal charge against him.

IV. The main thrust of defendants' defense in the trial court and on this appeal is that 'the law permits use of a spring gun in a dwelling or warehouse for the purpose of preventing the unlawful entry of a burglar or thief'. They repeated this contention in their exceptions to the trial court's instructions 2, 5 and 6. They took no exception to the trial court's statement of the issues or to other instructions.

In the statement of issues the trial court stated plaintiff and his companion committed a felony when they broke and entered defendants' house. In instruction 2 the court referred to the early case history of the use of spring guns and stated under the law their use was prohibited except to prevent the commission of felonies of violence and where human life is in danger. The instruction included a statement breaking and entering is not a felony of violence.

Instruction 5 stated: 'You are hereby instructed that one may use reasonable force in the protection of his property, but such right is subject to the qualification that one may not use such means of force as will take human life or inflict great bodily injury. Such is the rule even though the injured party is a trespasser and is in violation of the law himself.'

Instruction 6 stated: 'An owner of premises is prohibited from willfully or intentionally injuring a trespasser by means of force that either takes life or inflicts great bodily injury; and therefore a person owning a premise is prohibited from setting out 'spring guns' and like dangerous devices which will likely take life or inflict great bodily injury, for the purpose of harming trespassers. The fact that the trespasser may be acting in violation of the law does not change the rule. The only time when such conduct of setting a 'spring gun' or a like dangerous device is justified would be when the trespasser was committing a felony of violence or a felony punishable by death, or where the trespasser was endangering human life by his act.'

Instruction 7, to which defendants made no objection or exception, stated: 'To entitle the plaintiff to recover for compensatory damages, the burden of proof is upon him to establish by a preponderance of the evidence each and all of the following propositions:

'1. That defendants erected a shotgun trap in a vacant house on land owned by defendant, Bertha L. Briney, on or about June 11, 1967, which fact was known only by them, to protect household goods from trespassers and thieves.

'2. That the force used by defendants was in excess of that force reasonably necessary and which persons are entitled to use in the protection of their property.

'3. That plaintiff was injured and damaged and the amount thereof.

'4. That plaintiff's injuries and damages resulted directly from the discharge of the shotgun trap which was set and used by defendants.'

The overwhelming weight of authority, both textbook and case law, supports the trial court's statement of the applicable principles of law.

Prosser on Torts, Third Edition, pages 116–118, states: '* * * the law has always placed a higher value upon human safety than upon mere rights in property, it is the accepted rule that there is no privilege to use any force calculated to cause death or serious bodily injury to repel the threat to land or chattels, unless there is also such a threat to the defendant's personal safety as to justify a self-defense. * * * spring guns and other mankilling devices are not justifiable against a mere trespasser, or even a petty thief. They are privileged only against those upon whom the landover, if he were present in person would be free to inflict injury of the same kind.'

Restatement of Torts, section 85, page 180, states: 'The value of human life and limb, not only to the individual concerned but also to society, so outweighs the interest of a possessor of land in excluding from it those whom he is not willing to admit thereto that a possessor of land has, as is stated in s 79, no privilege to use force intended or likely to cause death or serious harm against another whom the possessor sees about to enter his premises or meddle with his chattel, unless the intrusion threatens death or serious bodily harm to the occupiers or users of the premises. * * * A possessor of land cannot do indirectly and by a mechanical device that which, were he present, he could not do immediately and in person: Therefore, he cannot gain a privilege to install, for the purpose of protecting his land from intrusions harmless to the lives and limbs of the occupiers or users of it, a mechanical device whose only purpose is to inflict death or serious harm upon such as may intrude, by giving notice of his intention to inflict, by mechanical means and indirectly, harm which he could not, even after request, inflict directly were he present.'

In Volume 2, Harper and James, *The Law of Torts,* section 27.3, pages 1440, 1441, this is found: 'The possessor of land may not arrange his premises intentionally so as to cause death or serious bodily harm to a trespasser. The possessor may of course take some steps to repel a trespass. If he is present he may use force to do so, by only that amount which is reasonably necessary to effect the repulse. Moreover if the trespass threatens harm to property only—even a theft of property—the possessor would not be privileged to use deadly force, he may not arrange his premises so that such force will be inflicted by mechanical means. If he does, he will be liable even to a thief who is injured by such device. . . .

In *Hooker v. Miller,* 37 Iowa 613, we held defendant vineyard owner liable for damages resulting from a spring gun shot although plaintiff was a trespasser and there to steal grapes. At pages 614, 615, this statement is made: 'This court has held that a mere trespass against property other than a dwelling is not a sufficient justification to authorize the use of a deadly weapon by the owner in its defense; and that if death results in such a case it will be murder, though the killing be actually necessary to prevent the trespass. *The State v. Vance,* 17 Iowa 138.' At page 617 this court said: '(T)respassers and other inconsiderable violators of the law are not to be visited by barbarous punishments or prevented by inhuman inflictions of bodily injuries.'

The facts in *Allison v. Fiscus,* 156 Ohio 120, 110 N.E.2d 237, 44 A.L.R.2d 369, decided in 1951, are very similar to the case at bar. There plaintiff's right to damages was recognized for injuries received when he feloniously broke a door latch and started to enter defendant's warehouse with intent to steal. As he entered a trap of two sticks of dynamite buried under the doorway by defendant owner was set off and plaintiff seriously injured. The court held the question whether a particular trap was justified as a use of reasonable and necessary force against a trespasser engaged in the commission of a felony should have been submitted to the jury. The Ohio Supreme court recognized plaintiff's right to recover punitive or exemplary damages in addition to compensatory damages.

In *Starkey v. Dameron,* 96 Colo. 459, 45 P.2d 172, plaintiff was allowed to recover compensatory and punitive damages for injuries received from a spring gun which defendant filling station operator had concealed in an automatic gasoline pump as protection against thieves.

In *Wilder v. Gardner,* 39 Ga.App. 608, 147 S.E. 911, judgment for plaintiff for injuries received from a spring gun which defendant had set, the court said: 'A person in control of premises may be responsible even to a trespasser for injuries caused by pitfalls, mantraps, or other like contrivances so dangerous in character as to imply a disregard of consequences or a willingness to inflict injury.'

In *Phelps v. Hamlett,* Tex.Civ.App., 207 S.W. 425, defendant rigged a bomb inside his outdoor theater so that if anyone came through the door the bomb would explode. The court reversed plaintiff's recovery because of an incorrect instruction but at page 426 said: 'While the law authorizes an owner to protect his property by such reasonable means as he may find to be necessary, yet considerations of humanity preclude him from setting out, even on his own property, traps and devices dangerous to the life and limb of those whose appearance and presence may be reasonably anticipated, even though they may be trespassers.'

In *United Zinc & Chemical Co. v. Britt,* 258 U.S. 268, 275, 42 S.Ct. 299, 66 L.Ed. 615, 617, the court states: 'The liability for spring guns and mantraps arises from the fact that the defendant has * * * expected the trespasser and prepared an injury that is no more justified than if he had held the gun and fired it.'

In addition to civil liability many jurisdictions hold a land owner criminally liable for serious injuries or homicide caused by spring guns or other set devices. See *State v. Childers,* 133 Ohio 508, 14 N.E.2d 767 (melon thief shot by spring gun); *Pierce v. Commonwealth,* 135 Va. 635, 115 S.E. 686 (policeman killed by spring gun when he opened unlocked front door of defendant's shoe repair shop); *State v. Marfaudille,* 48 Wash. 117, 92 P. 939 (murder conviction for death from spring gun set in a trunk); *State v. Beckham,* 306 Mo. 566, 267 S.W. 817 (boy killed by spring gun attached to window of defendant's chili stand); *State v. Green,* 118 S.C. 279, 110 S.E. 145, 19 A.L.R. 1431 (intruder shot by spring gun when he broke and entered vacant house. Manslaughter conviction of owner-affirmed); *State v. Barr,* 11 Wash. 481, 39 P. 1080 (murder conviction affirmed for death of an intruder into a boarded up cabin in which owner had set a spring gun).

In Wisconsin, Oregon and England the use of spring guns and similar devices is specifically made unlawful by statute. . . .

The legal principles stated by the trial court in instructions 2, 5 and 6 are well established and supported by the authorities cited and quoted supra. There is no merit in defendants' objections and exceptions thereto. Defendants' various motions based on the same reasons stated in exceptions to instructions were properly overruled.

* * *

Study and careful consideration of defendants' contentions on appeal reveal no reversible error.

Affirmed.

Media reports of this case reflected that the entry was into the Brineys' home rather than into an abandoned farmhouse. As a result, public outcry regarding the decision resulted in the introduction of "Briney Bills" in several state legislatures. These bills legalized the use of any means necessary to protect one's person, family, or property from intrusion.

If an owner intends to use some nondeadly mechanical device, such as barbed wire, he must post some type of warning that will put others on notice that the device is present. Even a warning will not suffice, however, in the case of a mechanical device that constitutes the use of deadly force. No warning of the spring gun, for example, would have relieved the defendants in *Katko* of liability.

[You may find it interesting to know that the Brineys were forced to sell 80 acres of their 120-acre farm in order to satisfy the judgment in this case.

Because no bids above the minimum price of $10,000 were made, three neighbors purchased the land for a dollar more, expecting to hold it for the Brineys until they won their appeal. After the Brineys lost their appeal, the neighbors leased the land back to them for enough money to pay their taxes and the interest on the money they had borrowed. Years later the neighbors decided to sell the property; one of them bought it for $16,000 and sold it to his son for $16,500. Briney and Katko then joined together and jointly sued the neighbors. Just before the case came to trial it was settled for a large enough sum that the Brineys were able to pay the remainder of their judgment to Katko.]

PUTTING IT INTO PRACTICE 3.8

1. Summarize the facts that are critical to an understanding of the *Katko* case.
2. According to Prosser, why is there no privilege to use force intended to cause death or serious physical injury in order to protect property? Under what conditions may such force be used?
3. Explain this: A possessor of land cannot do indirectly what he could not if he were present.
4. Summarize the theme of the civil cases cited by the *Katko* court.
5. Can a landowner be held criminally liable for serious injuries or homicide caused by a spring gun?

Regaining Possession of Chattels

Under limited circumstances a property owner may use force to regain possession of chattels taken from her by someone else. Because the owner becomes an aggressor by her use of force, she is not given the same latitude by the courts as one who is taking a less aggressive stance in defending her possession of chattels.

Reasonable Force

To claim this defense, the owner must first show that she used reasonable force in securing the chattels. Deadly force is never allowable unless justified under the doctrine of self-defense.

Property Wrongfully Taken

Second, the property must have been wrongfully taken. If the owner willingly gives up possession and is later entitled to repossession of the property, she cannot use force to regain it. A seller who attempts to repossess a stereo unit sold to a consumer who has missed several payments cannot break into the consumer's house to regain possession. If, however, the consumer uses fraud to gain possession and the seller promptly discovers the fraud, she may use reasonable force to recover possession (Restatement (Second) of Torts §§ 101(1)(a) and 106). No greater force than that required can be used and deadly force is impermissible unless necessary for the defendant to protect herself against ensuing violence.

Fresh Pursuit

Third, the property owner must be in "fresh pursuit." Therefore, if the owner delays for a substantial period of time before attempting to get her property back, she may no longer use reasonable force to secure possession. Instead she must turn to the courts for redress. Although the courts have never clearly defined the meaning of *fresh pursuit*, it appears that prompt and persistent efforts must be made to reclaim the property. Owners are privileged to use force to recapture property only because of the concern for the delay created by the cumbersome, time-consuming legal process. If, however, they fail to make timely efforts to regain possession, they will be relegated to the legal process.

Mistake

Any mistakes on the part of the owner will cause her to lose the privilege. If, for example, she mistakenly (albeit reasonably) believes that someone is in possession of her goods, she will not be justified in using force to retake the goods. Similarly, if she reasonably but mistakenly believes that force is necessary to reclaim the goods, she will lose the privilege. The owner is expected to bear the consequences of any mistakes.

Detention of Shoplifters

The issue of recapture of goods most frequently occurs in the context of merchants detaining suspected shoplifters. As discussed earlier in this chapter, many courts have granted merchants the privilege of temporarily detaining any person they reasonably suspect of shoplifting. As you will recall, the detention must be relatively short in duration and the merchant or its agent must not attempt to coerce a payment or a confession from the suspect, nor may the merchant or its agent purport to arrest the suspect.

PUTTING IT INTO PRACTICE 3.9

Read over the facts in the Putting It Into Practice question 3.2 for false imprisonment and consider the following additional facts:

The man being interrogated asked to call his employer and/or his wife and his request was denied.

One of the store detectives walked around the room repeatedly slapping his gun during the investigation.

After more than an hour of questioning, the detectives asked the man to sign a civil release form, threatening him with jail if he refused to sign. After he reluctantly signed the form, he was told not to mention this incident to anyone.

Did the detectives exceed their authority in their detention of the suspected shoplifter?

Reentry on Land

The issue of reentry on land typically occurs in the case of a landlord who attempts to forcibly evict a tenant who overstays his lease (referred to as a *holdover tenant*). The majority of American courts do not permit the use of force by landlords. Landlords, it is felt, should be restricted to the legal process to resolve these disputes because the law typically provides procedures allowing for expeditious resolutions. In short, landlords are discouraged from taking the law into their own hands. A landlord may, however, enter the land if she does so without force. Furthermore, if a provision in the lease allows for reentry through the use of force, some courts will uphold a forcible entry as long as only reasonable force is used.

Necessity

In the privileges discussed thus far, the defendant has prevailed in her cause of action because of some wrongdoing on the plaintiff's part. In some circumstances, however, the defendant is privileged not because the plaintiff has done anything wrong but because of unusual circumstances that justify the defendant's actions. The privilege of **necessity** justifies the defendant's harming of the plaintiff's property in emergencies. For example, a person who trespasses on another's land in an attempt to avoid a criminal attack can claim the privilege of necessity.

Distinction Between Public and Private Necessity

Cases involving necessity fall into two categories: public necessity and private necessity. The conduct of a defendant protecting only her own interests or those of a few private citizens falls into the realm of *private necessity.* By contrast, if the class of persons being protected is the public as a whole or a substantial number of persons, the privilege is referred to as *public necessity.* The only reason for distinguishing between these two kinds of necessities is that the defendant does not have to pay for damages caused in cases of public necessity but is required to do so in cases involving private necessity.

Public Necessity

The privilege of public necessity arises when interference with the land or chattels of another is required to avert a disaster to the community. In one case, for example, the defendant sprayed fire-retardant chemicals on the plaintiff's land while fighting a forest fire that threatened the entire county. When the plaintiff sued for the damage incurred by his trees, the court permitted the defendant to raise the privilege of necessity (*Stocking v. Johnson Flying Service,* 387 P.2d 312 (Mont. 1963)). The defendant who successfully claims the privilege of public necessity will not be required to reimburse the plaintiff for the damages he suffers. Although the common law does not require the community as a whole to compensate the victim, several states have enacted statutes that provide for such compensation.

Private Necessity

A person may claim the privilege for private necessity when she damages the property of another to prevent injury to herself or her property. The privilege also extends to the protection of a third person or the property of that person. Furthermore, the privilege requires that no less damaging way of preventing the harm exist. In contrast to cases of public necessity, private necessity applies even when the danger is not severe. A driver, for example, can claim the privilege of private necessity if she is forced to trespass on private land because the public roadway on which she is traveling is obstructed and the only conceivable path of avoidance is through the adjoining land of a private owner.

Damages

In determining whether a privilege exists, the harm to the plaintiff's property must be weighed against the severity and likelihood of the danger the defendant is seeking to avoid (Restatement (Second) of Torts § 263, cmt. d). If the defendant causes no substantial harm to the plaintiff's property, the privilege of private necessity is a complete defense. If, however, the defendant causes actual damage to the plaintiff's property, the privilege will be limited and the defendant will be required to pay for the damages caused. Suppose a man is lost in the forest and comes upon someone's cabin. If he enters the cabin and takes food because he is starving, he will not be liable for the trespass. He will, however, be required to compensate the owner of the cabin for the food he takes.

One of the benefits of invoking the privilege of private necessity is that the person whose property has been harmed has no right to use reasonable force to prevent the exercise of the privilege. Furthermore, one who resorts to such retaliatory force will be liable for any damages she causes (Restatement (Second) of Torts § 263, cmt. b).

PUTTING IT INTO PRACTICE 3.10 □

A fireman arrives at the scene of a raging blaze and removes Maryann's lawfully parked car from the highway to gain access to a fire hydrant. Is the fireman privileged to move the car? Is he liable to Maryann for any unavoidable damages to her vehicle?

Maryann's next-door neighbor, Liz, is bleeding profusely after being hit by flying debris from chemical-containing cans that exploded in the fire. Liz asks Maryann to use her scarf as a tourniquet until the ambulance arrives. Maryann refuses because the scarf is an heirloom and says she will look for something else to use as a tourniquet. Afraid that she will bleed to death before Maryann finds something acceptable, Liz grabs Maryann's scarf. Is Liz privileged to do so? Will she be liable to Maryann for the bloodstains on the scarf?

SUMMARY

An intentional tort requires that the tortfeasor intend or have a desire to bring about a particular consequence. The fact that the defendant wishes no harm to the plaintiff has no bearing on whether he acted intentionally. If he knows with substantial certainty that a result will occur, he will be liable for an intentional tort. Under the transferred intent doctrine, a tortfeasor's intent with respect to one person may be transferred to the person who is actually injured.

The intentional infliction of a harmful or offensive contact upon a person's body or anything attached to or identified with the body is referred to as *battery.* The plaintiff need not suffer actual pain or bodily injury nor even be aware of the contact at the time it occurs.

If a tortfeasor intentionally causes an apprehension of a harmful or offensive contact, he commits assault. Assault requires an intent either to commit a battery or to frighten the plaintiff. The victim of assault, unlike the victim of battery, must be aware of the threatened contact. The plaintiff need not actually fear that he will be harmed but he must believe that the defendant has the present ability to carry out the threatened contact.

The tortfeasor who intentionally confines another commits the tort of false imprisonment. The plaintiff must be aware of his confinement at the time it occurs

but is not required to subject himself to any risk of harm in order to extricate himself from his confinement. As with assault and battery, the doctrine of transferred intent is applicable and threats of harm must be imminent.

The tort of infliction of mental distress can be committed either intentionally or recklessly, but in either case the defendant's conduct must be "extreme and outrageous." The peculiar characteristics of the plaintiff may be taken into consideration in evaluating the defendant's conduct. Generally, the doctrine of transferred intent is not applicable although some exceptions exist. A plaintiff must prove she actually suffered severe emotional distress and in some courts must prove she experienced some kind of actual physical harm.

A person who enters or wrongfully remains on another's land commits the tort of trespass. The defendant's only intent must be to make physical contact with the plaintiff's land. He need not intend any harm to the plaintiff's property nor be aware that any harm might occur. An indirect invasion of the land is sufficient, as is an invasion of the airspace above or the surface below the plaintiff's property. A defendant who refuses to leave the plaintiff's land when permission has been terminated also commits trespass.

Intentional interference with the plaintiff's use or possession of chattels constitutes trespass to chattels. As with trespass, the only intent required is the intent to interfere. The defendant need not intend to cause harm to the property. As with trespass, the mistaken belief that the property is his own is not a defense. In contrast with trespass, the plaintiff is required to prove actual harm.

If the defendant's interference with the plaintiff's property is so substantial that the defendant must compensate the plaintiff for the full value of the property, the defendant has committed the tort of conversion. The defendant need not desire to harm the plaintiff's property. With trespass to chattels, the defendant has a right to return the goods to mitigate the plaintiff's damages, but the defendant in a conversion action is required to pay the full value of the property.

One of the defenses that can be raised in response to an intentional tort is consent. If a plaintiff implicitly or explicitly consents to the defendant's intentional interference, the defendant is not liable for his conduct. Consent is determined by objective manifestations of the plaintiff but can be inferred from custom. The plaintiff must be capable of giving consent and must do so voluntarily. If a defendant exceeds the scope of the plaintiff's consent, he will be liable for his conduct.

A defendant may use reasonable force to protect himself against threatened harmful or offensive bodily contact or threatened confinement. He cannot raise the defense in response to threats of future harm or when he is threatened with words alone, unless those words are accompanied by some kind of hostile act. Deadly force may be used only in response to a threat of death or serious bodily injury. A defendant who uses force to protect against the invasion of his home must show that he faced a threat of death or serious bodily harm and that no lesser degree of force was sufficient. The courts are split on whether a defendant has a duty to retreat before resorting to force.

If the circumstances would support a claim of self-defense and the defendant's intervention is immedi-ately necessary for the protection of a third person, a defendant may use reasonable force to protect another. If the person being rescued would not be privileged to act in self-defense, the defendant, according to most courts, will be precluded from claiming the privilege. A minority of courts, however, allow the privilege as long as the defendant reasonably believes that the person he is aiding would have been privileged to use self-defense.

A property owner may use only that degree of force that is reasonably necessary to protect his property. He must first verbally insist that an intruder stop unless it reasonably appears that the request to stop will be useless or that the harm will occur immediately. Mechanical devices used to protect property are generally considered deadly force and may be used only to prevent death, serious bodily harm, or the commission of certain felonies.

In some circumstances a property owner may use force to regain possession of chattels. Reasonable force is required and deadly force is never allowed unless justified under the doctrine of self-defense. Furthermore, the property must have been wrongfully taken and the property owner must be in fresh pursuit. If the property owner is mistaken in any way, he will lose the privilege even if his mistake is a reasonable one.

The use of force to gain reentry on land is usually not allowed by the courts. Landlords, who most frequently argue that force is necessary to evict a tenant, are generally restricted to the legal process to resolve their disputes.

A defendant who is justified in harming the plaintiff's property because of an emergency may claim the privilege of either public necessity or private necessity. Interference required to avert a disaster to the community is classified as a public necessity; interference necessary to prevent injury to a few private citizens is classified as a private necessity. In a case of public necessity the defendant is not required to reimburse the plaintiff for the damages he suffers.

PRACTICE POINTERS

Notice the key elements of the following complaint. The *caption* at the beginning of the complaint contains the names of the court, plaintiffs, and defendants. The caption also indicates that the type of pleading involved is a "complaint." Under the "General Allegations" the jurisdictional element of the complaint is satisfied by showing where the cause of action occurred and where the defendants are doing business. The "General Allegations" also contain a brief summary of the facts supporting the cause of action. Each "count" identifies a cause of action (intentional infliction of emotional distress and conversion) and the relief being sought (general, special, and punitive damages).

J. Stanley Edwards
P. O. Box 41033-371
Phoenix, Arizona 85000
Phone: (602) 466-9800
Fax: (602) 466-9900

State Bar No. 004190

Attorney for Plaintiffs

IN THE SUPERIOR COURT OF THE STATE OF ARIZONA
IN AND FOR THE COUNTY OF YAVAPAI

Morris Feldman and Sandra Feldman, husband and wife	)))	No. CV 97-00123
Plaintiffs	)	
vs.	))	**COMPLAINT** (Tort—Non-Motor Vehicle) (Conversion/Intentional Infliction of Emotional Distress)
Holly Hock Capital L.L.C., Mercy Limited Partnership, Sam Snow and Jane Doe Snow, husband and wife,	)))))	
Defendants,	))	

Continued on next page

Plaintiffs, by and through counsel undersigned, for their causes of action against the defendants, allege as follows:

GENERAL ALLEGATIONS

1. That plaintiffs are residents of Yavapai County, Arizona, and the cause of action referred to herein occurred in and is payable in Yavapai County, Arizona.

2. That defendant Holly Hock Capital L.L.C. is transacting business in Yavapai County, Arizona, and is or may be liable to plaintiffs as owner and/or as operator of the premises where plaintiff Morris Feldman was employed.

3. That defendant Mercy Limited Partnership is transacting business in Yavapai County, Arizona, and is or may be liable to plaintiffs as owner and/or operator of the premises where plaintiff Morris Feldman was employed.

4. That defendants Sam Snow and Jane Doe Snow are husband and wife; that the actions alleged herein on the part of Sam Snow were done on behalf of the marital community and as Managing Member of defendant Holly Hock Capital L.L.C., which upon information and belief, is the General Partner of defendant Mercy Limited Partnership; defendants Snow are liable to plaintiffs as perpetrators of the acts alleged; that leave of the court is requested to substitute Jane Doe Snow's true name when it becomes known to plaintiffs.

5. That on or about March 4, 1997, defendant Sam Snow entered the residence furnished plaintiffs as part of their employment with defendants, for reasons unknown to plaintiffs and without plaintiffs' permission; that later that day it was discovered by plaintiffs that some of the rent moneys collected by plaintiffs for the benefit of defendants, and which were in the residence prior to defendant Snow's unauthorized entrance, were missing.

6. That on March 15, 1997, defendants terminated plaintiff's employment.

7. That on or about March 23, 1997, the defendant removed and retained various items of personal property belonging to plaintiffs; that despite demand for return of plaintiffs' property defendants have refused to return the property to plaintiffs; that the acts of defendants represent conversion of plaintiffs' property.

8. That on or about March 23, 1997, defendants wrongfully attempted to force plaintiffs to vacate the premises in which they resided.

9. That the items converted by defendants include:

   1. scroll type jig-saw
   2. hand saws—2
   3. Skilsaw blades—approx. 12
   4. leaf rake
   5. box of drill bits, spacers, etc.
   6. drawer of plumbing supplies, solder gun and supplies
   7. framing square

Continued on next page

■   PRACTICE POINTERS—Continued   ☐

   8. caulking gun
   9. red and white Coleman cooler
  10. red dolly (belonging to Hubbell Apartment complex)
  11. aluminum ladder
  12. claw hammer
  13. various miscellaneous items

10. That the acts of defendants were intentional and done with the express purpose of humiliating plaintiffs in an attempt to wrongfully force them from their residence.

11. That as a result of defendants' acts plaintiffs have suffered extreme embarrassment and mental distress.

COUNT I

1. Plaintiffs reallege the allegations set forth in paragraphs 1 through 11.
2. That the acts alleged establish a cause of action for intentional infliction of emotional distress.
3. That the acts alleged show defendants acted with the requisite mental state to support an award of punitive damages.

  WHEREFORE, plaintiffs demand judgment against defendants, jointly and severally, as follows:

1. For general damages in an amount to be shown by the evidence;
2. For special damages in an amount to be shown by the evidence;
3. For punitive damages in an amount to be shown by the evidence;
4. For plaintiffs' costs incurred herein; and
5. For such other and further relief as the Court deems just and equitable.

COUNT II

1. Plaintiffs reallege the allegations set forth in paragraphs 1 through 11.
2. That the acts alleged establish a cause of action for conversion.
3. That the acts alleged show defendants acted with the requisite mental state to support an award of punitive damages.

  WHEREFORE, plaintiffs demand judgment against defendants, jointly and severally, as follows:

1. For general damages in an amount to be shown by the evidence;
2. For special damages in an amount to be shown by the evidence;
3. For punitive damages in an amount to be shown by the evidence;
4. For plaintiffs' costs incurred herein; and
5. For such other and further relief as the Court deems just and equitable.

  DATED this 12th day of April, 1997.

J. STANLEY EDWARDS
Attorney for Plaintiffs

1. What intentional torts were committed in the hypothetical scenario given at the beginning of this chapter? What defenses could have been raised by each of the actors who committed a tort?

2. In December, 1941, the United States Army destroyed vital parts of the plant of an oil company in Manila to prevent it from falling into the hands of the advancing Japanese Army. Was this conduct privileged? *United States v. Caltex, Inc.*, 344 U.S. 149 (1952).

3. An eighty-six-year-old member of a Catholic order experiences cardiac arrest subsequent to a hernia operation. Previously he had expressed a desire not to have his life artificially prolonged by use of a respirator if he were ever to become permanently unconscious. Should his request be granted? *In re Storar*, 420 N.E.2d 64 (N.Y. 1981).

4. Defendant sees Plaintiff break into a vending machine. He yells at Plaintiff to stop, drop his weapon, and wait for the police but Plaintiff and his companions continue to run. The thieves are carrying a money box, a tire tool, and a lug wrench. When they are seventy to seventy-five yards away Defendant fires three shots, one of which strikes Plaintiff in the back. Should Defendant be held liable? *Bray v. Isbell*, 458 So. 2d 594 (La. Ct. App. 1984), *cert. denied*, 462 So. 2d 210 (La. 1985).

5. Plaintiff is injured by Defendant's vicious dog when he trespasses on Defendant's land. Defendant has posted a sign warning outsiders of the presence of the dog. Should Defendant be held liable? *Hood v. Waldrum*, 434 S.W.2d 94 (Tenn. Ct. App. 1968).

6. Plaintiff takes a can of hair spray to the checkout counter but after she stands in line for several minutes decides to leave and puts the hair spray on a counter inside the store. After she leaves the store she is accosted by a security guard, who identifies herself by displaying a badge. When asked by the guard where the hair spray is, Plaintiff asks, "What hair spray?" At this point the security guard flips open Plaintiff's jacket and says,

"The hair spray you took out of the store." At the security guard's request, Plaintiff returns to the store and shows the guard where she put the can of hair spray. The security guard then just walks away. Is Defendant store entitled to detain Plaintiff to investigate the alleged shoplifting? Would Defendant store have been justified in using force had Plaintiff actually taken the can of hair spray out of the store? *Moore v. Pay'N Save Corp.*, 581 P.2d 159 (Wash. Ct. App. 1973).

7. What should the defendants in each of the following cases be found liable for?

a. Auctioneer sells stolen goods. *Judkins v. Sadler-MacNeil*, 376 P.2d 837 (Wash. 1962).

b. Plaintiff and Defendant are involved in an action to quiet title. Before any judgment is rendered Defendant forcibly breaks into the premises, which are occupied by Plaintiff, posts "No Trespassing" signs, and changes the locks. Defendant then removes Plaintiff's personal property and puts it in storage. Defendant informs Plaintiff that he can secure possession of his personal property by contacting his attorney but Plaintiff makes no response. Defendant never uses the goods during the four months they are kept in storage. *Zaslow v. Kroenert*, 176 P.2d 1 (Cal. 1946).

c. Plaintiff owns a tract of land on a hill. Defendant discovers the entrance to a cave on the land adjoining his own. The cave extends a considerable distance under Plaintiff's land. Defendant develops the cave, advertises it, and conducts tours through it. *Edwards v. Sims*, 232 Ky. 791, 24 S.W.2d 619 (1929).

d. A man touches a woman in an indecent manner. *Skousen v. Nidy*, 367 P.2d 248 (Ariz. 1961)

e. Defendant threatens Plaintiff with an unloaded gun. *Allen v. Hannaford*, 244 P. 700 (Wash. 1926).

f. Plaintiff is an eccentric old woman who believes that a pot of gold is buried in her back yard and is constantly digging for it. Defendants deliberately bury a pot filled with rocks and dirt in a place where they know she will dig it up. When she does so they escort her in a mock triumphal procession to City Hall where she opens the pot under circumstances causing her extreme public humiliation. *Nickerson v. Hodges,* 84 So. 37 (La. 1920).

g. Defendant, a police officer, observes Plaintiff's dog running loose in violation of the city's "dog leash" ordinance. When Defendant demands that Plaintiff produce her driver's license or go to jail, she refuses to do so, although she does volunteer her name and address. Defendant arrests her, charging her with a violation of the dog leash ordinance. *Enright v. Groves,* 567 P.2d 851 (Colo. Ct. App. 1977).

KEY TERMS

Assault
Intentional causing of an apprehension of harmful or offensive contact.

Battery
Intentional infliction of a harmful or offensive contact upon a person.

Chattels
Personal property.

Conversion
Substantial interference with another's property to the extent that justice demands payment for the full value of the property.

False imprisonment
Intentional confinement of another.

Intentional tort
Tort in which the tortfeasor intends to bring about a particular consequence or knows with substantial certainty that a result will occur.

Necessity
Privilege that justifies the defendant's harming of the plaintiff's property in an effort to prevent great harm to the defendant or others.

Transferred intent doctrine
Intent with respect to one person (or tort) is transferred to another person (or tort).

Trespass to chattels
Intentional interference with another's use or possession of chattels.

Trespass to land
Intentionally entering or wrongfully remaining on another's land.

Part Two

WHAT TO SUE FOR

CHAPTER

4

Negligence: An Overview

CHAPTER TOPICS

Definition of Negligence
Duty
Breach of Duty
Causation
Damages
Function of Judge and Jury
Application

CHAPTER OBJECTIVES

In this chapter you will learn to:
- Recognize the elements of negligence, which include duty, breach of duty, causation, and damages
- Recognize the concepts of negligence per se, res ipsa loquitur, and objective versus subjective standards
- Classify damages
- Recognize the mechanics of proving a case in terms of burdens of proof and functions of the judge and jury

One beautiful summer afternoon Jonathan and Teddy, both age six, were engaged in a particularly rollicking game of football in the backyard of Teddy's house. In an effort to emulate the quarterback hero of his fantasies, Jonathan took aim at Teddy and catapulted the ball into the air. Unfortunately, his aim was off and the ball landed in the backyard of Teddy's neighbors, Mr. and Mrs. Baxter. The Baxter backyard was surrounded by a six-foot wooden fence. Undeterred by this obstacle between him and his ball, Teddy attempted unsuccessfully to scale the fence. Jonathan, who was two months older than Teddy and, therefore, proportionately wiser, suggested that they try the gate to the yard.

Teddy knew that the Baxters always kept the gate locked and he also remembered that he had been warned repeatedly by both the Baxters and his parents that he should never enter the Baxter yard without supervision. Jonathan urged him to try the gate anyway but Teddy was hesitant. Other than his parents' and the Baxters' admonitions, he was circumspect about entering the yard because of the presence of Gertrude, the Baxters' German shepherd. Gertrude and Teddy had a somewhat strained relationship because Teddy, in some of his less enlightened moments, had taken a certain perverse pleasure in provoking Gertrude into a barking frenzy by teasing her through the gate. He was reluctant to test her capacity for forgiveness, but, egged on by Jonathan, he tried the gate latch and found, much to his surprise, that it was unlocked. Hesitantly, he opened the gate and peered inside. With Gertrude nowhere in sight he bolted across the yard to retrieve the ball.

Gertrude, her hearing somewhat impaired by advanced age, was deeply immersed in canine daydreams and was oblivious to Teddy's activities. Because of this Teddy might have escaped undetected had he not stubbed his toe on a sprinkler and let out a loud yell. The slumbering Gertrude, awakened by Teddy's cries, sprang to her feet. Somewhat disoriented but drawing on her instincts as a guard dog, Gertrude leaped off the porch in the direction of the unknown intruder. When she was within lunging distance of the now-panicked Teddy, vague memories of loathing filtered into Gertrude's consciousness as she began to recall the many indignities she had endured as a result of Teddy's tormenting.

Goaded by these memories, as well as her instinctual drive to protect her domain, Gertrude took aim for the hapless Teddy. When Teddy felt Gertrude grab hold of one of his pant legs he screamed in terror and tried desperately to kick Gertrude away. Incensed by the pummeling she received from Teddy, Gertrude plunged her teeth deeper, piercing Teddy's flesh. Teddy's continual thrashing about only made Gertrude more determined to maintain her viselike grip on Teddy's leg.

Meanwhile, Jonathan, who was a spectator to this whole drama, valiantly attempted to rescue his friend by pelting Gertrude with rocks he found in the Baxters' driveway. Unfortunately, the sting of the rocks further enraged Gertrude and, not realizing their source, she reinforced her grip on Teddy's leg.

Drawn by Jonathan's pleas for help and Teddy's screams of terror, a passerby, Mr. Goodright, came running into the Baxters' backyard. Immediately sizing up the situation, Mr. Goodright began kicking at Gertrude with all his might to induce her to release Teddy. Gertrude, stunned by his blows, let loose of Teddy to attack the object that was causing her pain. Seizing this opportunity to escape, Teddy dragged himself toward the gate and Jonathan pulled him to the safety of the driveway.

The courageous Mr. Goodright now pitted his wits against 120 pounds of wrath. Gertrude, enraged by the kicks she had received, lashed out wildly and caught Mr. Goodright's right hand. Pummeling Gertrude's head with his free arm, Mr. Goodright struggled desperately to free his hand from Gertrude's jaws.

The duo might have continued this struggle until one of them collapsed from exhaustion but, as fate would have it, Mr. Baxter arrived home early from work. As he drove in and caught sight of the fracas taking place in his backyard, he vaulted out of his car, yelling at Gertrude as he ran. When her master's commands finally penetrated her consciousness, Gertrude released her prey.

But the damage had already been wrought. Both Teddy and Mr. Goodright were bleeding profusely from their wounds and Teddy, his attention no longer diverted by the combat between Mr. Goodright and Gertrude, was beginning to become painfully aware of the full extent of his injuries. Both Mr. Goodright and Teddy sustained serious injuries from their battles with Gertrude.

Teddy would bear emotional as well as physical scars as a result of his encounter with Gertrude. In the future he would experience a phobic disorder connected to dogs, to the extent that the approach of any dog in his direction would trigger an anxiety attack. Mr. Goodright, a longtime animal lover and therefore more sympathetic to Gertrude's acts, would experience no emotional reactions from his trauma but would have to suffer the long-term consequences of his heroic efforts. He would endure several operations to repair the damage to his hand and would never gain full control of his hand again. As a result, his career as a much-heralded concert pianist would come to an untimely end and he would be relegated forever to the humble life of a piano teacher.

DEFINITION OF NEGLIGENCE

We will use the facts of this scenario throughout this and the next five chapters to illustrate the fundamental elements of negligence. Negligence involves conduct that creates an unreasonable risk of harm for another. It can be contrasted with an intentional tort, such as assault, where the tortfeasor's mental state must be such that the tortfeasor is aware of or actually intends that a certain result will occur. The mental state of a negligent tortfeasor is irrelevant.

There are four elements of negligence (see Figure 4-1), each of which will be discussed in detail in subsequent chapters. These elements are as follows:

1. *Duty:* A legal duty requiring the tortfeasor to conform to a certain standard of conduct in order to protect others from unreasonable risk of harm (Chapter 5).
2. *Breach of duty:* A failure of the tortfeasor to conform his or her conduct to the standard required (Chapter 6).
3. *Causation:* A causal connection between the tortfeasor's conduct and the resulting injury (Chapter 7).
4. *Damages:* The actual loss or damages resulting from the tortfeasor's conduct (Chapter 8).

Let us look briefly at each of these elements and see how they apply to the Gertrude/Teddy scenario.

FIGURE 4-1   Elements of Negligence

DUTY	BREACH OF DUTY	CAUSATION	DAMAGES
• Did the defendant, as a result of his relationship to the plaintiff, owe the plaintiff a duty of care?	• Did the defendant conduct himself as a reasonable person would have under similar circumstances?	• Was the defendant's conduct the actual cause of the plaintiff's injuries? (actual cause) • Was it reasonably foreseeable that the defendant's conduct would cause the plaintiff's injuries? (proximate cause)	• Did the plaintiff suffer compensable injuries as a result of the defendant's conduct?

DUTY

The notion of *duty* arises out of the legal obligations that result from our relationships with others. Parents, for example, owe a duty of care to their children; airline companies and their employees owe a duty of care to their passengers. The nature of this duty varies depending on the nature of the relationship. Landowners owe a different duty of care to trespassers than they do to those whom they invite on their premises. In some cases the tortfeasor may owe a duty of care to those with whom he has no direct contact, such as third parties that he could reasonably anticipate being injured by his conduct. A tavern owner, for example, could owe a duty of care to those injured by intoxicated patrons whom the tavern owner recognizes as being so intoxicated as to constitute a danger to those about him.

BREACH OF DUTY

As a practical matter, the key issue that arises in most negligence cases is not whether the defendant owed a duty of care to the plaintiff but whether she breached that duty. A key question that must be answered when dealing with **breach of duty** is whether the defendant conducted herself as a reasonable person would have under similar circumstances.

Objective versus Subjective Standard

In making this determination the courts use what is referred to as an **objective standard.** Under this standard the defendant's actions are compared to those of a hypothetical "reasonable person." In contrast, under a **subjective standard** one asks whether the tortfeasor herself believes she acted reasonably.

Suppose, for example, a woman believes that she is about to be burglarized and, fearing for her own safety, shoots a would-be burglar. Using an objective standard one would ask whether the woman acted as a reasonable person would have in that same situation. Using a subjective standard one would question whether the woman herself believed that she had acted in a reasonable fashion.

The difference in outcome resulting from using two different standards is most evident if the woman in question were unusually fearful of being attacked. Suppose the woman, having been burglarized several times in the past, became hysterical when she saw a man's outline in her window and shot him through the window before he made any actual attempt to enter her home. Under an objective standard her actions probably would not qualify as reasonable. A reasonable person in those circumstances most likely would have waited to ascertain whether the individual outside the window actually posed a threat. From a reasonable person's standpoint, it would have been just as likely that the person was a solicitor or a friend as a burglar. Under a subjective standard, however, the only question would be whether the woman herself in fact believed that her life was in danger.

Even under an objective standard, however, the physical characteristics of the tortfeasor are taken into consideration. A defendant who is blind, for example, is held to the standard of care expected of persons similarly impaired and not to the standard of care of sighted persons. The circumstances in which the defendant acts are also taken into consideration. The rescuer who responds in an emergency situation is not held to the same standard of care as one who acts under less demanding conditions.

PROFESSIONALS

Those blessed with a higher degree of knowledge, skill, or experience are held to a higher standard of care than the ordinary reasonable person. Because police officers, for example, have received training and presumably have experience in the handling of firearms, they are held to a higher standard of care when they discharge their weapons than the average person. Police officers are held to a "reasonable police officer" standard rather than a reasonable person standard. Therefore, a civilian might be justified under the reasonable person standard in taking another's life whereas a police officer under equivalent circumstances might not be. Specialists in a particular field are held to an even higher standard. A police officer trained as a hostage negotiator, for instance, is held to a higher standard of care in a hostage situation than the average police officer.

Negligence Per Se

In some cases statutes will determine the reasonable standard of care. Statutes that set forth safety standards, for example, in essence define minimal standards of reasonable conduct. Violation of those statutes will be treated as **negligence per se** (negligence in itself). A traffic ordinance mandating a speed of fifteen miles per hour in school crossing zones sets forth the standard of conduct expected of a reasonable driver in a school crossing zone. A driver who injures someone in the crossing zone as a result of violating the ordinance is negligent per se. In other words, the driver's negligence is presumed. Note that several factors limit this general rule; they are discussed in Chapter 6.

Res Ipsa Loquitur

In some cases the plaintiff is unable to prove the defendant's negligence because she is unable to gain access to information regarding the defendant's conduct. In such cases the plaintiff can rely on the doctrine known as **res ipsa loquitur,** which means "the thing speaks for itself." To utilize this doctrine, the plaintiff must show: (1) the event that injured the plaintiff was one that does not ordinarily happen except through negligence; (2) the instrument that caused the plaintiff's injury was under the exclusive control of the defendant; and (3) the plaintiff's injuries were not due to her own actions. In some courts, the plaintiff must further show that the explanation underlying the events that occurred is more readily accessible to the defendant than to the plaintiff.

A plaintiff injured in a modern-day airplane crash could use this doctrine to allow the jury to infer that negligence was more than likely the cause of the crash. Notice how the elements mentioned earlier are applicable to such a case. (1) Airplane crashes do not normally occur except through negligence. (2) Planes are under the exclusive control of the defendant airline company. (3) The plaintiff in such instances does not ordinarily contribute to the cause of the crash. (4) Finally, the defendant airline company is generally more capable of assessing the cause of the accident than the plaintiff.

CAUSATION

Actual Cause

The third element the plaintiff must prove is causation. Causation is divided into two categories: actual cause and proximate cause. **Actual cause,** or causation in fact, is a factual question that asks whether the defendant's conduct was the actual, factual cause of the plaintiff's injuries. Actual causation is not generally a legal problem unless there are multiple causes of the plaintiff's injuries. Suppose, for example, three different assailants throw rocks at the plaintiff. Only one of the rocks hits its mark, causing the plaintiff to sustain a serious eye injury. The question in this case would be which of the three assailants actually caused the plaintiff's injury. In the event of concurrent causes, as illustrated in this example, the courts generally find that each of the events was a cause of the injury, thereby forcing the defendants to apportion the damages. Further discussion of proof of actual cause is found in Chapter 7.

Proximate Cause

Proximate cause, referred to by some writers as "legal cause," revolves around the issue of foreseeability. The concept arises from the notion that even the most negligent defendant should not be responsible for consequences that are too remotely connected to his or her conduct. Suppose the plaintiff is knifed by the defendant and is hospitalized for his injuries. If the plaintiff refuses medical treatment, contracts gangrene, and dies from wounds that, under the ordinary course of treatment, would have been minimal, should the defendant be held responsible for his death? In other words, was the defendant in this case the proximate cause of the plaintiff's death or was the plaintiff's death due to some intervening factor, namely, the plaintiff's decision to reject medical care?

Another example of a situation in which proximate cause is an issue is one in which the plaintiff dies as a result of an injury that, if sustained by an ordinary person, would have resulted in only minor injuries. In these "eggshell skull" cases, so-called because the plaintiff has a skull of eggshell thinness, the rule often expressed by the courts is that the defendant must "take his plaintiff as he finds him." In other words, the defendant is responsible for the full extent of the plaintiff's injuries even if the average person in the same circumstances would have sustained far less serious injuries.

The issue of foreseeability also arises in what is sometimes referred to as the "unforeseeable plaintiff" problem. The question in this case is whether the defendant's conduct posed any foreseeable risk of harm to the plaintiff. Suppose the defendant's conduct is unquestionably negligent in reference to a third party but the plaintiff, rather than the third party, is injured as a result of the defendant's conduct. Should the defendant be held liable for the plaintiff's injury even if she did not act negligently in reference to the plaintiff?

That question was posed in one of the most famous American tort cases, *Palsgraf v. Long Island Railroad,* 162 N.E. 99 (N.Y. 1928). The defendant in that case negligently caused a passenger to drop a package of fireworks, which, through a series of bizarre events, caused injury to the plaintiff. Although the defendant was undeniably negligent toward the passenger, at issue was whether such negligence could give rise to liability to the plaintiff. The court, in a decision written by Judge Cardozo, held that the defendant was not liable because the plaintiff was not a foreseeable plaintiff, in that it was not reasonably foreseeable that she would be injured by the defendant's misconduct. Judge Andrews, in his dissent, argued that the defendant owed a duty of care to everyone in society to protect them from unnecessary danger. Everyone, he said, has a duty to refrain from any acts that unreasonably threaten the safety of others.

Foreseeability or Duty of Care?

The question of foreseeability is often phrased in terms of duty of care. Both revolve around the question of "whether the interests of the plaintiff are to be protected against the particular invasion of the defendant's conduct" (Prosser & Keeton, The Law of Torts § 53 (5th ed. 1984)). As a result, the elements of proximate cause and duty are often interwoven in a court's analysis. The majority in *Palsgraf* phrased the question of liability in terms of whether the defendant had a duty of care to the plaintiff. In essence, this question is the same as asking whether the plaintiff is a foreseeable plaintiff, i.e., one to whom the defendant's conduct poses a foreseeable risk. This and other interesting issues arise under the subject of proximate cause and are discussed in great detail in Chapter 7.

DAMAGES

The final issue that must be addressed in any tort case is that of damages. Damages can be classified using a variety of labels, but we will lump all damages into one of three categories: compensatory damages, nominal damages, and punitive damages (see Figure 4-2). **Compensatory damages,** as the name implies, are designed to compensate the plaintiff for her actual loss or injury. Compensatory damages can be further divided into two subcategories, general damages and special damages.

General damages are those damages that typically result from the kind of conduct the defendant engaged in. Monetary compensation for the loss of a leg resulting from a traffic accident falls into the category of general damages. Compensation for the plaintiff's pain and suffering resulting from her injuries is also classified as general damages.

Special damages, in contrast, are specifically tied to the plaintiff. Damages resulting from loss of earnings and medical expenses are examples of special damages.

Nominal damages are awarded when the plaintiff has proved to the jury's satisfaction that a tort was committed but has not been able to prove that any

FIGURE 4-2 Classification of Damages

PUNITIVE	COMPENSATORY	NOMINAL
• Designed to punish the defendant	• **General** Compensation for damages anticipated as a result of conduct defendant engaged in • **Special** Compensation for damages specially tied to plaintiff	• Awarded when tort was committed but no actual loss occurred

actual loss occurred. Nominal damages are not allowed in negligence actions because the plaintiff must prove the existence of an actual loss in a negligence case.

Punitive damages are designed to punish the defendant. Unlike compensatory damages, the purpose of punitive damages is not to make the plaintiff whole but to deter future, undesirable conduct of the defendant and similarly situated individuals. Punitive damages are reserved for those situations in which the defendant acted with particular ill will toward the plaintiff or in conscious disregard for the well-being of others. Pure negligence by itself will not support an award of punitive damages.

The computation of damages is a highly complex process and is dealt with only at an elementary level in this text. We will discuss the classification and computation of damages in Chapter 8. Although punitive damages and nominal damages cannot be awarded in pure negligence cases, for organizational reasons, they are discussed in the chapter addressing damages in negligence cases (Chapter 8).

FUNCTION OF JUDGE AND JURY

Consider the role of the judge and the jury in a negligence case. The judge decides all questions of law, whereas the jury is the finder of fact. In a negligence claim the judge determines as a matter of law what the defendant's duty was to the plaintiff. So in a suit by a plaintiff who was a social guest of a defendant, the court will instruct the jury regarding the duty of care owed by the defendant to a social guest. Based on that instruction, the jury will determine whether the defendant breached that duty of care.

If, however, the judge decides that reasonable persons could not differ in their decision as to whether the defendant breached his duty of care, she will instruct the jury as to the finding of fact they must make. By making such an instruction the judge, in essence, takes the case out of the jury's hands. If the judge decides that, as a matter of law, the plaintiff failed to prove one of the elements of his case, the judge may remove the case from the jury by directing a verdict.

Therefore, even though the jury is considered the finder of facts, it may do so only when the facts are such that reasonable persons could differ as to the nature of those facts. If a case does go to the jury, the jury determines whether the defendant breached his duty of care to the plaintiff, if he did so in such a way that proximately caused the plaintiff's injuries, and what damages the plaintiff is entitled to receive.

As you might recall from some of your other law-related classes, the plaintiff in a civil case bears two burdens of proof: the burden of production and the burden of persuasion. The **burden of production** requires the plaintiff to come forward with sufficient evidence to avoid a directed verdict. He must show in a negligence claim, therefore, that the defendant owed a duty of care to the plaintiff, that he breached that duty, that the plaintiff suffered an injury, and that the defendant's negligence was the proximate cause of that injury. In some states if the plaintiff can invoke the doctrine of res ipsa loquitur, the burden of production will shift to the defendant, who will be presumed negligent unless he can offer some rebuttal evidence. Ordinarily, however, at the end of the plaintiff's case, the defendant will usually move for a directed verdict, in essence requesting the court to declare that the plaintiff failed to meet the burden of production.

If the plaintiff manages to hurdle the evidentiary obstacle of the burden of production, he must then meet the **burden of persuasion** by convincing the jury that it is more likely than not that the plaintiff's injuries were due to the defendant's negligence. In other words, he must prove his case by a preponderance of the evidence. In quantitative terms this means that the plaintiff must convince the jury that there is more than a 50 percent chance that the defendant caused his injuries.

The burden of persuasion generally rests on the plaintiff throughout the case but, in a few jurisdictions, the courts have shifted this burden to the defendant in cases involving the doctrine of res ipsa loquitur. In other words, in those jurisdictions once the plaintiff establishes the elements of res ipsa loquitur, the burden of persuasion shifts and the defendant must prove by a preponderance of the evidence that he was not negligent.

APPLICATION

Let us now examine the basic elements of a negligence claim in the context of the hypothetical confrontation involving Gertrude, Teddy, and Mr. Goodright. If Teddy and Mr. Goodright decided to sue the Baxters for their damages, they would have to prove by a preponderance of the evidence that the Baxters owed them a duty of care, that they breached that duty, that they sustained injuries, and that the

Baxters' negligence was the proximate and actual cause of their injuries.

The first question that we would have to answer if we represented the Baxters is whether they owed any duty of care to the two people who trespassed on their property. We would also want to find out whether the duty of care owed to Mr. Goodright was different from that owed to Teddy, in light of the fact that Mr. Goodright's presence at the scene was directly linked to his commendable efforts to rescue a boy who was only a stranger to him.

Once we determined what, if any, standard of care the Baxters owed to Teddy and Mr. Goodright, we would have to ascertain whether they breached that duty in their failure to lock their gate on the occasion of Gertrude's attack. We would want to find out if there were any applicable statutes, the violation of which would make the Baxters negligent per se. We would also want to research case law in our jurisdiction to determine what precautions the courts thought were necessary for dog owners to take to protect others from being victimized by their pets.

We would also have to resolve whether the defendants' negligence was the actual and proximate cause of the plaintiff's injuries. Although there is no doubt that Gertrude was the actual cause of Teddy's and Mr. Goodright's injuries, proximate cause could be disputed. The Baxters, for example, might argue that Mr. Goodright would not have been injured had he not blindly dived in to rescue Teddy and that it was, in fact, his own gross negligence in carrying out his rescue mission that caused his injuries.

Causation is not to be confused with the defenses of contributory and comparative negligence, either of which is likely to be raised by the Baxters. Note that proximate cause is one of the elements of negligence for which the plaintiff bears an affirmative burden of proof. Contributory or comparative negligence, however, must be raised by the defendant. The argument made by one who raises the defense of contributory negligence is that even though the defendant was negligent, the plaintiff's own negligence contributed to his injuries to the extent that he should be barred from recovering. If a defendant successfully raises the defense of comparative negligence, the plaintiff's recovery will be reduced in proportion to his own negligence. Defenses to negligence are covered in Chapter 9.

Although it would be relatively straightforward to prove that Teddy and Mr. Goodright sustained injuries as a result of Gertrude's attack, we would need to go to considerable effort to compute the value of the appropriate damages. In essence, we would have to quantify the extent of emotional harm that Teddy sustained as well as the physical scarring he suffered. With both parties we would have to assign a numerical value to the pain and suffering they endured as a result of their traumatic experiences. In addition to assessing medical expenses we would need to project the potential lost earnings suffered by Mr. Goodright. Assigning a value to the loss of limbs, bodily disfigurement, or emotional pain and suffering may seem cold and calculating, but must be done so that some quantifiable amount of damages can be suggested to the jury.

SUMMARY

Any conduct that creates an unreasonable risk of harm for another is called negligence. The mental state of a negligent tortfeasor is irrelevant in that he or she need not intend nor be aware that the conduct will result in a particular consequence. Negligence consists of four elements: duty, breach of duty, causation, and damage.

The duty of care depends on the relationship between the plaintiff and the defendant. In some cases the tortfeasor may even owe a duty of care to one with whom he or she has had no direct contact.

In determining whether the defendant breached the duty of care, the question asked is whether the defendant conducted himself or herself as a reasonable person would have under similar circumstances. An objective standard is used in assessing the defendant's conduct. Some physical characteristics of the defendant, however, are taken into consideration, as are the circumstances in which the defendant acted. Those with a higher degree of knowledge, skill, or experience than the ordinary person are held to a higher standard of care. A defendant who violates a statute may be considered negligent per se. If the plaintiff is unable to prove the defendant's negligence because he or she lacks access to information regarding the defendant's conduct, the plaintiff may be able to rely on the doctrine of res ipsa loquitur.

The plaintiff must also prove actual cause and proximate cause. The defendant must be the actual, factual cause of the plaintiff's injuries. If there are concurrent or multiple causes of the plaintiff's injuries, the courts will generally find that each of the defendants was the actual cause of the plaintiff's injuries, forcing the defendants to apportion the damages.

Proximate cause, however, revolves around the issue of foreseeability. The question is whether the consequences of the conduct are so remote that the defendant should not be held responsible for his or her actions. If the plaintiff's injuries were really caused by some intervening factor other than the defendant's negligence, the defendant will be excused from liability. The question that often arises under the issue of proximate cause is whether the plaintiff was a foreseeable plaintiff. Under the "eggshell skull" rule, a defendant is required to take his plaintiff as he finds him.

The final issue is that of damages. The three categories of damages are compensatory damages, nominal damages, and punitive damages. Compensatory damages can be divided into two subcategories of general and special damages. General damages are those that typically result from the kind of conduct the defendant engaged in and include compensation for pain and suffering. Special damages are more specifically tied to the plaintiff and include compensation for medical expenses. Nominal damages are awarded if the jury is convinced of the defendant's liability but not of the occurrence of any actual loss. Punitive damages are designed to punish the defendant.

Questions of law are decided by the judge; factual questions are resolved by the jury. In certain circumstances the judge has the right to instruct the jury as to the finding of fact it must make. If the plaintiff fails to bear the burden of production, he or she faces a directed verdict imposed by the judge. The plaintiff also bears the burden of persuasion.

PRACTICE POINTERS

As a practical matter, the attorneys representing Teddy and Mr. Goodright, after having conducted their preliminary investigations, will contact the insurance adjustor representing the Baxters' insurance carrier and attempt to settle the case as soon as possible. In their ensuing conversations both sides will attempt to represent the facts known to them at that time in a light that best supports their position. The purpose of settlement, of course, is to avoid litigation, which is both expensive and burdensome to all involved. Most cases are, in fact, settled before trial, but it is advantageous to both sides to resolve disputes before entering into the costly discovery process.

At some point in this preliminary negotiation process the attorneys for Teddy and Mr. Goodright will write a demand letter to the insurance carrier. In this demand letter they will set forth the elements of the tort they claim the defendant committed and they will also spell out the damages to which their client is entitled as a result of the defendant's actions. Figure 4-3 is an example of a demand letter that might be written in this case.

FIGURE 4-3 Demand Letter

Digger Odell
Attorney at Law
62 Happy Trail
Gotcha, AZ 85034

Ms. Agnes Pain, Esq.
Happy Days Insurance Company
298 Refusal Way
Why, AZ 85602

Dear Ms. Pain:

I represent Teddy Jones with respect to the incident that occurred between Teddy Jones and your insured, Mr. & Mrs. Stephen Baxter. The attack occurred on June 6, 1990. Teddy was severely mauled by the Baxters' German shepherd, Gertrude. Gertrude attacked Teddy by seizing his right leg and inflicting serious physical injury. Teddy's injuries would have been even worse, and perhaps even fatal, had he not been rescued by a passerby. Teddy was only six years old and did nothing to provoke the attack.

The severity of the tissue damage caused by Gertrude's mauling necessitated surgical repair. Two surgical operations plus ongoing medical care resulted in total medical costs of over twenty-five thousand dollars ($25,000.00). Despite having received excellent medical care, Teddy must endure permanent and extensive scarring.

The emotional scars, however, run much deeper. Teddy now suffers from a severe panic disorder which was initiated by Gertrude's savageness. This disorder is triggered by the sight of any dog. Although he has received extensive psychiatric counseling to control this disorder, he continues to have an uncontrollable fear of dogs. This disorder is extremely debilitating to Teddy and has caused him extensive mental pain and anguish as well as much

Continued on next page

PRACTICE POINTERS—Continued

FIGURE 4.3 Demand Letter–Continued

embarrassment. He continues to be fearful of walking the streets alone and absolutely refuses to ride his bicycle for fear of being chased by a dog. Teddy's psychiatrist feels that over time and with the use of drug therapy, Teddy will eventually be able to function relatively normally but that he will most likely retain an abnormal fear of dogs for life.

Teddy's counseling fees amount to twelve thousand one hundred dollars ($12,100.00) as of this date. His treating psychiatrist, Dr. Harmony, estimates that he will have to spend at least another two years in counseling, at an additional cost of fifteen thousand dollars ($15,000.00).

Although the extensive pain and suffering already experienced by Teddy, as well as the pain and suffering it can be anticipated he will suffer, cannot be justly quantified with only a monetary award, we demand the sum of one hundred thousand dollars ($100,000.00) in compensation to settle Teddy's claim. Failure to pay this amount will result in our immediately filing suit against your insured.

I expect prompt payment of our very reasonable settlement proposal. If the funds demanded are not paid within ten (10) days from the date of this letter, I will assume that this settlement proposal is unacceptable to you and this offer will be deemed withdrawn. I am enclosing copies of all of Teddy's medical records and billings as well as narratives from Teddy's treating physicians.

Sincerely,

Digger Odell, Esq.

TORT TEASERS

Which of the four elements (duty, breach, causation, damages) would be at issue in each of the following cases?

1. Defendant negligently runs into Plaintiff with his taxicab. Plaintiff, an alcoholic, dies from delirium tremens, a condition associated with alcoholism but whose development was hastened by the accident. *McCahill v. New York Transportation Co.,* 94 N.E. 616 (N.Y. 1911).

2. Plaintiff is a passenger in a car driven by Defendant. Defendant runs into a tree, resulting in injuries to Plaintiff. Defendant renders no aid to Plaintiff and Plaintiff claims that this lack of assistance aggravated her injuries. *Tubbs v. Argus,* 225 N.E.2d 841 (Ind. 1967).

3. Defendant ophthalmologists routinely administer eye exams to Plaintiff over a period of years but never test her for glaucoma. When Plaintiff is 32 years old she develops glaucoma. Because the chances of anyone under the age of 40 developing glaucoma is 1:25,000, the test is not routinely given to those under the age of 40. *Helling v. Carey,* 519 P. 2d 981 (Wash. 1974).

4. Plaintiff experiences numbness, weakness, and pain in her left arm after having surgery that does not involve her left arm. Her expert testifies that this condition does not usually occur in the absence of negligence. Defendant doctors vehemently maintain that nothing unusual occurred during surgery. *Marrero v. Goldsmith,* 486 So. 2d 538 (Fla. 1986).

KEY TERMS

Actual cause
Cause in fact of the plaintiff's injuries.

Breach of duty
Failure to conform to the required standard of care.

Burden of persuasion
Burden of proving the elements of a case by a preponderance of the evidence.

Burden of production
Burden of producing sufficient evidence to avoid a directed verdict.

Compensatory damages
Damages designed to compensate the plaintiff; consist of both general and special damages.

General damages
Compensatory damages that can generally be anticipated to result from the type of conduct the defendant engaged in.

Negligence per se
Presumed negligence that arises from the unexcused violation of a statute.

Nominal damages
Damages awarded when liability is shown but no actual damages are proved.

Objective standard
Comparison of a defendant's conduct to that of a reasonable person.

Proximate cause
Legal cause of the plaintiff's injuries; emphasis is on the concept of foreseeability.

Punitive damages
Damages designed to punish the defendant (also referred to as *exemplary damages*).

Res ipsa loquitur
Doctrine the plaintiff can turn to in proving negligence when it is difficult to obtain information about the defendant's conduct.

Special damages
Compensatory damages specifically linked to the plaintiff.

Subjective standard
Use of the defendant's own subjective perceptions to determine whether the defendant behaved reasonably.

CHAPTER

5

Negligence: Duty

CHAPTER TOPICS

CHAPTER OBJECTIVES

In this chapter you will learn to:

- Describe the standard of care expected of a possessor of land toward those who enter her land
- Describe the standard of care that arises out of certain special relationships (e.g., employer-employee) and special situations (e.g., rendering emergency care)
- Describe the standard of care expected of landlords, tenants, and sellers of land
- Recognize the concepts of vicarious liability and the family purpose doctrine

One of the first questions that the attorneys representing Teddy and Mr. Goodright in our hypothetical case will have to consider is the question of duty. Did the Baxters owe a duty of care to one who trespassed on their land? Did they owe a different duty of care to a child than to an adult? Did they owe a higher duty of care to a rescuer than they did to an ordinary trespasser?

OVERVIEW OF DUTY

In any negligence claim, the concept of duty raises the question of whether the defendant is under any obligation to act for the benefit of the plaintiff. In general terms, the defendant's duty is to act reasonably. In other words, the defendant must exercise the degree of care that any reasonable person would exercise under similar circumstances. You will notice when you read cases that most courts spend relatively little time addressing the question of duty but, instead, jump directly into an analysis of breach of duty. Nevertheless, duty is a threshold question in every negligence case because a defendant is not liable, no matter how reckless his conduct, unless he owes a duty to the plaintiff. Therefore, we will explore the concept of duty in some depth in this chapter.

The question of duty is essentially a question of whether a defendant is under an obligation to protect the plaintiff. Some courts use the relational approach to answer this question. Under this approach the nature of the relationship between the parties determines whether the defendant has a duty to protect the plaintiff. An owner of land, for example, owes a different duty of care to a trespasser than to someone invited onto the premises, because of the difference in their relationships. Other courts analyze the existence of duty in the context of foreseeability. Under this analysis, a defendant owes a duty only to those persons the defendant could reasonably foresee would be endangered. This was the approach advocated by Justice Cardozo in *Palsgraf v. Long Island Railroad* (described briefly in Chapter 4 and discussed in more detail in Chapter 6).

Because the foreseeability approach seems to add to the confusion surrounding the duty question, and because foreseeability is also used to analyze breach of duty and proximate cause, we will rely on the relational approach in this text. Although this approach is based on the concept of relationship between plaintiff and defendant, that relationship need not be a personal or ongoing one. A reckless driver who runs over a pedestrian in a crosswalk owes a duty of care to that pedestrian even though the two have never seen one another before their unfortunate interaction.

Generally, a legal obligation exists only when a direct relationship between the defendant and the plaintiff exists. A duty to the plaintiff may also arise, however, if a relationship exists between the defendant and a third party whose negligence causes injury to the plaintiff. For example, a defendant who loans her automobile to someone who is intoxicated and who injures others could, under certain conditions, be found liable for the injuries caused by the intoxicated individual.

In this chapter we examine the duty of care owed by possessors of land and the duty of care arising out of certain special relationships, such as landlord-tenant, seller-buyer, and lessor-lessee. Be aware, however, that a legal duty arises out of many relationships, such as doctor-patient, parent-child, and employer-employee. We also touch lightly on the issue of vicarious liability (although that subject is discussed in greater detail in Chapter 15) and consider how that doctrine affects employers and car owners.

POSSESSORS OF LAND

Throughout this chapter we refer to "possessors" rather than owners of land. The possessor, not the landowner, was the focus of protection under the common law. The purpose of limiting the liability of possessors was to encourage full utilization of the land, unhampered by burdensome legal obligations to others. For that reason it was the tenant, not the landlord, who generally benefited from the common law rules.

Under the common law the duty of care owed by a possessor was determined by the class into which the plaintiff fell (see Figure 5-1). The three classes of plaintiffs were trespassers, licensees, and invitees. A trespasser was one who had no right to be on the defendant's land, a licensee was one who came on the land as a social guest and hence with the owner's consent, and an invitee was one who came on the land with a business purpose. The owner owed the highest duty of care to the invitee and the lowest duty of care to the trespasser. Note that although most courts continue to apply these classifications, the differences between the classes have blurred over time. Some courts have abandoned these distinctions altogether.

TRESPASSERS

Early common law established the principle that possessors of land could not deliberately set traps or spring guns with the intent of injuring a trespasser. From this principle evolved the rule that possessors of land must refrain from willfully or intentionally injuring trespassers. A trespasser assumes the risks inherent in entering the land and is responsible for her own safety.

In general, a possessor owes no duty of care to a trespasser to make the land safe or to protect the trespasser in any way. If the possessor is pursuing dangerous activities on the property, he or she need not warn the trespasser of such dangers nor avoid carrying on such activities (Restatement (Second) of Torts § 333). There are four exceptions, however, to this general rule (see Figure 5-2). Some duty of care is owed when the plaintiffs are (1) trespassing children, (2) individuals known to be trespassers, (3) rescuing someone in danger as a result of the defendant possessor's negligence, or (4) trespassing on a very limited portion of the possessor's land. We will discuss each of these exceptions in more depth in the following sections.

Attractive Nuisance

The notion that children who are trespassers should be entitled to greater protection than adults evolved from the **attractive nuisance** doctrine. Under this doctrine a possessor is liable if he or she maintains a dangerous condition on the land that induces children to enter the premises because it is an enticing item on which to play. A construction site might be considered an attractive nuisance. It is usually replete with lumber, ladders, and other items that make wonderful props for fertile imaginations.

Under the Restatement, a possessor can be found liable to a trespassing child if the following conditions are met (Restatement (Second) of Torts § 339):

• The possessor has reason to know that the condition is on a place on the land where children are likely to trespass.

• The possessor must have reason to know of the condition and to know that it poses an unreasonable risk of serious injury or death to trespassing children.

• Because of their youth, the children must not have discovered the condition or realized the danger posed by coming into the area made dangerous by the condition.

• The benefit to the possessor in maintaining the condition in its dangerous form must be slight in comparison to the risk posed to the children.

• The possessor must fail to use reasonable care to eliminate the danger or to protect the children.

FIGURE 5-1 Duties of Possessor of Land

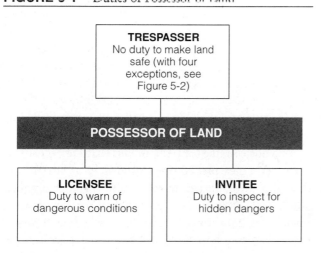

TRESPASSER
No duty to make land safe (with four exceptions, see Figure 5-2)

POSSESSOR OF LAND

LICENSEE
Duty to warn of dangerous conditions

INVITEE
Duty to inspect for hidden dangers

FIGURE 5-2 Exceptions to No Duty Rule for Trespassers

ATTRACTIVE NUISANCE	RESCUERS	KNOWN TRESPASSER	LIMITED TRESPASS
• Knows children are likely to trespass • Knows condition poses unreasonable risk of injury to children • Chlid is unaware of danger posed by condition • Benefit in maintaining condition is slight compared to risk posed • Possessor fails to use reasonable care to protect children	• Possessor negligently causes harm to person or property • Harm must be imminent, real, and require immediate action	• Possessor is aware of trespasser • Possessor is aware of dangerous condition	• Trespasser uses only limited portion of land

Suppose a two-year-old child, left unattended for approximately ten minutes, wanders into a neighbor's backyard, falls into the pool, and drowns. Assume the backyard is inadequately fenced and that the owner is aware that on previous occasions children have climbed over the fence into the backyard. Does the swimming pool meet the criteria of an attractive nuisance as set forth in the Restatement? Yes. The owner knows that children are likely to trespass, as he is aware they have trespassed in the past. A swimming pool certainly poses an unreasonable risk of serious injury or death to very young children, as they are not usually fully cognizant of the danger posed. The owner has failed to use reasonable care by failing to provide adequate fencing. Any benefit the owner gains from not expending the money to install safe fencing is slight when weighed against the risk of injury posed to trespassing children.

The age, experience, and intelligence of the child may determine whether the attractive nuisance doctrine applies. The question is whether the child is able to appreciate the risk of the condition involved. Even a relatively young child may be expected to understand the risk of drowning or the risk of falling from a great height. If the defendant can show that the injured child, because of her experience or intelligence, was aware of and appreciated the danger, even if other children of her age might not have been so appreciative, the child will be barred from recovery.

If the condition causing the injury is a "natural" rather than an "artificial" condition, the courts are less likely to allow the child to recover. The reasoning seems to be that it is prohibitively expensive to protect children from a natural condition such as a lake; also, a natural condition is one for which children are more likely to be familiar with the risk involved. The distinction, however, between a natural and an artificial condition is a stilted one and should not be relied on as the sole basis for denying liability.

The bottom line for possessors is that they must take reasonable measures to prevent harm to children. This does not mean that they need to make their premises childproof. Nor does it mean they are required to inspect for dangerous conditions of which they would otherwise have been unaware. Posting a warning may in many instances be sufficient.

PUTTING IT INTO PRACTICE 5.1

1. Is an objective or subjective standard used in assessing whether the attractive nuisance applies to a particular child?

2. Suppose a manufacturing company uses a pulley to hoist raw material up to a fifth story of its factory. The company is aware that children like to visit its open yard and its employees actively try to drive the children away. One day an employee forgets to shut off the engine that operates the pulley. A group of children who walk by and see the ball and hook on the pulley going up and down dare one another to grab hold of the pulley and be carried up to the fifth floor. Jed, an eight-year-old, accepts the dare and is being carried up by the pulley when he becomes frightened and lets go of the pulley, falling to the ground and sustaining serious injuries. Does the company owe Jed a duty under the attractive nuisance doctrine?

3. The owner of a small artificial pond is aware that children in the day care center next to him often wander away from the center and go near the pond. The owner could prevent this by closing and locking his gate. Marie, a three-year-old child, falls into the pond while attempting to catch some goldfish and almost drowns. Does the pond owner owe Marie a duty of care? Would your answer change if Marie were ten years old?

4. A railroad company has a turntable that it knows creates a risk of unreasonable harm to children and the company is aware the children often trespass in the area to play on the turntable. The company could easily prevent harm to children by installing a locking device on the turntable, which would make it difficult for children to set it in motion. Micki, who is nine, is injured when his foot gets caught in the turntable. Is the railroad company liable to Micki? Would your answer change if installing such a locking device would have prevented its effective operation? What if Micki's father were a railroad engineer and had repeatedly warned Micki about the dangers of playing on the turntable?

Rescue Doctrine

Under the rescue doctrine anyone who negligently causes harm to a person or property may be liable to one who is injured in an effort to rescue the imperiled person or property. The rationale is that the rescuer would not have been injured were it not for the negligence of the tortfeasor. This doctrine prevents a plaintiff from being found contributorily negligent for voluntarily placing herself in a dangerous situation in order to save another. Often dubbed the "danger invites rescue" doctrine, it stems from an opinion written by Judge Cardozo: "Danger invites rescue. . . . The wrong that imperils life is a wrong to the imperiled victim; it is wrong also to his rescuer" (*Wagner v. International Railway,* Co., 133 N.E. 437 (N.Y. 1921)).

Suppose, for example, a motorist were to negligently run into a bicyclist, knocking him to the ground. If another driver who stopped to render aid were run over in the process of helping the bicyclist, the motorist causing the accident would be liable for the injuries of the Good Samaritan. The rationale behind this liability is that the negligent motorist created a chain of events that foreseeably resulted in injury to the rescuer of the tortfeasor's victim. Restatement (Second) of Torts § 294, illus. 1, provides a slightly different example involving a person sitting on the curb watching children play ball on the sidewalk. A motorist driving down the street sees the children but fails to slow down or take any preventive measures. One of the children darts in front of the vehicle while in pursuit of the ball and the observer on the sidewalk lunges forward to pull the child to safety, meanwhile slipping and falling under the car. The motorist is liable for the broken leg sustained by the rescuer even though the motorist was not driving in a negligent manner in relationship to the rescuer. The driver's negligence in failing to anticipate the actions of the child created a situation that foreseeability justified the intervention of the rescuer.

The rescue doctrine is warranted only when the threatened danger is both imminent and real and requires immediate action if the victim is to be saved. If the defendant's conduct is neither negligent nor intentionally tortious, the doctrine is inapplicable.

Known Trespassers

Another exception to the general rule regarding trespassers involves those trespassers of whom the possessor is aware. Once a possessor knows that a particular person is trespassing on her property, she owes a duty of reasonable care to that person. This duty clearly applies when the danger to the trespasser arises out of something the possessor has done, such as excavate her land. The nature of the duty is less clear, however, when the condition is a natural one. (According to the Restatement (Second) of Torts § 337, cmt. b, the duty to exercise reasonable care should still apply when the condition is natural.)

The justification given for the imposition of this duty is that the possessor's continuing tolerance of the trespass constitutes implied permission to use the land. Thus, the trespasser is elevated to the status of a licensee. As a practical matter, however, defendants often do not attempt to thwart trespassing because to do so would be expensive and probably unproductive. Imagine the futility of a railroad company spending time and money trying to deter trespassers from using

its tracks. Nevertheless, possessors have been shifted from a position of complete exemption from liability to a more moderate position of limited liability when dealing with known trespassers.

When a possessor knows or has reason to know that trespassers are in dangerous proximity to a hazard and has reason to believe that the trespassers will either not discover the hazard or not realize its hazardous nature, the possessor has a duty to use reasonable care to warn the trespassers of the hazard. In one case, for example, in which the plaintiff ran into an unmarked barbed wire fence while riding on the defendant's land, a court found that the evidence justified a finding that the fence was "dangerously invisible" and could not reasonably be discovered by trespassers (*Webster v. Culbertson,* 761 P.2d 1063 (Ariz. 1988)).

Limited Trespass

Possessors of land also owe a limited duty of care to frequent trespassers who use only a very limited area of their land. Suppose a farmer knows of a well-worn path across the edge of his property created by children taking a shortcut to school. In such a case he would be expected to anticipate the traversal of these children and would be required to use reasonable care in his activities for their protection.

LICENSEES

A **licensee** is one step up from a trespasser. She has the possessor's consent to be on the property but does not have a business purpose for being there. Most licensees are social guests. The duty a possessor owes to a licensee is to warn her of any dangerous conditions if the possessor is aware of that condition and should reasonably anticipate that the licensee may not discover it. Suppose your dinner guest, for example, trips on a toy left unattended by one of your children. If you failed to warn your guest of the presence of the toy and the lighting conditions were such that he could not reasonably be expected to see it, you could be held liable for his injuries.

The most frequently litigated issue in reference to licensees pertains to the obviousness of a hazardous condition and the warning that is required to prevent harm. A warning that is adequate for an adult, for example, may be inadequate for a child, as a peril that is obvious to an adult may not be so to a child. A posted notice warning of danger is not sufficient when the possessor knows that a licensee is unable to read (e.g., a child, a blind person, or someone from a foreign country) and the possessor may thus be required to use reasonable care to warn in some other way.

The possessor is, however, under no duty to inspect for unknown dangers when dealing with a licensee. As with trespassers, the courts are more likely to find a higher duty of care if the possessor is carrying out activities on the land than if the danger arises out of some natural condition on the land.

Social guests in an automobile are due the same standard of care as are licensees on land. Unless there is a statute to the contrary, most courts have held that the guest is owed no duty of inspection. Therefore, if the owner of a vehicle fails to inspect the car's brakes, which ultimately fail and cause injuries to the guest, the owner will not be liable for the failure to inspect.

INVITEES

Invitees are those persons invited by the possessor onto her land to conduct business. An invitee can be either a public invitee or a business invitee. A *public invitee* is a member of the public invited to enter for a purpose for which the land is held open to the public. If a business owner maintains a free telephone for public use, anyone who enters the premises for purposes of using the telephone is a public invitee. If the land is held open to the public, the visitor need not pay admission to be considered a public invitee. Someone who attends a free public lecture is just as much an invitee as someone who pays admission to an exhibit. A *business invitee* is one who enters the land for a purpose connected with the business dealings of the possessor. A grocery shopper is an invitee, as is a worker who enters to make repairs.

Even if the plaintiff is not engaged in business at the time of his injury, he is considered an invitee so long as he has a general business relationship with the possessor. In *Campbell v. Weathers,* 111 P.2d 72 (Kan. 1941) the plaintiff had been a longstanding customer of the defendant, who operated a lunch counter and cigar stand in an office building. After standing next to the cigar stand for several minutes, the plaintiff used the toilet in the back of the building. On the way he fell into an open trap door in the dark hallway. The defendant argued that the plaintiff was not an invitee because he had made no purchases on the day of his injury and because the toilet was intended for the defendant's employees and not the general public. The court classified the plaintiff as an invitee and pointed out that anyone who goes into a store with the intent of doing business at the present or in the future is an invitee. The court noted that many people shop for hours without making any purchases. Could they be denied invitee status in light of the fact that owners implicitly invite them for their potential business purpose? The *Campbell* court thought not.

A social guest does not rise to the status of an invitee even by performing an incidental service for her host, such as repairing a broken faucet. The host must gain some type of economic benefit before the guest can be considered an invitee. By the same token, a salesperson making an unsolicited call to a private home is not an invitee unless she is invited in (Restatement (Second) of Torts § 332, cmt. b). By contrast, a salesperson who calls on a business where she reasonably believes that door-to-door salespeople are typically received is considered an invitee.

The majority of "slip and fall" cases involve invitees. In such cases the question is whether the store owner should be held liable for a customer's slip and fall caused by an unreasonably dangerous condition, such as the proverbial banana peel. The plaintiff must establish that the proprietor either caused the condition (by placing the banana peel on the floor) or that the proprietor was aware of the condition (caused by a third party, such as another customer) and failed to take reasonable measures to remove the hazard.

Losing Invitee Status

An invitee may become a licensee or trespasser if she goes to parts of the premises that extend beyond her invitation. So long as the visitor reasonably believes that the premises are open to the public, however, she will be treated as an invitee even if, unknown to her, the possessor intends that the area be off limits to the general public. However, even if a visitor receives explicit authorization from the possessor to go onto a private portion of the premises, she will lose her invitee status if she enters purely for her own benefit. In one such case a customer who came to a store with the intent of shopping was given permission, in her search for a particular saleswoman, to enter an alteration room reserved for employees. When she entered the room she fell down a stairway. The court held that she was a licensee because she entered the room for her own benefit and without invitation by the owner (although she had its permission to enter). As a licensee she was required to take the premises as she found them (*Lerman Bros. v. Lewis,* 277 Ky. 334, 126 S.W.2d 461 (1939)).

Compare this case with *Campbell v. Weathers,* in which the plaintiff retained his invitee status because he entered an area that reasonably appeared to him to be open to the public. Reasonable belief of the plaintiff appears to be the operative fact on which the courts focus in these cases.

An invitee also loses her status if she stays on the premises for longer than is reasonably necessary to conduct her business. Once her purpose becomes social rather than business she becomes a licensee.

Nature of Duty to Invitee

A possessor owes a higher duty of care to an invitee than he does to either a licensee or a trespasser. Most importantly, he has a duty to inspect his premises for hidden dangers when dealing with invitees. Although he has no duty to ferret out all hidden dangers, he must use reasonable care in making his inspection (Restatement (Second) of Torts § 343). He may even be liable for a dangerous condition resulting from faulty construction or design, even if the condition existed before he came into possession of the property.

The definition of *reasonable care* varies depending on the use of the premises. The possessor of a shopping mall, who may readily anticipate the passage of thousands of customers, is held to a higher duty of inspection than the owner of a private home who invites an insurance salesperson in for the purpose of discussing coverage. In some cases the use of a warning of a dangerous condition will meet the requirements of reasonable care, but in other situations affirmative action will be required. If a store owner knows, for example, that customers will be distracted by goods on display and probably will not notice a sign warning them of danger, then a warning will not be sufficient (Restatement (Second) of Torts § 343A, illus. 2).

Even if an invitee is aware of and appreciates the danger involved, the possessor may be obligated to take reasonable steps to reduce the danger. In *Wilk v. Georges,* 514 P.2d 877 (Or. 1973), the plaintiff and her husband were shopping for Christmas trees in a nursery operated by the defendant. On the day of the plaintiff's visit it had been raining and the walkways, put together using planks, were slippery and dangerous. The defendant had posted a sign that read:

> Please watch where you are going. This is a nursery where plants grow. There is four seasons: summer and winter, cold and hot, rain, icey spots. Flower petals always falling on the floor, leaves always on the floor.
>
> We are dealing with nature and we are hoping for the best. We are not responsible for anyone get hurt on the premises.
>
> Thank you.

The court found that the defendant should have anticipated an unreasonable risk of harm to the plaintiff despite the posted signs. The defendant, according to the court, had an obligation to take reasonable steps to prevent the harm that occurred to the plaintiff.

In some cases reasonable care may require the possessor to exercise control over third persons. As a tavern owner, for example, he may be obligated to prevent his patrons from becoming so intoxicated that they cause injury to others. This is discussed more in the section dealing with the duty to protect others, later in this chapter.

COMMON LAW DISTINCTIONS TODAY

It is interesting to note that several states have rejected the rigid distinction between invitee, licensee, and trespasser and have instead adopted a reasonable person standard of liability. Some states have abolished the invitee/licensee distinction but continue to apply the old rules of liability regarding trespassers. The majority, however, still adhere to the common law classifications.

OUTSIDE THE POSSESSOR'S PROPERTY

The reasons underlying the limitations on landowner liability are less persuasive when the dangerous condition affects those outside the possessor's property. Possessors are generally found liable for conditions that pose an unreasonable risk of harm to persons outside the premises (Restatement (Second) of Torts §§ 364–365). This is particularly true where the hazardous condition is artificially created by the possessor. Artificial conditions include manmade structures; additions to the land, such as trees; and alterations to the land, such as excavations.

If a possessor of land, for example, alters the condition of the premises so that the normal course of surface water is altered and it flows out onto a highway, she may be held liable for injuries caused by her negligence. Courts are less likely to impose liability, however, if the offending object is something like a telephone pole or mailbox, which are necessities and are also above-ground objects.

In contrast, if the hazardous condition is a natural one, the possessor is under no duty to remove it or protect others from it even if it poses an unreasonable danger of harm to people outside the property (Restatement (Second) of Torts § 363(1)). This general rule becomes more complicated when dealing with trees. In urban and suburban areas the courts have obligated possessors to prevent trees from exposing people outside the premises to an unreasonable risk of harm. They have also required the removal of rotten trees and have imposed an affirmative duty to inspect to discover potential defects in trees. In rural areas no duty to remove rotten trees or to inspect for defects has been imposed. Some modern courts have rejected the rural/urban distinction in the case of fallen trees and have held possessors to a reasonable care standard.

PUTTING IT INTO PRACTICE 5.2

1. How would you classify the following:
   a. A salesman soliciting magazines from door-to-door
   b. Children playing on a vacant lot where the landowner is aware that the children use the lot to play ball and does nothing to chase them away
   c. Children playing on a vacant lot where the landowner has installed playground equipment and has posted a sign welcoming children to play there
   d. A truck driver who delivers goods that have been ordered by the homeowner
   e. A customer who goes behind the counter in a department store without receiving permission to do so
2. A nineteen-month-old child falls into a pool and is seriously injured while her parents are houseguests of the homeowner. The parents have been warned about the pool. Is the homeowner liable for the child's injuries? What duty of care is owed the child?
3. A department store has a weighing scale that protrudes into the aisle. Although the scale is obvious to anyone who is looking, it is surrounded by displays of goods. A customer who is intent on looking at the displays fails to see the scale and trips over it, falling to the ground and injuring her arm. What duty does the department store owe to a customer? Could the store be subject to liability?

LANDLORD/TENANT LIABILITY

Under the common law the reason for limiting a possessor's liability was to promote the possessor's right to use the land to its fullest potential with minimal interference from others. Therefore, protection was given to the actual possessor of the land and not the abstract legal owner. As a result of this principle a tenant who is in possession of the property is entitled to the protection of the common law rules. In addition, members of the tenant's household, as well as those in his employ or working the land for him as independent contractors, are also entitled to the protection of the common law rules. A landlord, accordingly, was relieved of liability under the traditional common law once she surrendered possession of her property to the tenant. (See Figure 5-3.)

Tenant's Duties

A tenant is held to the same duty of inspection in reference to invitees as is a landowner. Consequently, a tenant is liable for the injuries to an invitee resulting from a defect that could have been discovered using reasonable care even if the tenant did not in fact discover it. This liability does not extend, however, to common areas such as elevators, stairways, and corridors if the building is an office building or a dwelling with multiple tenants.

Landlord's Duties

The general rule of nonliability of landlords has been significantly altered today by modern social policy concerns. A landlord is liable, for example, to the tenant and to the tenant's invitees and licensees for those dangers that the landlord knows or should know about and that the tenant has no reason to know about (Restatement (Second) of Torts § 358). Most courts do not interpret this as requiring the landlord to inspect the premises. The thrust of this rule is to protect the tenant from hidden dangers of which the landlord is aware or should reasonably anticipate. The landlord has a higher duty if he has reason to believe that the tenant is planning on holding the premises open to the public. In such cases the landlord has an affirmative duty to inspect the premises to find and repair any damages.

What happens if the landlord contracts with the tenant to keep the premises in good repair? Certainly the tenant can sue for breach of contract if the landlord fails to make timely repairs. The question is, however, whether the tenant can sue in tort as well. The majority of courts allow a tort claim to anyone injured as a result of the landlord's breach of his covenant to repair. In such a case the plaintiff must show that the landlord failed to use reasonable care in performing his contractual duties. The landlord, of course, must be given a reasonable time to correct a condition once he has been notified of it.

Even if a landlord has no contractual duty to perform repairs, once he begins performance he must do so reasonably. If he initiates repairs and then fails to complete them, he in effect makes the situation worse because tenants are implicitly led to believe that the

FIGURE 5-3

TENANT'S DUTIES	LANDLORD'S DUTIES
• Same duties as possessor of land • Duty does not extend to common areas	• Liable for dangers he knows or should know about and tenant has no reason to know about • Duty to inspect for dangers when landlord knows property is to be held open to public • Must use reasonable care if he contracts with tenant to keep premises in good repair • If landlord begins to make repairs he must perform reasonably • In some cases has duty to take security precautions to protect tenants from criminal activity

dangerous condition no longer exists. In such a case anyone on the premises with the tenant's consent who is injured by the landlord's negligence will be allowed to recover against the landlord. However, if the tenant is aware that the repairs were incomplete or were done in a negligent manner, the tenant and not the landlord will be held liable. If the landlord hires an independent contractor to carry out the repairs he will usually be held liable for the contractor's negligence. The reasoning is that a landlord cannot delegate his responsibility to a third party.

Does a landlord have a duty to take security precautions to make the premises as safe as possible for tenants? Such a duty was imposed in the landmark decision *Kline v. 1500 Massachusetts Avenue Apartment Corp., 439 F.2d 477 (D.D.C. 1970)*. Note in reading this case the analogy the court draws between the duty of innkeepers to protect their guests from attacks and the duty owed by landlords to protect their tenants.

CASE

Sarah B. Kline, Appellant, v.
1500 Massachusetts Avenue Apartment Corp. et al.
439 F.2d 477 (D.D.C. 1970)

WILKEY, Circuit Judge:

The appellee apartment corporation states that there is "only one issue presented for review * * * whether a duty should be placed on a landlord to take steps to protect tenants from foreseeable criminal acts committed by third parties". The District Court as a matter of law held that there is no such duty. We find that there is, and that in the circumstances here the applicable standard of care was breached. We therefore reverse and remand to the District Court for the determination of damages for the appellant.

I

The appellant, Sarah B. Kline, sustained serious injuries when she was criminally assaulted and robbed at approximately 10:15 in the evening by an intruder in the common hallway of an apartment house at 1500 Massachusetts Avenue. This facility, into which the appellant Kline moved in October 1959, is a large apartment building with approximately 585 individual apartment units. It has a main entrance on Massachusetts Avenue, with side entrances on both 15th and 16th Streets. At the time the appellant first signed a lease a doorman was on duty at the main

entrance twenty-four hours a day, and at least one employee at all times manned a desk in the lobby from which all persons using the elevators could be observed. The 15th Street door adjoined the entrance to a parking garage used by both the tenants and the public. Two garage attendants were stationed at this dual entranceway; the duties of each being arranged so that one of them always was in position to observe those entering either the apartment building or the garage. The 16th Street entrance was unattended during the day but was locked after 9:00 P.M.

By mid-1966, however, the main entrance had no doorman, the desk in the lobby was left unattended much of the time, the 15th Street entrance was generally unguarded due to a decrease in garage personnel, and the 16th Street entrance was often left unlocked all night. The entrances were allowed to be thus unguarded in the face of an increasing number of assaults, larcenies, and robberies being perpetrated against the tenants in and from the common hallways of the apartment building. These facts were undisputed and were supported by a detailed chronological listing of offenses admitted into evidence. The landlord had notice of these crimes and had in fact been urged by appellant Kline herself prior to the events leading to the instant appeal to take steps to secure the building.[3]

Shortly after 10:00 P.M. on November 17, 1966, Miss Kline was assaulted and robbed just outside her apartment on the first floor above the street level of this 585 unit apartment building. This occurred only two months after Leona Sullivan, another female tenant, had been similarly attacked in the same commonway.

II

At the outset we note that of the crimes of violence, robbery, and assault which had been occurring with mounting frequency on the premises at 1500 Massachusetts Avenue, the assaults on Miss Kline and Miss Sullivan took place in the hallways of the building, which were under the exclusive control of the appellee landlord. Even in those crimes of robbery or assault committed in individual apartments, the intruders of necessity had to gain entrance through the common entry and passageways.[4] These premises fronted on three heavily traveled streets, and had multiple entrances. The risk to be guarded against therefore was the risk of unauthorized entrance into the apartment house by intruders bent upon some crime of violence or theft.

While the apartment lessees themselves could take some steps to guard against this risk by installing extra heavy locks and other security devices on the doors and windows of their respective apartments, yet this risk in the greater part could only be guarded against by the landlord. No individual tenant had it within his power to take measures to guard the garage entranceways, to provide scrutiny at the main entrance of the building, to patrol the common hallways and elevators, to set up any kind of a security alarm system in the building, to provide additional locking devices on the main doors, to provide a system of announcement for authorized visitors only, to close the garage doors at appropriate hours, and to see that the entrance was manned at all times.

The risk of criminal assault and robbery on a tenant in the common hallways of the building was thus entirely predictable; that same risk had been occurring with increasing frequency over a period of several months immediately prior to the incident giving rise to this case; it was a risk whose prevention or minimization was almost entirely within the power of the landlord; and the risk materialized in the assault and robbery of appellant on November 17, 1966.

III

In this jurisdiction, certain duties have been assigned to the landlord because of his *control* of common hallways, lobbies, stairwells, etc., used by all tenants in multiple dwelling units. This Court in *Levine v. Katz,* 132 U.S.App.D.C. 173, 174, 407 F.2d 303, 304 (1968), pointed out that:

It has long been well settled in this jurisdiction that, where a landlord leases separate portions of property and reserves under his own control the halls, stairs, or other parts of the property for use in common by all tenants, he has a duty to all those on the premises of legal right to use ordinary care and diligence to maintain the retained parts in a reasonably safe condition.

While *Levine v. Katz* dealt with a physical defect in the building leading to plaintiff's injury, the rationale as applied to predictable criminal acts by third parties is the same. The duty is the landlord's because by his control of the areas of common use and common danger he is the only party who has the *power* to make the necessary repairs or to provide the necessary protection.

As a general rule, a private person does not have a duty to protect another from a criminal attack by a third person. We recognize that this rule has sometimes in the past been applied in landlord-tenant law, even by this court. Among the reasons for the application of this rule to landlords are: judicial reluctance to tamper with the traditional common law concept of the landlord-tenant relationship; the notion that the act of a third person in

---

3. Appellant Kline testified that one could hardly fail to notice the police cars about the building after each reported crime. She further testified that in 1966, before her assault, she herself had discussed the crime situation with Miss Bloom, the landlord's agent at the premises, and had asked her 'why they didn't do something about securing the building'. Moreover, the record contains twenty police reports of crimes occurring in the building in the year 1966, showing that in several instances these crimes were an almost daily occurrence. Such reports in themselves constitute constructive notice to the landlord.

4. The plaintiff testified that she had returned to her apartment after leaving work at 10:00 p.m. We are in agreement with the trial court that her assailant was an intruder. . . .

That such intruders did enter apartments from the hallways is substantiated by the Police reports which appear in the Record. In a number of instances doors are described as having been forced; in another instance, a tenant surprised a man standing in his front hallway; and there are still more instances of female tenants being awakened in the early morning hours to find an intruder entering their front doors. We also take notice of the fact that this apartment building is of the high rise type, with no easily accessible means of entry on the floors above the street level except by the hallways.

committing an intentional tort or crime is a superseding cause of the harm to another resulting therefrom; the oftentimes difficult problem of determining foreseeability of criminal acts; the vagueness of the standard which the landlord must meet; the economic consequences of the imposition of the duty; and conflict with the public policy allocating the duty of protecting citizens from criminal acts to the government rather than the private sector.

But the rationale of this very broad general rule falters when it is applied to the conditions of modern day urban apartment living, particularly in the circumstances of this case. The rationale of the general rule exonerating a third party from any duty to protect another from a criminal attack has no applicability to the landlord-tenant relationship in multiple dwelling houses. The landlord is no insurer of his tenants' safety, but he certainly is no bystander. And where, as here, the landlord has notice of repeated criminal assaults and robberies, has notice that these crimes occurred in the portion of the premises exclusively within his control, has every reason to expect like crimes to happen again, and has the exclusive power to take preventive action, it does not seem unfair to place upon the landlord a duty to take those steps which are within his power to minimize the predictable risk to his tenants.

This court has recently had occasion to review landlord-tenant law as applied to multiple family urban dwellings. In *Javins v. First National Realty Corporation*, the traditional analysis of a lease as being a conveyance of an interest in land—with all the medieval connotations this often brings—was reappraised, and found lacking in several respects. This court noted that the value of the lease to the modern apartment dweller is that it gives him "a well known package of goods and services—a package which includes not merely walls and ceilings, but also adequate heat, light and ventilation, serviceable plumbing facilities, *secure windows and doors,* proper sanitation, and proper maintenance." It does not give him the land itself, and to the tenant as a practical matter this is supremely unimportant. Speaking for the court, Judge Wright then went on to state, "In our judgment the trend toward treating leases as contracts is wise and well considered. Our holding in this case reflects a belief that leases of urban dwelling units should be interpreted and construed like any other contract."

Treating the modern day urban lease as a contract, this court in *Javins, supra,* recognized, among other things, that repair of the leased premises in a multiple dwelling unit may require access to equipment in areas in the control of the landlord, and skills which no urban tenant possesses. Accordingly, this court delineated the landlord's duty to repair as including continued maintenance of the rented apartment throughout the term of the lease, rightfully placing the duty to maintain the premises upon the party to the lease contract having the capacity to do so, based upon an implied warranty of habitability.

In the case at bar we place the duty of taking protective measures guarding the entire premises and the areas peculiarly under the landlord's control against the perpetration of criminal acts upon the landlord, the party to the lease contract who has the effective capacity to perform these necessary acts.

As a footnote to *Javins, supra,* Judge Wright, in clearing away some of the legal underbrush from medieval common law obscuring the modern landlord-tenant relationship, referred to an innkeeper's liability in comparison with that of the landlord to his tenant. "Even the old common law courts responded with a different rule for a landlord-tenant relationship which did not conform to the model of the usual agrarian lease. Much more substantial obligations were placed upon the keepers of inns (the only multiple dwelling houses known to the common law)."

Specifically, innkeepers have been held liable for assaults which have been committed upon their guests by third parties, if they have breached a duty which is imposed by reason of the inkeeper-guest relationship. By this duty, the innkeeper is generally bound to exercise reasonable care to protect the guest from abuse or molestation from third parties, be they innkeeper's employees, fellow guests, or intruders, if the attack could, or in the exercise of reasonable care, should have been anticipated.

Liability in the innkeeper-guest relationship is based as a matter of law either upon the innkeeper's supervision, care, or control of the premises, or by reason of a contract which some courts have implied from the entrustment by the guest of his personal comfort and safety to the innkeeper. In the latter analysis, the contract is held to give the guest the right to expect a standard of treatment at the hands of the innkeeper which includes an obligation on the part of the latter to exercise reasonable care in protecting the guest.

Other relationships in which similar duties have been imposed include landowner-invitee, businessman-patron, employer-employee, school district-pupil, hospital-patient, and carrier-passenger. In all, the theory of liability is essentially the same: that since the ability of one of the parties to provide for his own protection has been limited in some way by his submission to the control of the other, a duty should be imposed upon the one possessing control (and thus the power to act) to take reasonable precautions to protect the other one from assaults by third parties which, at least, could reasonably have been anticipated. However, there is no liability normally imposed upon the one having the power to act if the violence is sudden and unexpected provided that the source of the violence is not an employee of the one in control.

We are aware of various cases in other jurisdictions following a different line of reasoning, conceiving of the landlord and tenant relationship along more traditional common law lines, and on varying fact situations reaching a different result from that we reach here. Typical of these is a much cited (although only a 4–3) decision of the Supreme Court of New Jersey, *Goldberg v. Housing Authority of Newark, supra* relied on by appellee landlord here. There the court said:

> Everyone can foresee the commission of crime virtually anywhere and at any time. If foreseeability itself gave rise to a duty to provide "police" protection for others, every residential curtilage, every shop, every store, every manufacturing plant would have to be patrolled by the private arm of the owner. And since hijacking and attack upon occupants of motor vehicles are also foreseeable, it would be the duty of every motorist to provide armed protection for his passengers and the property of others. Of course, none of this is at all palatable.

This language seems to indicate that the court was using the word *foreseeable* interchangeably with the word *possible*. In that context, the statement is quite correct. It would be folly to impose liability for mere possibilities. But we must reach the question of liability for attacks which are foreseeable in the sense that they are *probable* and *predictable*. Thus, the United States Supreme Court, in *Lillie v. Thompson* encountered no difficulty in finding that the defendant-employer was liable to the employee because it "was aware of conditions which created a likelihood" of criminal attack.

In the instant case, the landlord had notice, both actual and constructive, that the tenants were being subjected to crimes against their persons and their property in and from the common hallways. For the period just prior to the time of the assault upon appellant Kline the record contains unrefuted evidence that the apartment building was undergoing a rising wave of crime. Under these conditions, we can only conclude that the landlord here "was aware of conditions which created a likelihood" (actually, almost a certainty) that further criminal attacks upon tenants would occur.

Upon consideration of all pertinent factors, we find that there is a duty of protection owed by the landlord to the tenant in an urban multiple unit apartment dwelling.

Summarizing our analysis, we find that this duty of protection arises, first of all, from the logic of the situation itself. If we were answering without the benefit of any prior precedent the issue as posed by the appellee landlord here, "whether a duty should be placed on a landlord to take steps to protect tenants from foreseeable criminal acts committed by third parties," we should have no hesitancy in answering it affirmatively, at least on the basis of the facts of this case.

As between tenant and landlord, the landlord is the only one in the position to take the necessary acts of protection required. He is not an insurer, but he is obligated to minimize the risk to his tenants. Not only as between landlord and tenant is the landlord best equipped to guard against the predictable risk of intruders, but even as between landlord and the police power of government, the landlord is in the best position to take the necessary protective measures. Municipal police cannot patrol the entryways and the hallways, the garages and the basements of private multiple unit apartment dwellings. They are neither equipped, manned, nor empowered to do so. In the area of the predictable risk which materialized in this case, only the landlord could have taken measures which might have prevented the injuries suffered by appellant.

We note that in the fight against crime the police are not expected to do it all; every segment of society has obligations to aid in law enforcement and to minimize the opportunities for crime. The average citizen is ceaselessly warned to remove keys from automobiles and, in this jurisdiction, may be liable in tort for any injury caused in the operation of his car by a thief if he fails to do so, notwithstanding the intervening criminal act of the thief, a third party. . . . In addition, auto manufacturers are persuaded to install special locking devices and buzzer alarms, and real estate developers, residential communities, and industrial areas are asked to install especially bright lights to deter the criminally inclined. It is only just that the obligations of landlords in their sphere be acknowledged and enforced.

Secondly, . . . there is implied in the contract between landlord and tenant an obligation on the landlord to provide those protective measures which are within his reasonable capacity. Here the protective measures which were in effect in October 1959 when appellant first signed a lease were drastically reduced. She continued after the expiration of the first term of the lease on a month to month tenancy. As this court pointed out in *Javins, supra,* "Since the lessees continue to pay the same rent, they were entitled to expect that the landlord would continue to keep the premises in their beginning condition during the lease term. It is precisely such expectations that the law now recognizes as deserving of formal, legal protection."

Thirdly, if we reach back to seek the precedents of common law, on the question of whether there exists or does not exist a duty on the owner of the premises to provide protection against criminal acts by third parties, the most analogous relationship to that of the modern day urban apartment house dweller is not that of a landlord and tenant, but that of innkeeper and guest. We can also consider other relationships, cited above, in which an analogous duty has been found to exist.

IV

We now turn to the standard of care which should be applied in judging if the landlord has fulfilled his duty of protection to the tenant. Although in many cases the language speaks as if the standard of care itself varies, in the last analysis the standard of care is the same—reasonable care in all the circumstances. The specific measures to achieve this standard vary with the individual circumstances. It may be impossible to describe in detail for all situations of landlord-tenant relationships, and evidence of custom amongst landlords of the same class of building may play a significant role in determining if the standard has been met.

In the case at bar, appellant's repeated efforts to introduce evidence as to the standard of protection commonly provided in apartment buildings of the same character and class as 1500 Massachusetts Avenue at the time of the assault upon Miss Kline were invariably frustrated by the objections of opposing counsel and the impatience of the trial judge. At one point during appellant's futile attempts, the judge commented with respect to the degree of proof required to show a custom: "I think the old proverb that one swallow does not make a summer applies. If you can get 100 swallows, you say this must be summertime."

Later, but still during appellant's efforts on this point, the judge commented to opposing counsel,

[M]ay I remind you that it is very dangerous to win a case by excluding the other side's testimony because the Court of Appeals might say that testimony should have been admitted even though you might have won the case with the testimony in.

Appellant then attempted to offer evidence of individual apartment houses with which she was familiar. The trial judge became impatient with the swallow by swallow approach, and needled by opposing counsel's objections, disregarded his own admonition and cut short appellant's efforts in this direction. The record as to custom is thus unsatisfactory, but its deficiencies are directly chargeable to defendant's counsel and the trial judge, not appellant.

We therefore hold in this case that the applicable standard of care in providing protection for the tenant is that standard which this landlord himself was employing in October 1959 when the appellant became a resident on the premises at 1500 Massachusetts Avenue. The tenant was led to expect that she could rely upon this degree of protection. While we do not say that the precise measures for security which were then in vogue should have been kept up (e.g., the number of people at the main entrances might have been reduced if a tenant-controlled intercom-automatic latch system had been installed in the common entryways), we do hold that the same relative degree of security should have been maintained.

The appellant tenant was entitled to performance by the landlord measured by this standard of protection whether the landlord's obligation be viewed as grounded in contract or in tort. As we have pointed out, this standard of protection was implied as an obligation of the lease contract from the beginning. Likewise, on a tort basis, this standard of protection may be taken as that commonly provided in apartments of this character and type in this community, and this is a reasonable standard of care on which to judge the conduct of the landlord here.

V

Given this duty of protection, and the standard of care as defined, it is clear that the appellee landlord breached its duty toward the appellant tenant here.[24] The risk of

---

24. In an apparent attempt to show that, regardless of the amount of care exercised, the landlord here could not possibly have prevented an assault such as that which had befallen the plaintiff, the following cross examination of Miss Kline was undertaken:

criminal assault and robbery on any tenant was clearly predictable, a risk of which the appellee landlord had specific notice, a risk which became reality with increasing frequency, and this risk materialized on the very premises peculiarly under the control, and therefore the protection, of the landlord to the injury of the appellant tenant. The question then for the District Court becomes one of damages only. To us the liability is clear.

Having said this, it would be well to state what is *not* said by this decision. We do not hold that the landlord is by any means an insurer of the safety of his tenants. His duty is to take those measures of protection which are within his power and capacity to take, and which can reasonably be expected to mitigate the risk of intruders assaulting and robbing tenants. The landlord is not expected to provide protection commonly owed by a municipal police department; but as illustrated in this case, he is obligated to protect those parts of his premises which are not usually subject to periodic patrol and inspection by the municipal police. We do not say that every multiple unit apartment house in the District of Columbia should have those same measures of protection which 1500 Massachusetts Avenue enjoyed in 1959, nor do we say that 1500 Massachusetts avenue should have precisely those same measures in effect at the present time. Alternative and more up-to-date methods may be equally or even more effective.

Granted, the discharge of this duty of protection by landlords will cause, in many instances, the expenditure of large sums for additional equipment and services, and granted, the cost will be ultimately passed on to the tenant in the form of increased rents. This prospect, in itself, however, is no deterrent to our acknowledging and giving force to the duty, since without protection the tenant already pays in losses from theft, physical assault and increased insurance premiums.

The landlord is entirely justified in passing on the cost of increased protective measures to his tenants, but the rationale of compelling the landlord to do it in the first place is that he is the only one who is in a position to take the necessary protective measures for overall protection of the premises, which he owns in whole and rents in part to individual tenants.

Reversed and remanded to the District Court for the determination of damages.

Q. Is it also correct that this apartment building also houses office apartments?

A. As the years went by they were putting more and more offices into the building, yes, sir.

Q. What type of offices would they be?

A. Well, I understood they were supposed to be professional offices because I tried to get my name listed once.

Q. Irrespective of whether you tried to get your name listed or not, did you observe the offices?

A. Yes, I worked for some of them.

Q. What type of organizations had their offices there?

A. Manufacturing representatives; there was a lawyer's office, maybe two; there were some engineers; there were some tour salesmen. That is all I can think of right now.

Q. So that there would be then in the course of a normal day clients going in and out of the lawyers' offices or customers going in and out of the other type offices, would that be correct?

A. Yes.

Q. And they would be able to walk in even if there was a doorman there?

A. Yes.

Q. And one would only speculate as to whether or not anyone could ever leave or not leave, isn't that also correct?

A. What do you mean, speculate if one could leave or not leave?

To which the trial court commented:

THE COURT: Well, we assume the general public would come into any office building or in any big apartment house.

* * *

THE COURT: The point is though that an intruder who commits this kind of an assault is apt to act a little different from the rest of the public although it does not always follow, you never know. Of course an intruder is not likely to come in through a public entrance either.

To this we add our own comment that it is unlikely in any case that a patron of one of the businesses, even if disposed to criminal conduct, would have waited for five hours after the usual closing time to perpetrate his crime—especially one of a violent nature. Further, although it is not essential to our decision in this case, we point out that it is not at all clear that a landlord who permits a portion of his premises to be used for business purposes and the remainder for apartments would be free from liability to a tenant injured by the criminal act of a lingering patron of one of the businesses. If the risk of such injury is foreseeable, then the landlord may be liable for failing to take reasonable measures to protect his tenant from it.

We note parenthetically that no argument regarding any change in the character of the building or its tenants was pursued on appeal.

PUTTING IT INTO PRACTICE 5.3

1. Summarize the key facts, i.e., those facts the court relied on in rendering its decision, in *Kline*.
2. What is the issue in this case?
3. Does a private person have a duty to protect another person from criminal attacks? Do innkeepers? What accounts for the difference in duty?
4. Did the court find the criminal attack upon the plaintiff foreseeable? Why?
5. What reasoning does the court use to arrive at its conclusion regarding the duty landlords owe tenants in reference to preventing criminal attacks?
6. What standard of care does the court apply to landlords in reference to protecting tenants?
7. Suppose that the plaintiff was assaulted when she left her job at an agency of the federal government and that she argues that the assault occurred because the entrance to the building was left unguarded and because the lights were lowered for energy conservation purposes. Further suppose that the agency was in a high-crime area but that no crimes against persons except those involving employees had occurred in the building in the several months preceding the assault on the plaintiff. Do you think a court would find that the agency had a duty to protect the plaintiff from criminal assault if the agency could show that it complied with the community standard of care? In other words, do you think the factual differences between this case and *Kline* would justify a finding of no duty of care?

SELLERS OF LAND

In general, a seller of land is released from tort liability once the buyer takes possession of the property. If, however, the seller fails to disclose a dangerous condition of which she is or should be aware and which she should realize that the buyer will not discover, she will be liable to anyone injured as a result of that condition (Restatement (Second) of Torts § 353). Her liability ceases when the buyer has a "reasonable opportunity" to find and correct the defect, even if the buyer does not in fact discover it (Restatement (Second) of Torts § 353(2)). If the seller hides the defect or intentionally misleads the buyer into not looking for it, the seller's liability will continue until the buyer actually discovers the condition and has a reasonable time to correct it.

If the seller of a house is also its builder, some courts hold the seller liable for any injuries caused by defects in the house. The courts in such cases analogize to product liability cases, in which both negligence and strict liability theories are utilized. See Chapter 13 for a discussion of liability in this area.

DUTY TO PROTECT OR AID OTHERS
Common Law No-Duty Rule

Under the common law a defendant has no legal obligation to aid a plaintiff in distress unless a special relationship exists between the plaintiff and the defendant. This rule applies even though the defendant could assist the plaintiff without causing any harm to himself. The extent to which this doctrine can be taken is illustrated dramatically in *Yania v. Bigan,* 155 A.2d 343 (Pa. 1959). In this case the defendant enticed his friend to jump into a trench containing eight to ten feet of water and then refused to rescue his friend when it became obvious that he was drowning. The court found that the defendant was not liable for his friend's death even though he could have easily saved him. For obvious reasons this doctrine has been subject to scathing criticism by legal commentators and seems to be unique to Anglo/American law.

Special Relationships

More imposing than the duty to rescue others is the duty to protect plaintiffs from the negligent, intentional, or criminal acts of third parties—and the law is loathe to impose this duty. Generally speaking, such a duty arises only in the context of special relationships, such as between parent and child, jailor and prisoner, carrier and passenger, or employer and employee (see Figure 5-4). Common carriers such as airline, railroad, and bus companies have a duty to protect their passengers. A bus company may be liable, for example, if a brawl breaks out on a bus, resulting in injury to sev-

eral passengers, and the bus driver does nothing to intervene. An employer also has a duty to protect employees from those dangers from which they are not able to protect themselves. Such duty is limited to situations within the scope and course of the employees' responsibilities.

In some situations a special relationship may exist even between a university and a student. A court is likely to impose a duty of care on a university, for example, when the harm involved is that of a physical nature, such as a criminal attack. A court is most unlikely, however, to hold a university responsible for the private affairs of its students, particularly when the harm that occurs is of a moral nature.

Defendant's Relationship with Third Parties

In some cases the duty to protect owed by the defendant to the plaintiff arises out of a special relationship

FIGURE 5-4

SPECIAL RELATIONSHIPS CREATING DUTY OF CARE	
Parent	Child
Husband	Wife
Teacher	Pupil
Jailor	Prisoner
Common Carrier	Passenger
Employer	Employee
University	Student
Possessor of Land	Licensee/Invitee
Innkeeper	Guest
Rescuer	Victim

DEFENDANT'S RELATIONSHIP WITH THIRD PARTY CREATING DUTY OF CARE TO PLAINTIFF	
Attorney	Client
Doctor	Patient
Guardian	Mentally Ill Person
Tavern Owner	Intoxicated Patron
Car Owner	Intoxicated Driver

the defendant has with a third party. For instance, the guardian of a mentally ill patient who is potentially dangerous may be held liable for injuries inflicted by his dangerous charge.

The obligation to control a third party becomes particularly problematic when the relationship between the defendant and the third party is that of attorney–client or doctor–patient. In the controversial case of *Tarasoff v. Regents of University of California*, 529 P.2d 553 (Cal. 1974), a patient told his psychotherapist that he intended to kill the plaintiff (whom he did, in fact, kill). The court held that the defendant psychotherapist had a duty to warn the plaintiff of the patient's intentions if a reasonable person in those circumstances would have done so. Admittedly, the doctor–patient privilege was inapplicable in this case because disclosure was necessary to prevent threatened danger. Nevertheless, the *Tarasoff* holding blurs the line between professionals' obligation to protect others and their need to promote open communication between themselves and their clients.

An area in which the defendant's relationship with a negligent third party is becoming increasingly significant involves situations in which the third party is intoxicated. A defendant who loans her vehicle to an intoxicated person, for example, may be liable for injuries caused by that person. Similarly, under the so-called "dram shop" laws, a tavern owner who sells liquor to an obviously intoxicated patron may be liable for injuries inflicted as a result of the patron's negligence. An increasing number of states are extending such liability to social hosts, especially those who violate statutes prohibiting the sale of liquor to minors. As the public becomes more conscious of the potential dangers associated with the immoderate consumption of alcohol (and other drugs), the courts appear to be more inclined to elevate the standard of care to which providers of alcohol are held.

Emergency Assistance

Duty also arises out of the special relationship that is created when a defendant begins to render assistance to a person in need. Once assistance is begun it must be administered using reasonable care. Every reasonable means possible must be utilized to keep the plaintiff safe. Part of the rationale underlying this rule is that once a party has begun helping another, others will be less likely to provide aid themselves. Also, if the defendant discontinues aid or gives it in an unreasonable manner, the plaintiff is essentially in a worse position than had the defendant done nothing at all.

One hospital, for example, was found liable for the injuries sustained by a child who was turned away and whose condition was worsened as a result (*Wilmington General Hospital v. Manlove,* 174 A.2d 135 (Del. 1961)). The court reasoned that by maintaining an emergency ward the hospital had in effect induced the plaintiff to forgo other forms of medical assistance. Thus, the hospital was liable for the injuries it created by the delay it had indirectly caused.

Pursuant to the Good Samaritan statutes in many jurisdictions, anyone providing emergency medical assistance is not liable for damages arising from that assistance as long as care is provided in good faith and does not constitute gross negligence. The intent of such statutes is to encourage people to render emergency assistance.

Voluntary Undertaking Doctrine

A defendant may be found liable even though it has no legal duty to protect the plaintiff. In one case the defendant railroad company established a watchman at a street crossing to warn drivers of approaching trains. When the watchman failed to give a warning and a driver, who was aware of the practice and relied on it in crossing the track, was injured, the defendant was found liable (*Erie Railroad v. Stuart,* 40 F.2d 855 (6th Cir. 1930)). Once the defendant undertook to protect drivers, the court reasoned, it induced reliance and was therefore liable when it discontinued its practice.

Some courts have applied this so-called "voluntary undertaking" doctrine even when the plaintiff did not rely on the defendant's undertaking of services. In one Illinois case, for example, the court found an insurance company liable for negligently carrying out a gratuitously undertaken safety inspection and concluded that liability was not restricted to those who relied upon the inspection, but extended to "such persons as defendant could reasonably have foreseen would be endangered as the result of negligent performance." *Nelson v. Union Wire Rope Corp.,* 199 N.E.2d 769, 779 (Ill. 1964).

Some modern courts have allowed a plaintiff who relied on a defendant's promise to recover even if the defendant made no overt act of assisting the plaintiff. In one case the sheriff's department was found liable for failing to live up to its promise to warn the plaintiff's wife when a dangerous prisoner, whom she had assisted in having arrested, was released. Shortly after his release he killed her. By inducing the plaintiff's wife to rely on its promise to warn her, the defendant was held liable even though it had done nothing overtly to assist her *(Morgan v. County of Yuba,* 41 Cal. Rptr. 508 (1964)).

Defendants may be liable to third parties as well when they undertake a service they have no legal duty to perform and perform the service negligently. Once again, it is the third party's reliance on the reasonable performance of that service that imposes liability on the defendant. Suppose a business hires a company, for example, to inspect its elevators and the company negligently reports that the elevators are in good condition when they are not. If someone is injured when one of the elevators falls, the company owes a duty of care to the injured person.

Public Entities

The same theory of duty that applies to private individuals also applies to public entities. In other words, the analysis of duty for a public body is essentially the same as it is for private persons. A state may be liable to an invitee just as if it were a private landowner. Cities, of course, have unique duties, such as providing police and fire protection and keeping the streets safe for purposes of transportation. The limited sovereign immunity (a tort defense that absolves the defendant of liability because of the defendant's status as a governmental entity, discussed in greater detail in Chapter 9) of a governmental body can create some interesting twists, however.

In one fascinating New York case, *Riss v. New York,* 22 N.Y.2d 579 (1968), the court used the doctrine of sovereign immunity to exempt the City of New York from liability even though the plaintiff had begged the New York City Police Department to protect her from the man who ultimately maimed her. The dissent's eloquent rebuttal to the majority's rather curt finding of nonliability is excerpted here. Interestingly, the point of contention between the majority and dissent is largely factual and the dissent carefully presents facts as well as reasoning to support its conclusion that the city should be liable for providing negligent police protection. You might be interested to know that Burton Pugach, the attorney who hired the man who maimed Linda Riss, served a fourteen-year sentence. After his release he proposed to Ms. Riss and they were ultimately married.

CASE

Linda Riss, Appellant, v.
City of New York, Respondent
22 N.Y.2d 579 (N.Y. 1968)

KEATING, Judge (dissenting).

Certainly, the record in this case, sound legal analysis, relevant policy considerations and even precedent cannot account for or sustain the result which the majority have here reached. For the result is premised upon a legal rule which long ago should have been abandoned, having lost any justification it might once have had. Despite almost universal condemnation by legal scholars, the rule survives, finding its continuing strength, not in its power to persuade, but in its ability to arouse unwarranted judicial fears of the consequences of over-turning it.

Linda Riss, an attractive young woman, was for more than six months terrorized by a rejected suitor well known to the courts of this State, one Burton Pugach. This miscreant, masquerading as a respectable attorney, repeatedly threatened to have Linda killed or maimed if she did not yield to him: "If I can't have you, no one else will have you, and when I get through with you, no one else will want you". In fear for her life, she went to those charged by law with the duty of preserving and safe-guarding the lives of the citizens and residents of this State. Linda's repeated and almost pathetic pleas for aid were received with little more than indifference. Whatever help she was given was not commensurate with the identifiable danger. On June 14, 1959 Linda became engaged to another man. At a party held to cel-ebrate the event, she received a phone call warning her that it was her "last chance". Completely distraught, she called the police, begging for help, but was refused. The next day Pugach carried out his dire threats in the very manner he had foretold by having a hired thug throw lye in Linda's face. Linda was blinded in one eye, lost a good portion of her vision in the other, and her face was per-manently scarred. After the assault the authorities con-cluded that there was some basis for Linda's fears, and for the next three and one-half years, she was given around-the-clock protection.

No one questions the proposition that the first duty of government is to assure its citizens the opportunity to live in personal security. And no one who reads the record of Linda's ordeal can reach a conclusion other than that the City of New York, acting through its agents, completely and negligently failed to fulfill this obligation to Linda.

Linda has turned to the courts of this State for redress, asking that the city be held liable in damages for its neg-ligent failure to protect her from harm. With compelling logic, she can point out that, if a stranger, who had absolutely no obligation to aid her, had offered her assis-tance, and thereafter Burton Pugach was able to injure her as a result of the negligence of the volunteer, the courts would certainly require him to pay damages. (Restatement, 2d, Torts, § 323.) Why then should the city, whose duties are imposed by law and include the prevention of crime . . . and, consequently, extend far beyond that of the Good Samaritan, not be responsible? If a private detective acts carelessly, no one would deny that a jury could find such conduct unacceptable. Why then is the city not required to live up to at least the same

minimal standards of professional competence which would be demanded of a private detective?

Linda's reasoning seems so eminently sensible that surely it must come as a shock to her and to every citi-zen to hear the city argue and to learn that this court decides that the city has no duty to provide police pro-tection to any given individual. What makes the city's position particularly difficult to understand is that, in con-formity to the dictates of the law, Linda did not carry any weapon for self-defense. . . . Thus, by a rather bitter irony she was required to rely for protection on the City of New York which now denies all responsibility to her.

It is not a distortion to summarize the essence of the city's case here in the following language: "Because we owe a duty to everybody, we owe it to nobody." Were it not for the fact that this position has been hallowed by much ancient and revered precedent, we would surely dismiss it as preposterous. To say that there is no duty is, of course, to start with the conclusion. The question is whether or not there should be liability for the negligent failure to provide adequate police protection.

The foremost justification repeatedly urged for the existing rule is the claim that the State and the munici-palities will be exposed to limitless liability. The city invokes the specter of a "crushing burden" . . . if we should depart from the existing rule and enunciate even the limited proposition that the State and its municipali-ties can be held liable for the negligent acts of their police employees in executing whatever police services they do in fact provide. . . .

The fear of financial disaster is a myth. The same argument was made a generation ago in opposition to proposals that the State waive its defense of "sovereign immunity". The prophecy proved false then, and it would now. The supposed astronomical financial burden does not and would not exist. No municipality has gone bank-rupt because it has had to respond in damages when a policeman causes injury through carelessly driving a police car or in the thousands of other situations where, by judicial fiat or legislative enactment, the State and its subdivisions have been held liable for the tortious con-duct of their employees. Thus, in the past four or five years, New York City has been presented with an aver-age of some 10,000 claims each year. The figure would sound ominous except for the fact the city has been pay-ing out less than $8,000,000 on tort claims each year and this amount includes all those sidewalk defect and snow and ice cases about which the courts fret so often. . . . Court delay has reduced the figure paid somewhat, but not substantially. Certainly this is a slight burden in a budget of more than six billion dollars (less than two tenths of 1 percent) and of no importance as compared to the injustice of permitting unredressed wrongs to continue to go unrepaired. That Linda Riss should be asked to bear the loss, which should properly fall on the city if we assume, as we must, in the present posture of the case, that her injuries resulted from the city's failure to provide sufficient police to protect Linda is contrary to the most elementary notions of justice.

The statement in the majority opinion that there are no predictable limits to the potential liability for failure to provide adequate police protection as compared to other areas of municipal liability is, of course, untenable. When immunity in other areas of governmental activity was removed, the same lack of predictable limits existed. Yet, disaster did not ensue.

Another variation of the "crushing burden" argument is the contention that, every time a crime is committed, the city will be sued and the claim will be made that it resulted from inadequate police protection. Here, again, is an attempt to arouse the "anxiety of the courts about new theories of liability which may have a far-reaching effect". . . . And here too the underlying assumption of the argument is fallacious because it assumes that a strict liability standard is to be imposed and that the courts would prove completely unable to apply general principles of tort liability in a reasonable fashion in the context of actions arising from the negligent acts of police and fire personnel. The argument is also made as if there were no such legal principles as fault, proximate cause or foreseeability, all of which operate to keep liability within reasonable bounds. No one is contending that the police must be at the scene of every potential crime or must provide a personal bodyguard to every person who walks into a police station and claims to have been threatened. They need only act as a reasonable man would under the circumstances. At first there would be a duty to inquire. If the inquiry indicates nothing to substantiate the alleged threat, the matter may be put aside and other matters attended to. If, however, the claims prove to have some basis, appropriate steps would be necessary.

The instant case provides an excellent illustration of the limits which the courts can draw. No one would claim that, under the facts here, the police were negligent when they did not give Linda protection after her first calls or visits to the police station in February of 1959. The preliminary investigation was sufficient. If Linda had been attacked at this point, clearly there would be no liability here. When, however, as time went on and it was established that Linda was a reputable person, that other verifiable attempts to injure her or intimidate her had taken place, that other witnesses were available to support her claim that her life was being threatened, something more was required—either by way of further investigation or protection—than the statement that was made by one detective to Linda that she would have to be hurt before the police could do anything for her.

In dismissing the complaint, the trial court noted that there are many crimes being committed daily and the police force is inadequate to deal with its "tremendous responsibilities". The point is not addressed to the facts of this case. Even if it were, however, a distinction must be made. It may be quite reasonable to say that the City of New York is not required to hire sufficient police to protect every piece of property threatened during mass riots. The possibility of riots may even be foreseeable, but the occurrence is sufficiently uncommon that the city should not be required to bear the cost of having a redundancy of men for normal operations. But it is going beyond the bounds of required judicial moderation if the city is permitted to escape liability in a situation such as the one at bar. If the police force of the City of New York is so understaffed that it is unable to cope with the everyday problem posed by the relatively few cases where single, known individuals threaten the lives of other persons, then indeed we have reached the danger line and the lives of all of us are in peril. If the police department is in such a deplorable state that the city, because of insufficient manpower, is truly unable to protect persons in Linda Riss' position, then liability not only should, but must be imposed. It will act as an effective inducement for public officials to provide at least a minimally adequate number of police. If local officials are not willing to meet even such a low standard, I see no reason for the courts to abet such irresponsibility.

It is also contended that liability for inadequate police protection will make the courts the arbiters of decisions taken by the Police Commissioner in allocating his manpower and his resources. We are not dealing here with a situation where the injury or loss occurred as a result of a conscious choice of policy made by those exercising high administrative responsibility after a complete and thorough deliberation of various alternatives. There was no major policy decision taken by the Police Commissioner to disregard Linda Riss' appeal for help because there was absolutely no manpower available to deal with

Pugach. This "garden variety" negligence case arose in the course of "day-by-day operations of government". . . . Linda Riss' tragedy resulted not from high policy or inadequate manpower, but plain negligence on the part of persons with whom Linda dealt. . . .

More significant, however, is the fundamental flaw in the reasoning behind the argument alleging judicial interference. It is a complete oversimplification of the problem of municipal tort liability. What it ignores is the fact that indirectly courts are reviewing administrative practices in almost every tort case against the State or a municipality, including even decisions of the Police Commissioner. Every time a municipal hospital is held liable for malpractice resulting from inadequate record-keeping, the courts are in effect making a determination that the municipality should have hired or assigned more clerical help or more competent help to medical records or should have done something to improve its record-keeping procedures so that the particular injury would not have occurred. Every time a municipality is held liable for a defective sidewalk, it is as if the courts are saying that more money and resources should have been allocated to sidewalk repair, instead of to other public services.

The situation is nowise different in the case of police protection. Whatever effects there may be on police administration will be one of degree, not kind. . . .

The truth of the matter, however, is that the courts are not making policy decisions for public officials. In all these municipal negligence cases, the courts are doing two things. First, they apply the principles of vicarious liability to the operations of government. Courts would not insulate the city from liability for the ordinary negligence of members of the highway department. There is no basis for treating the members of the police department differently.

Second, and most important, to the extent that the injury results from the failure to allocate sufficient funds and resources to meet a minimum standard of public administration, public officials are presented with two alternatives: either improve public administration or accept the cost of compensating injured persons. Thus, if we were to hold the city liable here for the negligence of the police, courts would no more be interfering with the operations of the police department than they "meddle" in the affairs of the highway department when they hold the municipality liable for personal injuries resulting from defective sidewalks, or a private employer for the negligence of his employees. In other words, all the courts do

in these municipal negligence cases is require officials to weigh the consequences of their decisions. If Linda Riss' injury resulted from the failure of the city to pay sufficient salaries to attract qualified and sufficient personnel, the full cost of that choice should become acknowledged in the same way as it has in other areas of municipal tort liability. Perhaps officials will find it less costly to choose the alternative of paying damages than changing their existing practices. That may be well and good, but the price for the refusal to provide for an adequate police force should not be borne by Linda Riss and all the other innocent victims of such decisions.

What has existed until now is that the City of New York and other municipalities have been able to engage in a sort of false bookkeeping in which the real costs of inadequate or incompetent police protection have been hidden by charging the expenditures to the individuals who have sustained often catastrophic losses rather than to the community where it belongs, because the latter had the power to prevent the losses.

Although in modern times the compensatory nature of tort law has generally been the one most emphasized, one of its most important functions has been and is its normative aspect. It sets forth standards of conduct which ought to be followed. The penalty for failing to do so is to pay pecuniary damages. At one time the government was completely immunized from this salutary control. This is much less so now, and the imposition of liability has had healthy side effects. In many areas, it has resulted in the adoption of better and more considered procedures just as workmen's compensation resulted in improved industrial safety practices. To visit liability upon the city here will no doubt have similar constructive effects. No "presumed cure" for the problem of crime is being "foisted" upon the city as the majority opinion charges. The methods of dealing with the problem of crime are left completely to the city's discretion. All that the courts can do is make sure that the costs of the city's and its employees' mistakes are placed where they properly belong. Thus, every reason used to sustain the rule that there is no duty to offer police protection to any individual turns out on close analysis to be of little substance.

* * *

The Appellate Division did not adopt the "no duty" theory, but said there was no negligence here because the danger was not imminent. Despite the fact that the majority of the Appellate Division "agree[d] that certain rulings, and particularly the manner in which they were made, did not add to the appearance of a fair trial", and which, in fact, resulted in a wholly inadequate hearing, the majority found that the "facts brought out on this trial do not show the presence of such imminent danger that extraordinary police activity was so indicated that the failure to take it can be deemed unreasonable conduct." This finding does not stand examination and to its credit the city does not argue that this record would not support a finding of negligence. The danger to Linda was indeed imminent, and this fact could easily have been confirmed had there been competent police work.

Moreover, since this is an appeal from a dismissal of the complaint, we must give the plaintiff the benefit of every favorable inference. The Appellate Division's conclusion could only have been reached by ignoring the thrust of the plaintiff's claim and the evidence in the record. A few examples of the actions of the police should suffice to show the true state of the record. Linda Riss received a telephone call from a person who warned Linda that Pugach was arranging to have her beaten up. A detective learned the identity of the caller. He offered to arrest the caller, but plaintiff rejected that suggestion for the obvious reason that the informant was trying to help Linda. When Linda requested that Pugach be arrested, the detective said he could not do that because she had not yet been hurt. The statement was not so. It was and is a crime to conspire to injure someone. True there was no basis to arrest Pugach then, but that was only because the necessary leg work had not been done. No one went to speak to the informant, who might have furnished additional leads. Linda claimed to be receiving telephone calls almost every day. These calls could have been monitored for a few days to obtain evidence against Pugach. Any number of reasonable alternatives presented themselves. A case against Pugach could have been developed which would have at least put him away for a while or altered the situation entirely. But, if necessary, some police protection should have been afforded.

Perhaps, on a fuller record after a true trial on the merits, the city's position will not appear so damaging as it does now. But with actual notice of danger and ample opportunity to confirm and take reasonable remedial steps, a jury could find that the persons involved acted unreasonably and negligently. Linda Riss is entitled to have a jury determine the issue of the city's liability. This right should not be terminated by the adoption of a question-begging conclusion that there is no duty owed to her. The order of the Appellate Division should be reversed and a new trial granted.

PUTTING IT INTO PRACTICE 5.4

1. According to the dissent in *Riss,* what is the essence of the majority's argument?
2. What is the "crushing burden" argument?
3. How does the dissent counter the "crushing burden" argument?
4. How does the dissent respond to the argument that allowing liability for inadequate police protection will make the courts the arbiters of decisions made by the police commissioner in allocating manpower and resources?
5. Of what kind of false bookkeeping does the dissent accuse the City of New York?
6. What is the "normative" aspect of tort law to which the dissent refers?

UNBORN CHILDREN

An area that has been subject to considerable controversy of late is whether a duty of care is owed to an unborn child. Suppose a defendant assaults a pregnant woman, recklessly injuring the fetus and causing defects that manifest physically when the child is born.

PUTTING IT INTO PRACTICE 5.5

Ms. Figueroa is abducted at gunpoint in the parking lot of the Child Care Center, where she has just dropped her child off. She is sexually assaulted and slashed with a knife. The parking lot is owned by North Park College, which both informally and formally (via a letter written to the parents of children attending the Child Care Center) allows parents to use the parking lot. North Park employs off-duty police officers to patrol its campus, including the parking lot. Before this incident only minor crimes had occurred anywhere on campus.

Ms. Figueroa sues North Park for negligent failure to provide adequate security in the parking lot. Should Ms. Figueroa be treated as an invitee or a licensee? Is there any other legal theory she might rely on to establish a duty of protection?

Under the common law the child could not recover for its injuries. Modern courts have reversed this no-duty rule and have allowed recovery in most instances where a causal link between the defendant's act and the fetus' injury can be proven. This causal link can be highly speculative with a recently conceived embryo and the Restatement suggests that courts require "convincing evidence" of causation in these circumstances (Restatement (Second) of Torts, § 869, cmt. d).

Some cases have implied in dicta that only fetuses that were viable (capable of surviving outside the uterus) at the time of injury could recover, but all courts directly confronted with the issue have allowed recovery even when the fetus was only a few weeks old at the time of injury. Such reasoning has permitted recovery in cases such as those involving fetuses suffering serious defects in the initial stages of development as a result of their mothers' ingestion of drugs, such as Thalidomide (a medication designed to prevent morning sickness that was later discovered to cause devastating birth defects).

Considerable controversy continues around the question of whether a wrongful death action can be brought if a fetus is stillborn as a result of its injuries. The Restatement suggests that recovery should not be allowed "unless the applicable wrongful death statute so provides" (Restatement (Second) of Torts § 869(2)). The issue in these wrongful death cases is whether the statutes, which usually refer to "persons," were intended to apply to fetuses. The courts are divided on this issue although more courts allow recovery than deny it.

VICARIOUS LIABILITY

Under the principle of **vicarious liability** a defendant may be liable for the tortious acts of another even though he is not at fault. An employer is vicariously liable for the tortious acts of her employees under the doctrine of respondeat superior. Vicarious liability also arises under the "family purpose" doctrine. Because these doctrines impose a duty of care on people who are not directly at fault, we discuss them in this chapter even though they are discussed in greater depth in other chapters.

Respondeat superior means, literally, "Let the superior respond." Under this doctrine the employer is liable for any torts committed by an employee during the scope and furtherance of his employment. An employer can escape liability if she can prove that the employee was acting on his own behalf and not the employer's when he committed the tortious act. Suppose an employee is instructed to use a vehicle to run an errand for his employer but, in the course of running the errand, he deviates substantially from his route to see his girlfriend. If the employee negligently causes a vehicular accident upon leaving his girlfriend's house, his employer will be absolved of liability because the employee was acting outside the scope of his employment.

The rationale underpinning this doctrine is that employers, rather than employees, should bear the expense of any accidents resulting from doing business. Such expense, it is reasoned, should be considered part of the price of doing business. The bottom line is that an employer owes a duty of care to any plaintiff injured by an employee acting in the scope and furtherance of his duties as an employee.

The **family purpose doctrine** holds the owner of a car vicariously liable for the torts committed by those members of his household whom he allows to drive his car. If a father loans his car to his daughter and she negligently injures someone, the father will be vicariously liable for his daughter's negligence. Some states have extended this liability by statute and have provided that the owner of an automobile is vicariously liable for the negligence of anyone who uses his car with his permission.

APPLICATION

In the case involving Teddy, Mr. Goodright, and Gertrude, several questions come to mind in reference to duty. Did the Baxters, for example, owe any duty of care to Teddy, who was a trespasser on their land? To answer that question Teddy's attorney will have to determine if Teddy was a known trespasser. Also she will want to consider whether Gertrude is an attractive nuisance. In answering this question she will have to ask whether the Baxters had reason to know that children were likely to trespass in their backyard and whether Gertrude posed an unreasonable risk of injury to trespassing children. Most importantly, she will have to argue that the Baxters failed to use reasonable care

in protecting children from Gertrude by failing to keep the gate locked. She will also have to be able to prove that Teddy was not aware of the danger posed by Gertrude and that children of his age, intelligence, and experience would not have perceived the danger.

Another question to be addressed is whether the Baxters owed any duty of care to Mr. Goodright. At first it may appear that Mr. Goodright was a trespasser; however, because he entered the land with the express purpose of rescuing another, he would not be considered a trespasser. Consequently, Teddy's attorney would have to research the standard of care accorded rescuers under the case law in her state.

Mr. Baxter did, in fact, have a duty to assist Mr. Goodright once he saw him being attacked by Gertrude. Remember that although generally there is no duty to render assistance to one in need, an exception exists when the danger has been created by the defendant's own conduct or by an instrument under his control. In this case, because Gertrude was legally under Mr. Baxter's control, Mr. Baxter had a duty to aid Mr. Goodright.

SUMMARY

The first question that arises in any negligence case is one of duty. Generally, a defendant is expected to exercise the same degree of care that any reasonable person would use under similar circumstances. The nature of the relationship between the defendant and the plaintiff is important in determining the duty owed.

The duty owed by possessors of land to those on their land depends on the latter's status as either a trespasser, licensee, or invitee. No duty of care is owed to a trespasser to make the land safe or to protect the trespasser in any way. There are four exceptions, however, to this general rule. Some duty of care is owed to trespassing children, to rescuers, to known trespassers, and to those trespassers using only a very limited portion of the possessor's land. A possessor has the duty to warn a licensee of any dangerous conditions of which the possessor is aware and should reasonably anticipate that the licensee will not discover. Invitees are owed the highest duty of care. A possessor has a duty to inspect her premises for hidden dangers when dealing with invitees. Possessors may be liable for those conditions that pose an unreasonable risk of harm to persons outside their premises, especially if the hazardous condition was artificially created by the possessor. The analysis of duty for public entities is essentially the same as the analysis for private individuals except when the doctrine of sovereign immunity is applicable.

In the special relationship of the landlord and tenant, the tenant is the one entitled to the protection of the common law rules. Although the landlord generally escaped liability under the common law once he transferred possession to the tenant, today he is liable for failure to keep premises in good repair and is liable for those dangers that he knows or should know about and about which the tenant has no reason to know.

Like landlords, sellers of land are released from tort liability once they turn the property over to the buyers. However, if a seller fails to disclose a dangerous condition of which he is or should be aware and which he should realize that the buyer will not discover, he will be liable for any injuries resulting from that dangerous condition.

In Anglo/American law people generally have no obligation to assist others in danger. However, when a special relationship exists between plaintiff and defendant, liability may be found for failure to act. A duty of care may also arise out of a special relationship between the defendant and a third party. Those who render aid to others in need or voluntarily undertake to render services to another establish a temporary special relationship. Once they initiate assistance or perform services, they have an obligation to use every reasonable means possible to keep the plaintiff safe.

Under the common law children could not recover for injuries sustained by them while *in utero*. Modern courts are more inclined to allow recovery.

The doctrine of respondeat superior and the family purpose doctrine are examples of vicarious liability, in which the defendant is liable for the tortious acts of another even though the defendant was not at fault. The doctrine of respondeat superior pertains primarily to employers, whereas the family purpose doctrine applies to car owners who allow members of their household to drive.

PRACTICE POINTERS

Jury instructions may be the deciding factor in a case—not because of the influence they have on jurors (most jurors have made up their minds long before they are read the jury instructions), but because of the impact they may have on appeal. Jury instructions that incorrectly state the law may provide grounds for reversal. Therefore, judges are well aware of the significance of jury instructions at the appellate level and place the burden on the attorneys for both sides to draft proposed instructions. These proposals are usually submitted before trial, giving the judge (and opposing counsel) ample time to review them and do any necessary research. After hearing the evidence presented at trial and listening to the arguments of both attorneys regarding jury instructions, the judge prepares instructions that most clearly and accurately present the law as it pertains to the case at hand.

Continued on next page

■   PRACTICE POINTERS—Continued   □

Jury instructions are the definitive statement of the elements of the plaintiff's case. Plaintiff's counsel must make sure that the evidence presented covers each required element (as set forth in the jury instructions), whereas defense counsel must evaluate the weakest elements in the plaintiff's case and focus an attack on those elements. Therefore, from a trial preparation standpoint, jury instructions assist attorneys in focusing on the essential elements of a case and seeing its weakest points.

Attorneys often use legal assistants in the researching and drafting of jury instructions. Jury instructions for the most common causes of action (e.g., motor vehicle accidents and slip and fall cases) can be found in books of recommended jury instructions compiled by the court, state bar associations, or some other authoritative source.

An example of a jury instruction that might be used in the case involving Teddy and the Baxters is shown here.

NEGLIGENCE OF A CHILD
DUTY OF ADULT TO ANTICIPATE BEHAVIOR OF CHILDREN

A child is not held to the same standard of care as an adult.

A child who does not use the degree of care that is ordinarily exercised by children of the same age, intelligence, knowledge, and experience under the existing circumstances is negligent.

An adult must anticipate the ordinary behavior of children, and that children might not exercise the same degree of care for their own safety as adults.

■   TORT TEASERS   □

1. Do the courts in your state classify those who come onto land as invitees, licensees, and trespassers? If not, how are cases involving premises liability analyzed? Is this area of the law controlled by the common law, or statute, or both? What are the applicable statutes?

In each of the following cases, discuss whether a duty of care is owed by the defendant to the plaintiff.

2. Plaintiff, a sixteen-year-old boy, is visiting the home of a friend when he notices a cat at the top of a utility pole in a neighboring yard. He climbs the pole, in part to rescue the cat and in part to see if he can climb the pole. When he arrives at the top of the pole he receives an electric shock and falls, sustaining injuries. *Brown v. Arizona Public Service Co.,* 790 P.2d 290 (Ariz. Ct. App. 1990).

3. Plaintiff, who is a pedestrian walking by a baseball park, is hit on the head by a foul ball hit by one of the players. Plaintiff sues Defendant, the owner of the baseball park, for her injuries. *Salevan v. Willington Park, Inc.,* 72 A.2d 239 (Del. 1950).

4. Plaintiff, who was shopping in Defendant's store, is bitten by Defendant's cat. Defendant promises to lock up the cat for fourteen days so that he can be tested for rabies. Defendant fails to live up to his promise and the cat disappears for a month, requiring Plaintiff to undergo a series of painful rabies

shots. After Plaintiff completes the treatment the cat returns in perfect health. *Marsalis v. La Salle,* 90 So. 2d 120 (La. 1957).

5. Plaintiff and Defendant are officers of a Masonic lodge. Plaintiff comes to Defendant's house to discuss lodge business. Defendant's mentally ill son stabs Plaintiff while he is in the home. Although Defendant is aware that his son committed some violent acts approximately ten years prior to this incident, he has no knowledge at the time of this incident that his son is likely to be violent to Plaintiff or anyone else. *Barmore v. Elmore,* 403 N.E.2d 1355 (Ill. App. Ct. 1980).

KEY TERMS

Attractive nuisance
Dangerous condition on the defendant's property that is likely to induce children to trespass.

Family purpose doctrine
Doctrine that makes the owner of a car liable for the tortious acts of family members committed while driving.

Invitee
Person invited by possessor of land onto her property for the purpose of conducting business.

Licensee
Person who has possessor's consent to be present on land.

Respondeat superior doctrine
Doctrine that makes employer liable for the tortious acts of employees committed in the scope and furtherance of their employment.

Vicarious liability
Liability for the tortious acts of others.

CHAPTER

6

Negligence: Breach of Duty

CHAPTER TOPICS

CHAPTER OBJECTIVES

In this chapter you will learn to:
- Identify the criteria used to assess the reasonableness of a person's conduct
- Distinguish between objective and subjective standards
- Use the Learned Hand formula
- Apply the concepts of negligence per se and res ipsa loquitur

If it can be established that the Baxters owed a duty of care to Teddy and to Mr. Goodright, the next question is whether they breached that duty. Because the duty required in most instances is to use reasonable care, that duty is breached by engaging in unreasonable conduct. Did the Baxters exercise the precautions expected of a reasonable person in their maintenance of Gertrude? Was she adequately confined for a dog of her size and temperament? Did the Baxters create an unreasonable risk of harm for Teddy and other children by failing to lock the latch on their gate?

WHAT IS REASONABLE CONDUCT?

Determining whether a breach of duty has occurred requires (1) a determination of the relevant standard of care and (2) an evaluation of the defendant's conduct in light of that standard. In other words, if the plaintiff is able to prove that she was owed a duty of care by the defendant, that duty gives rise to a general standard of conduct—to use reasonable care. Using reasonable care requires the defendant to recognize the risks created by his actions (or omissions) and to act reasonably in light of those risks. The general standard must then be applied to the specific circumstances of the case to determine the specific standard of care governing the defendant's conduct. The jury is asked to establish this specific standard of care, usually guided by only very general jury instructions defining negligence.

The question of reasonable care boils down to what a reasonable person would have done under similar circumstances. As Prosser and Keeton explain:

> The standard of conduct which the community demands must be an external and objective one, rather than the individual judgment, good or bad, of the particular actor; and it must be, so far as possible, the same for all persons, since the law can have no favorites. At the same time, it must make proper allowance for the risk apparent to the actor, for his capacity to meet it, and for the circumstances under which he must act.
>
> The courts have dealt with this very difficult problem by creating a fictitious person, who never

has existed on land or sea: the "reasonable man of ordinary prudence." Sometimes he is described as a reasonable person, or a person of ordinary prudence, or a person of reasonable prudence, or some other blend of reason and caution.

Prosser & Keeton, *The Law of Torts* § 32, 173 (5th ed. 1984).

A defendant's conduct must be evaluated at the time of the plaintiff's injury. "Monday-morning quarter-backing" is not allowed. What is important is how reasonable people would perceive the defendant's acts at the time they occurred. The plaintiff, consequently, is not permitted to use the self-serving argument that he or she was injured as a direct result of the defendant's conduct and, therefore, the defendant must have been unreasonable.

The characteristics of the proverbial "reasonable person" will be discussed shortly. But first we must consider how our reasonable person decides what to do in a predicament. We can assume that any reasonable person will avoid creating an unreasonable risk of harm for others. The tough question is how he or she calculates such risks and avoids actions that create unreasonable risks.

LEARNED HAND FORMULA

Judge Learned Hand, an influential jurist who is well known for his pragmatic approach to the resolution of this problem, advocated a type of cost/benefit analysis (see Figure 6-1). The judge asked the court to consider the probability that harm would occur as a result of the defendant's conduct (P), the gravity of the potential harm (L), and the burden of precautions that would have to be borne by the defendant to avoid the possible risk (B). He reduced these considerations into a formula and concluded that a defendant breached his duty if:

$$P \times L > B$$

In other words, according to this equation the defendant would be liable if the probability of harm occurring (P) multiplied by the gravity of such harm (L)

FIGURE 6-1 Learned Hand Formula

exceeded the defendant's burden of taking precautions to avoid the harm (*B*).

In considering *B*, the burden of precautions, the courts not only look at the cost involved in taking precautions, but also look at the social utility of the defendant's conduct. What is the social value of the defendant's conduct? If society would be better served by allowing all defendants in the defendant's position to act as he or she did, the courts are less likely to require the defendant to alter that course of conduct.

Application of Learned Hand Formula

Let us apply this equation to a hypothetical problem. Suppose an automobile manufacturer discovers a defect in the design of its automobile, which under certain circumstances has the potential of creating harm to the occupants of the vehicle. Will the manufacturer be acting unreasonably if it fails to alter this defective design?

In answering that question, one would have to calculate the statistical likelihood that accidents resulting in injury to a vehicle's occupants would occur. Next, one would have to consider the gravity of the types of injuries that would most likely occur, as well as the burden to the manufacturer of altering the design. Suppose it can be anticipated that 100 of those vehicles having

this defect will be involved in serious accidents within one year and those accidents will result in injuries costing an average of $1 million in medical expenses. If altering the design would cost the manufacturer $1 million, the manufacturer would be obligated to make the alteration because 100 × $1 million > $1 million.

Notice that under the Learned Hand formula, the more serious the potential injury that could be incurred, the less probable its occurrence must be before the defendant will be obligated to guard against the anticipated injury. Suppose, for example, the risk of injury were less than 20 percent and yet the type of injury likely to occur was death or serious physical injury. The court would be more likely to find the defendant negligent for failure to redesign the vehicle under those circumstances than if there were a 40 percent chance of an accident but the anticipated injuries were relatively minor.

In assigning a value to *B* the courts would not only calculate the cost of altering the design but would also consider the social consequences of not requiring similarly situated defendants to alter their comparably defective designs. If consumers could no longer afford a redesigned vehicle, the new design would have little social utility. Suppose the court in our hypothetical case concludes that the cost of redesigning the vehicle would be prohibitive and that the likelihood and gravity of injuries resulting from the defect would be relatively slight. The court would then conclude that the defendant manufacturer had not breached its duty of care to its consumers. Note, however, that the plaintiffs in such cases could still opt for strict liability and warranty causes of action (both of which are discussed in Chapter 13).

To see the Learned Hand formula applied in an actual case, read *Eimann v. Soldier of Fortune Magazine,* 880 F.2d 830 (5th Cir. 1989), excerpted here. In deciding whether the son and mother of a murder victim should be able to bring a wrongful death action against the magazine that published an ad through which the victim's husband hired an assassin to kill her, the Texas Court applied the Learned Hand risk-utility analysis.

CASE

Eimann v. Soldier of Fortune Magazine, Inc.
880 F.2d 830 (5th Cir. 1989)

W. EUGENE DAVIS, Circuit Judge:

Soldier of Fortune Magazine, Inc. appeals a $9.4 million jury verdict against it in a wrongful death action brought by the son and mother of a murder victim. The jury found that Soldier of Fortune acted with negligence and gross negligence in publishing a personal services classified advertisement through which the victim's husband hired an assassin to kill her. We reverse the judgment entered on the jury's verdict.

I. Facts

John Wayne Hearn shot and killed Sandra Black at the behest of her husband, Robert, who offered to pay Hearn $10,000 for doing so. Robert Black contacted Hearn through a classified advertisement that Hearn ran in Soldier of Fortune Magazine, Inc. (SOF), a publication that focuses on mercenary activities and military affairs.

The ad, which ran in the September, October and November 1984 issues of SOF, read:

EX-MARINES- -67-69 'Nam Vets, Ex-DI, weapons specialist- -jungle warfare, pilot, M.E., high risk assignments, U.S. or overseas. (404) 991-2684.

Hearn testified that "Ex-DI" meant ex-drill instructor; "M.E." meant multi-engine planes; and "high risk assignments" referred to work as a bodyguard or security specialist. Hearn testified that he and another former Marine placed the ad to recruit Vietnam veterans for work as bodyguards and security men for executives. Hearn's partner testified that they also hoped to train troops in South America. This partner never participated in any ad-related jobs and quit the venture shortly after the ad first ran.

Hearn and his partner testified that they did not place the ad with an intent to solicit criminal employment. However, Hearn stated that about 90 percent of the callers who responded to the ad sought his participation in illegal activities including beatings, kidnappings, jailbreaks, bombings and murders. It also generated at least one lawful inquiry from an oil conglomerate in Lebanon seeking ten bodyguards; Hearn received a commission for placing seven men with the company.

Between 1982 and January 1984, Black had asked at least four friends or coworkers from Bryan, Texas to kill Sandra Black or help him kill her. All four refused. Black called Hearn in October 1984 after seeing his ad in SOF.

Hearn testified that his initial conversations with Black focused on Black's inquiries about getting bodyguard work through Hearn. In later calls they discussed the sale of Black's gun collection to Hearn. Hearn testified that he traveled from his home in Atlanta to Black's home in Bryan on January 9, 1985 to look at Black's gun collection. Hearn stated that Black discussed his plans for murdering his wife during the meeting and "hinted" that he wanted Hearn to participate, but did not ask Hearn directly to kill his wife. Hearn did not act on the hint and returned to Atlanta.

Black called Hearn repeatedly after Hearn returned to Atlanta. During one call Black spoke with Hearn's girlfriend, Debbie Bannister. Hearn and Bannister met after she called him in response to his SOF ad.

Black proposed directly that Hearn kill his wife during the call to Bannister. She passed the proposal on to Hearn, who called Black and said he would consider doing it. The two talked by phone several times in the following weeks. After an aborted murder attempt about three weeks later—during which Hearn was to help Black himself kill his wife—Hearn killed Sandra Black on February 21, 1985. By that time Hearn also had killed the ex-husband of Bannister's sister on January 6, 1985 and Bannister's husband on February 2, 1985.

Neither Hearn, who was sentenced to concurrent life sentences for the murders, nor his partner had criminal records when they placed their ad in SOF. Neither had received a dishonorable discharge from the Marines. Further, Hearn included his real name and correct address in submitting the ad to SOF; the ad itself listed Hearn's correct home telephone number.

Sandra Black's son, Gary Wayne Black, and her mother, Marjorie Eimann, sued SOF and its parent, Omega Group, Ltd., for wrongful death under Texas law on the theory that SOF negligently published Hearn's classified ad.

Eimann introduced into evidence about three dozen personal service classified ads selected from the 2,000 or so classified ads that SOF had printed from its inception in 1975 until September 1984. Some ads offered services as a "Mercenary for Hire," "bounty hunter" or "mechanic"; others promised to perform "dirty work," "high risk contracts" or to "do anything, anywhere at the right price."

Eimann presented evidence that seven and perhaps as many as nine classified ads had been tied to crimes or criminal plots. Eimann introduced stories from sources including the Associated Press, United Press International, The Rocky Mountain News, The Denver Post, Time and Newsweek that reported on links between SOF classified ads and at least five of these crimes.

Eimann also presented evidence that law enforcement officials had contacted SOF staffers during investigations of two crimes linked to SOF personal service classifieds. In one case, SOF had provided correspondence from its files—along with two affidavits signed by SOF's managing editor—that were used in the 1982 criminal trial of a Houston man who was convicted of soliciting the murder of his wife; during his effort the man had tried to hire a poisons expert by placing a classified ad in the October 1981 issue of SOF. Eimann also presented testimony from a New Jersey detective, who stated that in April 1984, SOF's advertising manager had helped him to identify a man who placed a classified ad in SOF.

In addition, Eimann presented expert testimony from Dr. Park Dietz, a forensic psychiatrist who had studied SOF, its ads and readership. Dietz testified that an average SOF subscriber—a male who owns camouflage clothing and more than one gun—would understand some phrases in SOF's classified ads as solicitations for illegal activity given the "context" of those ads.

The context included other classified ads in SOF, display ads for semiautomatic rifles and books with titles such as "How to Kill," and SOF articles including "Harassing the Bear, New Afghan Tactics Stall Soviet Victory," "Pipestone Canyon, Summertime in 'Nam and the Dyin' was Easy," and "Night Raiders on Russia's Border." Dietz also described his visit to a SOF convention in summer 1987, where he photographed exhibits of weapons and tactical gear.

Based on his studies, Dietz concluded that the Hearn ad "or any other personal service ad in Soldier of Fortune in 1984 foreseeably is related to the commission of domestic crimes." He suggested that classified ads such as Hearn's would not carry such connotations if they appeared in Esquire or Vanity Fair.

Dietz conceded, however, that he had abandoned an effort to distinguish lawful SOF classified ads from criminal ones on the basis of specific code words such as "gun for hire," "mechanic" and "hunter" because some ads were too ambiguous to assign an illegal meaning to them with any certainty. He also noted that crimes had been linked to SOF classified ads that "seemed relatively innocuous." For example, one ad tied to a kidnapping and extortion plot read:

Recovery and collection. International agents guarantee results on any type of recover[y]. Reply to Delta Enterprises, P.O. Box 5241, Rockford, Illinois 61125.

As Dietz stated, "The code system doesn't work."

SOF relied primarily on the testimony of its president, Robert K. Brown, who stated he did not know or suspect in 1984 that some of the SOF classified ads had been linked to criminal plots. Other SOF staffers and readers echoed these denials. SOF's advertising manager, Joan Steele, testified that she understood the phrase "high risk assignments" in Hearn's ad to mean "gun for hire," but in the sense of a professional bodyguard or security consultant rather than a contract killer.

The district court's first special interrogatory asked the jury whether Hearn's ad "related to" illegal activity. The court's second interrogatory asked, "Did [SOF] . . . know or should it have known from the face or the context of the Hearn advertisement that the advertisement could reasonably be interpreted as an offer to engage in illegal activity?"

The court's instructions charged SOF with knowledge that Hearn's ad reasonably could be interpreted as such an offer when (1) the relation to illegal activity appears on the ad's face; or (2) "the advertisement, embroidered by its context, would lead a reasonable publisher of ordinary prudence under the same or similar circumstances to conclude that the advertisement could reasonably be interpreted" as an offer to commit crimes. The court went on to define "context" as the magazine's (1) "nature"; (2) other advertisements; (3) articles; (4) readership; and (5) knowledge, if any, that other advertisements in the magazine could reasonably be interpreted as an offer to engage in illegal activity.

The jury answered "yes" to the first two interrogatories, and found that SOF's negligence was a proximate cause of Sandra Black's death in response to Interrogatory Three. The court then asked the jury whether SOF's negligence constituted "gross negligence," defined as "conscious indifference." The jury answered "yes" to this interrogatory as well. The jury awarded Eimann $1.9 million in compensatory damages and $7.5 million in punitive damages; the district court entered judgment on the verdict. SOF appeals.

II. ANALYSIS
A. Overview

Eimann presented this case as a straightforward negligence action revolving around one primary issue: whether SOF knew or should have known from the face or context of Hearn's ad that it represented an offer to perform illegal acts. Based on evidence that SOF knew of links between other classified ads and other criminal plots, she contends that SOF owed a duty to recognize ads such as Hearn's that reasonably might be interpreted as criminal solicitations and refrain from publishing them.

SOF argues first that no liability can attach under these facts because the criminal activities of Hearn and Robert Black, rather than Hearn's ad, were the proximate cause of Sandra Black's murder. SOF also argues that imposition of tort liability here contravenes first amendment protection for commercial speech because (1) the judgment below impermissibly imposed a duty on publishers to investigate its advertisers and their ads; and (2) the district court's all-encompassing definition of "context," combined with Dietz's testimony, allowed the jury to penalize SOF for the mercenary and military focus of the magazine's articles and other ads.

We need not address SOF's first amendment attacks on the judgment to resolve this appeal. Assuming without deciding that a Texas court would apply general negligence principles to this case, we conclude that no liability can attach under these principles as a matter of law. SOF owed no duty to refrain from publishing a facially innocuous classified advertisement when the ad's context—at most—made its message ambiguous.

Under Texas law, negligence liability requires the existence of a duty, breach of that duty, and an injury proximately resulting from that breach. The existence of a duty presents a threshold question of law for the court; the jury determines breach and proximate cause only after the court concludes that a duty exists. Our resolution of this case hinges on the initial duty question.

B. Duty

In essence, a duty represents a legally enforceable obligation to conform to a particular standard of conduct. Whether the defendant in a negligence action owes a duty involves consideration of two related issues: (1) whether the defendant owes an obligation to this particular plaintiff to act as a reasonable person would in the circumstances; and (2) the standard of conduct required to satisfy that obligation.

Texas courts have applied risk-utility balancing tests in resolving both aspects of the duty question. Thus, in deciding whether an actor owes a duty of reasonable care to the public at large, the Supreme Court of Texas has weighed the risk, foreseeability and likelihood of injury from certain conduct against the conduct's social utility and the burden of guarding against injury.

Similarly, Texas courts have applied risk-utility analysis in determining the second duty issue—whether a defendant who owes an established duty of reasonable care to specified parties must take precautions against particular dangers. Courts have described this aspect of duty as the defendant's obligation to protect those parties against unreasonable risks. A risk becomes unreasonable when its magnitude outweighs the social utility of the act or omission that creates it.

Our analysis here assumes that SOF owes a duty of reasonable care to the public; we focus on the second prong of the duty issue: whether SOF's decision to print Hearn's ad violated the standard of conduct.

In answering this question we look to Judge Learned Hand's concise expression of these balancing principles in *United States v. Carroll Towing,* 159 F.2d 169, 173 (2d Cir.1947). As he described it in algebraic terms, liability turns on whether the burden of adequate precautions, B, is less than the probability of harm, P, multiplied by the gravity of the resulting injury, L. In other words, an actor falls below the standard of conduct and liability attaches when B is less than PL. Conversely, the actor satisfies the obligation to protect against unreasonable risks when the burden of adequate precautions—examined in light of the challenged action's value—outweighs the probability and gravity of the threatened harm.

We now turn to these individual factors.

1. The Probability and Gravity of the Threatened Harm

In assessing the threatened harm we note that "nearly all human acts . . . carry some recognizable but remote possibility of harm to another." The SOF classified ads presented more than a remote risk. Of the 2,000 or so personal service classified ads that SOF printed between 1975 and 1984, Eimann's evidence established that as many as nine had served as links in criminal plots. Of these nine, the evidence revealed that SOF staffers had participated in at least two police investigations of crimes in which classified ads played a role; other crimes tied to the ads received varying amounts of media coverage.

As noted above, the gravity of the threatened harm may require precautions against even unlikely events. For example, the standard of care may require those who own oil storage tanks to take precautions against fires caused by an unpredictable lightning strike. The prospect of ad-inspired crime represents a threat of serious harm. Eimann presented evidence that SOF classified ads played a role in other crimes ranging from extortion to jail-breaks. Sandra Black's murder illustrates one aspect of the crime linked to SOF classified advertisements.

2. The Burden of Preventing the Harm

SOF contends that the standard of conduct applied by the district court impermissibly required the magazine to guard against criminal solicitation by investigating its advertisers and their ads. It relies on a series of cases holding that newspaper publishers owe no duty in tort to investigate their advertisers for the accuracy of ads placed for publication.

However, in our view the standard of conduct against which the jury measured SOF's actions was more exacting than a duty to investigate; it requires publishers to recognize ads that "reasonably could be interpreted as an offer to engage in illegal activity" based on their words or "context" and refrain from printing them. Based on evidence that SOF knew other ads had been tied to crimes, Eimann's counsel contended at oral argument that SOF should have refrained from publishing Hearn's ad and all other personal service classified ads—suggestive ones and bland ones alike. This represents an especially heavy burden given (1) the ambiguous nature of Hearn's ad; and (2) the pervasiveness of advertising in our society.

At most, the residence reveals that Hearn submitted a facially innocuous ad. Standing alone, the phrase "high risk assignments" plausibly encompassed Hearn's professed goal of recruiting candidates for bodyguard jobs. Hearn performed precisely that function for at least one client who contacted him through the ad.

Eimann's effort to portray Hearn's ad as a readily identifiable criminal solicitation falls with Dr. Dietz's repudiation of his effort to identify specific code words signalling criminal intent. At one point in his testimony, Dr. Dietz analyzed a classified ad from the February 1980 issue of SOF. In terms that parallel Hearn's ad, this 1980 ad recruited SOF readers for "exciting high risk undercover stateside work." A court later convicted the individual who submitted it of mailing a threatening communication after he sent a letter instructing someone who had responded to the ad to "terminate" a person in Oklahoma City. Dr. Dietz stated:

In 1984, in my opinion, someone familiar with the classified ads that have been run for years in Soldier of Fortune would be able to recognize from that ad that this is possibly someone who would be willing to be involved in criminal activity; but they might be wrong when they thought that. We knew that sometimes there were honest advertisers, and we know that some of the readers who responded to ads were honest too. . . .

Dr. Dietz's description applies with equal force to Hearn's ad. Its bare terms reveal no identifiable offer to commit crimes, just as a locksmith's ad in the telephone directory reveals nothing about that particular advertiser's willingness to commit burglaries or steal cars.

This ambiguity persists even if we assume that SOF knew other ads had been tied to criminal plots. No evidence linked the other ads and crimes to Hearn. And as Eimann conceded, even if SOF had investigated Hearn and his partner in 1984, it would have discovered no criminal records and no false information that might have aroused suspicion.

Further, Eimann's heavy reliance on "context" cannot compensate for the fundamental ambiguity of Hearn's ad even if we assume that the district court properly defined that context. The presence in SOF of other ads and articles with violent themes provides no realistic method for gauging the likelihood that a particular ad will foster illegal activity. Do ads touting high-performance cars become solicitations for illegal activity when buyers drive them beyond the speed limit? Only when the ads run in Car and Driver magazine? Or, only when the ads run in magazines that also contain ads for radar detectors?

While we do not reach SOF's first amendment arguments, the Supreme Court's recognition of limited first amendment protection for commercial speech nonetheless highlights the important role of such communication for purposes of risk-benefit analysis. As the Court has noted, "[T]he particular consumer's interest in the free flow of commercial information . . . may be as keen, if not keener by far, than his interest in the day's most urgent political debate" . . . .

Eimann seeks to discount the importance of SOF's classified ads by stressing that (1) SOF's publisher promoted the ads because they added to the "flavor and mystique" of the magazine; and (2) the jury found that Hearn's ad "relate[d] to" illegal activity. She notes that the Supreme Court has excluded advertising of illegal activity from the scope of first amendment protection. However, in the constitutional arena we have noted that the possibility of illegal results does not necessarily strip an ad of its commercial speech protection.

* * *

Similarly, a standard of conduct that imposes tort liability whenever the advertised product "could reasonably be interpreted as an offer to engage in illegal activity"—or might "relate to" criminal conduct—imposes an especially heavy burden.

3. Balancing the Burdens and Risks

We conclude that the standard of conduct imposed by the district court does not strike the proper balance between the risks of harm from ambiguous advertisement and the burden of preventing harm from this source under these facts. The appreciable risk that ads such as Hearn's will cause harm, combined with the gravity of that harm, does not outweigh the onerous burden Eimann asks us to endorse.

Hearn's ad presents a risk of serious harm. But everyday activities, such as driving on high-speed, closed access roadways, also carry definite risks that we as a society choose to accept in return for the activity's usefulness and convenience. To take a more extreme example, courts have almost uniformly rejected efforts to hold handgun manufacturers liable under negligence or strict liability theories to gunshot victims injured during crimes, despite the real possibility that such products can be used for criminal purposes. Given the pervasiveness of advertising in our society and the important role it plays, we decline to impose on publishers the obligation to reject all ambiguous advertisements for products or services that might pose a threat of harm.

III. CONCLUSION

The standard of conduct imposed by the district court against SOF is too high; it allows a jury to visit liability on a publisher for untoward consequences that flow from his decision to publish any suspicious, ambiguous ad that might cause serious harm. The burden on a publisher to avoid liability from suits of this type is too great: he must reject all such advertisements.

The range of foreseeable misuses of advertised products and services is as limitless as the forms and functions of the products themselves. Without a more specific indication of illegal intent than Hearn's ad or its context provided, we conclude that SOF did not violate the required standard of conduct by publishing an ad that later played a role in criminal activity.

The judgment of the district court is REVERSED and RENDERED.

PUTTING IT INTO PRACTICE 6.1

1. Of the 2,000 ads printed in *Soldier of Fortune* magazine (SOF) between 1975 and 1984, how many had served as links in criminal plots? What kinds of crimes did these include?
2. Did the Hearn ad indicate a clearly identifiable offer to commit crimes?
3. What did Dietz testify in regard to the "context" of some of the ads in SOF? Could he distinguish lawful from unlawful classified ads in the magazine?
4. What does the court hold?
5. How have the Texas courts used the risk-utility test in relationship to the question of duty? When does a risk become unreasonable under the risk-utility test?
6. Did SOF owe a duty of reasonable care to the public?
7. Did the SOF ads create more than a remote risk of harm? What evidence does the court use to support its answer to this question?
8. Against what standard of conduct does the court feel the jury measured SOF's actions? Why does the court feel that standard imposed too heavy a burden?
9. For what reason does the court conclude that the district court did not strike the proper balance between the risks of harm from ambiguous ads and the burden of preventing harm arising from these ads?

RESTATEMENT POSITION

The Restatement (Second) of Torts § 291 basically incorporates the Learned Hand formula and states that an act is negligent if "the risk is of such magnitude as to outweigh what the law regards as the utility of the act or of the particular manner in which it is done." The following factors are considered in determining the utility of the defendant's conduct:

a. "the social value which the law attaches to the interest which is to be advanced or protected by the conduct;

b. "the extent of the chance that this interest will be advanced or protected by the particular course of conduct;

c. "the extent of the chance that such interest can be adequately advanced or protected by another less dangerous course of conduct" (Restatement (Second) of Torts § 292).

The factors to be considered in determining the magnitude of the risk are:

a. "the social value which the law attaches to the interests which are imperiled;

b. "the extent of the chance that the actor's conduct will cause an invasion of any interest of the other or of one of the class of which the other is a member;

c. "the extent of the harm likely to be caused to the interests imperiled;

d. "the number of persons whose interest are likely to be invaded if the risk takes effect in harm" (Restatement (Second) of Torts § 293).

PUTTING IT INTO PRACTICE 6.2

David, who is fifteen years old, goes camping with his friends at a state park. On their third day, one of his friends tells the group about a cove located about sixty yards from their campsite. David and the others take a boat to the cove about 7:00 P.M. At least fifteen people are swimming and wading in the cove; one of David's friends dives into the cove and swims away unharmed. David then dives in and hits his head on a ledge or sandbar below the surface and is permanently paralyzed.

David had never seen the cove before he dove into it and did not check the depth of the water before diving into it because he saw his friend dive in without harm and because others had evidently used the diving spot before; there was a "well-worn" path leading up to it. He is an accomplished swimmer and testifies in his deposition that he would not have dived in without checking the depth of the water if he had seen any signs prohibiting diving or warnings of any kind that were posted in the area or at the park entrance.

If David is classified as an invitee, did the state take reasonable precautions to protect him from harm? Did the state have an obligation to discover the danger posed by the shallow waters of the cove? Would a reasonable landowner have posted signs prohibiting diving or would it have removed the danger? Use the criteria set forth in the Restatement (Second) of Torts in §§ 291–293 to help you answer these questions.

REASONABLE PERSON STANDARD—OBJECTIVE VERSUS SUBJECTIVE

In assessing whether the defendant imposed an unreasonable risk of harm to others, his or her conduct is compared to that of a reasonable person (see Figure 6-2). In essence, the question put before a jury in a negligence case is whether a reasonable person of ordinary prudence standing in the defendant's shoes would have done the same thing the defendant did. Phrasing the question this way requires the use of an objective standard, in that the defendant's conduct is compared to that of a hypothetical reasonable person. By contrast, if a subjective standard were used, the question would be whether the defendant believed that he or she behaved in a reasonable manner. Under a subjective standard the reasonableness of one's acts vary depending on one's perception.

Let us illustrate the difference in outcome of these two standards by using a hypothetical problem. Suppose a driver pulled out in front of oncoming traffic, causing an accident. The driver had poor depth perception and was unable to accurately estimate the distance between himself and other vehicles. If an objective standard were used, one would ask whether a reasonable driver of ordinary prudence would have pulled out in front of the traffic. If the driver did not conform to that reasonable standard, his conduct would be considered negligent. In contrast, under a subjective standard, one would ask whether the driver himself perceived any risks. If he did not, he would be deemed to have used reasonable care and, hence, would not be negligent.

From this example you can probably deduce why the objective and not the subjective standard is used in most instances in tort law. To reduce the uncertainty in our legal system and to maximize safety to members of society, the peculiar frailties and idiosyncrasies of defendants generally are not taken into consideration in assessing the reasonableness of their conduct. With few exceptions, then, in tort law we use an objective standard.

WHAT THE REASONABLE PERSON IS EXPECTED TO KNOW

If the reasonable person standard serves as the barometer for all negligence cases, just what can we expect from the reasonable person? Reasonable persons are expected to know the "qualities and habits of human beings and animals and the qualities, characteristics, and capacities of things and forces in so far as

FIGURE 6-2   Factors Taken into Consideration in Determining Reasonableness

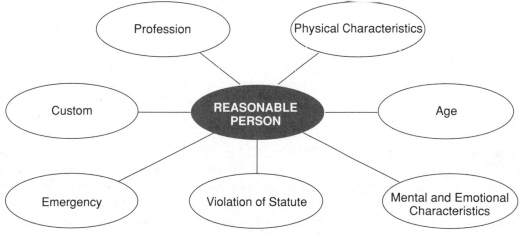

they are matters of common knowledge at the time and in the community" as well as "common law, legislative enactments, and general customs in so far as they are likely to affect the conduct of the other or third persons" (Restatement (Second) of Torts § 290).

Reasonable persons are assumed to possess a knowledge of scientific and natural laws that is common to laypersons in the community. They are, for example, presumed to be aware of the poisonous qualities of certain animals, insects, drugs, and chemicals; to appreciate the explosive nature of certain compounds and dangerous potential of high-voltage power lines and to anticipate basic weather phenomena (frigid weather in the Northeast in the winter and extremely hot temperatures in the deserts of the Southwest in the summer). Even if he has never been on a farm, the reasonable person is presumed to understand that stallions and bulls are potentially dangerous, that horses are likely to be frightened by certain objects and actions, and that even the most gentle of bitches may bite an intruding hand while she is nursing her pups. He should also be aware of the peculiarities and behavioral traits of particular groups of people. He should anticipate, for example, that children may behave recklessly and should take precautions when driving to prevent injury to them. He should be aware that foreign visitors and immigrants are likely not to speak English and realize that warnings written in English will not be adequate. Furthermore, the reasonable person is expected to conform to statutory law and judicial decisions and cannot claim ignorance of the law even if the standard of conduct required by the law contradicts the custom of the community. In short, ignorance of the law is no excuse under the reasonable person standard.

PUTTING IT INTO PRACTICE 6.3

1. Grant drives his car at high speeds on an icy road. Having lived in the tropics all his life, he is totally oblivious to the dangerousness of what he is doing and is shocked when he loses control of his car and careens into a parked vehicle. Has he behaved negligently?
2. Margaret detects an odor of gas in her basement and lights a match to look for the leak. She is unaware of the danger of explosion until she wakes up in the emergency room. Do her visitors at the time of the explosion have grounds to recover damages for the injuries they sustain?
3. A city ordinance requires trolley cars to stop at the near side of every boulevard crossing. Susan is following behind a trolley car and intends to pass between the trolley and the curb. As the trolley approaches the boulevard crossing, Susan speeds up to pass. As a visitor to the city, she is unaware of the ordinance and sees no evidence that the trolley is preparing to stop. When she is suddenly aware of the trolley stopping and a passenger stepping out of the car, she is going too fast to stop and runs over the trolley passenger. Is she negligent?
4. Frank invites Carole to ride his daughter's 11-year-old show horse, "Blue." Carole tells Frank she is a novice rider, so Frank gives her some basic riding instructions before she mounts Blue, but does not explain how to mount, sit, use the reins, turn, stop, or dismount. Allison observes Carole as she rides Blue around the ring; Frank is riding another horse in the same ring. After about 25 minutes Carole brings Blue over to Allison to dismount and as she does she drags her right foot over Blue's rump and jabs her foot into his left side. Blue suddenly bolts, runs through an open gate, and knocks off Carole (who has since regained her seat) as he runs beneath a metal overhang. Carole sues. Frank argues that he used reasonable care in assisting Carole to ride and that it was unforeseeable that Blue, a previously gentle, predictable horse, would suddenly bolt. Do you agree?

DEFENDANTS WITH SPECIAL CHARACTERISTICS

Special allowances are not made for defendants who are emotionally unstable or of substandard intelligence. The Restatement (Second) of Torts maintains this position even for persons whose intelligence is so low that they are not even aware that their conduct creates any danger. The majority rule is, however, at odds with the Restatement and does not impose liability where there is an extreme mental deficiency. An intoxicated person is held to the standard of a reasonable sober person (Restatement (Second) of Torts § 283C, cmt. d). For policy reasons a person who voluntarily consumes alcohol or becomes intoxicated, and thereby deliberately risks creating harm to others, cannot be absolved of liability simply because he lacks the physical and mental faculties of a sober person.

Even insane people are generally held to a reasonable person standard, although some courts are beginning to deviate from that standard when the insane person is unable to understand or avoid the danger. Three policy considerations are used to justify this apparently harsh rule. First, the allowance of an insanity defense would lead to fraudulent claims of insanity in an effort to avoid liability. Second, when injury results from an interaction between two innocent persons, the one causing the injury should bear the consequences. Third, the potential of liability provides an incentive to the wards of the mentally incompetent to supervise their charges closely and to prevent them from harming others.

In considering the attributes of the reasonable person the physical characteristics of the defendant are taken into consideration. A blind person, for example, is held to the standard of a reasonable blind person. Such a person may be expected to use a cane, a seeing eye dog, or some other form of assistance to make her way through town. If such a person fails to use any form of assistance and sues the city for injuries resulting from falling into a depression in the sidewalk, she may be precluded from recovering because of her own negligence.

This rule applies to known physical conditions. A defendant who suffers a heart attack while driving and has an accident will not be found negligent because he lost control of his car. If, however, he had had several previous heart attacks, he might be found to be negligent merely because he was driving a car (Restatement (Second) of Torts § 283C, cmt. c).

CHILDREN

Children are not held to the standard of care expected of an adult but instead are held to the standard of a "reasonable person of like age, intelligence, and experience under like circumstances" (Restatement (Second) of Torts § 283A). This is somewhat of a subjective standard because the intelligence and experience of the child, both of which are relative, are taken into consideration. Therefore, a ten-year-old child of above-average intelligence is held to a higher standard of conduct than a ten-year-old child of below-average intelligence.

Children are held to an adult standard when they engage in potentially dangerous activities that are normally reserved for adults. A child who drives a car is held to the standard of care expected of a reasonable adult driver. The courts are split as far as the standard of care to be applied when children engage in dangerous activities that are not necessarily pursued only by adults. For example, should a child who goes hunting be held to the standard of care of a child or an adult? Some courts reason that because we can reasonably anticipate that children will engage in this activity, they should be held to a standard of care of other children. Others emphasize the inherent dangerousness of the activity and hold children to an adult standard.

PUTTING IT INTO PRACTICE 6.4

1. A driver suddenly becomes convinced that God is taking control of her steering wheel, and as she nears a truck she accelerates "in order to become airborne because she knew she could fly because Batman does it." Will she be held liable for the injuries sustained by the truck driver?
2. A seventeen-year-old negligently shoots his minor companion while they are out deer hunting. To what standard of care should he be held?
3. A driver with a history of epilepsy, for which he has been successfully treated (seizure-free) for more than ten years, suffers an epileptic seizure and is involved in an accident. To what standard of care should he be held?

EMERGENCIES

In addition to considering the age and unique characteristics of the defendant, the courts also look at the circumstances in which the defendant was operating. In an emergency, for example, people are not expected to act with the same rational and calm consideration that one would expect in a less stressful situation. But even in an emergency a defendant is expected to act reasonably and if he does not, he can be found liable for his actions. For example, in the process of render-ing emergency medical assistance a person who takes no reasonable precautions in moving the victim from one position to another may be found negligent for any injuries he causes. A case that is illustrative (in content, not form) of the analysis employed by the courts in emergency situations is *Cordas v. Peerless Transportation Co.*, 27 N.Y.S.2d 198 (1941). The court's whimsical presentation of the facts makes this a particularly entertaining opinion to read.

CASE

Cordas v. Peerless Transportation Co.
27 N.Y.S.2d 198 (N.Y. City Ct. 1941)

CARLIN, Justice.

This case presents the ordinary man—that problem child of the law—in a most bizarre setting. As a lowly chauffeur in defendant's employ he became in a trice the protagonist in a breath-bating drama with a denouement almost tragic. It appears that a man, whose identity it would be indelicate to divulge was feloniously relieved of his portable goods by two nondescript highwaymen in an alley near 26th Street and Third Avenue, Manhattan; they induced him to relinquish his possessions by a strong argument ad hominem couched in the convincing cant of the criminal and pressed at the point of a most persuasive pistol. Laden with their loot, but not thereby impeded, they took an abrupt departure and he, shuffling off the coil of that discretion which enmeshed him in the alley, quickly gave chase through 26th Street toward 2d Avenue, whither they were resorting "with expedition swift as thought" for most obvious reasons. Somewhere on that thoroughfare of escape they indulged the strategem of separation ostensibly to disconcert their pursuer and allay the ardor of his pursuit. He then centered on for capture the man with the pistol whom he saw board defendant's taxicab, which quickly veered south toward 25th Street on 2d Avenue where he saw the chauffeur jump out while the cab, still in motion, continued toward 24th Street; after the chauffeur relieved himself of the cumbersome burden of his fare the latter also is said to have similarly departed from the cab before it reached 24th Street. The chauffeur's story is substantially the same except that he states that his uninvited guest boarded the cab at 25th Street while it was at a standstill waiting for a less colorful fare; that his "passenger" immediately advised him "to stand not upon the order of his going but to go at once" and added finality to his command by an appropriate gesture with a pistol addressed to his sacroiliac. The chauffeur in reluctant acquiescence proceeded about fifteen feet, when his hair, like unto the quills of the fretful porcupine, was made to stand on end by the hue and cry of the man despoiled accompanied by a clamourous concourse of the law-abiding which paced him as he ran; the concatenation of "stop thief", to which the patter of persistent feet did maddingly beat time, rang in his ears as the pursuing posse all the while gained on the receding cab with its quarry therein contained. The hold-up man sensing his insecurity suggested to the chauffeur that in the event there was the slightest lapse in obedience to his curt command that he, the chauffeur, would suffer the loss of his brains, a prospect as horrible to an humble chauffeur as it undoubtedly would be to one of the intelligentsia. The chauffeur apprehensive of certain dissolution from either Scylla, the pursuers, or Charybdis, the pursued, quickly threw his car out of first speed in which he was proceeding, pulled on the emergency, jammed on his brakes and, although he thinks the motor was still running, swung open the door to his left and jumped out of his car. He confesses that the only act that smacked of intelligence was that by which he jammed the brakes in order to throw off balance the hold-up man who was half-standing and half-sitting with his pistol menacingly poised. Thus abandoning his car and passenger the chauffeur sped toward 26th Street and then turned to look; he saw the cab proceeding south toward 24th Street where it mounted the sidewalk. The plaintiff-mother and her two infant children were there injured by the cab which, at the time, appeared to be also minus its passenger who, it appears, was apprehended in the cellar of a local hospital where he was pointed out to a police officer by a remnant of the posse, hereinbefore

mentioned. He did not appear at the trial. The three aforesaid plaintiffs and the husband-father sue the defendant for damages predicating their respective causes of action upon the contention that the chauffeur was negligent in abandoning the cab under the aforesaid circumstances. Fortunately the injuries sustained were comparatively slight. . . . In Steinbrenner v. M. W. Forney Co., [cite omitted] it is said, "The test of actionable negligence is what reasonably prudent men would have done under the same circumstances"; Connell v. New York Central & Hudson River Railroad Co. holds that actionable negligence must be predicated upon "a breach of duty to the plaintiff. Negligence is 'not absolute or intrinsic,' but 'is always relevant to some circumstances of time, place or person.' " In slight paraphrase of the world's first bard it may be truly observed that the expedition of the chauffeur's violent love of his own security outran the pauser, reason, when he was suddenly confronted with unusual emergency which "took his reason prisoner". The learned attorney for the plaintiffs concedes that the chauffeur acted in an emergency but claims a right to recovery upon the following proposition taken verbatim from his brief: "It is respectfully submitted that the value of the interests of the public at large to be immune from being injured by a dangerous instrumentality such as a car unattended while in motion is very superior to the right of a driver of a motor vehicle to abandon same while it is in motion even when acting under the belief that his life is in danger and by abandoning same he will save his life." To hold thus under the facts adduced herein would be tantamount to a repeal by implication of the primal law of nature written in indelible characters upon the fleshy tablets of sentient creation by the Almighty Law-giver, "the supernal Judge who sits on high". There are those who stem the turbulent current for bubble fame, or who bridge the yawning chasm with a leap for the leap's sake or who "outstare the sternest eyes that look, outbrave the heart most daring on the earth, pluck the young sucking cubs from the she-bear, yea, mock the lion when he roars for prey" to win a fair lady and these are the admiration of the generality of men; but they are made of sterner stuff than the ordinary man upon whom the law places no duty of emulation. The law would indeed be fond if it imposed upon the ordinary man the obligation to so demean himself when suddenly confronted with a danger, not of his creation, disregarding the likelihood that such a contingency may darken the intellect and palsy the will of the common legion of the earth, the fraternity of ordinary men,—

whose acts or omissions under certain conditions or circumstances make the yardstick by which the law measures culpability or innocence, negligence or care. If a person is placed in a sudden peril from which death might ensue, the law does not impel another to the rescue of the person endangered nor does it condemn him for his unmoral failure to rescue when he can; this is in recognition of the immutable law written in frail flesh. Returning to our chauffeur. If the philosophic Horatio and the martial companions of his watch were "distilled almost to jelly with the act of fear" when they beheld "in the dead vast and middle of the night" the disembodied spirit of Hamlet's father stalk majestically by "with a countenance more in sorrow than in anger" was not the chauffeur, though unacquainted with the example of these eminent men-at-arms, more amply justified in his fearsome reactions when he was more palpably confronted by a thing of flesh and blood bearing in its hand an engine of destruction which depended for its lethal purpose upon the quiver of a hair? When Macbeth was cross-examined by Macduff as to any reason he could advance for his sudden despatch of Duncan's grooms he said in plausible answer "Who can be wise, amazed, temperate and furious, loyal and neutral, in a moment? No man". Macbeth did not by a "tricksy word" thereby stand justified as he criminally created the emergency from which he sought escape by indulgence in added felonies to divert suspicion to the innocent. However, his words may be wrested to the advantage of the defendant's chauffeur whose acts cannot be legally construed as the proximate cause of plaintiff's injuries, however regrettable, unless nature's first law is arbitrarily disregarded. * * * 'The law presumes that *an act or omission done or neglected under the influence of pressing danger was done or neglected involuntarily.*' It is there said that this rule seems to be founded upon the maxim that self-preservation is the first law of nature, and that, where it is a question whether one of two men shall suffer, each is justified in doing the best he can for himself." Laidlaw v. Sage. (Italics ours.) Kolanka v. Erie Railroad Co. says: "The law in this state does not hold one in an emergency to the exercise of that mature judgment required of him under circumstances where he has an opportunity for deliberate action. He is not required to exercise unerring judgment, which would be expected of him, were he not confronted with an emergency requiring prompt action". The circumstances provide the foil by which the act is brought into relief to determine whether it is or is not negligent. If under normal circumstances an act is done which might be considered negligent it does not follow as a corollary that a similar act is negligent if performed by a person acting under an emergency, not of his own making, in which he suddenly is faced with a patent danger with a moment left to adopt a means of extrication. The chauffeur—the ordinary man in this case—acted in a split second in a most harrowing experience. To call him negligent would be to brand him coward; the court does not do so in spite of what those swaggering heroes, "whose valor plucks dead lions by the beard", may bluster to the contrary. The court is loathe to see the plaintiffs go without recovery even though their damages were slight, but cannot hold the defendant liable upon the facts adduced at the trial. Motions, upon which decision was reserved, to dismiss the complaint are granted with exceptions to plaintiffs. Judgment for defendant against plaintiffs dismissing their complaint upon the merits.

In some situations the reasonable person will be expected to anticipate the actions of others. A driver making her way down a residential street where children are playing will be expected to anticipate that children may run into the street. She will be expected to exercise special care to guard against their carelessness. A reasonable person is not, however, expected to anticipate the crimes or intentional torts of another unless her relationship with that person is such that she should reasonably anticipate such behavior.

CUSTOM

Custom may also be considered in determining reasonable care. Courts will look at the standard practices of a trade or community in assessing the reasonableness of the defendant's conduct. Adherence to custom is persuasive evidence of the reasonableness of conduct but is not necessarily conclusive. It is possible, although not likely, that a court might conclude that an entire industry is negligent if it fails to adopt certain safety precautions.

PROFESSIONS

A defendant who possesses a higher degree of knowledge or skill as a result of training or experience will be held to a higher standard of care. Lawyers, doctors, accountants, and police officers, among others, are held to the standard of care commonly exercised by members in good standing of their profession (Restatement (Second) of Torts § 299A). A medical doctor who administers first aid to someone injured on the street is held to a higher standard of care than someone lacking that training. Professionals who have specialized in a particular area are held to a specialist's standard of care, which exceeds that of the minimal standard of care expected of other members of the profession.

The standard of care applied to professionals is an objective one. Therefore, the question in malpractice cases is whether the professional met the standard of care expected of members of the profession. Relative inexperience is not taken into consideration. Novices in the profession are held to the same standard of competence as more experienced members of the profession. We discuss malpractice in greater depth in Chapter 10.

NEGLIGENCE PER SE

In some cases reasonable conduct is established by statute. A statute mandating that freeway drivers are limited to speeds under 65 mph establishes a safety standard. A defendant who violates this statute and who injures someone as a result of this violation will be considered *negligent per se* ("negligent in itself") in most courts. This doctrine, as applied by the majority of the courts, requires that (1) the violated statute be applicable to the facts of the case and that (2) a causal link between the act constituting a violation of the statute and the plaintiff's injury be established (see Figure 6-3). In a few courts, however, a statutory violation is considered mere evidence of negligence and may be outweighed by other evidence of due care.

To prove negligence per se the plaintiff must first show that he or she is a member of the class of persons whom the statute was intended to protect. The plaintiff must also show that the statute was designed to protect against the kind of harm that was sustained.

"Reasonable Person" Defined

It is impossible to travel anywhere or to travel for long in that confusing forest of learned judgments which constitutes the Common Law of England without encountering the Reasonable Man . . . The Reasonable Man is always thinking of others; prudence is his guide, and "Safety First," if I may borrow a contemporary catchword, is his rule of life. All solid virtues are his, save only that peculiar quality by which the affection of other men is won . . . While any given example of his behavior must command our admiration, which taken in the mass his acts create a very different set of impressions. He is one who invariably looks where he is going, and is careful to examine the immediate foreground before he executes a leap or a bound; who neither star-gazes nor is lost in meditation when approaching trap doors or the margin of a dock; who records in every case upon the counter-foils of checks such ample details as are desirable, scrupulously substitutes the word "Order" for the word "Bearer," crosses the instrument "a/c Payee only" and registers the package in which it is dispatched; who never mounts a moving omnibus and does not alight from any car while the train is in motion; who investigates exhaustively the bona fides of every mendicant before distributing alms, and will inform himself of the history and habits of a dog before administering a caress; who believes no gossip, nor repeats it, without firm basis for believing it to be true; who never drives his ball till those in front of him have definitely vacated the putting-green which is his own objective; who never from one year's end to another makes an excessive demand upon his wife, his neighbors, his servants, his ox, or his ass . . . Devoid, in short, of any human weakness, with not one single saving vice, sans prejudice, procrastination, ill-nature, avarice, and absence of mind, as careful for his own safety as he is for that of others, this excellent but odious character stands like a monument in our courts of Justice, vainly appealing to his fellow-citizens to order their lives after his own example. (*Newman v. Maricopa County,* 808 P.2d 1253 (Ariz. Ct. App. 1991), quoting from A.P. Herbert, *Uncommon Law* (1955).)

FIGURE 6-3 Questions Relating to Negligence Per Se

NEGLIGENCE PER SE

- Is violated statute applicable to facts of case?
- Is plaintiff member of class protected by statute?
- Is act causing injury a violation of the statute?
- Is harm that occurred intended to be prevented by statute?

The following case illustrates these two requirements. Plaintiffs were driving along a country dirt road when they approached an intersection. At the intersection they looked for cars and when they saw none they proceeded through the intersection; there they were hit by an oncoming car. The plaintiffs claimed that their view was obstructed by weeds growing in a ditch along the roadway. Pointing to a statute criminalizing the "shipping, selling or permitting [of] growing of noxious weeds," they sued the county for negligence per se.

They argued that the county had violated the statute by permitting weeds to grow in the ditch. The court, however, held that the defendants were not negligent per se because the plaintiffs did not belong to the class of persons whom the statute was designed to protect. The statute, the court reasoned, was designed to protect farmers and ranchers from an infestation of weeds and was not designed to protect travelers on the highway (*Hidalgo v. Cochise County,* 13 Ariz. App. 27 (1970)). Note also that the harm the statute was intended to protect against was the spread of weeds and not accidents on the highways.

The determination as to whether the type of harm that occurred was that anticipated by statute has been particularly problematic in cases involving keys left in cars. In such cases someone usually uses the keys to steal the car and ultimately becomes involved in an accident. The question then becomes whether the driver who left the keys in the car should be liable for the injuries caused by the person who stole the car. Plaintiffs in states having statutes that prohibit the leaving of keys in a car have argued negligence per se in these cases. If the purpose of the statute is to prevent

reckless driving by thieves, plaintiffs making this argument should prevail, but if there is some other purpose for the statute, the elements of negligence per se are not satisfied. Even if negligence per se cannot be proved, however, plaintiffs can cite statutory violations as evidence of negligence.

In some cases the statute in question is a criminal one. Some penal statutes specifically provide that their violation will result in civil liability, but ambiguity exists when no reference to civil liability is made. Under the majority rule and out of deference to the legislature, the courts will apply the criminal statutory standard to civil cases as a matter of law.

Defenses to Negligence Per Se

In rare instances courts have found an absolute duty to comply with a statute and have refused to accept even reasonable excuses for failure to comply. A defendant violating a statute prohibiting the sale of firearms to minors would likely be found negligent despite his good faith argument that he believed the minor to be an adult.

For the most part, however, statutes are not deemed to impose an absolute duty of compliance. In some jurisdictions the violation of a statute is construed as setting forth a presumption of negligence, which the defendant can rebut by introducing evidence of reasonable care. Other courts treat a statutory violation as negligence per se but accept excuses for noncompliance. Under the Restatement (Second) of Torts "excuse" approach, violation of a statute is excused for the following reasons:

a. "the violation is reasonable because of the actor's incapacity;

b. "he neither knows nor should know of the occasion for compliance;

c. "he is unable after reasonable diligence or care to comply;

d. "he is confronted by an emergency not due to his own misconduct;

e. "compliance would involve a greater risk of harm to the actor or to others"

(Restatement (Second) of Torts § 288A(2)).

Even if negligence per se is established, the defendant can still assert the defenses of contributory negligence and assumption of risk so long as the statute does not impose an absolute duty on the defendant.

One might conclude from the foregoing discussion that compliance with a statute establishes that a defendant was not negligent. But that is not true. The trier of fact is always free to conclude that a reasonable person would have taken precautions beyond those mandated by statute. A reasonable person, for example, would be expected to drive below the speed limit on icy roads.

PUTTING IT INTO PRACTICE 6.5

1. A statute requires railroads to fence their tracks. The ABA railroad fails to fence its track; as a result two of a rancher's cows wander onto the track. One is killed by a train and the other is poisoned by weeds growing next to the track. The purpose of the statute is to prevent animals that stray onto the track from being hit. Is the railroad negligent per se?

2. A man holds himself out as being able to diagnose and treat disease, but he is in fact not licensed to practice medicine as required by the New York Public Health Law. He gives a woman chiropractic treatment, after which she suffers paralysis, allegedly resulting from the treatment. Is the man negligent per se?

3. Marjorie, an employee, and her friend Helena, who is visiting Marjorie at her workplace, are both injured when an elevator falls because of the lack of a safety device. A statute requires all factory elevators to have a particular safety device for the express purpose of protecting employees from injury. Can Marjorie and Helena rely on this statute to establish the standard of care?

4. Harold is shot six times when police officers burst into his house in an effort to serve a search warrant. The officers claim that they acted in self-defense when Harold picked up a rifle, but Harold claims he picked up the rifle because the officers startled him from his sleep when they burst into his house unannounced and without identifying themselves.

   At trial the police argue that Harold is negligent per se if the jury finds he violated the criminal statutes regarding assault (whose definition is similar to that of civil assault). Their reasoning is that the plaintiff's negligent conduct in assaulting the police caused the police to shoot him and that, therefore, he was injured as a result of his own negligent conduct. Do you think the assault statute was intended to protect the police or Harold? In other words, who was intended to be protected from the harm of assaultive behavior, Harold or the police?

AUTOMOBILE GUEST STATUTES

Whereas some statutes have been used to establish a minimal standard of care, other statutes, specifically the automobile guest statutes, have been used to limit the duty of care. Such statutes hold a driver of a vehicle liable to a guest in his or her car only under circumstances of extreme misconduct. Typically such statutes require that the driver's misconduct be willful and wanton, grossly negligent, or reckless before he or she will be held liable.

The rationale underlying these statutes was twofold. First, at the time these statutes were enacted, automobile liability insurance was not widely available and drivers who were successfully sued by their guests had to bear the cost themselves. Many legislatures thought that such "ingratitude" should be discouraged. Second, when insurance was available, collusion between driver and guest (who were most likely friends or relatives) was feared. In other words, some thought that the owner (defendant) of the vehicle might concede negligence to assist the guest (plaintiff) in recovering damages.

In an effort to evade these statutes plaintiffs have spent considerable effort in litigating the question of who is a "guest," as well as what specific acts by the driver constitute the conduct defined by statute. Beginning in the 1970s a number of automobile guest statutes were either repealed or found unconstitutional. Today only a few states still have such statutes in effect.

RES IPSA LOQUITUR

Suppose the plaintiff in a medical malpractice case is injured while on the operating table. If several doctors and nurses are present during the operation and could contribute to the plaintiff's injuries, the plaintiff, because she was unconscious, will have difficulty proving who did and who did not act negligently. A court-developed doctrine that makes the plaintiff's task easier is the doctrine of *res ipsa loquitur,* which means, literally, "the thing speaks for itself." This doctrine allows the plaintiff to create an inference that the defendant was negligent without actually providing direct evidence of that negligence (see Figure 6-4).

Before a plaintiff can rely on the doctrine of res ipsa loquitur, he or she must prove the following:

• The instrument that caused the plaintiff's injury was under the exclusive control of the defendant or, stated another way, the negligence was probably due to the defendant.

• The injury suffered by the plaintiff was of a type that does not ordinarily occur except as a result of someone's negligence.

• The plaintiff did not voluntarily contribute to his or her own injuries.

• Some courts also require that the defendant is better able to explain the events that transpired than the plaintiff.

Let us examine each of these factors in some detail.

FIGURE 6-4   Elements of Res Ipsa Loquitur

• Event that resulted in plaintiff's injuries does not usually happen except as a result of negligence
• Instrument that caused plaintiff's injury was under the defendant's exclusive control
• Plaintiff did not cause his own injuries
• Defendant is in better position to explain events causing plaintiff's injuries than is plaintiff*

*Not all courts require proof of this element.

Defendant in Control or Cause of Injuries

Older cases required the plaintiff to show that the instrumentality that caused the harm was under the exclusive control of the defendant. Modern courts have required instead that the plaintiff show that the negligence was due to the defendant and not to someone else. To do this the plaintiff must often produce evidence demonstrating that it is more probable that the defendant caused the plaintiff's injuries than that someone else did. If it is just as likely that someone other than the defendant caused the injury, res ipsa loquitur will not apply.

A classic "falling chair" case is often used to illustrate the importance of the defendant having exclusive control. In this case the plaintiff was hurt when she was struck by a falling armchair that hit her when she was walking near the St. Francis Hotel during a particularly exuberant celebration of V-J day on August 14, 1945. The court concluded that res ipsa loquitur was inapplicable because the hotel did not have exclusive control over its furniture and that the "mishap would quite as likely be due to the fault of a guest or other person" as to hotel employees. (*Larson v. St. Francis Hotel,* 188 P.2d 513 (Cal. 1948)). In contrast, in a later case, the same court allowed the doctrine to apply when the plaintiff slipped and fell on garbage lying on the sidewalk at the rear of the defendant's restaurant. The court reasoned that the employees were in a position to have caused the accident and the probability of anyone else causing it was very remote. (*Noble v. Cavalier Restaurant*, 235 P.2d 396 (Cal. 1951)).

Proving responsibility becomes particularly problematic in cases involving multiple defendants. In such cases the plaintiff may be able to demonstrate that the injury was caused by the negligence of at least one of the defendants but may not be able to show which defendant. In one famous case (*Ybarra v. Spangard*, 154 P.2d 687 (Cal. 1944)), for example, a man had an appendectomy and after the surgery suffered pains in his right shoulder, having sustained injuries while being operated on that he could not explain. He sued the surgeon, attending physician, anesthesiologist, and owner of the hospital, claiming that at least one of them (or a nurse they were supervising) must have been negligent. The court held that res ipsa loquitur applied because it was unreasonable to require someone who was unconscious to identify the negligent defendant. In this case each of the defendants had interrelated responsibilities and therefore a concomitant duty to prevent harm to the plaintiff. The courts seem less willing, however, to apply res ipsa loquitur if the defendants are strangers to one another and act independently of one another.

Injury Is Consequence of Negligence

The plaintiff must demonstrate that the accident would have been unlikely to occur in the absence of negligence. He or she is not required to show that only negligence is the cause of such events but must prove that such events are generally a consequence of negligence. In some cases that awareness will lie within the experience of the jury and will not have to be proved explicitly by the plaintiff.

In a case in which an airplane disappeared over the Pacific Ocean, leaving no debris that was ever found, the plaintiff (suing on behalf of one of the deceased passengers) was unable to produce evidence of actual negligence. Even though the defendant airline produced evidence that the plane was properly maintained, that the weather was normal, and that the personnel were adequately trained, the court allowed the factfinder the right to infer that negligence was

more probably than not the cause of the accident. The plaintiff was not required to disprove every possible cause of the accident in order for the inference of negligence to be allowed. (*Cox v. Northwest Airlines, Inc.*, 379 F.2d 893 (7th Cir. 1967)).

Lack of Contributory Negligence

The plaintiff must also provide evidence showing that he or she acted properly. If the plaintiff was contributorily negligent, the doctrine is probably not applicable. Suppose, for example, that a boiler on a locomotive explodes, killing the engineer whose job includes keeping the right amount of water in the boiler. If testimony is offered that the engineer properly tended the boiler and did nothing to cause the explosion, the doctrine of res ipsa loquitur may apply; in the absence of such testimony, the doctrine may not apply. (Restatement (Second) of Torts § 328D, illust. 11.) In contrast, if the engineer were negligent in running the train at an unsafe speed but that negligence had nothing to do with the explosion, the doctrine could still apply. In the latter case, the plaintiff's contributory negligence would do nothing to reduce the likelihood that the defendant was also negligent.

Evidence More Available to Defendant

Some courts also require the plaintiff to show that evidence of negligence was more available to the defendant(s) than to the plaintiff. Most courts, however, apply the doctrine of res ipsa loquitur even when evidence is no more available to the defendant than to the plaintiff. This element seems to be more of a rationale for applying the doctrine than an evidentiary requirement.

This rationale was used in *Ybarra v. Spangard*, involving the doctors who testified that they knew no reason why the plaintiff's shoulder became painful after his appendectomy. Application of the doctrine in cases such as this requires the defendants either to explain what happened or to risk being found liable.

Procedural Consequences

The procedural consequence in most courts of the plaintiff's use of res ipsa loquitur is that the jury is allowed to infer negligence. In some courts, meeting the requirements of the doctrine creates a presumption of negligence, which the defendant must rebut to avoid a directed verdict. In a few courts, once res ipsa loquitur applies, the defendant must prove by a preponderance of the evidence that he or she did not act negligently.

APPLICATION

Breach of duty is the key question in the case against the Baxters. Teddy and Mr. Goodright will have to prove that the Baxters acted unreasonably by failing to lock the gate to their backyard. If statutes or ordinances within their jurisdiction mandate that dogs be confined in an area that is inaccessible to children, the Baxters could be found negligent per se. At the very least, statutes and ordinances could be used to establish the reasonable standard of care expected of dog owners. Compliance with these statutory requirements would not necessarily absolve the Baxters, however, because their conduct could still be deemed unreasonable. Even if found negligent per se, they could assert that the defendants were contributorily negligent or assumed the risk.

The plaintiffs could integrate the Learned Hand formula into any arguments before the court by showing that the probability of harm occurring if Gertrude was not locked in the yard and the gravity of injuries that would occur if she attacked someone greatly outweighed the minimal inconvenience of ensuring that the gate was locked. They would have to assign numerical figures to these factors to make this formula meaningful. This formula is somewhat esoteric and is designed to provide a guideline to the courts in assessing the defendants' conduct, so the attorneys would present the formula in arguments to the court and not to the jury.

The Baxters would argue that Teddy fell short of the conduct expected of a child of his age, intelligence, and experience. They would especially want to emphasize that Teddy was aware of Gertrude's propensity to defend her domain and that, having been forewarned

to stay out of the Baxters' yard, he was aware of the danger inherent in entering that yard without the Baxters being present. If the Baxters tried to argue that Mr. Goodright behaved negligently by interjecting himself in the altercation between Teddy and Gertrude, they would probably fail. As long as Mr. Goodright acted reasonably considering the frightening circumstances in which he became involved, he would not be found negligent. Reasonableness does not preclude acts of heroism.

SUMMARY

Breach of duty raises the question of whether the defendant engaged in unreasonable conduct. We presume that a reasonable person will avoid creating an unreasonable risk of harm for others. Under the Learned Hand formula, a defendant has breached his or her duty if the probability of the harm his or her act presents multiplied by the gravity of such harm exceeds the defendant's burden of taking precautions to avoid the harm. An objective standard is used in assessing the defendant's conduct.

Generally, special allowances are not made for defendants who are emotionally unstable, of substandard intelligence, or insane. The physical characteristics of a defendant are, however, taken into consideration. Children are held to the standard of care of a child of similar age, intelligence, and experience. The fact that a defendant acted in an emergency situation is taken into consideration in determining the reasonableness of the conduct. The custom of a particular industry or community is looked at in reviewing the reasonableness of a defendant's conduct. Professionals are held to the standard of care commonly exercised by members in good standing of their profession, whereas specialists are held to a specialist's standard of care.

If a defendant violates a statute that is applicable to the facts of the case and if someone is injured as a result of that violation, the defendant will be considered negligent per se. The plaintiff must show that he or she is a member of the class of persons whom the statute is intended to protect and that the statute was designed to protect against the type of harm sustained. Criminal as well as civil statutes may be used to prove negligence per se. Generally, however, statutes do not impose an absolute duty of compliance and their violation may be excused for a number of reasons.

In contrast to the doctrine of negligence per se, automobile guest statutes absolve defendants of liability unless their conduct is willful and wanton, grossly negligent, or reckless. Few states still have such statutes in operation.

In some cases the plaintiff is unable to prove negligence because he or she lacks any direct evidence. The doctrine of res ipsa loquitur allows the plaintiff to create an inference of negligence. Under this doctrine the plaintiff must prove that: (1) the negligence was due to the defendant and not to someone else; (2) the experience suffered by the plaintiff was of a sort that does not ordinarily occur except as a result of negligence; (3) the plaintiff did not voluntarily contribute to his or her own injuries, and, in some courts; (4) the defendant is better able to explain the event that occurred than is the plaintiff.

PRACTICE POINTERS

In cases of negligence per se, the task of locating the appropriate statutory standard may fall to the paralegal. Therefore, you should be aware of the most common sources of statutory law. When laws are first enacted they are published separately as "slip laws"; at the end of a legislative session the slip laws for that session are bound in volumes referred to as "session laws." The official source of session laws is a government publication, *United States Statutes at Large*, which orders the session laws by public law numbers (e.g., Pub. L. No. 97-334). Session laws are difficult to access because they are arranged chronologically rather than by subject. Therefore, federal statutes are easier to locate using arrangements of laws by subject matter, referred to as "codes." Unless you are looking for a recently enacted law, you will begin statutory research at the federal level using one of three federal codes: *United States Code* (the official version published by the government), *United States Code Annotated* (published by West Publishing); or *United States Code Service* (published by Lawyers Cooperative Publishing). The official version contains only the text of the federal code, but the two unofficial versions also contain annotations (information about decisions that have applied or discussed certain sections of the code), historical notes, and references to other sources that interpret and analyze the code.

Codes are updated using supplementary volumes or pamphlets or by pocket parts (annual supplements found in the back inside cover of the hardbound volume). Codes can be accessed using the index, which lists statutes alphabetically according to subject matter, or the titles listed in the front of each volume. The United States Code is divided into fifty titles and then further subdivided into chapters and subchapters.

All states have subject compilations of state statutes; these compilations may be referred to as "Statutes," "Codes," Revisions," "Compilations," or by other terms. All state codes are organized based on subject matter but the numbering schemes vary from state to state. Many jurisdictions have both official and unofficial codes; some have annotated codes and others are unannotated. Consult your law librarian to familiarize yourself with the organizational structure, frequency of updates, and research features of the codes published in your state.

1. How would you go about determining whether the Baxters had breached their duty to Teddy and Mr. Goodright? Suppose in your research you found a statute in your state that read as follows: "Owners of dogs known to have dangerous propensities must adequately restrain such dogs so as to prevent injury to others." The Restatement (Second) of Torts § 509 provides that:

> A possessor of a domestic animal that he knows or has reason to know has dangerous propensities abnormal to its class, is subject to liability for harm done by the animal to another, although he has used the utmost care to prevent it from doing the harm.

What arguments would you make on behalf of the Baxters? On behalf of Teddy and Mr. Goodright?

2. If you were to interview Teddy and his parents, what questions would you ask them to help establish that the Baxters had violated their duty of care?

3. Suppose the Baxters alleged that Teddy and Mr. Goodright were both contributorily negligent. If you were representing the Baxters, what arguments would you raise to show that Teddy's conduct was unreasonable? What arguments would you make to show that Mr. Goodright's actions were unreasonable?

4. Plaintiff and Defendant are both driving down the road when Defendant attempts to pass Plaintiff's vehicle. In doing so his left rear tire blows out, causing him to swerve into Plaintiff's vehicle. Testimony is presented showing that the tire was very worn but Defendant claims that he was unaware of the dangerous condition of the tire. Was Defendant's failure to examine his tire unreasonable conduct? *Delair v. McAdoo,* 188 A.181 (Pa. 1936).

5. Defending attorney represents a wife in a divorce proceeding. Under California community property law she is entitled to a claim to her husband's retirement benefits. Defendant fails to make this claim for his client because he erroneously believes that the wife is not entitled to the benefits. The law, in fact, is relatively clear on this issue and provides that retirement rights are community property. Defendant does not research the issue. Was Defendant negligent? How would you assess the reasonableness of his actions? *Smith v. Lewis,* 530 P.2d 589 (Cal. 1975).

6. A statute requires that the seller of a "deadly weapon" receive positive identification "of the purchaser from two residents of the state" and that he keep a record of the name, age, address, and other details pertaining to the purchaser. Defendant sells a gun and fails to comply with the statute. The purchaser uses it on Plaintiff in the course of committing an armed robbery. Was defendant negligent per se? *Hetherton v. Sears, Roebuck & Co.,* 593 F.2d 526 (3d Cir. 1979).

7. Plaintiff drinks from a bottle of Coca-Cola he purchased from the drugstore and spits up a fly. Defendant introduces evidence that the bottling plant was operated under sanitary conditions and that Coca-Cola bottles can be opened and their caps replaced without any obvious indication of tampering. Is the doctrine of res ipsa loquitur applicable? *Crystal Coca-Cola Bottling Co. v. Cathey,* 317 P.2d 1094 (Ariz. 1957).

CHAPTER

7

Negligence: Causation

CHAPTER TOPICS

Actual Cause
Proximate Cause
Exceptions to the Cardozo Rule
Intervening Causes
Jury Question
Application

CHAPTER OBJECTIVES

In this chapter you will learn to:
- Distinguish between actual cause and proximate cause
- Prove the element of actual cause
- Distinguish between the Cardozo and Andrews approaches to proximate cause
- Identify the exceptions to the Cardozo rule of foreseeability
- Distinguish between an intervening and a superseding cause

If Teddy and Mr. Goodright are able to hurdle the "duty" and "breach of duty" obstacles, they must then set their sights on the element of causation. Causation entails two separate considerations: actual cause (sometimes referred to as causation in fact) and proximate cause (or legal cause). **Actual cause** means, quite literally, that the defendant's actions were the actual and factual cause of the plaintiff's injuries. **Proximate cause,** in contrast, means that the defendant's conduct was so closely connected to the plaintiff's injuries that the defendant should be held liable. If the plaintiff is injured by a bizarre and extraordinary chain of events that is only remotely connected to the defendant's negligence, proximate cause is lacking.

ACTUAL CAUSE

But-For Test

The question of whether the defendant was the actual cause of the plaintiff's injuries is usually a factual one (see Figure 7-1). The "but-for" or "sine qua non" test is usually used to determine actual cause. Under this test, if the plaintiff's injuries would not have occurred *but for* the defendant's negligence, the defendant will be deemed the actual cause of the plaintiff's injuries (Restatement (Second) of Torts § 432).

Let us apply this test to an actual situation. The mate of the defendant's steam trawler falls overboard and disappears immediately. The defendant's lifeboat is equipped with only one oar, which is lashed to the deck instead of being suspended from the davits. As a result, the lashings have to be cut before the boat can be launched. Is the defendant's negligence the actual cause of the plaintiff's death (*Ford v. Trident Fisheries Co.,* 232 Mass. 400, 122 N.E. 389 (1919))? Because the plaintiff disappeared immediately after falling overboard and no evidence shows that the defendant's negligence in any way contributed to the plaintiff's death, the defendant would not be considered the actual cause of the plaintiff's death.

In a more modern context, actual cause arises in cases involving tavern owners who negligently serve liquor to patrons who are obviously intoxicated. If those patrons drive and injure someone, the question is whether the tavern owner's serving of liquor was the actual cause of the harm done to the injured person. In a case that is excerpted later in this chapter (*Ontiveros v. Borak,* 667 P.2d 200 (Ariz. 1983)), the court allowed a jury to find actual causation when a tavern owner served at least thirty beers to a patron who was involved in an accident after he left the bar. The court reasoned that a "defendant may be held liable if his conduct contributed to the result and if that result would not have occurred 'but for' defendant's conduct." The court noted, however, that some factual scenarios would not support a finding of actual causation. If, for example, the patron had consumed thirty beers at the defendant's bar and then had gone across the street for "one for the road," the court opined that "it would be difficult to argue that the accident would not have happened 'but for' the last drink."

FIGURE 7-1   Actual Cause

BUT-FOR TEST	SUBSTANTIAL FACTOR TEST	BURDEN OF PROOF
But for defendant's negligence plaintiff would not have been injured.	Two or more concurrent or successive events combine to cause the plaintiff's injury and each of them is a substantial factor in producing the injury.	Plaintiff bears burden of proof **Except:** 1. Alternate liability (*Summers v. Tice*) 2. Market share liability (*Sindell v. Abbott Labs*) 3. Concerted action

Substantial Factor Test

Notice that the but-for test makes for an extremely broad net into which many a defendant can be snared. But as sweeping as the but-for test is, it does not encompass situations involving concurrent causes of harm to the plaintiff. *Concurrent causes* are those events that combine (concur) to cause the plaintiff's harm, although either one of them alone could cause the harm without any contribution from the other. Under the substantial factor test, an alternative to the but-for test, the question is whether the defendant was a substantial factor in producing the plaintiff's injury. If the concurrent causes produce a single, indivisible harm in which the damage from one event cannot be separated from that caused by the other, the courts have generally found both events to be a substantial factor in producing the plaintiff's injuries.

To illustrate the application of this test, suppose the plaintiff is riding down a narrow road in his horse-drawn wagon when two motorcycles roar around him, one on each side. The frightened horse bolts and the plaintiff is injured. Although either motorcycle by itself would have been sufficient to frighten the horse, the harm created by both of the motorcycles produces a single, indivisible harm. Consequently, both motorcyclists are the actual cause of the plaintiff's injuries (*Corey v. Havener*, 65 N.E. 69 (Mass. 1902)).

Modern courts have struggled with the concept of causation in "toxic tort" cases and have often adopted the less stringent substantial factor test in concurrent cause cases. In one case the plaintiffs, who lived downwind from a nuclear test site, alleged that their exposure to radioactive fallout had caused them to develop various forms of cancer. The court adopted a substantial factor test. In rejecting the but for test, the court reasoned that the "use of any kind of 'but for' analysis—whether plaintiff's injury would not have occurred but for the conduct of the defendant—to determine factual causation is problematical at best; where likely 'causes' co-exist [such as fallout exposure, background radiation, medical x-rays, etc.], it is wholly inadequate to the task." In considering whether the radiation was a substantial factor in causing the cancers suffered by the plaintiffs, the court looked at whether the plaintiffs' injuries were consistent with the harm caused by exposure to radiation, the length of time the plaintiffs had lived near the test site, the probability that they were exposed to radiation in excess of natural background radiation, the estimated dose of radiation they had received, and whether the statistical incidence of cancer in the plaintiffs was greater than the expected incidence of cancer. *Allen v. United States*, 588 F. Supp. 247 (D. Utah 1984).

The problem in cases of this sort is proving that the toxin at issue, and not some other factor, was the cause of the plaintiff's injury. To illustrate, in another radiation case the plaintiffs were unable to prove causation because the defense produced evidence that one plaintiff's smoking of 1.5 packs of cigarettes per day for 45 years was just as much a cause of his lung cancer as the radiation to which he had been exposed, and that another plaintiff's high-cholesterol/low-fiber diet was just as likely a cause of his colon cancer as his exposure to radiation. *Prescott v. United States*, 858 F. Supp. 1461 (D. Nev. 1994).

To prove causation, plaintiffs in toxic tort cases must often rely on expert testimony, epidemiological studies (studies that demonstrate a statistical association between a disease and a toxic substance), and experimental studies conducted on humans and animals that measure and observe the effects of exposure to chemicals. The evidence presented by plaintiffs must not only prove that the toxin in question is capable of producing the type of injury suffered by the plaintiffs but also that each individual plaintiff's injury was caused by that particular toxin. The evidentiary rules governing the admissibility of such evidence go beyond the scope of this text, but suffice it to say that plaintiffs must surmount a number of evidentiary obstacles before they can introduce evidence to prove their allegations of causation.

Proof of Actual Cause

The plaintiff bears the burden of proving actual causation by a preponderance of the evidence. In other words, she must prove that it is probable that the injury would not have occurred but for the defendant's acts. Suppose, however, the defendant argues that the plaintiff would have been injured even if the defendant had not been negligent. The plaintiff must then show that the defendant's negligence greatly enhanced the chances of harm occurring, in order to sustain the burden of proof.

If two defendants are negligent but only one could have caused the plaintiff's injury, the burden of proof will be thrust back on the defendants to show who actually caused the harm (Restatement (Second) of Torts § 433B(3)). Under the theory of alternate liability, as developed in *Summers v. Tice,* 199 P.2d 1 (Cal. 1948), each negligent tortfeasor must prove that his or her actions did not cause the plaintiff's injuries. If one fails to make such proof both defendants will be found liable. In *Summers v. Tice* the plaintiff and the two defendants went hunting together. The defendants simultaneously shot at a quail and the plaintiff was struck by one of the shots. Because it could not be determined from which gun the bullet was fired, the court held that each of the defendants had the burden to show that it was the other's shot that wounded the plaintiff.

This theory has been expanded to encompass three or more defendants in the area of product liability. The so-called "market share liability" theory was developed in *Sindell v. Abbott Laboratories,* 607 P.2d 924 (Cal. 1980), to allow recovery to the plaintiff who can show only that the defendants were negligent but cannot prove which of the defendants caused the injury. In *Sindell* at least 200 manufacturers used an identical formula to produce diethylstilbestrol (DES). The plaintiff, whose mother took the drug during pregnancy, alleged that her cancer was a direct result of her mother's consumption of DES. The plaintiff sued five drug companies, which she maintained manufactured 90 percent of the DES ever marketed, but was unable to show which of the manufacturers produced the drug that her mother actually took.

The court concluded that it was impossible for the plaintiff to provide such proof, in part because the ill effects caused by the drug did not become apparent for many years after consumption. The court reasoned that when it came down to a conflict between an innocent plaintiff and negligent defendants, the latter should bear the cost of any injuries. The court also opined that the defendants were better able to bear the cost of injury, as they could discover and guard against any defects and could also warn consumers of potential harmful effects. Any defendant unable to prove that it did not produce the particular dosages consumed by the plaintiff's mother would be liable for the portion of the judgment that represented the defendant's share of the overall DES market at the time of the mother's consumption.

Notice that market share liability differs from res ipsa loquitur in that the latter is used when a plaintiff has no way of proving the nature of the defendant's conduct. If the plaintiff can meet the proof requirements of res ipsa loquitur the defendant's negligence will be inferred. With market share liability the plaintiff can show that all of the defendants were negligent (or produced a dangerous product) but is unable to pin the injuries on one specific defendant.

Other courts, when confronted with multiple defendants, have imposed liability using a concerted action theory set forth in the Restatement (Second) of Torts § 876. Under this theory plaintiffs must show that a tacit agreement existed among the defendants to perform a tortious act. To do this the plaintiff must show the existence of a common plan or that the defendants assisted or encouraged each other in accomplishing a tortious result. Regardless of which theory the court relies on, clearly a defendant may be considered the actual cause of the plaintiff's injury even if another defendant's negligence also contributed to that harm.

Proof of actual cause can be particularly problematic in medical malpractice cases in which a doctor's failure to diagnose may have contributed to a patient's death. One such case (*Wollen v. DePaul Health Center,* 828 S.W.2d 681 (Mo. 1992)), in which the doctors failed to diagnose gastric cancer, is excerpted here. Note the court's rejection of both the but-for and substantial factor tests because of the impossibility of the plaintiff being able to prove causation under either of these tests. The court develops an alternate theory of recovery—the "lost chance of recovery" theory. This theory allows medical malpractice plaintiffs to recover if they can prove a loss of the chance to recover, even if they cannot prove that the doctor's negligence resulted in a loss of life.

CASE

Wollen v. DePaul Health Center
828 S.W.2d 681 (Mo. 1992)

BENTON, Judge.

Linda F. Wollen appeals the dismissal, for failure to state a cause of action, of her petition for damages filed under the wrongful death statute, [Mo. Rev. Stat.] § 537.080 [1986]. The decision below is vacated; and this case is remanded for further proceedings in accordance with this opinion.

I.

Assuming for the purposes of appellate review that the allegations in appellant's pleadings are true, the facts of this case are: On January 26, 1988, David L. Wollen went to respondent Richard F. Jotte, Sr., M.D., for medical treatment. Dr. Jotte referred Mr. Wollen to the other respondents, DePaul Health Center, Ernst Radiology Clinic, Inc., and Edwin Ernst, III, M.D., for tests. If respondents had performed appropriate tests, or had correctly interpreted the tests that they had conducted, respondents would have diagnosed that Mr. Wollen was suffering from gastric cancer on January 28, 1988. If Mr. Wollen had been correctly diagnosed, and given appropriate treatment, he would have "had a thirty percent (30%) chance of survival and cure."

Mr. Wollen died from gastric cancer on July 2, 1989. On January 17, 1990, Linda F. Wollen, Mr. Wollen's widow, filed a wrongful death action against respondents. Each respondent filed a motion to dismiss the action on the ground that the petition failed to plead a causal connection between respondents' negligence and the death of Mr. Wollen. The circuit court sustained respondents' motions, and appellant refused leave to file an amended petition on May 7, 1990. After appeal to the Court of Appeals, Eastern District, and on application by appellant, this Court ordered this case transferred here on September 10, 1991.

II.

This case turns on the issues of proof and causation. At this initial stage of the case, courts are required to assume that the evidence introduced at the trial will prove the facts as pled by the plaintiff. The question remains, however, whether the ultimate legal fact of causation can be inferred from those facts.

As in the case with most petitions, in addition to pleading the alleged facts, the petition before this Court pleads, as facts, elements of the cause of action—negligence, causation, and damages. Such "facts"/elements are, in reality, merely legal conclusions. In the simple negligence case, the inference from the real pleadings of fact to these legal conclusions is simple and straightforward. A statement that the plaintiff slipped on a patch of ice creates an inference that the ice caused the plaintiff to slip. The inference in this case is not that easy.

In the failure-to-diagnose case, the fact pleaded to show causation often has to be a statistic. This problem can be avoided if the plaintiff can plead that there is a reasonable medical or scientific certainty that defendant's negligence caused the harm.

The cases on reasonable medical certainty, however, reflect the lack of clarity that can occur when the legal profession tries to impose its terms on other professions. In this Court's understanding of the medical issues involved, there are three possibilities: two of which involve "reasonable medical certainty," and a third that does not.

The first possibility is the circumstance that could be phrased as "but for" causation. In this circumstance, the patient has a disease for which, at the stage the patient seeks diagnosis, there is a cure that works in the overwhelming majority of cases. Death from this type of disease caught at this stage is rare unless either the patient or the doctor is negligent at some stage of the treatment process.

The second possibility is exactly the opposite. In this circumstance, there is no known cure for the disease. Medical science can only, at best, extend the patient's life a short time. In the overwhelming majority of cases, the disease is fatal except for a small number of spontaneous remissions or cures.

The third possibility is the one that appears in this case. Doctors have a treatment that works in a large number of cases and fails in a large number of cases. Because there is a real chance that the patient will survive and a real chance that the patient will die from the disease—even if it is diagnosed—it is impossible for a medical expert to state with "reasonable medical certainty" the effect of the failure to diagnose on a specific patient, other than the fact that the failure to diagnose eliminated whatever chance the patient would have had.

III.

Appellant proposes analyzing this case under the theory that respondents' negligence was a "substantial factor" that contributed to Mr. Wollen's death. Prior cases do not support appellant's interpretation of the substantial factor theory.

In this case, appellant can only allege that, even when all of the tortfeasors are taken together, the negligence of the respondents might have contributed to the death of Mr. Wollen. In these circumstances, the petition fails to allege facts that indicate that respondents' negligence was a substantial factor in causing the death of Mr. Wollen.

IV.

In argument before this Court, all parties have discussed whether this Court should recognize an alternative theory of recovery based on the Restatement (Second) of Torts, section 323(a). As Missouri is a fact-pleading state, this Court will consider whether the facts as pled entitle appellant to relief under a "lost chance of recovery" theory.

In the past this Court has recognized that section 323 creates a duty of care. In creating this duty, this section of the Restatement defines a type of negligent behavior but does not alter the rules of causation. For the reasons discussed in Parts III and V, the petition fails to allege facts that show that respondents' alleged negligence caused Mr. Wollen's death. The petition does, however, allege facts that would support an action for lost chance of recovery.

* * *

The arguments against recognizing such a cause of action, however, are not totally without merit. Tradition-ally, causation has been treated as a "yes-or-no" or "all-or-nothing" question. There has been a trend towards apportioning fault among various parties in law suits but such apportionment occurs only after the jury has decided that the evidence shows causation. This traditional view of causation does aid the goal—which should be shared by the entire legal profession—of avoiding unnecessary barriers to ordinary people understanding their rights and responsibilities under the law.

On the other hand, there are compelling reasons for granting compensation in this type of cause of action. The traditional yes-no view of the world in causation theory does not match the "maybe" view of the world found in probability, statistics, and everyday life. To both the statistician and the patient seeking care from a doctor, there is no meaningful difference between a 50.001% and a 49.999% chance of recovery.

Medical science has given patients real chances to recover, sometimes only a small chance, but still a chance, in circumstances that used to be hopeless. When patients go to doctors with serious illnesses, they expect to have those chances that medical science has provided. To the individual patient, if the doctor's negligence destroys the chance of recovery, it is irrelevant what that chance originally was. The courts of this state implicitly recognized this fact as far back as 1923.

A patient with cancer, like Mr. Wollen, would pay to have a choice between three unmarked doors—behind two of which were death, with life the third option. A physician who deprived a patient of this opportunity, even though only a one-third chance, would have caused her real harm.

In light of this reality, the patient does suffer a harm when the doctor fails to diagnose or adequately treat a serious injury or disease. The harm suffered is not, however, the loss of life or limb. The harm is the loss of the chance of recovery. While, in the end, damages can only be expressed by multiplying the value of a lost life or limb by the chance of recovery lost, the proper place for such an inquiry is in the damages stage rather than in the liability/causation determination. Therefore, rather than adopting a theory of proportional causation, this Court chooses to recognize a cause of action for lost chance of recovery in medical malpractice cases.

PUTTING IT INTO PRACTICE 7.1

1. A buyer purchases a condominium based on a false statement by the bank's broker that the association dues are $100 per month, when they are in fact $500 per month. One month after purchase the plumbing breaks down and the buyer has to pay $25,000 to replace the pipes. The buyer says she relied on the statement about the dues in purchasing the condominium and would not have bought it had it not been for the broker's misrepresentation. Does the buyer have a claim against the bank for the broken pipes?
2. Ford Dealers Advertising Association sponsors a $1 million drag race. Although its logo is used in promotional materials, Ford takes no part in preparing the materials nor in making any of the representations that are made in the materials. The winner of the race sues Ford when the promoters of the race refuse to give him his prize money. Does he have a valid claim against Ford?
3. Veterans of the Vietnam War sue the government for damages they claim to have suffered as a result of exposure to Agent Orange. What problems in relationship to actual causation do you anticipate they will have? What types of evidence will they have to present?

PROXIMATE CAUSE

If the plaintiff is successful in showing that the defendant's negligence was the actual cause of the injury, he or she must then show that the defendant proximately caused the injury. Some writers feel that the term *legal cause* is more descriptive because it reflects a judicial concern that limits should be put on a defendant's liability. This judicial constraint arises from a sense that a defendant should not be liable for a highly improbable or extraordinary consequence stemming from his or her negligence—to do so would be unfair. In reading cases you will discover that some courts blur the concepts of actual causation and proximate cause. For example, if a court finds that a defendant's conduct was not the actual cause of the plaintiff's harm, it may label this a failure of proximate cause. Throughout this text, however, we treat these two concepts separately.

Foreseeability

The question of proximate cause basically boils down to a question of foreseeability. Was the plaintiff's injury a reasonably foreseeable consequence of the defendant's conduct? The difficulty that the courts grapple with is where to draw the line in holding defendants liable.

Suppose a defendant and plaintiff are playing around and the defendant accidentally but negligently cuts the plaintiff with a knife, causing relatively mild injuries. In which of the following circumstances do you think the defendant should be held liable for the plaintiff's death?

a. The plaintiff panics at the sight of blood, blindly runs in front of a car, and is killed.
b. The plaintiff contracts gangrene and dies as a result of negligence on the part of the doctor who treats him.
c. The ambulance transporting the plaintiff to a hospital is involved in an accident in which the plain-tiff dies.
d. The plaintiff refuses medical care, contracts an infection that can be traced to the injuries he received from the defendant, and dies as a result of that infection.

We will deal with these situations later on in this chapter. But be aware only limited consensus exists in the area of proximate cause. The courts have struggled, and continue to struggle, with their determination of what is fair to a defendant.

Palsgraf

The most famous case dealing with the issue of fore-seeability is *Palsgraf v. Long Island Rail Co.*, 162 N.E. 99 (N.Y. 1928). In *Palsgraf* one of the defendant railroad's employees, attempting to assist a man running to board the defendant's train, accidentally dislodged a package from the passenger's arm. Unbeknownst to anyone, the package contained fireworks, which ex-ploded when they fell. As a result of the shock of the explosion some scales at the other end of the platform fell and hit the plaintiff. Arguably, the defendant's employee was negligent in pushing the passenger in the effort to assist him. The real question, however, was whether the defendant's negligence toward the passen-ger should give rise to liability to the plaintiff, who was injured by a series of fluke events.

CASE

Palsgraf v. Long Island Rail Co.
162 N.E. 99 (N.Y. 1928)

CARDOZO, C.J. Plaintiff was standing on a platform of defendant's railroad after buying a ticket to go to Rockaway Beach. A train stopped at the station, bound for another place. Two men ran forward to catch it. One of the men reached the platform of the car without mishap, though the train was already moving. The other man, carrying a package, jumped aboard the car, but seemed unsteady as if about to fall. A guard on the car, who had held the door open, reached forward to help him in, and another guard on the platform pushed him from behind. In this act, the package was dislodged, and fell upon the rails. It was a package of small size, about fif-teen inches long, and was covered by a newspaper. In fact it contained fireworks, but there was nothing in its appearance to give notice of its contents. The fireworks when they fell exploded. The shock of the explosion threw down some scales at the other end of the platform many feet away. The scales struck the plaintiff, causing injuries for which she sues.

The conduct of the defendant's guard, if a wrong in its relation to the holder of the package, was not a wrong in its relation to the plaintiff, standing far away. Relatively to her it was not negligence at all. Nothing in the situation gave notice that the falling package had in it the potency of peril to persons thus removed. Negligence is not actionable unless it involves the invasion of a legally pro-tected interest, the violation of a right. "Proof of negli-gence in the air, so to speak, will not do." . . . "Negligence is the absence of care, according to the circumstances." . . . The plaintiff, as she stood upon the platform of the station, might claim to be protected against intentional invasion of her bodily security. Such invasion is not charged. She might claim to be protected against unin-tentional invasion by conduct involving in the thought of reasonable men an unreasonable hazard that such inva-sion would ensue. These, from the point of view of the law, were the bounds of her immunity, with perhaps some rare exceptions, survivals for the most part of ancient forms of liability, where conduct is held to be at the peril of the actor. . . . If no hazard was apparent to the eye of ordinary vigilance, an act innocent and harmless, at least to outward seeming, with reference to her, did not take to itself the quality of a tort because it happened to be a wrong, though apparently not one involving the risk of bodily insecurity, with reference to some one else. "In every instance, before negligence can be predicated of a given act, back of the act must be sought and found a duty to the individual complaining, the observance of which would have averted or avoided the injury." . . . "The ideas of negligence and duty are strictly correlative." . . . The plaintiff sues in her own right for a wrong personal to her, and not as the vicarious beneficiary of a breach of duty to another.

* * *

A different conclusion will involve us, and swiftly too, in a maze of contradictions. A guard stumbles over a pack-age which has been left upon the platform. It seems to be a bundle of newspapers. It turns out to be a can of dyna-mite. To the eye of ordinary vigilance, the bundle is aban-doned waste, which may be kicked or trod on with impunity. Is a passenger at the other end of the platform protected by the law against the unsuspected hazard concealed beneath the waste? If not, is the result to be any different, so far as the distant passenger is con-cerned, when the guard stumbles over a valise which a truckman or a porter has left upon the walk? The passenger far away, if the victim of a wrong at all, has a cause of action, not derivative, but original and primary. His claim to be protected against invasion of his bodily security is neither greater nor less because the act resulting in the invasion is a wrong to another far removed. In this case, the rights that are said to have been violated, the interests said to have been invaded, are not even of the same order. The man was not injured in his person nor even put in danger. The purpose of the act, as well as its effect, was to make his person safe. If there was a wrong to him at all, which may very well be doubted, it was a wrong to a property interest only, the safety of his package. Out of this wrong to property, which threatened injury to nothing else, there has passed, we are told, to the plaintiff by derivation or succession a right of action for the invasion of an interest of another order, the right to bodily security. The diversity of interests emphasizes the futility of the effort to build the plaintiff's right upon the basis of a wrong to some one else. The gain is one of emphasis, for a like result would follow if the interests were the same. Even then, the orbit of the danger as disclosed to the eye of reasonable vigilance would be the orbit of the duty. One who jostles one's neighbor in a crowd does not invade the rights of others standing at the outer fringe when the unintended contact casts a bomb upon the ground. The wrongdoer as to them is the man who carries the bomb, not the one who explodes it without suspicion of the danger. Life will have to be made over, and human nature transformed, before prevision so extravagant can be accepted as the norm of conduct, the customary standard to which behavior must conform.

* * *

The argument for the plaintiff is built upon the shifting meanings of such words as "wrong" and "wrongful," and shares their instability. What the plaintiff must show is "a wrong" to herself; i.e., a violation of her own right, and not merely a wrong to some one else, nor conduct "wrongful" because unsocial, but not "a wrong" to any one. We are told that one who drives at reckless speed through a crowded city street is guilty of a negligent act and therefore of a wrongful one, irrespective of the consequences. Negligent the act is, and wrongful in the sense that it is unsocial, but wrongful and unsocial in relation to other travelers, only because the eye of vigilance perceives the risk of damage. If the same act were to be committed on a speedway or a race course, it would lose its wrongful quality. The risk seasonably to be perceived defines the duty to be obeyed, and risk imports

relation; it is risk to another or to others within the range of apprehension. . . . This does not mean, of course, that one who launches a destructive force is always relieved of liability, if the force, though known to be destructive, pursues an unexpected path. "It was not necessary that the defendant should have had notice of the particular method in which an accident would occur, if the possibility of an accident was clear to the ordinarily prudent eye." . . . Some acts, such as shooting are so imminently dangerous to any one who may come within reach of the missile however unexpectedly, as to impose a duty of prevision not far from that of an insurer. Even to-day, and much oftener in earlier stages of the law, one acts sometimes at one's peril. . . . Under this head, it may be, fall certain cases of what is known as transferred intent, an act willfully dangerous to A resulting by misadventure in injury to B. . . . These cases aside, wrong is defined in terms of the natural or probable, at least when unintentional. . . . The range of reasonable apprehension is at times a question for the court, and at times, if varying inferences are possible, a question for the jury. Here, by concession, there was nothing in the situation to suggest to the most cautious mind that the parcel wrapped in newpaper would spread wreckage through the station. If the guard had thrown it down knowingly and willfully, he would not have threatened the plaintiff's safety, so far as appearances could warn him. His conduct would not have involved, even then, an unreasonable probability of invasion of her bodily security. Liability can be no greater where the act is inadvertent.

Negligence, like risk, is thus a term of relation. Negligence in the abstract, apart from things related, is surely not a tort, if indeed it is understandable at all. . . . Negligence is not a tort unless it results in the commission of a wrong, and the commission of a wrong imports the violation of a right, in this case, we are told, the right to be protected against interference with one's bodily security. But bodily security is protected, not against all forms of interference or aggression, but only against some. One who seeks redress at law does not make out a cause of action by showing without more that there has been damage to his person. If the harm was not willful, he must show that the act as to him had possibilities of danger so many and apparent as to entitle him to be protected against the doing of it though the harm was unintended. Affront to personality is still the keynote of the wrong. . . .

The law of causation, remote or proximate, is thus foreign to the case before us. The question of liability is always anterior to the question of the measure of the consequences that go with liability. If there is no tort to be redressed, their is no occasion to consider what damage might be recovered if there were a finding of a tort. We may assume, without deciding, that negligence, not at large or in the abstract, but in relation to the plaintiff, would entail liability for any and all consequences, however novel or extraordinary. . . . There is room for argument that a distinction is to be drawn according to the diversity of interests invaded by the act, as where conduct negligent in that it threatens an insignificant invasion of an interest in property results in an unforeseeable invasion of an interest of another order, as, e. g., one of bodily security. Perhaps other distinctions may be necessary. We do not go into the question now. The consequences to be followed must first be rooted in a wrong.

* * *

The Judgment of the Appellate Division and that of the Trial Term should be reversed, and the complaint dismissed, with costs in all courts.

ANDREWS, J. (dissenting). Assisting a passenger to board a train, the defendant's servant negligently knocked a package from his arms. It fell between the platform and the cars. Of its contents the servant knew and could know nothing. A violent explosion followed. The concussion broke some scales standing a considerable distance away. In falling, they injured the plaintiff, an intending passenger.

Upon these facts, may she recover the damages she has suffered in an action brought against the master? The result we shall reach depends upon our theory as to the nature of negligence. Is it a relative concept—the breach of some duty owing to a particular person or to particular persons? Or, where there is an act which unreasonably threatens the safety of others, is the doer liable for all its proximate consequences, even where they result in injury to one who would generally be thought to be outside the radius of danger? This is not a mere dispute as to words. We might not believe that to the average mind the dropping of the bundle would seem to involve the probability of harm to the plaintiff standing many feet away whatever might be the case as to the owner or to one so near as to be likely to be struck by its fall. If, however, we adopt the second hypothesis, we have to inquire only as to the relation between cause and effect. We deal in terms of proximate cause, not of negligence.

Negligence may be defined roughly as an act or omission which unreasonably does or may affect the rights of others, or which unreasonably fails to protect one's self from the dangers resulting from such acts. Here I confine myself to the first branch of the definition. Nor do I comment on the word "unreasonable." For present purposes it sufficiently describes that average of conduct that society requires of its members.

There must be both the act or the omission, and the right. It is the act itself, not the intent of the actor, that is important. . . . In criminal law both the intent and the result are to be considered. Intent again is material in tort actions, where punitive damages are sought, dependent on actual malice—not on merely reckless conduct. But here neither insanity nor infancy lessens responsibility. . . .

As has been said, except in cases of contributory negligence, there must be rights which are or may be affected. Often though injury has occurred, no rights of him who suffers have been touched. A licensee or trespasser upon my land has no claim to affirmative care on my part that the land be made safe. . . . Where a railroad is required to fence its tracks against cattle, no man's rights are injured should he wander upon the road because such fence is absent. . . . An unborn child may not demand immunity from personal harm. . . .

But we are told that "there is no negligence unless there is in the particular case a legal duty to take care, and this duty must be one which is owed to the plaintiff himself and not merely to others." . . . This I think too narrow a conception. Where there is the unreasonable act, and some right that may be affected there is negligence whether damage does or does not result. That is immaterial. Should we drive down Broadway at a reckless speed, we are negligent whether we strike an approaching car or miss it by an inch. The act itself is wrongful. It is a wrong not only to those who happen to be within the radius of danger, but to all who might have been there— a wrong to the public at large. Such is the language of the street. Such is the language of the courts when speaking of contributory negligence. Such again and again their language in speaking of the duty of some defendant and discussing proximate cause in cases where such a discussion is wholly irrelevant on any other theory.

Due care is a duty imposed on each one of us to protect society from unnecessary danger, not to protect A, B, or C alone.

It may well be that there is no such thing as negligence in the abstract. "Proof of negligence in the air, so to speak, will not do." In an empty world negligence would not exist. It does involve a relationship between man and his fellows, but not merely a relationship between man and those whom he might reasonably expect his act would injure; rather, a relationship between him and those whom he does in fact injure. If his act has a tendency to harm some one, it harms him a mile away as surely as it does those on the scene. We now permit children to recover for the negligent killing of the father. It was never prevented on the theory that no duty was owing to them. A husband may be compensated for the loss of his wife's services. To say the wrongdoer was negligent as to the husband as well as to the wife is merely an attempt to fit facts to theory. An insurance company paying a fire loss recovers its payment of the negligent incendiary. We speak of subrogation—of suing in the right of the insured. Behind the cloud of words in the fact they hide, that the act, wrongful as to the insured, has also injured the company. Even if it be true that the fault of father, wife, or insured will prevent recovery, it is because we consider the original negligence, not the proximate cause of the injury. . . .

In the well-known Polhemis Case, . . . Scrutton, L. J., said that the dropping of a plank was negligent, for it might injure "workman or cargo or ship." Because of either possibility, the owner of the vessel was to be made good for his loss. The act being wrongful, the doer was liable for its proximate results. Criticized and explained as this statement may have been, I think it states the law as it should be and as it is. . . .

The proposition is this: Every one owes to the world at large the duty of refraining from those acts that may unreasonably threaten the safety of others. Such an act occurs. Not only is he wronged to whom harm might reasonably be expected to result, but he also who is in fact injured, even if he be outside what would generally be thought the danger zone. There needs be duty due the one complaining, but this is not a duty to a particular individual because as to him harm might be expected. Harm to some one being the natural result of the act, not only that one alone, but all those in fact injured may complain. We have never, I think, held otherwise. . . .

If this be so, we do not have a plaintiff suing by "derivation or succession." Her action is original and primary. Her claim is for a breach of duty to herself—not that she is subrogated to any right of action of the owner of the parcel or of a passenger standing at the scene of the explosion.

The right to recover damages rests on additional considerations. The plaintiff's rights must be injured, and this injury must be caused by the negligence. We build a dam, but are negligent as to its foundations. Breaking, it injures property down stream. We are not liable if all this happened because of some reason other than the insecure foundation. But, when injuries do result from our unlawful act, we are liable for the consequences. It does not matter that they are unusual, unexpected, unforeseen, and unforeseeable. But there is one limitation. The damages must be so connected with the negligence that the latter may be said to be the proximate cause of the former.

These two words have never been given an inclusive definition. What is a cause in a legal sense, still more what is a proximate cause, depend in each case upon many considerations, as does the existence of negligence itself. Any philosophical doctrine of causation does not help us. A boy throws a stone into a pond. The ripples spread. The water level rises. The history of that pond is altered to all eternity. It will be altered by other causes also. Yet it will be forever the resultant of all causes combined. Each one will have an influence. How great only omniscience can say. You may speak of a chain, or, if you please, a net. An analogy is of little aid. Each cause brings about future events. Without each the future would not be the same. Each is proximate in the sense it is essential. But that is not what we mean by the word. Nor on the other hand do we mean sole cause. There is no such thing.

Should analogy be thought helpful, however, I prefer that of a stream. The spring, starting on its journey, is joined by tributary after tributary. The river, reaching the ocean, comes from a hundred sources. No man may say whence any drop of water is derived. Yet for a time distinction may be possible. Into the clear creek, brown swamp water flows from the left. Later, from the right comes water stained by its clay bed. The three may remain for a space, sharply divided. But at least inevitable no trace of separation remains. They are so commingled that all distinction is lost.

As we have said, we cannot trace the effect of an act to the end, if end there is. Again however, we may trace it part of the way. A murder at Serajevo may be the necessary antecedent to an assassination in London twenty years hence. An overturned lantern may burn all Chicago. We may follow the fire from the shed to the last building. We rightly say the fire started by the lantern caused its destruction.

A cause, but not the proximate cause. What we do mean by the word "proximate" is that, because of convenience, of public policy, of a rough sense of justice, the law arbitrarily declines to trace a series of events beyond a certain point. This is not logic. It is practical politics. Take our rule as to fires. Sparks from my burning haystack set on fire my house and my neighbor's. I may recover from a negligent railroad. He may not. Yet the wrongful act as directly harmed the one as the other. We may regret that the line was drawn just where it was, but drawn somewhere it had to be. We said the act of the railroad was not the proximate cause of our neighbor's fire. Cause it surely was. The words we used were simply indicative of our notions of public policy. Other courts think differently. But somewhere they reach the point where they cannot say the stream comes from any one source.

Take an illustration given in an unpublished manuscript by a distinguished and helpful writer on the law of torts. A chauffeur negligently collides with another car which is filled with dynamite, although he could not know it. An explosion follows. A, walking on the sidewalk nearby, is killed. B, sitting in a window of a building opposite, is cut by flying glass. C, likewise sitting in a window a block away, is similarly injured. And a further illustration: A nursemaid, ten blocks away, startled by the noise, involuntarily drops a baby from her arms to the walk. We are told that C may not recover while A may. As to B it is a question for court or jury. We will all agree that the baby might not. Because, we are again told, the chauffeur had no reason to believe his conduct involved any risk of injuring either C or the baby. As to them he was not negligent.

But the chauffeur, being negligent in risking the collision, his belief that the scope of the harm he might do would be limited is immaterial. His act unreasonably jeopardized the safety of any one who might be affected by it. C's injury and that of the baby were directly traceable to the collision. Without that, the injury would not have happened. C had the right to sit in his office, secure from such dangers. The baby was entitled to use the sidewalk with reasonable safety.

The true theory is, it seems to me, that the injury to C, if in truth he is to be denied recovery, and the injury to the baby, is that their several injuries were not the proximate reason of the negligence. And here not what the chauffeur had reason to believe would be the result of his conduct, but what the prudent would foresee, may have a bearing—may have some bearing, for the problem of proximate cause is not to be solved by any one consideration. It is all a question of expediency. There are no fixed rules to govern our judgment. There are simply matters of which we may take account. We have in a somewhat different connection spoken of "the stream of events." We have asked whether that stream was deflected—whether it was forced into new and unexpected channels. . . . This is rather rhetoric than law. There is in truth little to guide us other than common sense.

There are some hints that may help us. The proximate cause, involved as it may be with many other causes, must be, at the least, something without which the event would not happen. The court must ask itself whether there was a natural and continuous sequence between cause and effect. Was the one a substantial factor in producing the other? Was there a direct connection between them, without too many intervening causes? Is the effect of cause on result not too attenuated? Is the cause likely, in the usual judgment of mankind, to produce the result? Or by the exercise of prudent foresight, could the result be foreseen? Is the result too remote from the cause, and here we consider remoteness in time and space. . . . Clearly we must so consider, for the greater the distance either in time or space, the more surely do other causes intervene to affect the result. When a lantern is overturned, the firing of a shed is a fairly direct consequence. Many things contribute to the spread of the conflagration—the force of the wind, the direction and width of streets, the character of intervening structures, other factors. We draw an uncertain and wavering line, but draw it we must as best we can.

Once again, it is all a question of fair judgment, always keeping in mind the fact that we endeavor to make a rule in each case that will be practical and in keeping with the general understanding of mankind.

Here another question must be answered. In the case supposed, it is said, and said correctly, that the chauffeur is liable for the direct effect of the explosion, although he had no reason to suppose it would follow a collision. "The fact that the injury occurred in a different manner than that which might have been expected does not prevent the chauffeur's negligence from being in law the cause of the injury." But the natural results of a negligent act—the results which a prudent man would or should foresee—do have a bearing upon the decision as to proximate cause. We have said so repeatedly. What should be foreseen? No human foresight would suggest that a collision itself might injure one a block away. On the contrary, given an explosion, such a possibility might be reasonably expected. I think the direct connection, the foresight of which the courts speak, assumes prevision of the explosion, for the immediate results of which, at least, the chauffeur is responsible.

It may be said this is unjust. Why? In fairness he should make good every injury flowing from his negligence. Not because of tenderness toward him we say he need not answer for all that follows his wrong. We look back to the catastrophe, the fire kindled by the spark, or the explosion. We trace the consequences, not indefinitely, but to a certain point. And to aid us in fixing that point we ask what might ordinarily be expected to follow the fire or the explosion.

This last suggestion is the factor which must determine the case before us. The act upon which defendant's liability rests is knocking an apparently harmless package onto the platform. The act was negligent. For its proximate consequences the defendant is liable. If its contents were broken, to the owner; if it fell upon and crushed a passenger's foot, then to him; if it exploded and injured one in the immediate vicinity, to him also as to A in the illustration. Mrs. Palsgraf was standing some distance away. How far cannot be told from the record— apparently 25 or 30 feet, perhaps less. Except for the explosion, she would not have been injured. We are told by the appellant in his brief, "It cannot be denied that the explosion was the direct cause of the plaintiff's injuries." So it was a substantial factor in producing the result— there was here a natural and continuous sequence—

direct connection. The only intervening cause was that, instead of blowing her to the ground, the concussion smashed the weighing machine which in turn fell upon her. There was no remoteness in time, little in space. And surely, given such an explosion as here, it needed no great foresight to predict that the natural result would be to injure one on the platform at no greater distance from its scene than was the plaintiff. Just how no one might be able to predict. Whether by flying fragments, by broken glass, by wreckage of machines or structures no one could say. But injury in some form was most probable.

Under these circumstances I cannot say as a matter of law that the plaintiff's injuries were not the proximate result of the negligence. That is all we have before us. The court refused to so charge. No request was made to submit the matter to the jury as a question of fact, even would that have been proper upon the record before us.

The judgment appealed from should be affirmed, with costs.

POUND, LEHMAN, and KELLOGG, JJ., concur with CARDOZO, C. J.

ANDREWS, J., dissents in opinion in which CRANE and O'BRIEN, JJ., concur.

Judgment reversed, etc.

The court, in an oft-quoted decision authored by Judge Cardozo, held that the defendant was not liable (see Figure 7-2). The court reasoned that the defendant's conduct did not create an unreasonable risk of harm to the plaintiff and that the injury she sustained was not a foreseeable one. "Proof of negligence in the air," the court said, "will not do." The wrong in relationship to the passenger holding the package did not extend to the plaintiff. According to the Cardozo rule, which is generally followed today, "[a] wrong is defined in terms of the natural and probable, at least when unintentional."

Judge Andrews, in his famous dissent, argued that the defendant had a duty to "protect society from unnecessary danger, not to protect A, B or C alone."

According to Andrews, "every one owes to the world at large the duty of refraining from those acts that may unreasonably threaten the safety of others. . . . Not only is he wronged to whom harm might reasonably be expected to result, but he also who is in fact injured, even if he be outside what would generally be thought the danger zone." (Cardozo's formulation of foreseeability is often referred to as the "zone of danger" test.) Judge Andrews did realize that liability must be cut off at some point. Although he fell short of defining the cutoff point, he did suggest that if the result were "too remote from the cause" in terms of time and space or if there were too many "intervening causes," the defendant's negligence should not be considered the proximate cause of the plaintiff's injuries.

FIGURE 7-2 Proximate Cause

MAJORITY RULE	MINORITY RULE
CARDOZO • Defendant is liable for all reasonably foreseeable consequences of his negligence. He owes a duty of care to the reasonably foreseeable plaintiff.	ANDREWS • Defendant owes a duty to world at large and not just to those in "danger zone." • Similar to "direct causation": defendant is liable for all consequences flowing directly from his actions no matter how unforeseeable.

EXCEPTIONS TO CARDOZO RULE
• "Eggshell skull" rule—defendant must take plaintiff as he finds him. • Defendant is liable for harm occurring in an unforeseen manner if harm is of the same general type that made defendant's conduct negligent. • Defendant is liable if plaintiff is member of class to which there is general foreseeability of harm even if plaintiff was not particularly foreseeable. • Defendant is liable even if there is an unforeseeable intervening cause leading to same type of harm threatened by defendant's negligence.

PUTTING IT INTO PRACTICE 7.2

1. In *Palsgraf,* was the defendant's conduct negligent in relationship to the passenger carrying the package? Did the negligence to this passenger transfer to Mrs. Palsgraf?
2. Before negligence can be found, what must be found "back of the act," according to Justice Cardozo?
3. According to the majority, what must a plaintiff show in reference to being "wronged"? How does the majority define a "wrong"?
4. When does negligence become a tort, according to the majority?
5. Does negligence at large or in the abstract "entail liability for any and all consequences, however novel or extraordinary"?
6. How does the dissent define "due care"?
7. How does the dissent view the duty to the world at large? Is this duty restricted to those within the "danger zone"?
8. How does the dissent define "proximate cause"? Is this definition a matter of logic or practical politics? Is proximate cause a matter of expediency or is it bound by fixed rules?

Continued on next page

---

9. According to the dissent, why might C and the baby in the hypothetical involving the chauffeur not be expected to recover? What argument does the dissent give to support C's recovery?
10. Can a clear line be drawn between proximate cause and causes that are too remote in time and space? What does the question of proximate cause ultimately boil down to, according to the dissent?
11. Was Mrs. Palsgraf's injury a natural and probable consequence of the explosion, according to the dissent?

Direct Causation

Andrews' position parallels that of a view commonly known as *direct causation.* Under this view a defendant is liable for all consequences of his or her negligent acts, no matter how unforeseeable those consequences may be, so long as they flow directly from his or her actions. A famous case that illustrates the direct causation view is *In re Polemis,* 3 K.B. 560 (Eng. 1921). In *Polemis,* while the defendants were unloading a ship, which they had chartered from the plaintiffs, they negligently dropped a plank into the hold. Somehow the plank struck a spark, which ignited petroleum the ship was carrying, and the resulting fire destroyed the ship. Although plainly no one could reasonably have foreseen that dropping a plank would strike a spark and destroy the entire ship, the defendants were held liable because the fire was the direct result of their negligent act.

Although the direct causation rule is commonly criticized because a logical extension of the rule would result in limitless liability, proponents of the view argue that a loss should be borne by the guilty rather than by the innocent. The courts that follow the direct causation rule will not take into account the extent of the harm, the foreseeability of the result, the manner in which the injury occurred, or the timing of the cause and effect.

Duty versus Proximate Cause

You will probably notice in the course of reading opinions that courts frequently blur the issues of duty and proximate cause together. In fact, the *Palsgraf* opinion itself was centered around a discussion of duty. The question, as posed by Cardozo, was whether the defendant had a duty of care to the plaintiff. Whether phrased in terms of duty or proximate cause, the question is essentially the same. A defendant is liable only if his or her conduct poses a foreseeable risk to the plaintiff. Similarly, a defendant owes a duty of care only if there is a foreseeable risk to the plaintiff. Keep in mind, however, that proximate cause is basically a policy question. It allows the courts to cut off liability in cases in which it would be inherently unfair to hold a defendant liable.

Read the facts for Putting It into Practice 6.2 (the boy who was paralyzed when he dove into the water without first checking its depth). Is the state's failure to post warning signs the cause of David's injuries? How would you analyze the question of actual cause? How would that analysis differ from an analysis of proximate cause?

EXCEPTIONS TO THE CARDOZO RULE

Although the Cardozo position has generally been followed by American courts, there are a few notable exceptions. Under these exceptions recovery is allowed even though the consequences are arguably unforeseeable.

"Eggshell Skull" Rule

The first exception requires that a defendant "take his plaintiff as he finds him." In *Watson v. Rinderknecht,* 84 N.W. 798 (Minn. 1901), the case that set forth this exception, the plaintiff, a sixty-year-old man who was receiving a pension resulting from injuries he had sustained during a war, was assaulted by a much younger and more vigorous defendant. The court held the defendant liable for the full extent of the plaintiff's injuries even though the average person in that same confrontation would have suffered much lesser injuries. Under the so-called "eggshell skull" rule, if the plaintiff suffers any foreseeable injury, the defendant is also liable for any additional unforeseen physical consequences. In other words, if a defendant inflicts a relatively minor impact on a plaintiff who dies because he has a skull of eggshell thinness, the defendant will be liable for his death. Suppose a defendant assaults a plaintiff who, unbeknownst to him, has AIDS. If the plaintiff dies from these injuries because of his weakened condition, the defendant will be liable for his death even though such injuries would have been minor to any healthy individual.

Same General Type of Harm But Unusual Manner

In the second exception to the *Palsgraf* general rule, a defendant is liable if the harm suffered by the plaintiff is of the general type that made the defendant's conduct negligent even if the harm occurs in an unusual manner. Suppose a defendant hands a loaded pistol to a small child, who carries it over to the plaintiff. In the process of handing the pistol to the plaintiff, if the child drops it and the gun goes off and wounds the plaintiff, the defendant is liable. The rationale is that the risk of accidental discharge is the same kind of general risk that made the defendant's conduct negligent initially. The fact that the discharge occurs by an unforeseeable means (dropping the gun) is irrelevant.

If, however, the child drops the gun on someone's foot, causing injuries, the defendant is not liable. The risk of injuring someone by dropping a gun on his foot is not one of the risks that makes the defendant's conduct negligent (Restatement (Second) of Torts § 281, illus. 3).

Plaintiff Member of Foreseeable Class

The same rationale is applicable when injury occurs to a plaintiff who is not a particularly foreseeable plaintiff. As long as the plaintiff is a member of a class to which there is a general foreseeability of harm, the defendant is liable. To illustrate, suppose a defendant's car carelessly collides with a car containing dynamite and the plaintiff, a pedestrian on a sidewalk near the collision point, is injured by the ensuing explosion. Even though there is no way she could have known the car contained dynamite, the defendant is liable because a reasonable driver should realize that careless driving can injure pedestrians. Therefore, the plaintiff is a member of a class (pedestrians) to whom harm is a foreseeable consequence of reckless driving. The fact that the harm occurs in a different manner than might be anticipated does not absolve the defendant of liability (Restatement (Second) of Torts § 281, illus. 2).

PUTTING IT INTO PRACTICE 7.4

1. As a result of a shipping company negligently mooring its ship, ice and debris cause the ship to run adrift and it collides with a properly moored ship. Both ships smash into a drawbridge, which is not raised in time because the employees who operate it are not on duty. The bridge topples and a dam is created by the collapsed bridge, the two ships, and ice. The resulting flood creates tremendous damage to the adjoining land. If the river-bank landowners bring suit against the shipping company and the City of Buffalo, which operates the drawbridge, will they be able to prove proximate cause in light of the bizarre turn of events?

2. Helen is a worker in a government munitions plant where she handles nitroglycerine. After working at the plant for a few months, Helen begins experiencing chest pains (on the weekends only), severe enough on one occasion to require hospitalization. Ultimately, she is diagnosed has having suffered a heart attack or coronary insufficiency (inadequate blood flow to the heart). After her return to work she experiences weekend chest pains with increasing frequency until she leaves her job four years later.

   Helen is convinced that her handling of nitroglycerine is causing her heart problems. Only one of the many doctors she consults agrees with her. Helen continues to experience health problems after she leaves the plant (continuing but less severe chest pains, dizziness, fatigue, high blood pressure, and coughing spells that lead to vomiting). At trial the district court judge finds the government to be negligent and the cause of her heart disease. She is awarded $53,000 in damages. The judge refuses, however, to make an award for what doctors determine to be hypochondriasis (a neurotic behavior that results in obsessive concern over the state of one's health). If the government's negligence is the actual cause of Helen's hypochondriasis, should the government be considered the proximate cause of her continuing poor health?

INTERVENING CAUSES

An **intervening cause** is anything that occurs after the defendant's negligent act and that contributes to the plaintiff's injury (Restatement (Second) of Torts § 441(1)). If the intervening cause rises to such a level of importance that it precludes the defendant's negligence from being the proximate cause of the plaintiff's injury, it becomes a superseding cause (Restatement (Second) of Torts § 440). A **superseding cause** supersedes or cancels out the defendant's liability. If the defendant should have foreseen the possibility that an intervening cause or one like it might occur, he or she remains liable (see Figure 7-3).

Examples of intervening forces can be seen in the hypothetical situations listed earlier in the section on foreseeability. In the scenario in which the wounded plaintiff died as a result of the doctor's malpractice, the doctor would be considered an intervening cause. Similarly, the person who caused the accident in which the plaintiff's ambulance was involved would also be an intervening cause. The question in these cases is whether the negligence of others was sufficiently foreseeable that the defendant was negligent in not anticipating and guarding against such negligence. If the negligence of third persons is not surprising, then any acts of the defendant that precipitate the third person's conduct will be considered a proximate cause of the plaintiff's injuries.

Is it surprising that an ambulance might be involved in an accident as a result of someone's negligence? Probably not, and if not, the defendant will remain the proximate cause of the plaintiff's injuries. Is it

FIGURE 7-3   Liability

DEFENDANT IS LIABLE	DEFENDANT IS NOT LIABLE
Intervening acts	Superseding acts
Accidents	"Acts of God"
Medical malpractice of doctor occurring after defendant's negligence	Gross medical malpractice of doctor occurring after defendant's negligence
Escape attempts	Bizarre escape response to defendant's negligence
Rescue	Grossly careless acts of rescuer
Foreseeable negligence of others	Unforeseeable negligence of others
Foreseeable criminal or intentionally tortious conduct	Unforeseeable criminal or intentionally tortious conduct

surprising that someone admitted to a hospital might be further injured as a result of the negligence of his caretaker? Most courts have found medical malpractice to be sufficiently foreseeable, as long as it is not gross malpractice, and therefore not a superseding cause. Similarly, if the defendant causes the plaintiff to be in a weakened state, making him susceptible to disease or accidents, he will be held liable for any subsequent disease or accidents the plaintiff suffers. In the scenario in which the plaintiff is killed in an attempt to flee from the defendant, the plaintiff's attempted escape will not be a superseding cause as long as the plaintiff's response was not totally extraordinary or bizarre. If someone attempts to rescue the plaintiff and causes part or all of the plaintiff's injuries, the defendant will be liable to the plaintiff and to the rescuer as well for any injuries sustained by either. However, if the rescuer is grossly negligent, his conduct will be considered a superseding cause.

The rationale that the foreseeable negligence of others will not be considered a superseding cause has been used to hold tavern owners liable for the negligence of their intoxicated patrons. Although courts are less

likely to impose such liability on social hosts, some courts have done so when the guest served was known to the host to be one who would be driving.

A third person's criminal conduct or intentional tortious act may also, in some cases, be sufficiently foreseeable that such conduct will not be considered a superseding cause. As a practical matter, however, proving that the risk of such criminal or tortious conduct was actually foreseeable is often difficult.

To illustrate foreseeable criminal conduct, consider the case in which an alarm company installed a burglar alarm in a pawnshop but, for the convenience of its maintenance people, left the key to the control box (which regulated the sensitivity of the alarm system) on top of the box. A burglar used the key to lower the sensitivity of the alarm so that he could carry out his illegal mission without detection. The court found the alarm company's negligence to be the proximate cause of the pawnshop's loss, refusing to classify the burglary as a superseding cause, in that the burglary was no doubt foreseeable considering that the whole purpose of the alarm system was to prevent such burglaries. *Central Alarm v. Ganem,* 567 P.2d 1203 (Ariz. 1977).

Superseding Causes

An "act of God," such as being struck by lightning, is considered a superseding cause, as it is an act of nature that is extraordinary and not foreseeable. If our plaintiff in the hypothetical case given earlier were killed by a bolt of lightning while in the process of running from the defendant, the lightning would be considered a superseding cause that would relieve the defendant of liability.

Another example of a superseding cause is a common carrier's negligent delay in the transporting of goods, resulting in the destruction of the goods by a natural catastrophe, such as a flood or fire. Even though the delay might clearly be the cause of the damage—the goods would not have been destroyed had there been no delay—most courts would consider the act of nature a superseding cause. To avoid this holding a plaintiff must show that an increase in the risk of such a catastrophe as a result of the delay was foreseeable.

A contemporary problem that aptly illustrates the issue of superseding causes is the liability of tavern owners for serving obviously intoxicated patrons who inflict injuries on others when they drink and drive. The question is whether the drinking by the patron supersedes the negligence of the tavern owner. As you read the excerpt from *Ontiveros v. Borak* note the policy concerns that drive the court to overrule the common law in Arizona. Some of these same policy concerns have prompted this court, as well as courts in some other states, to apply the same reasoning to cases involving social hosts.

CASE

Ontiveros v. Borak
667 P.2d 200 (Ariz. 1983)

FELDMAN, Justice.

Plaintiff brought this tort action for damages against the defendant, Peter Borak, Sr., d/b/a/ Max's Terminal Buffet (Borak), and others. The action against Borak, the owner of a tavern, was based on the claim that Borak's negligence in serving liquor to an intoxicated patron, Reuben Flores, had been a cause of a subsequent motor vehicle accident in which Flores had inflicted serious injuries on plaintiff. Flores was joined as a defendant.

* * *

This case presents the issue of a tavern owner's common law liability for negligence in serving his or her patrons. Believing the question is of considerable importance and that the public interest requires a speedy and final decision, we granted the petition for transfer in order to meet and finally resolve the issue so squarely presented by the facts of this case. While the evidence is conflicting, the case was decided on motion for a summary judgment and we are therefore required to review the facts in the light most favorable to the party against whom summary judgment was taken. Acknowledging this principle, defendant properly conceded in oral argument that for the purpose of deciding the question of law presented on this appeal the facts are as follows:

On May 22, 1975, Flores left work and, as was his custom, went to Borak's bar before going home. According to Flores' statement and deposition, he there had "quite a few" beers, which were served by the owner's son, and then went across the street to another bar for a short time. He returned to Borak's bar and remained there until closing time was announced at approximately 8:00 p.m. During the afternoon and early evening Flores consumed approximately 30 beers. Unfortunately, he was able to leave the bar and get in his car, which was parked in the bar's parking lot, and headed for home. A few blocks from the bar, he hit a fire hydrant, then swerved, saw cars from the other direction, swerved again, and then "all of a sudden a man was there and I hit him. I told the police officer there was no need to take a breath test because I was drunk." Nevertheless, the police did administer a breathalyzer test; the result was a reading of .33, more than triple the point at which the law now forbids driving.

Plaintiff survived the accident, but received a fractured skull, subdural hematomas and liver damage. These injuries allegedly resulted in partial paralysis and mental retardation. Plaintiff has been unable to work since the accident.

COMMON LAW

* * *

At common law, . . . a tavern owner is not liable for injuries sustained off-premises by third persons as the result of the acts of an intoxicated patron, even though the tavern owner's negligence in serving the patron was a contributing cause of the accident. The seminal cases in Arizona on tavern owner ("dram shop") liability are *Pratt v. Daly,* 55 Ariz. 535, 104 P.2d 147, and *Collier v. Stamatis,* 63 Ariz. 285, 162 P.2d 125, decided in 1940 and 1945, respectively. Plaintiff argues correctly that neither case explicitly held that a tavern owner could not be held liable under the common law in a fact situation similar to the one presented by the case at bench. We agree; however, implicit, if not explicit, in both *Pratt* and *Collier* is the acceptance of the common law rule. Thus, it was recognized both within and without Arizona that *Pratt v. Daly* had approved and adopted the common law rule of nonliability. . . . We conclude, therefore, that the rule of nonliability for tavern owners has been the common law in Arizona.

However, the common law, which is judge-made and judge-applied, can and will be changed when changed conditions and circumstances establish that it is unjust or has become bad public policy. In reevaluating previous decisions in light of present facts and circumstances, we do not depart from the proper role of the judiciary . . . .

We turn, therefore, to reexamine the present common law rule, its basis and its applicability under the present conditions. In doing so, we are mindful of our words in *Noland v. Wootan:* We take judicial notice of the terrible toll taken, both in personal injuries and property damage, by drivers who mix alcohol and gasoline . . . .

CAUSATION

All counsel agreed at oral argument that the common law rule was not a rule of immunity. Indeed, it is impossible to imagine why, of all occupations, those who furnish liquor should be singled out for a judicially conferred blessing of immunity to respond in damages for their wrongful acts. The common law rule was one of nonliability, founded, as indicated in both *Pratt* and *Collier,* upon concepts of causation. In *Pratt,* this court indicated

that the drinking of the liquor, and not the selling of it, is the act which causes the injury. We again acknowledge the obvious fact, mentioned in *Pratt,* that one cannot become intoxicated if one does not drink. However, the obverse is equally true: one cannot become intoxicated by drinking liquor unless someone furnishes it. Our common sense tells us that both the furnishing and the drinking are part of the chain of cause and effect that produces accidents such as the one in this case.

Arizona law holds that cause-in-fact exists if the defendant's act helped cause the final result and if that result would not have happened without the defendant's act. Defendant's act need not have been a "large" or "abundant" cause of the final result; there is liability if the result would not have occurred but for defendant's conduct, even if that conduct contributed "only a little" to plaintiff's injuries. Arizona also recognizes that more than one person may be liable for causing an injury and that a particular defendant may not avoid liability for his causative act by claiming that the conduct of some other person was also a contributing cause. . . .

Therefore, as far as causation-in-fact is concerned, the general rule is that a defendant may be held liable if his conduct contributed to the result and if that result would not have occurred "but for" defendant's conduct. There are some dram shop cases where it would be possible to say as a matter of law that the defendant's acts did not contribute to the result,[2] and there are other cases, such as this, where cause-in-fact remains a question for the jury. Certainly no court can say as a matter of law that there can never be a causal relation between serving liquor to an underaged, incompetent or already intoxicated patron and the subsequent accident in which that patron becomes involved when he or she leaves the premises. Insofar as *Pratt v. Daly* or *Collier v. Stamatis* stand for such a principle, they are wrong.

Another part of the causation question is the concept of superseding cause.

[This] is sometimes said to be a question of whether the [defendant's] conduct has been so significant and important a cause that the defendant should be legally responsible. But both significance and importance turn upon conclusions in terms of legal policy, so that this becomes essentially a question of whether the policy of the law will extend the

---

2. Suppose, for instance, that Flores had consumed 30 beers at Borak's and "one more for the road" at the bar across the street. Without specific evidence it would be difficult to argue that the accident would not have happened "but for" the last drink.

responsibility for the conduct to the consequences which have in fact occurred.

The basic issue of intervening and superseding causes is whether a defendant "is to be held liable for an injury to which he has in fact made a substantial contribution, when it is brought about by a later cause of independent origin, for which he is not responsible."

The common law rule of tavern owner nonliability was mainly based upon the concept that the chain of legal causation between the selling of the alcohol and the injury was broken or "superseded by the voluntary act of the purchaser in imbibing the drink." We acknowledge, of course, that the customer who drinks to excess or the underage patron who drinks at all is at fault. To say that the immediate actor is at fault, however, is not to say that there is no liability to be imposed upon the remote actor. The policy of the law on questions of intervening and superseding cause has evolved to the rule that the original actor is relieved from liability for the final result when, and only when, an intervening act of another was unforeseeable by a reasonable person in the position of the original actor and when, looking backward, after the event, the intervening act appears extraordinary. However, where the negligent conduct of the first actor increases the foreseeable risk of a particular harm occurring through the conduct of a second actor, the "fact that the harm is brought about through the intervention of another force does not relieve the [first] actor of liability."

The test, then, for whether the actions of a patron, such as Flores, constitute a superseding cause which relieves the tavern owner from liability is whether Flores' conduct was unforeseeable to one in Borak's position and whether the court can say with the benefit of hindsight that the occurrence of the harm through the conduct of the intervening actor was both unforeseeable and extraordinary. Even if there were no authority on the issue, we could find it neither unforeseeable nor unexpected that a patron who was served 30 beers over the space of five or six hours became quite drunk. The only thing extraordinary about the whole situation is that this patron, with a blood-alcohol level of .33, was able to walk to his car. It was certainly neither unforeseeable nor unexpected that once Flores began driving he would become involved in an accident likely to cause death or serious injury. This elemental point has not escaped other courts.

When alcoholic beverages are sold by a tavern keeper to a minor or to an intoxicated person, the unreasonable risk of harm . . . to members of the traveling public may readily be recognized and fore-

seen; this is particularly evident in current times when traveling by car to and from the tavern is so commonplace and accidents resulting from drinking are so frequent.

In fact, courts have recognized that the injury-producing conduct of the patron who has been served more alcohol while intoxicated is one of the very hazards which make the tavern owner's act negligent. The trend of modern authority is well summarized by the following words of the Supreme Court of Hawaii:

We hold that the consequences of serving liquor to an intoxicated motorist, in light of the universal use of automobiles and the increasing frequency of accidents involving drunk drivers, are foreseeable to a tavern owner . . . . The consumption, resulting inebriation and injurious conduct are therefore foreseeable intervening acts which will not relieve the tavern of liability.

Common sense, common experience and authority all combine to produce the irrefutable conclusion that furnishing alcohol, consumption of alcohol and subsequent driving of a vehicle which is then involved in an accident are all foreseeable, ordinary links in the chain of causation leading from the sale to the injury. Under the facts of this case, a jury could find that Borak's furnishing of additional liquor to Flores after he became intoxicated was a cause of the injuries sustained by plaintiff.

Borak argues, however, that as a matter of policy we should continue to hold that there is no "proximate cause" in dram shop cases. He contends that it will be difficult to sort out cause and effect in many cases since a patron who has already become intoxicated may be involved in an accident even without the "help" of the defendant who furnishes more alcohol. This contention is answered in the dissent in *Meade v. Freeman,* 93 Idaho 389, 462 P.2d 54 (1969). In criticizing the common law rule, Judge Prather stated:

It is quite ordinary to observe that persons who commence drinking intoxicants pass through various stages from complete sobriety to incapacitating intoxication and unconsciousness. . . . When the person has imbibed sufficient liquor that the effects thereof are becoming obvious to the ordinary person, the imbiber is still able to control himself and his actions sufficiently to avoid injury to others. If the imbiber continues to drink intoxicants, however, his condition will worsen until he reaches the point that he can not control his thought or muscular processes. After the first signs of apparent and obvious intoxication have begun to show on a person who is drinking, it is within the knowledge and experience of nearly all people that such person should not indulge in any further use of intoxicants until his body has rid itself of that which he has already imbibed. When so viewed, I perceive no difference in regarding the sale of further intoxicants to one already drunk as a proximate cause of ensuing injuries [as] in those cases wherein the sale of firearms to minors or incompetents, the sale of dangerous drugs to those known to be addicted, or the manufacture and release upon the market of dangerously defective commodities are held to form a basis for liability. The underlying principle of all of these cases is that the seller is sending out into the public a thing of danger which a reasonably prudent person under like circumstances would apprehend would be likely to cause injury to someone else.

When most people walked and few had horses or carriages, . . . it may have been that the common rule of law of non-liability arising from the sale of liquor to an intoxicated person was satisfactory. But the situation then and the problem in today's society of the imbiber going upon the public highways and operating a machine that requires quick response of mind and muscle and capable of producing mass death and destruction are vastly different.

Judge Prather's words are even truer today, fourteen years after they were written. The statistics cited in the concurring opinion in *State ex rel. Ekstrom v. Justice Court*, —- Ariz. —-, 663 P.2d 992 (1983), indicate a frightful toll—25,000 deaths and 650,000 injuries each year in motor vehicle accidents in which alcohol is a contributing cause. We believe, therefore, that the words of Division II of our Court of Appeals are correct:

It seems clear that the common law rule is an anachronism, unsuitable to our present society, and that its reasoning is repugnant to modern tort theories.

We agree with the Pennsylvania Supreme Court that "[t]o serve an intoxicated person more liquor is to light the fuse." Therefore, *Pratt v. Daly, supra,* and *Collier v. Stamatis, supra,* are overruled insofar as they stand for the proposition that the negligence of a tavern owner in continuing to serve liquor to a patron who is or has become intoxicated can never be the legal cause of a subsequent accident.

Unforeseeable Intervention

Thus far we have looked at cases in which the intervening cause was foreseeable. If the intervention was not foreseeable but, in fact, led to the same type of harm as that threatened by the defendant's negligence, the courts typically find the intervention not to be a superseding cause (Restatement (Second) of Torts § 442B). The reasoning is that the defendant exposed the plaintiff to an unreasonable risk of harm of the same type as that which occurred. Allowing the defendant to escape liability simply because the harm was produced by an unforeseeable intervention would be unfair.

Let us consider the case of *Derdiarian v. Felix Contracting Corp.,* 414 N.E.2d 666 (N.Y. 1981) as an illustration of this principle. In this case the plaintiff, an employee of a subcontractor, was sealing a gas main at a work site in the street when he was struck by a driver who had just suffered an epileptic seizure and lost control of his vehicle. When struck, the plaintiff was catapulted into the air and landed in 400° F liquid enamel, causing him to be ignited into a fireball, which he miraculously survived. The plaintiff alleged that the defendant contracting company had failed to take adequate measures to ensure the safety of workers on the excavation site. The defendant argued that the plaintiff was injured as a result of the driver's negligence and that there was no causal link between the defendant's breach of duty and the plaintiff's injuries. The court refused to find the driver's negligence a superseding cause, noting that an intervening act does not serve as a superseding cause "where the risk of the intervening act occurring is the very same risk which renders the actor negligent."

PUTTING IT INTO PRACTICE 7.5

1. Marilyn negligently runs over Lucinda, breaking her leg. While Lucinda is learning to walk on crutches, she slips, falls, and breaks her arm. Is Lucinda's fall a superseding cause of her broken arm? Would your answer change if you knew that at the time Lucinda was trying to walk across an extremely narrow walkway and that she was doing this on a dare from her friends?

2. Charles is in a phone booth making a call; he looks up and sees a vehicle coming toward him. He attempts to flee the booth but cannot because of the faulty design, maintenance, and repair of the booth by Pacific Telephone and Western Electric. At trial Charles also alleges that the telephone booth was too close to the stream of "habitually speeding, dangerous traffic." Will Pacific Telephone and Western Electric be successful in arguing that the intoxicated driver in the vehicle that hit Charles was the superseding cause of his injuries?

3. The Exxon tanker, the *Houston,* was delivering oil into a pipeline through two floating hoses when a storm arose, causing the line linking the tanker to the single point mooring system (SPM) to break. During this "breakout," when the hoses were disengaged from the SPM and threatening to damage the ship's propeller, another vessel arrived and helped the crew of the *Houston* to regain control of the hoses. The captain was able to safely navigate the ship back out to sea so that it was no longer in danger of being stranded. While the crew was working to disconnect the hoses, the captain negligently failed to have someone plot the ship's position. Without knowing this position the captain could not effectively use a navigational chart to check for hazards. Failure to fix the ship's position constituted gross and extraordinary negligence. When the captain did order someone to plot the ship's position, he noticed too late that the ship was heading for a reef and moments later the ship ran aground.

   Exxon sues the owner and operator of the mooring facility for the losses incurred by the loss of its ship. Do you think Exxon is likely to be successful in its suit?

JURY QUESTION

The issue of proximate cause is a jury question as long as there is a possibility that reasonable persons could differ on this issue. The judge must first formulate the appropriate legal rule in the form of a jury instruction. But once that standard has been formulated, the final decision is a factual one left to the jury.

APPLICATION

In the case of Gertrude's attack on Teddy and Mr. Goodright, Gertrude was unquestionably the actual cause of Teddy's and Mr. Goodright's injuries. Of course, the Baxters might argue that Mr. Goodright's injuries were due to Teddy's negligence in entering their backyard. Under the but-for test, however, the rebuttal would be that but for the Baxters' negligence in leaving their gate unlocked Teddy would not have been able to enter the yard. Even under the substantial factor test the Baxters' failure to lock their gate would be a significant factor in the cause of Mr. Goodright's injuries. Assuming that Teddy would not have been able to enter the Baxters' backyard except for the presence of the unlocked gate, both he and the Baxters would be considered causes of Mr. Goodright's injuries. As such they would both be liable for his injuries.

The Baxters would also be considered the proximate cause of Teddy's and Mr. Goodright's injuries. It is reasonably foreseeable that if a person fails to lock a gate to a yard housing a watchdog, someone, especially a child, will enter the yard and be attacked.

The Baxters might argue that Mr. Goodright's volunteering to rescue Teddy, which was of his own volition and not a duty imposed upon him, was a superseding cause that should absolve them of liability. Remember, however, that rescue is not considered an intervening cause unless it is performed in a grossly negligent manner. Based on the famous Cardozo rationale that "danger invites rescue," a rescue is foreseeable when the defendant's negligence has created a danger that could result in injury to somebody. An argument on the part of the Baxters that Teddy's negligence was a superseding cause would also fail. Such negligence was reasonably foreseeable if children were able to gain access to the Baxters' backyard via the unlocked gate.

SUMMARY

The issue of causation consists of two separate considerations—actual cause (causation of fact) and proximate cause (legal cause). If the plaintiff can prove that the defendant's actions were the actual and factual cause of her injuries, she has proven actual cause. If the plaintiff can further prove that her injuries were a reasonably foreseeable result of the defendant's conduct, she can show proximate cause.

The but-for and substantial factor tests are used in proving actual cause. The plaintiff bears the burden of proving actual cause and must do so by a preponderance of the evidence. If the plaintiff cannot prove which defendant actually caused his injuries, he can shift the burden back on the defendants to show who actually caused the harm using the theory of alternate liability or market share liability. If the tortfeasors are unable to prove that they did not cause the plaintiff's injuries, they will all be found liable. If a plaintiff can prove the existence of a common plan or that the defendants assisted or encouraged each other in accomplishing a tortious result, he has proved actual causation using the concerted action theory.

The purpose of proximate or legal cause is to restrict a defendant's liability by absolving him or her of liability when the plaintiff's injury occurred as a result of a series of highly improbable or extraordinary events stemming from the defendant's negligence. The question of proximate cause is a policy question; the question of actual cause is a factual one. The issue of foreseeability was addressed most notably in *Palsgraf*, in which Judge Cardozo denied recovery to the plaintiff because she was not a foreseeable one. Justice Andrews, in contrast, argued that one owes a duty to the "world at large" and not just to those in the "danger zone." Andrews' position parallels the view of courts that espouse the theory of direct causation.

The Cardozo position is generally followed by most American courts. There are, however, a few notable exceptions. First, under the so-called "eggshell skull" rule, if a plaintiff suffers any foreseeable injury, the defendant is liable for any additional unforeseeable physical consequences. Second, a defendant is liable if the harm suffered by the plaintiff is of the general type that made the defendant's conduct negligent, even if the harm occurs in an unanticipated manner. Third, a defendant is liable as long as the plaintiff is a member of a class to which there is a reasonable foreseeability of harm, even if the plaintiff herself is not a particularly foreseeable plaintiff.

■ PRACTICE POINTERS ☐

Plaintiffs are not entitled to compensation for *preexisting conditions,* i.e., physical or emotional conditions that existed prior to the damage inflicted by the defendant. Suppose, for example, the plaintiff were a horse trainer who had suffered a number of riding accidents prior to her vehicular accident involving the defendant. If the plaintiff were suffering from the pain of lower back injury due to these riding accidents, she could not recover damages for her lower back injuries from the defendant if the vehicular accident had not contributed in any way to her preexisting condition. If, however, the vehicular accident had aggravated her preexisting back condition or had caused additional injuries, she could still recover. Remember that under the "eggshell skull" rule she could recover for the full extent of her injuries even if she were more susceptible to injury than a normally healthy individual and even if the healthy individual might not have suffered similar injuries.

Paralegals are often assigned the task of determining the nature and extent of preexisting conditions. To do so they must meticulously review the medical records of the plaintiff. If their firm represents the plaintiff, they must interview the plaintiff to gain a clear comprehension of the plaintiff's preexisting complaints and distinguish them from the currently existing injuries. They will also need to examine employment records and any previous insurance or workers' compensation claims. All these records must be compiled in preparation for a review by the medical expert(s). Such careful preparation prevents surprise at subsequent depositions or at trial. Preexisting conditions are a hotly contested issue at all stages of a case and therefore must be carefully documented by both sides in personal injury cases.

A defendant is expected to foresee the possibility of an intervening cause. Even if the intervening cause is not foreseeable but the kind of harm suffered by the plaintiff is, the defendant will remain liable. If an intervening cause rises to such a level that it becomes a superseding cause, the defendant is absolved of liability. The foreseeable negligence of others is not considered a superseding cause. Neither is a person's criminal or intentionally tortious conduct considered a superseding cause if it is sufficiently foreseeable.

■ TORT TEASERS ☐

1. Plaintiff tries to put a can of freon in his automobile air conditioner. Defendant company, which produced the refrigerant, failed to put a warning on the can about the danger of attaching the can to the wrong side of the compressor. The evidence shows Plaintiff failed to read any instructions that were on the can. Is Defendant's failure to warn an actual cause of Plaintiff's injury? *Technical Chemical Co. v. Jacobs,* 480 S.W.2d 602 (Tex. 1972).

2. Just before Defendant's industrial "dinky" engine collides with a train on a crossing, the engineer of the "dinky" reverses the engine, shuts off the steam, and jumps. The collision causes the throttle to jar loose and the "dinky" engine backs up, gathers momentum,

and travels around a loop to a second crossing where it collides with a train. Plaintiff, who is a passenger on the train, is injured in the second collision. Even though the second collision occurred in an unforeseeable manner, should Defendant be held liable? *Bunting v. Hogsett,* 21 A.31 (Pa. 1890).

3. Suppose Defendant drives a truck at excessive speed. Which of the following consequences do you think are foreseeable?

a. The truck narrowly misses a pregnant woman, who is frightened into a miscarriage. *Mitnick v. Whelan Bros.,* 163 A. 414 (Conn. 1932).

b. Defendant injures a man who suffers a second accident six months later while he is walking on crutches as a result of the first accident. *Squires v. Reynolds,* 5 A.2d 877 (Conn. 1939).

c. A truck knocks a taxi cab up against a stone wall, the wall is weakened, and as a result a stone falls off the top of the wall as the taxi is being disengaged from the wall. A pedestrian is injured when the stone falls on her. *In re Guardian Casualty Co.,* 2 N.Y.S.2d 232 (N.Y. Sup. Ct. 1938).

4. A waitress employed at Defendant's restaurant spills hot coffee on Plaintiff's lap, resulting in first-degree burns. When Plaintiff jumps up she strikes her knee on an adjoining stool, requiring her leg to be put in a cast. Because of her obesity and neurotic anxiety, Plaintiff is disabled for eight months. If the normal recovery time is one to two weeks, should Defendant be held liable for the full extent of damages? *Thompson v. Lupone,* 62 A.2d 861 (Conn. 1948).

5. Defendant railroad company carries a young girl past her station and puts her off the train near a "hobo jungle," the favorite haunt of many unsavory criminal characters. On the way back to town she is raped by two unidentified persons. Is the defendant the proximate cause of the plaintiff's injuries? *Hines v. Garrett,* 108 S.E. 690 (Va. 1921).

6. A rock radio station with an extensive teenage audience sponsors a contest that rewards the first contestant to locate a particular disc jockey. Two minors, driving in separate automobiles in pursuit of the illustrious disc jockey, reach speeds of up to 80 mph. One of the minors negligently forces another car off the highway, killing the driver. A wrongful death action is filed against the radio station. Should the rock station be held liable, or is the negligence of the minor a superseding cause? *Weirum v. RKO General Inc.,* 539 P.2d 36 (Cal. 1975).

KEY TERMS

Actual cause
Cause in fact of the plaintiff's injuries.

Intervening cause
Act that contributes to the plaintiff's injuries but does not relieve the defendant of liability.

Proximate cause
Legal cause of the plaintiff's injuries, emphasis is on the concept of foreseeability.

Superseding cause
Act that contributes to the plaintiff's injuries to the extent that the defendant is relieved of liability.

CHAPTER

8

Negligence: Damages

CHAPTER TOPICS

CHAPTER OBJECTIVES

In this chapter you will learn to:

- Categorize damages
- Recognize the various components of damages
- Appreciate the practical problems inherent in calculating damages
- Recognize the limitations on what a plaintiff can recover
- Appreciate the controversy surrounding punitive damages
- Distinguish between wrongful death and survival actions

Liability without damages is like a car with no wheels. If the defendant is clearly liable but the plaintiff suffers minimal injuries, recovery will also be minimal. Clearly, if the attorney's fees exceed the anticipated recovery, the client cannot afford to have an attorney take the case. Therefore, the attorneys representing Teddy and Mr. Goodright will want to determine early if the anticipated damages warrant the expenditure of time and resources necessary to litigate the case. (For organizational purposes, damages are discussed throughout this chapter in the context of negligence only, even though damages can certainly be awarded in cases involving intentional torts and strict liability as well.)

CATEGORIES OF DAMAGES

Damages are generally divided into three categories: compensatory damages, punitive damages, and nominal damages (see Figure 8-1). **Compensatory damages** are designed to compensate the victim for her losses and restore her to the position she was in before she sustained her injuries. **Punitive damages** are intended to punish the defendant. **Nominal damages** are awarded when no actual damages are proved but a tort is shown to have been committed. Because actual damages must be proved in negligence cases, nominal damages are not available in negligence suits.

Compensatory damages are further divided into two categories: general damages and special damages. **General damages** are those that generally result from the kind of conduct engaged in by the defendant; **special damages** are specific or unique to the plaintiff. A good example of general damages is compensation for pain and suffering. Anyone injured in a motor vehicle accident, for example, will be expected to endure a certain amount of pain and suffering as a result of the injuries. Examples of special damages are medical expenses, lost wages, and future impairment of earnings. In most cases, special damages must be specifically pleaded in a complaint, whereas general damages need not be.

The purpose of punitive damages is to deter future misconduct by the defendant and similarly situated defendants. Punitive damages are not intended to make the plaintiff whole but instead are used to punish defendants who have acted with ill-will or in conscious disregard for the welfare of others. Such damage awards are reserved for defendants who act in a particularly egregious manner.

Nominal damages are awarded in intentional and strict liability cases in which liability is established but where no actual harm occurred. A jury could find the defendant liable for assaulting the plaintiff. But it could conclude that the plaintiff, although wronged, suffered no actual harm and could award nominal damages of $10. Nominal damages cannot be awarded in a negligence case because negligence requires proof of an actual injury. Nominal damages allow a plaintiff to be vindicated but do nothing in the way of compensating either the plaintiff or the attorneys involved. If nominal damages are anticipated, an hourly or set

FIGURE 8-1 Categories of Damages

COMPENSATORY	PUNITIVE	NOMINAL
• To compensate and restore. 1. Special damages are damages that are specific to plaintiff. 2. General damages are damages that are generally anticipated.	• Designed to punish.	• No actual damages.

fee will usually be the basis for an attorney's reimbursement rather than a contingency fee arrangement.

Figure 8-2 lists some questions plaintiffs and defendants may have about damages. The remainder of the chapter is structured around these questions.

ILLUSTRATION OF DAMAGES

Let us consider the facts of a real case to illustrate the various components of damages. In *Anderson v. Sears, Roebuck & Co.,* 377 F. Supp. 136 (E.D. La. 1974), the plaintiff was a young child who was severely burned in a house fire that was started by a heater negligently manufactured by the defendant. The child was burned over 40 percent of her body, with third-degree burns covering 80 percent of her scalp. She was hospitalized for twenty-eight days, during which time she developed infections and related problems and underwent repeated skin grafts. Furthermore, she had to undergo extensive subsequent operations and treatment.

The plaintiff's compensatory damages were divided into five categories: past and future medical expenses, past physical and mental pain, future physical and mental pain, permanent disability and disfigurement, and impaired earning capacity. Future medical expenses included the anticipated cost for plastic surgeons, psychiatrists, sociologists, and private tutors. The $250,000 allocated for these damages was also intended to cover the cost of future operations.

Pain and Suffering

The jury awarded the plaintiff $600,000 for past physical and mental pain. The pain included the pain she endured during her initial and subsequent hospitalizations as well as the mental and emotional trauma she underwent, manifesting in bedwetting, having nightmares, withdrawing, and developing speech impediments. She was further awarded $750,000 for future physical and mental pain. The pain anticipated here was that of an estimated twenty-seven future

---

FIGURE 8-2 Questions About Damages

QUESTIONS PLAINTIFFS ASK ABOUT DAMAGES

- Can they prove pain and suffering?
- Can they prove impaired present and future earning capacity?
- Are they entitled to recover for shortened life expectancy?
- Can they recover for expenses for which they have already been reimbursed?
- Can they recover attorney's fees?
- Are they entitled to punitive damages?
- What can they recover for property damage?
- Can spouses, parents, or children of victims recover for loss of consortium?
- Can spouses, parents, or children recover if the victim dies?

QUESTIONS DEFENDANTS ASK ABOUT DAMAGES

- Should plaintiffs be compensated for pain and suffering?
- Can an award be discounted to present value?
- Can an award be paid using a structured settlement?
- Did the plaintiff mitigate her damages?
- Did the plaintiff suffer actual physical harm?

operations along with the pain and crippling caused by the extensive scarring she had sustained. These damages were also intended to compensate her for the likely deprivation of social life that she would surely suffer.

The jury awarded $1 million for permanent disability and disfigurement. Examples of the types of permanent losses she was expected to suffer included permanent loss of use of her legs, permanent injury to the left elbow and left arm, permanent destruction of 40 percent of her skin, permanent impairment of speech, and permanent impairment of a normal social, recreational, and educational life. The obvious problem in awarding damages in this area is that no accurate monetary value can be affixed. How does one assign a monetary value to a person's suffering? Could $1 million, $2 million, or any amount of money compensate the plaintiff in this case for the excruciating pain she suffered and the social rejection she would experience in the future?

"Day in the life" videos are often used by plaintiffs' attorneys to graphically represent the plaintiff's suffering. These films document the everyday activities of the plaintiff and are designed to display in concrete and poignant terms the full extent of how the plaintiff's injuries have limited and complicated her life. Although criticized by defense attorneys as unfairly appealing to jurors' sympathies and prejudicing them against the defendant, they are generally admissible and often used by plaintiffs to buttress damage claims.

Some attorneys have attempted to concretize this process by assigning a numerical value to the amount of suffering experienced on a daily, hourly, or even minute-by-minute basis. That number is then multiplied by the total number of days, hours, or minutes the pain is expected to last. This so-called "per diem" technique has been disallowed by some courts because it can lead to deceptively high figures. The majority of courts have, however, allowed the use of this argument and leave it up to defendants to dissuade juries as to its reasonableness.

Melvin Belli, who first advocated the per diem argument, gave the following closing argument to illustrate how one might use this approach. The case involved a man with an irreparably injured back and a thirty-year life expectancy.

You are asked to evaluate in dollars and cents what pain and suffering is. This honorable court will instruct you that a man of this age has a life expectancy of thirty years. Let's put it to you bluntly, what's pain and suffering worth? You've got to answer this question. You've got to award for this as well as the special damages and loss of wages. Let's take Pat, my client, down to the waterfront. He sees Mike, an old friend. He goes up to him and says, "Mike, I've got a job for you. It's a perfect job. You're not going to have to work any more for the rest of your life. . . . you don't have to work even one second. All you have to do is to trade me your good back for my bad one and I'll give you $5.00 a day for the rest of your life. Do you know what $5.00 a day for the rest of your life is? Why, that's $60,000.00! Of course, I realize that you're not going to be able to do any walking, or any swimming, or driving an automobile, or be able to sit in a movie picture show; you're going to have excruciating pain and suffering with this job, 31,000,000 seconds a year, and once you take it on, you'll never be able to relieve yourself of this, but you get $60,000.00!" Do you think Mike would take on that job for $60,000.00?

M. Belli, *The Use of Demonstrative Evidence in Achieving "The More Adequate Award"* 33–34 (1952).

Criticism of Pain and Suffering Awards

The problem of subjectivity in reference to the awarding of damages for pain and suffering has been the subject of much debate. Quantification of such damages is often difficult. Nevertheless, some argue that if the law is able to redress a businessperson who sustains commercial damage, it can do no less for those who have suffered "a more poignant infliction" (*Gray v. Washington Power Co.,* 71 P. 206 (Wash. 1930)). Even though no gauge is available for measuring such damages, which are to some degree sentimental, sentiment, it has been observed, is an element in all damages. Furthermore, the reasoning goes, the lack of precision in assessing damages should not preclude their approximate measurement and they should be submitted to the best judgment of the jury.

The concept of compensating plaintiffs for their pain has been criticized, however. Some maintain that such damages should be allowed only when there is a physiological basis for the pain. Cornelius Peck, at the University of Washington Law School, argues that pain is a social and psychological as well as a physiological phenomenon (Peck, *Compensation for Pain: A Reappraisal in Light of New Medical Evidence,* 72 Mich. L. Rev. 1355 (1974)). One study he uses to illustrate his point involves a comparison between soldiers wounded in battle and civilians who had undergone surgery. Although the battle wounds probably provided a greater physiological basis for pain than did the incisions required by surgery, only a little more than 25 percent of the soldiers required relief for pain, whereas 87 percent of the civilians requested treatment for pain (Beecher, *Relationship of Significance of Wound to Pain Experienced,* 161 J.A.M.A. 1609 (1956)). This study seems to indicate that the cause of the injury creating the pain has some bearing on the individual's perception of that pain. Therefore, pain sustained as a result of some noble endeavor may be more easily borne than pain stemming from some capricious or inexplicable cause.

The usual argument given to justify compensation for pain is that compensation brings consolation to one who has suffered. Peck argues, however, that this consolation may actually provide a reinforcement for pain behavior and may serve to increase the pain of those who are to be consoled.

One of the objectives of tort law is to allocate risks to those who cause injury rather than to innocent victims. But Peck points to a study conducted by the U.S. Department of Transportation that indicates that compensation for pain and suffering fails to achieve this objective in any kind of equitable fashion. For example, the study shows that those persons suffering losses of less than $500 recovered 4.5 times more than the economic losses they suffered, whereas those victims who suffered economic losses of $25,000 or more recovered only 30 percent of their losses (1 U.S. Dept. of Transportation, *Economic Consequences of Automobile Accident Injuries,* 17 (1970)).

Equitable compensation of victims remains an illusory albeit noble goal of tort law. The struggle continues in the allocation of damages to balance the needs of plaintiffs, defendants, and the rest of society.

Impaired Earning Capacity

The last item addressed in *Anderson* is that of impaired earning capacity. The court concluded that the plaintiff's injuries would preclude her from earning a living for the rest of her life and that, therefore, the jury's award of $330,000 for impaired earning capacity was appropriate.

Two types of recovery fall under the category of impaired earnings: recovery for past earnings and recovery for prospective future losses. In dealing with past earnings, recovery is relatively simple to calculate if the plaintiff was employed at fixed wages. If he or she was unemployed or if the wages cannot be computed exactly, the plaintiff will have to use circumstantial evidence to show impairment of earning capacity.

Future loss of earning capacity is more difficult to compute. Jurors must first determine how long a plaintiff might be expected to live. Mortality tables published by insurance actuaries are used in this process. Jurors are also allowed to take into consideration the plaintiff's personal habits, prior health, and individual characteristics in determining the plaintiff's projected life span. Some creative attorneys use economists as experts to testify to a diminution of the plaintiff's earning capacity. Loss of future earnings is, of course, applicable only when the plaintiff can show that the injuries are permanent.

PUTTING IT INTO PRACTICE 8.1

A twenty-nine-year-old veteran is rendered paraplegic as a result of a negligently performed lung operation. Before his operation he had been pronounced completely cured of tuberculosis, for which he had previously been classified as 100 percent disabled. As a result of his injuries the man suffers frequent leg spasms, burning and swelling in his legs and feet, involuntary bowel movements, and occasional urinary accidents due to blockage in his catheter. His future medical treatment will include intensive rehabilitation, possible reconstructive procedures, and ongoing evaluations by neurologists, psychiatrists, urologists, and plastic surgeons. He runs the risk of kidney and bladder infections. He has become depressed, has lost his ability to procreate, his sleep is interrupted every night as he changes his position to prevent bed sores, and he has no hope of recovering the use of his legs. He has endured numerous operations stemming from his paraplegia and will probably have to have several more.

Prior to his lung operation he lived a normal social life, participated in athletics, had received a bachelor's degree in aeronautical engineering after receiving an honorable discharge from the Army, and was working as an associate engineer with a salary of $110 per week. With rehabilitation he could secure work in a related engineering field, and with intensive medical care he has a projected life expectancy of forty years. Had he not been injured he probably could have worked for thirty years. His medical expenses have been paid for by the government and he is receiving monthly VA disability payments.

What kinds of damages is he entitled to? How would you go about proving his damages?

SHORTENED LIFE EXPECTANCY

Although damages for loss of prospective earnings have been allowed, damages for the shortening of the plaintiff's life expectancy traditionally have been denied. Under the common law, damages for loss of life were precluded unless provided for by statute. The courts have reasoned that the same rule must be applicable to damages for a shortened life. Furthermore, there has been a desire to avoid an issue so fraught with incalculable variables as well as a fear that such compensation would result in a duplication of damages. A few courts have, however, considered shortening of life expectancy as a distinct compensable harm.

In one case, for example, a ten-month-old boy developed a severe case of meningitis after being negligently examined and treated at a military hospital. He subsequently became profoundly retarded and suffered severe physical disabilities. The court concluded that damages for shortened life expectancy were appropriate and awarded $900,000 for the child's reduced life expectancy as a separate element of damages. *McNeill v. United States,* 519 F. Supp. 283 (D.S.C. 1981).

COLLATERAL SOURCE RULE

A plaintiff is often reimbursed for her out-of-pocket expenses, including lost wages and payments for medical care, by her insurance company. Nevertheless, under the **collateral source rule** she is entitled to recover for these damages again from the defendant. Similarly, a plaintiff can recover for lost wages even if she has been reimbursed through sick pay provided by her employer or by disability benefits through worker's compensation. Social Security disability benefits and welfare payments also do not count against a plaintiff's recovery under this rule. Even if a plaintiff receives free services from friends or family members, she may recover the reasonable value of those services. In some cases, such as worker's compensation, statutory requirements mandate that the plaintiff pay back the benefits she receives.

The rationale underlying the collateral source rule is that the tortfeasor ought not to gain from benefits received by the plaintiff. Furthermore, in many cases the benefits received by the plaintiff are ones for which he has indirectly paid. If a plaintiff has paid premiums on an insurance policy, denying him double recovery would deprive him of the benefits of his investment. Furthermore, allowing the defendant to benefit from the plaintiff's investment would be unfair. In many cases the company making the plaintiff's payment has a right of reimbursement out of any judgment the plaintiff receives (known as the right of *subrogation*). A medical insurance plan typically requires that the plaintiff reimburse the company out of any judgment he receives, thereby precluding double recovery. Most courts have held that evidence of collateral benefits is inadmissible. (To read about the changes to the collateral source rule proposed by tort reform advocates, see Chapter 17.)

EXPENSES OF LITIGATION

Although in England the winning party is entitled to recover her expenses of litigation, including attorney's fees, such is not the case in the United States. Most personal injury cases are handled on a contingency fee basis, in which the attorney agrees to provide services for a fee based on a percentage of the client's recovery. If there is no recovery, the attorney receives nothing. Typically, the percentage of the fee depends on whether the case is settled or litigated. A common contingency fee arrangement provides for payment of 33⅓ percent of the settlement and 40 percent of a final judgment. Some have suggested that, as a practical matter, punitive damages and awards for pain and suffering in effect allow a plaintiff to pay attorney's fees and still retain compensation for his or her own losses.

The contingency fee arrangement has been the subject of frequent criticism. Some maintain that it creates a conflict of interest between the attorney and the client in reference to settlement offers. In some cases attorneys receive much more than would be considered a reasonable fee for the efforts they expended. However, such a fee arrangement allows those persons who would ordinarily be financially incapable of pursuing their claims to do so. Also, remember that attorneys do not win all their cases; therefore, cases in which they receive nothing may balance those for which they may be overcompensated.

DAMAGES FOR PHYSICAL HARM TO PROPERTY

Damages for physical harm to property are tied to the value of the property. If the property is completely destroyed, damages are measured according to the value of the property at the time and place the tort occurred. If the property is damaged but not destroyed, the damages are measured by the difference in value before and after the tort, although the amount cannot exceed the replacement cost. If the plaintiff is merely deprived of use of the property, damages consist of the value of the use of which the plaintiff was deprived.

When we refer to value of property we are alluding to its **fair market value.** *Fair market value* is defined as the amount that the property could have been sold for on the open market. The assumption in this definition is that it involves a voluntary sale by a leisurely seller to a willing buyer. Note that market value is usually determined on the basis of the market at the place and time that the wrong occurred. Furthermore, market value constitutes the highest price one seeking to sell the property could have realized and not the lowest price at which it could have been sold.

Market value does not always provide adequate compensation, particularly in cases in which the property has personal value to the plaintiff and no one else. In such cases the court considers the original cost of the property, the use made of the property, and its condition at the time of the tort. The mental distress that the plaintiff suffers as a result of being deprived of the property is, however, not usually compensable.

DAMAGES IN PRODUCT LIABILITY CASES

Damages in the context of product liability cases require special consideration and are treated separately in Chapter 13.

PUNITIVE DAMAGES

Punitive damages, which are sometimes referred to as *exemplary damages,* are designed to punish the tortfeasor and to deter similarly situated wrongdoers. In negligence cases they can be awarded only when the defendant's conduct is "reckless," "willful or wanton," or "with an evil mind." Punitive damages are also permitted when the defendant commits an intentional tort, such as assault or intentional infliction of emotional harm. Punitive damages are considered a windfall to the plaintiff and a jury can use its discretion to refrain from awarding them. These damages are often appealed and successfully reduced.

Punitive damages have been criticized as constituting undue compensation to the plaintiff. Some maintain that these damages are in essence criminal fines that should be paid to the state and not to the plaintiff. The counterargument is that such damages act as a deterrent to those with evil motivations. They also compensate plaintiffs for the expenses of litigation, such as attorney's fees, which they would normally have to bear themselves.

Punitive damages are more and more commonly being awarded in product liability cases. A defendant who knows of a defect and makes the product anyway is liable for punitive damages. As explained by the *Grimshaw* court (in the Ford Pinto case discussed later):

Punitive damages thus remain as the most effective remedy for consumer protection against defectively designed mass produced articles. They provide a motive for private individuals to enforce rules of law and enable them to recoup the expenses of doing so which can be considerable and not otherwise recoverable.

A problem in this area that has concerned some commentators and judges is that a defendant could be bankrupted if every jury that awarded compensatory damages were also to award significant punitive damages. Hundreds of potential victims might exist to whom the defendant might be liable for millions of dollars in punitive damages. As a result the defendant could become bankrupt and future plaintiffs could be precluded from recovering even compensatory damages.

One question that arises in the area of punitive damages is whether employers, who are generally liable for the torts of their employees, should be made to pay punitive damages. The courts are split in this area, but many follow the Restatement (Second) of Torts § 909, which requires the payment of punitive damages only in cases where the employer had personal culpability or where the employee was working in a managerial capacity.

Punitive damages have been the target of extensive criticism and tort reform advocates have focused their energies on remedying what they perceive as the excessiveness of many such awards. (For a more detailed consideration of the tort reform movement in reference to punitive damages, see the discussion in Chapter 17.) A comprehensive list of the pitfalls of punitive damages was outlined by a California superior court (in a case whose facts are the basis of Putting It into Practice 8.2):

The permissibility of punitive damages in negligence cases:

1. Inflames the cupidity of plaintiffs.
2. Adds a grossly intangible element to a negligence case grievously interfering with rational settlement negotiations.
3. Leads to lengthy and rancorous discovery process and disputes.
4. Places before the jury inflammatory evidence affecting their dispassionate judgment as to

negligence (often, this is its principal purpose) and compensatory damages.

5. Moreover, . . . if the plaintiff can inject the issue of punitive damages in a case, he can show the wealth of the defendant. This results in the trial of a negligence case becoming a field day with the issue of the defendant's wealth.

6. Places upon the defendants the risk of vast, unforeseeable damages for which usually no insurance protection is available (thus thwarting the policy of the law of spreading the risk and the cost thereof).

7. Places a social policy decision in the hands of a jury without giving them access to the huge and broad array of facts necessary to reach an intelligent and useful decision.

8. Outrageously gives a windfall to a few plaintiffs who are fortunate enough to be injured by a millionaire (or a billionaire corporation).

9. Imposes punishment for conduct (rather than reimbursement for loss), a decision usually, and better, left to the criminal law and the decision for the legislative, judicial or administrative representatives of the people, not a small group of haphazardly selected citizens.

10. Jury punitive damage awards of an unpredictable nature and appalling inconsistency continue to proliferate. Neither the Legislature nor the appellate courts have been able to formulate coherent, reasonable guidelines and limitations for the remedy. Perhaps the quest is utopian and unrealizable. In practice, it lacks any semblance of consistency between defendants, or even the same defendant, in cases tried by different juries.

Because the Legislature has not prescribed guidelines for punitive damages, they may be awarded by juries at whim. Those who favor abolishing the doctrine of punitive damages argue that the lack of clear standards governing the amount of punitive awards frees the jury to act irrationally, out of passion and prejudice.

11. The extreme unpredictability of punitive damages and the occasional crushing amount set by a vindictive jury approaches a due process violation because, in a practical sense, the defendant lacks notice [that] his conduct may result in loss of his entire assets.

12. To the extent that the defendant has been, or will be, punished for his conduct by the criminal process, the imposition of punitive damages constitutes double punishment.

13. If the punitive damage issue is injected into accident cases, the jury must be informed as to whether the compensatory award will come out of the defendant's pocket or be paid by an insurance carrier, for otherwise damages cannot be sensibly assessed. This has the evil of injecting the issue of insurance coverage in the case in violation of statutory policy.

14. Punitive damages awarded as a result of a fortuitous or accidental result rather than an intended result will have no deterrent effect, for the negligent actor just assumes they will not occur.

15. Because insurance carriers do not have to pay for injuries resulting from conduct that merits punitive damages, plaintiffs will only ask for punitive damages in negligence cases where defendant is uninsured or the defendant is wealthy. This will reduce the deterrent effect of permitting punitive damages in negligence cases.

16. The "punishment" of punitive damages is assessed without the constitutional safeguards of criminal punishment. The punishment is imposed by only a preponderance of the evidence. Although the remedy is quasi-criminal, the defendant does not have the protections of a criminal defendant, such as freedom from self-incrimination, prohibition of excessive fines, etc.

17. The doctrine developed in the common law to provide full compensation to the plaintiff. But now that the scope of damages has increased markedly in negligence cases to include compensation for various intangible injuries (including negligent infliction of emotional distress without proof of physical injury), the extra remedy is no longer necessary . . . .

18. Because compensatory damages include recovery for such intangibles as shock, loss of comfort

and society, loss of enjoyment of life, etc., they probably often contain an element of retribution.

19. A closely related argument is that civil juries are inexperienced and ill-equipped to mete out punishment that would be in the best interests of society.

The most frequently stated benefits of permitting punitive damage awards are:

1. To provide a plaintiff who has suffered only nominal damages with an incentive to litigate.

2. To punish the defendant for the transgression, and

3. To deter the defendant and others from committing similar acts in the future.

It is obvious that the first rationale does not apply to negligence cases, and the second and third should not apply to ordinary negligence cases, but only those with an element of outrageous conduct.

Moreover, the second rationale (punishment) infringes on the sphere of the criminal law and the third (deterrence) is wholly unsupported by any objective or scientific proof that it is effective.

Woolstrum v. Mailloux, 141 Cal. App. 3d Supp. 1 (1983) (citations omitted).

Ford Pinto Case

In the infamous Ford Pinto case, defendant Ford Motor Company argued that it should not be liable for punitive damages because no evidence of corporate ratification of the alleged misconduct was presented (*Grimshaw v. Ford Motor Co.,* 119 Cal. App. 3d 757, 174 Cal. Rptr. 348 (1981)). The facts are summarized by the court:

The Accident:

In November 1971, the Grays purchased a new 1972 Pinto hatchback manufactured by Ford in October 1971. The Grays had trouble with the car from the outset. During the first few months of ownership, they had to return the car to the dealer for repairs a number of times. Their car problems included excessive gas and oil consumption, down shifting of the automatic transmission, lack of

power, and occasional stalling. It was later learned that the stalling and excessive fuel consumption were caused by a heavy carburetor float.

On May 28, 1972, Mrs. Gray, accompanied by 13-year-old Richard Grimshaw, set out in the Pinto from Anaheim for Barstow to meet Mr. Gray. The Pinto was then six months old and had been driven approximately 3,000 miles. Mrs. Gray stopped in San Bernardino for gasoline, got back onto the freeway (Interstate 15) and proceeded toward her destination at 60–65 miles per hour. As she approached the Route 30 off-ramp where traffic was congested, she moved from the outer fast lane to the middle lane of the freeway. Shortly after this lane change, the Pinto suddenly stalled and coasted to a halt in the middle lane. It was later established that the carburetor float had become so saturated with gasoline that it suddenly sank, opening the float chamber and causing the engine to flood and stall. A car traveling immediately behind the Pinto was able to swerve and pass it but the driver of a 1962 Ford Galaxie was unable to avoid colliding with the Pinto. The Galaxie had been traveling from 50 to 55 miles per hour but before the impact had been braked to a speed of from 28 to 37 miles per hour.

At the moment of impact, the Pinto caught fire and its interior was engulfed in flames. According to plaintiffs' expert, the impact of the Galaxie had driven the Pinto's gas tank forward and caused it to be punctured by the flange or one of the bolts on the differential housing so that fuel sprayed from the punctured tank and entered the passenger compartment through gaps resulting from the separation of the rear wheel well sections from the floor pan. By the time the Pinto came to rest after the collision, both occupants had sustained serious burns. When they emerged from the vehicle, their clothing was almost completely burned off. Mrs. Gray died a few days later of congestive heart failure as a result of the burns. Grimshaw managed to survive but only through heroic medical measures. He has undergone numerous and extensive surgeries and skin grafts and must undergo additional surgeries over the next 10 years. He lost portions of several fingers on his left hand and portions of his left ear, while his face required many skin grafts from various portions of his body. Because Ford does not contest the amount of compensatory damages awarded to Grimshaw and the Grays, no purpose would be served by further description of the injuries suffered by Grimshaw or the damages sustained by the Grays.

Design of the Pinto Fuel System:

In 1968, Ford began designing a new subcompact automobile which ultimately became the Pinto. Mr. Iacocca, then a Ford Vice President, conceived the project and was its moving force. Ford's objective was to build a car at or below 2,000 pounds to sell for no more than $2,000.

Ordinarily marketing surveys and preliminary engineering studies precede the styling of a new automobile line. Pinto, however, was a rush project, so that styling preceded engineering and dictated engineering design to a greater degree than usual. Among the engineering decisions dictated by styling was the placement of the fuel tank. It was then the preferred practice in Europe and Japan to locate the gas tank over the rear axle in subcompacts because a small vehicle has less "crush space" between the rear axle and the bumper than larger cars. The Pinto's styling, however, required the tank to be placed behind the rear axle leaving only 9 or 10 inches of "crush space," far less than in any other American automobile or Ford overseas subcompact. In addition, the Pinto was designed so that its bumper was little more than a chrome strip, less substantial than the bumper of any other American car produced then or later. The Pinto's rear structure also lacked reinforcing members known as "hat sections" (2 longitudinal side members) and horizontal cross-members running between them such as were found in cars of larger unitized construction and in all automobiles produced by Ford's overseas operations. The absence of the reinforcing mem-

bers rendered the Pinto less crush resistant than other vehicles. Finally, the differential housing selected for the Pinto had an exposed flange and a line of exposed bolt heads. These protrusions were sufficient to puncture a gas tank driven forward against the differential upon rear impact.

Crash Tests:

During the development of the Pinto, prototypes were built and tested. Some were "mechanical prototypes" which duplicated mechanical features of the design but not its appearance while others, referred to as "engineering prototypes," were true duplicates of the design car. These prototypes as well as two production Pintos were crash tested by Ford to determine, among other things, the integrity of the fuel system in rear-end accidents. Ford also conducted the tests to see if the Pinto as designed would meet a proposed federal regulation requiring all automobiles manufactured in 1972 to be able to withstand a 20-mile-per-hour fixed barrier impact without significant fuel spillage and all automobiles manufactured after January 1, 1973, to withstand a 30-mile-per-hour fixed barrier impact without significant fuel spillage.

The crash tests revealed that the Pinto's fuel system as designed could not meet the 20-mile-per-hour proposed standard. Mechanical prototypes struck from the rear with a moving barrier at 21-miles-per-hour caused the fuel tank to be driven forward and to be punctured, causing fuel leakage in excess of the standard prescribed by the proposed regulation. A production Pinto crash tested at 21-miles-per-hour into a fixed barrier caused the fuel neck to be torn from the gas tank and the tank to be punctured by a bolt head on the differential housing. In at least one test, spilled fuel entered the driver's compartment through gaps resulting from the separation of the seams joining the rear wheel wells to the floor pan. The seam separation was occasioned by the lack of reinforcement in the rear structure and insufficient welds of the wheel wells to the floor pan.

Tests conducted by Ford on other vehicles, including modified or reinforced mechanical Pinto prototypes, proved safe at speeds at which the Pinto failed. Where rubber bladders had been installed in the tank, crash tests into fixed barriers at 21-miles-per-hour withstood leakage from punctures in the gas tank. Vehicles with fuel tanks installed above rather than behind the rear axle passed the fuel system integrity test at 31-miles-per-hour fixed barrier. A Pinto with two longitudinal hat sections added to firm up the rear structure passed a 20-mile-per-hour rear impact fixed barrier test with no fuel leakage.

The Cost to Remedy Design Deficiencies:

When a prototype failed the fuel system integrity test, the standard of care for engineers in the industry was to redesign and retest it. The vulnerability of the production Pinto's fuel tank at speeds of 20 and 30-miles-per-hour fixed barrier tests could have been remedied by inexpensive "fixes," but Ford produced and sold the Pinto to the public without doing anything to remedy the defects. Design changes that would have enhanced the integrity of the fuel tank system at relatively little cost per car included the following: Longitudinal side members and cross members at $2.40 and $1.80, respectively; a single shock absorbent "flak suit" to protect the tank at $4; a tank within a tank and placement of the tank over the axle at $5.08 to $5.79; a nylon bladder within the tank at $5.25 to $8; placement of the tank over the axle surrounded with a protective barrier at a cost of $9.95 per car; substitution of a rear axle with a smooth differential housing at a cost of $2.10; imposition of a protective shield between the differential housing and the tank at $2.35; improvement and reenforcement of the bumper at $2.60; addition of eight inches of crush space at a cost of $6.40. Equipping the car with a reinforced rear structure, smooth axle, improved bumper and additional crush space at a total cost of $15.30 would have made the fuel tank safe in a 34 to 38-mile-per-hour rear end collision by a vehicle the size of the Ford Galaxie. If, in addition to the foregoing, a bladder or tank within a tank were used or if the tank were protected with a shield, it would have been safe in a 40 to 45-mile-per-hour rear impact. If the tank had been located over the rear axle, it would have been safe in a rear impact at 50 miles per hour or more.

Management's Decision to Go Forward with Knowledge of Defects:

The idea for the Pinto, as has been noted, was conceived by Mr. Iacocca, then Executive Vice President of Ford. The feasibility study was conducted under the supervision of Mr. Robert Alexander, Vice President of Car Engineering. Ford's Product Planning Committee, whose members included Mr. Iacocca, Mr. Robert Alexander, and Mr. Harold MacDonald, Ford's Group Vice President of Car Engineering, approved the Pinto's concept and made the decision to go forward with the project. During the course of the project, regular product review meetings were held which were chaired by Mr. MacDonald and attended by Mr. Alexander. As the project approached actual production, the engineers responsible for the components of the project "signed off" to their immediate supervisors who in turn "signed off" to their superiors and so on up the chain of command until the entire project was approved for public release by Vice Presidents Alexander and MacDonald and ultimately by Mr. Iacocca. The Pinto crash tests results had been forwarded up the chain of command to the ultimate decision-makers and were known to the Ford officials who decided to go forward with production.

Harley Copp, a former Ford engineer and executive in charge of the crash testing program, testified that the highest level of Ford's management made the decision to go forward with the production of the Pinto, knowing that the gas tank was vulnerable to puncture and rupture at low rear impact speeds creating a significant risk of death or injury from fire and knowing that "fixes" were feasible at nominal cost. He testified that management's decision was based on the cost savings which would inure from omitting or delaying the "fixes."

Mr. Copp's testimony concerning management's awareness of the crash tests results and the vulnerability of the Pinto fuel system was corroborated by other evidence. At an April 1971 product review meeting chaired by Mr. MacDonald, those present received and discussed a report (Exhibit 125) prepared by Ford engineers pertaining to the financial impact of a proposed federal standard on fuel system integrity and the cost savings which would accrue from deferring even minimal "fixes" [footnote omitted]. The report refers to crash tests of the integrity of the fuel system of Ford vehicles and design changes needed to meet anticipated federal standards. Also in evidence was a September 23, 1970, report (Exhibit 124) by Ford's "Chassis Design Office" concerning a program "to establish a corporate (Ford) position and reply to the government" on the proposed federal fuel system integrity standard which included zero fuel spillage at 20 miles per hour fixed barrier crash by January 1, 1972, and 30 miles per hour by January 1, 1973. The report states in part: "The 20 and 30 mph rear fixed barrier crashes will probably require repackaging the fuel tanks in a protected area such as above the rear axle. This is based on moving barrier crash tests of a Chevelle and a Ford at 30 mph and other Ford products at 20 mph. Currently there are no plans for forward models to repackage the fuel tanks. Tests must be conducted to prove that repackaged tanks will live without significantly strengthening rear structure for added protection." The report also notes that the Pinto was the "(s)mallest car line with most difficulty in achieving compliance." It is reasonable to infer that the report was prepared for and known to Ford officials in policy-making positions.

The fact that two of the crash tests were run at the request of the Ford Chassis and Vehicle Engineering Department for the specific purpose of demonstrating the advisability of moving the fuel tank over the axle as a possible "fix" further corroborated Mr. Copp's testimony that management knew the results of the crash tests. Mr. Kennedy, who succeeded Mr.

Copp as the engineer in charge of Ford's crash testing program, admitted that the test results had been forwarded to the chain of command to his superiors.

Finally, Mr. Copp testified to conversations in late 1968 or early 1969 with the chief assistant research engineer in charge of cost-weight evaluation of the Pinto, and to a later conversation with the chief chassis engineer who was then in charge of crash testing the early prototype. In these conversations, both men expressed concern about the integrity of the Pinto's fuel system and complained about management's unwillingness to deviate from the design if the change would cost money.

The appellate court concluded that substantial evidence was presented from which the jury could reasonably have inferred that Ford's management went ahead with the production of the Pinto with full knowledge of the design defect. The defect rendered the fuel tank extremely vulnerable on rear impact at low speeds and endangered the safety and lives of its occupants. The court categorized Ford's executive decision-making process as corporate malice and the jury awarded $125 million in punitive damages, which was later reduced by the trial judge to $3.5 million.

One of the issues raised in this case was the propriety of the punitive damage award. Ford contended that the $3.5 million award exceeded, many times over, the highest award ever upheld in California as well as the maximum civil penalties that could be enforced under federal and state statutes against a manufacturer.

As can be seen, the court was unpersuaded by this argument:

In determining whether an award of punitive damages is excessive, comparison of the amount awarded with other awards in other cases is not a valid consideration. . . . Nor does "[t]he fact that an award may set a precedent by its size" in and of itself render it suspect; whether the award was excessive must be assessed by examining the circumstances of the particular case. . . . In deciding whether an award is excessive as a matter of law or was so grossly disproportionate as to raise the presumption that it was the product of passion or prejudice, the following factors should be weighed: The degree of reprehensibility of defendant's conduct, the wealth of the defendant, the amount of compensatory damages, and an amount which would serve as a deterrent effect on like conduct by defendant and others who may be so inclined. . . . Applying the foregoing criteria to the instant case, the punitive damage award as reduced by the trial court was well within reason.[14]

In assessing the propriety of a punitive damage award, as in assessing the propriety of any other judicial ruling based upon factual determinations, the evidence must be viewed in the light most favorable to the judgment. . . . Viewing the record thusly in the instant case, the conduct of Ford's management was reprehensible in the extreme. It exhibited a conscious and callous disregard of public safety in order to maximize corporate profits. Ford's self-evaluation of its conduct is based on a review of the evidence most favorable to it instead of on the basis of the evidence most favorable to the judgment. Unlike malicious conduct directed toward a single specific individual, Ford's tortious conduct endangered the lives of thousands of Pinto purchasers. Weighed against the factor of reprehensibility, the punitive damage award as reduced by the trial judge was not excessive.

Nor was the reduced award excessive taking into account defendant's wealth and the size of the compensatory award. Ford's net worth was 7.7 billion dollars and its income after taxes for 1976 was over 983 million dollars. The punitive award was approximately .005% of Ford's net worth and approximately .03% of its 1976 net income. The ratio of the punitive damages to compensatory damages was approximately 1.4 to one. Significantly, Ford does not quarrel with the amount of the compensatory award to Grimshaw.

Nor was the size of the award excessive in light of its deterrent purpose. An award which is so small that it can be simply written off as a part of the cost of doing business would have no deterrent effect. An award which affects the company's pricing of its product and thereby affects its competitive advantage would serve as a deterrent. The award in question was far from excessive as a deterrent against future wrongful conduct by Ford and others.

Ford complains that the punitive award is far greater than the maximum penalty that may be imposed under California or federal law prohibiting the sale of defective automobiles or other products. For example, Ford notes that California statutes provide a maximum fine of only $50 for the first offense and $100 for a second offense for a dealer who sells an automobile that fails to conform to federal safety laws or is not equipped with required lights or brakes . . .; that a manufacturer who sells brake fluid in this state failing to meet statutory standards is subject to a maximum of only $50 . . .; and that the maximum penalty that may be imposed under federal law for violation of automobile safety standards if $1,000 per vehicle up to a maximum of $800,000 for any related series of offenses. . . . It is precisely because monetary penalties under government regulations prescribing business standards or the criminal law are so inadequate and ineffective as deterrents against a manufacturer and distributor of mass produced defective products that punitive damages must be of sufficient amount to discourage

---

14. A quantitative formula whereby the amount of punitive damages can be determined in a given case with mathematical certainty is manifestly impossible as well as undesirable. . . . The authors advocate abandonment of the rule that a reasonable relationship must exist between punitive damages and actual damages. They suggest that courts balance society's interest against defendant's interest by focusing on the following factors: Severity of threatened harm; degree of reprehensibility of defendant's conduct, profitability of the conduct, wealth of defendant, amount of compensatory damages (whether it was high in relation to injury), cost of litigation, potential criminal sanctions and other civil actions against defendant based on same conduct . . . . In the present case, the amount of the award as reduced by the judge was reasonable under the suggested factors, including the factor of any other potential liability, civil or criminal.

such practices. Instead of showing that the punitive damage award was excessive, the comparison between the award and the maximum penalties under state and federal statutes and regulations governing automotive safety demonstrates the propriety of the amount of punitive damages awarded.

RECOVERY FOR LOSS OF CONSORTIUM

Under the common law, a husband and wife were considered one. Therefore, if the wife were injured the husband could recover for **loss of consortium,** which encompasses recovery for lost services, such as companionship, sex, earnings outside the home, and so on.

■   PUTTING IT INTO PRACTICE 8.2   ☐

1. A cow escapes from the defendant's enclosed pasture through an opening in the fence and strikes the plaintiffs' car, causing damage to the car and injury to the plaintiffs. Some of defendants' cows had escaped over the prior ten years but none had done so through this part of the fence. How the fence broke cannot be shown by either party. Ranchers are required by law to fence their land and to exercise ordinary care to keep their cattle inside. The defendants are found negligent despite their claims of diligence in repairing the fence. Are punitive damages justified in this case?
2. A workman, employed by a contractor hired by Standard Oil to repair a road on its refinery property, is injured by the explosive leaking of a sulfuric acid from the shallowly buried underground Standard Oil pipeline. The facts are summarized by the appellate court according to the plaintiff's testimony and then according to the defendant's testimony.

The plaintiff's testimony showed:
1. Fifty leaks had been reported in the pipeline throughout its life.
2. The line was 20 years old and its life expectancy at the time of the accident could have been measured in months.
3. The defendant knew the roadwork would be in the vicinity of the line.
4. A Standard Oil inspector had recommended replacement of the line.
5. But the company, because of the daily use of the pipe and the loss of profit if the line shut down, decided to "run it to failure."
6. That the defendant did not post a warning at the work site or place a guard there.
7. The sulfuric acid at the refinery had caused 20 to 25 injuries.

The defendant, on the other hand, showed:
1. That the previous leaks had occurred over a 20-year period and over a line 4 miles long.
2. That all leaks had been promptly repaired on the day of occurrence.
3. That all of the leaks except one or possibly two had occurred at valves or at defective welds, rather than pipe erosion, as in the present case.
4. That the line had a remaining life of four or five years and substantial loss would result from its being shut down for more than repair time.
5. That no leak had ever occurred near the section of the pipe where the plaintiff was injured.

Continued on next page

---

6. That in a far away area where the company had decided to "run to failure" rather than replace (after several ruptures), the company had placed a heavy redwood covering around the pipe.
7. That the defendant company had inspected the whole line with special equipment a few years before the accident and found no need of repair.
8. That in the area where the inspection showed a need for replacement, the company had been quite willing to shut down the line for several days.
9. That of the 32 sulfuric acid injuries in the plant in the preceding 10 years, only one or possibly two occurred because of leaks in the pipeline.

Colson v. Standard Oil, 60 Cal. App. 3d 913 (1976).

After reviewing these facts, do you think punitive damages are justified?

But because the wife had no right to services from her husband, she could recover nothing if he were injured. Evolution of the common law and equal protection attacks on statutes have resulted in both husbands and wives being entitled to recover for loss of services.

A loss of consortium claim is a **derivative claim** in that it is derived from the spouse's underlying claim. If a husband, for example, is injured in a motor vehicle accident and successfully sues the negligent driver, the wife can then sue for loss of her husband's consortium.

Because both spouses can recover, this leads to the possibility of double recovery. If the spouses were to sue in two separate actions, the wife might recover for medical expenses in one action and the husband might later recover for the same expenses by arguing that he was the one who in fact paid the expenses. To preclude double recovery, many states require that such actions be brought together.

In most jurisdictions parents can recover for medical expenses incurred as a result of injury to a child. They are also entitled to recovery for the lost services and earnings of a minor child. In cases in which the child has died, more and more courts are allowing recovery for loss of the child's companionship.

Typically, children have not been allowed to recover for loss of companionship of a parent who has been injured. More recently, however, a few courts have allowed such recovery when the child is a minor and is dependent on the parent for its nurturing and development. Courts have been reluctant to get involved in this area because of the difficulty in quantifying the damages. Furthermore, the potential for duplicative claims exists when the injured parent has several minor children.

ASSESSMENT OF DAMAGES

From a practical perspective, the evaluation of damages is a critical aspect of a plaintiff's case and of a defendant's response to a claim. What follows is a list of the types of questions plaintiffs' attorneys frequently ask when considering the value of a case:

Medical Expenses
1. What type of treatment was received?
2. For how long was the treatment received?
3. Was the treatment recognized in the medical community?

4. Who performed the treatment (e.g., a medical doctor, osteopath, chiropractor, physician's assistant, physical therapist, etc.)?

5. Was the treatment excessive considering the nature of the injuries?

6. Was the plaintiff hospitalized? If so, for how long?

7. Did the plaintiff have to be removed from the scene of the accident by an ambulance?

8. Was the plaintiff treated in the emergency room?

9. What percentage of medical expenses was devoted to diagnostics and what percentage to treatment?

10. Did the plaintiff suffer any permanent injuries, such as scarring, a limp, loss or impairment of a limb or organ? How serious are these injuries?

11. To what extent will these permanent injuries impair the plaintiff's ability to work, to exercise, to enjoy hobbies, and to otherwise enjoy life?

12. Did the plaintiff suffer any loss of mental function or emotional trauma and to what extent has this compromised her life?

13. To what extent will the plaintiff be prevented from pursuing interests or opportunities she had but had not yet pursued?

14. What is the nature and extent of rehabilitation the plaintiff has required?

15. What medical supplies and equipment, drugs, and nursing services has the plaintiff required?

16. In what ways have the plaintiff's injuries created a substantial impact on the plaintiff's family?

17. Is there a loss of consortium claim?

18. Will the plaintiff be a credible witness?

19. Has the plaintiff had prior claims? If so, what were they for?

Lost Wages

1. How much money would the plaintiff have earned but for being injured?

2. How much work has the plaintiff lost as a result of being injured, including vacation and sick time that was taken while recovering from the injuries?

3. Is the number of lost work hours reasonable in light of the nature and extent of the injuries sustained?

4. Has the plaintiff lost potential pay increases (e.g., promotions or bonuses) as a result of lost work?

Property Damage

1. What is the cost of repairing damaged property?

2. If a vehicle had to be rented while the plaintiff's vehicle was being repaired, what is the cost of that rental?

3. What personal items were lost or destroyed as a result of the defendant's actions and what is the cost of replacing those items based on their fair market value?

4. What is the fair market value of any items that cannot be replaced (i.e., heirlooms, paintings)?

5. How much did the plaintiff expend in sales taxes in replacing or repairing property?

Pain and Suffering

1. What is the nature and extent of injuries?

2. To what extent is the plaintiff incapacitated by permanent injuries or disfigurement?

3. To what extent are the plaintiff's daily activities curtailed or made more difficult as a result of being injured?

4. What kinds of recoveries have been awarded in cases involving injuries of comparable nature and degree?

To answer this last question, attorneys consider their own experience as well as the experiences of other litigators, which they can do by accessing the following:

a. Trial reporters (or jury reporters), which are issued weekly or biweekly and list the verdicts received in jury trials, arbitrations, mediations, nonjury trials, and other dispute resolution mechanisms, such as summary trials.

b. Compendiums, which are compilations of all dispute resolution mechanisms involving specific injuries for a designated period of time. Compilation can also be requested for verdicts and settlements for particular doctors, attorneys, firms, or judges.

c. Personal injury valuation programs, which are software programs that allow attorneys to input the data from their cases and help them compute the value of their case.

d. Journals published by the American Trial Lawyers Association, state trial lawyers associations, and defense organizations that list the verdicts for cases that went to trial or were settled. Attorneys can also place personal ads soliciting information from other attorneys who have tried or settled cases involving injuries similar to those implicated in the case the attorney is litigating.

e. Web sites on the Internet that provide access to forums, discussion groups, bulletin boards, and research tools, all of which can be used in evaluating cases.

To evaluate future medical expenses, attorneys usually consult with medical doctors to help assess what kinds of medical treatment and rehabilitation will be required in the future and to what extent that treatment will temporarily incapacitate the plaintiff. If, for example, the doctor projects that in twenty years the plaintiff will need another hip replacement, the attorney needs to know how much time the plaintiff will spend in the hospital and undergoing rehabilitation before being restored to relatively normal functioning. To assess future lost wages attorneys rely on the expertise of economists and vocational rehabilitation counselors, who help predict what the plaintiff will be able to do, whether special schooling will be required, and how much that schooling will cost. Less tangible factors that attorneys consider in evaluating cases are the experience and reputation of opposing counsel and the adjustor, as well as the policies and reputation of the insurance company against which they have a claim.

WRONGFUL DEATH AND SURVIVAL ACTIONS

Under the common law, when a plaintiff died as a consequence of injuries inflicted on him by the defendant his tort action died along with him. At that point his spouse and children also lost any right to recovery. The reasoning behind this rule was that it was immoral to put a monetary value on a human life. Unfortunately, this rule increased the likelihood that defendants would kill their plaintiffs, as it was cheaper for the defendant if the plaintiff died.

Lord Campbell's Act, passed in England in 1846 and after which most modern statutes are patterned, allowed recovery to families of individuals killed by tortious conduct. In accord with this act all states have passed some kind of **survival** statute which allows the injured party's claim to survive his or her death (see Figure 8-3). In most states the cause of death is irrelevant but in a few states if the death resulted from the defendant's tort, a wrongful death action and not a survival claim must be filed. All survival statutes provide that a cause of action for injury to tangible property survives the death of the plaintiff. The majority allows personal injury actions to survive as well. A few states permit claims pertaining to intangible interests, such as infliction of emotional distress and defamation, to survive. Most allow a tort action to be maintained or even initiated after the defendant's death as well. Similarly, **wrongful death** statutes have also been passed, which allow third persons, usually the decedent's spouse and children, to recover for losses they sustained as a result of the decedent's death.

The issue of wrongful death is unique in the field of tort law because it centers around the interpretation of statutes. Litigants in this area are forced to engage in statutory construction and determination of legislative intent. This is often onerous because most of the statutes were written more than 100 years ago.

Types of Recovery Allowed

When a survival action is filed separately from a wrongful death action, the possibility of double recovery exists. To preclude this from happening, many

FIGURE 8-3 Comparison of Survival Statutes and Wrongful Death Statutes

SURVIVAL STATUTES	WRONGFUL DEATH STATUTES
• Injured party's claim survives his death. • Damages awarded to deceased's estate.	• Third parties can recover for losses they sustain as a result of victim's death. • Proceeds go to spouses, parents, or children of deceased.

states limit survivor actions to those losses occurring prior to the decedent's death. Damages are restricted, therefore, to the decedent's medical expenses, lost earnings prior to death, and pain and suffering. Consequently, in such states, if the death is instantaneous no survival action exists at all because no damages occurred prior to death (see Restatement (Second) of Torts § 926, cmt. a).

Under Lord Campbell's Act and the wrongful death legislation patterned after that act, damages were to be limited to pecuniary or economic losses caused by the decedent's death. Typically, the loss is measured in terms of the monetary contributions that the decedent would have made during his or her lifetime to the plaintiff beneficiary. In more recent years a pecuniary value has been attached to the companionship, sexual relationship, and moral guidance provided by the decedent. Furthermore, several states allow recovery for grief and other mental suffering of the survivors. Some of those states have imposed a cap on those damages, however, to protect against runaway awards.

Recovery in this area becomes particularly problematic when parents bring a wrongful death action for a child's death. Usually the expense of raising a child far surpasses any earnings the child can be expected to bring home. Many courts allow recovery of a substantial reward for loss of companionship of the child. Other courts have allowed consideration of what the decedent child might have brought to his or her parents in terms of support in their old age. In one case, for example, $100,000 was allowed for loss of a very intelligent seven-year-old who exhibited talent as a cartoonist (*Haumerson v. Ford Motor Co.*, 257 N.W.2d 7 (Iowa 1977)).

Disclosure of Remarriage

Another issue that arises in wrongful death and survival actions is whether a surviving spouse who remarries is entitled to keep this information from the trier of the fact. The concern is that a jury in particular may be inclined to give a lower verdict if it learns of the remarriage. Of course, defendants are eager to disclose this information during voir dire and argue that they need to do so in case prospective jurors are acquainted with the new spouse. Most courts, however, refuse to allow evidence of remarriage even if used for this limited purpose.

Who Recovers?

Survival actions are usually brought by the executor or administrator of an estate. Recovery becomes an asset of that estate and may be reached by creditors. It is often distributed in accordance with state testacy and intestacy laws. Some argue that survival actions may result in a windfall to distant relatives who had little or no contact with the decedent. In contrast, relatives who were not named beneficiaries in a wrongful death action may be able to recover in a survival action. Recovery for pain and suffering in survival actions is allowed only if the decedent was conscious of pain. Courtroom battles often revolve, therefore, around the issue of the decedent's consciousness, particularly if he or she survived only a few seconds or minutes after being injured (such as in a mid-air collision of an aircraft).

Defenses

Although any defenses that could have been raised against the decedent are still available to the defendant in a survival action, considerable disagreement exists as to which defenses should be allowed in a wrongful death action. Most states resolve this by allowing the defendant to assert any defenses he or she would have been able to use against the decedent if the decedent were still alive. In such cases, for example, the defendant may argue that the decedent was contributorily negligent or that he or she assumed the risk.

Statutes of limitations are another concern in wrongful death and survival actions. Suppose, for example, the decedent failed to file an action until after the statute of limitations had run. Would a wrongful death or survival action be barred? Most courts have answered no and indicate that the death action begins to run from the date of death.

Remember that survival actions and wrongful death actions are statutory creatures and are therefore subject to statutory construction. Be sure to examine the statutory scheme in your state dealing with these types of claims.

■ PUTTING IT INTO PRACTICE 8.3 □

After buying a used vehicle that proved to be defective, Garcia returned the vehicle to the seller and refused to make further payments. After several unsuccessful attempts by a collection agency to collect payments, sheriff's deputies are sent to execute a writ of attachment on Garcia's mobile home. When they arrive Garcia kills one of the deputies and then engages in a shoot-out with the other deputy, resulting in the death of both Garcia and the deputy. A wrongful death action is filed alleging that the wrongful acts of the collection agency drove Garcia insane, and that while insane he engaged in a gunfight with the deputies, which was tantamount to suicide.

Consult the wrongful death and survival statutes in your states to determine who could bring this claim. What kinds of damages could be claimed? What would be the statute of limitations for this claim?

DISCOUNTING FUTURE DAMAGES

A plaintiff, in a sense, receives a windfall by collecting in the present for future losses. The rationale is that a lump sum paid now for future loss is worth more to the recipient than future payments because a lump sum has the potential of creating more money through investment. In practical terms, having $10,000 in the bank now, invested at a modest rate of return, is more advantageous than having $10,000 ten years from now. To illustrate, the present value of $1.00 payable at 5 percent compound interest in one year is $.95, whereas the present value of $1.00 in ten years is $.61 and the present value of $1.00 payable in twenty years is $.38. Recognition of the earning power of money has resulted in many courts requiring juries to reduce or **discount awards** to the **present value** of lost future earnings. Discounting an award prevents the plaintiff from realizing an unwarranted windfall and reduces losses to the defendant.

Life expectancy tables, annuity tables, and work expectancy tables are used for determining earning expectancy. The present value of anticipated earnings can be computed by calculating the present value of a dollar at a particular rate of interest and multiplying that by the average monthly earnings for the designated period of time. The present value, for example, of twenty-five annual payments of $10,000 per year ($250,000 total) would be $127,833 if an interest rate of 6 percent were assumed. As you can see, the defendant receives a type of "interest" on the advance payment when the plaintiff is awarded the present value of the losses (Restatement (Second) of Torts § 913A). See "Practice Pointers" at the end of this chapter for more details on the calculation of present values.

Some attorneys have argued that inflation offsets the discounting of present value awards. The argument is that claiming future damage for present value does not fully compensate the victim, as the upward movement of prices can generally be anticipated. In one case, for example, the court concluded that inflation and present value canceled each other out. (*Pierce v. New York Central Rail Co.*, 304 F. Supp. 44 (W.D. Mich. 1969)). The court noted that a dollar invested that would earn 5 percent per year now would increase in value to $2.30 after twenty-six years. However, if the purchasing power of that same dollar were reduced 5 percent per year, then in twenty-six years it would take $2.30 to purchase what it presently cost a dollar to buy. Other courts have rejected this argument as being too speculative.

STRUCTURED SETTLEMENTS

Traditionally under the common law past and future damages were paid in a single lump sum. More recently, large future damages have been paid using a periodic-payment settlement, often referred to as a **structured settlement.** Three reasons are generally given for the use of a structured settlement. First, the plaintiff does not have the responsibility of making arrangements to invest the money if he or she receives periodic payments over a long period of time. Money will be available to cover basic human needs. Second, a large amount of the money will be prudently invested and will not be squandered through ignorance, bad advice, or frivolity. Third, the income tax that the plaintiff has to pay is usually minimized using a structured settlement. Although tax need not be paid on a lump sum amount, it does have to be paid on any income resulting from an investment of a lump sum damage award.

The downside of these settlements from the plaintiff's perspective is the inability to freely spend the monies; the uncertainty of the real present cash value of the settlement (because the negotiated figure is in the hands of the defendant); the fixed nature of the payments, which cannot be modified over time; the possibility that the death of the recipient may terminate some payments; and the possibility of insolvency of the company responsible for the payments.

The structured settlement is widely used in products liability cases (such as in the cases involving thalidomide, a drug that was shown to cause severe birth defects) and can bridge the gap between a plaintiff's final settlement demand and a defendant's final offer. To illustrate the incentive for defendants to enter into such agreements, benefits worth $3 million over time could actually cost a defendant $2 million if made through a structured settlement. These settlements can also reduce defense costs by avoiding trial and appeal and can provide defense counsel more flexibility in the negotiating process. Agreements may provide for an up-front fixed payment, including an amount covering attorney's fees, and then guaranteeing specified payments over time. Payments for medical, hospital, nursing, therapy, prescription drugs, medical equipment, and supply needs can also be added. Structured settlements are limited only by the imagination and ingenuity of the parties and the rules and regulations imposed by the Internal Revenue Service.

We will not explore any of the intricacies involved in structuring such a settlement. Suffice it to say that federal tax law is crucial in shaping the form of a settlement. Some attorneys, however, feel that the advantages of structured settlements are illusory and that such arrangements better serve the interests of the insurance company than they do that of the plaintiff. (See A. Fuchsberg, "Pitfalls in Structured Settlements," *Trial* 42 (Sept. 1989).) Structured settlements are required by statute under certain circumstances in some states and are generally supported by the defense bar.

MITIGATION OF DAMAGES

The duty to mitigate damages required under contract law is also required under tort law. Under this rule, also referred to as the **avoidable consequences** rule, a plaintiff cannot recover for any damages he or she could reasonably have avoided. Recovery will not be allowed, for example, for the additional medical expenses necessary to treat an infection incurred by the plaintiff's failure to seek prompt medical care for a wound caused by the defendant's negligence. The burden would be on the defendant, however, to prove that the plaintiff could have avoided the harm.

Although this rule is usually applied to the plaintiff's conduct after the accident, in some states it has been used to argue that the plaintiff should have taken certain safety precautions before the accident. In states mandating the wearing of seat belts or motorcycle helmets, the argument has been made that the plaintiff suffered injuries that he would not have sustained had he or she taken the precautions required by statute. The defendant's argument in such cases is that passage of such statutes represents legislative recognition of the capacity to avoid injuries by the wearing of seat belts or motorcycle helmets. In other states, failure to take such safety precautions is considered contributory negligence.

MENTAL SUFFERING

In a typical negligence case the plaintiff must show that he suffered some kind of physical harm. If he sustained only mental harm with no physical symptoms, he will usually be precluded from recovering. Where there is physical injury, damages from mental suffering are often called **parasitic** because they attach to the physical injury.

When the plaintiff sustains no physical injury, the courts are reluctant to permit recovery for emotional suffering because of a fear that the suffering may be feigned. Suppose a woman eats cottage cheese containing broken glass. She is not cut nor in any way physically injured but she is frightened at the prospect of possibly having swallowed some glass. She is slightly nauseated and unable to sleep that evening. The vast majority of courts will deny her recovery if she is unable to point to any nontransitory (ongoing) physical symptoms of her emotional distress. The theory is that the lack of objective physical symptoms greatly increases the risk of fraudulent claims and therefore recovery is denied. (Restatement (Second) of Torts § 436A, cmts. b and c, illus. 1).

Many courts have allowed an exception to this general rule in cases involving the negligent mishandling of corpses (such as the misplacement or dismember-

ment of a corpse) or in cases involving the negligent transmission of a message by telegraph (such as an erroneous message regarding the death of a family member). Such cases are thought by their very nature to cause actual suffering and therefore minimize the risk of fake claims.

A small minority of courts follow the "impact rule," predicating recovery for mental suffering on the plaintiff experiencing some type of physical "impact." An impact could be an electric shock, a slight jarring, inhalation of smoke, dust in the eye, or any contact even of a trivial nature. Impact was achieved in a particularly novel way in one case in which a circus horse defecated in the plaintiff's lap (*Christy Bros. Circus v. Turnage,* 144 S.E. 680 (1928)). The vast majority of courts have abandoned the impact rule in favor of requiring the plaintiff to exhibit some physical manifestation if he or she is to recover for mental disturbances.

Attempts to Circumvent the Physical Harm Requirement

If the defendant's conduct was intentional or willful, the courts have been much more willing to allow recovery for pure emotional distress. If the plaintiff suffers emotional distress that subsequently manifests in the form of physical consequences, the vast majority of courts also allow recovery even if the manifestation of physical consequences is not immediate.

Some states have abandoned the rule altogether when the facts are such that one could readily believe there could have been actual mental distress. In one notable case a plaintiff was allowed to recover against the defendant doctors and hospital who had mistakenly told his wife that she had syphilis (*Molien v. Kaiser Foundation Hospitals,* 616 P.2d 813 (Cal. 1980)). As a result of this disclosure the plaintiff's wife became suspicious that the plaintiff was having an extramarital affair and their marriage broke up. The court rejected the artificial physical harm requirement for two reasons:

First, the classification is both overinclusive and underinclusive when viewed in the light of its purported purpose of screening false claims. It is overinclusive in permitting recovery for emotional distress when the suffering accompanies or results in any physical injury whatever, no matter how trivial. If physical injury, however slight, provides the ticket for admission to the courthouse, it is difficult for advocates of the "floodgates" premonition to deny that the doors are already wide open. . . . More significantly, the classification is underinclusive because it mechanically denies court access to claims that may well be valid and could be proved if the plaintiffs were permitted to go to trial.

The second defect in the requirement of physical injury is that it encourages extravagant pleading and distorted testimony. Thus it has been urged that the law should provide a remedy for serious invasions of emotional tranquillity, "otherwise the tendency would be for the victim to exaggerate symptoms of sick headaches, nausea, insomnia, etc., to make out a technical basis for bodily injury, upon which to predicate a parasitic recovery for the more grievous disturbance, the mental and emotional disturbance she endured."

The court concluded that the jurors were in the best position to determine whether the defendants' conduct could have caused emotional distress.

Some courts presented with the physical harm problem in the context of a plaintiff who has seen injury occur to others have taken the *Palsgraf* "zone of danger" approach. They have held that a plaintiff who is not within the "zone of danger" and who is therefore not endangered by the defendant's conduct is owed no duty. Such a plaintiff cannot recover for emotional distress as a result of another's injury even if this distress leads to physical harm.

A growing number of states have, however, begun to abandon the physical harm requirement if the plaintiff was near the scene of the accident, personally observed it, and was closely related to the victim. In one such case a young girl was run down by the defendant's automobile in front of her mother and her sister (*Dillon v. Legg*, 441 P.2d 912 (Cal. 1968)). The sister, who was standing a few feet away, was in the zone of danger; the mother, who was standing on the sidewalk, was still in view of the accident but was not in any direct danger and was therefore outside the zone of danger. The court, in allowing the mother to recover, pointed out the inconsistency that would arise if the sister were allowed to recover and the mother were denied recovery when both had experienced the same kind of distress.

Although modern courts have relaxed restrictions around physical harm requirements, most have restricted liability to experiences of serious emotional harm, such as neuroses, psychoses, chronic depression, phobia, or shock, and have refused to extend liability to plaintiffs who have experienced only transitory states of fright, disappointment, regret, nausea, grief, or humiliation.

PUTTING IT INTO PRACTICE 8.4

1. A mother watches from the front porch of her home as her son is killed by a negligent motorist. Does she have grounds for a claim of negligent infliction of emotional distress?
2. After being told that her child has been involved in an accident, a mother arrives moments later at the scene and sees her child's body in the street. Does she have grounds for a claim of negligent infliction of emotional distress?
3. A doctor incorrectly advises a patient that she has tested positive for AIDS when in fact her test results are invalid. Does she have a claim against the doctor for negligent infliction of emotional distress?

APPLICATION

Although neither Teddy nor Mr. Goodright would be entitled to recover for punitive damages, as the Baxters' negligence did not rise to the level of recklessness, they would both be entitled to compensatory damages if the Baxters were found liable. Both could certainly recover for their medical expenses and for their pain and suffering, both past and future. Proof of their past medical expenses would probably be relatively straightforward, but future medical expenses might be more difficult to quantify. Teddy, for example, might require ongoing psychiatric care as a result of his phobic disorder. Because estimating the length and cost of such treatment would be difficult, a concrete dollar figure would also be difficult to calculate. If Mr. Goodright might have to endure future operations, the expenses of those operations, along with all other future medical expenses, would have to be estimated. Remember, too, that Mr. Goodright's spouse and Teddy's parents could also file claims for loss of consortium.

The pain and suffering endured by this duo, though less tangible than their physical injuries, would be a crucial element in their recoveries. Teddy's attorney would want to point to the physical trauma that Teddy experienced as well as the ongoing psychological pain he could be expected to suffer for the remainder of his life in relationship to his fear of dogs. His attorney would want to paint a vivid picture of the limitations stemming from this emotional trauma. If Teddy were unable to secure a job as a paper carrier as a result of his phobia, or if he became so chronically anxious that his social life were disrupted, his attorney would point to this as evidence of the long-term effects of Gertrude's attack. Mr. Goodright's attorney, in contrast, would focus more on the life-changing consequences of Gertrude's actions in bringing Mr. Goodright's concert pianist career to an abrupt end. Again, the challenge in this case would be in converting the intangible but real suffering of a human being into a dollar figure. Both parties would also be able to recover for any permanent disfigurement, such as scarring, that they sustained.

At a more tangible level, Mr. Goodright's attorney would have to project Mr. Goodright's loss of income resulting from the termination of his career. Obviously, one could anticipate conflict between counsel in reference to the relative values of a concert pianist's career and a piano teacher's career. Both counsel would have to dig out as many facts as possible to substantiate their positions. This is what makes litigation so challenging! Any other limitations that Mr. Goodright suffered as a result of his disabled hand would also have to be quantified. Specific, concrete evidence illustrating such disability would be necessary.

The Baxters might argue that the plaintiffs in this case failed to mitigate their damages if, for example, they failed to seek immediate medical treatment. They would also want to minimize the pain and suffering experienced by the plaintiffs and would want to do everything in their power to present evidence that the plaintiffs had magnified their damages. They would argue that any recoveries by the plaintiffs should be discounted to present values and would likely push for some form of structured settlement.

SUMMARY

Damages can be divided into three categories: compensatory, punitive, and nominal. Compensatory damages are further divided into two categories: general and special.

The difficulty in assigning a monetary award for pain and suffering is in the assignment of a numerical value. Some attorneys, in an effort to quantify suffering, have used a per diem technique. Attempts to compensate plaintiffs for pain and suffering have been subject to criticism.

Plaintiffs can be compensated for loss of future earning capacity. In calculating these damages jurors are expected to project the anticipated life span of the plaintiff. Generally plaintiffs may not be directly compensated for their shortened life expectancy. Under the collateral source rule, plaintiffs are entitled to recover for damages for which they have been reimbursed by a collateral source, such as an insurance company.

Plaintiffs are not entitled to compensation for the expenses of litigation, although some have suggested that, as a practical matter, punitive damages and awards for pain and suffering in effect provide for such compensation.

Damages for physical harm to property are tied to the fair market value of the property. Fair market value is considered the highest price one seeking to sell the property could have realized and not the lowest price at which a sale could have been made.

Punitive damages are reserved for defendants who act in a particularly egregious manner. These damages have been criticized as constituting undue compensation to the plaintiff and as having the potential of bankrupting defendants, especially in product liability cases.

Spouses can recover for loss of consortium, which is considered a derivative claim. Parents are also entitled to recover for the lost services and earnings of their minor children. Some courts have allowed minor children to recover for loss of consortium when a parent on whom they were dependent dies or is seriously injured.

Survival statutes allow an injured party's claim to be sustained after his or her death. Wrongful death statutes allow third persons, usually a decedent's spouse and children, to recover for losses they sustained as a result of the decedent's death. Survival actions are typically brought by the executor or administrator of an estate and recovery becomes an asset of the estate, which may be reached by creditors. Although at one time wrongful death actions were limited to economic losses caused by the decedent's death, in more recent times they have been extended to the loss of companionship of the decedent. Most states have ruled that wrongful death and survival actions begin to run from the date of the decedent's death. Both survival and wrongful death actions are subject to statutory construction.

To prevent plaintiffs who recover for future losses from receiving a windfall, many courts require juries to discount awards to a present value. Some have argued that the discounting of awards is unfair to plaintiffs because inflation offsets the discounting of present value awards. Large future damages are frequently paid using a periodic-payment settlement called a structured settlement. Arguably, this type of settlement relieves the plaintiff of the responsibility of making arrangements to invest the money and minimizes the amount of income tax required.

Under the avoidable consequences rule, a plaintiff has a duty to mitigate his or her damages by avoiding any harm that reasonably could have been avoided. This rule has been used as a defense in seat belt and motorcycle helmet cases.

A plaintiff in a negligence claim must typically show that he or she suffered some kind of physical harm or, in a few states, some kind of impact. Some courts have abandoned this rule in circumstances where one could readily believe the plaintiff actually suffered mental distress. Some courts have denied compensation for emotional distress to any plaintiff not within the zone of danger, whereas others have allowed recovery when the plaintiff was near the scene of the accident, personally observed it, and was closely related to the victim.

PRACTICE POINTERS

As a paralegal you may be called on to provide the evidence necessary to prove or disprove a claim for damages (see Figure 8-4). Here we will consider the practical implications of proving past and future medical expenses, loss of earning capacity, and pain and suffering.

Continued on next page

PRACTICE POINTERS—Continued

Past Medical Expenses

In terms of proving past medical expenses, the plaintiff has the burden of proving the amount of the expenses and that the expenses were necessary and reasonable. The best way to prove past expenses is, of course, through the use of bills that reflect the charges made. Alternatively, the plaintiff can testify to the amount of the bill or have a doctor or the person who prepared the bill testify as to the amount of the charge made. It is important to keep a running account of all bills. These bills should be tabulated on a monthly basis and may be submitted to the insurance company and to defense counsel on an ongoing basis. Some plaintiffs' counsel feel that the continual amassing of medical expenses into an ever-burgeoning file has a psychological impact on the defendant. Defense counsel, for obvious reasons, deny this.

In most jurisdictions proof of medical bills plus proof of payment raises the presumption that the bill was necessary and reasonable. In some states, however, testimony from a doctor, druggist, or other expert is required. The reasonableness and necessity of treatment become particularly problematic when dealing with

FIGURE 8-4 Proving Damages

TYPES OF DAMAGES	EVIDENCE USED TO PROVE
PAST MEDICAL EXPENSES	• Bills from doctors, hospitals, radiology, etc. • Testimony from expert showing necessity of treatment.
FUTURE MEDICAL EXPENSES	• Expert testimony. • Award is discounted to present value.
LOSS OF EARNING CAPACITY	• Plaintiff's work record showing hours lost due to injuries. • Wage stubs, W-4 forms, or IRS records (showing value of lost earnings). • Evidence of lost profits and loss of fringe benefits. • Extent of plaintiff's education and training (showing earning potential).
PAIN AND SUFFERING	• Plaintiff's testimony. • Testimony of those who have observed plaintiff's suffering; day-in-the-life video.

Continued on next page

PRACTICE POINTERS—Continued

preexisting conditions. If the plaintiff was not suffering from the preexisting condition at the time of the injury, the expenses will probably be recoverable. If, however, the plaintiff was under treatment for that condition at the time of the injury, he or she will have difficulty proving which expenses were necessitated by the aggravation caused by the defendant's negligence and which expenses stemmed from the preexisting condition. The plaintiff may therefore be unable to recover any of the medical expenses.

Future Medical Expenses

Future medical expenses are much less subject to quantification. No doctor can state with absolute certainty how long future treatment will be needed nor what exact amount of future medical expenses will be incurred. Courts are aware of this ambiguity and do not require the same degree of mathematical proof that they do for past expenses. In some jurisdictions future medical expenses are left for the jury to determine based on the amount of past medical expenses, the nature of the plaintiff's injuries, and the condition of the plaintiff at the time of trial. Other jurisdictions require medical testimony regarding a dollar amount and do not allow a jury to award more than the amount supported by testimony.

As was noted in the text of this chapter, future awards are often discounted to present value. Discounting is based on the idea that a dollar today is worth more than a dollar ten years from now because of the investment potential of that dollar. Present value tables, an example of which is shown in this section, allow one to calculate the present value of future awards.

Let us use a hypothetical scenario to illustrate the use of these tables. Suppose $1,000 is to be awarded the plaintiff in year 1, $2,000 in year 2, and $3,000 in year 3. Using an interest rate of 10 percent, what would be the present value of that award? Locate 10 percent on the table. Notice that next to year 1 in the third column is the number 0.90909, which indicates that the value of a dollar received a year from now is worth $.90909 now. Therefore, $1,000 a year from now would be worth $909.09 today. By the same token $2,000 in year 2 would be worth $2,000 × .82645 or $1,652.90; $3,000 in year 3 would be worth $3,000 × .75132 or $2,253.96. Therefore, the total present value would be $4,815.95:

PRESENT VALUE OF $1

Paid at End of Year	8%	9%	10%	11%	12%
1	0.92593	0.91743	0.90909	0.90090	0.89286
2	0.85734	0.84168	0.82645	0.81162	0.79719
3	0.79383	0.77219	0.75132	0.73119	0.71178
4	0.73503	0.70843	0.68302	0.65873	0.63552
5	0.68058	0.64993	0.62092	0.59345	0.56743
6	0.63027	0.59627	0.56448	0.53464	0.50663
7	0.58349	0.54704	0.51316	0.48166	0.45235
8	0.54027	0.50187	0.46651	0.43393	0.40388

Continued on next page

PRACTICE POINTERS—Continued

Paid at End of Year	8%	9%	10%	11%	12%
9	0.50025	0.46043	0.42410	0.39093	0.36061
10	0.46319	0.42241	0.38555	0.35219	0.32197
15	0.31524	0.27454	0.23939	0.20901	0.18270
20	0.21455	0.17843	0.14865	0.12404	0.10367
25	0.14602	0.11597	0.09230	0.07361	0.05882
30	0.09938	0.07537	0.05731	0.04368	0.03338
35	0.06764	0.04899	0.03559	0.02592	0.01894
40	0.04603	0.03184	0.02210	0.01539	0.01075

$1,000 × .90909 = $ 909.09
$2,000 × .82645 = $1,652.90
$3,000 × .75132 = $2,253.96
Total Present Value = $4,815.95

Loss of Earning Capacity

To prove loss of earning capacity, you must first prove that the injuries creating the plaintiff's physical disability impaired his or her ability to work and earn money. Second, you must prove the value of that incapacity. To prove the latter you must obtain copies of the plaintiff's wage stubs, W-4 forms, and/or IRS records (not admissible in some states). The defense will want to show that the plaintiff's work record was sporadic, that the earnings for the years at issue were unusually high, or that for some reason the plaintiff would not have been able to earn comparable wages in the years ahead for reasons other than the disability sustained.

Proof of earning capacity becomes more problematic if the plaintiff was temporarily disabled prior to the injuries or was for some reason not able to work before sustaining the injuries. In such cases the jury will be left to determine the value of the lost earning capacity based on their own common sense and sense of fair play.

Proof of lost earning capacity can also be difficult when the plaintiff was self-employed. In such cases a difference in profits prior to and after the plaintiff's injuries is not considered a measure of damages because factors other than the plaintiff's incapacity, such as changes in the market, could account for the decrease in profits. The plaintiff is obligated to prove that it was inability to work rather than other economic factors that caused the loss of business income.

Other types of evidence you might want to consider using to show a plaintiff's earning potential would be evidence of education and on-the-job training, as well as evidence of fringe benefits, such as bonuses, insurance programs, tips, and pensions. Prospective earnings from reasonably anticipated promotions or advancements may also be submitted, as well as evidence that the plaintiff was studying or in other ways taking steps to advance into better paying work.

Continued on next page

Evidence of income that the plaintiff receives that is unrelated to work is inadmissible. The fact that the plaintiff receives Social Security benefits, worker's compensation benefits, welfare benefits, dividends from stocks, or monies from other investments is irrelevant and therefore inadmissible unless used to impeach the plaintiff.

Pain and Suffering

Damages for pain and suffering are by their very nature not amenable to quantification. Therefore, all a plaintiff can do is prove that the physical pain and mental anguish were in fact experienced. The most direct evidence of pain and suffering is testimony by the plaintiff as to objective symptoms, such as the actual injuries received, and subjective symptoms, such as headaches. Mental anguish may take the form of fear, worry, depression, or humiliation.

Elicit detailed descriptions from the plaintiff, complete with specific incidents that illustrate the nature and depth of the pain and anguish and the limitations such suffering imposed on his or her lifestyle. In major personal injury lawsuits plaintiffs' attorneys frequently use "day in the life of" videotapes to illustrate graphically to the jury the full extent of the plaintiff's injuries. Such videos chronicle in a simple but poignant way the everyday suffering of the plaintiff and those who care for him or her. If your firm is without such resources, the attorney must create vivid word pictures in the jurors' minds through the process of direct examination. In preparing the plaintiff for such testimony you must draw his or her attention to all those events in the course of a day that are rendered more difficult as a result of the injuries.

Doctors as well as others who are familiar with the plaintiff can testify regarding their observations that are indicative of pain and suffering. In working with these potential witnesses it is important to strive for detailed information that can be used to create a visual picture for the jury. Generalizations and vague statements are not helpful and will not create the kind of jury empathy plaintiff's counsel desires.

The defendant will want to rebut the plaintiff's claim of physical and mental anguish by presenting evidence that the plaintiff is pain-free and relatively happy or, alternatively, that the plaintiff's suffering is caused by factors other than the injuries. The courts are reluctant, however, to admit evidence of collateral events causing the plaintiff's suffering because such evidence may be highly prejudicial to the plaintiff. Therefore, a defendant who wants to introduce such evidence must show that the connection between the collateral event and the plaintiff's suffering is not purely conjectural.

TORT TEASERS

---

1. Suppose your firm represents Mr. Goodright and you have been asked to interview him to ascertain the full extent of his damages. Write down a list of the questions that you would want to ask him in reference to his medical expenses, lost income, lost future income, and pain and suffering.

2. If your firm were representing Teddy, what information would you want to elicit from the medical

doctors and psychologists who treated Teddy?

3. Your client is injured in an automobile accident and as a result suffers a fractured dislocation of his right ankle. He is determined to have a remaining work life of twenty-nine years. Medical testimony indicates that he will be unable to work from one to five years at anything other than a sedentary type of job that would require no prolonged walking, running, or heavy lifting. Your client receives a medical discharge from the Air Force after the accident, receiving a 60 percent disability compensation, 40 percent of which is attributed to his ankle and the remaining 20 percent to other medical problems not related to the accident. *Beaulieu v. Elliott,* 434 P.2d 665 (Alaska 1967).

a. What types of damages would you attempt to recover in this case?

b. How would you go about determining a monetary value for each of these damages?

c. What arguments do you anticipate your opponents will make in reference to the payment of damages?

4. A twenty-one-year-old college student dies allegedly as a result of improper diagnosis and care as well as the administration of unsafe drugs. Her parents bring a claim under the wrongful death statute on their behalf and under the survival statute on behalf of their daughter's estate. *Warner v. McCaughan,* 460 P.2d 272 (Wash. 1969).

a. What problems would you anticipate with the parents filing a wrongful death action?

b. What damages would you attempt to recover under the survival statute?

c. What arguments would you want to make if you were the defense in this case as to why the parents should not be able to recover for their daughter's pain and suffering?

5. An internationally known singer and recording artist, Connie Francis, is sexually assaulted in her motel room. After the assault she suffers from depression, social and sexual withdrawal, and traumatic phobia. Psychiatrists testify that she will probably have difficulty resuming her professional career for at least the next ten years and she testifies she is unable to perform because of her shame and humiliation. She sues the motel owner for pain and suffering, mental anguish, humiliation, and loss of earnings; her husband sues for loss of consortium. How would you go about determining the amount of their damages? *Garzilli v. Howard Johnson's Motor Lodges,* 419 F. Supp. 1210 (E.D.N.Y. 1976).

KEY TERMS

Avoidable consequences rule
Obligation of a plaintiff to minimize (mitigate) her damages.

Collateral source rule
Right of a plaintiff to recover twice for damages.

Compensatory damages
Damages designed to compensate the plaintiff; consist of both general and special damages.

Derivative claim
Claim derived from underlying claim (e.g., loss of consortium).

Discounting an award
Reducing an award to its present value.

Fair market value
Amount property could be sold for on the open market.

General damages
Damages that generally result from conduct engaged in by the defendant.

Loss of consortium
Loss of services, including companionship, sex, and earnings outside of the home.

Nominal damages
Damages awarded when liability is shown but no actual damages are proved.

Parasitic damages
Damages attached to physical injury, e.g., mental suffering.

Present value
Current value of money that is to be paid in the future, based on the assumption that money received today is worth more than money received in the future because of the investment potential of money.

Punitive damages
Damages designed to punish the defendant (also referred to as *exemplary damages*).

Special damages
Damages that are unique to the plaintiff.

Structured settlement
Agreement to pay damages in installments rather than a lump sum.

Survival action
Action that remains available the decedent's death.

Wrongful death action
Action brought by third parties to recover for losses they suffered as a result of the decedent's death.

CHAPTER

9

Negligence: Defenses

CHAPTER TOPICS

Contributory Negligence
Comparative Negligence
Assumption of Risk
Immunities
Statutes of Limitations and Statutes of Repose
Application

CHAPTER OBJECTIVES

In this chapter you will learn to:
- Identify the elements of contributory negligence, comparative negligence, and assumption of risk
- Recognize the exceptions to the contributory negligence rule
- Recognize the problems that arise in the administration of a comparative negligence system
- Differentiate between contributory negligence and assumption of risk
- Identify situations in which immunity can be raised as a defense
- Recognize the purpose behind the problems inherent in a statute of limitations defense

If Teddy and Mr. Goodright are able to prove their claims of negligence against the Baxters, the Baxters will certainly want to raise some form of defense (see Figure 9-1). The three defenses they will consider are contributory negligence, comparative negligence, and assumption of risk. If Teddy and Mr. Goodright were **contributorily negligent**—if they contributed in some way to their own injuries—they would be totally barred from recovery. If the state in which the suit is filed has adopted a **comparative negligence** rather than a contributory negligence system, their recovery will be reduced in direct proportion to their own degree of negligence. For example, suppose Teddy suffered damages of $10,000 and was shown to be 20 percent negligent. His recovery would be reduced to $8,000, i.e., $10,000 – $2,000 (20 percent of $10,000). Under the doctrine of **assumption of risk,** if it can be shown that Teddy and Mr. Goodright voluntarily consented to take the chance that harm would occur, they might, at the worst, be precluded from recovery and, at best, have their recovery reduced.

Before diving into this chapter, be aware of two things. First, the area of defenses is largely controlled by statute. Therefore, this chapter is merely a general description of the subject and an overview of approaches followed across the United States; to be knowledgeable about defenses as they are applied in your jurisdiction, you must consult the relevant statutes and case law in your state. Second, at the time of this writing all but five states have adopted some form of comparative negligence. Nevertheless, contributory negligence and its exceptions are discussed in some detail so that you may better appreciate the historical roots of and justifications for comparative negligence.

CONTRIBUTORY NEGLIGENCE

The defense of contributory negligence in essence shifts the loss from the defendant to the plaintiff by totally barring the negligent plaintiff from recovery. The plaintiff is barred even though the defendant was negligent and, in most cases, was more negligent than the plaintiff.

The rationale for this judge-created rule stems from the notion that negligent plaintiffs should be punished for failing to protect their own safety. Additionally,

FIGURE 9-1 Defenses to Negligence

CONTRIBUTORY NEGLIGENCE	Plaintiff barred from recovery.
COMPARATIVE NEGLIGENCE	Plaintiff's recovery reduced.
ASSUMPTION OF RISK	Plaintiff either barred from recovery or recovery is reduced.
IMMUNITY	Plaintiff barred from recovery.
STATUTE OF LIMITATIONS AND STATUTE OF REPOSE	Plaintiff barred from recovery.

some courts have argued that the plaintiff's negligence becomes the proximate cause of his or her injuries, thus removing the defendant as the proximate cause. This argument does not hold water, however, in light of the principles of proximate cause discussed in Chapter 7. Remember that if several events contribute to the plaintiff's injuries, each of them will be considered a distinct proximate cause. A more practical explanation of the judicial creation of contributory negligence lies in judges' historical distrust of juries and their fear that, given free rein, juries would hamper the growth of industry by awarding huge awards to injured plaintiffs.

Exceptions to the Contributory Negligence Rule

The results rendered by the rule of contributory negligence are often harsh and unjust. Worthy plaintiffs are often denied recovery and blameworthy defendants go unscathed. As a result the courts have developed various escape mechanisms by which plaintiffs can avoid this rule. One way, which has been adopted in every jurisdiction that adheres to the contributory negligence system, is the requirement that contributory negligence be proved and specifically pleaded by the defendant. Additionally, in most jurisdictions the question of contributory negligence is left to the jury. Arguably juries have an opportunity to apply a comparative negligence standard in those cases in which application of a contributory negligence standard would lead to unfair results.

Most states require that the plaintiff's negligence meet the standards of the but-for or substantial factor test of actual causation in order to be barred from recovering. A few courts, however, bar the plaintiff's recovery if his or her negligence contributed in any way to the result, no matter how slight that contribution might have been.

In most cases, the same rules that apply in determining proximate cause in terms of the defendant's conduct also apply to the plaintiff. In one instance, however, proximate cause is construed more narrowly

in the case of contributory negligence than it is in the case of the defendant's negligence. If the harm that is likely to occur as a result of the plaintiff's negligence occurs in some unforeseen manner, the plaintiff's conduct is usually held not to be the proximate cause of the harm. Suppose a pedestrian crosses a street without looking and is injured, not by an oncoming vehicle, but by an explosion that occurs when a truck carrying dynamite strikes an automobile. In such a case the plaintiff's negligence would not be considered the proximate cause of the injuries because the injury came about as a result of an unforeseen risk (an explosion) and not the foreseeable risk of being run over. Because the harm that occurred came about in a different way than the harm that was threatened, the plaintiff would not be barred from recovery (Restatement (Second) of Torts § 468).

Last Clear Chance Doctrine

The most significant way in which the contributory negligence defense has been limited has been through the use of the **last clear chance doctrine.** Under this doctrine, if the defendant has an opportunity that is unavailable to the plaintiff to prevent the harm that occurs and does not take advantage of it, the defendant will remain liable despite the plaintiff's contributory negligence. In essence the defendant's failure to take advantage of an opportunity to prevent the harm negates or wipes out the plaintiff's contributory negligence. Although the courts have used various explanations to rationalize this doctrine, it most likely stems from an attempt to mitigate the harshness of the contributory negligence defense.

The last clear chance doctrine, which is essentially a defense of the plaintiff, was first utilized in the case of *Davies v. Mann,* 152 Eng. Rep. 588 (1842), in which the plaintiff had chained up his donkey and left it blocking the roadway; the defendant ran his wagon into the animal. Because the defendant could have taken measures to avoid the collision and the plaintiff was at a loss to do anything at the time of the accident, the defendant was held liable.

The courts have struggled with the variations to this last clear chance doctrine (see Figure 9-2). The courts are unanimous in holding the defendant liable if the plaintiff is unable to avoid the predicament and the defendant is aware of but negligently fails to circumvent the harm. Less consensus exists, however, if the plaintiff is helpless and the defendant negligently fails to discover the plaintiff's situation because the defendant is inattentive. Suppose the plaintiff negligently turns her vehicle in front of the defendant and the defendant, who could have avoided the accident had he been paying attention instead of talking with his passenger, is unable to avoid the plaintiff by the time he sees her. Most, but not all, courts would apply the last clear chance doctrine, thereby holding the defendant liable.

Suppose the plaintiff is inattentive rather than helpless and negligently fails to extricate himself from the danger. If the defendant discovers the plaintiff's predicament but negligently fails to respond to it, most courts will adhere to the last clear chance doctrine. A train engineer, for example, may be liable if she fails to blow the train's whistle a second time or slow the train down once she becomes aware that a person standing on the track has not heard or has disregarded the first blow of the whistle (Restatement (Second) of Torts § 480, cmt. b).

When the Last Clear Chance Doctrine Is Not Applicable. When is the last clear chance doctrine not applicable? If both the defendant and the plaintiff are inattentive so that neither discovers the danger, the last clear chance doctrine is not applicable. Also, if the defendant discovers the plaintiff's peril but cannot avoid it because of the defendant's earlier negligence, the majority of courts will not allow the last clear chance

FIGURE 9-2   Last Clear Chance Doctrine Variations

PLAINTIFF IS HELPLESS AND:
    1. Defendant discovers danger but negligently fails to avoid it.
    2. Defendant fails to discover danger because he is inattentive.
	Plaintiff can recover in all courts.
	
	Plaintiff can recover in most courts.

PLAINTIFF IS INATTENTIVE BUT NOT HELPLESS AND:
    1. Defendant discovers danger but negligently fails to avoid it.
    2. Defendant fails to discover danger because he is inattentive.
	Plaintiff can recover in most courts.
	
	Plaintiff cannot recover.

DEFENDANT IS UNABLE TO AVOID HARMING PLAINTIFF (even though he is aware of danger) because of defendant's earlier negligence ("first clear chance doctrine").	Plaintiff cannot recover in most courts.

doctrine. Suppose the defendant is driving a car with defective brakes and as a result, although he sees the plaintiff turning in front of him, he cannot stop in time. Should the last clear chance doctrine be applied? Most courts have refused to apply the doctrine in this so-called "first clear chance" case. The general rule is that the last clear chance doctrine is inapplicable when the defendant's original act of negligence precludes her from avoiding the accident after she discovers the

plaintiff's peril (Restatement (Second) of Torts § 479, illus. 3).

In other words, if because of his prior negligence (such as driving with defective brakes) the defendant does not have an opportunity to avoid the accident, the plaintiff cannot allege that the defendant had the last clear chance to avert that accident. That opportunity was not in fact available to the defendant.

PUTTING IT INTO PRACTICE 9.1

Assume that contributory negligence is the rule in each of the following questions.

1. Jeff is speeding down the highway when Josie, who is putting on her makeup at the time, crosses slightly over the center line, scraping the side of Jeff's car. As a result Jeff loses control of his car and careens into a ditch. Expert testimony shows that Jeff's excessive speed did not contribute to the collision but did contribute to his losing control of his car. Can Jeff recover for the damage to his vehicle and for his personal injuries?

2. Because of her negligent driving, Geraldine gets involved in a collision and her car is thrown to the opposite side of the road. Corinne, who is approaching the scene in her vehicle, sees Geraldine's car and unreasonably believes she can cut around it. She is wrong and ends up overturning Geraldine's car, causing Geraldine to fracture her back. Is Corinne liable to Geraldine for the fractured back?

   a. Would your answer change if Corinne had tried to stop but in her confusion hit the accelerator rather than the brake?

   b. Would your answer change if Corinne had tried to stop but could not do so because her brakes were not operating properly?

3. Margaret's car becomes disabled. She pulls over to the side of the road but negligently fails to put her lights on so that other drivers can see her vehicle. The headlights on Christy's vehicle go out, but she decides to drive home anyway. Because of her lack of headlights she is unable to detect Margaret's car in time and runs into the vehicle. Can Margaret recover for the damage to her vehicle?

When Contributory Negligence Is Not a Defense

Contributory negligence is not a defense to an intentional tort (see Figure 9-3). A defendant in a battery case cannot, for example, argue that the plaintiff was negligent in failing to duck. Similarly, contributory negligence is not allowed as a defense if the defendant's conduct was "willful and wanton" or "reckless"

unless the plaintiff's conduct was also willful and wanton or reckless. The rationale for these rules is that defendants who intentionally or recklessly harm others should not be able to escape liability simply because those whom they harmed are negligent.

A defendant who is negligent per se might not be able to raise the defense of contributory negligence. If the statute upon which the defendant's negligence is

FIGURE 9-3 Exceptions to Contributory Negligence Rule

- Plaintiff's negligence does not meet standards of but-for or substantial factor tests.
- Harm likely to occur as a result of plaintiff's negligence occurs in unforeseen manner.
- Last clear chance doctrine—defendant did not take advantage of opportunity to avoid accident and plaintiff had no such opportunity. (Not applicable if neither plaintiff nor defendant discovers danger due to inattentiveness or if defendant's original act of negligence made it impossible for him to avoid accident.)
- Defendant committed an intentional tort.
- Defendant was "willful and wanton" or "reckless."
- Defendant was negligent per se. (If statute's intent was to place sole responsibility on defendant and was enacted to protect class of people to which plaintiff belongs.)

based was enacted for the sole purpose of protecting a class of persons of which the plaintiff was a member and the statute's intent was to place sole responsibility upon the defendant, contributory negligence is not a viable defense. Such a statute is one prohibiting the sale of liquor to minors.

Finally, some kinds of contributory negligence are not considered defenses in strict liability actions. A consumer, for example, who fails to inspect a defective product before using it and is injured as a result will not be prevented from recovering damages even though he or she was contributorily negligent. (See Chapter 13, "Product Liability," for further discussion of this topic.) Some statutes explicitly abolish the defense of contributory negligence and others do so implicitly by imposing a strict liability standard.

COMPARATIVE NEGLIGENCE

Comparative negligence was created as an alternative to the all-or-nothing approach of the contributory negligence system (see Figure 9-4). In one of the more famous cases in which a court adopted the doctrine of comparative negligence (*Li v. Yellow Cab Co.,* 532 P.2d 1226 (Cal. 1975), the court explained why it felt that use of the contributory negligence rule undermined confidence in the jury system:

It is unnecessary for us to catalogue the enormous amount of critical comment that has been directed over the years against the "all-or-nothing" approach of the doctrine of contributory negligence. The essence of that criticism has been constant and clear: the doctrine is inequitable in its operation because it

FIGURE 9-4 Comparative Negligence

TYPES OF COMPARATIVE NEGLIGENCE	PROBLEMS RELATED TO COMPARATIVE NEGLIGENCE
• Pure • 50% Approach 1. Not as great as 2. Not greater than	• How is fault assigned, especially where there are multiple defendants? • Is the last clear chance doctrine applicable? • Should a negligent plaintiff's recovery be reduced if the defendant was negligent per se?

fails to distribute responsibility in proportion to fault.[3] Against this have been raised several arguments in justification, but none have proved even remotely adequate to the task. The basic objection to the doctrine—grounded in the primal concept that in a system in which liability is based on fault, the extent of fault should govern the extent of liability—remains irresistible to reason and all intelligent notions of fairness.

For a more in-depth discussion of the reasons supporting the adoption of comparative negligence, read *McIntyre v. Balentine,* 833 S.W.2d 52 (Tenn. 1992). Contained within the original opinion was a listing of the states that have adopted comparative negligence along with the applicable statutes in those that have done so by legislative action. The appendix to the opinion contains sample jury instructions and a verdict form that you might find interesting.

---

3. Dean Prosser states the kernel of critical comment in these terms: "It [the rule] places upon one party the entire burden of a loss for which two are, by hypothesis, responsible." [cite omitted] Harper and James express the same basic idea: "[T]here is no justification—in either policy or doctrine—for the rule of contributory negligence, except for the feeling that if one man is to be held liable because of his fault, then the fault of him who seeks to enforce that liability should also be considered. But this notion does not require the all-or-nothing rule, which would exonerate a very negligent defendant for even the slight fault of his victim. The logical corollary of the fault principle would be a rule of comparative or proportional negligence, not the present rule." [cite omitted]

. . . "[P]ractical experience with the application by juries of the doctrine of contributory negligence has added its weight to analyses of its inherent shortcomings: "Every trial lawyer is well aware that juries often do in fact allow recovery in cases of contributory negligence, and that the compromise in the jury room does result in some diminution of the damages because of the plaintiff's fault. But the process is at best a haphazard and most unsatisfactory one." [cite omitted] It is manifest that this state of affairs, viewed from the standpoint of the health and vitality of the legal process, can only detract from public confidence in the ability of law and legal institutions to assign liability on a just and consistent basis.]

 CASE

McIntyre v. Balentine
833 S.W.2d 52 (Tenn. 1992)

DROWOTA, Justice.

In this personal injury action, we granted Plaintiff's application for permission to appeal in order to decide whether to adopt a system of comparative fault in Tennessee. We are also asked to determine whether the criminal presumption of intoxication is admissible evidence in a civil case. We now replace the common law defense of contributory negligence with a system of comparative fault. Additionally, we hold that the criminal presumption of intoxication established by T.C.A. § 55-10-408(b) (1988) is admissible evidence in a civil case.

In the early morning darkness of November 2, 1986, Plaintiff Harry Douglas McIntyre and Defendant Clifford Balentine were involved in a motor vehicle accident resulting in severe injuries to Plaintiff. The accident occurred in the vicinity of Smith's Truck Stop in Savannah, Tennessee. As Defendant Balentine was traveling south on Highway 69, Plaintiff entered the highway (also traveling south) from the truck stop parking lot. Shortly after Plaintiff entered the highway, his pickup truck was struck by Defendant's Peterbilt tractor. At trial, the parties disputed the exact chronology of events immediately preceding the accident.

Both men had consumed alcohol the evening of the accident. After the accident, Plaintiff's blood alcohol level was measured at .17 percent by weight. Testimony suggested that Defendant was traveling in excess of the posted speed limit.

Plaintiff brought a negligence action against Defendant Balentine and Defendant East-West Motor Freight, Inc. . . . Defendants answered that Plaintiff was contributorially negligent, in part due to operating his vehicle while intoxicated. After trial, the jury returned a verdict stating: "We, the jury, find the plaintiff and the defendant equally at fault in this accident; therefore, we rule in favor of the defendant."

After judgment was entered for Defendants, Plaintiff brought an appeal alleging the trial court erred by (1) refusing to instruct the jury regarding the doctrine of comparative negligence, and (2) instructing the jury that a blood alcohol level greater than .10 percent creates an inference of intoxication. The Court of Appeals affirmed, holding that (1) comparative negligence is not the law in

Tennessee, and (2) the presumption of intoxication provided by T.C.A. § 55-10-408(b) (1988) is admissible evidence in a civil case.

I.

The common law contributory negligence doctrine has traditionally been traced to Lord Ellenborough's opinion in *Butterfield v. Forrester,* 11 East 60, 103 Eng.Rep. 926 (1809). There, plaintiff, "riding as fast as his horse would go," was injured after running into an obstruction defendant had placed in the road. Stating as the rule that "[o]ne person being in fault will not dispense with another's using ordinary care," plaintiff was denied recovery on the basis that he did not use ordinary care to avoid the obstruction . . . .

The contributory negligence bar was soon brought to America as part of the common law . . . and proceeded to spread throughout the states . . . . This strict bar may have been a direct outgrowth of the common law system of issue pleading; issue pleading posed questions to be answered "yes" or "no," leaving common law courts, the theory goes, no choice but to award all or nothing . . . . A number of other rationalizations have been advanced in the attempt to justify the harshness of the "all-or-nothing" bar. Among these: the plaintiff should be penalized for his misconduct; the plaintiff should be deterred from injuring himself; and the plaintiff's negligence supersedes the defendant's so as to render defendant's negligence no longer proximate . . . .

In Tennessee, the rule as initially stated was that "if a party, by his own gross negligence, brings an injury upon himself, or contributes to such injury, he cannot recover;" for, in such cases, the party "must be regarded as the author of his own misfortune." In subsequent decisions, we have continued to follow the general rule that a plaintiff's contributory negligence completely bars recovery . . . .

Equally entrenched in Tennessee jurisprudence are exceptions to the general all-or-nothing rule: contributory negligence does not absolutely bar recovery where a defendant's conduct was intentional; where defendant's conduct was "grossly" negligent; where defendant had the "last clear chance" with which, through the exercise of ordinary care, to avoid plaintiff's injury; or where plaintiff's negligence may be classified as "remote."

In contrast, comparative fault has long been the federal rule in cases involving injured employees of interstate railroad carriers and injured seamen . . . .

Similarly, by the early 1900s, many states, including Tennessee, had statutes providing for the apportionment of damages in railroad injury cases . . . . While Tennessee's railroad statute did not expressly sanction damage apportionment, it was soon given that judicial

construction. In 1856, the statute was passed in an effort to prevent railroad accidents; it imposed certain obligations and liabilities on railroads "for all damages accruing or resulting from a failure to perform said dut[ies]." . . . Apparently this strict liability was deemed necessary because "the consequences of carelessness and want of due skill [in the operation of railroads at speeds previously unknown] . . . are so frightful and appalling that the most strict and rigid rules of accountability must be applied." The statute was then judicially construed to permit the jury to consider "[n]egligence of the person injured, which caused, or contributed to cause the accident . . . in determining the amount of damages proper to be given for the injury." This system of comparative fault was utilized for almost a century until 1959 when, trains no longer unique in their "astonishing speeds," the statute was overhauled, its strict liability provision being replaced by negligence per se and the common law contributory negligence bar . . . .

Between 1920 and 1969, a few states began utilizing the principles of comparative fault in all tort litigation . . . . Then, between 1969 and 1984, comparative fault replaced contributory negligence in 37 additional states . . . . In 1991, South Carolina became the 45th state to adopt comparative fault . . . . leaving Alabama, Maryland, North Carolina, Virginia, and Tennessee as the only remaining common law contributory negligence jurisdictions.

Eleven states have judicially adopted comparative fault.[3] Thirty-four states have legislatively adopted comparative fault.[4]

---

3 In the order of their adoption, these states are Florida, California, Alaska, Michigan, West Virginia, New Mexico, Illinois, Iowa, Missouri, Kentucky, and South Carolina. Nine courts adopted pure comparative fault . . . In two of these states, legislatures subsequently enacted a modified form. . . . Two courts adopted a modified form of comparative fault. . . . The "pure" and "modified" forms are discussed in Part III infra.
4. Six states have legislatively adopted pure comparative fault: Mississippi, Rhode Island, Washington, New York, Louisiana, and Arizona; eight legislatures have enacted the modified "49 percent" rule (plaintiff may recover if plaintiff's negligence is less than defendant's): Georgia, Arkansas, Maine, Colorado, Idaho, North Dakota, Utah, and Kansas; eighteen legislatures have enacted the modified "50 percent" rule (plaintiff may recover so long as plaintiff's negligence is not greater than defendant's): Wisconsin, Hawaii, Massachusetts, Minnesota, New Hampshire, Vermont, Oregon, Connecticut, Nevada, New Jersey, Oklahoma, Texas, Wyoming, Montana, Pennsylvania, Ohio, Indiana, and Delaware; two legislatures have enacted statutes that allow a plaintiff to recover if plaintiff's negligence is slight when compared to defendant's gross negligence: Nebraska and South Dakota . . . .

II.

Over 15 years ago, we stated, when asked to adopt a system of comparative fault: "We do not deem it appropriate to consider making such a change unless and until a case reaches us wherein the pleadings and proof present an issue of contributory negligence accompanied by advocacy that the ends of justice will be served by adopting the rule of comparative negligence . . . ." Such a case is now before us. After exhaustive deliberation that was facilitated by extensive briefing and argument by the parties, amicus curiae, and Tennessee's scholastic community, we conclude that it is time to abandon the outmoded and unjust common law doctrine of contributory negligence and adopt in its place a system of comparative fault. Justice simply will not permit our continued adherence to a rule that, in the face of a judicial determination that others bear primary responsibility, nevertheless completely denies injured litigants recompense for their damages.

We recognize that this action could be taken by our General Assembly. However, legislative inaction has never prevented judicial abolition of obsolete common law doctrines, especially those, such as contributory negligence, conceived in the judicial womb . . . . Indeed, our abstinence would sanction "a mutual state of inaction in which the court awaits action by the legislature and the legislature awaits guidance from the court," thereby prejudicing the equitable resolution of legal conflicts.

Nor do we today abandon our commitment to stare decisis. While "[c]onfidence in our courts is to a great extent dependent on the uniformity and consistency engendered by allegiance to stare decisis, . . . mindless obedience to this precept can confound the truth and foster an attitude of contempt." . . .

III.

Two basic forms of comparative fault are utilized by 45 of our sister jurisdictions, these variants being commonly referred to as either "pure" or "modified." In the "pure" form,[5] a plaintiff's damages are reduced in proportion to the percentage negligence attributed to him; for example, a plaintiff responsible for 90 percent of the negligence that caused his injuries nevertheless may recover 10

percent of his damages. In the "modified" form,[6] plaintiffs recover as in pure jurisdictions, but only if the plaintiff's negligence either (1) does not exceed ("50 percent" jurisdictions) or (2) is less than ("49 percent" jurisdictions) the defendant's negligence . . . .

Although we conclude that the all-or-nothing rule of contributory negligence must be replaced, we nevertheless decline to abandon totally our fault-based tort system. We do not agree that a party should necessarily be able to recover in tort even though he may be 80, 90, or 95 percent at fault. We therefore reject the pure form of comparative fault.

We recognize that modified comparative fault systems have been criticized as merely shifting the arbitrary contributory negligence bar to a new ground . . . . However, we feel the "49 percent rule" ameliorates the harshness of the common law rule while remaining compatible with a fault-based tort system . . . . Therefore we hold that so long as a plaintiff's negligence remains less than the defendant's negligence the plaintiff may recover; in such a case, plaintiff's damages are to be reduced in proportion to the percentage of the total negligence attributable to the plaintiff.

In all trials where the issue of comparative fault is before a jury, the trial court shall instruct the jury on the effect of the jury's finding as to the percentage of negligence as between the plaintiff or plaintiffs and the defendant or defendants . . . . The attorneys for each party shall be allowed to argue how this instruction affects a plaintiff's ability to recover.

IV.

Turning to the case at bar, the jury found that "the plaintiff and defendant [were] equally at fault." Because the jury, without the benefit of proper instructions by the trial court, made a gratuitous apportionment of fault, we find that their "equal" apportionment is not sufficiently trustworthy to form the basis of a final determination between these parties. Therefore, the case is remanded for a new trial in accordance with the dictates of this opinion.

---

5. The 13 states utilizing pure comparative fault are Alaska, Arizona, California, Florida, Kentucky, Louisiana, Mississippi, Missouri, Michigan, New Mexico, New York, Rhode Island, and Washington . . . .

6. The 21 states using the "50 percent" modified form: Connecticut, Delaware, Hawaii, Illinois, Indiana, Iowa, Massachusetts, Minnesota, Montana, Nevada, New Hampshire, New Jersey, Ohio, Oklahoma, Oregon, Pennsylvania, South Carolina, Texas, Vermont, Wisconsin, and Wyoming. The 9 states using the "49 percent" form: Arkansas, Colorado, Georgia, Idaho, Kansas, Maine, North Dakota, Utah, and West Virginia. Two states, Nebraska and South Dakota, use a slight-gross system of comparative fault.

V.

We recognize that today's decision affects numerous legal principles surrounding tort litigation. For the most part, harmonizing these principles with comparative fault must await another day. However, we feel compelled to provide some guidance to the trial courts charged with implementing this new system.

First, and most obviously, the new rule makes the doctrines of remote contributory negligence and last clear chance obsolete. The circumstances formerly taken into account by those two doctrines will henceforth be addressed when assessing relative degrees of fault.

Second, in cases of multiple tortfeasors, plaintiff will be entitled to recover so long as plaintiff's fault is less than the combined fault of all tortfeasors . . . .

Further, because a particular defendant will henceforth be liable only for the percentage of a plaintiff's damages occasioned by that defendant's negligence, situations where a defendant has paid more than his "share" of a judgment will no longer arise, and therefore the Uniform Contribution Among Tort-feasors Act, T.C.A. §§ 29-11-101 to 106 (1980), will no longer determine the apportionment of liability between codefendants.

Fourth, fairness and efficiency require that defendants called upon to answer allegations in negligence be permitted to allege, as an affirmative defense, that a nonparty caused or contributed to the injury or damage for which recovery is sought. In cases where such a defense is raised, the trial court shall instruct the jury to assign this nonparty the percentage of the total negligence for which he is responsible. However, in order for a plaintiff to recover a judgment against such additional person, the plaintiff must have made a timely amendment to his complaint and caused process to be served on such additional person. Thereafter, the additional party will be required to answer the amended complaint. The procedures shall be in accordance with the Tennessee Rules of Civil Procedure.

Fifth, until such time as the Tennessee Judicial Conference Committee on Civil Pattern Jury Instructions promulgates new standard jury instructions, we direct trial courts' attention to the suggested instructions and special verdict form set forth in the appendix to this opinion . . . .

Suggested Jury Instructions

[The following instructions should be preceded by instructions on negligence, proximate cause, damages, etc.]

1. If you find that defendant was not negligent or that defendant's negligence was not a proximate cause of plaintiff's injury, you will find for defendant.

2. If you find that defendant was negligent and that defendant's negligence was a proximate cause of plaintiff's injury, you must then determine whether plaintiff was also negligent and whether plaintiff's negligence was a proximate cause of his/her injury.

3. In this state, negligence on the part of a plaintiff has an impact on a plaintiff's right to recover damages. Accordingly, if you find that each party was negligent and that the negligence of each party was a proximate cause of plaintiff's damages, then you must determine the degree of such negligence, expressed as a percentage, attributable to each party.

4. If you find from all the evidence that the percentage of negligence attributable to plaintiff was equal to, or greater than, the percentage of negligence attributable to defendant, then you are instructed that plaintiff will not be entitled to recover any damages for his/her injuries. If, on the other hand, you determine from the evidence that the percentage of negligence attributable to plaintiff was less than the percentage of negligence attributable to defendant, then plaintiff will be entitled to recover that portion of his/her damages not caused by plaintiff's own negligence.

5. The court will provide you with a special verdict form that will assist you in your duties. This is the form on which you will record, if appropriate, the percentage of negligence assigned to each party and plaintiff's total damages. The court will then take your findings and either (1) enter judgment for defendant if you have found that defendant was not negligent or that plaintiff's own negligence accounted for 50 percent or more of the total negligence proximately causing his/her injuries or (2) enter judgment against defendant in accordance with defendant's percentage of negligence.

Special Verdict Form

We, the jury, make the following answers to the questions submitted by the court:

1. Was the defendant negligent?

Answer: _____ (Yes or No)

(If your answer is "No," do not answer any further questions. Sign this form and return it to the court.)

2. Was the defendant's negligence a proximate cause of injury or damage to the plaintiff?

Answer: _____ (Yes or No)

(If your answer is "No," do not answer any further questions. Sign this form and return it to the court.)

3. Did the plaintiff's own negligence account for 50 percent or more of the total negligence that proximately caused his/her injuries or damages?

Answer: _____ (Yes or No)

(If your answer is "Yes," do not answer any further questions. (Sign this form and return it to the court.)

4. What is the total amount of plaintiff's damages, determined without reference to the amount of plaintiff's negligence?

Amount in dollars: $_____

5. Using 100 percent as the total combined negligence, which proximately caused the injuries or damages to the plaintiff, what are the percentages of such negligence to be allocated to the plaintiff and defendant?

Plaintiff _____%

Defendant _____%

(Total must equal 100%)

_____

Signature of Foreman

Under the comparative negligence doctrine, the plaintiff's recovery is reduced in direct proportion to her degree of negligent contribution to her own injuries. Therefore, if a plaintiff is found to be responsible for 20 percent of her injuries and suffers damages of $1,000,000, her recovery will be reduced by 20 percent of the $1,000,000 or $200,000. Today all but five states have adopted a comparative negligence system by statute or through a state court decision.

The states that have adopted comparative negligence have, for the most part, adopted either a pure comparative negligence standard or a 50 percent approach. (See the listing of these states in part III of the *McIntyre* opinion.) Under the pure system the plaintiff can recover no matter how extensive his negligence. For example, if the plaintiff is found to be 80 percent negligent by the jury, under a pure comparative negligence system he can still recover 20 percent of his damages. Contrast this with the 50 percent approach, in which such a plaintiff would be precluded from recovering because he was more than 50 percent responsible for his own injuries.

Two subsystems of the 50 percent approach have been developed: the "not as great as" and the "not greater than" (referred to as "49 percent rule" in the *McIntyre* decision) approaches. Although subtle in terms of language, the differences in these two systems can have a profound impact on the plaintiff. Under the "not as great as" approach the plaintiff's claim is barred

as soon as her negligence is as great as the defendant's negligence; under the "not greater than" approach the plaintiff is barred only when her negligence is greater than the defendant's. The reason this subtle distinction can give rise to tremendous differences in outcome results from juries' tendency to assign a 50–50 apportionment in terms of blame. In a 50–50 apportionment the plaintiff would be barred under the "not as great as" approach (because her negligence would be as great as the defendant's) but would not be barred under the "not greater than" approach (because her negligence would not be greater than the defendant's).

Administrative Problems

The administration of the comparative fault system creates some practical problems. For example, how should the percentage of fault be assigned to the plaintiff and defendant? Should fault be based on the extent that the party's conduct contributed to the resulting harm, as suggested by the Uniform Comparative Fault Act? Or should fault be based on the extent to which the plaintiff's conduct deviated from a reasonable standard of care? Both methods are used and can lead to different outcomes.

What if some persons are not parties to an action? Should fault be assigned to their actions? How is negligence assigned if there are more parties than just the plaintiff and defendant? Under a pure comparative negligence system the answer is simple: the negligence of all parties will be considered and the plaintiff will be allowed to recover in direct proportion to the negligence of those parties.

Suppose, for example, the jury determines the damages to be $100,000 and allocates the fault as follows:

Plaintiff	25%
Defendant 1	20%
Defendant 2	30%
Nonparty	25%

The plaintiff would receive a judgment of $50,000, for which defendant 1 would be liable for $20,000 and defendant 2 would be liable for $30,000. (This allocation is based on the assumption that the jury determined that the plaintiff's fault should be applied to reduce the plaintiff's damages.)

A problem arises, however, in jurisdictions where the plaintiff may recover only if her negligence is less than that of the defendants. Should such a plaintiff be allowed to recover if her negligence is less than that of all the defendants combined but greater than that of a particular defendant? Suppose, for example, the plaintiff is responsible for 40 percent of her injuries, Defendant A is 30 percent responsible, Defendant B is 20 percent responsible, and Defendant C is 10 percent responsible. Should the plaintiff be able to recover when her negligence exceeds that of each individual defendant, even though she is less negligent than all of the defendants combined? Most state statutes do not answer this question.

Other Issues Affecting Comparative Negligence

Is the last clear chance doctrine applicable in a comparative negligence system? The majority of states has not recognized the last clear chance doctrine after adopting comparative negligence and a few have abolished the last clear chance doctrine altogether. A minority of states, however, has retained the last clear chance doctrine as a distinct doctrine, either reasoning that last clear chance is not incompatible with comparative negligence or not questioning the compatibility. The Uniform Comparative Fault Act expressly rejects its use.

Comparative negligence generally is not used in reference to intentional torts to reduce the plaintiff's damages; thus, a defendant who commits an intentional tort may not use the argument that the plaintiff contributed to his own injuries. The defendant whose conduct is willful and wanton or reckless, however, may still rely on the defense of comparative negligence to reduce the plaintiff's recovery.

Most states adopting the comparative negligence approach have allowed for the reduction of the negligent plaintiff's recovery in cases in which the defendant violated a safety statute and was therefore negligent per se. Unlike contributory negligence, the same stance is taken even when the statute is designed to protect members of the plaintiff's class and to place all responsibility on the defendant. Some states, however, have denied apportionment, arguing that it would defeat the purpose of the statute in question.

The Minnesota courts, for example, have grappled with this issue. In one case the court refused to apply comparative negligence when a minor died after using glue given him by another minor, who had bought the glue from a retailer. The court reasoned that certain statutes, such as child labor statutes, statutes prohibiting the sale of dangerous articles to minors, and statutes protecting intoxicated persons, impose absolute liability because the purpose of these statutes is to protect certain classes of people from their inability to protect themselves. *Zerby v. Warren,* 210 N.W.2d 58 (Minn. 1973). Later, however, the court allowed comparative negligence when a minor was involved in a single-car accident after being served liquor at a party hosted by the defendants. Although the defendants had violated a statute prohibiting the furnishing of liquor to minors, the court deferred to legislative intent to allow the defense of contributory negligence in certain actions involving violations of statutes regulating liquor, including the statute prohibiting the furnishing of alcohol to persons under the age of twenty-one. *VanWagner v. Mattison,* 533 N.W.2d 75 (Minn. Ct. App. 1995).

To see how one court addressed some of the administrative concerns and legal questions outlined in this section, read the excerpt from *Li v. Yellow Cab Co.*

CASE

Li v. Yellow Cab Co.
532 P.2d 1226 (Cal. 1975)

We are thus brought to the second group of arguments which have been advanced by defendants and the amici curiae supporting their position. Generally speaking, such arguments expose considerations of a practical nature which, it is urged, counsel against the adoption of a rule of comparative negligence in this state even if such adoption is possible by judicial means.

The most serious of these considerations are those attendant upon the administration of a rule of comparative negligence in cases involving multiple parties. One such problem may arise when all responsible parties are not brought before the court: it may be difficult for the jury to evaluate relative negligence in such circumstances, and to compound this difficulty such an evaluation would not be res judicata in a subsequent suit against the absent wrongdoer. Problems of contribution and indemnity among joint tortfeasors lurk in the background.

A second and related major area of concern involves the administration of the actual process of fact-finding in a comparative negligence system. The assigning of a specific percentage factor to the amount of negligence attributable to a particular party, while in theory a matter of little difficulty, can become a matter of perplexity in the face of hard facts. The temptation for the jury to resort to a quotient verdict in such circumstances can be great . . . . These inherent difficulties are not, however, insurmountable. Guidelines might be provided the jury which will assist it in keeping focussed upon the true inquiry . . . and the utilization of special verdicts or jury interrogatories can be of invaluable assistance in assuring that the jury has approached its sensitive and often complex task with proper standards and appropriate reverence . . . .

The third area of concern, the status of the doctrines of last clear chance and assumption of risk, involves less the practical problems of administering a particular form of comparative negligence than it does a definition of the theoretical outline of the specific form to be adopted. Although several states which apply comparative negligence concepts retain the last clear chance doctrine . . . , the better reasoned position seems to be that when true comparative negligence is adopted, the need for last clear chance as a palliative of the hardships of the "all-or-nothing" rule disappears and its retention results only in a windfall to the plaintiff in direct contravention of the principle of liability in proportion to fault . . . . As for assumption of risk, we have recognized in this state that this defense overlaps that of contributory negligence to some extent and in fact is made up of at least two distinct defenses. "To simplify greatly, it has been observed . . . that in one kind of situation, to wit, where a plaintiff unreasonably undertakes to encounter a specific known risk imposed by a defendant's negligence, plaintiff's conduct, although he may encounter that risk in a prudent manner, is in reality a form of contributory negligence . . . . Other kinds of situations within the doctrine of assumption of risk are those, for example, where plaintiff is held to agree to relieve defendant of an obligation of reasonable conduct toward him. Such a situation would not involve contributory negligence, but rather a reduction of defendant's duty of care." . . . We think it clear that the adoption of a system of comparative negligence should entail the merger of the defense of assumption of risk into the general scheme of assessment of liability in proportion to fault in those particular cases in which the form of assumption of risk involved is no more than a variant of contributory negligence . . . .

Finally there is the problem of the treatment of willful misconduct under a system of comparative negligence. In jurisdictions following the "all-or-nothing" rule, contributory negligence is no defense to an action based upon a claim of willful misconduct . . . and this is the present rule in California . . . .[19] As Dean Prosser has observed, "[this] is in reality a rule of comparative fault which is being applied, and the court is refusing to set up the lesser fault against the greater." . . . The thought is that the difference between willful and wanton misconduct and ordinary negligence is one of kind rather than degree in that the former involves conduct of an entirely different order,[20] and under this conception it might well be urged that comparative negligence concepts should have no application when one of the parties has been guilty of willful and wanton misconduct. It has been persuasively argued, however, that the loss of deterrent effect that would occur upon application of comparative fault concepts to willful and wanton misconduct as well as ordinary negligence would be slight, and that a comprehensive system of comparative negligence should allow for the apportionment of damages in all cases involving misconduct which falls short of being intentional . . . . The law of punitive damages remains a separate consideration . . . .

The existence of the foregoing areas of difficulty and uncertainty (as well as others which we have not here mentioned . . . has not diminished our conviction that the time for a revision of the means for dealing with contributory fault in this state is long past due and that it lies within the province of this court to initiate the needed change by our decision in this case. Two of the indicated areas (i.e., multiple parties and willful misconduct) are not involved in the case before us, and we consider it neither necessary nor wise to address ourselves to specific problems of this nature which might be expected to arise.

---

19. BAJI No. 3.52 (1971 re-revision) currently provides: "Contributory negligence of a plaintiff is not a bar to his recovery for an injury caused by the wilful or wanton misconduct of a defendant. ( ) Wilful or wanton misconduct is intentional wrongful conduct, done either with knowledge, express or implied, that serious injury to another will probably result, or with a wanton and reckless disregard of the possible results. An intent to injure is not a necessary element of wilful or wanton misconduct. ( ) To prove such misconduct it is not necessary to establish that defendant himself recognized his conduct as dangerous. It is sufficient if it be established that a reasonable man under the same or similar circumstances would be aware of the dangerous character of such conduct."
20. "Disallowing the contributory negligence defense in this context is different from last clear chance; the defense is denied not because defendant had the last opportunity to avoid the accident but rather because defendant's conduct was so culpable it was different in 'kind' from the plaintiff's. The basis is culpability rather than causation."

As the Florida court stated with respect to the same subject, "it is not the proper function of this Court to decide unripe issues, without the benefit of adequate briefing, not involving an actual controversy, and unrelated to a specific factual situation." Our previous comments relating to the remaining two areas of concern (i.e., the status of the doctrines of last clear chance and assumption of risk, and the matter of judicial supervision of the finder of fact) have provided sufficient guidance to enable the trial courts of this state to meet and resolve particular problems in this area as they arise. As we have indicated, last clear chance and assumption of risk (insofar as the latter doctrine is but a variant of contributory negligence) are to be subsumed under the general process of assessing liability in proportion to fault, and the matter of jury supervision we leave for the moment within the broad discretion of the trial courts.

Our decision in this case is to be viewed as a first step in what we deem to be a proper and just direction, not as a compendium containing the answers to all questions that may be expected to arise. Pending future judicial or legislative developments, we are content for the present to assume the position taken by the Florida court in this matter: "We feel the trial judges of this State are capable of applying (a) comparative negligence rule without our setting guidelines in anticipation of expected problems. The problems are more appropriately resolved at the trial level in a practical manner instead of theoretical solution at the appellate level. The trial judges are granted broad discretion in adopting such procedures as may accomplish the objectives and purposes expressed in this opinion." . . .

It remains to identify the precise form of comparative negligence which we now adopt for application in this state. Although there are many variants, only the two basic forms need be considered here. The first of these, the so-called "pure" form of comparative negligence, apportions liability in direct proportion to fault in all cases. This was the form adopted by the Supreme Court of Florida in *Hoffman v. Jones,* and it applies by statute in Mississippi, Rhode Island, and Washington. Moreover it is the form favored by most scholars and commentators . . . . The second basic form of comparative negligence, of which there are several variants, applies apportionment based on fault up to the point at which the plaintiff's negligence is equal to or greater than that of the defendant—when that point is reached, plaintiff is barred from recovery. Nineteen states have adopted this form or one of its variants by statute. The principal argument advanced in its favor is moral in nature: that it is not morally right to permit one more at fault in an accident to recover from one less at fault. Other arguments assert the probability of increased insurance, administrative, and judicial costs if a "pure" rather than a "50 percent" system is adopted, but this has been seriously questioned . . . .

We have concluded that the "pure" form of comparative negligence is that which should be adopted in this state. In our view the "50 percent" system simply shifts the lottery aspect of the contributory negligence rule[21] to a different ground. As Dean Prosser has noted, under such a system "[i]t is obvious that a slight difference in the proportionate fault may permit a recovery; and there has been much justified criticism of a rule under which a plaintiff who is charged with 49 percent of a total negligence recovers 51 percent of his damages, while one who is charged with 50 percent recovers nothing at all."[22] . . . In effect "such a rule distorts the very principle it recognizes, i.e., that persons are responsible for their acts to the extent their fault contributes to an injurious result. The partial rule simply lowers, but does not eliminate, the bar of contributory negligence." . . .

We also consider significant the experience of the State of Wisconsin, which until recently was considered the leading exponent of the "50 percent" system. There

21. "The rule that contributory fault bars completely is a curious departure from the central principle of nineteenth century Anglo-American tort law—that wrongdoers should bear the losses they cause. Comparative negligence more faithfully serves that central principle by causing the wrongdoers to share the burden of resulting losses in reasonable relation to their wrongdoing, rather than allocating the heavier burden to the one who, as luck would have it, happened to be more seriously injured." . . .

22. This problem is compounded when the injurious result is produced by the combined negligence of several parties. For example in a three-car collision a plaintiff whose negligence amounts to one-third or more recovers nothing; in a four-car collision the plaintiff is barred if his negligence is only one-quarter of the total . . . .

that system led to numerous appeals on the narrow but crucial issue whether plaintiff's negligence was equal to defendant's . . . . Numerous reversals have resulted on this point, leading to the development of arcane classifications of negligence according to quality and category . . . . This finally led to a frontal attack on the system . . . wherein the state supreme court was urged to replace the statutory "50 percent" rule by a judicially declared "pure" comparative negligence rule. The majority of the court rejected this invitation, concluding that the Legislature had occupied the field, but three concurring justices and one dissenter indicated their willingness to accept it if the Legislature failed to act with reasonable dispatch. The dissenting opinion of Chief Justice Hallows . . . stands as a persuasive testimonial in favor of the "pure" system. We wholeheartedly embrace its reasoning . . . .

For all of the foregoing reasons we conclude that the "all-or-nothing" rule of contributory negligence as it presently exists in this state should be and is herewith superseded by a system of "pure" comparative negligence, the fundamental purpose of which shall be to assign responsibility and liability for damage in direct proportion to the amount of negligence of each of the parties. Therefore, in all actions for negligence resulting in injury to person or property, the contributory negligence of the person injured in person or property shall not bar recovery, but the damages awarded shall be diminished in proportion to the amount of negligence attributable to the person recovering. The doctrine of last clear chance is abolished, and the defense of assumption of risk is also abolished to the extent that it is merely a variant of the former doctrine of contributory negligence; both of these are to be subsumed under the general process of assessing liability in proportion to negligence. Pending future judicial or legislative developments, the trial courts of this state are to use broad discretion in seeking to assure that the principle stated is applied in the interest of justice and in furtherance of the purposes and objectives set forth in this opinion . . . .

Your client, a motorcyclist, was involved in a motor vehicle accident in which he was seriously injured. He was not wearing a helmet at the time of the accident.

1. Under the laws of your state, could he recover damages if he was found to be contributorily negligent?
2. Could he recover if a jury found him to be 50 percent responsible for his injuries?
3. If another vehicle were involved as well, could your client recover if a jury found him to be 40 percent responsible and the other two defendants each 30 percent responsible for his injuries?
4. How would the jury be instructed if a nonparty were partially responsible for your client's injuries?
5. Will the jury be instructed that your client's contribution should be determined on the basis of how much his conduct contributed to his injuries or on the basis of how much his conduct deviated from a reasonable standard of care?
6. Could the defendant claim comparative negligence if his lack of care in driving was considered willful and wanton?
7. Could your client use the last clear chance doctrine?

ASSUMPTION OF RISK

A plaintiff who volunteers to take the chance that harm will occur is said to have *assumed the risk*. Under the common law such a plaintiff was completely barred from recovery. Most courts today have discontinued that practice but do take into account the plaintiff's assumption of risk when determining how to apportion damages.

Comparison to Contributory Negligence

Some states have in effect abolished the doctrine and consider assumption of risk to be a form of contributory negligence. The justification behind this merger is that often a plaintiff who has assumed the risk has also been contributorily negligent. A plaintiff who voluntarily but unreasonably decides to take a risk can also be said to have behaved in a negligent manner.

In some situations, however, a plaintiff is not negligent simply because he has assumed the risk. If the plaintiff's decision to entertain a risk is reasonable in light of the circumstances, he will not be considered negligent, particularly if few options are available to him other than engaging in risky behavior. Suppose a father uses a car with defective brakes because it is the only car available to him and he must use it to get his seriously injured child to the hospital. He has assumed the risk even though he has not acted negligently. In situations such as this, the defense of assumption of risk can be raised even though the defense of contributory negligence cannot.

Differences Between Contributory Negligence and Assumption of Risk

Some states have extended assumption of risk to any situation in which the plaintiff voluntarily exposes herself to a known risk. The definition of voluntary exposure goes beyond the concept of consenting to a risk and further blurs the distinction between assumption of risk and contributory negligence (see Figure 9-5). To get around this ambiguity some courts have characterized

FIGURE 9-5 Differences Between Assumption of Risk and Contributory Negligence

CONTRIBUTORY NEGLIGENCE	ASSUMPTION OF RISK
Characterized as "recklessness."	Characterized as "adventurousness."
Plaintiff compared to reasonable person. (objective standard)	Did plaintiff understand risk? (subjective standard)
Not a defense to reckless conduct.	Is a defense to reckless conduct.
Not generally a defense in strict liability cases.	Is a defense in strict liability cases.

contributory negligence as "carelessness" and assumption of risk as "adventurousness." A plaintiff who deliberately walks down defective steps when others, only slightly more inconvenient, are available may voluntarily assume the risk of confronting a known hazard, even though she exercises due care on the stairs. Such a plaintiff is said to assume the risk but not to be contributorily negligent if assumption of risk is defined as adventurousness (*Hunn v. Windsor Hotel Co.,* 119 W. Va. 215, 193 S.E. 57 (1937)).

If the plaintiff's conduct constitutes both assumption of risk and contributory negligence, the defendant can choose to assert either defense or, in some jurisdictions, both. In deciding which of the defenses to raise, the defendant should consider the standards used to assess the plaintiff's conduct. An objective standard is used to assess the reasonableness of the plaintiff's conduct in the case of contributory negligence. A subjective standard is used in cases involving assumption of risk. It requires that the plaintiff actually have understood the risk that he undertook and not merely that a reasonable person would have understood.

Contributory negligence cannot be raised as a defense if the defendant is reckless and cannot generally be used as a defense in strict liability cases. Conversely, assumption of risk can be used as a defense of reckless conduct and in strict liability cases.

Comparative Negligence and Assumption of Risk

Those states that have adopted comparative negligence statutes have, for all intents and purposes, removed assumption of risk as a separate defense and have merged it, in part at least, into the defense of comparative negligence. Therefore, a plaintiff who unreasonably places himself in danger is considered negligent and his recovery is reduced although not barred completely. If his conduct in exposing himself to the danger is reasonable, he is not considered negligent at all.

Express Assumption of Risk

A plaintiff can either expressly or impliedly assume the risk. A plaintiff who signs a release in which she agrees to assume all risk of injury to herself and her property has expressly assumed the risk. Even an express agreement, however, may not be enforced by the courts if the defendant has unusual bargaining power, if she is the sole or unique provider of a service, and if she uses her power to compel the plaintiff to waive liability.

By the same token, agreements involving common carriers, public utilities, or other regulated industries are unlikely to be enforced. The courts usually feel that such entities are obligated to provide reasonable service and will not allow them to escape their responsibility through the use of waivers.

A plaintiff must actually be aware of any risk he is said to have assumed. If a limitation on liability is buried in fine print where the plaintiff is unlikely to see it, it will not be binding on him. Additionally, waivers of liability are valid only in reference to the defendant's negligence and not for his intentional tortious acts nor for his gross or willful and wanton negligence. One area in which the courts are unwilling to uphold a waiver, no matter how well informed that waiver is, is in the field of medical care. Agreements, for example, in which patients waive potential malpractice claims in exchange for reduced fees are unenforceable.

A release must be expressed in clear, unequivocal language. To see how the enforceability of releases is generally viewed, consider *Gross v. Sweet,* 400 N.E.2d 306 (N.Y. 1979), in which the plaintiff signed a release prior to his first practice jump while enrolled in the defendant's parachute training school:

I, the undersigned, hereby and by these covenants, do waive any and all claims that I, my heirs, and/or assignees may have against Nathaniel Sweet, the Stormville Parachute Center, the Jumpmaster, and the Pilot who shall operate the aircraft when used for the purpose of parachute jumping for any personal injuries or property damage that I may sustain or which may arise out of my learning, practicing or actually jumping from an aircraft. I also assume full responsibility for any damage that I may do or cause while participating in this sport.

The Gross court explained that the intention of the parties must be expressed in "unmistakable language" for an exculpatory clause to insulate a party from liability for his own negligent acts. For a release to be enforceable, the court said it must be expressed in "unmistakable language," and it must be plainly and precisely apparent that "the limitation of liability extends to negligence or other fault of the party attempting to shed his ordinary responsibility." Although the term negligence need not be used, words conveying a similar meaning must appear. The court found the quoted release to be unenforceable because its "opaque terminology" did not reveal that plaintiff released defendant from liability for injury that might result from defendant's failure to use due care.

Implied Assumption of Risk

A plaintiff is said to have impliedly assumed the risk when her conduct shows that she was aware of the risk in question and voluntarily agreed to bear that risk herself. Suppose a plaintiff watches as her friend mounts the defendant's horse and is subsequently bucked off. If the plaintiff then climbs aboard the same horse she will have impliedly assumed the risk for any injuries she sustains.

For this principle to be applicable the plaintiff must actually be aware of the particular risk in question. It is not enough that the plaintiff merely should have known of the risk involved. The plaintiff must also voluntarily consent to the risk. Consent is not voluntary if the plaintiff had no reasonable choice but to confront a danger.

The consent principle is colorfully illustrated in a case in which the plaintiff, who was a tenant of the defendant, fell through a hole in the outhouse floor when she submitted to a "call of nature." The court held that the plaintiff did not voluntarily assume the risk, even though she was aware of the defective floor, because she had no choice but to use the facilities at her disposal. The court concluded that she was under no legal obligation to seek other facilities (*Rush v. Commercial Realty Co.,* 145 A. 476 (N.J. 1929)). If the plaintiff in this case had had a reasonable alternative, such as another intact outhouse on the same property, she might have been held to have assumed the risk.

In sports and recreation the inherent risks involved are known by the parties, who are free to either engage in the activity or not. Those who sponsor or organize such activities are obligated to use reasonable care to make conditions as safe as they appear, but as long as the risks are fully understood or perfectly obvious, the plaintiff will be deemed to have assumed the risk. Furthermore, professional athletes are assumed to be more cognizant of the risks and more willing to accept them (because of the monies involved) than amateurs. Therefore, when a professional jockey was severely injured when his horse tripped over the heels of another horse, causing the jockey to be thrown, the court concluded that the jockey had assumed the risk and did not allow him to recover from the jockey of the other horse or the track owner. The court found that the jockey was aware of the dangers of speeding horses changing position and bumping each other during a race and of the track conditions and the dangers associated with them, especially as he had participated in three prior races at the track on the day of the accident. *Turcotte v. Fell,* 502 N.E.2d 964 (N.Y. 1986).

What if a plaintiff protests against being asked to assume a risk but ultimately agrees to do so? In most cases the courts will hold that he waived his objection and assumed the risk. Even if the risk the plaintiff is exposed to is not created by the defendant, he is still considered to have voluntarily accepted the risk. A plaintiff who is badly injured in an accident and who requests that the defendant drive him to the hospital, despite his knowledge that the defendant's car has bad brakes, assumes the risk of injury caused by the defective brakes. Although the risk involved is not due to the defendant's wrongdoing, the plaintiff is still deemed to have assumed the risk (Restatement (Second) of Torts § 496E, illus. 1).

PUTTING IT INTO PRACTICE 9.3

1. Why are the waivers on the back of event tickets generally not enforceable?
2. A tennis umpire is struck on the head by a ball during a match. A wrongful death suit is filed alleging that the rules required the umpire to stand in a position of danger and thereby increased his risk of being injured. Did the umpire assume the risk?
3. Do you think someone who flails around in the mosh pit (an area in the front of the stage where concert attendees engage in various types of wild activities, such as body slamming) should be able to recover for his injuries, or has he assumed the risk of injury?
4. In 1993 several former waitresses at the restaurant "Hooters" sued the chain for sexual harassment, alleging that Hooters established a work environment in which its customers felt free to make sexual comments and advances to the waitresses. Examples of the offensive nature of the work environment included the name of the restaurant ("Hooters," a slang term for women's breasts) as well as the sexually provocative uniforms the waitresses were required to wear. Do you think assumption of risk should be allowed as a defense to hostile work environment sexual harassment claims such as these?

IMMUNITIES

Immunity is a complete defense to tort liability in that it completely absolves the defendant of all liability. It is granted to those entities that bear a particular relationship to the plaintiff, such as a spouse, or who occupy a status, such as that of a governmental or charitable entity (see Figure 9-6).

Govermental Immunity

Federal Government

Under the common law the immunity of the king was based on the precept that "the king can do no wrong." American courts applied this adage early by adopting the principle that the United States government could not be sued without its consent. To get around this principle Congress passed private bills authorizing particular plaintiffs to sue on certain claims. Obviously this process created considerable inconvenience for Congress. The fear of being inundated by thousands of private bills upon the return of servicemen after World War II prompted Congress in 1946 to pass the Federal Tort Claims Act (FTCA).

In general the FTCA provides that money damages can be recovered against the United States "for injury or loss of property or personal injury or death caused

FIGURE 9-6 Immunities

GOVERNMENTAL IMMUNITIES	PARENT-CHILD IMMUNITY
• Federal government immunity (limited by Federal Tort Claims Act) • State government immunity • Local government immunity (for governmental but not proprietary functions) • Public official immunity	• Abolished in majority of states and limited in others today

INTERSPOUSAL IMMUNITY	CHARITABLE IMMUNITY
• Abolished by majority of states today	• Abolished in some states and limited in others today

by the negligent or wrongful act or omission of any employee of the government while acting within the scope of his office or employment, under circumstances where the United States, if a private person, would be liable to the claimant" (28 U.S.C. § 1346(B)). Thousands of claims are filed against the federal government each year, more than half of which arise out of automobile accidents.

Several exceptions limit the scope of the FTCA. The United States is not liable, for example, for intentional torts, such as assault, battery, false imprisonment, false arrest, abuse of process, or malicious prosecution except when they are committed by federal law enforcement officials. Questions regarding interpretation often arise when construing what types of claims should and should not be permitted under the FTCA. In one case, for example, a surgeon in a veterans hospital operated on the wrong hip and leg of the plaintiff and the court found no liability under the FTCA because, technically, under the law of Minnesota, the surgeon had committed a battery, which is excluded under the FTCA (*Moos v. United States*, 118 F. Supp. 275 (D. Minn. 1954)).

One of the most troubling exclusions to the FTCA pertains to a federal agency's or federal employee's exercise or failure to exercise a **discretionary function** or duty. No liability exists when a discretionary function is involved, even if that discretion is abused (28 U.S.C. § 2680(A)). Deciding what constitutes a discretionary function has caused the courts considerable grief. The United States Supreme Court has provided some guidance by indicating that discretion is involved "where there is room for policy judgment and decision" (*Dalehite v. United States*, 346 U.S. 15, 34–36 (1953)).

Furthermore, discretionary functions occur at the planning stages. In *Dalehite* an explosion occurred at a fertilizer exportation program run by the government. The Court held that decisions about how fertilizer was to be bagged and how the bags were to be labeled and transported were made at the planning level. Therefore, those who did the planning could have been found liable for negligence but the underlings who carried out the plans could not.

State Government

Traditionally, state governments enjoyed sovereign immunity as well, but today most of them have abolished it to some extent, either by statute or judicial decision. Many courts that have abolished governmental immunity have done so because of the availability of public liability insurance. Some have viewed taking responsibility for the torts of public employees as being part of the cost of administering a government. Regardless of the state's stance toward immunity, judges and legislators are almost never liable for their acts. Similarly, the making of "basic policy decisions" rarely results in liability (Restatement (Second) of Torts § 895B(3)).

States usually replace complete sovereign immunity with a statutory form of immunity, through some form of state tort claims act. Statutory limits are often placed on damages, thereby limiting plaintiffs' recovery. Many statutes require any person claiming to have been injured as a result of tortious conduct by a public entity or employee to file a written notice of the claim within a designated time period after the date of discovering the injury. Failure to comply with such notice requirements may forever bar any claim.

Local Government

Local governmental entities, such as police and fire departments, school systems, and public hospitals, have traditionally enjoyed at least partial immunity. The key legal argument that arises in the context of local government is whether the function being performed is a **governmental** or a **proprietary function.** A proprietary function is one that could be performed as well by a private corporation as by the government. A proprietary function is usually being performed in activities that produce revenue for the government, such as those carried out by gas and water utilities and city airports. Police and fire departments and school systems, in contrast, are almost exclusively involved in governmental functions.

Governmental functions are subject to immunity whereas proprietary functions are not. To date, many courts have abolished local government immunity or have allowed suit when liability insurance is available. Administrative policy decisions as well as judicial and legislative actions still enjoy immunity.

Public Officials

Legislators and judges, as well as some other public officials, receive complete immunity so long as the act complained of is within the scope of their duties. The rationale for this immunity is that a public official must be given free rein to carry out the difficult tasks of his or her office, unfettered by fear of being sued. Furthermore, by granting immunity competent people are not deterred from seeking public office out of fear of being sued. This protection extends even to those officials who are obviously operating out of a sense of greed or malice toward the plaintiff. Exception is made only when the official's act is outside the jurisdiction of the office.

To illustrate the extremes to which this doctrine can be taken, consider the Supreme Court decision involving a judge who ordered a fifteen-year-old plaintiff to be sterilized. The order was given as a result of a peti-

tion by the plaintiff's mother. No notice was given to the plaintiff nor did any statutory authorization exist for such a judicial order. Nevertheless, the court held that the judge did not act wholly beyond his jurisdiction and he was therefore immune from suit (*Stump v. Sparkman,* 435 U.S. 349 (1978)).

In some states high-ranking administrative officials receive the same complete immunity that legislators and judges do. In others they have limited immunity, which protects them only if they do not act in bad faith.

A public official's immunity is separate from governmental immunity. Therefore, if governmental immunity is abolished, the public official may still be protected by his or her own immunity. In contrast, even if the government is immune, the public official may still be liable. To illustrate, consider the amendments made by Congress to the Federal Tort Claims Act, making it the exclusive remedy for plaintiffs alleging torts committed by federal officers and employees, including those in the legislative and judicial branches, acting within the scope of their employment. Under these provisions plaintiffs must file suit against the United States only and not the employees individually, thus effectively rendering the employees immune from suit. Although these provisions do not prevent plaintiffs from suing, they substantially limit any chance of recovery because of the United States' immunity for "discretionary" functions.

Another provision of the Federal Tort Claims Act that limits recovery is one that limits liability of the government (and renders the employee immune) for any injuries arising out of a federal employee's operation of a motor vehicle. However, a very important act that *promotes* recovery when individuals' civil rights have been violated is the Civil Rights Act of 1871 (42 U.S.C. § 1983). Under this so-called *1983 action,* anyone who "under color of any statute, ordinance, regulation . . . of any state" violates the federal civil rights of any person "shall be liable to the party injured in an action at law." An inmate of a correctional institution, for example, may file a 1983 action against the state government, the correctional institution, and its employees if he is not provided adequate medical care while institutionalized. He must show that the employees were acting "under the color of state law," that they violated his constitutional right (in this case, the right to be protected from cruel and unusual punishment under the Eighth Amendment), that he suffered damages as a result of the employee's actions, and that the employees were not immune. Such 1983 actions are often relied upon when suing governmental officials like police officers and correctional officers.

The subject of immunity is a crucial one when deciding whom to sue. It is imperative before filing suit that you review applicable state or federal statutes as well as any case decisions pertaining to immunity. A case involving the state as a defendant that looks particularly appealing under the "deep pocket" theory (the theory that one should go after the defendant with the most money) can take on a different light when the issue of immunity is considered.

Interspousal Immunity

Under the common law spouses were immune from suit by their spouses and parents were immune from suit by their children. Spousal immunity arose out of the precept that a husband and wife were one entity and could not therefore sue each other. Consequently, a wife, for example, could not sue her husband if she was injured while a passenger in a car that he negligently drove.

The majority of states have now abolished interspousal immunity, rejecting the common law notion of the unity of the husband and wife as well as the arguments that allowing such suits would create family discord and encourage fraud. The claim that abolition of this immunity would result in a flood of litigation has not materialized. Some fraudulent cases have arisen in which the defendant spouse has failed to fully litigate a claim against him or her so that the other spouse could collect the insurance. But most courts have chosen to weed out those claims from the meritorious claims rather than bar all interspousal cases.

Even those states that have not completely abolished interspousal immunity have applied certain limitations. Some, for example, have abolished immunity in reference to automobile accidents or when the tort committed was intentional.

Parent-Child Immunity

Some of the same reasons given to justify interspousal immunity were also given under the common law to bar suits by children against their parents and vice versa. Briefly, the fear was that such suits would breed disharmony in the family, encourage collusion and fraud among family members, and create a flood of litigation.

Some states have chosen to abolish this immunity, particularly in cases involving motor vehicle accidents. The reason commonly given is that most suits are between a family and its insurance company and not between individual members of a family. Even in those states that have not abolished such immunity, many have allowed suit when the tort was intentional, when it involved loss of property or other pecuniary loss, when the injury occurred in the course of a business activity, when the child was legally emancipated or was a stepchild of the defendant, or when the parent-child relationship was terminated by the death of one of the parties prior to the suit. No immunity exists between siblings or in other family relationships.

One of the problems that can arise in the context of parent-child suits is the matter of negligent supervision. Consider the case of a child left unsupervised by her mother and who, as a result of this lack of supervision, is run over by the defendant. Should the defendant be allowed to bring a third-party claim against the plaintiff's mother for negligent failure to supervise the child? Some courts have said no, arguing that permitting such claims would in effect reduce the child's compensation by allowing the defendant to obtain contribution from the parent. Others have allowed such claims and have created a "reasonable parent" standard in determining the duty of supervision owed to a child.

Charitable Immunity

Charitable organizations, including educational and religious organizations, received immunity under the common law. The purpose of such immunity was to protect charitable institutions from tort claims and thereby promote their existence. Some courts have argued that the beneficiaries of charitable organizations impliedly waive their right to sue when they accept the benefits offered by that organization. Other courts have characterized this so-called *implied waiver theory* as a legal fiction that has no relevance in emergency situations, such as the receipt of emergency aid from a charitable hospital.

The other rationale used to justify charitable immunity is sometimes referred to as the *trust fund theory*. This theory is based on the premise that funds given for charitable purposes should not be used to pay judgments resulting from tort claims. The refutation of this argument is that the trust fund theory refers to how a judgment should be satisfied and not to the root question of whether an individual has a right to bring an action. In short, the argument goes, the question of liability should not be based on the charity's ability to satisfy a judgment.

The majority of states have abolished charitable immunity altogether; others have abolished it only in reference to charitable hospitals. Some, in deference to the trust fund theory, have allowed liability when liability insurance is available but have denied it when a judgment would have to be paid out of trust funds. Still others, relying on the rationale of the implied waiver theory, have allowed those who are not beneficiaries of the charity, such as employees or visitors, to sue.

■ PUTTING IT INTO PRACTICE 9.4 □

1. The coaches of a school athletics program are alleged to be negligent in causing injury and death to some football players as a result of heat prostration during team practice. The school charges admission to football games but the program has been operating at a net loss for the past five years. Can negligence actions be filed against the school district and the coaches?
2. An indigent defendant believes that his public defender failed to adequately represent him and that because of this lack of competent representation he was convicted. Can he sue the public defender under a § 1983 claim or, alternatively, under a theory of negligence (malpractice)?
3. An action is brought against the archdiocese of Newark for the reckless and negligent hiring of a priest who forced a child to engage in sexual conduct with him while attending a camp sponsored by the church. The child ultimately commits suicide and his brother, who attended the same camp, suffers medical problems as a result of feeling responsible for his brother's death. Can the parents recover for their damages and their children's damages?
4. A minor suffers mental and emotional harm as a result of being sexually assaulted by his father. Can he sue his father?

STATUTES OF LIMITATIONS AND STATUTES OF REPOSE

A **statute of limitations,** as the name indicates, is a statute limiting the time in which an action can be brought. Any action not commenced within that time period is barred. The purpose of such statutes is to protect individuals from having to defend stale claims. They also allow people to have some measure of stability and predictability in their lives by limiting the time frame in which they can anticipate being sued.

Because most statutes of limitations begin to run when a cause of action **accrues,** the question is when accrual takes place. Most courts have held that accrual occurs when there has been an actual injury to the plaintiff's person or property. Problems arise, however, when the plaintiff could not reasonably have discovered her injury until after the statute had run. Suppose, for example, that the statute of limitations on medical malpractice claims is five years but that the plaintiff did not begin to suffer complications from the medical procedures she underwent until six years later. By the time she discovered she had a cause of action she would be barred from pursuing it.

To mitigate the harshness of a statute that precludes recovery in a case such as this, many courts have created the so-called *discovery doctrine,* which provides that the statute does not begin to run until the injury is, or should have been, discovered. Many states apply this rule to all surgical cases, but some have limited it to claims that an object was left in the patient's body. Still others have held that the statute begins to run when the doctor-patient relationship terminates, regardless of whether the plaintiff has discovered her injury at that time.

Some have argued that the discovery doctrine contributes to the rising cost of medical malpractice insurance. Many policies cover a physician's conduct during a particular year even though a claim based on that conduct may not arise for several years. As a result of the actuarial projections necessitated by this type of policy, premiums are very high. Arguably, premiums could be reduced if policies were issued on a claims-made basis so that only those claims filed against the physician that year, regardless of when the act of malpractice occurred, would be covered. Alternatively, some argue that a maximum time limit should be set for discovery under the discovery doctrine.

A similar issue arises in the case of malpractice by lawyers and other professionals. When should the statute of limitations begin to run when a lawyer negligently prepares a will? What if a latent construction defect does not show up until many years after the completion of construction? In some states the discovery doctrine has been applied.

It is important to consult the statutes in your state to determine the applicable statute of limitations and to ascertain when a cause of action accrues. This is one of the first questions that an attorney must answer when deciding whether to take a case. Failure to determine the appropriate statute of limitations could be grounds for malpractice.

Whereas the statute of limitations begins to run at the time of injury, a **statute of repose** begins to run at the date of sale of a product. Such statutes are designed to limit a manufacturer's liability, to lower insurance costs for manufacturers, and to introduce a sense of certainty in the area of product liability litigation. Most statutes of repose are five to twelve years and in some cases may bar suit even before injury occurs. As a practical matter, however, few suits are actually prevented, as few plaintiffs are injured by old, defective products. The effects are devastating, however, to certain victims, such as those who were injured by DES or asbestos or by some kinds of long-lasting machinery. Some courts have found statutes of repose to be constitutionally impermissible.

■ PUTTING IT INTO PRACTICE 9.5 □

1. Pam consults with an attorney after she is severely injured in an automobile accident. The attorney convinces her to settle out of court for $100,000. Ten years later, when she is having her will done by another attorney, she mentions her personal injury case and the name of the attorney who represented her. She

Continued on next page

PUTTING IT INTO PRACTICE 9.5—Continued

discovers that the attorney was subsequently disbarred for unethical conduct, specifically relating to his collusive agreements with a particular insurance company. She also finds out that the actual value of her case was probably closer to $1 million. Under the statute of limitations in your state, can she sue her former attorney and the firm for which he worked?

2. John buys a defective airgun and is injured. He does not realize until ten years later that he has a claim against the manufacturer. Under the laws of your state, can he still sue?

APPLICATION

The Baxters will likely claim that Teddy and Mr. Goodright were contributorily negligent. If they prevail in this claim and they live in a contributory negligence state, both Teddy and Mr. Goodright will be precluded from recovering. If, however, they live in a comparative negligence state, their recoveries will be reduced in direct proportion to their percentage of negligence. Whereas Teddy would likely be found negligent, Mr. Goodright would probably not be found negligent as long as he acted reasonably in rescuing Teddy. The last clear chance doctrine is inapplicable because the Baxters were not present during the time of the attack on Teddy and Mr. Baxter did everything he could to rescue Mr. Goodright when he became aware of Gertrude's attack.

Arguably Teddy impliedly assumed the risk by going into the Baxter's backyard, as he was aware of Gertrude's presence and of her propensity to attack. The defendants will have to prove, however, that Teddy actually knew that there was a risk and not merely that he ought to have known. Again, because of his classification as a rescuer, Mr. Goodright will probably be successful in rebutting any claim that he assumed the risk.

As a result of the consideration of the defenses that can be raised in this case, it is likely that Teddy's attorney will opt for a strict liability claim if at all possible.

Remember that contributory negligence is generally not a defense to strict liability, although assumption of risk will usually be a complete defense. Nevertheless, assumption of risk requires subjective proof, putting the burden on the Baxters to show that Teddy knew the risk that he was confronting. The Baxters' task in proving assumption of risk would be more difficult than proving contributory negligence, in which an objective standard would be used to evaluate Teddy's conduct.

Although no immunities could be raised as defenses, consideration of the applicable statute of limitations would be important. If Teddy and Mr. Goodright "sat" on their cases for a considerable period of time, their attorneys would be required to conduct their initial investigations expeditiously and file immediately before the statute of limitations ran. If the attorneys failed to file in a timely manner and their clients were precluded from filing due to the statute of limitations, the attorneys would be subject to malpractice claims.

SUMMARY

The three defenses most commonly raised in negligence cases are contributory negligence, comparative negligence, and assumption of risk. Because the contributory negligence rule is sometimes viewed as harsh and unjust, courts have developed various escape mechanisms by which plaintiffs can avoid this rule.

The most significant exception to the contributory negligence defense is the last clear chance doctrine. This doctrine does not apply if neither the defendant nor the plaintiff discovers the danger as a result of their inattentiveness. The doctrine is also inapplicable if the defendant's act of negligence precedes the plaintiff's predicament and precludes him or her from avoiding the accident after discovering the plaintiff's peril.

Contributory negligence cannot be used as a defense against an intentional tort. Nor is it allowed if the defendant's conduct was willful and wanton or reckless unless the plaintiff's conduct was also willful and wanton or reckless. Contributory negligence can be raised in the case of negligence per se unless the statute on which the defendant's negligence is based was enacted solely to protect a class of persons of which the plaintiff is a member and the statute's intent was to place sole responsibility on the defendant.

All but a few states have adopted a comparative negligence system. Under a pure comparative negligence system the plaintiff recovers regardless of the extent of his or her negligence. Under the 50 percent approach, a plaintiff's claim is barred if his or her negligence is either as great as or not greater than the defendant's negligence. Difficulty is often encountered in assigning fault to the parties, particularly when there are more parties involved than just the plaintiff and defendant.

As with contributory negligence, comparative negligence cannot be raised as a defense to an intentional tort. It can be raised if the defendant's conduct was willful and wanton, reckless, or negligent per se. Some jurisdictions continue to apply the last clear chance doctrine, although the Uniform Comparative Fault Act expressly rejects its use in a comparative negligence system.

The distinction between contributory negligence and assumption of risk is often blurred. Contributory negligence is sometimes characterized as "carelessness" whereas assumption of risk is sometimes perceived as "adventurousness." In the defense of contributory negligence, an objective standard is used; in assumption of risk a subjective standard is relied on. Assumption of risk, unlike contributory negligence, can be used as a defense to reckless conduct and in a case of strict liability.

A plaintiff can either expressly or impliedly assume the risk. An express waiver will not be enforced if the defendant has unusual bargaining power or if the plaintiff is unaware of the risk. In terms of implied consent the plaintiff will not be considered to have acted voluntarily if she had no reasonable choice but to confront the danger. Those states that have adopted comparative negligence have, to some degree, removed assumption of risk as a separate defense.

Immunity is a complete defense to tort liability. Immunity of federal government officials has been curtailed by the Federal Tort Claims Act. Federal officials performing discretionary functions are immune from suit. State governments traditionally enjoyed sovereign immunity although most states have abolished it to some extent. Local governmental entities have enjoyed at least partial immunity. Immunity is typically granted for governmental functions but not allowed for proprietary functions. Legislators, judges, and some other public officials receive complete immunity as long as they are acting within the scope of their duties.

The majority of states have now abolished interspousal immunity, or at the least have imposed various limitations on such immunity. Similarly, some states have chosen to abolish parent-child immunity. Charitable immunity has been abolished altogether in the majority of states. Some courts have adhered to the trust fund theory and have denied liability if the judgment would have to be paid out of trust funds. Still other courts have adhered to the implied waiver theory and have allowed recovery only to those who are not beneficiaries of the charity.

Statutes of limitations and statutes of repose prevent the bringing of stale claims and allow some measure of stability and predictability in people's lives. The key question that arises in reference to these statutes is the question of accrual. Under the discovery doctrine a statute does not begin to run until the injury is or should have been discovered. A statute of repose begins to run at the date of sale of a product.

PRACTICE POINTERS
PREPARING A DEFENSE

Paralegals often participate in the discovery process, which (if you represent the defendant) involves gathering information that supports your client's defense. This process includes:

- Sending out interrogatories and requests for production of documents
- Setting up depositions
- Interviewing witnesses
- Requesting the plaintiff to sign medical release authorizations (which allow the release of medical records by doctors and other medical providers)
- Checking with the county recorder's office and the clerk's office to determine if the plaintiff has been involved in other suits
- Checking Motor Vehicle Department records (to determine vehicle ownership, for example)

Once the requested records are assembled, medical records, accident reports, repair records and the records of the major medical insurance carrier must be reviewed to determine:

- The nature, type, and extent of the plaintiff's injuries
- The existence of preexisting injuries and any claims relating to those injuries
- The names, addresses, and phone numbers of potential witnesses
- The treatments the plaintiff has received and the prognosis for recovery

Medical Records

To secure medical records and the records of the plaintiff's medical insurance carrier, interrogatories must be sent out to identify the plaintiff's treating physicians both before and after the accident. These doctors are then contacted to find out if any advance fees are required before the records will be copied. Medical authorization requests are sent to the plaintiff's attorney with a request to have the plaintiff sign them. If the plaintiff complies, these forms are submitted to the appropriate physicians. If the plaintiff refuses to sign the medical authorization requests and the procedural rules permit such a refusal, the records are subpoenaed using a subpoena duces tecum and a notice of deposition, which are sent to the custodian of the medical records. A notice of deposition follows, along with a letter stating that if the custodian voluntarily agrees to submit the records, he or she need not appear at the deposition. The custodian must sign an affidavit affirming that all of the requested records have been sent and must return the affidavit along with the records (all of which must be returned before the date of the deposition).

Police Records and Other Official Records

To obtain accident reports, you must send a written request to the law enforcement agency and enclose any required fees. Many agencies require forms to be filled out and some require that a need be established before the records will be provided, because the records may not be available to the public. A similar process must

Continued on next page

PRACTICE POINTERS—Continued

often be followed to secure death certificates (usually from a department of health services), motor vehicle registration records, and driver's license information.

County Recorder's Office and Court Clerk's Office

Become familiar with the location, procedures, and personnel in the county recorder's office and the court clerk's office. Paralegals often are asked to obtain records and file documents with these offices. Find out if the records in these offices are available online and whether this service is free or subscription-based.

TORT TEASERS

1. The so-called "seat belt defense" is used by defense counsel to argue that the plaintiff was contributorily negligent or negligent per se in his failure to wear a seat belt. Assume you are representing a defendant in a motor vehicle accident case and argue: (a) the plaintiff was contributorily negligent; (b) the plaintiff was comparatively negligent; (c) the plaintiff assumed the risk; (d) the plaintiff failed to mitigate his damages; and (e) the plaintiff was negligent per se. Be as specific as possible in terms of the type of legal argument you would want to make and the type of evidence that you would want to introduce. Would you rather argue that the plaintiff contributed to his own injuries or that he assumed the risk? Why?

Then assume you are representing the plaintiff and argue that the seat belt defense is inappropriate. In your arguments consider whether the plaintiff has a duty to use a seat belt and whether his failure to do so constitutes the proximate cause of the accident. Furthermore, you might want to consider when the plaintiff's duty to mitigate his damages arises.

2. A state Board of Pardons and Paroles grants parole to an individual despite information that he is an extremely dangerous person and has a definite potential for violence. The parolee subsequently kills one person and seriously injures another. The injured man and the parents of the deceased file a personal injury and wrongful death suit against the Board of Pardon and Paroles. The board argues that it and its individual members enjoy absolute immunity from civil suit for decisions granting parole. In the alternative the board argues for qualified immunity. Discuss whether the same type of immunity that is given to judges should be granted to a Board of Pardons and Paroles. If granted qualified immunity, should such immunity extend to the grossly negligent release of a highly dangerous prisoner? *Grimm v. Arizona Board of Pardons & Paroles,* 564 P.2d 1227 (Ariz. 1977).

3. The plaintiff, a participant in a "National Lap Sitting Contest" promoting wrinkle-free slacks, is injured when the chair in which he is sitting collapses because he was holding fourteen girls on his lap. What defenses do you think should be raised in this case and why? *Wyly v. Burlington Industries,* 452 F.2d 807 (5th Cir. 1971).

KEY TERMS

Accrual
Time at which a statute of limitations begins to run, usually at the time the plaintiff is injured.

Assumption of risk
Defense that the plaintiff voluntarily consented to take the chance that harm would occur if he or she engaged in certain conduct.

Comparative negligence
Defense that the plaintiff's recovery should be reduced in direct proportion to the plaintiff's percentage of contribution to his or her own injuries.

Contributory negligence
Defense that the plaintiff contributed to his or her own injuries and should therefore be barred from recovery.

Discretionary function
Act of a government employee requiring the use of judgment.

Governmental function
Task typically performed by a governmental entity.

Immunity
Absolute defense derived from the defendant's status (e.g., a government official) or relationship to the plaintiff (e.g., spouse of the plaintiff).

Last clear chance doctrine
Doctrine that allows the plaintiff to recover in a contributory negligence system despite the plaintiff's negligence.

Proprietary function
Function performed by the government that could just as easily be performed by a private entity.

Statute of limitations
Statute that limits the time period in which a claim can be filed.

Statute of repose
Statute of limitations in product liability cases that limits the time period during which suit can be filed.

CHAPTER

10

Malpractice

CHAPTER OBJECTIVES

In this chapter you will learn to:
- Explain the standard of care to which a professional is held
- Identify ways in which professional negligence is committed
- Explain the informed consent doctrine
- Recognize defenses that can be raised in response to a professional negligence claim
- Appreciate the reasons for the increase in professional negligence claims

The attorney by whom you have just been hired is a recent law school graduate. Early in his career, he discovers, through personal experience, many of the legal land mines on which an attorney can step. First, he advises a woman who was injured in an automobile accident that she has no viable cause of action. Two days after the statute of limitations runs out, she consults with another attorney on a separate matter. This attorney advises her that she did indeed have a good cause of action for which she probably could have netted a considerable recovery.

Next, unaware of the malpractice noose now dangling over his head, your attorney blithely decides not to relay a settlement offer to another client because in his opinion the client should not accept the offer. When the case goes to trial the client is awarded less than he would have received under the terms of the offer. The client is most displeased when he discovers that the terms of the settlement offer were never relayed to him.

Finally, you forget to file a list of exhibits and witnesses on the date it is due. As a result, the judge refuses to allow your key witness to testify and the case is lost when it goes to trial. What will clients in each of these cases have to prove if they allege professional negligence? What might the attorney argue in his defense?

WHAT IS REASONABLE CARE?

As we discussed in Chapter 6, the duty of care required of professionals is one of reasonableness. A professional is required to have the skill and learning commonly possessed by members in good standing within that profession. The question that frequently arises is whether professionals should be required to meet national or local standards. For example, should a physician who practices in a rural area be held to the same standard of care as one who practices in an urban, high-tech office? In the medical area many states have opted for a local standard, apparently with an implicit

acknowledgment that expectations of reasonableness are dependent on locale. Some courts, however, influenced by the elevated expectations of professionals resulting from enhanced communications, have discarded the "locality rule" in favor of a national standard.

Negligence is not necessarily equated with unfavorable outcome. Simply because a course of action ultimately yields undesirable results does not make it negligent. Hindsight, as we all know, is perfect, but reasonable foresight is all that is required of a professional. A veterinarian, for instance, may recommend surgery for an ailing dog, but if the dog dies from complications, the veterinarian is not necessarily negligent even though the outcome proves the prognosis incorrect. The veterinarian's recommendation need only be reasonable, not accurate.

In many instances several possible options are available to the professional. The rule of reasonable care does not require that all other professionals would have chosen the same course of action as that decided upon by the defendant professional. The fact that other dentists, for example, might testify that they personally would have opted for a different procedure than that used by the defendant does not necessarily make the defendant's conduct negligent. If, however, only one recognized method of treatment is used by dentists in good standing in the profession and the defendant dentist chooses another course of action, the choice will likely be considered negligent.

HOW NEGLIGENCE CAN OCCUR

Professional negligence, like any other type of negligence, can occur in a number of ways (see Figure 10-1). A professional may lack the requisite training to perform a given task. He or she may fail to ask for the information necessary to make an informed recommendation to the plaintiff, or may fail to refer his or her client to a specialist when the situation dictates such a referral. An attorney in general practice with

FIGURE 10-1   What Constitutes Professional Negligence

- Failure to have skills and learning commonly possessed by members in good standing within a profession.
- Failure to use good judgment in choosing course of action, to the extent that the action chosen constitutes a deviation from the standard of care reasonably expected of professionals in the field.
- Failure to ask for essential information from client.
- Failure to make referrals when appropriate.
- Failure to keep abreast of changes in profession.
- Failure to follow up on client's progress, condition, or status.
- Failure to adhere to specialist's standard of care when appropriate.
- Failure to provide informed consent.

no training or experience in securities fraud, for example, could be negligent if she represented a client in a securities fraud case to the detriment of that client.

Even if a professional chooses an appropriate course of conduct, he may be negligent if he fails to use due diligence and care. Professionals who resort to unorthodox procedures are more likely to be found negligent if the client ultimately suffers some kind of damage than professionals who rely on more conventional techniques. The degree of innovation that will be considered legally acceptable will be determined largely by the seriousness of the situation. If a physician uses a method unknown or disapproved of by her peers when dealing with a critically ill patient, she is more likely to be found negligent than if she is dealing with someone suffering a minor illness. In extremely difficult cases the professional may be expected to consult with someone else in the field. A general physician, for example, who identifies a condition that he is ill equipped to handle has an obligation to consult with a specialist.

A professional is obligated to keep abreast of new developments in the field. Accountants are expected to be aware of recent changes in tax law. Physicians are expected to be aware of innovations in medications and procedures.

Professionals are obligated to pay attention to their clients' complaints and feedback. A physician who fails to remain apprised of her patient's change in condition may be negligent. In one case a patient with a history of attacking women was involuntarily committed to a mental hospital where, several years later, a committee of three psychiatrists decided to discharge him. After this decision was made, but before he was released, he had to be put in restraints because he went berserk. The psychiatrists failed to reevaluate him and when he was released on schedule he attacked two women within twenty minutes of his release. The court held that the psychiatrists' failure to reexamine him constituted negligence. (*Homere v. New York,* 361 N.Y.S.2d 820 (1974)).

The elements of a malpractice claim are set forth in *Togstad v. Vesely, Otto, Miller & Keefe,* 291 N.W.2d 686 (Minn. 1980). Notice that even when the defendant professional is negligent, if the plaintiff cannot prove that the negligence was the proximate cause of her injuries, no malpractice claim exists. Furthermore, in *Togstad,* because the legal malpractice claim arose out of a medical malpractice claim, the plaintiff bore the burden of proving that she would have been successful had she been able to pursue the medical malpractice claim.

CASE

Togstad v. Vesely, Otto, Miller & Keefe
291 N.W.2d 686 (Minn. 1980)

Heard, considered and decided by the court en banc.

PER CURIAM.

This is an appeal by the defendants from a judgment of the Hennepin County District Court involving an action for legal malpractice. The jury found that the defendant attorney Jerre Miller was negligent and that, as a direct result of such negligence, plaintiff John Togstad sustained damages in the amount of $610,500 and his wife, plaintiff Joan Togstad, in the amount of $39,000. Defendants (Miller and his law firm) appeal to this court from the denial of their motion for judgment notwithstanding the verdict or, alternatively, for a new trial. We affirm.

In August 1971, John Togstad began to experience severe headaches and on August 16, 1971, was admitted to Methodist Hospital where tests disclosed that the headaches were caused by a large aneurysm[1] on the left internal carotid artery.[2] The attending physician, Dr. Paul Blake, a neurological surgeon, treated the problem by applying a Selverstone clamp to the left common carotid artery. The clamp was surgically implanted on August 27, 1971, in Togstad's neck to allow the gradual closure of the artery over a period of days.

The treatment was designed to eventually cut off the blood supply through the artery and thus relieve the pressure on the aneurysm, allowing the aneurysm to heal. It was anticipated that other arteries, as well as the brain's collateral or cross-arterial system would supply the required blood to the portion of the brain which would ordinarily have been provided by the left carotid artery. The greatest risk associated with this procedure is that the patient may become paralyzed if the brain does not receive an adequate flow of blood. In the event the supply of blood becomes so low as to endanger the health of the patient, the adjustable clamp can be opened to establish the proper blood circulation.

In the early morning hours of August 29, 1971, a nurse observed that Togstad was unable to speak or move. At the time, the clamp was one-half (50%) closed. Upon discovering Togstad's condition, the nurse called a resident physician, who did not adjust the clamp. Dr. Blake was also immediately informed of Togstad's condition and arrived about an hour later, at which time he opened the clamp. Togstad is now severely paralyzed in his right arm and leg, and is unable to speak.

Plaintiffs' expert, Dr. Ward Woods, testified that Togstad's paralysis and loss of speech was due to a lack of blood supply to his brain. Dr. Woods stated that the inadequate blood flow resulted from the clamp being 50% closed and that the negligence of Dr. Blake and the hospital precluded the clamp's being opened in time to avoid permanent brain damage. Specifically, Dr. Woods claimed that Dr. Blake and the hospital were negligent for (1) failing to place the patient in the intensive care unit or to have a special nurse conduct certain neurological tests every half-hour; (2) failing to write adequate orders; (3) failing to open the clamp immediately upon discovering that the patient was unable to speak; and (4) the absence of personnel capable of opening the clamp.

Dr. Blake and defendants' expert witness, Dr. Shelly Chou, testified that Togstad's condition was caused by blood clots going up the carotid artery to the brain. They both alleged that the blood clots were not a result of the Selverstone clamp procedure. In addition, they stated that the clamp must be about 90% closed before there will be a slowing of the blood supply through the carotid artery to the brain. Thus, according to Drs. Blake and Chou, when the clamp is 50% closed there is no effect on the blood flow to the brain.

About 14 months after her husband's hospitalization began, plaintiff Joan Togstad met with attorney Jerre Miller regarding her husband's condition. Neither she nor her husband was personally acquainted with Miller or his law firm prior to that time. John Togstad's former work supervisor, Ted Bucholz, made the appointment and accompanied Mrs. Togstad to Miller's office. Bucholz was present when Mrs. Togstad and Miller discussed the case.

Mrs. Togstad had become suspicious of the circumstances surrounding her husband's tragic condition due to the conduct and statements of the hospital nurses shortly after the paralysis occurred. One nurse told Mrs.

---

1. An aneurism is a weakness or softening in an artery wall which expands and bulges out over a period of years.
2. The left internal carotid artery is one of the major vessels which supplies blood to the brain.

Togstad that she had checked Mr. Togstad at 2 a.m. and he was fine; that when she returned at 3 a.m., by mistake, to give him someone else's medication, he was unable to move or speak; and that if she hadn't accidentally entered the room no one would have discovered his condition until morning. Mrs. Togstad also noticed that the other nurses were upset and crying, and that Mr. Togstad's condition was a topic of conversation.

Mrs. Togstad testified that she told Miller "everything that happened at the hospital," including the nurses' statements and conduct which had raised a question in her mind. She stated that she "believed" she had told Miller "about the procedure and what was undertaken, what was done, and what happened." She brought no records with her. Miller took notes and asked questions during the meeting, which lasted 45 minutes to an hour. At its conclusion, according to Mrs. Togstad, Miller said that "he did not think we had a legal case, however, he was going to discuss this with his partner." She understood that if Miller changed his mind after talking to his partner, he would call her. Mrs. Togstad "gave it" a few days and, since she did not hear from Miller, decided "that they had come to the conclusion that there wasn't a case." No fee arrangements were discussed, no medical authorizations were requested, nor was Mrs. Togstad billed for the interview.

Mrs. Togstad denied that Miller had told her his firm did not have expertise in the medical malpractice field, urged her to see another attorney, or related to her that the statute of limitations for medical malpractice actions was two years. She did not consult another attorney until one year after she talked to Miller. Mrs. Togstad indicated that she did not confer with another attorney earlier because of her reliance on Miller's "legal advice" that they "did not have a case."

On cross-examination, Mrs. Togstad was asked whether she went to Miller's office "to see if he would take the case of (her) husband . . . ." She replied, "Well, I guess it was to go for legal advice, what to do, where shall we go from here? That is what we went for." Again in response to defense counsel's questions, Mrs. Togstad testified as follows:

Q: And it was clear to you, was it not, that what was taking place was a preliminary discussion between a prospective client and lawyer as to whether or not they wanted to enter into an attorney-client relationship?
A: I am not sure how to answer that. It was for legal advice as to what to do.

Q: And Mr. Miller was discussing with you your problem and indicating whether he, as a lawyer, wished to take the case, isn't that true?
A: Yes.

On re-direct examination, Mrs. Togstad acknowledged that when she left Miller's office she understood that she had been given a "qualified, quality legal opinion that (she and her husband) did not have a malpractice case."

Miller's testimony was different in some respects from that of Mrs. Togstad. Like Mrs. Togstad, Miller testified that Mr. Bucholz arranged and was present at the meeting, which lasted about 45 minutes. According to Miller, Mrs. Togstad described the hospital incident, including the conduct of the nurses. He asked her questions, to which she responded. Miller testified that "(t)he only thing I told her (Mrs. Togstad) after we had pretty much finished the conversation was that there was nothing related in her factual circumstances that told me that she had a case that our firm would be interested in undertaking."

Miller also claimed he related to Mrs. Togstad "that because of the grievous nature of the injuries sustained by her husband, that this was only my opinion and she was encouraged to ask another attorney if she wished for another opinion" and "she ought to do so promptly." He testified that he informed Mrs. Togstad that his firm "was not engaged as experts" in the area of medical malpractice, and that they associated with the Charles Hvass firm in cases of that nature. Miller stated that at the end of the conference he told Mrs. Togstad that he would consult with Charles Hvass and if Hvass's opinion differed from his, Miller would so inform her. Miller recollected that he called Hvass a "couple days" later and discussed the case with him. It was Miller's impression that Hvass thought there was no liability for malpractice in the case. Consequently, Miller did not communicate with Mrs. Togstad further.

On cross-examination, Miller testified as follows:

Q: Now, so there is no misunderstanding, and I am reading from your deposition, you understood that she was consulting with you as a lawyer, isn't that correct?
A: That's correct.
Q: That she was seeking legal advice from a professional attorney licensed to practice in this state and in this community?
A: I think you and I did have another interpretation or use of the term "Advice." She was there to see

whether or not she had a case and whether the firm would accept it.

Q: We have two aspects; number one, your legal opinion concerning liability of a case for malpractice; number two, whether there was or wasn't liability, whether you would accept it, your firm, two separate elements, right?

A: I would say so.

Q: Were you asked on page 6 in the deposition, folio 14, "And you understood that she was seeking legal advice at the time that she was in your office, that is correct also, isn't it?" And did you give this answer, "I don't want to engage in semantics with you, but my impression was that she and Mr. Bucholz were asking my opinion after having related the incident that I referred to." The next question, "Your legal opinion?" Your answer, "Yes." Were those questions asked and were they given?

MR. COLLINS: Objection to this, Your Honor. It is not impeachment.

THE COURT: Overruled.

THE WITNESS: Yes, I gave those answers. Certainly, she was seeking my opinion as an attorney in the sense of whether or not there was a case that the firm would be interested in undertaking.

Kenneth Green, a Minneapolis attorney, was called as an expert by plaintiffs. He stated that in rendering legal advice regarding a claim of medical malpractice, the "minimum" an attorney should do would be to request medical authorizations from the client, review the hospital records, and consult with an expert in the field. John McNulty, a Minneapolis attorney, and Charles Hvass testified as experts on behalf of the defendants. McNulty stated that when an attorney is consulted as to whether he will take a case, the lawyer's only responsibility in refusing it is to so inform the party. He testified, however, that when a lawyer is asked his legal opinion on the merits of a medical malpractice claim, community standards require that the attorney check hospital records and consult with an expert before rendering his opinion.

Hvass stated that he had no recollection of Miller's calling him in October 1972 relative to the Togstad matter. He testified that:

A: . . . when a person comes in to me about a medical malpractice action, based upon what the individual has told me, I have to make a decision as to whether or not there probably is or probably is not, based upon that information, medical malpractice.

And if, in my judgment, based upon what the client has told me, there is not medical malpractice, I will so inform the client.

Hvass stated, however, that he would never render a "categorical" opinion. In addition, Hvass acknowledged that if he were consulted for a "legal opinion" regarding medical malpractice and 14 months had expired since the incident in question, "ordinary care and diligence" would require him to inform the party of the two-year statute of limitations applicable to that type of action.

This case was submitted to the jury by way of a special verdict form. The jury found that Dr. Blake and the hospital were negligent and that Dr. Blake's negligence (but not the hospital's) was a direct cause of the injuries sustained by John Togstad; that there was an attorney-client contractual relationship between Mrs. Togstad and Miller; that Miller was negligent in rendering advice regarding the possible claims of Mr. and Mrs. Togstad; that, but for Miller's negligence, plaintiffs would have been successful in the prosecution of a legal action against Dr. Blake; and that neither Mr. nor Mrs. Togstad was negligent in pursuing their claims against Dr. Blake. The jury awarded damages to Mr. Togstad of $610,500 and to Mrs. Togstad of $39,000.

On appeal, defendants raise the following issues:

(1) Did the trial court err in denying defendants' motion for judgment notwithstanding the jury verdict?

(2) Does the evidence reasonably support the jury's award of damages to Mrs. Togstad in the amount of $39,000? . . .

In a legal malpractice action of the type involved here, four elements must be shown: (1) that an attorney-client relationship existed; (2) that defendant acted negligently or in breach of contract; (3) that such acts were the proximate cause of the plaintiffs' damages; (4) that but for defendant's conduct the plaintiffs would have been successful in the prosecution of their medical malpractice claim. . . .

This court first dealt with the element of lawyer-client relationship in the decision of *Ryan v. Long,* 35 Minn. 394, 29 N.W. 51 (1886). The *Ryan* case involved a claim of legal malpractice and on appeal it was argued that no attorney-client relation existed. This court, without stating whether its conclusion was based on contract principles or a tort theory, disagreed:

(I)t sufficiently appears that plaintiff, for himself, called upon defendant, as an attorney at law, for "legal advice," and that defendant assumed to give him a professional opinion in reference to the matter as to which plaintiff consulted him. Upon this state of facts the defendant must be taken to have acted as plaintiff's legal adviser, at plaintiff's request, and so as to establish between them the relation of attorney and client.

Id. (citation omitted). More recent opinions of this court, although not involving a detailed discussion, have analyzed the attorney-client consideration in contractual terms. . . . For example, the *Ronnigen* court, in affirming a directed verdict for the defendant attorney, reasoned that "(u)nder the fundamental rules applicable to contracts of employment . . . the evidence would not sustain a finding that defendant either expressly or impliedly promised or agreed to represent plaintiff . . . ." The trial court here . . . applied a contract analysis in ruling on the attorney-client relationship question. This has prompted a discussion by the Minnesota Law Review, wherein it is suggested that the more appropriate mode of analysis, at least in this case, would be to apply principles of negligence, i.e., whether defendant owed plaintiffs a duty to act with due care. 63 Minn.L.Rev. 751 (1979).

We believe it is unnecessary to decide whether a tort or contract theory is preferable for resolving the attorney-client relationship question raised by this appeal. The tort and contract analyses are very similar in a case such as the instant one,[4] and we conclude that under either theory the evidence shows that a lawyer-client relationship is present here. The thrust of Mrs. Togstad's testimony is that she went to Miller for legal advice, was told there wasn't a case, and relied upon this advice in failing to pursue the claim for medical malpractice. In addition, according to Mrs. Togstad, Miller did not qualify his legal opinion by urging her to seek advice from another attorney, nor did Miller inform her that he lacked expertise in

the medical malpractice area. Assuming this testimony is true, as this court must do . . ., we believe a jury could properly find that Mrs. Togstad sought and received legal advice from Miller under circumstances which made it reasonably foreseeable to Miller that Mrs. Togstad would be injured if the advice were negligently given. Thus, under either a tort or contract analysis, there is sufficient evidence in the record to support the existence of an attorney-client relationship.

Defendants argue that even if an attorney-client relationship was established the evidence fails to show that Miller acted negligently in assessing the merits of the Togstads' case. They appear to contend that, at most, Miller was guilty of an error in judgment which does not give rise to legal malpractice. . . . However, this case does not involve a mere error of judgment. The gist of plaintiffs' claim is that Miller failed to perform the minimal research that an ordinarily prudent attorney would do before rendering legal advice in a case of this nature. The record, through the testimony of Kenneth Green and John McNulty, contains sufficient evidence to support plaintiffs' position.

In a related contention, defendants assert that a new trial should be awarded on the ground that the trial court erred by refusing to instruct the jury that Miller's failure to inform Mrs. Togstad of the two-year statute of limitations for medical malpractice could not constitute negligence. The argument continues that since it is unclear from the record on what theory or theories of negligence the jury based its decision, a new trial must be granted. . . .

The defect in defendants' reasoning is that there is adequate evidence supporting the claim that Miller was also negligent in failing to advise Mrs. Togstad of the two-year medical malpractice limitations period and thus the trial court acted properly in refusing to instruct the jury in the manner urged by defendants. One of defendants' expert witnesses, Charles Hvass, testified:

Q: Now, Mr. Hvass, where you are consulted for a legal opinion and advice concerning malpractice and 14 months have elapsed (since the incident in question), wouldn't and you hold yourself out as competent to give a legal opinion and advice to these people concerning their rights, wouldn't ordinary care and diligence require that you inform them that there is a two-year statute of limitations within which they have to act or lose their rights?

A: Yes. I believe I would have advised someone of the two-year period of limitation, yes.

---

4. Under a negligence approach it must essentially be shown that defendant rendered legal advice (not necessarily at someone's request) under circumstances which made it reasonably foreseeable to the attorney that if such advice was rendered negligently, the individual receiving the advice might be injured thereby. . . . Or, stated another way, under a tort theory, "(a)n attorney-client relationship is created whenever an individual seeks and receives legal advice from an attorney in circumstances in which a reasonable person would rely on such advice." . . . A contract analysis requires the rendering of legal advice pursuant to another's request and the reliance factor, in this case, where the advice was not paid for, need be shown in the form of promissory estoppel . . . .

Consequently, based on the testimony of Mrs. Togstad, i.e., that she requested and received legal advice from Miller concerning the malpractice claim, and the above testimony of Hvass, we must reject the defendants' contention, as it was reasonable for a jury to determine that Miller acted negligently in failing to inform Mrs. Togstad of the applicable limitations period.

Defendants also indicate that at the time Mrs. Togstad went to another attorney (after Miller) the statute of limitations may not have run and thus Miller's conduct was not a "direct cause" of plaintiffs' damages. As they point out, the limitations period ordinarily begins to run upon termination of the treatment for which the physician was retained. . . . There is other authority, however, which holds that where the injury complained of consists of a "single act," the limitations period commences from the time of that act, even though the doctor-patient relationship may continue thereafter. . . . Consequently, the limitations period began to run on either August 29, 1971, the date of the incident in question, or October 6, 1971, the last time Dr. Blake treated Mr. Togstad. Mrs. Togstad testified that she consulted another attorney "a year after (she) saw Mr. Miller." Thus, since she visited with Miller on October 2, or 3, 1972, if Mr. Togstad's injuries resulted from a "single act" . . . the limitations period had clearly run by the time Mrs. Togstad consulted another attorney. If, as defendants argue, the statutory period commenced on the date of last treatment, October 6, and Mrs. Togstad's testimony is taken literally, she would have met with a different attorney at a time when perhaps three days of the limitations period remained.

Defendants' contention must be rejected for two reasons. First, at trial defendants apparently assumed that the limitations period commenced on August 29, 1971, and thus did not litigate the instant issue below. Accordingly, they cannot raise the question for the first time on appeal. . . . Further, even assuming the limitations period began on October 6, 1971, it is reasonably inferable from the record that Mrs. Togstad did not see another attorney until after the statute had run. As discussed above, Mrs. Togstad testified that she consulted a lawyer a year after she met with Miller. This statement, coupled with the fact that an action was not brought against Dr. Blake or the hospital but instead plaintiffs sued defendants for legal malpractice which allegedly caused Mrs. Togstad to let the limitations period run, allows a jury to draw a reasonable inference that the statutory period had, in fact, expired at the time Mrs. Togstad consulted another lawyer. Although this evidence is weak, it constitutes a prima facie showing, and it was defendants' responsibility to rebut the inference.

There is also sufficient evidence in the record establishing that, but for Miller's negligence, plaintiffs would have been successful in prosecuting their medical malpractice claim. Dr. Woods, in no uncertain terms, concluded that Mr. Togstad's injuries were caused by the medical malpractice of Dr. Blake. Defendants' expert testimony to the contrary was obviously not believed by the jury. Thus, the jury reasonably found that had plaintiff's medical malpractice action been properly brought, plaintiffs would have recovered.

Based on the foregoing, we hold that the jury's findings are adequately supported by the record. Accordingly we uphold the trial court's denial of defendants' motion for judgment notwithstanding the jury verdict. . . .

PUTTING IT INTO PRACTICE 10.1

1. Why did Mrs. Togstad not pursue a claim against the doctors who had treated her husband?
2. Why did Mrs. Togstad not seek another attorney until one year after she had consulted with Miller?
3. How did Miller's recollection of events differ from Mrs. Togstad's?
4. What are the four elements of a malpractice claim?

Continued on next page

PUTTING IT INTO PRACTICE 10.1—Continued

5. Did Mrs. Togstad and Miller have an attorney-client relationship?
6. Why was Miller's assessment of the Togstad claim more than a "mere error of judgment"?
7. Were there grounds for a jury to conclude that Miller was negligent in failing to tell Mrs. Togstad about the two-year statute of limitations for medical malpractice claims?
8. Why did the court reject the defendants' contention that the statute may not have run when Mrs. Togstad contacted another attorney and that Miller's conduct was not therefore the direct cause of Mrs. Togstad's damages?
9. Was there sufficient evidence in the record to show that but for Miller's negligence, the Togstad medical malpractice claim would have been successful?

PUTTING IT INTO PRACTICE 10.2

1. Before, during, and after her mastectomy, Helen is transfused with blood. Some of the blood with which she is transfused is drawn from someone who is HIV-positive. As a result, Helen contracts and eventually succumbs to AIDS. Her estate sues the surgeon and her attending physician for negligence. The following is an excerpt from the testimony of the medical expert who testifies regarding the care of Helen's attending physician:

   To review, it is my opinion that Dr. Eck did not meet the standard of care for a family physician in the treatment of his patient, Helen Perpinka, from the time that she was discovered to be HTLV III (HIV) positive to the time that she was referred to an infectious disease specialist. . . . It is my opinion that because he chose not to refer Mrs. Perpinka to an infectious disease specialist that he undertook these awesome responsibilities on his own and he was ill-prepared to carry them out. This in all likelihood delayed the administration of anti-viral medication, which may have hastened the onset of opportunistic disease in Mrs. Perpinka and caused her illness to progress sooner than it might have.

   Does Helen's estate have a viable claim for medical malpractice based on this testimony?

2. Following surgery for an enlarged prostate, Herman suffers from abdominal myoclonus, which results in violent, jerking abdominal contractions. His medical malpractice claim is dismissed because his attorney fails to make proper service of process. Herman is prepared to introduce expert medical testimony that the anesthesiologist's failure to wait for more than ten minutes before administering a second dose of anesthetic deviated from accepted practice and that the resulting overdose of anesthetic was the proximate cause of Herman's myoclonus. His medical expert will admit, however, that he has never previously seen a case of abdominal myoclonus, that he does not know of any reported cases of abdominal

Continued on next page

---

myoclonus caused by the spinal anesthetic used in this case, and that the studies he will rely upon (involving 65,000 cases) report only one or two cases of myoclonus, but only in the legs rather than in the abdomen. The doctor will also testify that abdominal myoclonus can occur spontaneously, without any drugs, trauma, or evidence of disease.

Do you think Herman will be able to prevail in a legal malpractice claim against the attorney, based on the failure to make proper service of process? (To answer this question you must decide whether the underlying medical malpractice claim is viable.)

SPECIALISTS

Specialists are held to a higher standard of care than generalists. They must adhere to the standard of the "reasonably careful and prudent specialist" in that field. Therefore, a neurosurgeon is held to the standard of care of the average neurosurgeon rather than the average physician. As a result, a specialist may be found negligent in a situation in which a general practitioner doing the same thing might not.

Specialists are typically required to adhere to a national standard of care in their field rather than a local one. The reasoning is that clients particularly seek out a specialist because they want someone who is aware of advances in the field. A pediatrician, for example, who failed to make a standard PKU test on a newborn was found negligent even though the hospitals in his community did not use such a test. Because these tests were in general use by pediatricians throughout the rest of the country, the defendant's conduct was held against the national standard of care and he was found negligent (*Naccarato v. Grob,* 180 N.W.2d 788 (Mich.1970)).

Attorneys are held to a general standard of care unless they present themselves as certified specialists. Those who set themselves out through their advertising as certified specialists are held to the standard of care of a specialist.

INFORMED CONSENT

Professionals have a **fiduciary relationship** with their clients in that the relationship is one of trust and confidence. Therefore, they have an obligation to disclose all relevant facts to their clients so that the clients can make informed decisions. The principle of autonomy underlying the **informed consent** doctrine requires clients to be given ultimate dominion over their bodies and those events that affect their lives.

Particularly in the area of medical treatment, the issue of consent is very important. Certainly every human being has a right to determine what is to be done with his or her body and no physician may force unwanted treatment on anyone. Under the doctrine of informed consent a physician has a duty to warn patients of possible hazards, complications, and expected and unexpected results of treatment, as well as risks of any alternative treatments. Particularly if a therapy is new or experimental, the physician has a duty to warn the patient that all side effects of the treatment are not completely known. The duty to warn increases as the probability or severity of risk to the patient increases. Any patient who is unaware of the inherent risk of a proposed procedure cannot voluntarily consent to that procedure.

If alternative treatments exist, a physician is obligated to advise a patient about those alternatives. Failure to explain an alternative may in itself constitute negligence. If a physician does not think that an alternative would work in a particular patient's case, however, he or she has no obligation to suggest that alternative. In emergency situations when a patient is unconscious or so ill that he or she is unable to comprehend what is being said, the physician has a right to render treatment without informing the patient of the risks involved.

In determining what should and should not be disclosed to a patient, some courts look to the expectations of a reasonable layperson and ask what a patient in that position would reasonably need to know to make an informed decision. In the words of one court, informed consent should be judged by

> whether the physician disclosed all those facts, risks and alternatives that a reasonable man in the situation which the physician knew or should have known to be the plaintiff's would deem significant in making a decision to undergo the recommended treatment. This gives maximum effect to the patient's right to be the arbiter of the medical treatment he will undergo without either requiring the physician to be a mindreader into the patient's most subjective thoughts or requiring that he disclose every risk lest he be liable. . . . The physician is bound to disclose only those risks which a reasonable man would consider material to his decision whether or not to undergo treatment. This standard creates no unreasonable burden for the physician. . . . This formulation has been described as the "prudent patient" standard. It attempts to reconcile the tension between the patient's right to self-determination and the physician's responsibility to exercise sound medical judgment.

Cooper v. Roberts, 286 A.2d 647 (Pa. 1971). Under this standard the question boils down to whether a reasonable patient in that situation would have submitted to the procedure had he or she been advised of the risks involved.

Other courts rely on the "professional" standard, under which a physician must disclose only those risks and alternatives that the reasonable medical practitioner in the community would disclose under similar circumstances. Some consider this a paternalistic standard that leaves the choice to the medical community, rather than the patient whose life is most intimately affected by the choices made.

■ PUTTING IT INTO PRACTICE 10.3 □

1. Leslie has a CT scan under his doctor's orders. Prior to the test, he is given no information about the risks of the procedure, which include the injection of a contrast dye. He does answer routine questions by the hospital staff regarding allergies, illnesses, medications, and previous reactions to contrast materials. Later he develops thrombophlebitis at the site of the injection. Does Leslie have a claim for lack of informed consent?
2. Hazel has a heart valve replacement. Before the surgery her doctor tells her that mechanical valves (like the Beall valve which is to be implanted in her) outlast natural-tissue valves. She is not told about the danger of the development of thromboemboli and strokes nor about the need for a lifelong regimen of anticoagulants. After the surgery Hazel suffers multiple episodes of thromboemboli, leaving her with severe, permanent brain damage. Later a natural-tissue implant is used to replace the Beall valve. Does Hazel have a claim for lack of informed consent?

Nature of Risk Involved

A physician must, however, balance the need to provide information versus the effect such information will have on the patient's morale. Studies show a close connection between a patient's mental state and his or her response to treatment, so physicians naturally want to avoid doing anything to jeopardize the healing process. If a risk is highly improbable and advising the patient of this risk would in the physician's opinion induce the patient to forego necessary treatment or would severely reduce the efficacy of any treatment, the physician may not be compelled to disclose this information. If the probability of the risk is statistically high, however, the patient should be informed regardless of the effect it might have on his or her morale. Even if the probability of the risk is statistically low but the consequence is extremely severe, the patient should be informed. If the probability of harm is statistically low and its severity is relatively minor, the physician can tailor the warning to avoid unnecessarily exciting the patient.

BATTERY VERSUS NEGLIGENCE

Plaintiffs alleging lack of consent may sue on a theory of either battery or negligence (based on lack of informed consent). If a patient is in total ignorance of what is to be done or if the physician obtains consent for one procedure and then performs another, an action for battery will lie. In the more typical case, however, the patient is aware of the procedure and in fact signs a consent form but does not clearly understand some of the risks inherent in the procedure. In this case a more appropriate cause of action is negligence. Today negligence has for the most part displaced battery as a basis for liability. The practical difference between the two theories is that if battery is alleged, lay witness testimony is sufficient. In cases of negligence, however, expert witnesses are required to testify to the standard of care and the fact that it was breached. Also, the statute of limitations for battery is typically longer than the statute for negligence.

If the cause of action is for negligence, the primary issue is whether the risks that were not disclosed were material risks. In determining what is and is not material, the courts consider the severity of the consequences and the probability of their occurrence, as well as the feasibility of any alternatives. The plaintiff is also required to prove that the outcome was a foreseeable risk and not an unpredictable consequence. If the risk pertaining to that outcome is remote, recovery will not be allowed.

■   PUTTING IT INTO PRACTICE 10.4   ☐

Patricia is under the care of a doctor for the treatment of trichomonas vaginitis, an infection of the female reproductive tract. She is admitted to the hospital and treated intravenously with the antibiotic Flagyl. She develops peripheral neuropathy as a result of the Flagyl treatment and argues that her doctor failed to inform her of the risks of this antibiotic. Does the doctrine of informed consent apply to the intravenous administration of a therapeutic drug in a state that has a battery standard, rather than a negligence standard, for informed consent?

DEFENSES TO PROFESSIONAL NEGLIGENCE

A plaintiff attempting to prove professional negligence must prove both the standard of care expected within the profession and the defendant's deviation from that standard. To do this requires expert testimony, which is usually provided by a professional in that same area of practice. If the defendant is a specialist, the expert is typically a specialist in the same area. The expert witness must be familiar with the procedures or techniques used in the case, although he or she need not follow the same practices. In courts that follow the locality rule the expert must be familiar with the standard of care in the relevant community or similar communities. The plaintiff also has the burden of proving that his or her injuries more probably than not resulted from the negligence of the professional.

The professional can then choose either to refute the plaintiff's factual allegations of negligence or to raise the affirmative defenses of contributory negligence, comparative negligence, or assumption of risk. To allege contributory negligence, the defendant must show that the plaintiff's negligence was concurrent with his or her own. If the plaintiff's negligence merely added to the effects of the defendant's negligence, the defendant will not be relieved of liability. The damages awarded to the plaintiff, however, may be reduced. Figure 10-2 lists defenses to the charge of professional negligence.

Contributory Negligence

Typically, when the defense of contributory negligence is raised, the defendant argues that the client refused to comply with his or her instructions or was otherwise uncooperative. If a client lies to his attorney about the facts of the case, he cannot later claim that the attorney was negligent, because the attorney relied on the client's veracity in making strategic decisions. If, however, the client's negligence merely compounded the attorney's negligence, the attorney will remain liable and the plaintiff's damages will simply be reduced. In the medical arena, a physician may argue that the patient contributed to her injuries by delaying so long in seeking medical attention that the condition became untreatable. The physician would then have to prove that the untoward effects suffered by the patient were the sole result of the patient's procrastination and that the physician was not in any way negligent himself.

Assumption of Risk

Related to the issue of informed consent is the doctrine of assumption of risk. A patient who understands the risk involved in treatment and knowingly consents to that treatment can be said to have assumed the risk. Of course, if those risks are not carefully explained or the plaintiff does not clearly understand them, this defense is inapplicable. No client can assume the risk of negligent care. For example, a physician who advises

FIGURE 10-2   Defenses to Professional Negligence

- Rebut plaintiff's factual allegations.
- Prove plaintiff was negligent and that plaintiff's negligence was concurrent with professional's.
- Prove plaintiff assumed the risk by knowingly and voluntarily consenting to risks involved in treatment.
- Prove state of emergency (in medical situations).

a patient regarding the risk involved if given improper care and then provides improper care cannot claim that the patient assumed the risk.

Emergency Situations

In medical situations the defense of emergency can also be used. Treatment given during a life-and-death emergency is not required to be of the same level of care as that provided under less stressful circumstances. If death is imminent and treatment is absolutely necessary for the patient's protection, the defense of emergency may be a viable defense to a claim of negligent treatment. A patient who suffers brain damage subsequent to being treated for a cardiac arrest, for example, may file a negligence claim for her damages, but will most likely meet with the defense of emergency. However, if the emergency is caused by the physician's negligence, he cannot use it as a defense. The physician in such cases bears the burden of proving that an emergency in fact existed and that it was not due to any fault of his.

What constitutes adequate care in an emergency depends on the circumstances in which the emergency occurs. A doctor intent on treating a severe head injury who fails to notice a fractured arm may or may not be considered negligent for her failure to diagnose the fracture. Such a question would be submitted to the jury for its determination of whether the doctor's conduct conformed to the expectations for a reasonable doctor working under those conditions.

MAINTAINING ADEQUATE RECORDS

Maintenance of adequate records on a client's case may be of critical importance in proving that no negligence occurred. Professionals should therefore allocate time for the completion of such records even though it may seem a frivolous expenditure of valuable time when being done. The passage of time weakens our memories. Therefore, a professional confronted with a lawsuit one, two, or more years after he has last seen the client may not remember anything about the case. He will be grateful in that circumstance if he can locate records that can be used to refresh his recollec-

tion and that he can use to establish his defense. Of course, such records can also be used to build the plaintiff's case.

Acquiring medical records may present a problem, because the physical record itself is considered the property of the health care provider. The content of the record, however, is usually considered to be the patient's property and if the patient will waive the physician-patient privilege, most state laws require that the record be released to him or her. Trial courts have uniformly ordered the release of such records. In a personal injury case in which the plaintiff has made his or her medical problems the subject of litigation, all relevant medical records are subject to subpoena by the defendant. If the defendant professional, for example, claims that the plaintiff's injuries preceded the damages the plaintiff alleges were caused by the defendant, the defendant has a right to subpoena the records of physicians who previously treated the plaintiff for related complaints.

UNDERLYING CAUSES OF PROFESSIONAL NEGLIGENCE SUITS

Professional negligence claims appear to be on the rise, particularly those involving attorneys. Mandatory continuing legal education programs in almost every state and the increasing cost of malpractice insurance premiums attest to the increased incidence of professional negligence suits against attorneys.

As of 1992, malpractice claims cost lawyers and their insurers over $4 billion each year, and these costs were projected to increase, according to Robert O'Malley of Attorneys' Liability Assurance Society, the nation's largest malpractice insurance carrier. The annual claims for doctors is on par with that for attorneys, although the per-capita amount paid for malpractice claims is significantly higher for lawyers than doctors (because at least 40 percent of the nation's lawyers are uninsured). Although much press has been devoted to exorbitant jury awards, legal malpractice costs are greater than what is collected annually from punitive and compensatory damages awarded by juries nationwide (in 1992 about $5.8 billion was awarded in total damages by juries, of which approximately $580 million was due to punitive damages). The reported number of malpractice claims represents only the tip of the iceberg; it is estimated that only 10 percent of legal malpractice ever becomes an insurance claim. (For references to the statistics cited here and for further reading, *see* Manuel Ramos, "Legal Malpractice: Reforming Lawyers and Law Professors," 70 *Tulane L. Rev.* 2583 (June 1996).)

Today's lawyer can anticipate having three or more claims filed against her before she finishes her career. The attorney most likely to be sued is the litigator. The statistics from about 30,000 legal malpractice claims gathered by the American Bar Association's Standing Committee on Lawyers' Professional Liability show that plaintiffs' personal injury lawyers account for about 25 percent of all claims nationwide and as high as 31 percent in California (taken from a 1986 study conducted by the ABA National Data Center for Malpractice). When claims against lawyers arising out of litigation in other areas of law, such as business, property, and family law, are included, the allegations against litigation attorneys account for almost 50 percent of all claims.

Furthermore, these same statistics document that the greatest number of errors committed by litigators are administrative errors. Interestingly, such errors are 100 percent greater for plaintiffs' personal injury lawyers than for lawyers in general. (Administrative errors constitute 26 percent of all claims in general and 50 percent of all claims against plaintiffs' personal injury lawyers.) Forty percent of the administrative errors involve failure to file actions in a timely manner, usually because of missed statutes of limitation. Surprisingly, experienced lawyers account for a disproportionate number of these claims.

Although the public has become more sophisticated in terms of its legal rights, the primary culprit behind many malpractice claims is a breakdown in communication. Poor client relations is probably the single most important factor contributing to these claims. The most common complaint levied against attorneys, according to most state bar organizations, is lack of communication. Many attorneys are notoriously bad about returning telephone calls to clients or advising clients about the status of their case. The failure of lawyers to communicate with their clients has resulted in so many disciplinary and civil complaints that the American Bar Association's Model Rules of Professional Conduct now include Rule 1.4, which requires clients to be kept "reasonably informed about the status" of the case and lawyers to promptly respond to reasonable requests for information. Failure to return phone calls when there are overt requests for help or information is considered particularly egregious and may be grounds for a negligence claim.

Professionals can maintain a good rapport with their clients by talking openly with clients about their problems, listening to their complaints, and behaving in a manner that indicates they respect their clients. Those who do so are far less likely to be sued for negligence, even when they make mistakes, than are those who treat clients in a paternalistic, disdainful manner.

Another possible explanation for the increase in malpractice claims is the unreasonable expectations many plaintiffs have as a result of what they hear from friends and what they learn from the media. The media tend to overglamorize any personal injury cases, for example, by heavily publicizing large jury awards and then only casually mentioning when those awards are reduced or the verdicts are overturned. People compare these multimillion-dollar awards to their own claims and unrealistically extrapolate what their damages should be. Those watching television shows about life in the medical and legal fields may expect professionals they deal with to have the same charismatic personas and demonstrate the same infallibility they see depicted on television. When reality does not conform to their expectations, some seek recourse by filing suit.

HOW TO PREVENT PROFESSIONAL NEGLIGENCE SUITS

Although professionals can do little to counteract this sort of publicity, they can take several steps to improve client relations (see Figure 10-3). First, they can ensure that their workload does not exceed their capacity to perform. Many professionals, fearful of experiencing a dearth of clients in the future, take on more clients than they can possibly handle at one time. Juggling an unrealistic workload forces them to cut corners and the corner usually cut is client communication. Therefore, professionals should accept no more clients than they can reasonably handle.

Second, professionals need to learn how to manage their businesses. Most have dedicated many years of their lives to honing their technical skills, but few have allocated much time or attention to consideration of the management of their practices. Simple, inexpensive management devices that would make them more efficient and less likely to commit silly errors of omission are often overlooked.

Third, professionals must be willing to dedicate the amount of time necessary to handle a client's problem competently. Consequently, if research should be done or if other practitioners should be consulted, the professional must be willing to expend the time and money necessary to do this. Professionals who constantly take shortcuts in this area are flirting with the specter of malpractice claims.

FIGURE 10-3 Ways to Avoid Malpractice Exposure

- Maintain a reasonable workload
- Calendar deadlines; maintain a back-up calendar
- Maintain client confidences
- Be alert to client dissatisfaction
- Keep clients well informed
- Return client phone calls and respond to client correspondence in a timely fashion
- Keep client files well organized
- Use management techniques and devices that enhance efficiency
- Allocate the time necessary to complete tasks completely
- Bill periodically and in detail; monitor accounts receivable on a regular basis

Role of Legal Assistants

Confidentiality

One way to prevent malpractice claims is to ensure that client confidences are maintained. In accordance with the attorney-client privilege, confidential information between an individual and his or her attorney cannot be disclosed unless the individual consents to the disclosure. Any information exchanged between a client and his or her attorney that is not disclosed to a third person is considered confidential. Disclosure to a third person does not waive the privilege if the person to whom the information is disclosed receives it for the purpose of furthering the client's interest or the disclosure is necessary for the communication of information. If, for example, an attorney writes a letter to a private investigator outlining the case so that the investigator has sufficient information to begin work, the letter is considered privileged because the information is intended to further the client's interest. Once a privilege is lost it cannot be regained. Therefore, a legal assistant must never do anything that could jeopardize the attorney-client privilege.

This privilege may be claimed by the individual, his or her attorney, or anyone authorized to claim the privilege on behalf of the individual, such as a representative of the client's estate. All employees of an attorney or law firm are subject to any prohibitions regarding disclosure and must not disclose privileged information to spouses or anyone else. As the intermediary between support staff and lawyers, the legal assistant is often in the best position to ensure that client confidences are maintained. Therefore, it is often up to the legal assistant to make sure that faxes and computer-generated information are reviewed periodically to ensure confidentiality and that client conferences are conducted in places where privacy is protected.

Unauthorized Practice of Law

One of the axioms by which the paralegal profession operates is that legal assistants cannot give legal advice. Doing so constitutes the unauthorized practice of law and can be the basis of a malpractice claim. The question, however, is: "What constitutes legal advice?" Does suggesting to a client that she might want to consider filing a particular motion constitute legal advice? What about conducting research to determine the meaning of a particular statute? Case law is generally not helpful in answering these types of questions. You may find it more enlightening to consult attorney general and ethics committee opinions rendered in your state.

Most importantly, consult with your attorney as to what tasks you should perform. Clarify, for example, what your role should be in dealing with clients. Determine what types of questions you should answer yourself and which ones you should refer to the attorney. Most attorneys are careful about supervising the work of their legal assistants because they are aware that the ultimate responsibility for any work product lies with them. Nevertheless, some attorneys, because of their workload or outright carelessness, are less than diligent in carrying out their supervisorial tasks. In some cases you may have to insist that an attorney review your work. If an attorney should ever gloss over his refusal to carry out his review responsibilities by assuring you of his implicit trust in you, do not be appeased. For the protection of all concerned, it is imperative that you work under the auspices of an attorney.

The question regarding the appropriate scope of duties of legal assistants is further complicated by the close working relationship legal assistants often establish with clients. Some clients have more contact with the legal assistant than with the attorney, so these clients may naturally turn to the legal assistant for legal advice. Even though the legal assistant may know the answer, he or she must confirm the answer with an attorney. Failure to do so can result in problems for the attorney, the legal assistant, and the client. Furthermore, incorrect advice may lead to a malpractice claim against the attorney and the firm and an ethics complaint against the attorney who allowed the legal assistant to engage in the unauthorized practice of law.

Client Relations

Despite the caveat against giving legal advice, legal assistants can do their part to prevent professional negligence claims by improving client relations. A legal assistant can maintain close contact with clients, informing them of the progress of their cases, listening to their concerns, and answering their questions. By doing these things he can shield the attorney from some of the time-consuming interpersonal tasks that make for good rapport with clients but are often avoided by attorneys because of their limited time.

Making clients aware of the strengths and weaknesses of their case and keeping them apprised as to the status of their case minimizes exposure to malpractice claims. Additionally, regular communication helps create realistic expectations on the part of the client and reassures the client that her case is important to the firm.

Maintenance of Documents and Files

Because legal assistants often bear the responsibility for maintaining documents and files, they can make sure files are well organized so that information can be easily retrieved. Having information but not being able to access it is almost as bad as not having the information at all. Client relations suffer when a client comes to the office to discuss her case and the attorney cannot locate relevant documents in the file. All files should be reviewed periodically to ensure that all necessary documents are included and that they are organized logically. Although document control has been made more efficient with computer technology, the legal assistant should still back up all information in the computer so that data is not lost if the computer malfunctions.

Legal assistants must also ensure that information requested on behalf of a client is received in a timely manner. If, for example, medical records are requested from health care providers, the legal assistant should track these records to make sure they have been received and appropriately filed.

Trust Accounts

Although attorneys cannot delegate ultimate responsibility for client trust accounts to anyone, legal assistants can make sure that the trust account can be quickly and accurately reviewed by the attorney each month. Legal assistants must exhibit great care in dealing with clients' money and remember that they are doing so on behalf of the client and under the direction of the attorney. Courts show no mercy when discrepancies concerning trust accounts arise, even when the attorney was merely sloppy.

Filing and Court Date

Legal assistants can also assume responsibility for meeting filing dates. By using management tools, such as "tickler" systems, to alert them to upcoming deadlines, they can minimize the chances of missing important filing and court dates, (including trial dates, trial setting conferences, depositions, and brief due dates). Because legal assistants must be intimately familiar with the procedural rules and customs of the courts in their jurisdiction, you should pay special attention to procedural law courses in your program of study.

MEDICAL MALPRACTICE CRISIS

Because of the perceived current "medical malpractice crisis," most legislatures have passed statutes that affect medical malpractice litigation in some way. This crisis has arisen because of the increase in the amount of litigation since the 1960s, the size of the judgments sometimes awarded, and the concomitant increase in the cost of medical malpractice insurance.

More recent studies, however, indicate a leveling-off of claims since 1985. In 1994, the American Medical Association reported that since the large increases of the early 1980s, the number of claims against hospitals and physicians dropped at an average rate of 1.9 percent per year. Martin L. Gonzalez, *Socioeconomic Characteristics of Medical Practice* 41 (1994). Some attribute this decrease to the high procedural cost associated with filing a medical malpractice claim, which includes outlays for medical reports, second opinions, and expert witnesses.

Legislators attempting to slay the "malpractice dragon" have enacted legislation resulting in modification of the informed consent doctrine, the burden of proof, evidentiary rules, statutes of limitation, the awarding of punitive damages, and the setting of the standard of care. You would be prudent, therefore, to consult the statutes in your state when getting involved in a medical malpractice case.

Some statutes imposing limitations on the damages recoverable in medical malpractice cases have been challenged as a denial of equal protection and held invalid. One court, for example, concluded that a limitation on recovery not only created an arbitrary classification between malpractice victims and denied full recovery to the most seriously injured malpractice victims, but also constituted special legislation that violated the equal protection provision of the state's constitution.

Some states require pretrial review panels to hear malpractice claims, providing that these claims must be submitted to a panel for findings on the issues of liability or damages or both before proceeding to trial. Some of these statutory provisions, which are designed to encourage settlement, have been attacked as a denial of the constitutional right of access to the courts.

A few states have enacted legislation called *practice guidelines,* which define the standard of care to be used in certain clinical situations. The standardization of minimal actions necessary for care protects physicians from malpractice suits and discourages physicians from practicing defensive medicine (i.e., ordering additional and arguably unnecessary tests and procedures to minimize the chances of being sued for malpractice). Under this system, doctors need only demonstrate that they have complied with the guidelines to avoid litigation. How much weight at trial is given to these guidelines, however, is up to the trier of fact.

SUMMARY

Professionals are held to a reasonable standard of care, in that they are required to have the skill and learning commonly possessed by members in good standing within their profession. Choosing a course of action that other professionals might not have chosen or that results in an undesirable outcome does not necessarily make a professional negligent. Lack of proper training, failure to refer to a specialist when necessary, failure to stay abreast of new discoveries, and failure to follow up on a client's progress may all constitute negligence. Specialists are held to the standard of care of a "reasonably careful and prudent specialist." Unlike generalists, specialists must adhere to a national standard of care rather than a local one.

The doctrine of informed consent requires that a physician warn patients of possible hazards, complications, and expected and unexpected results of treatment as well as possible risks of alternative treatments.

This duty increases as the probability or severity of risk to the patient increases. How much information must be disclosed to the patient depends on the situation, but sufficient information must be given so that the patient can make an informed decision. If no information is disclosed or if the physician obtains consent for one procedure and then opts to perform another, the patient may sue for battery. If, however, the patient is simply uninformed as to the nature of the risks involved, he or she may sue for negligence. With the latter cause of action, the key question is whether the risks that were not disclosed were material risks. Adequate records should always be maintained so that the professional's memory can be refreshed in the event of a lawsuit.

PRACTICE POINTERS

The defendant in a malpractice case may request that the plaintiff submit to an independent physical or mental examination to verify injuries claimed and to justify expenses and suffering alleged. In most jurisdictions, however, the plaintiff is required to submit to only one examination. The examination cannot take place at a location unduly far from the plaintiff's residence and must not include any procedure that is particularly painful or intrusive. Physical examinations must be conducted by a licensed physician or health care professional and mental examinations must be conducted by a licensed physician or clinical psychiatrist.

Typically, the defendant submits a written demand for physical examination to the plaintiff. Such a demand must include the time and location that the examination is to take place, the identity and specialty of the examining physician, and a description of the conditions, scope, and nature of the examination. This demand is served on all other parties to the action but is not filed with the court. The plaintiff must then file a response to the demand indicating whether he or she will comply with the terms of the demand. Alternatively, the plaintiff can insist that certain modifications be made, such as a change in the time or location of the examination. If the defendant then concludes that the plaintiff's request for changes or refusal to appear is unwarranted, he or she may move the court for an order compelling compliance with the demand.

If a physical examination of someone other than the plaintiff is requested or if a mental examination of any person is demanded, a court order must be obtained unless all other parties stipulate to allowing an examination. A motion for medical examination must include the same elements as a demand for physical examination. Additionally, it must contain a declaration showing that the parties have attempted to resolve the issue by stipulation. If an examination is held a long way from the plaintiff's residence (more than seventy-five miles, according to federal rules), a court will order attendance only if the requesting party can

Continued on next page

PRACTICE POINTERS—Continued

show good cause for requesting an examination at this distance and if the moving party agrees to advance travel expenses. If a party seeking recovery for personal injuries stipulates that no claim is being made for mental or emotional distress (other than that normally anticipated to arise from a physical injury) and that no expert testimony will be used to show unusual mental and emotional distress, a court may not order a psychological examination.

Most states prohibit the presence of anyone other than the examinee at a psychological examination. In many cases, however, the examiner or the examinee may tape-record a mental examination. An attorney for the examinee does, however, have a right to attend a physical examination as well as to tape-record that examination. The attorney has a right to suspend the examination if, in his or her opinion, the physician uses tests or procedures that were not included in the order for physical examination. Either the physician or the attorney may suspend an examination if they believe it necessary to secure a protective order.

After submitting to a medical examination, the party may, by written demand, obtain a written report setting forth the findings of the examiner. This report should include the examiner's conclusion, the results of all tests, and copies of any previous reports prepared by the examiner in reference to the examinee. If the demanding party fails to receive these reports in a timely manner, it may move the court for an order compelling delivery. If a party fails to comply with this court order, the court must exclude the testimony of the examiner whose report was not delivered. By the same token, the party who conducts the examination, at the time it serves the demanded report, is entitled to any reports prepared as a result of an examination of the same condition. Additionally, that party is entitled to the identity of any physician who conducts an examination but does not prepare a report, as well as the identification of any physician who later examines the patient.

Demand for Physical Examination

Carbuncle and Boyle
1620 Blissful Lane
Suite 6200
Carefree, Arizona 85254
(602) 897-1334
Alma Carbuncle
Steven Boyle
Attorneys for the Defendants

     Superior Court for the State of _____
        For the County of _____

	CASE NUMBER C 6096-ABC
THEODORE JONES, et al., Plaintiffs	
v.	DEMAND FOR PHYSICAL EXAMINATION

STEVEN AND MILDRED BAXTER,
    husband and wife
    Defendants	

Continued on next page

TO ALL PARTIES AND TO THEIR ATTORNEYS OF RECORD HEREIN:

A demand is hereby made upon Plaintiff THEODORE JONES to submit to a physical examination.

The examination will take place on April 4, 19___ at 10:30 am at the office of Dr. Bryon Happytimes, Do It Now Medical Center, 4700 Harmony Lane, Suite 200, Scottsdale, Arizona.

The examination will be conducted by Dr. Happytimes, a board certified dermatologist.

February 22, 19___

Carbuncle and Boyle

Alma Carbuncle
Attorney for Defendants

---

1. Review the hypothetical scenario at the beginning of this chapter. Has professional negligence been committed? What defenses can be raised?

2. An attorney in general practice tries but fails to create a trust that would have given his client a tax advantage. Though conceding his inexperience, the attorney argues that he did a fair job of working on the matter and that he did not have a duty to refer the client to a tax specialist. Do you think the attorney should be found negligent for his failure to seek assistance? *Horne v. Peckham,* 158 Cal. Rptr. 714 (Ct. App. 1979).

3. The father of a small child takes the child to an emergency room and tells the attendants that the child has ingested a large quantity of aspirin. The attendants specifically tell the father to advise the physician of this fact but the father fails to make mention of it. The physician diagnoses the child as having the flu. The child dies shortly thereafter and the parents sue the physician for negligence. Should the parents be able to recover? What defense might the physician raise? *Hudson v. St. Paul Mercury Insurance Co.,* 219 So. 2d 524 (La. 1969).

4. A physician tells his patient he is going to perform a biopsy on her breast and in fact performs a mastectomy. Before performing surgery he specifically indicates that he is not going to perform a mastectomy. On what theory should the patient base her cause of action and why? *Corn v. French,* 289 P.2d 173 (Nev. 1955).

5. A troubled twenty-four-year-old man consults the head pastor of a church and several of its pastoral counsel. Severely depressed, he tells them he has contemplated suicide. Defendants advise him that suicide is an acceptable alternative in some cases. Defendants visit him in the hospital after he unsuccessfully attempts suicide and he tells them that he will reattempt suicide when he is released. Defendants do not advise the doctors or the young man's family about this conversation. Two weeks after he is released from the hospital, the young man commits suicide. Plaintiffs, the parents of the young man, sue for wrongful death, alleging, among other things, "clergy malpractice." How would you go about determining whether Defendants were negligent? *Nally v. Grace Community Church,* 763 P.2d 948 (Cal.), *cert. denied,* 109 S. Ct. 1644 (1989).

KEY TERMS

Fiduciary relationship
Relationship based on trust and confidence that imposes an obligation to act in good faith; an example is the attorney-client relationship.

Informed consent
Knowledgeable consent based on disclosure of all relevant facts that allows one to make an informed decision.

CHAPTER

11

Misrepresentation, Nuisance, and Other Torts

CHAPTER TOPICS

Development of Misrepresentation and Its Relationship to Other Torts
Intentional Misrepresentaation
Negligent Misrepresentation
Innocent Misrepresentation
Nuisance
Interference with Business Relations
Misuse of Legal Process

CHAPTER OBJECTIVES

In this chapter you will learn to:
- Distinguish among intentional, negligent, and innocent misrepresentation and identify the elements of each
- Identify situations in which one is entitled to rely on the representations of another
- Identify the two ways in which a plaintiff's damages can be measured
- Distinguish between public and private nuisance and identify the elements of both
- Identify the elements of the torts involving interference with business relations
- Distinguish among the torts involving misuse of legal process and identify the elements of each

After meeting your sister's fiancé, you suspect that he is not all he pretends to be. You ask a friend of yours, who is a private investigator, to conduct a background check on him. You discover, among other things, that your prospective brother-in-law had an affair with a woman who was married to a prominent businessman. When the husband discovered their relationship and terminated their affair, your sister's boyfriend sought revenge. First he went to the attorney general's office and tried to convince an attorney to prosecute the husband for price fixing, even though he was aware that such claims were utterly false. In a further act of petulance, he sent the husband materials advertising a get-rich-quick scheme that your future relation knew was bogus and included several fake endorsements by well-known people, in an effort to capture the husband's interest. Not being one to forgive and forget, your brother-in-law-to-be is currently trying to purchase property next to the husband's business. He plans to open a bookstore that features pornographic materials. Because the husband operates a religious bookstore, he is confident that this will, at the very least, have a detrimental effect on the husband's business and, more likely, he hopes, contribute to its demise.

What torts has this potential bane of your existence committed? Has he committed nuisance, interference with business relations, misrepresentation, or misuse of legal process? Let us see.

DEVELOPMENT OF MISREPRESENTATION AND ITS RELATIONSHIP TO OTHER TORTS

Misrepresentation (which is basically the making of false representations) can be found interwoven among other types of tortious behavior. A conversion, for example, can be committed by making false representations. A battery can be committed by a person who uses deceit to induce the plaintiff to consent to physical contact. A claim for intentional infliction of emotional distress may arise out of a maliciously spread lie.

Misrepresentation as a distinct cause of action arose out of the common law action of **deceit.** Typically, in a case of deceit the plaintiff lost money or property as a result of reliance on the defendant's representations. Today, however, the law of misrepresentation is broader than an action for deceit. Although deceit was usually based on an intent to deceive, misrepresentation can be based on intentional deception, negligent deception, or innocent deception (strict liability).

INTENTIONAL MISREPRESENTATION

Intentional misrepresentation corresponds to what was known as "deceit" or "fraud" under the common law. The elements of intentional misrepresentation are as follows (see Figure 11-1):

- The defendant misrepresents something with the intent of inducing the plaintiff's reliance on that misrepresentation.
- The defendant knows that the representation is false or acts with reckless indifference to the truth.
- The plaintiff justifiably relies on the defendant's misrepresentation.
- The plaintiff suffers damages stemming from this reliance.

What Constitutes a Misrepresentation?

A defendant commits misrepresentation by affirmatively making a false statement. Alternatively, he or she can intentionally conceal a fact from the plaintiff. A seller of a house, for example, who deliberately paints the ceiling to conceal from the plaintiff-buyer the fact that the roof is leaking commits misrepresentation. Actions alone may constitute misrepresentation. The seller of a car who turns back the odometer misrepresents the mileage on that car even though he says nothing (Restatement (Second) of Torts § 525, illus. 1).

Under the common law, mere failure to disclose a material fact (as opposed to deliberate concealment) was not considered a misrepresentation. Until the 1950s, the doctrine of caveat emptor ("let the buyer beware") reigned and sellers of real estate had virtually

FIGURE 11-1   Elements of Intentional Misrepresentation

- Defendant makes a misrepresentation with intent of inducing plaintiff's reliance.
- Defendant knows the misrepresentation is false or acts with reckless indifference to truth or falsity of representation.
- Plaintiff justifiably relies on misrepresentation.
- Plaintiff suffers damages as a result of reliance.

no duty to disclose what they knew about the condition of their property to potential purchasers. Courts premised this doctrine on the fact that buyers and sellers of comparable power, skill, and experience were conscious of the risks they assumed and could protect themselves against those risks. In the modern view, however, nondisclosure may be considered concealment under certain circumstances, especially when the defect is **latent** (not visible to the buyer). A duty to disclose, for example, is frequently set forth in the so-called "termite" cases, in which the homeowner fails to tell the purchaser that the house has been infested with termites.

Similarly, liability may be imposed if a defendant presents a "half-truth," a statement that although literally true tends to be misleading. A statement such as "We have no termites in this house" is a half-truth if the termites have been long-term residents up until a month before the statement was made. If a **fiduciary relationship** exists between the parties, such as that between parent and child or attorney and client, the law imposes a more demanding obligation to disclose than if a transaction occurs at *arm's length* (i.e., no special relationship exists between the parties). For example, a businessman selling property to his business partner (assuming they have a fiduciary relationship for purposes of the transaction involved) has an obligation to disclose information that he would not be required to disclose if he were conducting an arm's-length transaction with a stranger.

The courts are more likely to find misrepresentation if a nondisclosed fact is essential to the transaction. If a seller of land fails to disclose to a buyer that nothing can be grown on the land even though she is aware that the buyer intends to use the land to grow crops, she is likely to be found liable for misrepresentation. Even if a plaintiff is unable to recover damages for nondisclosure, he can get rescission (which results in the canceling of the contract) if the nondisclosed fact is a material one.

Today, a small but rapidly growing number of states has enacted legislation or created regulations that require sellers of residential property to disclose certain aspects of the property's physical condition to potential purchasers. A copy of the mandatory disclosure form used in Ohio is shown in Figure 11-2.

To Whom Must the Misrepresentation Be Made?

Under the traditional common law, a defendant was liable only to those persons whom he or she intended to influence by the misrepresentation. A debtor, for example, who misrepresented his credit record to a creditor and then failed to make payments was not liable to a party who bought the debtor's note from the creditor. The requirement has been relaxed in recent times. Presently a plaintiff can recover if he or she is a member of a class whom the defendant could reasonably expect to learn of and rely on the misrepresentation.

Additionally, the plaintiff's reliance must occur in the "type of transaction" the defendant could reasonably expect the plaintiff to engage in as a result of the reliance (Restatement (Second) of Torts §§ 531 and

FIGURE 11-2 Residential Property Disclosure Form (Ohio)

DEPARTMENT OF COMMERCE
RESIDENTIAL PROPERTY DISCLOSURE FORM

Pursuant to Ohio Revised Code Section 5302.30

TO BE COMPLETED BY OWNER (Please Print)

Property Address:

Owners Name(s):

Date: , 19

Owner ( ) is ( ) is not occupying the property. If owner is occupying the property, since what date   .

Purpose of Disclosure Form: This is a statement of the condition of the property and of information concerning the property actually known by the owner as required by Ohio Revised Code Section 5302.30. Unless otherwise advised in writing by the owner, the owner, other than having lived at or owning the property, possesses no greater knowledge than that which could be obtained by a careful inspection of the property by a potential purchaser. Unless otherwise advised, owner has not conducted any inspection of generally inaccessible areas of the property. THIS STATEMENT IS NOT A WARRANTY OF ANY KIND BY THE OWNER OR BY ANY AGENT OR SUBAGENT REPRESENTING THE OWNER OF THE PROPERTY. THIS STATEMENT IS NOT A SUBSTITUTE FOR ANY INSPECTIONS. POTENTIAL PURCHASERS ARE ENCOURAGED TO OBTAIN THEIR OWN PROFESSIONAL INSPECTION.

Owner's Statement: The representations contained on this form are made by the owner and are not the representations of the owner's agent or subagent. This form and the representations contained in it are provided by the owner exclusively to potential purchasers in a transfer made by the owner, and are not made to purchasers in any subsequent transfers. The information contained in this disclosure form does not limit the obligation of the owner to disclose an item of information that is required by any other statute or law to be disclosed in the transfer of residential real estate.

Instructions to Owner: (1) Answer ALL questions. (2) Identify any material matters in the property that are actually known. (3) Attach additional pages with your signature if additional space is needed. (4) Complete this form yourself. (5) If some items do not apply to your property, write NA (not applicable). If the item to be disclosed is not within your actual knowledge, indicate Unknown.

THE FOLLOWING STATEMENTS OF THE OWNER ARE BASED ON OWNER'S ACTUAL KNOWLEDGE

A) WATER SUPPLY: The source of water supply to the property is (check appropriate boxes):

( ) Public Water Service   ( ) Private Water   ( ) Well Service   ( ) Holding Tank

( ) Cistern   ( ) Spring   ( ) Pond   ( ) Unknown   ( ) Other

If owner knows of any current leaks, backups or other material problems with the water supply system or quality of the water, please describe:

B) SEWER SYSTEM: The nature of the sanitary sewer system servicing the property is (check appropriate boxes):

( ) Public Sewer   ( ) Private Sewer   ( ) Septic Tank   ( ) Leach Field

( ) Aeration Tank   ( ) Filtration Bed   ( ) Unknown   ( ) Other

If not a public or private sewer, date of last inspection.

If owner knows of any current leaks, backups or other material problems with the sewer system servicing the property, please describe:

C) ROOF: Do you know of any current leaks or other material problems with the roof or rain gutters?
( ) Yes   ( ) No

If "YES," please describe:

If owner knows of any leaks or other material problems with the roof or rain gutters since owning the property (but not longer than the past 5 years), please describe and indicate any repairs completed:

D) BASEMENT/CRAWL SPACE: Do you know of any current water leakage, water accumulation, excess dampness or other defects with the basement/crawl space?   ( ) Yes   ( ) No

If "YES," please describe:

If owner knows of any repairs, alterations or modifications to the property or other attempts to control any water or dampness problems in the basement or crawl space since owning the property (but not longer than the past 5 years), please describe:

E) STRUCTURAL COMPONENTS (FOUNDATIONS, FLOORS, INTERIOR AND EXTERIOR WALLS): Do you know of any movement, shifting, deterioration, material cracks (other than visible minor cracks or blemishes) or other material problems with the foundation, floors, or interior/exterior walls?   ( ) Yes   ( ) No

If "YES," please describe:

If you know of any repairs, alterations or modifications to control the cause or effect of any problem identified above, since owning the property (but not longer than the past 5 years), please describe:

F) MECHANICAL SYSTEMS: Do you know of any current problems or defects with the mechanical systems?
( ) Yes   ( ) No

If "YES," please describe:

For purposes of this section, mechanical systems include electrical, plumbing (pipes), central heating and air conditioning, sump pump, fireplace/chimney, lawn sprinkler, water softener, security system, central vacuum, or other mechanical systems that exist on the property.

G) WOOD BORING INSECTS/TERMITES: Do you know of the presence of any wood boring insects/termites in or on the property or any existing damage to the property caused by wood boring insects/termites?
( ) Yes   ( ) No

If "YES," please describe:

If owner knows of any inspection or treatment for wood boring insects/termites, since owning the property (but not longer than the past 5 years), please describe:

H) PRESENCE OF HAZARDOUS MATERIALS: Do you have actual knowledge of the presence of any of the below identified hazardous materials on the property?

	Yes	No	Unknown
1) Lead-Based Paint	( )	( )	( )
2) Asbestos	( )	( )	( )
3) Urea-Formaldehyde Foam Insulation	( )	( )	( )
4) Radon Gas	( )	( )	( )

    4a) If YES, indicate level of gas if known

	Yes	No	Unknown
5) Other toxic substances	( )	( )	( )

If the answer to any of the above questions is "YES," please describe:

I) DRAINAGE: Do you know of any current flooding, drainage, settling or grading problems affecting the property? ( ) Yes ( ) No

If "YES," please describe:

If owner knows of any repairs, modifications or alterations to the property or other attempts to control any flooding, drainage, settling or grading problems since owning the property (but not longer than the past 5 years), please describe:

J) CODE VIOLATIONS: Have you received notice of any building or housing code violations currently affecting the use of the property? ( ) Yes ( ) No

If "YES," please describe:

K) UNDERGROUND STORAGE TANKS/WELLS: Do you know of any underground storage tanks, oil or natural gas wells (plugged or unplugged), or abandoned water wells on the property? ( ) Yes ( ) No

If "YES," please describe:

L) OTHER KNOWN MATERIAL DEFECTS: The following are other known material defects currently in or on the property:

For purposes of this section, material defects would include any non-observable physical condition existing on the property that could be dangerous to anyone occupying the property or any non-observable physical conditions that would inhibit a person's use of the property.

Owner represents that the statements contained in this form are made in good faith based on his/her actual knowledge as of the date signed by the Owner.

OWNER: DATE:

OWNER: DATE:

RECEIPT AND ACKNOWLEDGEMENT OF POTENTIAL PURCHASERS

Potential purchasers are advised that the owner has no obligation to update this form but may do so according to Revised Code Section 5302.30(G). Pursuant to Ohio Revised Code Section 5302.30(K), if this form is not provided to you prior to the time you enter into a purchase contract for the property, you may rescind the purchase contract by delivering a signed and dated document of rescission to Owner or Owner's agent, provided the document of rescission is delivered prior to all three of the following dates: 1) the date of closing; 2) 30 days after the Owner accepted your offer; and 3) within 3 business days following your receipt or your agent's receipt of this form or an amendment of this form.

I/WE ACKNOWLEDGE RECEIPT OF A COPY OF THIS DISCLOSURE FORM AND UNDERSTAND THAT THE STATEMENTS ARE MADE BASED ON THE OWNER'S ACTUAL KNOWLEDGE AS OF THE DATE SIGNED BY THE OWNER.

My/Our Signature below does not constitute approval of any disclosed condition as represented herein by the owner.

PURCHASER: DATE:

PURCHASER: DATE:

533). Suppose an architect supplies erroneous specifications to a builder, who in turn subcontracts the electrical work. If the subcontractor suffers pecuniary (monetary) damages because of the faulty specifications, the subcontractor will be allowed to recover from the architect. Recovery will be allowed even if the architect is unaware of the identity of the subcontractor when he gives the specifications to the builder (Restatement (Second) of Torts § 531, illus. 5).

Another exception to the rule requiring intent to induce reliance occurs in the context of commercial documents. Those who incorporate misstatements into commercial documents are liable to persons who suffer as a result of their justifiable reliance on the truth of those statements. A company that markets clover seed intentionally mislabeled as alfalfa seed is liable to those who plant the seeds in reliance on the label and consequently suffer a loss. Again it does not matter whether the seed company intended to make contact with those buyers (Restatement (Second) of Torts § 532, illus. 2).

Required State of Mind

Proof of intentional misrepresentation also requires showing that the defendant knew of the falsity of the statement or acted with reckless disregard to the truth. A defendant who lacks grounds for his representation or confidence in its accuracy possesses the state of mind required for intentional misrepresentation. State of mind is what distinguishes intentional misrepresentation from negligent misrepresentation.

A defendant is also culpable if he makes a statement that is merely a belief but represents it as being actual knowledge. In one case the officers of a corporation told one of the company's creditors that the company was making money. They also sent him some erroneous financial statements. In reliance on the officers' statements, the plaintiff refrained from collecting his debt. In fact, the company was losing money and when the plaintiff finally sought reimbursement he was unable to collect the monies owed him. The defendant officers were found liable in this case, not because their statements were false but because they made statements regarding the solvency of the company without

knowing whether the company was making money or not. Their culpability lay in their representation of belief as knowledge (*Sovereign Pocohontas Co. v. Bond*, 120 F.2d 39 (D.C. Cir. 1941)).

Reliance on the Misrepresentation

A plaintiff must also show that she relied on the defendant's misrepresentation. The question that commonly arises is whether the plaintiff made any independent investigation of her own and whether her reliance was on the misrepresentation, her investigation, or both. Suppose the seller of a horse fraudulently misrepresents the breeding potential of the horse and the plaintiff, wishing to confirm these representations, checks with other experienced horse breeders. If the plaintiff relies totally or almost totally on her own investigation, she will be deemed not to have relied on the seller's misrepresentation. If, however, the seller's misrepresentation is a substantial factor in inducing the plaintiff's reliance, the reliance requirement will be fulfilled and the seller will be found liable.

Was the Reliance Justifiable?

A related question is whether the plaintiff's reliance was justifiable. Is a plaintiff entitled to rely on an opinion offered by the defendant? Traditionally, courts have been reluctant to allow plaintiffs to recover on the basis of any of the defendant's statements that could be characterized as opinion.

In some circumstances, however, such reliance may be justified. If a defendant and plaintiff have a fiduciary relationship or if the defendant has worked to secure the confidence of the plaintiff, the plaintiff may be justified in relying on the defendant's opinion. Also, if the defendant purports to have special knowledge that the plaintiff does not have, the plaintiff may be justified in relying on the defendant. Similarly, if the defendant is aware that the plaintiff is particularly gullible or unintelligent and will be easily misled by any kind of opinion, a justifiable reliance will more likely be found. A horse trader, for example, who tells an ignorant investor that a particular horse is worth $500,000 may be found liable for misrepresentation if, in fact, any knowledgeable investor would recognize that figure as being wholly unrealistic (Restatement (Second) of Torts § 542).

"Puffing"

Mere "puffing" is not actionable. A used car dealer who tells a customer that this car is "the best deal you will ever make" is not liable for the statement even though the dealer does not actually believe that the car is a particularly good deal (Restatement (Second) of Torts § 542, cmt. e).

As Justice Learned Hand once commented, "Such statements, like the claims of campaign managers before election, are rather designed to allay the suspicion which would attend their absence than to be understood as having any relation to objective truth." *Vulcan Metals Co. v. Simmons Manufacturing Co.,* 248 F. 853, 856 (2d Cir. 1918).

Opinion of Disinterested Party

The result may be different if the plaintiff reasonably perceives that the opinion is being expressed by a "disinterested" party. In that case the plaintiff's reliance is more likely to be considered reasonable. If a consumer advocacy group indicates that a particular brand of off-road vehicle is safe and the plaintiff is injured in that vehicle, the consumer group's argument that its endorsement was merely an opinion is likely to fail. By holding itself out as a disinterested party that examined and ultimately endorsed the product, the group likely will be deemed as possessing special information upon which the public was reasonably justified in relying.

Opinion Implying Facts

If a defendant renders an opinion implying that no facts incompatible with that opinion exist, the plaintiff may be able to recover if he or she can show that the defendant was aware of such incompatible facts. For example, a corporation president who, in an effort to sell stock, represents his company as being a "gold mine" when in fact he knows the company to be losing money may be found liable for misrepresentation

(*Ragsdale v. Kennedy,* 209 S.E.2d 494 (N.C. 1974)).

Remember that the line between fact and opinion is a tenuous one at best—but if the defendant crosses over that line by making a statement of fact that she knows to be false, she can be found liable. A statement of value that would normally be considered opinion may become a factual statement because of the context in which it is expressed. A defendant who says "The land across the street sold for $10,000 an acre last year" has made a statement of fact for which he will be liable if he is aware that the land actually sold for much less.

Predictions

A prediction that a certain event is bound to happen will almost always be regarded as an opinion. If, however, the defendant knows of facts inconsistent with that prediction, he or she may still be found liable for misrepresentation. A landowner who predicts that the value of her land will increase 10 percent a year for the next five years could be held liable if the plaintiff could show that the landowner was aware that the property was about to be condemned.

Statement of Intentions

If a defendant makes a statement as to her own intentions, a plaintiff's reliance on that statement will frequently be considered justifiable. If a party to a contract is unable to sue for breach of contract because the opposing party can raise a contract defense, such as the Statute of Frauds, the party wanting to sue may be able to claim misrepresentation if she relied on the defendant's statements. Suppose a defendant promises to buy the plaintiff's house for $50,000 but at the time she makes this promise she actually has no intention of buying the house. When the plaintiff sues for breach of contract, if the defendant raises a Statute of Frauds defense (because the contract was not in writing), the plaintiff can sue on the basis of misrepresentation, arguing that the defendant never intended to keep her contract. If the plaintiff can prove this was the defendant's intent, most courts will not allow the defendant to raise the Statute of Frauds, the parol evidence rule, lack of consideration, or any other contract defense to bar liability.

Proximate Cause

The plaintiff in a suit for misrepresentation must prove that he or she sustained actual damages that were proximately caused by the defendant's misrepresentation. In other words, the loss must be a "reasonably foreseeable" result of the misrepresentation. Suppose, for example, the plaintiff purchases stock in reliance on the defendant's misrepresentation. If the market value of the stock declines due to causes unrelated to those misrepresentations, the defendant will not be considered the proximate cause of the plaintiff's losses (Restatement (Second) of Torts § 548A, illus. 1).

Damages

Damages for misrepresentation may be measured in two ways. First, the plaintiff may be asked to be put in the position he or she was in before the misrepresentation (referred to as the *reliance measure*). Alternatively, the plaintiff may be asked to be put in the position he or she would have been had the misrepresented facts been true (referred to as the *benefits of the bargain measure*). The majority of courts use the latter measure of damages.

To exemplify these approaches, suppose that a plaintiff pays $20,000 for a horse that is actually worth $10,000. If the horse would have been worth $50,000 if the misrepresentation about the horse had actually been true, under the benefit of the bargain approach the plaintiff will receive $40,000 (the difference between the actual value of the horse, $10,000, and what it would have been worth if it had been as it was represented, $50,000). Under the reliance method of measurement the plaintiff will recover $10,000 (the difference between the actual value of the horse, $10,000, and what the plaintiff paid, $20,000). Note that in assessing damages the fact that the plaintiff would have made a bad bargain even if the defendant had made no misrepresentations is irrelevant.

Figure 11-3 lists the aspects of misrepresentation we have been discussing.

PUTTING IT INTO PRACTICE 11.1

1. Lucille, a blackjack dealer in Lake Tahoe, has a "tummy tuck" operation to lower the scar from a previous tummy tuck. She says the surgeon assured her there were no risks involved, that her skin "would be as smooth as a baby's," and that she would be pleased with the results. After the operation Lucille's scar is lowered but her skin blisters and she experiences severe pain in an area above the stitches. The doctor promises either to resolve the problem himself or to pay for another doctor to do so. He continues to treat Lucille and never refuses to answer her questions or respond to her requests for treatment.

   Lucille decides to consult with other physicians and then hires an attorney to litigate her grievance. At trial, Lucille's expert witness speculates that the burn could be due to a chemical or "cast" burn, a minor injury, or, as the defense expert testifies, due to liquid silicone that had been injected into Lucille's breast years earlier and that had migrated to the abdomen.

   Do you think Lucille has a cause of action for misrepresentation based on any of the doctor's representations to her?

2. Barbara files suit for misrepresentation after suffering an ectopic pregnancy resulting from intercourse with her attorney (who is representing her in a domestic relations matter). The attorney vowed to her that "I

Continued on next page

---

can't possibly get anyone pregnant." Does she have a viable claim?

Suppose Barbara had delivered a healthy child after falsely telling the attorney before they engaged in intercourse that she was a on birth control pills. If she had sued him for child support, would the attorney have a viable claim for misrepresentation?

3. Maria and Martin are Polish prisoners of war who meet in a displaced persons camp. He proposes to her and she signs what she believes to be an application for a marriage certificate but later discovers she has entered into a civil marriage. Martin promises her a church marriage. Because she refuses to have marital relations with him until they are properly married, Martin locks her in a room and rapes her. After several days of confinement she escapes but he induces her to return, again promising a church marriage. Once again she escapes, only to return reluctantly when Martin promises her they will be married in the church.

Should Maria be granted an annulment on the basis of Martin's false representation? Is her reliance on Martin's promises justifiable?

4. Peter claims that the school district he attended for twelve years and from which he graduated deprived him of basic academic skills in reading and writing. Part of his complaint alleges that the district "allowed him 'to pass and advance from a course or grade level' with knowledge that he had not achieved either its completion or the skills 'necessary for him to succeed or benefit from subsequent courses,' . . . assigned him to classes in which the instructors were unqualified or which were not 'geared' to his reading level, and . . . permitted him to graduate from high school although he was 'unable to read above the eighth grade level.' " Peter claims that as a result of the district's and its employees' fraudulent representations that he was "performing at or near grade level in basic academic skills," he has suffered a loss of earning capacity. Should Peter be allowed to recover for intentional misrepresentation?

5. Florence brings suit against Kaiser Health Plan for malpractice because of the delay of her husband's doctor in ordering a biopsy in the diagnosis of her husband's condition. Florence maintains that when Kaiser represented that it would provide "high standards" of medical service, it promised a "standard higher than nonnegligence." She also points out that although Kaiser claimed to be a "nonprofit" organization, it was actually built around a system that encouraged doctors to be conservative in ordering tests and treatments. Because she and her husband were not told about Kaiser's policies, she alleges that they were fraudulently led to believe they would receive "the best quality of care and treatment." Do you think Florence has a viable claim for misrepresentation?

NEGLIGENT MISREPRESENTATION

Although historically recovery for negligent misrepresentation was not permitted, today most American courts allow such a claim. Other than intent, the requirements for an action of negligent misrepresentation are essentially the same as those for intentional misrepresentation.

The courts are most inclined to allow recovery for negligent misrepresentation when the defendant makes false statements during the course of his or her

FIGURE 11-3 Misrepresentation

WHAT IS A MISREPRESENTATION?

- False statement.
- Concealment by actions.
- Failure to disclose material fact that is essential to transaction.
- Telling of half-truth.

TO WHOM MUST MISREPRESENTATION BE MADE?

- Plaintiff belongs to class of persons that defendant could reasonably expect to learn of and rely on misrepresentation.
- Plaintiff is involved in the type of transaction defendant could reasonably expect plaintiff to engage in as a result of reliance.
- Defendant incorporates misstatements into commercial documents.

DEFENDANT'S STATE OF MIND

- Is aware of falsity of representation.
- Acts with reckless disregard for truth or falsity of representation.
- Has mere belief but acts as if he or she has actual knowledge.

WHAT IS JUSTIFIABLE RELIANCE?

Defendant offers an opinion and:
- Defendant and plaintiff have fiduciary relationship.
- Defendant has worked to gain plaintiff's confidence.
- Defendant is aware plaintiff is gullible or unintelligent.
- Plaintiff is likely to perceive that opinion is offered by "disinterested" party.
- Defendant suggests no facts incompatible with opinion exist when he or she is aware such facts exist.
- Defendant makes prediction and is aware of facts inconsistent with prediction.
- Defendant states what his or her intentions are, knowing the actual intentions are different.

HOW ARE DAMAGES PROVED?

Reliance: Putting plaintiff in position he or she was in prior to misrepresentation.
Benefit of the bargain: Putting plaintiff in position he or she would have been in had the misrepresented facts been true.

business or profession or has a pecuniary interest in the transaction at hand. A real estate broker, for example, may be liable for negligent misrepresentation by failing to use reasonable care in ascertaining the truth of a representation made by a seller, even if the broker honestly believes it to be true.

The defendant is not required to receive compensation directly. If a prospective client comes to an attorney's office and the attorney negligently gives him incorrect advice as part of a "free first consultation," the defendant attorney is still liable for the misrepresentation (Restatement (Second) of Torts § 552, cmt. d).

One who negligently misrepresents something, however, is liable to a narrower class of third persons than is one who intentionally misrepresents something. One who makes an *intentional* misrepresentation is liable to anyone whom he or she reasonably expects to learn about the statement (under the modern view). One who makes a *negligent* misrepresentation is liable only to those whom he or she intends to reach with the information or knows the recipient of the information intends to reach.

Nevertheless, as long as the defendant is aware that a negligent misrepresentation will be passed on to a limited number of people, he or she will be liable even if unaware of their precise identity. Suppose a surveyor negligently provides a landowner with an erroneous description of her land. If the surveyor is aware that the owner is planning to sell her land, he will be liable to the purchaser for his errors even though he does not know the name of the purchaser. By the same token, a lawyer who negligently drafts a will may be liable to the beneficiaries even though he may be unaware of the identity of those beneficiaries.

The courts deny recovery, however, when the class of people intended to be reached by the negligent misrepresentation is not limited. Suppose a stock ticker service negligently reports information to its customer brokers. The plaintiff, a stock owner, reads the news at his broker's office and immediately sells his stock because he expects stock prices to fall. The stock ticker service is not liable because the plaintiff did not subscribe directly to its service; therefore, the "limited number of persons" requirement is not met (*Jaillet v. Cashman,* 139 N.E. 714 (N.Y. 1923)).

To see an interesting application of the law regarding intentional and negligent misrepresentaiton in the context of adoptions, read *Gibbs v. Ernst,* 647 A.2d 882 (Pa. 1994). Notice how, and for what social policy reasons, the court allows the common law tort of misrepresentation to be applied to an area of law that is wholly created by statute. Note, too, how courts are more reluctant to hold adoption agencies liable for their negligent misrepresentations than for their intentional misrepresentations, out of a fear that imposing too heavy a burden on adoption agencies will unduly hamper their ability to place children in homes.

PUTTING IT INTO PRACTICE 11.2

William has an ankle replacement after fracturing his right ankle. Before the surgery he is told by his physician that the physician has performed three successful ankle replacements. When William asked the doctor what would happen if the ankle replacement did not work, the doctor responded, "The worse that could happen is that we will just take that out and fuse it." The doctor also assures him that amputation is "not a problem" and "not something to worry about." Based on the doctor's representations, Williams agrees to the ankle replacement. After the surgery, the ankle becomes infected; the infection does not respond to antibiotics and William's leg has to be amputated below the knee by another doctor. At trial the doctor testifies that he had never personally performed an ankle replacement, although members of his medical group had.

Do you think William has a claim for negligent misrepresentation? Are there any other grounds upon which William might be able to sue?

CASE

Gibbs v. Ernst
647 A.2d 882 (Pa. 1994)

MONTEMURO, Justice.

This is an appeal by Concern Professional Services for Children and Youth; Concern's Director, Paul Ernst; Concern Adoption Specialist, Marsha S. Hiester (hereinafter collectively Concern); and Northhampton County Children and Youth; its Executive Director, R. Nancy Haley; and its Caseworker, Brenda Messa (hereinafter collectively Children and Youth) from an Order of the Commonwealth Court reversing the trial court's grant of demurrers to counts of Wrongful Adoption and Negligent Placement of Adoptive Child in the complaint filed by appellees Frank A. and Jayne Gibbs, and Michael J. Gibbs.

Appellees initiated this action in the Court of Common Pleas of Bucks County against Concern and Children and Youth arising out of the adoption of Michael J. Gibbs on October 21, 1985. Children and Youth is an agency of the Commonwealth of Pennsylvania and, pursuant to law, is responsible for placing children who are wards of the Commonwealth with agencies for the purposes of adoption. Concern is a private child placement agency, licensed by the Commonwealth.

The sole issue presented before this Court is whether the law of the Commonwealth recognizes as causes of action Wrongful Adoption and Negligent Placement of Adoptive Child. For the reasons set forth below, we affirm in part the decision of the Commonwealth Court and hold that traditional common law causes of action sounding in fraud and negligence apply in the adoption context.

The Complaint alleges the following facts: in early 1983, appellees Jayne and Frank Gibbs, who were already foster parents, inquired of Concern about the availability of a healthy Caucasian infant for adoption, and were informed that there was a two year waiting list for healthy Caucasian infants. Appellees were actively encouraged by agency representatives to apply for the adoption of an older child, and were told that it would be easier to adopt a "hard to adopt due to age" child, and that if the child had been physically or sexually abused, Concern would disclose fully the history of these occurrences. Appellees were invited to look through a book containing photographs of older children available for adoption, along with brief positive descriptions of the children.

In May of 1983, appellees submitted a dual application for adoption of a healthy Caucasian infant and a "hard to adopt due to age" child. After a home-study by Marsha Hiester, Concern's adoption specialist, appellees reviewed the book of waiting children approximately twice a month at Concern's offices. On each occasion they completed a form for the child they wanted to adopt, and on each occasion they specifically requested a child who was "hard to place due to age," but who had no history of sexual or physical abuse or any mental or emotional problems.

In late August or early September 1984, appellees were informed by Concern that they had been chosen to adopt Michael, a five year old boy from Northhampton County.[1] In addition to his age, appellees were told by Concern that Michael was presently repeating kindergarten, that he was Caucasian, and that he had been in foster care, but for only two years and only with one family. Appellees were further informed by Concern that Michael was hyperactive, behind in his school work, had been verbally abused by his mother and that the major problem was neglect by his mother. Concern specifically denied any history of physical or sexual abuse. In October of 1984, appellees were introduced to Michael and his caseworkers at Concern. They were given information about Michael's foster family, and were once again informed by Concern that there was no history of sexual or physical abuse. Later that same afternoon, appellees met with Brenda Messa, a caseworker at Children and Youth's offices in Easton, Pennsylvania where they requested a more detailed social and medical history of Michael.

During the first weekend of November, 1984, Michael was placed for adoption with appellees who filed a Report of Intention to Adopt with the Orphan's Court of Berks County. Shortly thereafter, Concern forwarded certain documents identified as Michael's medical file, consisting of records of Michael's birth and the medical history of his natural mother. Appellees once again

---

1. We note that Michael was born on May 21, 1977, making him, in fact, more than seven years old in August/September of 1984.

requested more information about Michael's psychological and emotional history.

Concern supervised Michael's placement with appellees and although he had educational problems, Michael seemed much calmer and passed first grade. In September of 1985, Concern consented to the finalization of the adoption. Prior to finalization, appellees met with Concern and specifically asked whether there was anything in Conern's file that had not been disclosed to them. They were assured by Concern that they had been given everything Children and Youth had provided to Concern; but were told that Children and Youth had "promised additional information," and that there was a "communication problem" with Children and Youth. Concern agreed to check all records to make sure everything was made available to appellees prior to the finalization of the adoption.

On October 21, 1985, a final order was entered in the Court of Common Pleas of Berks County granting the adoption of Michael J. Gibbs. Immediately thereafter, Michael began experiencing severe emotional problems. He became violent and aggressive toward younger children, attempting to amputate the arm of a five year old; attempting to suffocate his younger cousin; attempting to kill another cousin by hitting him over the head with a lead pipe; deliberately placing Clorox in a cleaning solution, causing Ms. Gibbs to burn her hands badly; and starting a fire which seriously injured a younger cousin.

After Michael's admission and evaluation at the Philadelphia Child Guidance Center, appellees were advised that little chance existed of any change in his violent behavior. Michael's conduct deteriorated further, and he was admitted to a special program for adopted children at the Northwestern Institute where he remained until he was transferred by court order to the Eastern State School and Hospital. On or about September 15, 1989, Michael was declared dependent by the Family Division of the Philadelphia Court of Common Pleas, and was placed in the custody of the Department of Human Resources.

In September of 1989, a caseworker from the Department of Human Services informed appellees for the first time that Michael had been severely abused, both physically and sexually, as a young child. Records in the possession of Northwestern Institute revealed that Michael had been in ten different foster placements before he was freed for adoption; that during his first six years Michael's mother repeatedly placed him in and then removed him from foster care; that there was a long, serious history of abuse, both physical and sexual, by his biological parents; that Michael had been neglected by his biological mother; that Michael had an extensive history of aggressiveness and hostility towards other children; and that Michael's mother at one time attempted to cut off his penis. At no time prior to the finalization of the adoption did Concern or Children and Youth disclose this information although it was in their possession and had been requested.

In April of 1990, appellees commenced this action in the Court of Common Pleas of Bucks County, setting forth in Count I of their complaint a cause of action for Wrongful Adoption and in Count II a cause of action for Negligent Placement of Adoptive Child. Appellants, Concern and Children and Youth, filed preliminary objections in the nature of a demurrer to these counts which the trial court granted. The Commonwealth Court reversed, *Gibbs v. Concern Professional Services,* 150 Pa. Commw. 154, 160, 615 A.2d 851, 854 (1991), and in June of 1993, we granted allocatur on the sole question of whether the Commonwealth Court was correct in its conclusion that appellees could maintain their action for Wrongful Adoption and Negligent Placement of Adoptive Child.

The Commonwealth Court's standard of review in assessing the propriety of a common pleas court decision is limited to a determination of whether constitutional rights have been violated or whether the common pleas court abused its discretion or committed an error of law. . . . We agree with the Commonwealth Court that the Court of Common Pleas erred in sustaining appellants' demurrer.

In examining appellees' claims, we do not believe that we are considering novel theories of recovery, since the terms employed by appellees are somewhat of a misnomer. The proper focus of this case is whether long-standing common law causes of action should be applied to the adoption context.

Most authorities have recognized that causes of action for wrongful adoption are no more than an extension of common law principles to the adoption setting.

In determining whether these traditional common law causes of action should be applied to the adoption context in our Commonwealth, we are well aware of the competing interests involved. On one side is the interest of prospective parents in obtaining as much information as possible about the child they are to adopt. Adoption experts are virtually unanimous in the belief that complete and accurate medical and social information should be communicated to adopting patents. Providing full and complete information is crucial because the consequences of non-disclosure can be catastrophic; ignorance of medical or psychological history can prevent the adopting parents and their doctors from providing effective treatment, or any treatment at all. Moreover, full and accurate disclosure ensures that the adopting parents are emotionally and financially equipped to raise a child with special needs. Failure to provide adequate background information can result in the placement of children with families unable or unwilling to cope with physical or mental problems, leading to failed adoptions.[6]

On the other side of the ledger, adoption agencies and intermediaries are justifiably concerned lest any undue burden placed upon them should ultimately reduce the number of successful adoptions. In deciding to apply traditional common law causes of action to the adoption context, we have paid particular attention to the obligations placed upon adoption agencies so as not to diminish their effectiveness in placing children. We are convinced that the vast majority of adoption agencies in this Commonwealth conduct the adoption process with the utmost professionalism. However, we are also convinced that agencies, on occasion, do fail to provide prospective parents with complete and accurate information, and worse, occasionally supply information which is both false and misleading.[8] Mindful of the seriousness of this problem and its potentially devastating consequences, we hold that the traditional common law causes of action grounded in fraud and negligence to apply to the adoption setting.

---

6. . . . It can be argued that adoptive parents are entitled to no notice of medical problems, since natural parents receive no advance warning of a child's special needs. However, the risks assumed by adoptive parents are, in truth, very different from those of [natural] parents. Biological parents, theoretically at least, are aware of their medical histories and can decide to have a child with knowledge of, e.g., an increased risk of genetic abnormality. Adoptive parents, without full and accurate information, have no way of knowing if the adoptee has a risk of a genetic problem. This Court is also mindful that adoptive parents are performing a valuable social service in providing a family to otherwise unwanted children. In light of this contribution to society, it is only equitable to conclude that adoptive parents should not be asked to assume unwittingly the same risks as natural parents. For these reasons, a policy in favor of full and accurate disclosure of a child's medical history improves the chances of a successful placement and promotes public confidence in the institution of adoption.

8 . Research reveals that one third of the parents who had adopted physically abused children, and one half of those adopting sexually abused children were not informed of the abuse.

The Adoption Act of 1970, codified at 23 Pa.C.S. §§ 2101–2901, sets forth the steps which must be taken to realize an adoption, and the responsibilities and duties of adoption intermediaries in the process. Any person intending to adopt a child must file a Report of Intention to Adopt, 23 Pa.C.S. § 2531, within six months of which the intermediary must respond by reporting to the court information specifically required by 23 Pa.C.S. § 2533. Under Section 2533 (b) (12), the intermediary must include as part of its report "[a] statement that medical history was obtained and if not obtained, a statement of the reason therefor." Medical history information is defined as:

[m]edical records and other information concerning an adoptee or an adoptee's natural family which is relevant to the adoptee's present or future health care or medical treatment. The term includes otherwise confidential or privileged information providing that identifying contents have been removed pursuant to section 2909 (relating to medical history information).

23 Pa.C.S. § 2102.

Section 2909 sets forth medical history requirements and states in pertinent part that "[m]edical history information shall, where practicable, be delivered by the attending physician or other designated person to the intermediary who shall deliver such information to the adopting parents or their physician." 23 Pa.C.S. § 2909(a).

Appellants argue that the Commonwealth Court exceeded its authority and encroached upon the province of the legislature in recognizing appellees' action for Wrongful Adoption and Negligent Placement of Adoptive Child because they are not mentioned in the Adoption Act. Although the Act, . . . sets forth the duties of an adoption intermediary with regard to providing the medical history of an adoptive child, it provides no sanction against an intermediary who fails to meet that obligation.

Appellants correctly assert that adoption is a statutorily created mechanism, unknown at common law. It is also true that the Adoption Act must be strictly construed . . . and that exceptions to the Act may not be judicially created. However, we find nothing in the Act to be inconsistent with the application of traditional common law principles to the adoption setting.

In *Roe v. Catholic Charities*, the Illinois Appellate Court considered precisely the question of whether common law causes of action were disallowed where the adoption statute did not provide for them. There, the court analogized adoption to corporations, which are also creatures of statute, but which are bound by both statutory and common law. After noting that, for example, a corporation may be sued in tort, the court concluded that "[p]rivate adoption agencies and agencies of not-for-profit corporations in particular, are bound by all the law . . . both statute and common law."

We are in full accord with the reasoning of the court in *Roe*. The Adoption Act establishes the procedures that govern the adoption process, and the cases cited by appellants properly stand for the notion that these procedures are to be strictly construed. However, the Act is silent on whether adoption intermediaries are liable for the commission of torts. It is our opinion that this silence evidences the legislature's intention that adoption agencies be liable under the long-established common law of Pennsylvania. Had the legislature intended for the Adoption Act to provide intermediaries with immunity from common law sanctions, it would have said so explicitly. The causes of action we address today are so well established that we find affirmative action by the legislature, rather than silence, would be necessary to prevent their application in the adoption context. Until such legislative action is forthcoming, we hold that adoption intermediaries are subject to all the law of this Commonwealth, both statutory and common law.

The complaint suggests several common law theories of recovery. The first such cause of action is intentional misrepresentation or fraud, which contains the following elements: (1) a representation; (2) which is material to the transaction at hand; (3) made falsely, with knowledge of its falsity or recklessness as to whether it is true or false; (4) with the intent of misleading another into relying on it; (5) justifiable reliance on the misrepresentation; and (6) the resulting injury was proximately caused by the reliance.[12]

---

12. The tort of intentional non-disclosure has the same elements as the tort of intentional misrepresentation except that in a case of intentional non-disclosure the party intentionally conceals a material fact rather than making an affirmative misrepresentation. . . . The tort of intentional non-disclosure has been recognized in the adoption setting by other state courts. We have recognized that concealment or non-disclosure is an actionable tort in this Commonwealth . . . . Such fraud arises where there is an intentional concealment calculated to deceive. . . . We need not decide whether actions for the closely related tort of intentional non-disclosure or concealment should be allowed in the adoption setting, since close examination of appellees' complaint reveals that they have not pleaded such a cause of action.

Our sister states have unanimously applied the theory of intentional misrepresentation to the adoption context. . . . In *Burr*, the adopting parents were told that the adoptee was born in a hospital to an eighteen year old unwed mother who gave up the child to move to Texas in search of a better job. The agency stated that the child was a "nice, big, healthy, baby boy." The child later developed severe medical problems requiring twenty-four hour nursing care, and was eventually institutionalized for the remainder of his life. The adopting parents later learned that the child had, in fact, been born in a mental institution to a mentally retarded woman and had previously been placed with several foster families. The adoption agency was well aware of these facts and that the child was developing slowly, but provided the adopting parents a fictional story about the child's medical history. The parents sued the adoption agency for intentional misrepresentation, and the Ohio Supreme Court upheld an award of damages, concluding that "[i]t would be a travesty of justice and a distortion of the truth to conclude that deceitful placement of this infant, known by [the adoption agency] to be at risk, was not actionable when the tragic, but hidden realities of the child's infirmities finally came to light."

The law of this Commonwealth has long recognized fraud or intentional misrepresentation as actionable conduct in other settings. . . . We now hold, in accord with the unanimous decisions of our sister jurisdictions, that the cause of action for intentional misrepresentation is equally applicable in the adoption context. Such application will further the goal of providing prospective parents with full and accurate information about the child, and, at the same time will inhibit adoption agencies from providing false information. Adopting parents will then be able to make informed choices about adoption, ensuring that they have the emotional and financial resources to care properly for the child they have consented to adopt. This truthfulness in the adoption process will, thus, result in fewer failed adoptions and enhance public confidence in the process. We, like the court in *Burr*, believe that it would be a "travesty of justice" to allow adoption agencies to engage in deceitful and fraudulent conduct with impunity. . . . Few would argue that the knowing provision of false information by adoption intermediaries to prospective parents so as to induce them to accept a particular child is not reprehensible and blameworthy conduct. Still, we have carefully considered the interests of adoption intermediaries so as not to place an undue burden on them. We find that the only burden placed upon agencies arising from the application of this tort is the obligation to refrain from fraudulent and deceitful tactics. We require no less from every other business or non-profit organization in this Commonwealth, and see no valid reason to release adoption intermediaries from the burden of truth in their daily operations. Indeed, we find it particularly apposite in this context because of the potentially devastating consequences that can result from fraudulent conduct here.

Upon review of the complaint, we find that appellees clearly plead the elements of intentional misrepresentation . . ., and we hold that they should be able to proceed to trial on this cause of action.

The complaint also suggests that negligent misrepresentation provides grounds for recovery. The elements which must be proven for such a wrong to be shown are: (1) a misrepresentation of a material fact; (2) the representor must either know of the misrepresentation, must make the misrepresentation without knowledge as to its truth or falsity or must make the representation under circumstances in which he ought to have known of its falsity; (3) the representor must intend the representation to induce another to act on it; and (4) injury must result to the party acting in justifiable reliance on the misrepresentation . . . . Thus, negligent misrepresentation differs from intentional misrepresentation in that to commit the former, the speaker need not know his or her words are untrue, but must have failed to make reasonable investigation of the truth of those words.

Several of our sister states have recognized the tort of negligent misrepresentation in the adoption context . . . .

Any action in negligence is premised on the existence of a duty owed by one party to another. . . . In a claim for negligent misrepresentation, the adoption agency has assumed a duty to tell the truth when it volunteers information to prospective parents, but has failed to perform that duty. . . . In *Meracle,* the adoption agency informed the prospective parents that the adoptee's paternal grandmother had died from Huntington's Disease. The parents asserted that the agency told them that the child's natural father had tested negative for the disease, and that, therefore, the child had no greater chance of developing the illness than any other child. The parents later learned that, in fact, there was no test to determine whether the father had inherited Huntington's. When the child developed the disease, the adopting parents sued the agency for negligently misrepresenting to them the

father's condition. The court concluded that the parents' claim was not barred by public policy, and that "[s]uch a conclusion does not expose adoption agencies to potentially unlimited liability nor does it make such agencies the guarantors of the health of adoptive children. To avoid liability agencies simply refrain from making affirmative representations about a child's health."

In *Caritas,* the adopting parents were told that a slight possibility of incest in the child's background existed, but that the child was otherwise in good health. When serious behavioral and emotional problems developed after adoption, the child's psychologists contacted the agency for more information regarding the child's genetic background. The agency provided a document revealing that the child's biological parents were a 17 year old boy and his 13 year old sister, and that the father was hyperactive with a history of psychological problems. The parents sued the agency maintaining that it had made negligent misrepresentations about the child's background. The court held that public policy did not preclude a negligent misrepresentation action against an adoption agency, finding instead that "our decision will give potential parents more confidence in the adoption process and in the accuracy of the information they receive. Such confidence would be eroded if we were to immunize agencies from liability for false statements made during the adoption process."

Pennsylvania has long recognized the common law tort of negligent representation . . . and there is no reason why this cause of action should not be recognized in the adoption context.

We are fully aware that application of the tort of negligent misrepresentation presents more of a burden on adoption agencies than the tort of intentional misrepresentation, which requires only that adoption agencies refrain from fraudulent and deceitful conduct. Negligent misrepresentation, however, requires that the adoption agency make reasonable efforts to determine whether its representations are true. . . . Nevertheless, we believe that this admittedly heavier burden is tempered in several ways. First, agencies are only under the obligation to make reasonable efforts to determine if their statements are true. Thus, adoption agencies need not offer warranties or guarantees as to the information they provide. Second, as aptly stated by the court in *Meracle,* agencies may refrain from making any representations at all if they find that the burden of reasonable investigation is too harsh. While we adopt the traditional common-law cause of action of negligent misrepresentation in the adoption setting today, we in no way imply that adoption agencies are insurors or warrantors of a child's health. The tort we now recignize is not similar to, nor can it be compared with products liability or contractual warranties. Adoption agencies must merely use reasonable care to insure that the information they communicate is accurate, and the parents must show that any negligently communicated information is causally related to their damages. We believe that this tort is sufficiently restricted by the common law notion of foreseeability as found in the concepts of duty and proximate cause to prevent it from becoming in any way a guarantee or warranty of a child's future health.

An important element of duty is foreseeability; thus, the liability of adoption agencies is limited to those conditions reasonably predictable at the time of placement. . . . As the court in *Foster* held, "[a] duty does not exist if the defendant could not reasonably foresee any injury as the result of his acts or if his conduct was reasonable in light of what he could anticipate—no one is expected to guard against events which are not reasonably to be anticipated or that are so unlikely that the risks would be commonly disregarded." Accordingly, under the traditional principles of negligence, the duty of adoption agencies for the purposes of negligent misrepresentation will only apply where the condition of the child was foreseeable at the time of placement so that the agency is blameworthy in making a misrepresentation. . . .

Upon reviewing appellees' complaint we find that they have pleaded a cause of action for negligent misrepresentation. In Count I, ¶ 53, they aver that appellants "should have known" the statements and representations they made were false. Thus ¶¶ 52–59 state a cause of action for negligent misrepresentation as well as intentional misrepresentation. We therefore hold that appellees should be able to proceed to trial on the theory of negligent misrepresentation. . . .

For the reasons set forth above, we affirm the order of the Commonwealth Court to the extent that it allows appellees to proceed to trial on claims of intentional misrepresentation [and] negligent misrepresentation.

■ PUTTING IT INTO PRACTICE 11.3 □

1. What is the issue in *Gibbs*?
2. What are the competing interests implicated in deciding how much information should be revealed to prospective adoptive parents?
3. Does an adoption intermediary have an obligation under the Adoption Act of 1970 to provide prospective parents with the medical history of adoptees and their natural family?
4. Is adoption a statutorily created mechanism that was unknown under the common law? Does this mean that common law principles cannot be applied to the adoption setting?
5. What does the Adoption Act indicate about whether adoption intermediaries can be held liable for the commission of a tort? What does the court believe the legislature would have to do to indicate that common tort law is not applicable in the adoption context?
6. How does the tort of intentional non-disclosure differ from intentional misrepresentation?
7. How have other states treated the issue of intentional misrepresentation in the context of adoption? How have they treated negligent misrepresentation?
8. What does the court hold in reference to whether the parents in this case should be able to proceed to trial on the intentional misrepresentation claim? What about the negligent misrepresentation claim?
9. Why does the court believe that the additional burden imposed on adoption agencies by allowing suit for negligent misrepresentation is not unreasonable?

INNOCENT MISREPRESENTATION

Until relatively recently, the courts have been unwilling to impose liability for innocent misrepresentations, which are, in effect, representations for which a defendant is strictly liable. At least two circumstances exist, however, in which many courts are now willing to allow recovery. (See Figure 11-4.) If a party involved in a sale, rental, or exchange transaction makes a material misrepresentation to the other in an effort to close a deal, he or she will be liable even if the misrepresentation is innocent (Restatement (Second) of Torts § 552C (1)). If a seller of land, for example, represents in good faith that he is selling property that he in fact does not own, he will be liable to the purchaser for his misrepresentation even though it is perfectly innocent. The sale, rental, or exchange must be directly between the plaintiff and the defendant. Suppose a manufacturer makes a representation to a retailer, who in turn passes it on to the plaintiff to induce her to buy the product. In that case strict liability does not apply (Restatement (Second) of Torts § 552C).

Cases involving innocent misrepresentations can also be brought on the basis of an implied or express warranty theory. The plaintiff may opt for the strict liability theory because certain contract defenses that can be raised in a warranty suit are inapplicable in a strict liability suit. The parol evidence rule, for example, which precludes the admission of oral and written evidence external to a contract, is inapplicable in a strict liability suit but is certainly appropriate in a warranty suit.

Innocent misrepresentation also arises in the context of product liability. Similar to the "express warranty" provisions of the Uniform Commercial Code (UCC), a seller of goods that makes misrepresentations on a label or through public advertising is strictly liable for any physical injury that results from such misinformation. Even if the plaintiff does not buy the product from the defendant, the defendant remains liable. (See discussion on warranty in Chapter 13.)

FIGURE 11-4   Recovery for Negligent and Innocent Misrepresentation

WHEN IS RECOVERY ALLOWED FOR NEGLIGENT MISREPRESENTATION?	WHEN IS RECOVERY ALLOWED FOR INNOCENT MISREPRESENTATION?
• Misrepresentation is made during course of defendant's business or profession. • Misrepresentation is made during transaction in which defendant has a pecuniary interest. • Plaintiff is someone defendant intends to reach with representation or knows recipient of representation intends to reach. • Defendant is aware misrepresentation will be passed on to limited number of persons although he does not know their identities.	• Defendant makes misrepresentation during course of sale, rental, or exchange in effort to close the deal. • Defendant makes misstatement on product label or in course of public advertising.

PUTTING IT INTO PRACTICE 11.4

The Ballards are interested in buying a lot with an unfinished dwelling and a well. The sellers' listing mentions a 100-foot well and their real estate broker, believing the well to be good based on representations made to him by the sellers, tells the Ballards the well is adequate. Based on their belief in the sufficiency of the well, the Ballards buy the property. They are forced, however, to haul water when the well fails to provide sufficient water and then have to deepen the well so that its water production is adequate. Do the Ballards have a claim of innocent misrepresentation against the broker?

NUISANCE

A precise definition of the term **nuisance** has eluded the courts for centuries. In fact, one of the foremost scholars of tort law, William Prosser, refers to nuisance as "a sort of legal garbage can." The most that can be said is that a defendant's interference with a plaintiff's interest constitutes nuisance. A nuisance can be either a public nuisance or a private nuisance. The essence of a *public nuisance* is an interference with "a right common to the general public" (Restatement (Second) of Torts § 821B(1)). A *private nuisance,* in contrast, is an unreasonable interference with the plaintiff's use and enjoyment of his or her land (Restatement (Second) of Torts § 822). The key to private nuisance is the need for the plaintiff to have an interest in the land that has been affected by the defendant's activities. The maintenance of a feedlot or a house of prostitution in close proximity to a residential area are examples of public nuisance; the playing of extremely loud music at 2:00 A.M. in a residential area exemplifies a private nuisance. Figure 11-5 defines the aspects of public and private nuisances.

Public Nuisance

To sustain a claim for public nuisance, the plaintiff must show that the public at large was actually injured or was exposed to the possibility of injury. It is not sufficient if only the plaintiff is injured, even if he or she is injured in a public place. Furthermore, the harm

FIGURE 11-5   Nuisance

PUBLIC NUISANCE	PRIVATE NUISANCE
•Substantial interference. • Affects right common to general public. • Public must be injured or exposed to injury. • Plaintiff need not have interest in land. • Plaintiff must suffer damages peculiar to him.	• Substantial interference. • Affects plaintiff's use and enjoyment of land. • Plaintiff must suffer substantial interference with use or enjoyment of land. • Plaintiff must have interest in land.

must be a substantial one. Under the common law, only conduct that constituted a crime met the requirement of a public nuisance. Most modern courts no longer require conduct to be criminal, although such conduct is still more likely to be deemed a public nuisance than conduct that is not.

The plaintiff must also show that he suffered damage peculiar to him that was not shared by the rest of the public. Suffering the same inconvenience or being exposed to the same threat as everyone else in the community is not sufficient. The rationale for this rule is that wrongs to the community as a whole should be redressed by the community's representatives to avoid duplication of legal actions. The government, however, can bring an action on behalf of the public without this showing. This special-injury element requires that the injuries of a private plaintiff be "different in kind" from the injuries suffered by the general community, but that they be incurred in the plaintiff's exercise of the common right enjoyed by the community. This special-injury requirement has raised a barrier to potential private plaintiffs bringing nuisance claims relating to environmental hazards.

The courts, however, have struggled with this notion of "particular damage." Some have allowed recovery if the plaintiff suffered greater economic loss than others in the community; others have denied recovery in similar cases. If the plaintiff's pecuniary loss precludes him from performing on a contract or causes him additional expense in his performance, many courts have allowed the plaintiff to recover. Similarly, if the defendant has interfered with the plaintiff's commercial use of his land, many courts allow recovery for public nuisance. Commercial fisheries, for example, have been allowed to recover for losses due to pollution even though ordinary citizens who used the polluted waters could not recover.

A legislature can, by virtue of its police power, declare uses of property or conduct that are detrimental to the health, morals, peace, or general welfare of its citizens to be a nuisance. Because neighbors are more likely to spot nuisances in their community than are local officials, some states have set up administrative systems in which citizens can alert government officials about a nuisance property in their neighborhood. A Texas statute, for example, allows the district attorney to call public meetings to identify public nuisances after receiving a request for such a meeting by a certain percentage of the registered voters in the area. At the meeting, neighbors may, in front of the property owner, voice their complaints about the alleged nuisance. After the meeting, the district attorney may elect to take legal action if she determines that sufficient evidence exists. Florida law provides for the creation of local administrative boards that receive neighbors' complaints and conduct hearings regarding alleged public nuisances. These boards have the authority to declare a property to be a public nuisance, to prohibit further operation of the premises for one year, and/or to seek court injunctions.

Private Nuisance

The key to suing on the basis of private nuisance, as mentioned earlier, is the plaintiff's ability to show that she has an interest in the affected land. Tenants, as well as family members of an owner or tenant, are considered to have such an interest. The plaintiff must prove that the use and enjoyment of her land was substantially interfered with and that the defendant's conduct was either negligent, intentional, or abnormally dangerous.

Nuisance versus Trespass

The difference between a private nuisance and trespass is subtle. A trespass consists of an interference with the plaintiff's right to *possession* of his or her property; nuisance consists of an interference with the plaintiff's right to *enjoy* and *use* his or her property. Nuisance can occur, therefore, even if nothing physically enters the plaintiff's property. Furthermore, the fact that the interference must be substantial also differentiates nuisance from trespass. Recall that a plaintiff may recover for trespass even though suffering no substantial harm, as the tort requires only an intentional invasion of the plaintiff's property. Most conduct that constitutes a trespass typically meets the criteria for a nuisance as well. Blasting activities in the vicinity of the plaintiff's land, for example, obviously create a nuisance in light of the noise and vibrations that are produced. But if rocks and other debris are cast on the plaintiff's land, a trespass is also committed.

What Constitutes Substantial Interference

Substantial interference undoubtedly occurs when the plaintiff is injured or her property is damaged. The interference may also be substantial if the plaintiff is inconvenienced or subjected to unpleasant sensory awarenesses, such as obnoxious odors or blaring sounds. The plaintiff must show that a person of normal sensitivity would be seriously bothered by the defendant's conduct. An abnormally sensitive plaintiff, therefore, will be precluded from recovery. What constitutes substantial interference will, of necessity, hinge on the type of neighborhood in which the activity occurs. Activities that constitute a nuisance in a quiet suburban area might not qualify as a nuisance in a densely populated urban area.

Intentional and Unreasonable Interference

Although a defendant's conduct can be either negligent, intentional, or abnormally dangerous, most private nuisance claims arise out of intentional conduct. A defendant must, in other words, know with substantial certainty that interference will occur even if he has no desire to interfere with the plaintiff's use and enjoyment of his land.

If the defendant's interference is intentional, the plaintiff must also prove that such interference is unreasonable. To determine whether interference is unreasonable, some courts have balanced the utility of the defendant's conduct against the plaintiff's harm. In accordance with this test a plaintiff may be barred from recovery, even though she suffered substantial harm, if the utility of the defendant's conduct exceeds the harm the plaintiff suffered.

The Restatement (Second) has rejected this balancing test for reasonableness and deemed that interference is unreasonable if one of two things is true. Either the plaintiff's harm must outweigh the utility of the defendant's conduct, or, alternatively, the harm caused by the conduct must be substantial and greater than anything any individual should be required to bear without compensation (Restatement (Second) of Torts § 829A). Under this criterion, even if the defendant's activity is socially useful he will be required to compensate the plaintiff, unless so many people are affected by the defendant's conduct that requiring the defendant to pay damages would make it impossible for him to continue the activity.

In one case a coal-burning electric generating plant emitted 90 tons of sulphur-dioxide gas into the atmosphere each day, causing extensive crop damage and other harm. The defendant claimed it had used due care in constructing and operating the plant. Nevertheless, the emissions from the plant were determined to be a nuisance. Even though the economic and social utility of the plant outweighed the harm to the farmers, the court required the plant to compensate the farmers for their damages (*Jost v. Dairy Cooperative*, 172 N.W.2d 647 (Wis. 1970)).

Remedies

A plaintiff alleging private nuisance may seek either compensatory damages or an injunction. If the nuisance is likely to be permanent, she can recover for both past and prospective damages in the same action. However, if it is unclear whether the harm will be an ongoing one, she can recover only for those damages sustained at the time of suit and must bring future actions for subsequent harm.

If damages would be an insufficient remedy, the plaintiff may be entitled to an injunction. If she seeks an injunction, she must prove that the harm to her outweighs the utility of the defendant's conduct. Compare this to the Restatement approach discussed earlier, in which a plaintiff can recover damages even if the harm to her does not outweigh the utility of the defendant's conduct as long as it would be unfair to deprive her of payment.

Defenses

Both contributory negligence and assumption of risk can be raised as defenses in private nuisance claims. One way a plaintiff can assume the risk is if he "comes to the nuisance" by purchasing property while having advance notice that the nuisance exists. A plaintiff who purchases a home adjacent to an industrial plant that is in full operation and spewing gases and waste into the environment is said to have come to the nuisance. Although at one time the courts treated coming to the nuisance as an absolute defense, modern courts look at that fact as merely one of many factors to be considered in deciding whether the plaintiff should be allowed to recover. To bar recovery to all plaintiffs who come to the nuisance would allow defendants, in essence, to condemn the land in their vicinity so that the land would become valueless to others. The courts expect defendants to contemplate the possibility that others will eventually want to settle in the area and to anticipate that nuisance claims may arise in the future.

This point is illustrated in one interesting case involving a defendant cattle feedlot that produced "over a million pounds of wet manure per day" in a rural area outside of Phoenix. The plaintiff developer constructed a retirement development, "Sun City," one portion of which adjoined the feedlot. The plaintiff alleged that the flies and odor from the feedlot rendered this portion of the development unhealthy and virtually uninhabitable. The court concluded that the plaintiff had indeed come to the nuisance in its building of a subdivision in the vicinity of an already existing feedlot. Nevertheless, the court enjoined the defendant from operating the feedlot because the rights of innocent third parties, the residents of Sun City, were also involved. Because the plaintiff had come to the nuisance, however, the court required the plaintiff to indemnify the defendant for its moving costs (*Spur Industries, Inc. v. Del E. Webb Development Co.*, 494 P.2d 700 (Ariz. 1972)).

Environmental Law

Currently, nuisance law is enjoying a resurgence, especially in environmental law. Most claims for money damages for pollution brought under state common law include a claim for nuisance. Nuisance laws are resorted to because of some of the advantages they have over statutory remedies. Public nuisance claims provide environmental plaintiffs with a cause of action that is both flexible and powerful.

At one time plaintiffs rarely prevailed in hazardous waste cases, because they could not prove that the harm hazardous waste sites caused was greater than the necessity and utility of most of the polluting activities. Today most courts find polluters' conduct to be unreasonable because they conclude that hazardous waste contamination interferes with the use and enjoyment of land, and in most cases, causes substantial harm (see discussion in *Wood v. Picillo*).

In 1986 Congress passed the Comprehensive Environmental Response, Compensation and Liability Act (CERCLA), which authorizes the Environmental Protection Agency to clean up sites contaminated by toxic wastes. When Congress passed CERCLA, many observers anticipated that nuisance law would become outmoded. Instead, common law actions have emerged as potent weapons for recovering damages caused by hazardous wastes.

Plaintiffs have found several advantages in pursuing nuisance claims instead of filing actions under CERCLA: they can recover more in damages, resulting in significantly higher awards; they can obtain injunctions more easily; and they enjoy the common law's broader parameters of liability. For example, CERCLA excludes petroleum and petroleum byproducts in its definition of "hazardous substances" and exempts the normal application of fertilizer and the release of nuclear materials from its definition of "release." These products are not exempted under nuisance law. Furthermore, under traditional public nuisance law there is no statute of limitations, and the plaintiff need not show that his property was physically harmed.

Defendants also enjoy advantages under the common law tort of nuisance. First, under nuisance law defendants are liable only for the contamination they cause. Thus, under nuisance, if a defendant is responsible for 70 percent of a site's contamination, she need pay for only 70 percent of cleanup costs, whereas she might have to pay for 100 percent under CERCLA. Second, the original owner of a contaminated site can, under nuisance law, defeat liability claims by subsequent owners by asserting caveat emptor ("buyer beware") as a defense. In contrast, under CERCLA, the original parties remain liable for cleanup costs to those who buy the site at a later date. Third, common law defendants can avoid long-term cleanup costs by arguing that a site is "permanently contaminated," thereby being required to pay only the difference between the original land value and the current value of the contaminated land. Such cleanup can be very expensive and take decades. Fourth, remedies under nuisance law are contingent on balancing the costs and benefits of the nuisance, whereas remedies under CERCLA can require defendants to carry heavy burdens regardless of the costs or benefits.

Despite the advantages to both plaintiffs and defendants, common law actions are not a panacea. Designing and monitoring cleanup is easier under CERCLA; also, because the outcome of litigation is more predictable with CERCLA, settlement is more likely with CERCLA than with nuisance claims. Furthermore, relying on state-by-state adjudication inhibits efforts to create a uniform national campaign to clean up hazardous wastes. Also, common law actions require a plaintiff to file a lawsuit, whereas under CERCLA the Environmental Protection Agency may initiate an enforcement action any time there is "a release, or threatened release" of a hazardous substance. If individual injuries are slight and large numbers of people are affected by a hazardous waste, individuals have little incentive to file nuisance suits.

An illustration of litigation involving a hazardous waste site is *Wood v. Picillo,* 443 A.2d 1244 (R.I. 1982). This case chronicles the evolution of nuisance law in the context of environmental concerns. Notice how the court acknowledges and conforms to changes in societal attitudes and scientific knowledge.

 CASE

Wood v. Picillo
443 A.2d 1244 (R.I. 1982)

WEISBERGER, Justice

This is an appeal from a judgment of the Superior Court entered after trial without the intervention of a jury. Finding that the defendants created a public and private nuisance in maintaining a hazardous waste dump site on their Coventry farm, the trial justice enjoined further chemical disposal operations at the defendants' property and ordered the defendants to finance cleanup and removal of the toxic wastes. The defendants now contend that the trial justice erred in finding the disposal operation to be a public and private nuisance. We strongly disagree. Accordingly, the judgment of the Superior Court is affirmed.

This testimony elicited during the extensive hearings conducted on this case revealed the following dramatic events. On September 30, 1977, an enormous explosion erupted into fifty-foot flames in a trench on defendants' Coventry property. Firefighters responded to the blaze but could not extinguish the flames. As the fire raged within the trench, additional explosions resounded. From the conflagration billowed clouds of thick black smoke that extended "as far as the eye could see on the Eastern horizon."

Not unexpectedly, the extraordinary blaze aroused the interest of various state officials. The state fire marshal declared the dump site a fire hazard and ordered defendants to cease disposal activity and to remove all flammable wastes. Personnel from the Department of Environmental Management (DEM) also investigated the dumping operation, conducting soil, water, chemical, and topographical analyses of defendants' property and adjacent areas. Despite the fire marshal's order and the ongoing official investigations, the dumping and burying of chemical wastes continued.

A general description of the Picillo property and adjacent lands is helpful in evaluating the evidence. According to the testimony of various witnesses, the Picillos owned acreage on Piggy Hill Lane in Coventry, Rhode Island. Piggy Hill Lane, which serves only the Picillos' property, is a winding dirt road running from Perry Hill Road. Near the entrance to the property defendants maintain pigs, and two houses are located in this general area. A three- to five-acre clearing in once-wooded land lies approximately 800 feet uphill from the two homes. It is this clearing that houses the chemical dump site. About 600 feet downhill to the north-northwest of the clearing is a marshy wetland. The wetland is part of the Quinabog River Basin; the wetland waters drain in a gradual southwesterly flow into the Quinabog River, Wickford Pond, the Roaring Brook, and Arnold Pond. These fish-inhabited waters are utilized both by the general public and by a commercial cranberry grower.

The dump site proper might best be described in the succinct expression of the trial justice as "a chemical nightmare." John Quinn, Jr., chief of the DEM's solid-waste management program, visited defendants' property on October 13, 1977 and testified to what he saw. Quinn stated that at one side of the clearing lay a huge trench which he estimated to be 200 feet long, 15 to 30 feet wide, and 15 to 20 feet deep. A viscous layer of pungent, varicolored liquid covered the trench bottom to a depth of six inches at its shallowest point. Along the periphery of the pit lay more than 100 fifty-five gallon drum-type and five-gallon pail-type containers. Some of the containers were upright and sealed, some tipped, and some partially buried; some were full, some partially full, and some empty. An official from the state fire marshal's office also visited the dump site. He testified that on October 15, 1977, he observed a truck marked "Combustible" offloading barrels of chemical wastes. The truck operator knocked the barrels off the truck's tailgate directly onto the earth below, and chemicals poured freely from the damaged barrels into the trench. In 1979 state officials discovered a second dump site when "sink holes" emitting chemical odors opened in the earth at some distance from the previously described pit.

Several witnesses testified at trial to the immediate and future effects of the chemical presence. Neighbors of the Picillos reported that in the year preceding the fire, tractor-trailer traffic to and from defendants' property greatly increased. According to the testimony many of the trucks bore "Flammable" warnings and the name of a chemical company. The neighbors also testified that on several occasions during the summer of 1977 pungent odors forced them to remain inside their homes. The odors were described variously as "sickening," "heavy," "sweet," "musky," "terrible," and like "plastic burning." One neighbor testified that the odors induced in her severe nausea and headaches, while another stated that on one occasion fumes from the Picillo property caused her to cough severely and to suffer a sore throat that lasted several days.

At trial expert witnesses developed a scientific connection between the neighbors' experiences and the Picillos' operations. Laboratory analyses of samples taken from the trench, monitoring wells, and adjacent waters revealed the presence of five chemicals: toluene, xylene, chloroform, III trichloroethane, and trichloroethylene.[2] Doctor Nelson Fausto, a professor of medical sciences in the pathology division of the Department of Biological and Medical Sciences at Brown University, described the toxic effects of the five discovered chemicals. Doctor Fausto testified that chloroform is a narcotic and an anesthetic that will induce vomiting, dizziness, and headaches in some persons exposed to it. Trichloroethane and trichloroethylene, according to Dr. Fausto, are similar to chloroform in chemical structure and in toxic effect. Toluene and xylene are also toxins, Dr. Fausto testified, that may cause irritation of the mucous membranes in the upper respiratory tract.

Doctor Fausto explained that the chemicals in question also exert chronic or long-term effects on animals and humans. According to the professor, chloroform, trichloroethane, and trichloroethylene are strong carcinogens that cause cirrhosis (cell death) of the liver and hepatoma (cancer of the liver). Doctor Fausto asserted that there is no safe level of human or animal exposure to these chemicals. Regarding toluene and xylene, Dr. Fausto testified that neither is as yet known to be carcinogenic, but both exert a toxic effect on bone marrow, causing anemia in susceptible persons. Additionally, Dr. Fausto stated, the presence of chloroform in areas where it might be heated presents further potential danger. Heated to sixty-eight degrees Fahrenheit, chloroform converts to phosgene gas, a nerve gas of the type utilized in World War I. Doctor Fausto stated that direct sunlight would provide sufficient heat to turn chloroform present in surface water into phosgene.

According to the experts, the chemicals present on defendants' property and in the marsh, left unchecked, would eventually threaten wildlife and humans well downstream from the dump site. Mr. Frank Stevenson, the principal sanitary engineer for the DEM, and Dr. William Kelly, an Associate Professor of civil and environmental engineering at the University of Rhode Island, testified as experts in soil mechanics and groundwater hydrology. The experts established that the soil at the dump site consisted of an unstratified composition of sand, gravel, and silt of varying sizes. The permeable

2. These were the only chemicals for which tests were conducted.

nature of this soil would allow any liquid or chemical in or on it to percolate down to the water table and to travel with the groundwater in a northerly flow. The opinion of the experts was buttressed by the documented presence of toluene, xylene, chloroform, trichloroethane, and trichloroethylene in the northern marsh and in several monitoring wells.[3] The only possible source of the pollutants, according to Dr. Kelly, was the Picillo dump site.

Expert testimony further revealed that the chemicals had traveled and would continue to travel from the dump site into the marsh at the rate of about one foot per day. From the marsh, predicted the experts, the chemicals would flow in a southwesterly direction into the Quinabog River and its tributaries Moosup River and Roaring Brook, and Wickford Pond. These waters are inhabited by fish and used by humans for recreational and agricultural purposes.

On these and other facts the trial justice determined the dump site to be a public and private nuisance. He found also that the current danger to the public health and safety posed by the chemical presence would worsen unless effective remedial action was quickly taken. The trial judge thus permanently enjoined disposal operations on defendants' property and ordered that all chemicals and contaminated earth be removed to a licensed disposal facility. Because defendants had in the past displayed an unwillingness or inability to remedy the danger, the Superior Court justice authorized plaintiffs to effectuate cleanup of defendants' property at defendants' expense.

The defendants contend that the evidence adduced at trial was insufficient to support a finding of public and private nuisance. The defendants point to two alleged evidentiary inadequacies: (1) that plaintiffs failed to establish any significant injury to persons or to natural wildlife and (2) that plaintiffs failed to meet their obligation to show that defendants acted negligently in disposing chemical wastes on their property. We find both assertions to be without merit.

The essential element of an actionable nuisance is that persons have suffered harm or are threatened with injuries that they ought not have to bear. . . . Distinguished from negligence liability, liability in nuisance is predicated upon unreasonable injury rather than upon unreasonable conduct. . . . Thus, plaintiffs may recover in nuisance despite the otherwise nontortious nature of the conduct which creates the injury.

In his brief defendant has accurately stated that the injury produced by an actionable nuisance "must be real and not fanciful or imaginary." . . . The defendant next suggests that the injuries in the case at bar are of the insubstantial, unactionable type. It is this statement, however, rather than the purported injuries, that is fanciful. The testimony to which reference is made in this opinion clearly establishes that defendants' dumping operations have already caused substantial injury to defendants' neighbors and threaten to cause incalculable damage to the general public. The Picillos' neighbors have displayed physical symptoms of exposure to toxic chemicals and have been restricted in the reasonable use of their property. Moreover, expert testimony showed that the chemical presence on defendants' property threatens both aquatic wildlife and human beings with possible death, cancer, and liver disease. Thus, there was ample evidence at trial to support the finding of substantial injury implicit in the trial justice's finding of public and private nuisance.

The defendants' remaining contention is that Rhode Island case law requires plaintiffs to prove negligence as an element of the nuisance case and that plaintiffs failed to do so. Generally, this court has not required plaintiffs to establish negligence in nuisance actions. . . . In one case, however, the Rhode Island Supreme Court refused to impose nuisance liability upon an oil refining company absent proof of negligence. The defendant asserts that the *Rose* case is apposite to and controls the case at bar. We disagree.

Whether or not a nuisance is actionable absent proof of negligence depends upon the nature of the nuisance and the facts of the particular case. . . .

The facts of *Rose* are somewhat similar to the facts of the present case. The plaintiff, Manuel Rose, owned a fifty-seven-acre farm in East Providence, Rhode Island, on which he maintained a piggery and hennery. Rose drew drinking water for his family and for the hens from a fresh-water well dug on the property, and the pigs drank from a stream that traversed the farm. The well and the stream were fed by waters that percolated from an underground source.

The defendant in *Rose* was the owner of a large oil refinery and several storage tanks situated directly across the street from the plaintiff's farm. The refinery

---

3. The chemicals were detectable not only through laboratory processes but also by gross visual inspection. Experts reported a reddish discoloration and an oily surface in one section of the wetland, along with a pungent chemical odor. Doctor Kelly stated also that at one location chemicals seeped out of the ground as if from a spring.

and the storage tanks discharged and leaked petroleum, gasoline, and waste products into basins, streams, and ponds on the defendant's property. These substances, however, did not remain in their natural repositories. Rather, the oil products percolated through the soil into the groundwater and discharged into the plaintiff's well and stream. The pollutants contaminated the plaintiff's drinking water, killing 700 hens and 75 breeding sows. The plaintiff instituted suit against Socony-Vacuum, alleging private nuisance but not negligence.

The Superior Court sustained defendant's demurrer. On appeal, the Supreme Court framed the issue in the following terms:

> "While the defendant could appropriate to its own use the percolating waters under its soil—providing that in so doing it was not actuated by an improper motive and was not negligent—can it, by the use to which it puts its land, deprive the plaintiffs of such waters by rendering them unfit for plaintiffs' use by contamination?" 54 R.I. at 418–19, 173 A. at 630.

The court held that the defendant could with inpunity contaminate the plaintiff's drinking water if the defendant polluted nonnegligently. . . . The court reasoned that because "courses of subterranean waters are . . . indefinite and obscure," rights to them are less easily definable than riparian rights to surface streams. Suggesting that it might be unjust to subject landowners to liability for the unforeseeable consequences of legitimate land uses, the court looked to the teaching of other courts that had considered the issue. Examination of the cases disclosed a split of authority; jurisdictions with primarily agricultural economies imposed nuisance liability without proof of negligence, whereas jurisdictions with primarily industrial economies required a negligence showing. The *Rose* court determined that petroleum products were vital to the highly developed industrial economy of the local area, and held as a matter of policy that injury of the type occasioned by the defendant's percolating pollutants was, absent negligence, "damnum absque injuria."

Since this court decided *Rose v. Socony-Vacuum* in 1934, the science of groundwater hydrology as well as societal concern for environmental protection has developed dramatically. As a matter of scientific fact the courses of subterranean waters are no longer obscure and mysterious. The testimony of the scientific experts in this case clearly illustrates the accuracy with which scientists can determine the paths of groundwater flow. Moreover, decades of unrestricted emptying of industrial effluent into the earth's atmosphere and waterways has rendered oceans, lakes, and rivers unfit for swimming and fishing, rain acidic, and air unhealthy. Concern for the preservation of an often precarious ecological balance, impelled by the spectre of "a silent spring," has today reached a zenith of intense significance. Thus, the scientific and policy considerations that impelled the *Rose* result are no longer valid. We now hold that negligence is not a necessary element of a nuisance case involving contamination of public or private waters by pollutants percolating through the soil and traveling underground routes.

For the reasons stated, the defendants' appeal is denied and dismissed. The judgment of the Superior Court is affirmed.

PUTTING IT INTO PRACTICE 11.5

1. What facts support a finding that the defendants' dump site constitutes a nuisance?
2. How does a negligence claim differ from a nuisance claim?
3. What facts support the plaintiffs' contention that they were injured by the chemical wastes harbored by the defendants?
4. On what basis does the court distinguish *Rose*?
5. Must negligence be shown in a nuisance case involving contamination of public or private waters by pollutants percolating through soil and traveling underground? ·

PUTTING IT INTO PRACTICE 11.6

1. Seventy-five neighbors of an apartment complex sue the landlords of the complex for failure to combat a drug-dealing operation on the property. The neighbors assert they have been confronted by drug dealers, drug customers, and prostitutes and that such confrontations, along with the sounds of gunshots, fighting, and yelling, have made them fear for their lives. Neither the dealers, their customers, nor the neighbors are tenants of the landlords. Do the neighbors have grounds for a nuisance action?
2. A local health club employs female masseuses who, while completely nude, provide body massages consisting of genital stimulation. Do the neighbors of this "health club" have grounds for a public nuisance suit?
3. Property owners whose properties are not subject to groundwater contamination emanating from the defendants' property argue that even though no contaminants had reached their properties, the defendant should be held liable "for any loss in property values due to public concern about the contaminants in the general area." Do the property owners have grounds for a private nuisance claim?
4. Jet noise from an airport is described by residents as being comparable to the "noise of a riveting machine or steam hammer." The noise interrupts residents' sleep, makes it difficult for them to converse on the phone, and causes their windows to vibrate and plaster to fall. What relief, if any, are the residents entitled to?

INTERFERENCE WITH BUSINESS RELATIONS

Two tort actions specifically protect business interests. They are interference with existing contractual relations and interference with prospective contractual relations.

Interference with Existing Contractual Relations

One commits interference with existing contractual relations by inducing another to breach a contract with the plaintiff. The defendant's interference must be intentional (negligence is not sufficient) and improper. Several factors are taken into consideration when deciding if a tort has been committed. They include the purpose and motive of the defendant, the means used to create the interference, and the type of interest with which the defendant interferes, as well as the social interest involved in protecting both the defendant's freedom of action and the contractual interest of

the plaintiff (Restatement (Second) of Torts §§ 766 and 767).

One of the first and certainly most famous decisions imposing liability for intentional inducement of a breach of contract was *Lumley v. Gye,* 118 Eng. Rep. 749 (Q.B. 1853). In *Lumley,* the plaintiff's theater entered into a contract with an opera singer in which she agreed she would not perform for anyone else during a period of time. The defendant deliberately enticed the singer to refuse to perform and was held liable for improper interference with a contractual relationship.

In more modern times, liability for contractual interference was found in a case in which an attorney, after terminating his employment with a law firm, actively engaged in an attempt to procure business for his new law firm. He contacted some of the first firm's clients with whom he had been working and advised them that he was leaving the firm and that they could choose to be represented by him, the firm, or any other firm or attorney. Additionally, he mailed these clients form letters that could be used to discharge the firm as counsel and create a contingency fee agreement between him and the client. The court reasoned that the attorney had used his position of trust and responsibility to unfairly prejudice the firm. The court also concluded that no public interest was served in allowing such use of confidential information (*Adler, Barish, Daniels, Levin & Creskoff v. Epstein*, 393 A.2d 1175 (Pa. 1978)).

Active Interference

The defendant must actively interfere with the contract. Merely offering a better price to a third person, knowing that this might cause the third person to breach his contract with the plaintiff, is not sufficient. However, suppose the defendant says "I'll give you a better price than the plaintiff is offering and if you accept my offer you'll save enough money to afford to break your contract with the plaintiff and still come out ahead." By this statement the defendant actively induces a breach of contract (Restatement (Second) of Torts § 766, illus. 3).

Kind of Contract Involved

Some kinds of contracts cannot serve as a basis for this tort. The plaintiff cannot recover if a contract that is illegal or contrary to public policy is breached. Similarly, most courts will not hold the defendant liable if he or she induces the breach of a contract that is terminable at will. An **at-will employee** is one who, because of the employment agreement into which he entered with his employer, can be discharged at any time for any reason. The Restatement (Second) and a growing number of courts, however, do consider the inducing of a breach of an at-will contract to be contractual interference. The reasoning behind this approach is that a plaintiff has a right to expect that the contract will not be tampered with until it is in fact terminated. Contracts that are unenforceable for other reasons, such as lack of consideration or because they are not in conformance with the Statute of Frauds, can serve as a basis for contractual interference.

Remedies

The plaintiff may certainly recover for pecuniary losses he or she sustains as a result of the interference and also, according to some courts, may be allowed to recover for emotional harm. The plaintiff can recover for breach of contract against the person the defendant induced to breach the contract.

In one case, the plaintiffs, a black family that had contracted to buy a house in a white neighborhood, were allowed to recover for mental suffering from the defendants, their would-be neighbors, who induced the owner not to go through with the sale. They were also allowed to seek specific performance from the seller as well as incidental expenses they incurred as a result of the breach. The plaintiffs were not, however, entitled to recover twice for the same damages. They could not, for example, recover from the seller the interest they had to pay while waiting for their suit and then recover that sum again from the defendants who induced the breach (*Duff v. Engelberg*, 47 Cal. Rptr. 114 (Ct. App. 1965)).

Privileges

If a defendant merely tries to protect his own existing contractual rights, he will be privileged to induce a breach as long as his motive is not to gain business for himself. If a buyer is aware, for example, that a manufacturer of goods has promised to deliver goods to both himself and another buyer, he can ask that the manufacturer fulfill his contract even if he is aware that the manufacturer will be unable to fulfill both contracts.

If an individual induces a breach for the purpose of promoting social interests, she will also be privileged. One unusual case illustrating this point involved a burlesque troupe known as the Wu Tut Tut Revue, whose manager so underpaid the performers that they were forced to eke out an existence by resorting to prostitution. The defendant persuaded the theater owners with whom the troupe had contracted to perform to cancel the contract unless higher wages were paid to the performers. The defendant's action was considered justified and therefore not tortious (*Brimelow v. Casson,* 1 Ch. 302 (1924)).

Interference with Prospective Contractual Relations

Essentially the same rules apply to interference with prospective contractual relations as to interference with existing contractual relations, except for one major difference. Because no contract actually exists, the defendant is given greater leeway as to what he can do to interfere. Although a defendant cannot interfere with an existing contract for the purpose of obtaining business for himself, he is privileged to do so when only a potential contract is involved. He is even privileged to drive a plaintiff out of business, as long as he does not use unlawful means such as price fixing or monopolization. But if he acts out of sheer malice, his conduct will not be privileged.

Interference with a plaintiff's nonbusiness expectations of financial gain can be the basis for this tort. If the defendant induces a testator to leave the plaintiff out of her will, he can be held liable. Interference with a plaintiff's potential legal claim can also be tortious. A defendant may be liable if he tampers with medical records or conceals facts from the plaintiff that if known would reveal a cause of action.

PUTTING IT INTO PRACTICE 11.7

1. Pro-Image and University Graphics are business competitors. Pro-Image has leased space from a commercial landlord when it discovers that University Graphics is negotiating to rent space in the same location. Representives for Pro-Image express their concern about the landlord renting space to their "fierce competitor"; the landlord decides not to lease space to University Graphics to avoid conflict between tenants. Does University Graphics have grounds for a claim of interfrence with existing contractual relations against Pro-Image? Does it have grounds for a claim of interference with prospective contractual relations?
2. An attorney represents a proprietary court-reporting school student who is being sued by the school to collect unpaid fees. The student counterclaims for fraud and misrepresentation. In the course of representing the student, the attorney contacts several students at the school and discovers that many of them are dissatisfied with the court-reporting program. Some of the students approach the attorney and indicate that they might be interested in suing the school. The attorney takes the names of the students and contacts them when the collection case is settled. The attorney holds three meetings in his office with the students. After the third meeting, approximately thirty-five students withdraw from the program. The school files a claim for interference with contractual relations against the attorney. Does the school have a viable claim?

MISUSE OF LEGAL PROCESS

A plaintiff who has been subjected to unwarranted judicial proceedings may sue on the basis of malicious prosecution, wrongful institution of civil proceedings, or abuse of process (see Figure 11-6). Notice that the plaintiff in these cases was originally the defendant in the cause of action leading to the suit involving the misuse of legal process. Suppose an individual became the target of a criminal investigation that resulted in his becoming the defendant in a criminal trial. If the individual believed the prosecutor's chief witness fabricated the story involving the defendant and actively

FIGURE 11-6 Misuse of Legal Process

MALICIOUS PROSECUTION	WRONGFUL INSTITUTION OF CIVIL PROCEEDINGS
Defendant institutes criminal proceedings against plaintiff but has no probable cause and acts out of motives other than a sense of bringing plaintiff to justice.	Defendant institutes civil proceedings against plaintiff but has no probable cause and acts out of motives other than seeking compensation for wrong suffered.

ABUSE OF PROCESS
Defendant uses litigation devices for improper purposes.

sought to bring criminal proceedings against the defendant out of vengeance because of a squabble the two had had years earlier, the defendant in the criminal action could sue the prosecutor's witness, who would become the defendant in the malicious prosecution suit.

Malicious Prosecution

A defendant whose motives are for some purpose other than bringing the plaintiff to justice and who, without probable cause, institutes criminal proceedings against another commits *malicious prosecution* (Restatement (Second) of Torts § 653). For the plaintiff to recover, the proceedings must conclude in the plaintiff's favor and the defendant must actively participate in instigating the prosecution. A defendant who leaves the decision in the hands of the prosecutor is not considered to have actively participated in the prosecution. Rather, the defendant must have lied to the prosecutor or attempted in some way to influence his decision to prosecute. The proceedings are deemed to have concluded in favor of the plaintiff if the prosecutor decides not to prosecute, the grand jury refuses to indict, or the case is dismissed because of the weakness of the case. A plaintiff's plea of guilty in acceptance of a plea bargain is not considered a favorable conclusion for the plaintiff.

The most difficult hurdle for plaintiffs to overcome in malicious prosecution cases is the probable cause requirement. If a defendant reasonably believes that the plaintiff committed certain acts, he will be deemed to have probable cause. If it turns out that the defendant's belief is mistaken, his mistake will not constitute lack of probable cause as long as the mistake is a reasonable one. An acquittal does not necessarily indicate a lack of probable cause, because an acquittal may occur on the basis of reasonable doubt rather than lack of probable cause. Therefore, even if the plaintiff is acquitted, the defendant has a right to, in essence, retry the plaintiff. If he can show by a preponderance of the evidence that the plaintiff was guilty, he can establish the existence of probable cause.

In showing improper purpose, the plaintiff must show that the defendant acted out of malice or for some reason other than seeing justice done. A creditor, for example, who uses the criminal process to compel a debtor to pay her debt has an improper purpose (Restatement (Second) of Torts § 668, cmt. g).

Prosecutors are almost always immune from malicious prosecution suits. Immunity is also generally given to police officers as long as they are acting within the general scope of their duties.

Wrongful Institution of Civil Proceedings

Although the tort of malicious prosecution normally applies to criminal proceedings, most states allow similar actions for *wrongful institution of civil proceedings.* The elements are essentially the same as for malicious prosecution, although civil proceedings may encompass administrative proceedings, bankruptcy proceedings, and insanity proceedings as well as ordinary civil lawsuits. Proving lack of probable cause in a civil case is more difficult than in a criminal case because one can initiate civil proceedings with far less certainty of the facts than in a criminal proceeding. A suit brought merely to harass an opponent or to extort a settlement when the defendant is aware there is no real chance of succeeding exemplify wrongful institution of civil proceedings. A counterclaim brought solely for the purpose of delaying proceedings is another example.

Abuse of Process

If an individual initiates a criminal or civil proceeding based on probable cause and on the basis of permissible motives, he may still be liable for **abuse of process** if he uses certain litigation devices for improper purposes. Using a subpoena, for example, to harass someone or to induce her to settle rather than for its practical purpose of obtaining testimony could be considered abuse of process (Restatement (Second) of Torts § 682, illus. 3). As long as the primary purpose for the proceeding is justified the fact that the defendant has an ulterior motive or that the proceedings may be of some incidental benefit to her is irrelevant. If the instigation of bankruptcy proceedings is justified, it does not become abuse of process merely because the instigator of those proceedings hopes she will gain some benefit from the closing down of her competitor's business. Typically, abuse of process involves situations in which a party puts undue pressure on another to induce her to engage in or refrain from a particular action.

PUTTING IT INTO PRACTICE 11.8

1. Robert, a free-lance reporter and owner of a helicopter news service, films a night-time air hoist rescue of a stranded fisherman. One of the firefighters involved in the rescue claims that Robert shone a bright spotlight from his helicopter during the rescue, causing the firefighter to momentarily lose control of the hoist, thereby endangering his crew and the fisherman. The firefighter brings his complaint to the Federal Aviation Administration (FAA), which exonerates Robert after an investigation. The firefighter then goes to the city attorney's office. The prosecutor brings charges against Robert but drops them after learning of the FAA adjudication and the exonerating evidence presented. Robert files a claim for malicious prosecution. Do you think a court would uphold his claim?
2. Rosemary is dismissed from her job at Nursefinders. Later she returns to Nursefinders to discuss vacation pay she thought might be due her and tells her former supervisor that she has been contacted by someone from Norrell Health Care Services regarding potential employment there. After consulting with an attorney, who tries to contact Rosemary numerous times without success, Nursefinders seeks and obtains a temporary restraining order. The order prevents Rosemary from accepting employment from any of Nursefinders' competitors, in conformance with a two-year noncompetition clause in her contract with Nursefinders. After a hearing, the trial court dissolves the temporary restraining order and denies the request for a preliminary injunction. Rosemary then files suit, claiming malicious prosecution and abuse of process. Does she have a viable suit?

SUMMARY

Misrepresentation arose out of the common law action of deceit. Intentional misrepresentation, corresponding to fraud under the common law, requires (1) that the defendant makes a misrepresentation with the intent of inducing the plaintiff's reliance on that misrepresentation, (2) that the defendant knows the representation is false or acts with reckless indifference to the truth, (3) that the plaintiff justifiably relies on the defendant's misrepresentation, and (4) that the plaintiff suffers damages stemming from his or her reliance.

A misrepresentation may consist of a false statement or an intentional concealment of a fact or an action by itself. Under modern law, mere failure to disclose a material fact may be considered concealment under certain circumstances.

A plaintiff can recover if he or she is a member of the class whom the defendant can reasonably expect to learn of and rely on the misrepresentation. The plaintiff must also show that his or her reliance occurred in the type of transaction the defendant could reasonably expect the plaintiff to engage in as a result of the reliance. A defendant must know that his or her statement is false or act with reckless disregard to the truth or falsity of the statement. In reference to the issue of reliance, the question is whether the plaintiff made any independent investigation of his or her own and whether reliance was on the misrepresentation, the investigation, or both.

The plaintiff is not usually entitled to rely on an opinion offered by the defendant. If, however, the defendant and plaintiff have a fiduciary relationship, or if the defendant has worked to secure the plaintiff's confidence or purports to have special knowledge, the plaintiff may be justified. Mere "puffing" is not actionable unless the plaintiff reasonably perceives that the opinion being offered is being made by a disinterested party. Predictions are almost always considered opinion unless the defendant is aware of facts inconsistent with that opinion.

To recover for misrepresentation, the plaintiff must show that the losses suffered were the reasonably foreseeable results of the misrepresentation. A plaintiff may ask either to be put into the position he or she was in before the misrepresentation (reliance measure) or to be put in the position he or she would have been in had the misrepresented facts been true (benefit of the bargain measure).

Most courts today allow a claim for negligent misrepresentation. Recovery is most likely to be allowed when a defendant makes false statements during the course of his or her business or profession or has a pecuniary interest in the transaction in which he or she is involved. One who makes a negligent misrepresentation is liable only to those he intends to reach with his information or whom he knows the recipient of his information intends to reach.

Recovery for innocent misrepresentation is allowed if a party makes an innocent but material misrepresentation in the course of a sale, rental, or exchange transaction. The seller of goods who makes misrepresentations on a label or through public advertisement is also liable for any innocent misrepresentations resulting in physical injury.

A public nuisance requires interference with a right common to the general public; a private nuisance is an unreasonable interference with the plaintiff's use and enjoyment of his or her own land. To prove public nuisance a plaintiff must show that the public at large was injured or exposed to the possibility of injury, and the harm must be a substantial one. The harm suffered by the plaintiff must be peculiar to her and not shared by the rest of the public. Some courts allow recovery, however, if the plaintiff suffers greater economic loss than others in the community.

Private nuisance, in contrast, requires only that the plaintiff's use and enjoyment of his or her land be substantially interfered with and that the defendant's conduct be negligent, intentional, or abnormally dangerous. Interference is considered substantial if the plaintiff is inconvenienced or subjected to unpleasant sensory awarenesses. A plaintiff may seek either compensatory damages or an injunction. If he seeks an injunction, however, he must prove that his harm outweighs the utility of the defendant's conduct.

Contributory negligence and assumption of risk can be raised as defenses in private nuisance claims.

Two tort actions that specifically protect business interests are interference with existing contractual relations and interference with prospective contractual relations. Intentionally and actively inducing another to breach a contract with the plaintiff constitutes interference with existing contractual relations. When deciding if this tort has been committed, the courts will consider the defendant's motive and purpose, the means he uses to create the interference, the type of interest with which he interferes, and the social interest involved in protecting both the defendant's freedom of action and the contractual interest of the plaintiff. Greater latitude is allowed defendants charged with interference with prospective contractual relations.

Anyone subjected to unwarranted judicial proceedings may recover on the basis of malicious prosecution, wrongful institution of civil proceedings, or abuse of process. Malicious prosecution occurs when a defendant actively participates in instituting criminal proceedings against another, lacks probable cause, and has motives other than bringing the plaintiff to justice. Wrongful institution of civil proceedings is comparable to malicious prosecution except that it involves the initiation of civil proceedings. Abuse of process occurs when an individual institutes criminal or civil proceedings on the basis of permissible motives and with probable cause but uses litigation devices for improper purposes.

PRACTICE POINTERS

Summarizing Depositions

Legal assistants are often asked to summarize depositions. A well-composed deposition summary can provide an attorney with easy access to testimony in the form of a compact document. Not only are deposition summaries usually included in trial notebooks, they are also used to prepare for subsequent depositions and pretrial motions such as motions for summary judgment. They are helpful when compiling discovery documents such as interrogatories and requests for admissions, and when preparing witnesses for trial. These summaries analyze testimony by breaking it down into its relevant components and restructuring it in a form that highlights the significant issues. The writing style must be concise and clear.

Before attempting to summarize a deposition, you should be familiar with the case file. If you must summarize a deposition for an unfamiliar case, you should read the pleadings and motions in the case file and develop a sense of the chronology of the pertinent events. You should also write out the legal issues you believe are at stake and then verify these with your supervising attorney.

Several different methods can be used to summarize depositions; your choice should be dictated by your attorney's preference. One straightforward method requires a *page-by-page summary* of the witness's testimony. This is really nothing more than a condensed version of the original transcript, but it allows the attorney who took the deposition to follow the summary easily. Reference to the page and line number where the testimony can be found in the transcript is provided in the left-hand column. A brief summary of the testimony is recorded at the right.

Continued on next page

Page:Line	Summary
6:02	*Work History:* Worked as teaching assistant from 9/83 to 5/87. Private piano lessons from 6/85 to 9/88. Music consultant for theatre from 4/88 to present. Went on concert tour 1986.
8:22	*Work History:* Part of string ensemble that went on tour in 1982.
10:01	Explanation of activities involved in teaching piano.
12:22	*Damages to career as result of injury:* Unable to perform as concert pianist. Unable to participate in upcoming competition for which he had spent a year preparing. Restricted now to consultant work and giving piano lessons. No possibility of recording contract.

A *topical index* of the main subjects covered during the witness's testimony is another organizational method used in deposition summaries. Less detailed than the previous method, it provides a list of the main subjects designated by page and line number. This method is especially helpful when it is necessary to cross-reference numerous deposition summaries. For example, if an attorney wants to review all the testimony pertaining to a particular exhibit, he or she can use this type of summary to locate the relevant testimony quickly.

Topic	Transcript Page:Line
Work history	6:02
Damages due to injury	12:22
Medical expenses	32:07
Pain and suffering	36:15

Issues can be used as a means of structuring a deposition summary. In this method all testimony relating to a particular subject matter is grouped together. This method is useful for impeaching witnesses if complete quotations of significant testimony are included. Because this method sometimes requires reorganization of the material, a word processor is useful. If a word processor is not available, you might consider photocopying the deposition and using a cut-and-paste technique to group related statements together.

Subject	Page:Line
Work History	
Worked as teaching assistant, gave piano lessons, and served as music consultant to a theater. Went on concert tour in 1986.	6:02
Was part of a string ensemble that went on tour in 1982.	8:22
Worked as assistant in recording studio.	20:19

The writing style used in deposition summaries is also a matter of choice. Some attorneys prefer a terse writing style in which all nonessential words, such as "a," "and," and "the" are eliminated; others prefer complete sentences. Regardless of the summarizing method you use, your summary should include the following information:

- Name of the deponent.
- Time, date, and location of deposition.
- Names of those in attendance at deposition.
- Case name and number.

1. Answer the questions posed in the hypothetical scenario given at the beginning of this chapter.

2. A law firm writes an opinion letter for its client in which it indicates that the client is a general partnership. In fact, some of the members claim to be limited partners and are therefore not subject to full liability. Does the law firm have a duty to disclose this information to Plaintiff, who is contemplating making loans to the partnership? *Roberts v. Ball, Hunt, Hart & Barerwitz,* 57 Cal. App. 3d 104, 128 Cal. Rptr. 901 (1976).

3. An attorney negligently gives erroneous "curbstone advice" to his client. Can he be held liable for misrepresentation? *Buttersworth v. Swint,* 186 S.E. 77 (Va. 1936).

4. Plaintiff, who is interested in buying a boiler, requests that Defendant inspect the boiler. Defendant negligently provides Plaintiff with a report that the boiler is in good condition when in fact it is not. Defendant is aware that his report is to be passed on to the seller, who can be expected to rely on the report in giving warranties. When the seller does sell the boiler, it proves to be defective and the seller suffers pecuniary loss when he incurs liability for breach of warranty. Is Defendant liable for misrepresentation? *Du Rite Laundry v. Washington Electric Co.,* 263 A.D. 396, 33 N.Y.S.2d 925 (1942).

5. Plaintiff is a strong believer in spiritualism. She receives a "Spanish prisoner" letter from Mexico, which states that the writer is unjustly imprisoned and that he has a draft for $20,000 that he has been unable to cash, located in a New York bank. He promises Plaintiff that this draft will be turned over to her if she will deliver $8,500 to a designated agent of the writer. Plaintiff consults Defendant, a spiritualist medium, who tells Plaintiff that the letter is legitimate. Relying on this assurance, Plaintiff mortgages her house, pays the $8,500, and loses it. Should Plaintiff be allowed to recover from Defendant? *Hyma v. Lee,* 60 N.W.2d 920 (Mich. 1953).

6. A violin expert tries to sell an instrument purported to be a genuine Stradivarius to a purchaser who is also a violin expert. Should the seller be liable for his misrepresentation? *Banner v. Lyon & Healy Co.,* 249 A.D. 569, 293 N.Y.S. 236 (1937).

Decide which tort you think would be appropriate to allege in each of the following cases.

7. Defendant purchases a home in a residential area and uses it to operate a funeral home. *Williams v. Montgomery,* 186 So. 302 (Miss. 1939).

8. A bitter dispute arises between Plaintiff school district and Defendant teachers' association. The teachers' association subpoenas eighty-seven teachers and refuses to stagger their appearances, thereby requiring the school district to hire substitutes to avoid a total shutdown of the schools. *Board of Education v. Farmingdale Classroom Teachers' Ass'n, Inc.,* 343 N.E.2d 278 (N.Y. 1975).

9. Pennzoil Company (Plaintiff) and Getty Oil negotiate a contract involving the sale of Getty Oil to Pennzoil. After a press release is issued by both parties, Getty Oil's investment banker continues to contact other companies, looking for a higher price than Pennzoil offered. While Pennzoil's attorneys work on a draft of a formal transaction agreement, Getty Oil accepts an offer from Texaco (Defendant). Pennzoil immediately contacts Getty and demands that Getty honor its agreement with Pennzoil. Evidence exists that Texaco had a strong motivation to acquire the oil reserves of Getty and that it deliberately formulated and implemented a strategy to acquire Getty Oil. *Texaco, Inc. v. Pennzoil Co.,* 729 S.W.2d 768 (Tex. Ct. App. 1987).

KEY TERMS

Abuse of process
Use of litigation devices for improper purposes.

At-will employee
Employee who, because of the nature of his or her employment contract, can be discharged at any time for any reason.

Deceit
Common law cause of action equated with intentional misrepresentation; also referred to as fraud.

Fiduciary relationship
Relationship based on trust and confidence imposing an obligation to act in good faith.

Latent defect
Defect that is invisible or not readily discoverable.

Nuisance
Substantial and unreasonable interference with a plaintiff's intent; includes public and private nuisance.

Patent defect
Defect that is visible or readily discoverable.

CHAPTER

12

Strict Liability

CHAPTER TOPICS

CHAPTER OBJECTIVES

In this chapter you will learn to:
- Identify those circumstances in which animal owners are held strictly liable for damages caused by their animals
- Describe abnormally dangerous activities
- Describe the defenses that can be raised in response to a strict liability claim

In this high-tech era of powerful but potentially dangerous sources of energy, we are now faced with the problem of waste disposal. We are just beginning to awaken to the horrendous potential posed by hazardous chemicals and are taking our first faltering steps toward safeguarding future generations. But some in our society have already begun to experience the repercussions of our ignorance. Suppose a woman comes to your supervising attorney and claims she has contracted cancer as a result of the leakage of toxic chemicals into her home. She wants to sue the city for approving the construction of the housing development in which she lives. She tells you that fifteen years before the land was developed into a residential area, it was used as a disposal site for chemical wastes. Is the city liable for the residents' injuries, even if those who allowed the dumping of wastes were, at the time, completely unaware of the potential medical dangers posed by such wastes?

OVERVIEW OF STRICT LIABILITY

In such a case your attorney might choose a theory of strict liability as an alternative to a negligence theory. **Strict liability** is applicable even when a defendant is neither negligent nor has any intent of wrongdoing (see Figure 12-1). It is a particularly useful theory in situations involving **abnormally dangerous** activities. Injuries involving defective products and dangerous animals are two other areas in which strict liability is imposed. An in-depth discussion of product liability is presented in Chapter 13.

In cases involving strict liability, defendants who engage in particularly dangerous kinds of activities must pay for any damage that results even if they carry

FIGURE 12.1 Strict Liability

ANIMALS	• Trespassing • Wild
PRODUCT LIABILITY	
ABNORMALLY DANGEROUS ACTIVITIES*	**Abnormally dangerous acts** • Crop dusting • Storage of flammable liquids (urban areas) • Toxic waste disposal • Use of poisonous gas exterminators • Testing of rocket fuel **Not Abnormally Dangerous Acts** • Airplane flight (except ground damage) • Defective electrical wiring • Water damage from burst dam • Defective plumbing • Household use of gas, water, or electricity

*The courts do not agree on what does or does not constitute an abnormally dangerous activity. The examples given are representative of the majority position but should not be considered definitive.

out those activities in the most careful manner possible. Liability is imposed even though a defendant is not at fault. This lack of fault is what distinguishes strict liability from negligence.

Some courts refer to strict liability as "absolute liability." The latter description, however, is somewhat misleading because defenses to strict liability actions can be raised; therefore, liability is not absolute. Others refer to strict liability as "liability without fault." This term is also a misnomer because liability without fault exists under an intentional tort basis of liability. Therefore, we use the term *strict liability* throughout this text.

Remember that the key distinction between negligence and strict liability lies in the area of fault. In a strict liability cause of action, a defendant may be liable even if he or she did not intentionally injure the plaintiff and adhered to an objective standard of reasonable care.

STRICT LIABILITY FOR HARM CAUSED BY ANIMALS

Trespassing Animals

Under the English common law, owners of animals were liable for property damage caused when animals trespassed on another's land. Owners could not escape liability even if they used the utmost care to prevent their animals from escaping. Luckily for animal owners, the rule applied only to animals likely to roam, such as cattle, horses, sheep, and goats, and not to household animals such as dogs and cats.

Most American jurisdictions follow the English rule of strict liability in reference to trespassing animals. Historically, the Western states, whose economic base relied on cattle that were customarily allowed to graze at large on open range, rejected the common law rule. Many of these states have, however, adopted "fencing in" statutes, which provide that an owner is not strictly liable if he or she attempts to fence in the animals but is strictly liable if he or she does not. Under "fencing out" statutes, property owners who properly fence their land have a strict liability claim against those whose animals trespass onto their land.

Nontrespassing Animals

One who keeps *dangerous animals* is strictly liable for the harm done by those animals. The definition of dangerous depends on whether the animal is considered wild or domesticated. A domesticated animal, according to the Restatement (Second) of Torts § 506(2), "is by custom devoted to the service of mankind." Under this definition, the courts have generally held that bulls and stallions, though often very dangerous, are domesticated. The apparent reasoning is that ownership of animals serving a valid social purpose should not be discouraged.

According to the Restatement (Second) of Torts, people who keep wild animals are strictly liable for all damage caused by such animals if the damage results from a "dangerous propensity" typical of that particular species (Restatement (Second) of Torts § 507). Javelinas and foxes are examples of animals that are considered wild. Liability also exists when the damage stems from a dangerous tendency of the particular animal in question of which the owner is or should be aware. Some courts have moved away from a strict liability standard to a negligence standard when dealing with those who display wild animals to the public (as in a zoo, for example).

Strict liability is imposed in the case of domestic animals when the owner knows or has reason to know that the animal has vicious propensities. If an animal has unsuccessfully attempted to bite someone in the past or in general has a vicious temperament, the owner will be deemed to have reason to know of the pet's dangerous tendencies and will be held liable for any damage caused. The oft-repeated phrase "Every dog is entitled to one free bite" is an illusion and should not be relied on to evade liability. Note, too, that the common law regarding liability for dog bites has been changed by statute in many states. Furthermore, statutory provisions, such as those requiring dogs to be leashed or muzzled, may also affect liability. Failure to comply with such statutes may render an owner negligent per se.

PUTTING IT INTO PRACTICE 12.1

1. Two-year-old Jessica is bitten by Smokey, a seventy-five-pound German shepherd, when he tries to get away from her hugging him and she will not let go. She has bites under and over one eye and over her lip. Smokey has played with other children with no problems, but did bite one man who had kicked him on three occasions. Should Smokey's owner be held strictly liable for Jessica's $20,000 in medical care?

2. Ruth, a Jehovah's Witness, is going house to house to discuss the Bible with those who might be interested. When she passes by one house, Bandit, a sixty-five-pound pit bull, runs toward her, jumps on her, and causes her to break her hip. Bandit is restrained by a 100-foot chain at the time but has access to the driveway where Ruth is at the time. Bandit has never bitten anyone and is generally considered a well-behaved dog, but does have a tendency to jump on people. Is Bandit's owner strictly liable for Ruth's injuries?

ABNORMALLY DANGEROUS ACTIVITIES

Doctrine of *Rylands v. Fletcher*

The path to strict liability for abnormally dangerous activities was paved in the English case of *Rylands v. Fletcher*, L.R. 3 H.L. 330 (1868). In *Rylands* the defendants hired an engineer and contractors to plan and construct a reservoir to supply their mill with water. When the defendants filled the reservoir, the water broke through into some abandoned mine shafts and then flooded adjacent mine shafts owned by the plaintiffs. An arbitrator found that although the defendants themselves were not guilty of any negligence, the engineer and contractors were negligent in their failure to use proper care. The case reached the House of Lords, the final appellate tribunal in England. The court, in finding for the plaintiff, established the rule that "the person who for his own purposes brings on his lands and collects and keeps there any thing likely to do mischief if it escapes, must keep it in at his peril, and if he does not do so, is prima facie answerable for all the damage which is the natural consequence of its escape."

The majority of American courts, along with the Second Restatement, have adopted the rationale of *Rylands* and imposed strict liability in cases involving abnormally dangerous activities. Restatement (Second) of Torts § 520 suggests consideration of six factors in determining whether an activity is abnormally dangerous:

- High degree of risk: "High degree of risk of some harm to the person, land or chattel of others."
- Risk of serious harm: "Likelihood that the harm that results from it will be great."
- Cannot be eliminated even by due care: "Inability to eliminate the risk by the exercise of reasonable care."
- Not a matter of common usage: "Extent to which the activity is not a matter of common usage."
- Inappropriateness: "Inappropriateness of the activity to the place where it is carried on."
- Value: "Extent to which its value to the community is outweighed by its dangerous attributes."

In determining whether strict liability should be imposed, the courts consider all of these factors (see Figure 12-2). Read *Yukon Equipment, Inc. v. Fireman's Fund Insurance Co.* to see an application of the six-factor test (although observe that the court ultimately rejects this test). Any one factor alone is generally not sufficient to warrant strict liability; however, all of the

FIGURE 12-2   Six-Factor Test for Abnormally Dangerous Activity (Restatement (Second) of Torts)

- Is there a high degree of risk of harm to person or property?
- Is any harm that results from the activity likely to be serious?
- Can the risk of harm be eliminated by exercising reasonable care?
- Is the activity a matter of common usage?
- Is the activity inappropriate in reference to the place where it is carried on?
- Is the value of the activity to the community outweighed by its dangerousness?

---

factors need not be present to find strict liability. The essential question is whether the risk created is so unusual (either because of its magnitude or because of the circumstances surrounding it) to justify strict liability even though the activity was carried out with all reasonable care. An example of such an activity is the transportation of nuclear materials. This activity necessarily involves a major risk of harm to others no matter how carefully it is carried out. (Note: Federal statutes impose a ceiling on liability for any nuclear mishaps.)

Be aware that the following examples of activities the courts have or have not considered abnormally dangerous are highly fact-specific. In other words, if the fact pattern had varied slightly in any of these cases, the court could have arrived at a different conclusion. Therefore, do not categorize certain activities as being either abnormally dangerous or not. Rather, look at these cases as illustrative of the courts' reasoning in the context of specific fact patterns.

CASE

Yukon Equipment, Inc. v. Fireman's Fund Insurance Co.
585 P.2d 1206 (Alaska 1978)

MATTHEWS, Justice.

A large explosion occurred at 2:47 A.M. on December 7, 1973, in the suburbs north of the city of Anchorage. The explosion originated at a storage magazine for explosives under lease from the federal government to petitioner E. I. du Pont de Nemours and Company, which was operated by petitioner Yukon Equipment, Inc. The storage magazine is located on a 1,870 acre tract of federal land which had been withdrawn by the Department of the Interior for the use of the Alaska Railroad for explosive storage purposes by separate orders in 1950 and 1961. The magazine which exploded was located 3,820 feet from the nearest building not used to store explosives and 4,330 feet from the nearest public highway. At the time of the explosion it contained approximately 80,000 pounds of explosives. The blast damaged dwellings and other buildings within a two-mile radius of the magazine and, in some instances, beyond a two-mile radius. The ground concussion it caused registered 1.8 on the Richter scale at the earthquake observation station in Palmer, some 30 miles away.

The explosion was caused by thieves. Four young men had driven onto the tract where the magazine was located, broken into the storage magazine, set a prepared charge, and fled. They apparently did so in an effort to conceal the fact that they had stolen explosives from the site a day or two earlier.

This consolidated lawsuit was brought to recover for property damage caused by the explosion. Cross-motions for partial summary judgment were filed, and summary judgment on the issue of liability was granted in favor of the respondents. Respondents presented alternative theories of liability based on negligence, nuisance, absolute liability, and trespass. The court's order granting partial summary judgment did not specify the theory on which the liability was based.

Petitioners contend that none of the theories may be utilized to fix liability on them by summary judgment and further that the intentional detonation of the magazine is a superseding cause relieving them of liability under any theory. Respondents argue that the summary judgment is sustainable under the theory of absolute liability and that the intentional nature of the explosion is not a defense. We agree with respondents and affirm.

I

The leading case on liability for the storage of explosives is *Exner v. Sherman Power Constr. Co.,* 54 F.2d 510 (2d Cir. 1931). There dynamite stored by the defendant exploded causing personal injury and property damage to the plaintiffs who resided some 935 feet away from the storage site. A distinguished panel of the Circuit Court of Appeals for the Second Circuit held the defendant liable regardless of fault:

> Dynamite is of the class of elements which one who stores or uses in such a locality, or under such circumstances as to cause likelihood of risk to others, stores or uses at his peril. He is an insurer, and is absolutely liable if damage results to third persons, either from the direct impact of rocks thrown out by the explosion (which would be a common law trespass) or from concussion.

Id. at 512–13. The court pointed out that while the general principle of absolute liability expressed in the English case of *Rylands v. Fletcher* had been accorded a mixed reception at best in United States courts, there had been no such reluctance to impose absolute liability in blasting cases. The court then noted that some authorities had made a distinction between damage done by rocks or debris hurled by an explosion, as to which there would be absolute liability, and damage caused by a concussion, as to which a negligence stan-

dard applied. The court concluded that such a distinction was without a logical basis and rejected it. *Id.* at 514. The court also determined that there was no reason for attaching different legal consequences to the results of an explosion "whether the dynamite explodes when stored or when employed in blasting." The court expressed the policy behind the rule of absolute liability as follows:

> The extent to which one man in the lawful conduct of his business is liable for injuries to another involves an adjustment of conflicting interests. . . . When, as here, the defendant, though without fault, has engaged in the perilous activity of storing large quantities of a dangerous explosive for use in his business, we think there is no justification for relieving it of liability, and that the owner of the business, rather than a third party who has no relation to the explosion, other than that of injury, should bear the loss.

Id. at 514. *Exner* has been widely followed, and was based on many earlier authorities imposing absolute liability for explosions. . . .

> The storage and transportation of explosive substances are ultra-hazardous activities because no precautions and care can make it reasonably certain that they will not explode and because the harm resulting from their explosion is almost certain to be serious.

Comment (e) addresses the question of common usage, stating:

> While blasting is recognized as a proper means of clearing woodlands for cultivating and of excavating for building purposes, the conditions which require its use are usually of brief duration. It is generally required because of the peculiar character of the land and it is not a part of the customary processes of farming or of building operations. Likewise, the manufacture, storage, transportation and use of high explosives, although necessary to the construction of many public and private works, are carried on by a comparatively small number of persons and, therefore, are not matters of common usage.

Thus the particular rule of *Exner,* absolute liability for damage caused by the storage of explosives, was preserved by the Restatement and a general rule, inferred from *Exner* and the authorities on which it was based, and from *Rylands v. Fletcher* and its antecedents, was stated which imposed absolute liability on any other activity which met the definition of ultra-hazardous.

The Restatement (Second) of Torts (1977), adopted by the ALI after the explosion in this case, does not reflect a *per se* rule of liability for the storage of explosives. Instead it lists six factors to be considered in determining whether an activity is "abnormally dangerous" and therefore subject to the rule of absolute liability. The factors are:

(a) existence of a high degree of risk of some harm to the person, land or chattels of others;
(b) likelihood that the harm that results from it will be great;
(c) inability to eliminate the risk by the exercise of reasonable care;
(d) extent to which the activity is not a matter of common usage;
(e) inappropriateness of the activity to the place where it is carried on; and
(f) extent to which its value to the community is outweighed by its dangerous attributes.

Id. § 520.

Based in large part on the Restatement (Second), petitioners argue that their use was not abnormally dangerous. Specifically they contend that their use of the magazine for the storage of explosives was a normal and appropriate use of the area in question since the storage magazine was situated on lands set aside by the United States for such purposes and was apparently located in compliance with applicable federal regulations. They point out that the storage served a legitimate community need for an accessible source of explosives for various purposes. They contend that before absolute liability can be imposed in any circumstance a preliminary finding must be made as to whether or not the defendant's activity is abnormally dangerous, that such a determination involves the weighing of the six factors set out in section 520 of the Restatement (Second) of Torts, and that an evaluation of those factors in this case could not appropriately be done on motion for summary judgment.

If we were to apply the Restatement (Second)'s six-factor test to the storage of explosives in this case we would be inclined to conclude that the use involved here was an abnormally dangerous one. Comment (f) to section 520 makes it clear that all of the factors need not be present for an activity to be considered abnormally dangerous:

In determining whether the danger is abnormal, the factors listed in clauses (a) to (f) of this Section are all to be considered, and are all of importance. Any one of them is not necessarily sufficient to itself in a particular case, and ordinarily several of them will be required for strict liability. On the other hand it is not necessary that each of them be present, especially if others weigh heavily.

The first three factors, involving the degree of risk, harm, and difficulty of eliminating the risk, are obviously present in the storage of 80,000 pounds of explosives in a suburban area. The fourth factor, that the activity not be a matter of common usage, is also met. Comment (i) states:

Likewise the manufacture, storage, transportation and use of high explosives, although necessary to the construction of many public and private works, are carried on by only a comparatively small number of persons and therefore are not matters of common usage.

The fifth factor, inappropriateness of the activity, is arguably not present, for the storage did take place on land designated by the United States government for that purpose. However, the designation took place at a time when the area was less densely populated than it was at the time of the explosion. Likewise, the storage reserve was not entirely appropriate to the quantity of explosives stored because the explosion caused damage well beyond the boundaries of the reserve. The sixth factor, value to the community relates primarily to situations where the dangerous activity is the primary economic activity of the community in question. Thus comment (k) states that such factor applies

particularly when the community is largely devoted to the dangerous enterprise and its prosperity largely depends upon it. Thus the interests of a particular town whose livelihood depends upon such an activity as manufacturing cement may be such that cement plants will be regarded as a normal activity for that community notwithstanding the risk of serious harm from the emission of cement dust.

The comment further states that

in Texas and Oklahoma, a properly conducted oil or gas well, at least in a rural area, is not regarded as abnormally dangerous, while a different conclusion has been reached in Kansas and Indiana. California, whose oil industry is far from insignificant, has concluded that an oil well drilled in a thickly settled residential area in the City of Los Angeles is a matter of strict liability.

Since five of the six factors required by section 520 of the Restatement (Second) are met and the sixth is debatable, we would impose absolute liability here if we were to use that approach.

However, we do not believe that the Restatement (Second) approach should be used in cases involving the use or storage of explosives. Instead, we adhere to the rule of *Exner v. Sherman Power Constr. Co.* and its progeny imposing absolute liability in such cases. The Restatement (Second) approach requires an analysis of degrees of risk and harm, difficulty of eliminating risk, and appropriateness of place, before absolute liability may be imposed. Such factors suggest a negligence standard.[10] The six-factor analysis may well be necessary where damage is caused by unique hazards and the question is whether the general rule of absolute liability applies, but in cases involving the storage and use of explosives we take that question to have been resolved by more than a century of judicial decisions.

The reasons for imposing absolute liability on those who have created a grave risk of harm to others by storing or using explosives are largely independent of considerations of locational appropriateness. We see no reason for making a distinction between the right of a homesteader to recover when his property has been damaged by a blast set off in a remote corner of the state, and the right to compensation of an urban resident whose home is destroyed by an explosion originating in a settled area. In each case, the loss is properly to be regarded as a cost of the business of storing or using explosives. Every incentive remains to conduct such activities in locations which are as safe as possible,

because there the damages resulting from an accident will be kept to a minimum.

II

The next question is whether the intentional detonation of the storage magazine was a superseding cause relieving petitioners from liability. In *Sharp v. Fairbanks North Star Borough,* 569 P.2d 178 (Alaska 1977), a negligence case, we stated that a superseding cause exists where "after the event and looking back from the harm to the actor's negligent conduct, it appears to the court highly extraordinary that it should have brought about the harm." We further explained in *Sharp,*

> [w]here the defendant's conduct threatens a particular kind of result which will injure the plaintiff and an intervening cause which could not have been anticipated changes the situation but produces the same result as originally threatened, such a result is within the scope of the defendant's negligence.

Id. at 183 n. 9. The considerations which impel cutting off liability where there is a superseding cause in negligence cases also apply to cases of absolute liability.

Prior to the explosion in question the petitioners' magazines had been illegally broken into at least six times. Most of these entries involved the theft of explosives. Petitioners had knowledge of all of this.

Applying the standards set forth in *Sharp, supra,* to these facts we find there to have been no superseding cause. The incendiary destruction of premises by thieves to cover evidence of theft is not so uncommon an occurrence that it can be regarded as highly extraordinary. Moreover, the particular kind of result threatened by the defendant's conduct, the storage of explosives, was an explosion at the storage site. Since the threatened result occurred it would not be consistent with the principles stated in *Sharp* to hold there to have been a superseding cause. Absolute liability is imposed on those who store or use explosives because they have created an unusual risk to others. As between those who have created the risk for the benefit of their own enterprise and those whose only connection with the enterprise is to have suffered damage because of it, the law places the risk of loss on the former. When the risk created causes damage in fact, insistence that the precise details of the intervening cause be foreseeable would subvert the purpose of that rule of law.

The partial summary judgment is AFFIRMED.

---

10. In the analogous area of strict liability for defective products we have rejected the approach of § 402(a) of the Restatement (Second) of Torts which requires proof that a product is "unreasonably dangerous." "It represents a step backwards in the development of products liability cases. The purpose of strict liability is to overcome the difficulty of proof inherent in negligent and warranty theories, thereby insuring that the costs of physical injuries are borne by those who market defective products." *Butaud v. Suburban Marine & Sporting Goods, Inc.,* 543 P.2d 209, 214 (Alaska 1975).

RABINOWITZ, Justice, concurring.

Although I concur in the result reached by the court, I disagree with its adoption of the approach of *Exner v. Sherman Power Construction Co.,* 54 F.2d 510 (2d Cir. 1931), which imposes absolute or strict liability in all cases involving the use or storage of explosives. I am persuaded that sections 519 and 520 of the Restatement (Second) of Torts (1977) embody a sounder rule of law. On balance, I think it is preferable that the court, in making the determination whether an activity is "abnormally dangerous" and therefore subject to absolute liability, employ the criteria articulated in section 520 to analyze the particular acts and circumstances of the case. In my view, consideration of these criteria offers a rational solution to the problem of determining whether a particular activity is abnormally dangerous.

Despite the foregoing, I can agree with the court's overall disposition of this appeal since application of section 520 to the facts of the case leads to the conclusion that the activity in question was abnormally dangerous. Thus absolute liability was properly imposed.

Examples of Activities Some Courts Have Considered Abnormally Dangerous

Crop Dusting

The plaintiffs were organic farmers who used no nonorganic fertilizers, insecticides, or herbicides in their farming; they sold their produce to organic food buyers. The defendant, a crop duster, while spraying land adjoining the plaintiffs' land, during one spraying pass began spraying while over the plaintiffs' property. The residue rendered the plaintiffs' produce unfit to sell to buyers of organic food. The court, considering each of the six factors set forth in the Second Restatement, held that the defendant was strictly liable for the damage caused by his aerial spraying. The court emphasized that the risk of harm was accentuated by the fact that the drift of chemicals in aerial spraying is particularly unpredictable. The court also noted that the likelihood that harm would result was dependent upon what adjoining property owners did with their land. In balancing the risk of harm versus the utility of the activity, the court concluded that an equitable balancing of social interests could be attained only if the defendants were made to pay for the consequences of their acts (*Langan v. Valicopters, Inc.,* 567 P.2d 218 (Wash. 1977)).

Poisonous Gases

In an effort to kill cockroaches, the defendant, an exterminator, put hydrocyanic acid gas in the basement of a commercial building one evening while the building was unoccupied. The next morning the plaintiff was almost fatally poisoned because he was unable to smell the fumes (due to having a cold) and because he was unaware of the defendant's nocturnal activities. The court found that the defendant had engaged in an ultrahazardous activity that was likely to cause injury even though the utmost care was used. The court also concluded that the defendant knew or should have known injury might result and that the use of gas in this case was not "common usage"; even though the gas was commonly used by fumigators, it was not used generally by the public (*Luthringer v. Moore,* 190 P.2d 1 (Cal. 1948)).

Other activities the courts have held subject to strict liability include the following:

- Storage of flammable liquids in urban areas
- Disposal of hazardous waste
- Testing of rocket fuel

Examples of Activities Some Courts Have Considered Not Abnormally Dangerous

Airline Crash

An airline crash resulted in fire damage to a nearby apartment building. The court held for the defendant after concluding that flying is not an abnormally dangerous activity and that there was no intent to crash and no control over the plane after the mid-air collision preceding the crash (*Wood v. United Air Lines,*

Inc., 223 N.Y.S.2d 692, *aff'd,* 226 N.Y.S.2d 1022, *appeal dismissed,* 230 N.Y.S. 207 (1961)).

In the early days of commercial aviation, airlines were held to a strict liability standard. Modern safety records no longer warrant classifying flying as an abnormally dangerous activity and most courts have retreated to a negligence standard in this area. In many states strict liability continues to apply to ground damage caused by an airline crash, although an increasing number of states appear to be abandoning that position.

Irrigation Dam

A saboteur ruptured the defendant's irrigation dam, causing damage to the plaintiff's property. The appellate court held that reservoir owners are not absolutely liable for damage to the property of others caused by escaping waters if the breach is caused by an "act of God," a public enemy, or the malicious act of a third person. The court noted that in a semiarid climate an irrigation reservoir does not qualify as an uncommon usage or an ultrahazardous activity (*Wheatland Irrigation District v. McGuire,* 537 P.2d 1128, *reh'g granted in part,* 552 P.2d 1115, *reh'g,* 562 P.2d 287 (Wyo. 1975)).

Falling Tree

The plaintiff, a motorist, was injured when his automobile was struck by a falling tree. The plaintiff alleged that the defendant's construction of an irrigation canal was abnormally dangerous conduct that caused the roots of the tree to weaken. The court held that the defendant's acts were not abnormally dangerous because building an irrigation canal was not an uncommon activity in a rural area and did not involve an abnormally high degree of risk (*Stroda v. State Highway Commission,* 539 P.2d 1147 (Or. Ct. App. 1975)).

Other activities that the courts have concluded are not abnormally dangerous include:
• A defective lawn sprinkler that resulted in an automobile crash.
• Defective plumbing that caused damage to plaintiff's lower floor apartment.
• Defective electric wiring that resulted in property damage.

The courts do not agree as to what does or does not constitute an abnormally dangerous activity. Public policy appears to influence that determination; an overview of the cases in several jurisdictions indicates that courts are more likely to classify an activity as abnormally dangerous if the activity occurs in a highly populated area and less likely to do so if the activity occurs in an isolated area. Courts are more likely, for example, to hold strictly liable those who store flammable liquids or explosives in densely populated areas than they are those who store these materials in rural areas. By the same token, courts appear reluctant to classify the household use of gas, water, or electricity as an abnormally dangerous activity.

PUTTING IT INTO PRACTICE 12.2

1. A hotel guest is burned while watching a fire-eating act. He sues the hotel owner and the travel service that had arranged the "mystery tour" on the basis of strict liability, claiming that the act was an abnormally dangerous activity. Should he be allowed to recover?

Continued on next page

■ PUTTING IT INTO PRACTICE 12.2—Continued ☐

2. Mr. Warner is seriously injured when the truck in which he is a passenger is struck by a locomotive. He sues the railway on the basis of strict liability, arguing that the operation of a railway is an abnormally dangerous activity. Should he be able to recover on that basis?

3. The Tenneco Corporation operates a natural gas pipeline that includes 16,000 miles of pipe extending from Texas to New England. Compressor stations, which are necessary to compress and push the gas, are located at intervals along the pipeline. Since an air line explosion at compressor station 106, caused by the use of lubricants that lacked fire retardants, Tenneco began using a fire-retardant lubricant called Pydraul AC, which contains a polychlorinated biphenyl (PCB) called Aroclor 1254. In the late 1960s or early 1970s, Tenneco discontinued the use of Pydraul AC in favor of another non-PCB-containing lubricant. The use of PCBs was banned in 1976 by the Toxic Substances Control Act. Tenneco alleges it only recently discovered that PCBs were dumped directly onto the ground surrounding station 106 or into the station's drainage system.

   The Fletchers own a farm adjacent to station 106. PCBs have been detected in the soil of their property, in the water that drains onto their property, in their beef cattle, and in the blood of some members of the Fletcher family. Tenneco admits that its use of Pydraul AC is a source of the Fletchers' PCB contamination.

   Should Tenneco be held strictly liable for the Fletchers' injuries, even though it was unaware of the dangerousness of PCBs at the time it installed the compressor stations? Are there other torts the Fletchers might rely on to recover?

4. Danny's clothing is set on fire and he suffers facial burns and serious injury to his eyes when a shell from a firework display explodes nearby the crowd of onlookers of which Danny is a part. Should the company that is putting on the display be held strictly liable for Danny's injuries?

5. A service station owner sues the oil company for damage resulting from the leakage of gasoline from underground storage tanks. The tanks are in a state of preventable disrepair at the time of the leakage. Is the storage and removal of gasoline in underground storage tanks an abnormally dangerous activity for which the oil company should be strictly liable?

PRODUCT LIABILITY

The rationale underlying strict liability in the area of product liability is that it is easier for the defendant to bear the risk of loss than for the plaintiff. Advocates of strict liability reason that merchants and manufacturers have the ability to internalize the costs of accidental losses and can distribute such losses among the consumers who purchase their products.

Another reason given for imposing strict liability is that product safety is better promoted by a strict liability theory than by traditional negligence theory. Once courts render decisions imposing strict liability on defendants even though they were not negligent, defendants arguably have a strong incentive to prevent the occurrence of future harm. Preventing future harm is a primary goal for those who advocate strict liability. This theory of liability is discussed at length in Chapter 13.

LIMITATIONS ON STRICT LIABILITY

A defendant can raise either of two defenses in a strict liability case. First, a defendant can argue lack of proximate cause, i.e., that the damage that occurred was not the result of the kind of risk that made the activity abnormally dangerous. Second, a defendant can argue that a plaintiff who has "assumed the risk" should be barred from recovery.

Proximate Cause

A defendant is strictly liable only for damages that result from the kind of risk that made the activity abnormally dangerous. The Restatement (Second) of Torts illustrates this point using an example of a pedestrian run over by a truck transporting dynamite. Although transporting dynamite is an abnormally dangerous activity, the plaintiff will not be able to sue on the basis of strict liability because the risk of hitting pedestrians is not one of the things that makes such transportation abnormally dangerous.

A related rule is that a defendant will not be strictly liable if the harm occurred only because the plaintiff was conducting an "abnormally sensitive" activity. The case commonly used to illustrate this point is one in which the plaintiff's female minks killed their young as a result of being frightened by the defendant's blasting operation being conducted more than two miles from the plaintiff's mink ranch (*Foster v. Preston Mills Co.,* 268 P.2d 645 (Wash. 1954)). The court reasoned that blasting operations are unusually dangerous because of "the risk that property or persons may be damaged or injured by coming into direct contact with flying debris, or by being directly affected by vibrations of the earth or concussions of the air." Here, because the minks were harmed only because of their "exceedingly nervous disposition," the court held that the defendant was not strictly liable. Strict liability does not protect against "harms incident to the plaintiff's extraordinary and unusual use of land."

Some courts will also relieve defendants of liability if the harm occurred in an unforeseeable manner. An "act of God," for example, is often enough to relieve a defendant of strict liability. Although the Restatement (Second) of Torts rejects the "act of God" exception, many courts have been reluctant to impose liability when the harm that occurred was clearly out of the control of the defendant. Courts have refused to impose strict liability, for example, when extraordinary rainfall washed out a dam or when a hurricane caused water to overflow from a hydroelectric plant, resulting in flood damage.

Although the courts are not uniform in where they draw the line on strict liability, most courts impose liability for a narrower range of harm in cases involving strict liability than in cases involving negligence. That is, a court is more likely to find proximate cause in a negligence case than in a strict liability case. Likewise, a court is more likely to deny liability if there is an unforeseen, intervening cause in a strict liability case than in a negligence case. This willingness to curtail liability in strict liability cases is most likely due to the fact that the defendant is without fault.

Assumption of Risk

A plaintiff who knowingly, voluntarily, and either reasonably or unreasonably subjects himself or herself to danger is barred from recovering on the basis of strict liability. For example, a plaintiff who insists on driving through an area where blasting is being done, after seeing warning signs and being detained by a flagman, assumes the risk if he is injured by the blasting (Restatement (Second) of Torts § 523, illus. 2). Note, however, that contributory negligence usually will not bar a plaintiff from recovery. In the preceding example, if the driver had been merely inattentive and had missed the warning signs, this contributory negligence would not have barred him from recovery. Even though the driver in that situation did not discover a risk he should have discovered, full responsibility would lie with the party who created the abnormal risk (Restatement (Second) of Torts § 524, cmt. a).

PUTTING IT INTO PRACTICE 12.3

1. The owner of a food store sues an electric cooperative for a loss of food and equipment suffered as a result of a power outage. An expert for the defendant testifies that the power outage was due to the failure of an electrical transformer, which was caused by either an excessive load, lightning, or an internal problem. In the expert's opinion the most likely cause was lightning.

    The food store owner sues under a theory of strict liability. Is he likely to recover?

2. Kramer, a forklift driver, brings a strict liability action against a forklift manufacturer after he is injured in an accident involving the forklift. At the time of the accident, Kramer failed to look in the direction of travel and to keep his foot inside the operator's compartment (contrary to written warnings). Both of these actions may have contributed to the accident. The forklift is defective in that it fails to contain a guard on the operator's compartment; this defect makes the forklift dangerous.

    What defenses might the forklift manufacturer raise? Are these defenses likely to be successful?

3. Martin accepts a job hauling nitroglycerine. Because of the danger involved he is paid more than for hauling other types of loads. He is involved in a two-vehicle crash and is killed. Can his estate recover on the basis of strict liability?

4. Lynn tries to pass a truck on a narrow road. The truck is clearly marked "Danger, Dynamite" but Lynne, intent on passing the truck, fails to read the sign. She negligently runs into the truck and is killed in the ensuing explosion. Will her estate be barred from recovering if suit is filed on the basis of strict liability?

SUMMARY

Strict liability is a cause of action that can be used in cases involving abnormally dangerous activities, dangerous animals, and product liability. A plaintiff can recover damages even if the defendant acted without fault. The rationale underlying strict liability is that persons who engage in unusually dangerous activities must be responsible for any damages resulting from those activities.

Animal owners who are or should be aware of the vicious propensities of their domesticated pets are strictly liable for damages caused by those pets. Under the common law, owners were liable for property damage created by trespassing animals if those animals were likely to roam. This rule was modified by the "fencing in" and "fencing out" statutes adopted by many Western states.

Abnormally dangerous activities are those activities involving a high degree of risk of serious harm that cannot be eliminated with due care. Furthermore, the activity must not be a matter of common usage, must be inappropriate to the place where it is carried out, and its value to the community must be outweighed by its dangerous attributes. Crop dusting and the storage of flammable liquids are both examples of abnormally dangerous activities. Public policy concerns appear to affect the courts' classification of activities as being abnormally dangerous.

A defendant can be absolved of liability if the plaintiff assumes the risk by voluntarily and knowingly exposing himself or herself to the danger created by the defendant. If proximate cause is lacking, in that the damage that occurred did not result from the kind of risk making the activity abnormally dangerous, the defendant is not liable.

PRACTICE POINTERS

Evidence Collection and Preservation

Litigation in strict liability cases, as with negligence, is often fact-intensive—and though attorneys may be the masters of the law, legal assistants are the masters of the facts. Therefore, from the inception of a lawsuit until its resolution, a legal assistant can be invaluable to an attorney in performing factual research. Factual research involves interaction with such entities as government agencies, courts, corporations, fact witnesses, expert witnesses, other law firms, and computer database resources to obtain documentary evidence and witness statements.

In product liability cases, for example, product information and research data is essential and can be obtained from the governing organization for that product. The U.S. Patent Office is also an excellent source of documentary evidence. Patents usually contain detailed diagrams along with explanations of how the product works. Patents can be located using the patent number, which usually appears in the manufacturer's literature. Advertisements should also be consulted to determine claims made about the product, and the original product should be obtained along with any instructions, warranties, and warnings.

Other examples of documents that may be helpful in a case include telephone records (which can be subpoenaed) and records produced by city, county, and state street and highway departments. The latter show road conditions and construction projects, road maintenance, traffic signal sequence and pedestrian light timing, and, in some cases, histories of traffic accidents and traffic impact studies that record vehicle counts at a particular location. Before attempting to secure documents relevant to a case, you must determine the procedures and fees involved in obtaining records from a particular agency.

Witness Statements

Having interviewed a witness, you may decide that you want to take his statement. Several means can be used to do that. You may wish, with the permission of the witness, to tape-record his statement. Alternatively, you may ask him to write out his statement, although it is rare that individuals do an adequate job. Frequently, investigators write out the person's statement and have the witness sign it. The obvious drawback to this procedure is that the witness can later deny having made the statement or can say he signed it even though he was never given an opportunity to read it. In such cases the statement may be inadmissible and the investigator may be forced to take the stand to testify as to the witness's statement. Putting the statement in the words of the witness makes it more difficult for him later to deny having made the statement. In addition to having the witness sign the statement, have him initial each page, as well as sign a statement attesting to the truth and accuracy of the foregoing statement.

Although expensive, another alternative is the use of a court reporter. This method virtually precludes the witness from denying that he made the statement, but if he does a court reporter, who is a disinterested third party, rather than an investigator, will be called to testify.

Statements should be as specific as possible. Detailed, specific information rather than abstract generalizations are the goal. Be sure to get the witness's actual observations and not his opinions, because opinions of lay witnesses are generally not admissible.

Continued on next page

Witness statements may also be made from recorded telephone statements. When taking a statement over the telephone, identify yourself, the purpose of the phone call, the name of the person being interviewed, the date and time of the call, the telephone number of each party, and the fact that the conversation is being recorded and that the witness gave permission to record the statement. The witness should then be asked to give his full name, date of birth, address, driver's license number, and social security number. Having all of this information facilitates location of the witness two or three years later if the case ultimately goes to trial. This same identifying information should be obtained when recording a statement in person. During the conversation, be careful to avoid making extraneous comments or speaking while the witness is speaking. After the statement has been recorded, the tape should be labeled with the case name, witness name, and date of interview and should be transcribed as soon as possible after the interview.

If a witness is unwilling to be recorded or to sign an affirmative statement, he may be willing to sign a written "negative" statement. Such a statement denies any knowledge on the part of the witness (e.g., I did not see anything happen at location X at time Y). Having this statement in writing precludes the witness from coming back at a later date with new recollections.

Photographs

Photographs are extremely helpful in relating a story to a jury. Careful attention must be given to the photographic process. Keep in mind that the purpose of photographing evidence is for evidentiary and not aesthetic purposes. Therefore, black-and-white film rather than color film will be used in certain instances, because black-and-white produces sharper details. Always try to fill the frame as much as possible, blocking out any distracting background. Lighting is especially crucial. When photographing shoe prints or tire impressions, oblique (low-angle) lighting is essential to bring out the unique characteristics of the evidence.

Also be careful to make sure that the photographs accurately reflect the scene as it occurred. Distortions are easily created through the use of photography, so the attorneys who cross-examine you will be interested in finding out the precise manner in which you took each photograph. To help jog your memory, record details, such as camera speed, lighting conditions, and camera location for each photograph. Never alter any evidence in photographing it; such alterations will render the photograph inadmissible.

Sometimes a series of photographs will be necessary. For example, if the plaintiff has been bruised, the discoloration will not appear for a while, and the bruises will have to be photographed over time. Accident scenes should also be photographed in a series of shots, recreating the scene from the viewpoint of the drivers. Begin shooting from the direction of your client's vehicle about 500 feet from the point of impact and move progressively closer to the point of impact. Repeat this sequence from the viewpoint of the other driver. Take these photographs at the eye level of the driver so that they represent the scene from the driver's vantage point.

Remember that a photograph is indeed "worth a thousand words." Never skimp on film to save a little money. Photograph every square inch of an accident scene from every conceivable angle. Take several photographs of damaged areas of vehicles, including less visible damages such as scratches or paint scrapings. A

Continued on next page

---

piece of evidence that may at the time seem trivial to you may be the very evidence upon which the whole case hinges at trial. Taking photographs in the investigative process is an exacting science. If possible, you should consider taking courses or at least reading extensively in this area to enhance your expertise.

Aerial photographs can be helpful in orienting jurors to the conditions existing at a particular location, especially when presenting accident cases involving freeways, complicated intersections, or remote areas. Such photographs can often be obtained from the highway department, the U.S. Department of Agriculture, or the U.S. Army Corps of Engineers. Private companies also do aerial photographs and they are helpful in having photographs enlarged to scale.

In this era of television and movies, jurors are accustomed to seeing moving visual displays and often benefit from seeing videos. A video of how a product is made, how it works, and what it does, for example, can help focus jurors on key factual issues in a product liability case. Videos should be prepared professionally and should be done with a clear sense of purpose and direction.

■ TORT TEASERS □

1. Remembering the hypothetical scenario presented at the beginning of the chapter, what arguments would you make if you wanted to allege that those who dispose of hazardous wastes, such as toxic chemicals, are strictly liable for the consequences of their dumping? Analogize to the cases in this chapter, arguing that your case is most like those cases used to illustrate abnormally dangerous activities and unlike those cases used to illustrate activities that are not abnormally dangerous.

2. Plaintiff, while employed by defendants to look after their children, is startled by defendants' pet bird when it lights on her face. In trying to avoid the bird she steps back, falls, and fractures her hip. Defendants often let the bird out of its cage and do not lock the cage even though they are aware that they could do so. Should Defendants be held strictly liable? *Neagle v. Morgan*, 277 N.E.2d 483 (Mass. 1971).

3. Plaintiff boards his mare in a pasture with other horses. One day while trying to feed his mare Plaintiff leads the mare away from the other horses in the pasture. Defendant's colt approaches him in a menacing manner and Plaintiff, who is aware of the colt's vicious propensities, drives the colt away and returns to feeding his mare. The colt waits and then stealthily comes up behind Plaintiff and kicks him in the behind. Do you think this is a case of strict liability? What defenses might be raised and why? *Sandy v. Bushey*, 128 A. 513 (Me. 1925).

4. The court's synopsis of the facts in this particular case certainly bears repeating. "On September 14, 1907, the plaintiff was the owner of a thoroughbred Holstein-Friesian heifer, which was born on January 9, 1906, and had been thereafter duly christened 'Martha Pietertje Pauline.' The name is neither euphonious nor musical, but there is not much in a name anyway. Notwithstanding any handicap she may have had in the way of a cognomen, Martha Pietertje Pauline was a genuine 'highbrow,' having a pedigree as long and at

least as well authenticated as that of the ordinary scion of effete European nobility who breaks into this land of democracy and equality, and offers his title to the highest bidder at the matrimonial bargaining counter. The defendant was the owner of a bull about one year old, lowly born and nameless as far as the record discloses. This plebeian, having aspirations beyond his humble station in life, wandered beyond the confines of his own pastures, and sought the society of the adolescent and unsophisticated Martha, contrary to the provisions of Sec. 1482, . . . As a result of this somewhat morganatic mesalliance, a calf was born July 5, 1908." What would a court consider in deciding whether Defendant should be held strictly liable for Plaintiff's damages? *Kopplin v. Quade,* 130 N.W. 511 (Wis. 1911).

5. Plaintiff, a fireman, suffers severe chemical bronchitis as the result of inhaling antimony pentachloride gas when he responds to a call to give assistance to two men trapped in a tank. When Plaintiff arrives at the scene, he is told that the men have been extricated and that he should return to the station. While at the scene he encounters gas in the form of a haze or fog coming from an unknown source. Plaintiff never puts on a face mask to protect himself. Although Plaintiff experiences some irritation resulting from his contact with the gas, he is unaware of the potential danger created by exposure to the gas. Should Plaintiff be able to recover on the basis of strict liability? *Langlois v. Allied Chemical Corp.,* 249 So. 2d 133 (La. 1971).

6. Defendants' gasoline trailer breaks away from the truck towing it, leaves the highway, and falls onto a road below. Thousands of gallons of gasoline spill onto the road and a motorist driving across the road is killed when the gas explodes and his car is engulfed in flames. Plaintiff brings a wrongful death action against Defendants, one of whom is the owner of the truck and the other of whom is the driver. Do you think strict liability should be imposed? *Siegler v. Kuhlman,* 502 P.2d 1181 (Wash. 1973).

KEY TERMS

Abnormally dangerous activity
Activity for which a defendant is strictly liable if someone is injured; characterized as an activity having a high degree of risk of serious harm that cannot be eliminated with due care and whose value is outweighed by its dangerous attributes.

Strict liability
Liability imposed without a showing of intent or negligence.

CHAPTER

13

Product Liability

CHAPTER OBJECTIVES

In this chapter you will learn to:
- Differentiate among negligence, warranty, and strict liability causes of action
- Appreciate the importance of classifying losses as personal injury losses, property damage, or economic losses
- Identify characteristics and examples of manufacturing defects, design defects, and defective warnings
- Recognize when it is appropriate to sue on the basis of negligence, strict liability, and breach of warranty
- Identify the characteristics of express and implied warranties
- Explain the rationale behind strict liability
- Outline the elements of a strict liability claim
- Identify the defenses that can be raised in negligence, strict liability, and warranty causes of action

Having spent several years desperately trying to have children, Tom and Susan go to Dr. Payne to determine the reason for Susan's inability to conceive. After running several tests, Dr. Payne concludes that Tom's sperm count is so low that he probably will never be able to impregnate Susan. Dr. Payne suggests that they might be able to impregnate Susan using semen from a sperm bank. After studying in depth the procedures used in artificial insemination, Tom and Susan opt for this technique. Based on a list that Tom and Susan prepare as to the traits they wish their child to have, Dr. Payne selects a specific anonymous donor. Susan becomes pregnant as a result of the artificial insemination and delivers a boy. Unfortunately, when the child is quite young, it is discovered that he has a serious congenital birth defect. Tom and Susan sue Dr. Payne for the harm caused to their child.

Are Dr. Payne and the sperm bank negligent in supplying a defective product, i.e., sperm that contains faulty genetic coding? Did they breach any implied warranties? Should they be held strictly liable for the injuries sustained by the child? Can the child as well as the parents sue for his damages? What defenses can Dr. Payne and the sperm bank raise?

OVERVIEW OF PRODUCT LIABILITY

Product liability refers to the liability of a manufacturer, seller, or other supplier of a chattel which, because of a defect, causes injury to a consumer, a user, or in some cases a bystander. Liability can be based on any of three theories of recovery: (1) negligence; (2) warranty; or (3) strict liability.

THEORIES OF RECOVERY

Negligence

Anyone who negligently manufactures a product is liable for any personal injuries proximately caused by his or her negligence. A manufacturer may be negligent in the way it designs or manufactures its product. It may be negligent in its failure to conduct a reasonable inspection or test of its finished products. Fur-

thermore, a manufacturer may be negligent in its failure to package and ship its products in a reasonably safe manner.

Users and Makers of Components Parts

Similarly, the manufacturer of a component part may be liable for failure to use reasonable care. Additionally, a manufacturer that uses components prepared by others may be liable if it does not take reasonable care to obtain them from a reliable source or does not make a reasonable inspection of the components before incorporating them. Thus an automobile manufacturer who assembles a chassis using components prepared by other manufacturers is liable for any malfunctions that result from a defect in the component parts if the manufacturer does not make a reasonable inspection of those components before incorporating them.

Retailers

A manufacturer is liable if a retailer fails to make an inspection that it is under an obligation to make. If, however, the retailer learns of the defect either by inspection or through some other means and fails to warn the customer, many courts have found the chain of causation to be broken and have absolved the manufacturer of any liability.

Retailers as well as manufacturers may be found negligent, but suits against retailers on the basis of negligence are often unsuccessful. The sale of a negligently manufactured or designed product is not enough by itself to show negligence. Generally, a retailer has no duty to inspect goods unless it has reason to believe they may be dangerous because even if it did inspect it would have no chance of finding the defect. A retailer selling microwave ovens, for example, has no duty to break open the boxes in which the ovens are packaged to inspect the ovens. A majority of courts have, however, imposed a duty to make at least a superficial examination, especially when the retailer is a car dealer. The consequences of a defect in a car are likely to be severe and the retailer is much more likely than the buyer to discover any defects. If a retailer knows or should know that a product is unreasonably dangerous, it is negligent if it does not at least warn customers. Generally, plaintiffs suing retailers opt for warranty or strict liability theories for reasons we will discuss later in this chapter.

Lessors, Real Estate Agents, and Sellers of Services

Lessors of goods may also be liable in negligence for failing to discover defects. Rental car companies that lease defective cars, for example, may be found negligent. The sellers of real estate as well as suppliers of services (e.g., the providers of blood transfusions) may also be found negligent.

Privity

Formerly, a plaintiff in a negligence action was required to contract directly with the defendant. This so-called **privity** requirement was abolished in *MacPherson v. Buick Motor Co.,* 111 N.E. 1050 (N.Y. 1916), allowing a plaintiff who buys a product from a retailer and not directly from the defendant manufacturer to recover. Therefore, a plaintiff can sue the manufacturer, the retailer, or the lessor of a product. Users of products who do not purchase the products can also recover under a negligence theory if they are "reasonably foreseeable" plaintiffs. (See *Palsgraf* in Chapter 7 for a discussion of foreseeability.)

Damages in Negligence Cases

Although plaintiffs generally seek to recover damages resulting from personal injuries, they can also recover for property damage. Suppose a defendant fails to use due care in manufacturing a television set and the defect in the electrical wiring in the television causes it to catch fire and burn down the plaintiff's house. The plaintiff can recover for the resulting property damage.

Plaintiffs in negligence actions generally have a hard time recovering for pure economic loss. Breach of warranty, rather than negligence, is the preferred theory for use in recovering for economic damages. Also, the distinction between property damage and economic loss is not always clear. Is the destruction of the plaintiff's property or of the product itself considered property damage or economic loss? Similarly, does the fact that the product no longer works or is now worthless because of the defect constitute property damage or economic loss? Consult the case law in your state to see how the courts in your jurisdiction have resolved these issues.

Warranty

Combination of Tort and Contract Law

A cause of action based on breach of warranty is a hybrid one, containing characteristics of both tort and contract law. Originally the action was deemed a form of misrepresentation and was therefore considered a tort. But because most warranties arose under the common law in situations involving a contract of sale, contract law was also applicable. Today this amalgamated form of law is made even more confusing by the Uniform Commercial Code's efforts to deal with warranties on a statutory basis.

Pay particular attention to the fact that the public policy justifications underlying tort law and contract law are quite different. Tort remedies are designed to protect the public from dangerous products. The purpose of strict liability is to protect consumers and allocate the risk to manufacturers, who are better able than consumers to bear the risk of loss. Contract remedies, in contrast, are designed to compensate parties for the loss of the benefit of their bargain. Under the Uniform Commercial Code (UCC), the free flow of commerce is encouraged (*see* UCC § 1–102, Official Comment 2) and commercial parties of equal bargaining power are allowed to allocate the risk of loss between themselves. A party to a commercial contract may, for example, choose to forego a remedy in exchange for a lower purchase price. Presumably merchants are better able to protect themselves from economic loss than are consumers.

In deciding whether to apply contract law or tort law, a court must consider the nature of the defect in the product and the type of loss for which the plaintiff seeks compensation. In a tort claim the plaintiff is alleging that she has been exposed by means of a hazardous product to an unreasonable risk of injury. In a contract case, however, the plaintiff is alleging that the product failed to perform in accordance with the expectations one would have for a product of a particular quality and fit for ordinary use. Tort law, then, is reserved for defects that result in an unreasonably dangerous product. Contract remedies are more appropriate when the defect involves only the quality of the product and presents no unreasonable danger to persons or property.

The type of loss—personal injury, property damage, or economic loss—also determines whether the plaintiff will select a contract or tort claim. Although a majority of jurisdictions restrict contract liability to recovery for commercial or economic loss and restrict tort liability to recovery for damage to persons or property, this distinction has been challenged by several modern courts. Some, such as the Arizona courts, have reasoned that if the plaintiff's only loss is an economic one, the parties are best left to their commercial remedies. If the plaintiff's economic loss is accompanied by some physical damage to a person or other property, the party's interests are best protected via tort liability. Consult the case law in your state to determine how the courts in your jurisdiction have analyzed this issue.

Express Warranty

There are two types of warranties—express and implied. With an **express warranty** a seller expressly represents that the goods possess certain qualities. A description of a windshield by a manufacturer as being "shatterproof" is an example of an express warranty. If the purchaser can later show that the product does not possess such qualities (if, for example, the windshield shatters after being hit by a stone), she may sue for breach of warranty. An express warranty may be made in one of three ways:

• An "affirmation of fact or promise" regarding the goods
• A description of the goods

• Use of a sample or model of the goods (UCC § 2–313)

A seller might describe goods as being water-resistant, for example, or might use a model to demonstrate how the product works, thus suggesting to consumers that the product they buy is similar in nature.

Who May Recover? In a sense, breach of express warranty is a type of strict liability claim. The plaintiff need not show that she believed the seller's representations to be true nor, in most cases, that she was even aware of the express warranty. All the plaintiff need show is that the representation was in fact false. A drug company that produced a drug it believed to be nonaddictive and that it advertised as such was found liable when a consumer became addicted to the drug and ultimately died from his addiction (*Crocker v. Winthrop Laboratories,* 514 S.W.2d 249 (Tex. 1974)). The court discounted the reasonableness of the company's belief in the nonaddictiveness of the drug. It focused on the falsity of the company's representations and the disastrous results of the physician's misplaced reliance on such representations.

Plaintiffs may recover for breach of express warranty even when they are not in privity with the seller, in that they did not purchase directly from the seller. According to some courts, a plaintiff who is a user and not a purchaser of a product must show that he is a member of the general class of the public that the manufacturer expected or should have expected to be reached by the warranty. In many cases express warranties, such as the warranty of shatterproofness, would be considered to be addressed to the public at large. Therefore, a remote buyer, user, or even bystander would probably be held to be part of the general class to which the warranty was addressed.

What May Be Recovered? A plaintiff whose damages are solely economic, such as lost profits, can recover the difference between what the product would have been worth had it been as it was warranted and what it was in fact worth with its defect (UCC § 2–714(2)).

The buyer can also recover for incidental and consequential damages (UCC § 2–715). As in the case of negligence, plaintiffs can certainly recover for property damage and personal injuries resulting from the defective product.

Implied Warranty

A seller also makes certain **implied warranties** by virtue of offering a product for sale. The two most common types of implied warranties are the warranty of merchantability and the warranty of fitness for a particular purpose.

A **warranty of merchantability** is implied in a contract for the sale of goods if the seller is a merchant in the regular business of selling the kind of goods in question. According to UCC § 2–314, for goods to be merchantable they must (among other things):

- Be "fit for the ordinary purposes for which such goods are used."
- Be "within the variations permitted by the agreement, of even kind, quality and quantity within each unit and among all units involved."
- Be "adequately contained, packaged, and labeled as the agreement may require."
- "Conform to the promises or affirmations of fact made on the container or label, if any."

The courts have consistently held that retailers impliedly warrant the merchantability of their products. A few courts, however, have created what is known as the "sealed container" doctrine, which absolves retailers who sell sealed containers of any liability. Under the UCC, the merchantability warranty is applicable to the sale of food or drink. The code does not apply, however, to services and to real estate transactions, although some courts have creatively applied warranty theory to such transactions. Some courts, for example, have utilized an "implied warranty of habitability" in finding liability on the part of builders of homes when purchasers of the homes suffered injuries. The courts are in disagreement as to whether an implied warranty of merchantability exists for sellers dealing in used goods.

An implied **warranty of fitness for a particular purpose** is created when a seller who knows that a buyer wants goods for a particular (noncustomary) purpose makes a recommendation on which the buyer relies (UCC § 2–315). Suppose, for example, a consumer asks advice from a salesman at the hardware store regarding what type of lumber he should purchase for a particular construction project. If the type of lumber he purchases turns out to be unsuitable for such use, the consumer can sue the hardware store on the basis of breach of implied warranty.

What Can Be Recovered?　A direct purchaser, i.e., one who buys directly from the defendant, can certainly recover on the basis of breach of implied warranty for personal injury and property damage resulting from the product, and also for solely economic damages such as lost profits. As with express warranties, a direct purchaser can recover the difference between what the product would have been worth had it been as warranted and what it is worth with its defect. The direct buyer can also recover for incidental and consequential damages.

A purchaser can recover for personal injury on the basis of implied warranty even though he or she bought the product from a dealer and not the defendant manufacturer. Some states allow such remote purchasers to recover for property damage alone on the basis of breach of implied warranty. A remote purchaser, however, probably would not be able to recover for purely economic damages, such as lost profits. According to the majority position a nonprivity plaintiff should instead sue the immediate seller for economic damages resulting from a breach of an implied warranty. Many states permit a nonpurchaser (user), such as an employee of a purchaser, whose use of the product was foreseeable, to recover for personal injuries from the manufacturer or others in the distributive chain. There is a great deal of variation among states regarding privity requirements in reference to implied warranties. The UCC itself suggests three alternatives for dealing with privity requirements. Therefore, it is important that you check the case law and statutes in your state pertaining to recovery by remote purchasers and nonpurchasers.

Who Can Be Held Liable?   Breach of warranty actions can be brought against manufacturers, retail dealers, and component manufacturers (those who manufacture components that are incorporated into a larger product). Considerable controversy exists as to whether warranty liability can be imposed on the sellers of used goods, but by analogizing to the UCC, the courts do allow recovery on the basis of implied warranty in cases involving lessors of goods, sellers of real estate, and sellers of services. A mass producer of homes, for example, can be held liable for breach of an implied warranty of habitability for having installed faulty plumbing.

Comparison with Strict Liability Claims.   Many plaintiffs opt for strict liability over warranty claims because strict liability is easier to prove than breach of warranty and in many respects is virtually identical to warranty claims. In a few instances, however, the plaintiff may have an advantage in suing on a warranty theory. A plaintiff who is the direct purchaser and whose damages are solely economic will likely sue for breach of warranty rather than for strict liability or negligence because of the generosity of the UCC in providing for damages. Remember that under the UCC, whether a warranty is express or implied, a direct purchaser can recover the difference between what the product would have been worth had it been as warranted and what it is worth with its defect. The buyer can also recover for incidental and consequential damages. Under the UCC a remote purchaser who has suffered only economic harm may recover on the basis of breach of express warranty, whereas he or she would be precluded from doing so on the basis of strict liability or negligence. Furthermore, in many states the statute of limitations used in warranty actions is the contract statute of limitations, which is typically longer than the tort statute of limitations used in strict liability claims.

PUTTING IT INTO PRACTICE 13.1

1. Elite Professionals, Inc., a trucking company, sues Carrier Corporation for damages arising out of a truck refrigeration unit malfunction that resulted in the spoilage of a cargo of meat. Elite had bought the unit from Carrier. The incident giving rise to Elite's claim occurs when Elite is transporting a twenty-three-ton load of frozen hog sides from Vermont to California. The first evidence of a refrigeration problem is discovered by the driver when he stops in New Mexico to check out the truck. The "T-ticker" gauge on the outside of the refrigeration unit shows that the temperature inside the reefer is three to five degrees above zero (the temperature must be maintained at 0 degrees to preserve the meat). The driver turns the temperature control down and telephones Elite's headquarters to report the situation to Elite's president, who tells the driver to proceed and call back later. A few hours later the driver reports that the temperature has risen to 20 degrees. The president instructs the driver to continue, thinking this to be the most expedient decision and hoping that making a direct run to California will result in getting the cargo transported more quickly than getting assistance at a Carrier service facility. Unfortunately, when the refrigerator is opened the next morning, the temperature has risen to 60 degrees and the hog sides have spoiled. The truck is immediately taken to Carrier, whose mechanics identify and replace a defective solenoid coil.

Continued on next page

PUTTING IT INTO PRACTICE 13.1—Continued

The printed warranty and disclaimer that Elite received upon purchasing the refrigeration unit reads in part:

MANUFACTURER'S WARRANTY TRUCK/ TRAILER REFRIGERATION UNITS

Carrier . . . through its dealer organization shall, at their facility, during normal working hours, repair or replace with a new or remanufactured part, any parts or components of the [refrigeration unit] . . . which . . . malfunction as a result of defects in material or workmanship. . . .

THE FOREGOING OBLIGATION IS EXPRESSLY GIVEN IN LIEU OF ANY OTHER WARRANTIES, EXPRESSED OR IMPLIED, INCLUDING ANY IMPLIED WARRANTY OF MERCHANTABILITY OR FITNESS FOR PARTICULAR PURPOSE, WHICH EXCEEDS THE RESPONSIBILITIES SET FORTH HEREIN.

LIMITATION OF LIABILITY

Carrier . . . expressly disclaims and denies all liability for SPECIAL, INCIDENTAL, OR CONSEQUENTIAL DAMAGES or losses of a commercial nature arising out of a malfunctioning product or its parts or components thereof, as a result of defects in material or workmanship. THE OWNER'S SOLE AND EXCLUSIVE REMEDY AND [CARRIER'S] SOLE AND EXCLUSIVE LIABILITY SHALL BE LIMITED TO THE REPAIR OR REPLACEMENT OF PARTS OR COMPONENTS CONTAINED IN THE [REFRIGERATION UNIT] . . . WHICH . . . MALFUNCTION AS A RESULT OF DEFECTS IN MATERIAL OR WORKMANSHIP IN ACCORDANCE WITH THE APPLICABLE PROVISIONS AND LIMITATIONS STATED ABOVE.

Carrier argues that by replacing the defective solenoid coil it has satisfied its "repair or replace" obligation under the warranty. Elite responds that the remedy provided in the warranty failed and that under the UCC if "circumstances cause an exclusive or limited remedy to fail of its essential purpose, remedy may be had as provided in [the Uniform Commercial Code]."

a. Is the warranty at issue express or implied?

b. Did Carrier satisfy the requirements of the warranty?

2. Women whose mothers took DES (diethylstilbestrol) to prevent miscarriages are suing the manufacturers of the drug for injuries they have suffered. On what grounds might they sue under a theory of warranty?

3. A widower files a product liability action against some tobacco companies on the grounds that statements made by the companies about smoking and health were express warranties. These statements were made in a 1954 report entitled "Frank Statement to the Public by the Makers of Cigarettes" and "A Statement About Tobacco and Health."

Do you think representations by tobacco companies that cigarettes are safe to use constitute express warranties as to their safety? Does the fact that the plaintiff cannot show that his wife actually read these reports necessarily preclude his claim?

Strict Liability

Rationale Justifying Strict Liability

Strict liability theories now constitute the primary basis for liability for manufacturers of products. Three basic reasons are given to support the premise that manufacturers should be held strictly liable for defects in their products. Foremost is the idea that sellers of defective products, rather than consumers, should bear the cost of compensating tort victims for the injuries they sustain from defective products. Proponents argue that manufacturers are in a better economic position than consumers to bear such costs.

Second, some feel that sellers should be made to internalize the cost of any injuries their products inflict, forcing them to incorporate the cost of liability into the product itself and thereby raising the market price of the product. The reasoning is that consumers, when faced with the higher costs of such products, will purchase cheaper and presumably safer products.

The third argument is that the sophistication of modern products precludes the average consumer from pinpointing the act of negligence responsible for his or her injuries. When some of the evidentiary obstacles to recovery found under negligence analysis are removed, more consumers are able to recover under a strict liability theory and manufacturers are deterred from producing unsafe products.

Many courts and commentators refute these arguments, however. Some have pointed out that empirical evidence of strict liability's effect on product safety is lacking. Some feel that the pendulum has swung too far in favor of consumer protection and should reach a more moderate position, so that manufacturers are not unduly hampered in their efforts to meet consumer demands.

Section 402A of the Restatement

One of the first decisions dealing with strict liability was rendered by Justice Traynor, who was disenchanted with the warranty theory. In *Greenman v. Yuba Power Products, Inc.,* 377 P.2d 897 (Cal. 1963), Justice Traynor held that the plaintiff's failure to give timely notice of breach of warranty to the defendant, as required by California law, did not bar his recovery, because the defendant was strictly liable. (In *Greenman* the plaintiff was injured by a piece of wood that flew off a lathe he was using.) Traynor noted that "a manufacturer is strictly liable in tort when an article he places on the market, knowing that it is to be used without inspection for defects, proves to have a defect which causes injury to a human being." Traynor reasoned that manufacturers who put defective products on the market should bear the cost of injuries resulting from such defective products rather than the injured parties who, he believed, were powerless to protect themselves. Consumers, he concluded, were better protected under a strict liability theory than under a warranty theory.

Traynor's opinion laid the foundation for § 402A of the Restatement (Second) of Torts, which has been adopted by the majority of American jurisdictions. Section 402A reads as follows:

> Section 402A. Special liability of seller of product for physical harm to user or consumer.
>
> (1) One who sells any product in a defective condition unreasonably dangerous to the user or consumer or to his property is subject to liability for physical harm thereby caused to the ultimate user or consumer, or to his property, if
> > (a) the seller is engaged in the business of selling such a product, and
> > (b) it is expected to and does reach the user or consumer without substantial change in the condition in which it is sold.
> (2) The rule stated in subsection (1) applies although
> > (a) the seller has exercised all possible care in the preparation and sale of his product, and
> > (b) the user or consumer has not bought the product from or entered into any contractual relation with the seller.

Under § 402A, as interpreted by most courts, the plaintiff must prove five elements:

- A product was sold.
- The product was defective.
- The defective product was the cause in fact and proximate cause of the plaintiff's injuries.
- The defect existed at the time the product left the defendant's hands.
- The item was manufactured or sold by the defendant.

Unlike the plaintiff proving negligence, the plaintiff who has opted for a strict liability claim need not prove that the manufacturer or seller failed to use due care. In other words, the defendant in a strict liability case is liable even if he or she was not at fault (see Figure 13-1).

Sale of a Product. Section 402A applies only to the sale of products and not to the provision of services. A typical sale of a carpet, for example, involves a sales-service transaction. The actual sale of the carpet involves the sale of a product, but the installation involves a service. The seller need not be engaged solely in the business of selling products. The owner of a theater who sells popcorn and candy to patrons is engaged in the sale of products even though the sales are incidental to his primary business (Restatement (Second) of Torts § 402A, cmt. f.) In one case a patient sued the surgeon who had implanted his mandibular prosthesis, which later was found to be defective. The court refused to hold the doctor strictly liable because it found that the doctor was not a "seller" of a product. Refusing to analogize to the movie theater example in the Restatement, the court explained that although the

"implant was incidental to the surgical procedure . . . it was a necessary adjunct to the treatment administered, as were the scalpel used to make the incision, and any other material objects involved in performing the operation, all of which fulfill a particular role in provision of medical service, the primary activity." *Cafazzo v. Central Medical Health Services,* 668 A.2d 521 (Pa. 1995).

This sales-service dichotomy also used to be a point of contention, for example, in the so-called "bad blood" cases in which the plaintiffs contract a disease after receiving contaminated blood in the form of transfusions. The question is whether a transfusion involves the sale of a product (blood) or is part of the package of services provided by a hospital and is therefore not a sale but a service. (The same issue arises in the context of warranty cases because the UCC applies only to goods sold and not to services rendered.) Now most states have statutes protecting blood banks from being held strictly liable for "bad blood," so this issue is moot in most instances.

Defective Conditions. What constitutes a defective condition for purposes of strict liability? In most strict liability cases the courts focus on whether the product is in "a defective condition unreasonably dangerous." According to Restatement (Second) of Torts § 402A, cmt. i, a product is in a *defective condition unreasonably dangerous* if it is "dangerous to an extent beyond that which would be contemplated by the ordinary consumer who purchases it, with the ordinary

FIGURE 13-1 Elements of Strict Liability Claim

- Was a product sold (as opposed to a service)?
- Was the product defective (in a "defective condition unreasonably dangerous")?
- Was the defective product the proximate cause and cause in fact of the plaintiff's injuries?
- Did the defect exist at the time the product left the defendant's hands?
- Was the product manufactured or sold by the defendant?

knowledge common to the community as to its characteristics." Good whiskey, therefore, is not considered unreasonably dangerous merely because some people will become drunk and injure themselves. Bad whiskey containing a dangerous amount of isopropyl alcohol, however, is considered in a defective condition unreasonably dangerous. The phrase *defective condition unreasonably dangerous* is a term of art and so the words "defective condition" should not be separated from the words "unreasonably dangerous."

Some courts look at the acts of a reasonable consumer, using the consumer expectation test, to determine whether a product is in a defective condition unreasonably dangerous. Others look at the acts of a reasonable defendant, using what is commonly referred to as the risk-utility test. Under this test, the court imputes knowledge of a defective condition of the product to the defendant. The core inquiry is whether a reasonable person would conclude that the perceived risks created by the design and marketing of the product outweigh the benefits. Would the defendant, as a reasonable person, have put the product into the stream of commerce if he or she had knowledge of its defective condition? This test was used in *Turner v. General Motors Corp.,* 514 S.W.2d 497 (Tex. Civ. App. 1974), to determine whether General Motors' design of the Impala's roof was defective.

A defective condition unreasonably dangerous can arise not only from the characteristics of the product itself but also from foreign objects contained in the product, from decay or deterioration before sale, or from the way in which the product was prepared or packaged. A carbonated beverage that is bottled under excessive pressure and explodes upon being opened, or a beverage that contains bits of glass, is in a defective condition unreasonably dangerous.

Unavoidably Unsafe Products. **Unavoidably unsafe products** are those products that are incapable of being made safe for their intended and ordinary use. If the benefits of such products outweigh their risks, the courts will not hold their manufacturers strictly liable for harm coming to the consumers. Experimental drugs exemplify unavoidably unsafe products. Their absolute safety cannot be assured because of insufficient research data and lack of medical experience. Those who sell these drugs are not held strictly liable for any untoward consequences resulting from their use as long as they prepare and market the drugs properly and give adequate warnings to consumers (§ 402A, cmt. k). Note, however, that if a manufacturer were negligent in failing to make adequate tests before selling the drugs, a plaintiff could recover for negligence.

Many courts have classified blood as an unavoidably unsafe product. Additionally, many states have precluded by statute strict liability suits by those receiving "bad" blood. In one case in which the plaintiff contracted serum hepatitis as a result of receiving a blood transfusion, the court held that neither the hospital nor the blood bank was strictly liable (*Hines v. St. Josephs Hospital,* 527 P.2d 1075 (N.M. 1974)). No technology existed at the time to determine whether a particular specimen was infected with hepatitis, even though blood banks were aware that a percentage of all specimens would be infected with hepatitis. The court concluded that the blood was "incapable of being made safe for its intended and ordinary use." The defendants fulfilled their duty to warn of the defect by warning the doctor and the hospital (through labeling) even though they never warned the plaintiff herself.

Plaintiffs generally cannot introduce evidence that the defendant redesigned the product to make it safer. Such evidence is, however, admissible for the limited purpose of rebutting the defendant's argument that the product is unavoidably unsafe because of the extreme cost involved in removing the defect.

Causation. The plaintiff must also show that the product was the cause in fact and proximate cause of his or her injuries. Suppose, for example, that the plaintiff eats a food product manufactured by the defendant and becomes ill several hours later. He must establish that it was the defendant's product and not some other factor that caused his illness.

Frequently, defendants will argue that intervening events were the proximate cause of the plaintiff's injuries or that other factors were the sole cause in fact of the accident. Remember from our discussion on strict liability (Chapter 12) that the courts are more likely to find a superseding cause in a strict liability cause of action than in a negligence case. Generally, if the act was reasonably foreseeable, it will not be considered a superseding act. If the act was unforeseeable but caused the same type of harm that made the product dangerous, then once again the act will not be considered superseding.

Unique causation problems have been raised in the diethylstilbestrol (DES) litigation. In one of the first DES cases, *Sindell v. Abbott Laboratories,* 26 Cal. 3d 588, 607 P.2d 924, *cert. denied,* 101 S. Ct. 285 (1980), the plaintiff was unable to identify the manufacturer responsible for making the DES taken by her mother while the plaintiff was in utero. Sympathizing with the plaintiff's plight, the court determined that because the plaintiff had sued five of the manufacturers of DES, whom she asserted produced 90 percent of the DES marketed, the burden of proof shifted to the defendants to demonstrate that they could not have supplied the DES that caused the plaintiff's injuries. Furthermore, the court reasoned that each defendant that failed to make such a showing would be held liable for the proportion of the judgment represented by its share of the DES market.

The theory of alternate liability (see Chapter 7 for further discussion), adopted by Restatement (Second) of Torts § 433B(3), preceded the market share liability theory of *Sindell.* It has been used by at least one AIDS victim (a hemophiliac), who could not identify the manufacturer that made the blood product from which he contracted AIDS (*Poole v. Alpha Therapeutic Corp.,* 696 F. Supp. 351 (N.D. Ill. 1988)). Under this theory, if two or more persons have committed a tortious act and it can be proven that the harm done to the plaintiff was done by only one of them, but there is uncertainty as to which one did the harm, the burden is on each defendant to prove that he or she did not cause the harm. Any defendant that cannot prove his or her actions did not cause the plaintiff's injuries will be found liable. In *Poole,* once the plaintiff was able to identify all of the defendants that could possibly have caused him to contract AIDS, the burden of proof shifted to the defendants to prove that they were not responsible for the plaintiff's injuries.

When Defect Existed. Finally, the plaintiff must show that the defect existed at the time the product left the hands of the defendant manufacturer. If it is just as likely that the defect developed while the product was in the hands of an intermediate dealer, the plaintiff cannot sustain her burden of proof against the manufacturer. Proof of this is exacerbated in cases in which the product passed through several intermediaries before it was used by the plaintiff. Most courts, however, are fairly liberal in allowing the plaintiff to at least get to the jury on this issue.

Strictly speaking, res ipsa loquitur is not applicable in a strict liability case, but some of the inferences made under that doctrine are applicable. The fact that a product malfunctioned and no one else tampered with it may give rise to a permissible inference that the product was defective and that the defect existed when it left the hands of the defendant. The principles of res ipsa loquitur were successfully used in one strict liability case in which shortening exploded when the user drained it from a fryer into a can. In light of the fact that the plaintiff had properly handled and used the shortening, there was no possible explanation for the explosion other than a defect in the shortening, as shortening does not normally explode (*Franks v. National Dairy Products Corp.,* 414 F.2d 682 (5th Cir. 1969)).

Who May Be a Defendant?

Strict liability applies to anyone in the business of selling goods, whether or not he or she is the manufacturer. A retail dealer in the business of selling goods is therefore strictly liable for the sale of any defective goods even if the sale is not a predominant part of the business. An owner of a movie theater, for example, is strictly liable for any defective popcorn or candies he sells even though such sales are presumably a by-product of his main business. In contrast, a private individual who sells her furniture is not strictly liable because she is not in the business of furniture selling. Component manufacturers are usually held to a standard of strict liability if the plaintiff can show that the defect existed at the time the component left the manufacturer's shop. Many courts have been willing to impose strict liability on lessors of defective goods (when the lessor is in the business of leasing) as well as sellers of real estate and sellers of services. Those who sell used goods, however, generally are not held to a standard of strict liability unless the plaintiff can show that the defects were created by the seller.

Who May Be a Plaintiff?

Strict liability allows recovery for anyone who is the "ultimate user or consumer." Consumers include those who prepare a product for consumption (such as the husband who opens a bottle of beer for his wife to drink), those who passively enjoy the benefit of a product (such as passengers in an airplane), and those who use the product for the purpose of doing work on it (such as a serviceperson making repairs on an automobile). (Restatement (Second) of Torts § 402A, cmt. l.)

Many courts have been willing to extend strict liability protection to bystanders whose presence was reasonably foreseeable. One court reasoned that bystanders are entitled to greater protection than consumers or users because they do not have the same opportunity to inspect products for defects that consumers and users do (*Elmore v. American Motors Corp.*, 451 P.2d 84 (Cal. 1969)).

The courts have struggled with where to draw the line in reference to the protection of bystanders.

Should a father, for example, be able to sue a manufacturer of birth control pills on behalf of his twin Down's syndrome daughters, one of whom is living and one of whom is deceased, on the theory that the pills altered the mother's chromosome structure, causing the resultant birth defects (*Jorgensen v. Meade Johnson Laboratories, Inc.*, 483 F.2d 237 (10th Cir. 1973))? The *Jorgensen* court held that the plaintiffs' claim for pain and suffering, mental retardation, and deformity, all of which were prenatal injuries, could be maintained because the children were born alive. While recognizing the father's right to bring this cause of action, the circuit court saw the key problem as being one of causation, i.e., presenting sufficient medical evidence to prove that the contraceptives did in fact cause the Down's syndrome.

Damages

Plaintiffs suing under a strict liability cause of action may recover for property damage as well as damages resulting from personal injuries. Lost profits and other intangible economic harm are generally not recoverable under a strict liability theory unless the plaintiff can show that he or she also suffered injury or property damage.

A prime example of a case in which the court classified the plaintiff's losses as economic and therefore unrecoverable involved the purchase by the plaintiff cattle-breeding company of semen for its cattle (*Two Rivers Co. v. Curtis Breeding Service*, 624 F.2d 1242 (5th Cir. 1980)). The semen had a recessive genetic defect that resulted in some of the calves being still-born and lowered the market value of the calves that survived. The court reasoned that the policy reasons underlying strict liability were not compelling in a case in which the plaintiff's commercial expectations were not realized, and concluded that contract law (the UCC's warranty provisions) rather than tort law should be applied.

PUTTING IT INTO PRACTICE 13.2

1. If someone experiences serious and damaging consequences from being injected with a rabies vaccine, is the manufacturer strictly liable?

2. The parents of a child injured in a go-cart accident bring a strict liability action against the amusement park owner. They allege that the go-cart was defective because it inadequately absorbed the energy of rear-end collisions and inadequately protected the driver's neck in rear-end collisions. The owner claims he was providing a service and could not be subject to a strict liability claim. Do you think strict liability is an appropriate theory of recovery? What public policy reasons support a strict liability claim?

3. The parents of a child bring a strict liability suit against the manufacturer of BIC lighters after their child is seriously injured as a result of a fire ignited with the lighter by an older child. The parents argue that the lighter was defective because it was not designed to be "childproof." The manufacturer argues that it should not be held strictly liable because children were not the intended users of the lighter and that a product is defective only if it is unreasonably dangerous to its intended users. The parents claim that BIC designed a lighter unreasonably dangerous to foreseeable users, to whom the lighters were attractive and by whom they were easily lit. They are prepared to introduce evidence that thousands of children have been killed or seriously injured in childplay fires in the past twenty years. Based on this evidence they argue that BIC knew or should have known that a safer, child-resistant lighter design was feasible and should have been employed.

   Which side do you think has the better argument? Should the manufacturer be held liable under a theory of negligence even if it is not strictly liable?

4. The parents of a child who chokes to death on a toy building block sue the manufacturer and retailer for strict liability. The manufacturer argues that because the child was fifteen months old and that the box containing the blocks indicated that the blocks were for "Ages 1½–5," the child was not an intended user. Based on the results in the case in question 3, do you think the strict liability claim is likely to stand?

5. The manufacturers of DES (diethylstilbestrol), a drug used to prevent miscarriages, are sued under a theory of strict liability by the daughters of the women who ingested the drug. The plaintiffs argue that the drug is in a "defective condition unreasonably dangerous." How would their claim be analyzed on a consumer expectation standard versus a risk-utility test? For what public policy reasons might a court consider not applying a strict liability standard to a prescription drug like DES?

6. What considerations should a plaintiff make when deciding what theory of recovery to rely upon in a product liability case? Use Figure 13-2 to help you decide when you should sue under a theory of
   a. strict liability
   b. warranty
   c. negligence

FIGURE 13-2 Considerations for Theories of Recovery

WHO CAN SUE?	
NEGLIGENCE	Direct purchaser Remote purchaser User (if reasonably foreseeable)
EXPRESS WARRANTY	Direct purchaser Remote purchaser User (if member of general class expected to be reached by warranty)
IMPLIED WARRANTY	Direct purchaser Remote purchaser User (some courts)
STRICT LIABILITY	Direct purchaser Remote purchaser User Bystanders (some courts)
WHO CAN BE SUED?	
NEGLIGENCE	Manufacturer User or manufacturer of component part Retailer (difficult to prove) Lessor Seller of real estate Supplier of service
EXPRESS WARRANTY	Manufacturer User or manufacturer of component part Retailer Lessor Seller of real estate Supplier of service
IMPLIED WARRANTY	Manufacturer User or manufacturer of component part Retailer (except for sealed containers [in some courts]) Lessor Seller of real estate (in some courts) Seller of service (in some courts)
STRICT LIABILITY	Manufacturer User or manufacturer of component part Retailer Lessor Seller of real estate Supplier of service

Continued on next page

FIGURE 13-2 Considerations for Theories of Recovery—Continued

WHAT CAN PLAINTIFF RECOVER?
NEGLIGENCE	Personal injuries Property damage Economic loss (although pure economic loss is difficult to recover)
EXPRESS WARRANTY	Personal injuries Property damage Pure economic loss Incidental and consequential damages
IMPLIED WARRANTY	Personal injuries Property damage Pure economic loss Incidental and consequential damages (direct purchaser only)
STRICT LIABILITY	Personal injuries Property damage Economic loss if accompanied by personal injury or property damage

TYPES OF LOSSES

Defective products can cause three types of losses: personal injury, property damage, and economic loss. Injury to a person resulting from a defective product is, logically enough, referred to as *personal injury,* whereas physical injury to property is referred to as *property damage.* **Economic loss** is defined as a diminution in the value of the product and includes such items as the cost of repairs, the cost of replacement, and the loss of profits.

For example, if a computer in a car malfunctions, resulting in an explosion and ensuing fire, any damage to the car is classified as property damage, whereas any injuries to the driver of the car are considered personal injuries. If the computer malfunction results in the driver of the car being late for work and thereby losing his job, such loss is deemed an economic loss.

Most courts do not allow recovery under a strict liability theory for purely economic loss in the absence of personal injury or property damage. However, the method for categorizing a loss as either economic loss or property damage varies tremendously among the states. Some courts consider damage to the product itself as property damage; others consider such damage economic loss. If the computer malfunction mentioned earlier results in damage only to the computer and not to any other part of the car, the question is whether that constitutes property damage or economic loss. A claim classified as an economic loss in one state (and therefore not recoverable) may be classified as property damage (and therefore recoverable) in another state. Because the classification of economic loss is an unsettled area of the law, you should consult the case law in your state when dealing with damages of an economic nature.

PUTTING IT INTO PRACTICE 13.3

1. Review "Putting It Into Practice" exercise 13.1 in this chapter referring to the litigation between Elite and Carrier. What kind of damages is Elite seeking if it wants to recover for the loss of the meat in accordance with the preincident value of the meat?
2. A commercial chicken and egg producer loses more than 140,000 chickens who suffocate when a power failure interrupts the power supply to the ventilation system in the chicken houses. Is the loss of the chickens an economic loss?
3. A law firm is forced to close its offices because of a power failure. The firm sues the power company for its loss in billable hours, lost rental value, and lost use of parking facilities. The firm does not allege actual physical harm to persons or property but contends that "impairment of their opportunity to practice law, to provide time and advice for a fee, is tantamount to physical harm to property." Will the firm be allowed to recover under a theory of negligence?

TYPES OF DEFECTS

Most product liability causes of action involve products that are defective in some way. The three major defects plaintiffs typically allege are: (1) manufacturing defects; (2) design defects; and (3) defective warnings (see Figure 13-3). A **manufacturing defect** results from a deviation in the manufacturing process, which causes the item that injures the plaintiff to be different from others manufactured by the defendant. In a **design defect** case all products manufactured by the defendant are the same but possess a feature whose design is unreasonably dangerous. **Defective warning** cases involve a failure to give adequate warnings or directions for use.

The definition of *defective* lies at the core of all product liability cases, so we will examine the three categories of defects in some detail.

Manufacturing Defects

A classic example of a manufacturing defect is found in the landmark case of *MacPherson v. Buick Motor Co.,* 111 N.E. 1050 (N.Y. 1916). Buick Motor Company made a car that it sold to a retail dealer, who in turn sold it to the plaintiff. One of the wheels was made of defective wood and its spokes crumbled into fragments, causing injury to the plaintiff when the car suddenly collapsed. The defendant manufacturer was found liable even though it had not manufactured the wheel. The court reasoned that the manufacturer could have discovered this defect by reasonable inspection and that its failure to do so constituted a breach of its duty of care. Notice that what was at issue here was the faulty construction of one of the wheels and not the design of the wheel.

Whereas *MacPherson* was based on a theory of negligence, the famous case of *Henningsen v. Bloomfield Motors, Inc.,* 161 A.2d 69 (N.J. 1960), was based on a breach of warranty. In *Henningsen* defendant Chrysler Corporation produced a car with a defective steering mechanism. One of its dealers, defendant Bloomfield Motors, sold the car to Mr. Henningsen, who gave it to his wife. While Mrs. Henningsen was driving the car the steering mechanism failed, causing the car to veer sharply to the right and into a wall, resulting in her injury. The court held that Mrs. Henningsen could recover from Chrysler for breach of implied warranty of merchantability. As in *MacPherson,* the defect was peculiar to this particular car and was not inherent in the design of the car.

FIGURE 13-3 What Is a Defect?

MANUFACTURING DEFECT	Results from deviation in manufacturing process
DESIGN DEFECT	Feature in design of product is unreasonably dangerous Structural Safety feature Misuse of product
DEFECTIVE WARNING	Failure to give adequate warnings or directions

Manufacturing defects are not restricted to man-made products. They can also be found in food that is improperly produced, processed, or stored. A manufacturer or retailer, for example, can be found liable for a manufacturing defect if a consumer contracts botulism as a result of purchasing a can of improperly stored food.

Design Defects

The key issue in a design defect case is whether the defendant chose a design that posed an unreasonable danger to the plaintiff in light of the availability of some other design. For instance, a sanding machine that contains no guards or shields to protect the operator of the machine might be found defective if the manufacturer, with little cost or inconvenience, could have created a design that had a shield or guard.

Design defect claims can be cast in terms of a negligence or strict liability standard. The key issue in a negligence case is the reasonableness of the manufacturer in placing the product on the market. Is the product an essential item? Is it likely to cause injury and is any such injury likely to be serious? These questions are representative of the types of questions a court will contemplate in determining whether a manufacturer acted in a reasonable manner.

The key issue in a strict liability case is the consumer's expectations, i.e., whether the product performed as safely as an ordinary consumer would expect. A court will consider how much the consumer paid for the product in determining what the reasonable expectations should be. Use by the consumer extends to any reasonably foreseeable use even if it is not the use intended by the manufacturer. Whether phrased in negligence or strict liability terms, the key element in a design defect case is whether the defendant chose a design that posed an unreasonable danger to the plaintiff in light of the availability of affordable, safer alternative designs.

Defendants will often raise the "state-of-the-art" defense, in which they argue that the level of technology existing at the time they made the product precluded them from utilizing a safer design. Although courts generally allow such a defense, defendants relying on this argument will not necessarily be absolved of liability. A jury could conclude, for example, that even though no reasonable alternative design existed at the time, the risk created by producing such an item outweighed its utility.

In defective design cases the plaintiff will frequently try to bring out the fact that the defendant redesigned the product to make it safer after the plaintiff received injuries. Such evidence is generally inadmissible to prove defectiveness. The rationale underlying this rule is that the admission of this evidence would inhibit manufacturers from redesigning products to make them safer.

If the plaintiff does recommend an alternative design, the burden rests on him or her to show that the alternative is practicable. Plaintiffs must, in other words, conduct a type of cost-benefit analysis in which they produce evidence that their alternative design is an economically viable one.

Any design defect alleged by a plaintiff must fall into one of three categories: (1) structural defect; (2) absence of safety features; and (3) misuse of product.

Structural Defects

A *structural defect* exists when the defendant's choice of materials results in a structural weakness, causing the product to be dangerous. A stepladder that collapses when anyone of more than average weight steps on it might, for example, be structurally defective. Defendants are not, however, obliged to provide the most durable design. Nor are they expected to make products that last forever. Their only obligation is to make products that are reasonably safe.

Safety Features

In determining whether a *safety feature* must be installed, one must consider the expense of installation of the feature in comparison with the cost of the product and the magnitude of the danger that exists without such a safety feature. If the expense is relatively minimal, any design not incorporating the safety feature is likely to be considered defective.

Defendants often claim that their product is as safe as that of the competition. Although often successful, such a defense is unpersuasive in situations in which the entire industry has been negligent in the installation of safety devices.

A defendant may also argue that the danger was so obvious that the plaintiff could have protected himself or herself even in the absence of any safety device. Even though the obviousness of the danger is considered when determining the degree of dangerousness, most courts will not automatically dismiss the need for protective devices even though the defect is obvious. A manufacturer could, for example, be found liable for failing to provide protective guard rails for a machine even though the potential danger inherent in getting too close to the machine might be patently obvious.

Foreseeable Misuse.   One of the most common design defect arguments is that the product, though not dangerous when used in the manner intended by the manufacturer, becomes dangerous when put to some other use. If such misuse is reasonably foreseeable by the manufacturer, most courts will require the manufacturer to employ reasonable design precautions to protect the plaintiff from the danger resulting from that misuse.

The most common foreseeable misuse cases center around the production of "crashworthy" vehicles. Plaintiffs reason that manufacturers should protect vehicle occupants involved in "second collisions," the collisions that occur inside the vehicle following the initial accident. Most modern courts have found that secondary collisions are clearly foreseeable and that manufacturers have an obligation to take reasonable precautions to make their cars reasonably safe in the event of an accident.

CASE

Turner v. General Motors Corp.
514 S.W.2d 497 (Tex. Civ. App. 1974)

COULSON, Justice.
    This is an appeal from an order sustaining a plea of privilege in a products liability case. Appellant Robert Turner sued General Motors Corporation, appellee, and

Raymond Kliesing d/b/a Kliesing Motor Company in strict liability in tort for personal injuries received when his car rolled over in an accident. . . . Turner sued General Motors and Kliesing in strict liability in tort for a defectively designed roof on his automobile which enhanced his injuries, but did not cause the accident. The trial judge, in his findings of fact, found all the facts necessary for this alleged cause of action, if such a cause of action does exist; the sustaining of a plea of privilege was, in effect, a holding that no such cause of action exists in Texas.

The question here is whether a manufacturer and retailer may be held strictly liable in tort for a defectively designed automobile which enhances the injuries of plaintiff, but does not cause the accident.

At the plea of privilege hearing, Turner testified that in April of 1971 he was driving on a two-lane farm-to-market road in his 1969 four-door, Chevrolet Impala, hardtop sedan with a center post. He was following a truck, which started to pull onto the right shoulder. Turner accelerated to fifty or sixty miles per hour to pass the truck, but the truck attempted to make a left-hand turn when Turner came up to it. Turner pulled to the right to avoid a collision and left the road. When he attempted to return to the road, he overturned and the car landed on its top. Turner estimated his speed immediately before the roll-over at twenty to thirty miles per hour. Turner's seat belt was buckled, but the right-front portion of the roof collapsed and came into contact with his head. This contact paralyzed Turner's hands and legs.

Mr. James Barron, called as an expert witness by Turner, stated that he had worked as a design engineer for the Chevrolet Division of General Motors from 1963 to 1965, and had then worked in the same capacity for American Motors for over five years. Barron testified that General Motors designed for future production five years in advance and that he was involved in the design of the 1969 Impala. Barron informed his superiors at General Motors of the desirability of putting a roll bar in the roof of their cars, and Barron worked on a roll bar program. He testified that a roll bar would be expensive as an option, but relatively inexpensive if put on all cars at their birth on the assembly line. The roll bar program was discontinued, and Barron was told this was due "primarily [to] cost reasons and cost in conjunction with the fact that the consumer could not see what he was paying for." His supervisor told him that "it is difficult to pass on something to the consumer and charge him money for it if he cannot see it."

Barron testified that it would be impossible to design a crash proof car. He defined the term "crashworthiness" as the ability of a car "to withstand normal hazard conditions." Crashworthiness was broken down into the following categories: the structural integrity of the car's shell; the elimination of sharp or protruding objects in the interior; passenger restraint devices; and the elimination of post-crash fire. Barron estimated that, in the context of all possible types of accidents, roll-overs occur in twenty percent of all accidents involving "principal" injuries.

Barron drew a diagram of the Impala's roof structure and termed the roof "cosmetic," in that it provided protection from sun and rain, but it would not provide adequate protection in an overturn regardless of the speed. He categorized the roof as definitely defective, "uncommonly dangerous," and "unreasonably dangerous." The design of the Impala's roof was called perhaps the weakest way to design a roof, and Barron said that all of the roof structure in this Impala had collapsed. There was nothing in the roof of the car which would support the car in an overturn.

Barron suggested that there were many alternative ways to design a roof more safely and specifically proposed the roll bar or roll cage (the latter is, in effect, a connected double roll bar forming a rectangle with a bar at each corner attaching the frame to the body of the car). Roll bars and roll cages had been known to Barron since 1952, and he stated that General Motors put them on test cars and racing cars. In Mr. Barron's opinion, roll bars would greatly minimize roll-over injuries. Barron admitted that no mass-produced automobile in the United States had ever come equipped with a roll bar or roll cage and conceded that the Impala's roof was no more dangerous than the roof in any other car produced at that time. He frankly stated that he considered the roofs on all American cars defectively designed, including those currently manufactured (West Germany's Porsche Targa was the only production car cited by Barron as being equipped with a roll bar).

Raymond Kliesing, the defendant dealer, testified that, based upon his forty-five years of sales experience, the average consumer believes that a sedan vehicle will be a reasonably safe product in a roll-over.

The trial judge sustained General Motors' plea of privilege and filed findings of fact and conclusions of law. The trial judge found that Kliesing was an authorized General Motors dealer, that Turner's roof collapsed and injured him in the accident, and that the auto immediately before the accident was in substantially the same condition it was in when sold. The court's crucial finding is that the car was

defectively designed in that the roof was not a sufficient structural support to prevent the roof from collapsing and thereby injuriously encroaching into the passenger compartment in the event of an over-turn of the automobile and this defective design rendered the automobile unreasonably dangerous to the user or consumer, i.e., dangerous to an extent beyond that which would be contemplated by the ordinary user or consumer with the knowledge available to him as to the characteristics of a 1969 Chevrolet four-door sedan with a center post.

The defect was found by the trial judge to be a proximate and producing cause of the injuries, and the possibility of overturn accidents was held to be clearly foreseeable by General Motors.

The trial judge's sustaining of General Motor's plea of privilege was a ruling, in effect, that Turner had failed to prove a bona fide claim against Kliesing. In light of the trial judge's findings of fact, it is clear that his implicit conclusion of law was that strict tort liability in Texas does not encompass the liability of a manufacturer or retailer of a defective product when the defect enhances the injuries of a plaintiff, but plays no role in causing the accident. The question thus presented is one of first impression in Texas.

The genesis of this issue can be found in *Evans v. General Motors Corporation*. . . . There the plaintiff sued under general negligence, strict liability, and implied warranty principles with the argument that the manufacturer of his automobile should be liable for his enhanced injuries due to the "X" frame without side rails on his car, despite the fact that this defect had not caused the collision. The Seventh Circuit held that the manufacturer owed no duty to design or make an accident-proof or fool-proof car. The court also said that the intended purpose of a car does not include its participation in collisions. In *Larsen v. General Motors Corporation*, . . . the plaintiff claimed under negligence principles that his car was defectively designed in that the steering shaft protruded in front of the axle so that his injuries were enhanced when his car was struck in the left front. The Eighth Circuit said that an auto manufacturer has a duty to design and construct its product to be reasonably fit for its intended use and free of hidden defects which would render it unsafe for that use. The court found that the real issue was one of intended use and said that the intended use of an automobile necessarily entails the risk of injury-producing accidents; such injuries are foreseeable as an incident to the normal and expected use of a car. Since *Evans* and *Larsen*, more than twenty

jurisdictions have addressed the issue of crashworthiness and have split evenly. . . . We are persuaded by the logic of *Larsen*. . . .

Before addressing the merits of the *Evans-Larsen* controversy, it is necessary to discuss several Texas cases which General Motors feels have implicitly rejected the doctrine of crashworthiness. In *Muncy v. General Motors Corp.*, . . . an automobile was alleged to be negligently designed because the key could be removed from the ignition while the car was in gear and the engine was running. The court held that the appellant "was not using the car in the manner and for the purpose for which it was intended—at least appellants have failed to prove that the car was being so used." *Kahn v. Chrysler Corporation* . . . involved an allegation of negligent design in regard to sharp, protruding tailfins on a car. The plaintiff was a boy who had ridden his bicycle into a fin. The court, relying heavily on *Muncy*, held that the "duty of the automobile manufacturer extends to the ordinary use of the vehicle. . . . But the manufacturer has no obligation to so design his automobile that it will be safe for a child to ride his bicycle into it while the car is parked." . . . Because of the Supreme Court's decision in *Otis Elevator Company v. Wood*, we believe that both these decisions have taken an overly narrow and restrictive view of the standard of "intended use." General Motors also cites *Kerby v. Abilene Christian College*, . . . which involved a finding of contributory negligence on the part of the plaintiff in failing to close the sliding door of his van; this act had substantially increased the plaintiff's injuries but had played no part in causing the accident. The court held:

> We draw a sharp distinction between negligence contributing to the accident and negligence contributing to the damages sustained. Contributory negligence must have the causal connection with the accident that but for the conduct the accident would not have happened. Negligence that merely increases or adds to the extent of the loss or injury occasioned by another's negligence is not such contributory negligence as will defeat recovery.

This holding explicitly restricts the basic scope of contributory negligence, does not deal with actionable primary negligence, and we think, simply expresses the Court's rejection of the harsh doctrine of denying a plaintiff any recovery because of an omission playing no part in causing the accident from which his injuries flow. General Motors would construe *Kerby* to stand for the general proposition that pre-existing negligence which causes injury is not actionable if another's intervening negligence specifically sparks the accident. This is not the law of Texas. . . .

General Motors cites one case applying Texas law which does deal with the issue of defective design and crashworthiness. In *Willis v. Chrysler Corporation*, . . . plaintiff was traveling at seventy miles per hour and was struck head-on by another car moving at an undetermined but extremely high rate of speed. The plaintiff's auto broke completely in two, directly behind the front seat, and suit was brought for breach of the manufacturer's warranty. The court held that a manufacturer has "no duty to design an automobile that could withstand a high speed collision and maintain its structural integrity." The court then agreed with *Evans* that the intended purpose of a car does not include its participation in collisions. While we simply disagree with the court's acceptance of *Evans* as the law of Texas, we do not believe that *Larsen* imposes a duty to design an automobile which will withstand the type of high-speed, head-on collision described in *Willis*.

We find pertinent and agree with *South Austin Drive-In Theatre v. Thomison*. . . . In that case, the driver of a riding lawn mower backed the vehicle into a child and knocked him down. The driver attempted to pull the boy away, but found him pinned by the machine. The boy lost a leg. The court rejected the manufacturer's arguments of foreseeability, misuse, and industry custom. The manufacturer was held to have negligently designed the mower in failing to have a guard over the drive chain and gear sprocket, despite the fact that this design had not caused the accident. The court said, . . .

> We believe it is a correct statement of the law to say that [the manufacturer] owed a duty to use reasonable care in the design and manufacture of its power mower to prevent injury to the user and to persons [the manufacturer] should reasonably expect to be in the vicinity of the mower's probable use.

Preliminary to a discussion of the question of crashworthiness, it must be noted that the issues and arguments pertinent to the question are essentially the same whether suit is brought under general negligence or under strict tort liability. Most of the decisions from other jurisdictions involving crashworthiness were brought under negligence, but they are nevertheless applicable here. The issue of a manufacturer's exercise of due care under negligence becomes the issue of whether he has put an unreasonably dangerous product into the stream of commerce under strict liability, and the issues of foreseeability and intended use under negligence are transformed into the issue of normal use under strict liability.

General Motors concedes that it could foresee that its products would be involved in accidents of an infinite variety, including roll-overs. Its argument is that foreseeability cannot be equated with duty. General Motors characterizes the *Larsen* argument as being that, since car accidents can be foreseen, there is a duty to design cars to reduce the injuries from these accidents. If duty were commensurate with foreseeability, then an automobile manufacturer would be an insurer. . . . However, duty has never properly been defined solely by foreseeability. . . . This argument was expressed by the Seventh Circuit in *Evans* as follows:

> The intended purpose of an automobile does not include its participation in collisions with other objects, despite the manufacturer's ability to foresee the possibility that such collisions may occur. As defendant argues, the defendant also knows that its automobiles may be driven into bodies of water, but it is not suggested that defendant has a duty to equip them with pontoons.

We agree that foreseeability alone cannot define an automobile manufacturer's duty; this would create the duty to design a crash-proof car. However, *Larsen* seeks merely to hold the manufacturer to the duty of designing a crashworthy vehicle. While all agree that there is no duty to design a crash-proof car, one court has termed it a "non sequitur" to use this truism as a basis for thus saying there is no duty to design a crashworthy car. . . . The rule of *Larsen* is not grounded upon foreseeability, but upon the *unreasonable* risk of injury in the event of a collision. Under strict liability the question of liability in each case turns upon whether the product is in a defective condition which is "unreasonably dangerous."

The controlling issue in the crashworthiness inquiry is not foreseeability, but intended use. General Motors argues that the normal and proper use of an automobile does not include its participation in collisions. The *Evans* court said that collisions are not an intended purpose of the automobile even though the manufacturer may foresee the "possibility" of collisions. The *Larsen* court terms collisions a "probability;" the court stated that between one-fourth and two-thirds of all automobiles are involved during their life in a collision producing injury or death. . . . It is irrelevant whether the occurrence of an accident involving a particular car is a possibility or a probability. What is germane is the fact that collisions are so frequent and common that they must be considered an unavoidable incidence of the normal and proper use of automobiles. Misuse of an automobile may occur, such as the intentional use of a car as a bulldozer. However, the normal use of an automobile is to transport people *safely* over the public roads. It cannot be argued that a manufacturer should not be liable for a defect which causes an accident, and no logical distinction can be drawn between that situation and one in which a defect causes injury in a foreseeable accident. We hold that an automobile manufacturer may be held strictly liable for a defective design which produces injuries, but not the accident. . . .

The doctrine of crashworthiness does not make insurers of automobile manufacturers. The Fourth Circuit, in adopting *Larsen,* noted that the question of whether a manufacturer had created an unreasonable risk of injury involves a traditional balancing of the gravity and likelihood of harm against the burden of precautions to avoid the harm. *Dreisonstock v. Volkswagenwerk.* . . . The court stated that the burden of taking precautions included a consideration of the particular purpose of the vehicle, the style or aesthetic appeal of the model, and the cost of the change and of the vehicle. So viewed, it is obvious that manufacturers are not required to produce the safest possible car, but only a reasonably safe one. For instance, if a change in design would add little to safety, render the vehicle ugly or inappropriate for its particular purpose, and add a small fortune to the purchase price, then a court should rule as a matter of law that the manufacturer had not created an unreasonable risk of harm.

The same type of balancing of factors takes place under strict liability. Section 402A states that a manufacturer is strictly liable for a product in a defective condition "unreasonably dangerous" to the user or consumer. Comment i to § 402A defines "unreasonably dangerous" as "dangerous to an extent beyond that which would be contemplated by the ordinary consumer who purchases it, with the ordinary knowledge common to the community as to its characteristics." . . .

When Comment i is applied to crashworthiness, *Dreisonstok's* balancing test for negligence governs characteristics of a product which lie within the ordinary knowledge of the community. . . . This approach would reply to the *Evans'* pontoon argument that, while the average consumer as a matter of law does not expect his car to float, he may well expect the roof of

that car to maintain its structural integrity in a roll-over accident.

The moderate approach of *Dreisonstok* to the issue of crashworthiness should dispel General Motors' fears of absolute liability. This approach may be contrasted with that of *Cronin v. J. B. E. Olson Corporation.* . . . There, a clasp holding bread trays on a delivery truck failed to hold the trays in a collision, sending the driver through the windshield. The plaintiff recovered under his allegation of defective design in strict liability. The court adopted *Larsen* and then stated that it was not necessary for a plaintiff to establish that the product was unreasonably dangerous after he had shown a defect and causation, because such a requirement would place too onerous a burden upon plaintiffs. Such an approach to crashworthiness does indeed make insurers of manufacturers.

The courts adopting *Evans* often say that safety standards must be left to Congress, because courts lack the expertise for dealing with such complex matters, because sporadic and ad hoc court decisions will result in wrong and even contradictory standards, and because Congress had already proceeded to set safety standards. In 1966 (eighteen months before Larsen), Congress enacted the National Traffic and Motor Vehicle Safety Act, 15 U.S.C.A. §§ 1381–1431. Section 1392 instructs the Secretary of Transportation to establish motor vehicle safety standards.[1] Section 1397(a) prohibits the manufacture of vehicles not in compliance with these standards. However, § 1397(c) provides: "Compliance with any Federal motor vehicle safety standard issued under this subchapter does not exempt any person from any liability under common law." It is obvious from this language that the federal standards were meant to supplement rather than obviate the law of negligence and products liability. It has been suggested that, while the federal regulations propounded by the Secretary do not preempt the common law, they may serve as strong evidence of negligence, if not negligence per se, in regard to vehicles before the effective date of each regulation. . . . The question of whether safety standards *should* be left to federal regulation presents a separate question from that of congressional intent. However, we are not aware that the argument of the

---

1. The Secretary's Standard No. 216 ("roof crush resistance—passenger cars") provides that a force equal to one and one-half the weight of the vehicle or 5,000 pounds, whichever is less, applied to the corner of the roof must not move the roof more than five inches. 49 C.F.R. § 571.216 (1973).

necessity of federal regulation has been made in regard to design defects which cause accidents, and we cannot see any reason why design defects which cause injuries are any more in need of federal control. The danger that juries will arrive at conflicting conclusions is a hazard every manufacturer who distributes nationally runs. The complex, technical questions facing juries, aided by expert testimony, cannot be more difficult than the questions in such fields as medical malpractice. Finally, the argument that a single jury verdict may have profound consequences disrupting an essential industry has been characterized as contending that the desirability of immunity from liability is directly proportional to the magnitude of the risk created. . . .

Assuming the existence of liability for a design defect causing injuries, but not the accident, General Motors argues that the trial judge's finding of defective design is supported by no evidence, insufficient evidence, or is contrary to the great weight and preponderance of the evidence. The expert witness below admitted that no mass-produced automobile had ever been manufactured in the United States with a roll bar or roll cage, and he agreed that the roof of Turner's vehicle was no more unsafe than the roof on other vehicles of the same manufacturing era.

General Motors relies principally upon two cases for these evidence point. *Dyson v. General Motors Corporation* . . . involved roof deformation in the roll-over accident of a hardtop. General Motors argued that to require roofs which would be perfectly safe in a roll-over would be to declare convertibles unreasonably dangerous per se. The court adopted *Larsen* and said . . . ,

[T]he manufacturer was not necessarily under an obligation to provide a hardtop model which would be as resistant to roll-over damage as a four-door sedan; but the defendant was required, in my view, to provide a hardtop automobile which was a reasonably safe version of such model, and which was not substantially less safe than other hardtop models.

In *Dreisonstok*, a 1968 Volkswagen van was involved in a front-end collision. Such a vehicle does not have the engine in front, but plaintiff's experts declared the van to be defectively designed by comparing it to a 1966 mid-sized Ford passenger car. The Fourth Circuit, amplifying upon *Dyson*, held that this was impermissible; vehicles of the same type must be compared in order to determine defective design. These two cases do not stand for the proposition that defective design *must* be shown by comparing plaintiff's vehicle to similar vehicles. The expert below indicted the entire industry, a possibility which *Dreisonstok* does not foreclose. This is in accord with the law of Texas that, while conformance to industry custom is admissible on the question of negligence, the custom itself may be shown to be negligent. . . . We think the expert's condemnation of the industry for its failure to install roll bars constitutes a sufficient showing that the custom itself was unreasonably dangerous. General Motors' evidence points are overruled.

The judgment of the trial court is reversed, and judgment here rendered that General Motors' plea of privilege is overruled.

PUTTING IT INTO PRACTICE 13.4

1. What is the question in this case?
2. What is the alleged defect in the Impala's design?
3. What is the *Evans-Larsen* controversy?
4. Can the analysis regarding crashworthiness in the context of negligence be applied in the context of strict liability?
5. Does foreseeability alone define a manufacturer's duty? Does a manufacturer have a duty to design a crash-proof car?

Continued on next page

<table>
<tr><td>■</td><td style="text-align:center">PUTTING IT INTO PRACTICE 13.4—Continued</td><td>☐</td></tr>
</table>

6. Is the rule of *Larsen* grounded on foreseeabilty? What is it grounded on?
7. What is the issue in a crashworthiness inquiry?
8. Is a manufacturer strictly liable for a design that produces injuries even if it does not cause accidents?
9. Can the average consumer be expected to anticipate that the roof of a car will maintain its structural integrity in a rollover accident?
10. What reasons do the courts that have adopted *Evans* give for leaving the safety standards up to Congress?
11. At the time of this decision, had any mass-produced automobiles been manufactured with a roll bar or roll cage? What was the court's response to GMC's argument that it had conformed to the industry standard?

Turner v. General Motors Corp. contains an interesting analysis of the doctrine of crashworthiness. Note the court's conclusion that automobile manufacturers have an obligation to make cars reasonably safe in a collision. In arriving at this conclusion the court advocates the use of a balancing test in which the gravity and likelihood of harm resulting from a particular design are weighed against the burden of precautions necessary to avoid the harm. It is noteworthy that the *Turner* court found the General Motors car to be unreasonably unsafe even though no American car had ever been manufactured with the roll bar recommended by the design engineer. Clearly, industry custom itself may be found to be negligent.

The issue of crashworthiness has also arisen in the relatively new area of litigation surrounding airbags. Because automobile manufacturers have a duty to build reasonably safe cars based on state-of-the-art technology and feasibility considerations, the question exists as to whether manufacturers who have failed to install airbags have fully complied with that duty. The controversy centers around the question of whether airbags are necessary to make a car reasonably safe in case of an accident. Airbag proponents argue that airbag systems are within the realm of state-of-the-art protection; automobile manufacturers assert that airbags have not been proven to be reliable and might be potentially hazardous to car occupants (as evidenced by improperly deployed airbags that have caused accidents). Consumer advocates and representatives of the automobile industry also clash over the potential cost of airbag systems as well as the public's desire to have such systems.

To prevail at trial, a plaintiff must prove that the manufacturer's failure to install airbags rendered the vehicle's design defective. She proves this by showing that (1) an alternative, safer design (a design with airbags) was practicable and existed at the time of the accident; (2) the plaintiff's injuries would not have been as severe if the manufacturer had installed airbags; and (3) the extent of the enhanced injuries is attributable to the lack of airbags.

Airbag cases are not easy to win. Besides having to establish that a vehicle without an airbag is defective or unreasonably dangerous, plaintiffs have to show the technological and economic feasibility of airbags at the time the vehicle was manufactured. With earlier models this may be a difficult burden to bear. Furthermore, most jurisdictions require proof that the design defect enhanced the plaintiff's injuries, a rule that in effect shifts the burden of proof to the defendant to prove which portion of the injuries was due to the absence of the airbag.

In a few states, however, plaintiffs must distinguish the injuries that would have occurred despite an airbag from those than an airbag would have prevented. Finally, manufacturers can avail themselves of certain fact-specific defenses. They can argue, for example, that a plaintiff's failure to wear a lap belt or shoulder harness constituted contributory or comparative negligence.

Defective Warnings

The absence of a warning regarding the possible dangers of a product may also lay the groundwork for a defective product claim. A seller may be required to give directions or warnings on a container to keep the product from being deemed unreasonably dangerous. In determining what warnings or instructions will suffice, a court looks at the likely number and severity of accidents that could be avoided by having a warning or instruction. The court then weighs these factors against the difficulty of providing such warnings or instructions.

In cases involving the manufacture of drugs, courts look at whether the warnings clearly convey the nature, gravity, and likelihood of the known or knowable risks of the drugs. An advertising or publicity campaign for a drug, however, may dilute the warning to the point that it becomes inadequate. For example, a warning that blood disorders are a possible side effect of using a drug may in effect be canceled by the manufacturer's "detail men" who, when speaking with physicians, downplay the dangers of using the drug (*Incollingo v. Ewing,* 282 A.2d 206 (Pa. 1971)).

If the defendant can show that it neither knew nor should have known of the danger at the time of the sale of the product, most courts have held that the defendant has no duty to warn. Manufacturers are not to be the insurers of their products. So if a drug manufacturer can show that it had subjected a drug to reasonable testing procedures and did not discover any adverse side effects, it would escape liability for injuries to consumers resulting from long-term side effects not known to either the manufacturer or researchers at the time the drug was produced. In some rare cases, however, such as those involving asbestos, the defense of ignorance has failed. The courts have held asbestos manufacturers liable even if they were unaware of the danger, essentially holding them to a strict liability standard.

Obviousness of danger is a factor that is considered in determining the defendant's obligation to warn. But obviousness of danger alone does not preclude a duty to warn. Indeed, a product may be so dangerous that it should not be marketed at all. A light fixture with exposed (noninsulated) wiring, for example, is dangerous with or without a warning attached advising consumers of the danger. In such a case giving a warning would not protect the defendant from liability.

PUTTING IT INTO PRACTICE 13.5

1. A man commits suicide shortly after he begins taking Xanax, a prescription tranquilizer. His estate sues the drug manufacturer.
   a. Under what theories of recovery might the estate sue?
   b. What types of defects might the estate claim?
   c. Should the question of defect be analyzed using a reasonable consumer expectation or a reasonable doctor expectation standard?
   d. Given the social policy questions at stake, do you think the manufacturer should be held strictly liable? How would you use the Learned Hand formula to answer this question?

Continued on next page

PUTTING IT INTO PRACTICE 13.5—Continued

2. Review the facts in question 4 of "Putting It into Practice" exercise 13.2. What defense might the manufacturer raise in response to a defective warning claim?

3. Wilma sues the manufacturer of Halcion for the injuries she has sustained as a result of having been prescribed this drug between 1987 and 1992. Her claim includes an allegation that the manufacturer failed to "warn of the dangerous propensities of Halcion." If the same court that heard the DES case described in question 5 of "Putting It into Practice" exercise 13.2 hears this case, do you think Wilma will be allowed to recover?

4. The estate of a man who is alleged to have died as a result of being exposed to an herbicide sues the manufacturer of the herbicide. If the manufacturer were unaware of the potential dangers of the herbicide, what defense might it raise to avoid being held strictly liable?

5. The parents of children injured by blasting caps bring an action against several explosives manufacturers and their trade association. The manufacturers argue that under the "intended use" doctrine, they had a duty to exercise reasonable care only toward "those who use [the product] for a purpose for which the manufacturer should expect it to be used and . . . those whom [the manufacturer] should expect to be endangered by its probable use." How might the plaintiffs rebut this argument?

6. A widower sues a tobacco company after his wife dies from a cigarette-induced illness. He alleges a design defect and introduces a report issued by the Surgeon General of the United States that concludes that smoking lower-yield cigarettes seems to reduce the risk of lung cancer. This report was issued more than ten years after his wife had quit smoking. What additional evidence will the plaintiff have to muster to rebut a defense motion for summary judgment?

DEFENSES

Negligence

The plaintiff's contributory negligence, comparative negligence, or assumption of risk are defenses to product liability claims based on a theory of negligence (see Figure 13-4). For a complete discussion of those defenses see Chapter 9.

Warranty

The rules pertaining to contributory negligence are generally applicable to cases involving warranty claims. If a buyer discovers that a good is defective and uses it anyway, his or her action rather than the breach of warranty may be considered the proximate cause of the injuries. The buyer's unreasonable failure to examine goods before using them may also constitute a defense to a breach of warranty claim. The courts tend to be more lenient, however, with consumers than with merchants in terms of the obligation to examine goods.

If the plaintiff's negligence is due to his or her misuse or abnormal use of the product, many courts will analyze the warranty action as involving a proximate cause or duty problem rather than as involving an affirmative defense. If a plaintiff, for example, misuses a bottle in attempting to remove its cap, a court might hold that the defendant had no duty to produce a bottle that could withstand unreasonable handling or, alternatively, that the makeup of the bottle was not the proximate cause of the plaintiff's injuries. The only real significance in this difference in analysis lies in the burden of proof. If the court uses a duty or proximate

FIGURE 13-4 Defenses to Product Liability Claims

NEGLIGENCE	WARRANTY	STRICT LIABILITY
• Contributory negligence • Comparative negligence • Assumption of risk • Statute of limitations/Statute of repose	• Contributory negligence • Comparative negligence • Assumption of risk • Disclaimer of warranty • Limitation of remedies • Failure to discover breach in reasonable time • Statute of limitations/Statute of repose	• Contributory negligence (only if plaintiff misused product or used it in abnormal fashion) • Comparative negligence (subject to much controversy) • Assumption of risk • Statute of limitations/Statute of repose

cause analysis, then the burden of proof lies with the plaintiff. If, however, the court treats the misuse as an affirmative defense, then the burden of proving that misuse lies with the defendant.

In addition to contributory negligence, assumption of risk is also generally a valid defense in warranty actions.

Disclaimers

Under the UCC a seller can *disclaim* both implied and express warranties. To disclaim a warranty of merchantability the UCC requires that the seller use language that is conspicuous and that specifically mentions merchantability (UCC § 2–316). Alternatively, an implied warranty of merchantability is disclaimed if the product is sold "as is" or if the buyer has an opportunity to examine the goods but refuses to do so. Federal law (under the Magnuson-Moss Federal Trade Commission Improvement Act, 15 U.S.C. § 2301 *et seq.*) precludes any manufacturer that provides a consumer with a written warranty from disclaiming any implied warranty. Any written warranty provided by a manufacturer must therefore include the implied warranty of merchantability.

Limitations of Remedies

Sellers sometimes try to limit the remedies available to plaintiffs for breach of implied warranties by pro-viding that they (sellers) will not be liable for consequential damages. "[L]imitation of consequential damages for injury to the person in the case of consumer goods is prima facie unconscionable" (UCC § 2–719(3)). Therefore, provisions limiting the seller's liability to repair or replacement of goods will not be enforced in cases involving personal injuries resulting from defects in products designed for personal use. Limitation of damages is not unconscionable, however, when the loss is commercial, i.e., involving intangible economic loss (UCC § 2–719(3)).

Time Limits

A seller can also argue that a buyer must "within a reasonable time after he discovers or should have discovered any breach" notify the seller of the breach (UCC § 2–607(3)). Courts frequently refuse to enforce this requirement when the plaintiff is not in privity with the defendant.

Strict Liability

A plaintiff's contributory negligence is not a defense to a strict liability claim if the plaintiff fails to discover the defect or to guard against the possibility of its existence. A valid defense may exist, however, if the plaintiff misuses the product or uses it in an abnormal fashion. Examples of the misuse or abnormal use of a product include knocking a bottled beverage against a radiator to remove the cap and overeating a product to the point of becoming ill (Restatement (Second) of Torts § 402A, cmt. h). However, if the abuse or misuse is reasonably foreseeable, the manufacturer has a duty to anticipate such misuse and to make the product safe against it. Drivers inadvertently trying to start their vehicles from the "drive" position might, for example, be foreseeable. In that case manufacturers would have a duty to protect consumers from the consequences of their negligence. As discussed in the section on defenses to warranty actions, cases of misuse or abnormal use can be phrased in terms of a duty or proximate cause analysis rather than as an affirmative defense.

Suppose the manufacturing defect is not the sole proximate cause of the plaintiff's injuries, but, in fact, the plaintiff's own negligence is an additional proximate cause. The plaintiff can still recover if he or she can show that the acts were not so unforeseeable that they should be considered superseding acts.

In comparative negligence jurisdictions, considerable controversy exists as to whether a plaintiff suing on the basis of strict liability should have recovery reduced in proportion to his or her own negligence. Some courts have construed their comparative negligence statutes so as to find them applicable to strict liability situations, in effect reducing the plaintiff's recovery. The Uniform Comparative Fault Act suggests that the plaintiff's strict liability recovery should be reduced in proportion to the degree of fault.

Assumption of risk is basically treated in the same fashion in strict liability cases as it is in negligence cases. A plaintiff who discovers a defect and voluntarily and unreasonably proceeds to use the product is barred from recovery.

Statute of Limitations

A defendant must look at the plaintiff's pleadings to determine the appropriate statute of limitations. The general tort statutes, which are usually relatively short, are applicable to negligence claims. The UCC's statute of limitations (§ 2–725) usually applies to breach of warranty actions and gives the plaintiff four years from the time of sale of the product in which to sue. In strict liability cases the courts are in disagreement as to whether the UCC or the general tort statutes are applicable.

Some states have adopted **statutes of repose,** which provide a fixed period of time from the date of the original sale during which a product liability suit can be brought. Unlike a statute of limitations, which begins to run at the time of injury, a statute of repose begins to run at the date of sale. Consequently, some product liability suits may be barred by a statute of repose before the injury even occurs. Victims of DES or AIDS, whose injuries become apparent years after the initial exposure, will often be precluded from filing suit if a statute of repose exists. Because the majority of bodily injuries occur within five years of purchase, however, statutes of repose have little effect on most claims.

PREEMPTION

A state common law tort action cannot be brought if a federal statute expressly or impliedly **preempts** (prohibits) such an action. The roots of the federal preemption doctrine can be traced back to the framers of the Constitution, who foresaw the potential for conflict between the two separate law-making bodies of federal and state government. They addressed this problem by mandating within the Constitution that the laws of the United States "shall be the Supreme Law of the Land." Preemption, however, goes beyond the concept of supremacy. Under the supremacy doctrine, states are free to act as long as their laws do not conflict with federal law; under the rules of preemption, states lose their power to act at all, regardless of any conflict with federal law.

Federal preemption of state law can either be express or implied. Under express preemption Congress explicitly states the extent to which its enactments preempt state law. To illustrate, the Public Health Cigarette Smoking Act (15 U.S.C. §§ 1331–1340) specifically states "[n]o statement relating to smoking and health, other than the statement required by [the act] . . . shall be required on any cigarette package [or on advertising of labeled cigarettes]." In *Cipollone v. Liggett,* 112 S. Ct. 2608 (1992) (a suit against cigarette manufacturers based on design defect, failure to warn, express warranty, fraud, and conspiracy to defraud claims), the U.S. Supreme Court held that this preemption clause preempted state law claims based on failure to warn, but not claims based on breach of warranty, product liability, or intentional fraud, because Congress had expressly limited the scope of preemption.

Preemption can be implied in one of two ways— field preemption or conflict preemption. *Field preemption* occurs when a statute is in a field that Congress intended the federal government to occupy exclusively. In *Cipollone,* for example, a plurality of the Supreme Court reasoned that because Congress had expressly preempted failure-to-warn claims against cigarette manufacturers, preemption could not be implied with respect to the breach of warranty or fraud claims. In a later decision (*Myrick v. Freightliner,* 115 S. Ct. 1483 (1995), the Court clarified that express preemption did not necessarily foreclose the possibility of implied preemption, although it did support an inference of implied preemption. Under *conflict preemption* a state law is preempted to the extent that it actually conflicts with federal law. Such a conflict may arise when compliance with both state and federal law is impossible or when the purpose and objectives of Congress would be blocked by the state law.

To understand the impact of preemption on product liability cases, consider *Cipollone,* the much-publicized case involving a suit against the tobacco industry. *Cipollone* was initiated by Rose Cipollone and her husband against three cigarette manufacturers; they both died during the course of this protracted litigation and her son then represented their estate. Their suit alleged the following: cigarettes are defective because manufacturers failed to use a safer alternative design and because the dangers of cigarettes outweighed their social value; the manufacturers failed to provide adequate warnings of the health consequences of smoking; the manufacturers expressly warranted that smoking did not present any significant health risk (express warranty); the manufacturers tried to neutralize the warning labels through their advertising (fraudulent misrepresentation); and the manufacturers conspired to deprive the public of medical and scientific data (conspiracy to defraud).

The manufacturers claimed, among other things, that the Federal Cigarette Labeling and Advertising Act (1965) and its successor, the Public Health Cigarette Smoking Act of 1969, protected them from any liability based on their conduct after 1965. The district court ruled that the statutes did not preempt common law actions. The court of appeals reversed, the U.S. Supreme Court denied a petition for certiorari, and the case was remanded to the district court for trial. Complying with the court of appeals' mandate, the district court held that the failure-to-warn, express-warranty, fraudulent-misrepresentation, and conspiracy-to-defraud claims were barred to the extent that they relied on the manufacturers' advertising, promotional, and public relations activities after January 1, 1966 (the effective date of the 1965 Act). The court also ruled that the design defect claims were not preempted by federal law but were barred on other grounds. Following a four-month trial, the jury rejected the misrepresentation and conspiracy claims, but found that Liggett had breached its duty to warn in its express warranties before 1966. It found, however, that Rose Cipollone had "'voluntarily and unreasonably encounter[ed] a known danger by smoking cigarettes'" and that 80 percent of the responsibility for her injuries was attributable to her. The jury awarded $400,000 to Rose Cipollone's husband for losses attributed to the manufacturers' breach of warranty but awarded no damages to her estate. On cross-appeals from the final judgment, the court of appeals affirmed the district court's preemption rulings but remanded for a new trial on other issues. The preemption issue was then taken before the U.S. Supreme Court, whereupon the Court ruled that Congress had intended to preempt the failure-to-warn claims but not the other claims.

The Court's rulings in *Cipollone* muddied the waters concerning preemption, creating a patchwork of rulings among the lower courts. One area that has been affected by the uncertainty about preemption is airbag litigation. In a typical airbag case, the auto maker alleges that the National Traffic and Motor Safety Act of 1966 preempts the plaintiff's claim because the vehicle complies with Federal Motor Vehicle Safety Standard Act (Standard 208), which covers occupant crash protection. The car maker argues that between 1973 and 1986, Standard 208 gave a manufacturer three options for protecting front-seat automobile occupants, and that compliance with any one satisfied the federal standard. In accordance with this standard, the manufacturer chose to install manual seat belts rather than airbags. The manufacturer contends that imposing liability for failure to select one particular option undermines the legislative purpose of providing manufacturers the flexibility to choose among alternatives. The counterargument to this position is that the Safety Act expressly preserves common law tort claims, by virtue of a savings clause in the Act stating:

> Compliance with any Federal motor vehicle safety standard issued under this subchapter does not exempt any person from liability under common law.

Prior to *Cipollone,* courts that were inclined to find preemption relied on the concept of conflict preemption by finding that a tort claim was in conflict with the Safety Act. The courts began their analysis by acknowledging that the savings clause explicitly preserved liability under the common law and that the preemption clause was silent on the issue (hence no express preemption). The courts then found a conflict between the options of Standard 208 and the implications of a common law judgment for the plaintiff. Upon finding a conflict, the courts ruled that common law actions were impliedly preempted because state common law cannot prevent the exercise of a federally granted option. Because the preemption defense eliminates cases before plaintiffs can argue the merits of their cases, car manufacturers have frequently resorted to this defense.

A clear application of *Cipollone* has eluded the lower courts, even after the Supreme Court tried to clarify its *Cipollone* holding by revisiting the preemption issue (see *Myrick v. Freightliner,* 115 S. Ct. 1483 (1995)). Therefore, predicting how a court will resolve preemptive issues in the context of airbag cases or any other kind of product liability claim has become increasingly difficult. An in-depth discussion of preemption goes beyond the scope of this text, but the foregoing analysis, albeit superficial, reveals the pitfalls that preemption poses for plaintiffs in the realm of product liability.

PUTTING IT INTO PRACTICE 13.6

1. Your firm represents a manufacturer of blasting caps. This manufacturer is one of six manufacturers being sued by parents of children who were injured in blasting cap accidents. The blasting caps contained no warning labels and could easily be detonated by children. The plaintiffs are unable to prove which manufacturer made the caps that injured their children. They allege, however, that their children's injuries stemmed from the manufacturers' failure to warn and failure to design caps that were less easily detonated by children. They further allege that the manufacturers had actual knowledg of how frequently children were injured by blasting caps.

   What defenses should your firm suggest the manufacturer raise?
2. The parent of a teenager who was killed while using a shredder sues the manufacturer on the basis of strict liability. What defenses might the manufacturer consider raising?

Continued on next page

PUTTING IT INTO PRACTICE 13.6—Continued

3. Consider the facts in question 1 of "Putting It into Practice" exercise 13.1, involving the dispute between Elite and Carrier. What defenses might Carrier raise?

4. Joseph brings a product liability action against cigarette manufacturers, which move for summary judgment based on the statute of limitations. Joseph began smoking when he was thirteen or fifteen; he began experiencing breathing problems and a chronic cough in the early 1970s; his condition deteriorated through the 1980s; he was diagnosed with chronic obstructive pulmonary disease (COPD) in 1988. During this time, physicians repeatedly warned Joseph of the dangers of smoking, and when he was diagnosed with COPD, his doctors told him that his illness was caused by smoking. Joseph filed his action in July 1995. Joseph contends that his cause of action accrued when he discovered or should have discovered the "wrongful conduct" of the tobacco companies, such as their denial of the addictive nature of nicotine despite their internal research that proved otherwise and their manipulation of nicotine levels in cigarettes to increase their addictiveness. His complaint is based on strict liability, negligence, failure to warn, and defendants' wilful misrepresentation of the true nature of the health risks associated with cigarette use.

   When do you think his cause of action accrued? Joseph argues that his injury includes not only his COPD but also his addiction and that his addiction is due to the misconduct of the defendants in enhancing the addictive effects of nicotine. He maintains that his claim did not accrue until he knew the true cause of his addiction and that he could not have known that until November 1995, when a former tobacco research chief "let the cat out of the bag" while being deposed in another case. Are you persuaded by this argument?

5. The Federal Insecticide, Fungicide and Rodenticide Act (7 U.S.C. §§ 136–136y) expressly bars state labeling requirements additional to federal requirements. What defense can a manufacturer that complies with the federal regulations set forth in this Act raise if sued by a consumer for improper labeling?

SUMMARY

Product liability cases can be based on theories of negligence, breach of warranty, or strict liability. All three types of actions involve products in a defective condition, which can involve manufacturing defects, design defects, or defective warnings. Design defects include structural defects, absence of safety features, and misuse of a product if the misuse is reasonably foreseeable.

Plaintiffs recovering on the basis of negligence can sue the manufacturer, retailer, or lessor of a product whose defect was the proximate cause of their injuries. They can recover for personal injuries and property damage but will have difficulty recovering for pure economic loss.

Warranty actions, which are a hybrid of contract and tort law, can be based on breach of an express or implied warranty. The most common implied warranties are warranties of merchantability and warranties of fitness for a particular purpose. A plaintiff who is a direct purchaser will, because of the generosity of the UCC, likely opt for a warranty theory over a negligence or strict liability theory if the damages are solely economic. Privity requirements, which vary from state to state, dictate who may and may not be sued.

Strict liability is the most commonly used cause of action in product liability cases. Plaintiffs must prove that the product was in a "defective condition unreasonably dangerous," that the defect was the cause in fact and proximate cause of the plaintiff's injuries, that the defect existed at the time the product left the defendant's hands, and that the product was manufactured or sold by the defendant. Strict liability extends to the ultimate user or consumer of a product, including, for many courts, bystanders whose presence was reasonably foreseeable. Anyone in the business of selling goods, including manufacturers, retailers, and lessors can be held strictly liable for the defective products they pass on to others.

Contributory and comparative negligence and assumption of risk are defenses to negligence and warranty claims. With certain restrictions warranties can be disclaimed under the UCC and sellers can limit the remedies available in the event of a breach. Contributory negligence is not a defense in a strict liability case unless the plaintiff abused the product in an unforeseeable way. Assumption of risk is generally a defense to strict liability. Plaintiffs must determine the appropriate statute of limitations and must consider any statute of repose when filing claims. Some claims are preempted (expressly or impliedly) by actions of Congress.

PRACTICE POINTERS

Expert witnesses are an integral part of product liability suits because such suits are often complex and technical. At trial experts can offer their opinions on relevant issues (e.g., the defectiveness of the product) and can educate jurors on technical matters. Before trial they are even more invaluable, for they can:

- investigate facts
  —review medical and accident records
  —inspect the product
  —review records relating to the product's design or warnings
  —analyze literature relating to injuries sustained using the product
  —research industry standards
  —conduct experiments
- determine and evaluate alternate theories of defect or defenses
- identify sources of facts, experts, and references
- assist in preparation of and response to discovery
- review documents produced by the opponent
- assist in preparing for their own depositions as well as the depositions of witnesses called by the opposition
- attend depositions of opposing experts
- assist in attacking the credentials and methodology of the opposition's experts
- provide the factual basis for motions for summary judgment and motions to dismiss
- assist in preparing for cross-examination of the opposition's experts at trial
- assist in cross-examination of the opposition's experts at trial
- assist in preparing demonstrative evidence to be used at trial

Continued on next page

PRACTICE POINTERS—Continued

Legal assistants can help attorneys select and prepare experts. First, they can help the attorney identify a potential pool of experts by consulting trade journals, university rosters, client recommendations and recommendations from others in the profession or industry, and computer databases. The legal assistant can then review résumés and/or curricula vitae of candidates and weed out those who are unable to address the relevant issues. From this preliminary research, the legal assistant can recommend a list of potential candidates.

The legal assistant can also locate articles, case law, testimony from other lawsuits dealing with similar issues, and information about the opposition's expert witnesses. Once the expert has been retained, the legal assistant can compile relevant case materials on which the expert witness will base his or her opinion. Legal assistants can also help prepare the experts for their own depositions as well as for depositions of the opposition's expert witnesses.

The legal assistant should prepare a witness file in advance of trial. This file contains everything necessary to prepare the witness for testimony and to guide the attorney in examining the witness at trial. It should include the trial subpoena, deposition transcript and summary, attorney notes and memoranda of interviews, signed statements or affidavits, transcripts of deposition or trial testimony taken in other cases, and a memorandum that identifies the objectives of the examination and that arranges the areas within that examination in a logical sequence. This memorandum gives the attorney a starting point from which to prepare her examination of a witness and for her to prepare the witness for cross-examination by opposing counsel. An outline format enables the attorney to quickly read and grasp the key components of the examination.

To prepare the witness file, you need to outline the areas of inquiry during examination of the witness and attach the documents that are relevant to those areas. The headings of this outline should be succinct and should indicate the subjects and objectives of examination. Under each heading, list the subparts in their appropriate sequence and identify the exhibits (in sequence) by exhibit number and a brief description. Highlight critical passages in the documents, indicate the admissions and acknowledgments expected to be elicited on examination, and write a succinct description of the importance of the witness's statement. At the top of the page, identify the event to which the document relates or show the relationship between the document and preceding or subsequent exhibits. When preparing a file for a witness who is to be cross-examined include, for impeachment purposes, extracts from the witness's prior testimony.

TORT TEASERS

What type of defect would you argue exists in each of the following cases?

1. Plaintiff, a twenty-six-year-old woman, is given a prescription for oral contraceptives by her physician. The pill dispenser she receives is labeled with the warning "Oral contraceptives are powerful and effective drugs which can cause side effects in some users and should not be used at all by some women," and that "[t]he most serious known side effect is abnormal blood clotting which can be fatal." The warning also refers Plaintiff to a booklet that contains detailed information about the medication, including the increased

risk to vital organs. The booklet specifically notes the possibility of the brain being damaged by abnormal blood clotting. The word "stroke" does not appear on the dispenser warning or in the booklet. Three years after commencing use of the pills, Plaintiff suffers a disabling stroke. *MacDonald v. Ortho Pharmaceutical Corp.*, 475 N.E.2d 65 (Mass. 1985).

2. The petcock in the undercarriage of a bus is unprotected from debris on the road. One night while Plaintiff is driving his heavily overloaded bus down the highway, the petcock becomes disengaged by the debris, allowing the brakes to drain. The resultant brake failure causes an accident. *Carpini v. Pittsburgh & Weirton Bus Co.*, 216 F.2d 404 (3d Cir. 1954).

3. Plaintiff decides he wants to buy a Shopsmith, a combination power tool that can be used as a saw, drill, and wood lathe. He sees a Shopsmith demonstrated by a retailer and then studies a brochure prepared by the manufacturer. He buys the Shopsmith along with necessary attachments and uses the Shopsmith as a lathe. While making a chalice, Plaintiff is struck on the forehead by a piece of wood when it flies out of the machine, and he is seriously injured. Plaintiff had used the Shopsmith as a lathe on several previous occasions with no difficulties. *Greenman v. Yuba Power Products, Inc.*, 377 P.2d 897 (Cal. 1963).

In each of the following cases, which of the three theories of recovery (negligence, breach of warranty, or strict liability) would you use as a basis for recovery and why?

4. After being injured by an armed robber, Plaintiff brings suit against the manufacturer of "Saturday night specials." Such guns are characterized by "short barrels, light weight, easy concealability, low cost, use of cheap quality materials, poor manufacture, inaccuracy, and unreliability." These weapons are basically useless for legitimate purposes and are used mainly by criminals. *Kelley v. R.G. Industries*, 497 A.2d 1143 (Md. 1985).

5. After selling a plastic molding press to Company A, a manufacturer learns that the press has a dangerous tendency to crush the hands of people using it and that it violates state safety laws. When Company A sells the machine to Company B the manufacturer learns of this transaction through repair records and offers Company B a safety device for the machine for $500. Company B declines this offer and Plaintiff, one of its employees, gets her hand crushed. *Balido v. Improved Machinery, Inc.*, 105 Cal. Rptr. 890 (Ct. App. 1973).

6. Defendant manufacturer advertises its rifle as being suitable for "big game hunting." When Plaintiff uses this gun on a foreign safari and it fails, he sues the manufacturer for the cost of that safari. *Thomas v. Olin Mathieson Chemical Corp.*, 63 Cal. Rptr. 454 (Ct. App. 1967).

What would you argue as the defendant in the following cases? How would you, as the plaintiff, respond to the defendant's arguments?

7. Plaintiff buys a car with a defective seat belt from Defendant. When Plaintiff brings the car back for a new belt Defendant tells him that nothing can be done until a new one is received from the factory. While waiting for the new belt, Plaintiff drives without a belt and is involved in an accident. *DeVaney v. Sarno*, 311 A.2d 208 (N.J. 1973).

8. A strict liability claim is brought against the manufacturer of the Opel automobile on behalf of a driver who is killed as a result of an alleged defect in the door latch. The evidence shows that the driver was not using a shoulder harness, did not lock the door, and was intoxicated at the time of the accident. *Daly v. General Motors Corp.*, 575 P.2d 1172 (Cal. 1978).

9. Salt River Project (SRP), an electric utility company, purchases a gas turbine generator from Westinghouse. After a year of using the generator, SRP complains to Westinghouse about frequent computer malfunctions in the generator. In response to this complaint Westinghouse develops a Local Maintenance Controller (LMC) that permits manual operation of the turbine. SRP orders the LMC; Westinghouse responds with a standardized acceptance form containing the following warranty:

> This warranty . . . is exclusive and in lieu of any warranty of merchantability, fitness for purpose, or other warranty of quality, whether express or implied.

Limitation of Liability—Neither party shall be liable for special, indirect, incidental or consequential damages. The remedies of the purchaser set forth herein are exclusive, and the liability of Westinghouse with respect to any contract or sale or anything done in connection therewith, whether in contract, in tort, under any warranty or otherwise, shall not, except as expressly provided herein, exceed the price of the product or part on which such liability is based.

Two years after the LMC was installed, an explosion and fire occurred, which SRP alleges resulted from a malfunction in the LMC. *Salt River Project Agricultural Improvement & Power District v. Westinghouse Electric Corp.*, 694 P.2d 198 (Ariz. 1985).

10. Recall the hypothetical problem posed at the beginning of this chapter.

a. Which of the three theories of recovery would you use if you decided to sue the doctor and the sperm bank? What would be the reasoning underlying your choice?

b. Outline the elements you would have to prove if you decided to sue on the basis of negligence. Then do the same for warranty and strict liability.

c. Develop a list of questions you would want to ask your potential clients, Tom and Susan, at the initial interview.

d. Draft some interrogatories that you would want to submit to the sperm bank.

e. Compile a list of questions you would want to submit to a doctor you are thinking about using as an expert witness.

f. Prepare a list of the documents and correspondence you would want to request during discovery from Dr. Payne and the sperm bank.

KEY TERMS

Defective warning
Defect arising out of a manufacturer's failure to give adequate warnings or directions for use.

Design defect
Defect arising out of a manufacturer's use of an unreasonably dangerous design.

Economic loss
Diminution in the value of a product.

Express warranty
Express representation by a seller that a product possesses certain qualities.

Implied warranty
Representations as to a product's qualities that are implied by virtue of the product being offered for sale.

Manufacturing defect
Defect arising out of a deviation in the manufacturing process.

Preemption
Prohibition of a state tort law claim due to a federal enactment.

Privity
Requirement that the plaintiff must contract directly with the defendant in order to recover for losses.

Statute of repose
Statute of limitations in reference to sale of products.

Unavoidably unsafe products
Products incapable of being made safe for their ordinary and intended use.

Warranty of fitness for a particular purpose
Implied warranty that goods are suitable to be used for a particular (noncustomary) purpose.

Warranty of merchantability
Implied warranty that goods are fit for the ordinary purpose for which they are used.

CHAPTER

14

Defamation and Related Torts

CHAPTER TOPICS

Libel versus Slander
What Is a Defamatory Statement?
Privileges
Invasion of Privacy

CHAPTER OBJECTIVES

In this chapter you will learn to:
- Distinguish between libel and slander
- Identify the elements of defamation and the damages that can be recovered
- Recognize the importance of distinguishing between private and public figures
- Distinguish between absolute and qualified privileges of defendants
- Distinguish among the four torts that are considered an invasion of privacy and identify the elements of each
- Identify the tort of injurious falsehood and distinguish between slander of title and trade libel

The headlines of the *National Snoop* proclaim that the current "heartthrob" of a daytime soap opera has impregnated his co-star. In reality, the young lady with whom he is romantically linked on the show is in fact pregnant. Further adding fuel to this story is the fact that in real life the couple has been seen together on several occasions. The actor, however, vehemently denies that he is the father of the child. What would he have to show if he wanted to claim libel? Suppose that stories of his purported fatherhood circulate around the studio but are never published. Will he have any more difficulty proving slander than he will proving libel? Let us consider the elements of defamation and the distinction between libel and slander as we attempt to answer these questions.

LIBEL VERSUS SLANDER

Defamation, which is defined as an invasion of reputation of a person or group resulting from libel or slander (as defined in the following pages), is a complex tort. Some of its complexity stems from the courts' struggle to balance freedom of expression against protection of the individual's reputation. Before the key case in this area, *New York Times Co. v. Sullivan,* 376 U.S. 254 (1964), the U.S. Supreme Court had held that defamatory statements were outside the protection of the First Amendment and that defamation was primarily a matter of state law. In limiting states' power to establish their own defamation laws, *New York Times* dramatically shifted the course of defamation law and, in the opinion of some critics, struck a balance that gives too much latitude to media defendants.

The *New York Times* Court found "a profound national commitment to the principle that debate on public issues should be uninhibited, robust, and wide-open, and that it may well include vehement, caustic, and sometimes unpleasantly sharp attacks on government and public officials." Consequently, the Court created a federal rule that required public officials to prove that defamatory statements made relating to their official conduct were made with "actual malice" (knowledge that the statement was false or that it was made with reckless disregard for the truth). Under the

common law plaintiffs could essentially prove defamation if they could show that the defendant's statements were false. The Court's concern was that such a "rule compelling the critic of official conduct to guarantee the truth of all his factual assertions—and to do so on pain of libel judgments virtually unlimited in amount—leads to 'self-censorship.'"

Today the key features that shape defamation law are the status of the plaintiff (public official or public figure versus private individual) and the subject matter of the statement (public issue versus private). These features determine which standard of proof a plaintiff must meet to recover damages.

Keep in mind, however, that no matter how much controversy swirls around this area of the law, defamation is extremely difficult to prove and does not warrant litigation unless the damages are substantial. Few cases are actually litigated, and of those that are, especially those against media defendants, many are lost. In fact, the number of libel suits involving the media has declined in recent years and the rate of defense wins at trial has risen since 1990. (According to the *Libel Defense Resource Center Bulletin,* Jan. 31, 1994, media defendants won 26.3 percent of jury trials in the 1980s and 45.5 percent of jury trials in 1992–1993.) Although the media are concerned about what they perceive as the chilling effects of defamation reform, because they contend such reform will result in less aggressive reporting and the avoidance of controversial topics, the average American is unlikely ever to be involved in a defamation suit.

Defamation encompasses the two related torts of libel and slander (see Figure 14-1). **Libel** refers to written defamatory statements; **slander** refers to oral statements. Libel encompasses communications occurring in "physical form" (according to many modern courts and the Restatement (Second)). Under this definition defamatory statements on records and computer tapes are considered libel rather than slander. Spoken words that are intended to be written down, such as words dictated to a stenographer, are also categorized as libel. A radio or television program that originates from a written script is considered libel, but the courts do not agree about how to classify a program that is "ad-libbed."

FIGURE 14-1   Libel versus Slander

LIBEL	SLANDER
• Written statements (including records, computer tapes, dictation by stenographer). • No need to prove special harm. • Presumed damages awarded if: (a) actual malice is shown and matter involved is of public concern or (b) matter involved is a private concern and no actual malice is shown.	• Oral statements. • Must prove special harm unless slander per se. • Presumed damages not awarded.

PUTTING IT INTO PRACTICE 14.1

1. A news broadcaster falsely announces that a famous actor has AIDS. Has the actor been libeled or slandered?
2. A wax figure representing Sam is displayed in a "Chamber of Horrors," depicting figures of several famous murderers. The exhibition is shown for several months. Has Sam been libeled or slandered?
3. Louis makes a gesture at Andrew indicating that Shari carries the "evil eye," which is highly disparaged in their community. Has Louis libeled or slandered Shari?

Special Harm

The distinction between libel and slander is sometimes blurred, but it is a significant one. To prove slander a plaintiff must establish that he or she suffered some kind of **special harm.** Special harm need not necessarily be proved in the case of libel. The special harm that must be established generally involves harm of a **pecuniary** (monetary) nature. Loss of friendship and emotional upset are not generally considered to have pecuniary value. However, if a plaintiff is able to prove pecuniary loss she can attach any emotional damages to her pecuniary loss.

Four exceptions to the special harm requirement for slander exist. In these four cases of **slander per se**

pecuniary harm can be assumed. The four categories encompass statements alleging (1) that the plaintiff engaged in criminal behavior; (2) that the plaintiff suffers from some type of venereal or otherwise loathsome and communicable disease; (3) that the plaintiff is unfit to conduct his or her business, trade, or profession; and (4) that the plaintiff has engaged in sexual misconduct.

Under the common law special harm did not have to be proved and damages were presumed in cases of libel in which the defamatory nature of the statement was obvious. **Presumed damages** are those damages that ordinarily flow from defamation, thereby precluding the necessity of the plaintiff proving actual harm.

If damages are presumed, a plaintiff can recover an amount that approximates the damages that normally result from a defamatory statement like the one made by the defendant. Recovery is allowed even though the plaintiff produces no evidence of any actual harm, such as loss of business or friends.

Supreme Court decisions, however, have substantially limited the courts in their right to award presumed damages. In cases involving matters of public concern, a plaintiff cannot be awarded presumed damages if he or she is unable to prove "actual malice" (*Gertz v. Robert Welch, Inc.,* 418 U.S. 323 (1974)). A defendant who acts with **actual malice** knows either of the falsity of his statement or acts with reckless disregard in reference to the truth or falsity of his statement. If the plaintiff is able to prove actual malice, then presumed damages may be awarded. In matters involving purely private concerns, the plaintiff can recover presumed damages even without a showing of actual malice.

WHAT IS A DEFAMATORY STATEMENT?

The Restatement (Second) of Torts defines a statement as being defamatory if it tends to harm one's reputation, thereby lowering him or her in the estimation of the community or deterring others from associating with him or her (see Figure 14-2). Defamation requires proof that the defendant's statement was defamatory

FIGURE 14-2   Elements of Defamation

• Plaintiff's reputation is harmed or tended to be harmed.
• Statement is reasonably interpreted by at least one person as referring to plaintiff.
• At least one interpretation of statement could reasonably be considered defamatory.
• Statement is false.
• Statement is seen or heard by someone other than plaintiff (publication).
• Defendant acts with actual malice (if plaintiff is a public official or public figure).

and that it was *published,* that is, communicated to someone other than the plaintiff. Furthermore, the defendant must, at the very least, act negligently (although a greater degree of fault is required under certain circumstances).

Harm of Reputation

To be considered defamatory, a statement must have a tendency to harm the reputation of the plaintiff (Restatement (Second) of Torts § 559). The plaintiff's reputation need not actually be injured. A statement is sufficiently harmful if the plaintiff's reputation would have been injured if those who heard the statement had believed it. Therefore, even if everyone who hears a defamatory statement believes it to be false, this statement can still be considered defamatory.

A plaintiff may recover even if his or her reputation is tarnished in the eyes of only a certain segment of a community, as long as the segment consists of a significant and "respectable" minority of people. In one case, for example, the defendant mistakenly published the plaintiff's picture next to a testimonial signed by a nurse praising the medicinal merits of Duffy's pure malt whiskey. As Judge Holmes noted, "if the advertisement obviously would hurt the plaintiff in the estimation of an important and respectable part of the community, liability is not a question of majority vote" (*Peck v. Tribune Co.,* 214 U.S. 185, 190 (1909)). Nonetheless, the statement must contain some element of "disgrace." Although referring to a Democrat as a Libertarian, for example, might engender some feelings of hostility, such a statement could not be construed as defamatory.

Reasonable Interpretation

The plaintiff must also prove that the statement was reasonably understood by at least one person as referring to the plaintiff. The defendant need not refer to the plaintiff, but someone must interpret the statement as pertaining to the plaintiff. Furthermore, the defendant need not refer to the plaintiff by name as long as it is reasonably understood to whom the defendant is referring. A plaintiff will often have a difficult time recovering if the defendant's statement is made in reference to a group to which the plaintiff belongs. The statement probably will not be considered defamatory unless the group is a relatively small one.

■ PUTTING IT INTO PRACTICE 14.2 □

The *National Enquirer* publishes an article with the headline "Night That Turned Mom Into Killer." The article pertains to Susan Smith, the young mother who publicly maintained that her two young sons had been abducted and later admitted that she had drowned them by allowing her vehicle to roll down into a lake with her children strapped inside. A smaller headline reads "Shocking scene in bar with her lover just hours before she drowned her babies." A photo of the plaintiff appears above type that reads "BAR MANAGER Lorinda Robins says she knew something was wrong."

The article describes Smith's visit to the local bar where Lorinda was working, telling how Tom Findlay, Smith's former lover, had kidded with Lorinda in Smith's presence about a prior affair he and Lorinda had had. Lorinda is quoted as saying, "We were just cutting up. But I guess maybe Susan misunderstood. She abruptly got up and walked out." In the article Lorinda speculates that "when I think about that night, I'm convinced that's what pushed her over the edge." Two psychiatrists quoted in the article agree that the episode in the bar could have contributed to Smith's murder of her children the following day.

Lorinda argues that the article implicates her as being at least partially responsible for the deaths of Susan Smith's children. Do you think Lorinda has been defamed?

Burden of Proving Truth

Statements can often be interpreted in several different ways. The plaintiff must show that the statement is defamatory in accordance with at least one interpretation that a reasonable person might make, and must also prove that at least one person interpreted it in a defamatory way. Before the jury can declare a statement defamatory, a judge must first determine that the statement is subject to at least one reasonable interpretation that is defamatory.

To illustrate this point, consider the case involving the famous attorney Melvin Belli, in which a newspaper alleged that, while on an expense-paid appearance before the Florida bar, Belli "took" the bar by charging hundreds of dollars' worth of clothing to his hotel bill. The trial judge ruled that the statement was not defamatory and refused to submit the case to the jury. The appellate court, however, held that the statement had a clear defamatory meaning (indicating Belli was dishonest) as well as a nondefamatory meaning (indicating Belli was clever) and that the case should have been submitted to the jury (*Belli v. Orlando Daily Newspapers, Inc.,* 389 F.2d 579 (5th Cir. 1967)).

Contrast *Belli* with a case involving the ex-wife of Jerry Solomon, who later married Nancy Kerrigan, the well-known figure skater. The *National Enquirer* published an article entitled "Nancy Kerrigan in Love Nest with Married Man." The paper attributed the following quotation to the plaintiff: "Nancy Kerrigan stole my husband! She's a home-wrecker—a witch who deserves to burn in hell!" The plaintiff contended that the statements in the *Enquirer* portrayed her as a "woman who is so hateful, contemptuous, and bitter that she would blasphemously call forth damnation on another person." The court found the plaintiff's contention "far-fetched to say the least," noting that "it strains credulity to believe that others in the community would read the article as literally as Plaintiff apparently has." The court denied the plaintiff's claim, finding her interpretation of the published statement to be unreasonable as a matter of law (*Solomon v. National Enquirer,* 1996 WL 635384 (D. Md. 1996)).

Sometimes the defamatory content of a statement may not be recognizable unless certain extrinsic facts are known. A birth announcement, for example, may not be defamatory on its face, but if the recipient of that announcement is made aware that the plaintiff has been married for only six months then the defamatory implications become clearer. The plaintiff must specifically show in his or her pleadings the **innuendo,** which refers to the way in which the extrinsic facts convey a defamatory meaning. The plaintiff in the case pertaining to the birth announcement would be required to allege that because of the fact that the plaintiff had been married for only six months, the birth announcement created a false impression that the plaintiff had been unchaste prior to marriage.

A statement must be obviously false to be considered defamatory. A statement that is substantially true—even though it may not be literally true in all respects—is considered a true statement. Under the common law the defendant had the burden of proving the truth of his or her statement. Supreme Court decisions, however, have limited a state's ability to require the defendant to bear such a burden. Today the plaintiff bears the burden of proving that a statement was false if the statement involves a matter of "public interest" and the defendant is a media defendant (*Philadelphia Newspapers v. Hepps,* 106 U.S. 1558 (1986)). Even plaintiffs who are private figures must bear this burden of proof. Whether a defendant may be required to bear the burden of proving the truth of the statements if the statements are not of public interest and the plaintiff is a private figure is not clear.

Who Can Be Defamed?

Only living persons can be defamed. Therefore, survivors of the deceased may not sue for defamation because of statements made against the deceased. If the words defame a living person by implication, however, recovery is allowed. For example, a statement that the deceased was unwed when she gave birth to her child tends to defame that child. A corporation, partnership, or association may be defamed only if the statement "tends to prejudge it in the course of its business or to deter others from dealing with it" (Restatement (Second) of Torts §§ 561 and 562).

Opinion

Under the common law an opinion could be defamatory unless it fell under the privilege of "fair comment" i.e., the expression was an opinion on a matter of public concern. Supreme Court decisions point to the conclusion that a pure expression of opinion cannot be defamatory (Restatement (Second) of Torts § 566 cmt. c). A statement that implies factual matters, however, can be considered defamatory.

The difference between fact and opinion is not always clear, but the courts look at a number of factors in making that distinction. The more precise a statement is, the more likely a court will consider it a fact. A statement that is almost impossible to verify is likely to be considered an opinion. The literary context in which the statement is made is also considered. Readers are generally assumed to understand, for example, that statements made by reviewers constitute opinion rather than objectively verifiable facts. Statements implying undisclosed facts may be actionable even though they are opinions. A statement such as "I think George is an alcoholic" may be defamatory even though the declarant is apparently expressing an opinion. The implication from the statement is that the declarant knows or has factual information about George's alcohol consumption that would justify rendering an opinion as to George's alcoholic condition (Restatement (Second) of Torts § 566, illus. 3).

Suppose, however, someone says, "George has lived in this house for a year. Every night I see him with a drink in his hand. I think he must be an alcoholic." This statement offers facts upon which the opinion is based and does not imply other facts. Because the facts are not defamatory, the statement is not defamatory (Restatement (Second) of Torts § 566, illus. 4).

PUTTING IT INTO PRACTICE 14.3

Melba Moore, an entertainer, goes on the Maury Povich show and engages in a lively discussion with members of the panel (a divorce attorney, a marital counselor, and members of the studio audience). Povich introduces her by saying that she has recently come out of an acrimonious divorce and that she is now destitute and applying for welfare. The subject of the show is divorce and its financial aftermath. Some of the dialogue is as follows:

"(1) MAURY POVICH: Or you have applied for welfare, I don't know . . .
MELBA MOORE: I've, I've applied for welfare and I have been accepted and I just came from the Human Resources Office, where I put in a petition for child support enforcement, because my husband is, he's only been required to pay two hundred dollars a week, and it's very erratic. But I got to this position because my husband was my manager, we had a company called Hush Productions, and he got a fraudulent, secret divorce from me. . . .

* * *

(8) MELBA MOORE: Extremely well. My husband is a multi-millionaire.
MAURY POVICH: How do you know that?
MELBA MOORE: Well, I can't prove that, but we lived down the street from each other because he wasn't able to get me out of my apartment. We have a multi-million dollar building at 231 West 58th Street. That's just one asset.
MAURY POVICH: And that's supposed to be part of . . . that's supposed to be . . . are, are you on the deed for that, too . . . on the title for that?
MELBA MOORE: Well, as part of the, of the partnership, I should share in something . . .
MAURY POVICH: And you feel you're sharing in nothing?

Moore's husband sues her for defamation. Based on the preceding statements only, do you think he has a cause of action against her?

Publication

The term **publication,** when used in the context of defamation, is a term of art requiring that the statement be seen or heard by someone other than the plaintiff. The publication may be intentional or negligent. Merely overhearing a statement made by the defendant to the plaintiff does not constitute publication. The publication must also be understood by the person who hears it. A defamatory statement made in a language not understood to the person hearing it does not meet the requirement of publication.

Repetition of a defamatory statement is considered publication. One who repeats a statement is just as liable as if he or she were the first person to make the statement, even if the one repeating the statement does not believe it to be true (Restatement (Second) of Torts § 578 cmt. e). Those who distribute or sell defamatory matter, such as news dealers and libraries, are not liable if they can show they had no reason to believe that the materials were defamatory. Under the *single publication rule* most courts hold that an entire edition of a book or periodical should be treated as one publication. Therefore, even if several copies of a book are sold, only one defamation can be alleged.

Intent

Under the common law, defamation was essentially a strict liability tort, because defendants could be liable even if they had every reason to believe that a statement they made was true. That has changed, however, with U.S. Supreme Court decisions. Under the court's first landmark decision in this area, *New York Times Co. v. Sullivan,* 376 U.S. 254 (1964), the court held that if a plaintiff is a public official, he or she can recover only by showing that the defendant acted with actual malice. *Actual malice* is defined as having the knowledge that a statement is false or acting with "reckless disregard" for the truth or falsity of the statement. Actual malice differs from the lay definition of the term, which normally implies some type of ill will. *Reckless disregard* has been defined as evidence indicating that the defendant in fact "entertained serious doubts" as to the truth of his or her statements (*St. Amant v. Thompson,* 390 U.S. 727 (1969)).

The actual malice requirement was extended to public figures in a later case. The Supreme Court defined a **public figure** as "one who has achieved pervasive fame or notoriety" or who "voluntarily injects himself or is drawn into a particular public controversy" (*Gertz v. Robert Welch, Inc.,* 418 U.S. 323 (1974)). In *Gertz* the plaintiff was a locally well-known lawyer who represented the family of a young man killed by a policeman. The defendant, publisher of a John Birch Society magazine, falsely accused the plaintiff of being a criminal and a Communist. The court held that a person does not become a public figure merely because he becomes involved in a controversy of public interest. Therefore, the plaintiff in *Gertz* was not a public figure merely because the newspapers took an interest in the lawsuit. The *Gertz* court's reasoning for giving less protection to public figures was that those in the public eye "usually enjoy significantly greater access to the channels of effective communication and hence have a more realistic opportunity to counteract false statements than private individuals normally enjoy." Whether *New York Times* and *Gertz* apply to nonmedia defendants is not clear.

The public figure issue is discussed at length in *Street v. National Broadcasting Co.,* a historically interesting case that emanates from the famous "Scottsboro Boys" case involving the alleged rape of two white women by nine black youths. Once the *Street* court concludes that the plaintiff is a public figure, it is faced with the question of how long she retains that status. Pay particular attention to the court's public policy arguments and note its application of the actual malice standard.

If a plaintiff is neither a public official nor a public figure, the Constitution does not require that he or she prove actual malice. Strict liability, however, is not sufficient. The plaintiff must, at the very least, prove that the defendant acted negligently.

CASE

Street v. National Broadcasting Co. 645 F.2d 1227 (6th Cir. 1981).

MERRITT, Circuit Judge.

This is a Tennessee diversity case against the National Broadcasting Company for libel and invasion of privacy. The plaintiff-appellant, Victoria Price Street, was the prosecutrix and main witness in the famous rape trials of the Scottsboro boys, which occurred in Alabama more than forty years ago. NBC televised a play or historical drama entitled "Judge Horton and the Scottsboro Boys," dramatizing the role of the local presiding judge in one of those trials.

The movie portrays Judge Horton as a courageous and tragic figure struggling to bring justice in a tense community gripped by racial prejudice and intent on vengeance against nine blacks accused of raping two white women. In the movie Judge Horton sets aside a jury verdict of guilty because he believes that the evidence shows that the prosecutrix—plaintiff in this action—falsely accused the Scottsboro defendants. The play portrays the plaintiff in the derogatory light that Judge Horton apparently viewed her: as a woman attempting to send nine innocent blacks to the electric chair for a rape they did not commit.

This case presents the question of what tort and First Amendment principles apply to an historical drama that allegedly defames a living person who participated in the historical events portrayed. The plaintiff's case is based on principles of libel law and "false light" invasion of privacy[1] arising from the derogatory portrayal.

At the end of all the proof, District Judge Neese directed a verdict for defendant on the ground that even though plaintiff was not a public figure at the time of publication the defamatory matter was not negligently published. We affirm for the reason that the historical events and persons portrayed are "public" and distinguished from "private." A malice standard applies to public figures under the First Amendment, and there is no evidence that the play was published with malice.

___

1. False light invasion of privacy is one of four generally recognized forms of the tort of invasion of privacy. It differs from the other three forms in that falsity is one of its essential elements.

I. Statement of Facts

A. Historical Context

In April 1931, nine black youths were accused of raping two young white women while riding a freight train between Chattanooga, Tennessee, and Huntsville, Alabama. The case was widely discussed in the local, national, and foreign press. The youths were quickly tried in Scottsboro, Alabama, and all were found guilty and sentenced to death. The Alabama Supreme Court affirmed the convictions. . . . The United States Supreme Court reversed all convictions on the ground that the defendants were denied the right to counsel guaranteed by the Sixth Amendment. *Powell v. Alabama,* 287 U.S. 45, 53 S.Ct. 55, 77 L.Ed. 158 (1932). The defendants were retried separately after a change of venue from Scottsboro to Decatur, Alabama. Patterson was the first defendant retried, and this trial was the subject of the NBC production. In a jury trial before Judge Horton, he was tried, convicted, and sentenced to death. Judge Horton set the verdict aside on the ground that the evidence was insufficient. Patterson and one other defendant, Norris, were then tried before another judge on essentially the same evidence, convicted, and sentenced to death. The judge let the verdicts stand, and the convictions were affirmed by the Alabama Supreme Court. . . . The United States Supreme Court again reversed, this time because blacks were systematically excluded from grand and petit juries. . . . At his fourth retrial, Patterson was convicted and sentenced to seventy-five years in prison. . . . Defendants Weems and Andrew Wright were also convicted on retrial and sentenced to a term of years. Defendant Norris was convicted and his death sentence was commuted to life imprisonment by the Alabama governor. Defendants Montgomery, Roberson, Williams, and Leroy Wright were released without retrial. Powell pled guilty to assault allegedly committed during an attempted escape. The last Scottsboro defendant was paroled in 1950.

The Scottsboro case aroused strong passions and conflicting opinions in the 1930s throughout the nation. Several all white juries convicted the Scottsboro defendants of rape. Two trial judges and the Alabama

Supreme Court, at times by divided vote, let these verdicts stand. Judge Horton was the sole trial judge to find the facts in favor of the defendants. Liberal opinion supported Judge Horton's conclusions that the Scottsboro defendants had been falsely accused.

During the lengthy course of the Scottsboro trials, newspapers frequently wrote about Victoria Price. She gave some interviews to the press. Thereafter, she disappeared from public view. The Scottsboro trials and her role in them continued to be the subject of public discussion, but there is no evidence that Mrs. Street sought publicity. NBC incorrectly stated in the movie that she was no longer living. After the first showing of "Judge Horton and the Scottsboro Boys," plaintiff notified NBC that she was living, and shortly thereafter she filed suit. Soon after plaintiff filed suit, NBC rebroadcast the dramatization omitting the statement that plaintiff was no longer living.

B. The Dramatization

The script for "Judge Horton and the Scottsboro Boys" was based on one chapter of a book by Dr. Daniel Carter, an historian, entitled *Scottsboro: A Tragedy of the American South* (Louisiana State University Press, 1969). The movie is based almost entirely on the information in Dr. Carter's book, which, in turn, was based on Judge Horton's findings at the 1933 trial, the transcript of the trial, contemporaneous newspaper reports of the trial, and interviews with Judge Horton and others. NBC purchased the movie from an independent producer.

Plaintiff's major libel and invasion of privacy claims are based on nine scenes in the movie in which she is portrayed in a derogatory light. The essential facts concerning these claims are as follows:

1. After an opening prologue, black and white youths are shown fighting on a train. The train is halted, and the blacks are arrested. The next scene shows plaintiff standing next to Ruby Bates at the tracks. Plaintiff claims that this scene, in effect, makes her a perjurer because she testified at the 1933 trial and in this case that she fainted while alighting from the train and did not regain consciousness until she was taken to a local grocery store. Judge Horton, in his opinion sustaining the motion for a new trial, found that the observations of other witnesses and the testimony of the examining doctor contradicted her testimony in this respect. Horton concluded that it was unlikely that Victoria Price had fainted.

2. As plaintiff and Ruby Bates are led away from the tracks by the sheriff and his men, the sheriff in the play

calls the two women a "couple of bums." There is no indication in Judge Horton's opinion, in the 1933 trial transcript, or in Dr. Carter's book that this comment was actually made.

3. In a pretrial conversation between two lawyers representing the defendant, the play portrays one of them as advising restraint in the cross-examination of plaintiff Price. He says to the other defense lawyer: "The Scottsboro transcripts are really clear. . . . The defense at the last trial made one thing very clear, Victoria was a *whore,* and they got it in the neck for it. . . ." (Emphasis added.) There is no evidence that this specific conversation between the two defense lawyers actually occurred. Dr. Carter does state in his book that one of the purposes of the defense in cross-examining plaintiff was to discredit her testimony by introducing evidence that she was a common prostitute. . . .

4. Plaintiff in this action contends that the movie falsely portrays her as defensive and evasive during her direct and cross-examination. Judge Horton found in his 1933 opinion granting a new trial that plaintiff was not a cooperative witness: "Her manner of testifying and her demeanor on the stand militate against her. Her testimony was contradictory, often evasive, and time and again she refused to answer pertinent questions."

5. Plaintiff claims that the last question put to her on cross-examination in the play is inaccurate. In the movie the defense attorney asks: "One more question: have you ever heard of a white woman being arrested for perjury when she was the complaining witness against Negroes in the entire history of the state of Alabama?" According to the 1933 trial transcript, the actual question was, "I want to ask you if you have ever heard of any single white woman ever being locked up in jail when she is the complaining witness against Negroes in the history of the state of Alabama?" Plaintiff objects to the insertion of the word "perjury" in the play.

6. In the play, Dr. Marvin Lynch, one of the doctors who examined plaintiff after she alighted from the train, approaches Judge Horton outside the courtroom and confides that he does not believe that the two women were raped by the Scottsboro boys. Dr. Lynch refuses to go on the witness stand and so testify, however. Plaintiff argues that this scene is improper because it is not supported in the 1933 trial record. This is true. Neither the 1933 trial transcript nor Judge Horton's opinion make reference to this incident. The Carter book does state, however, that Judge Horton told the author in a later interview that this incident occurred. . . .

7. The play portrays events leading up to plaintiff's trip to Chattanooga with her friend, Ruby Bates. It was on the return trip to Alabama that the rape alleged occurred. Lester Carter, a defense witness in the play, testifies that he had intercourse with Ruby Bates on the night before the trip to Chattanooga and the plaintiff had intercourse with Jack Tiller. During the testimony there is a flashback that shows an exchange in a boxcar in which Ruby Bates suggests that they all go to Chattanooga and plaintiff says, "[m]aybe Ruby and me could hustle there while you two [Carter and Tiller] got some kind of fill-in work. What do you say?" This is an accurate abridgement of the substance of the actual testimony of Lester Carter at the 1933 trial, although Price denied, both at the 1933 trial and in the defamation trial below, that she had had intercourse with Tiller. Judge Horton specifically found that she did not tell the truth. The dramatization quoted or closely paraphrased substantial portions of Judge Horton's 1933 opinion. Judge Horton concluded that the testimony of Victoria Price "is not only uncorroborated, but is contradicted by other evidence," evidence that "greatly preponderates in favor of the defendant":

> When we consider, as the facts hereafter detailed will show, that this woman had slept side by side with a man the night before [the alleged rape] in Chattanooga, and had intercourse at Huntsville with Tiller on the night before she went to Chattanooga . . . the conclusion becomes clearer and clearer that this woman was not forced into intercourse with all of these Negroes upon the train, but that her condition [the presence of dead sperm in her vagina] was clearly due to the intercourse that she had on the nights previous in this time.

8. Lester Carter also testifies in the play that plaintiff urged him to say that he had seen her raped. The 1933 trial transcript reveals that Carter actually testified that he overheard plaintiff tell another white youth that "if you don't testify according to what I testify I will see that you are took off the witness stand. . . ." Judge Horton in his opinion observed that there was evidence presented at the trial showing that Price encouraged others to support her version of what had happened.

9. Another witness in the play, Dallas Ramsey, testifies that he saw plaintiff and Ruby Bates in a "hobo jungle" near the train tracks in Chattanooga the night before the train trip back to Alabama. Ramsey testifies that plaintiff states that she and her husband were looking for work and that "her old man" was uptown scrounging for food. The play dramatizes Ramsey's testimony while he is on the stand by a flashback to the scene at the "hobo jungle." The flashback gives the impression that plaintiff is perhaps inviting sexual advances from Ramsey, although the words used do not state this specifically. The substance of Ramsey's testimony, as portrayed in the play, is found in the 1933 trial transcript. The record provides no basis for the suggestive flashback.

The facts recited above illustrate that the play does cast plaintiff in an extremely derogatory light. She is portrayed as a perjurer, a woman of bad character, a woman who falsely accused the Scottsboro boys of rape knowing that the result would likely be the electric chair. The play is a gripping and effective portrayal of its point of view about her, the Scottsboro boys, and Judge Horton. As an effective dramatic production, the play has won many awards, including the George Foster Peabody Award for playwriting and awards from the Screenwriters' Guild and the American Bar Association. . . .

III. The First Amendment Defenses

A. Plaintiff was a Public Figure During the Scottsboro Trials

Since common law defenses do not support the directed verdict for NBC, we must reach the constitutional issues, particularly the question whether plaintiff should be characterized as a "public figure." In *Gertz,* the Supreme Court held that one characterized as a "public figure," as distinguished from a private individual, "may recover for injury to reputation *only on clear and convincing proof* that the defamatory falsehood was made *with knowledge of its falsity or with reckless disregard for the truth*." . . . (emphasis added). In balancing the need to protect "private personality" and reputation against the need "to assure to the freedoms of speech and press that 'breathing space' essential to their free exercise," the Supreme Court has developed a general test to determine public figure status.

Gertz establishes a two-step analysis to determine if an individual is a public figure. First, does a "public controversy" exist? Second, what is "the nature and extent of [the] individual's participation" in that public controversy? . . . Three factors determine the "nature and extent" of an individual's involvement: the extent to which participation in the controversy is voluntary, the extent to which there is access to channels of effective communication in order to counteract false statements, and the prominence of the role played in the public controversy. . . .

The Supreme Court has not clearly defined the elements of a "public controversy." It is evident that it is not simply any controversy of general or public interest. Not all judicial proceedings are public controversies. For example, "dissolution of a marriage through judicial proceedings is not the sort of 'public controversy' referred to in *Gertz*." *Time, Inc. v. Firestone* . . . (1976). Several factors, however, lead to the conclusion that the Scottsboro case is the kind of public controversy referred to in *Gertz*. The Scottsboro trials were the focus of major public debate over the ability of our courts to render even-handed justice. It generated widespread press and attracted public attention for several years. It was also a contributing factor in changing public attitudes about the right of black citizens to equal treatment under law and in changing constitutional principles governing the right to counsel and the exclusion of blacks from the jury.

The first factor in determining the nature and extent of plaintiff's participation is the prominence of her role in the public controversy. She was the only alleged victim, and she was the major witness for the State in the prosecution of the nine black youths. Ruby Bates, the other young woman who earlier had testified against the defendants, later recanted her incriminating testimony. Plaintiff was left as the sole prosecutrix. Therefore, she played a prominent role in the public controversy.

The second part of the test of public figure status is also met. Plaintiff had "access to the channels of effective communication and hence . . . a . . . realistic opportunity to counteract false statements." . . . The evidence indicates that plaintiff recognized her importance to the criminal trials and the interest of the public in her as a personality. The press clamored to interview her. She clearly had access to the media and was able to broadcast her view of the events.

The most troublesome issue is whether plaintiff "voluntarily thrust" herself to the forefront of this public controversy. It cannot be said that a rape victim "voluntarily" injects herself into a criminal prosecution for rape. . . . In such an instance, voluntariness in the legal sense is closely bound to the issue of truth. If she was raped, her participation in the initial legal proceedings was involuntary for the purpose of determining her public figure status; if she falsely accused the defendants, her participation in this controversy was "voluntary." But legal standards in libel cases should not be drawn so that either the courts or the press must first determine the issue of truth before they can determine whether an individual should be treated as a public or a private figure. The principle of libel law should not be drawn in such a way that it forces the press, in an uncertain public controversy, to guess correctly about a woman's chastity.

When the issue of truth and the issue of voluntariness are the same, it is necessary to determine the public figure status of the individual without regard to whether she "voluntarily" thrust herself in the forefront of the public controversy. If there were no evidence of voluntariness other than that turning on the issue of truth, we would not consider the fact of voluntariness. In such a case, the other factors—prominence and access to media—alone would determine public figure status. But in this case, there is evidence of voluntariness not bound up with the issue of truth. Plaintiff gave press interviews and aggressively promoted her version of the case outside of her actual courtroom testimony. In the context of a widely-reported, intense public controversy concerning the fairness of our criminal justice system, plaintiff was a public figure under *Gertz* because she played a major role, had effective access to the media and encouraged public interest in herself.

B. Plaintiff Remains a Public Figure for Purposes of Later Discussion of the Scottsboro Case

The Supreme Court has explicitly reserved the question of "whether or when an individual who was once a public figure may lose that status by the passage of time." *Wolston v. Reader's Digest Ass'n, Inc.,* 443 U.S. 157 (1979). In *Wolston* the District of Columbia Circuit found that plaintiff was a public figure and retained that status for the purpose of later discussion of the espionage case in which he was called as a witness. The Supreme Court found that the plaintiff's role in the original public controversy was so minor that he was not a public figure. It therefore reserved the question of whether a person retains his public figure status.

Plaintiff argues that even if she was a public figure at the time of the 1930s trial, she lost her public figure status over the intervening forty years. We reject this argument and hold that once a person becomes a public figure in connection with a particular controversy, that person remains a public figure thereafter for purposes of later commentary or treatment of *that controversy*. This rule finds support in both case law and analysis of the constitutional malice standard.

On this issue the Fifth Circuit has reached the same conclusion as the District of Columbia Circuit in *Wolston*. In *Brewer v. Memphis Publishing Co., Inc.,* 626 F.2d 1238 (5th Cir. 1980), plaintiff sued when a newspaper implied that she was reviving a long-dormant romantic relationship with Elvis Presley. The Fifth Circuit concluded that although the passage of time might narrow the range of topics protected by a malice standard, plaintiff remained a public figure when the defendant commented on her romantic relationship. The court noted that plaintiff's name continued to be connected with Presley even after her retirement from show business. . . .

Our analytical view of the matter is based on the fact that the Supreme Court developed the public figure doctrine in order that the press might have sufficient breathing room to compose the first rough draft of history. It is no less important to allow the historian the same leeway when he writes the second or the third draft.

Our nation depends on "robust debate" to determine the best answer to public controversies of this sort. The public figure doctrine makes it possible for publishers to provide information on such issues to the debating public, undeterred by the threat of liability except in cases of actual malice. Developed in the context of contemporaneous reporting, the doctrine promotes a forceful exchange of views.

Considerations that underlie the public figure doctrine in the context of contemporaneous reporting also apply to later historical or dramatic treatment of the same events. Past public figures who now live in obscurity do not lose their access to channels of communication if they choose to comment on their role in the past public controversy. And although the publisher of history does not operate under journalistic deadlines it generally makes little difference in terms of accuracy and verifiability that the events on which a publisher is reporting occurred decades ago. Although information may come to light over the course of time, the distance of years does not necessarily make more data available to a reporter: memories fade; witnesses forget; sources disappear.

There is no reason for the debate to be any less vigorous when events that are the subject of current discussion occurred several years earlier. The mere passage of time does not automatically diminish the significance of events or the public's need for information. A nation that prizes its heritage need have no illusions about its past. It is no more fitting for the Court to constrain the analysis of past events than to stem the tide of current news. From Alfred Dreyfus to Alger Hiss, famous cases have been debated and reinterpreted by commentators and historians. A contrary rule would tend to restrain efforts to shed new light on historical events and reconsideration of past errors.

The plaintiff was the pivotal character in the most famous rape case of the twentieth century. It became a political controversy as well as a legal dispute. As the white prosecutrix of nine black youths during an era of racial prejudice in the South, she aroused the attention of the nation. The prosecutions were among the first to focus on the conscience of the nation on the question of the ability of our system of justice to provide fair trials to blacks in the South. The question persists today. As long as the question remains, the Scottsboro boys case will not be relegated to the dusty pages of the scholarly treatise. It will remain a living controversy.

C. Evidence Insufficient to Support Malice[6]

A plaintiff may not recover under the malice standard unless there is "clear and convincing proof" that the defamation was published "with knowledge of its falsity or with reckless disregard for the truth." There is no evidence that NBC had knowledge that its portrayal of Victoria Price was false or that NBC recklessly disregarded the truth. The derogatory portrayal of Price in the movie is based in all material respects on the detailed findings of Judge Horton at the trial and Dr. Carter in his book. When the truth is uncertain and seems undiscoverable through further investigation, reliance on these two sources is not unreasonable.

We gain perspective on this question when we put to ourselves another case. Dr. Carter, in his book, persuasively argues, based on the evidence, that the Communist Party financed and controlled the defense of the Scottsboro boys. A different playwright might choose to portray Judge Horton as some Southern newspapers portrayed him at the time—as an evil judge who associated himself with a Communist cause and gave his approval to interracial rape in order to curry favor with the eastern press. The problem would be similar had Judge Horton—for many years before his death an obscure private citizen—sued the publisher for libel.

---

6. The District Court found that even if plaintiff was a public figure forty years ago, she no longer was a public figure at the time of publication. The court then directed a verdict for NBC on grounds that there was no evidence of negligence. The evidence indicates, however, that there is arguably some proof of negligence by NBC. NBC was notified between the first and second showings of the film that not only was plaintiff alive but that she objected to her characterization in the movie. NBC made no attempt to verify the factual presentation in the movie thereafter. This arguably presents a jury-submissible case of negligence, as Judge Peck's dissent points out.

Some controversial historical events like the Scottsboro trials become symbolic and take on an overlay of political meaning. Speech about such events becomes in part political speech. The hypothetical case and the actual case before us illustrate that an individual's social philosophy and political leanings color his historical perspective. His political opinions cause him to draw different lessons from history and to see historical events and facts in a different light. He believes the historical evidence he wants to believe and casts aside other evidence to the contrary. So long as there is no evidence of bad faith or conscious or extreme disregard of the truth, the speaker in such a situation does not violate the malice standard. His version of history may be wrong, but the law does not punish him for being a bad historian.

The malice standard is flexible and encourages diverse political opinions and robust debate about social issues. It tolerates silly arguments and strange ways of yoking facts together in unusual patterns. But it is not infinitely expandable. It does not abolish all the common law of libel even in the political context. It still protects us against the "big political lie," the conscious or reckless falsehood. We do not have that in this case.

Accordingly, the judgment of the District Court is affirmed.

PUTTING IT INTO PRACTICE 14.4

1. What is the issue in this case?
2. For what reason did the court conclude that no libel had been committed?
3. How was the plaintiff portrayed in the drama?
4. Under *Gertz,* what two factors determine whether an individual is a public figure?
5. Was the Scottsboro trial a "public controversy"?
6. How does the plaintiff meet the requirements of the three factors that determine the nature and extent of her participation in the controversy?
7. Why does the plaintiff remain a public figure fifty years after the trial?
8. Why is the malice standard not satisfied in this case?

PUTTING IT INTO PRACTICE 14.5

1. Carol Burnett decides to sue the *National Enquirer* for what she alleges are defamatory headlines and articles appearing about her in the magazine. What intent on the part of the *Enquirer* will she have to prove and why?
2. Charlotte White is employed by "Native America, Inc." as an organizer and promoter of Native American pow-wows across the country. An article is published referring to her first pow-wow in Florida, telling about how Ms. White left "a trail of bad checks" and was "briefly jailed on charges of fraud." The article states that "White is in hiding because of money she owes to Native American entertainers who came to Florida in January after being guaranteed up to $75,000 in fees" and that she left $10,000 in

Continued on next page

---

unpaid hotel expenses. Although she admits that rain hindered the success of the Florida pow-wow, she denies all the allegations made in the article.

Ms. White sues for defamation; the publication argues that she is a public figure because she appeared at a city council meeting requesting that the City of Manchester run additional water lines to the proposed pow-wow site. It maintains that this request for $10,000 in public funds to run the water lines satisfies the public controversy requirement for public figures. Should Ms. White be classified as a public figure?

3. Gerry Spence, a well-known attorney, represents a client (an activist engaged in a fight against pornography) in an action against *Hustler* magazine. In response to the litigation, Larry Flynt, owner of *Hustler,* refers to Spence as a "parasitic scum-sucker," a "reeking rectum," a "vermin-infected turd dispenser," a "hemorrhoidal type," and "Asshole of the Month for July." Some statements by Flynt are apparently false; he says, for example, that Spence stands to "fatten his wallet" by his litigation against *Hustler* when in fact Spence has assigned all of his proceeds to a charitable organization. Spence sues *Hustler* for defamation. Is he a public figure for purposes of this suit? If he is a public figure, can he recover damages for the statements that are clearly false?

Damages

A plaintiff who successfully proves defamation can recover for pecuniary as well as nonpecuniary losses, such as lost friendship, illness, and humiliation. As a constitutional matter, punitive damages may not be awarded to private figures in suits involving matters of public interest unless the plaintiff is able to prove that the defendant acted with actual malice (*Dun & Bradstreet, Inc. v. Greenmoss Builders, Inc.,* 472 U.S. 749 (1985)). Punitive damages may still be awarded, however, in matters pertaining to issues of merely private concern when only negligence is shown.

Recall that under the common law presumed damages were allowed in most cases of libel and in cases involving slander per se. Thus, the plaintiff could recover even if she could not prove that she suffered any actual harm, because she could recover for the harm that "ordinarily" stems from a defamatory statement. U.S. Supreme Court decisions, however, cut back on this allowance by requiring the plaintiff to prove that the defendant acted at least with reckless

disregard of the truth if she is to recover presumed damages. Therefore, in those states requiring plaintiffs to prove mere negligence, plaintiffs are constitutionally precluded from recovering presumed damages. If a matter is not one of public interest, however, presumed damages may be awarded even if the plaintiff proves only mere negligence.

Even though a plaintiff suffers no quantifiable loss he may still be motivated to go to court in an effort to clear his name. Such a plaintiff is often willing to accept only nominal damages just to be given the opportunity to have his day in court.

The majority of states, in an effort to discourage defamation suits, have enacted *retraction statutes.* These statutes essentially bar a plaintiff from recovery if a defendant retracts a defamatory statement within a certain time period. Other statutes merely require the defendant to provide the plaintiff with response time and do not bar the plaintiff's recovery.

To illustrate how such statutes function, consider the Uniform Correction or Clarification of Defamation

Act, which serves as a model for states to enact. This Act requires that either the plaintiff request a correction or clarification from the defendant within ninety days after learning of the publication or that the defendant voluntarily make a correction or clarification. Plaintiffs requesting a correction after the ninety-day period are limited to recovering economic losses only and cannot recover for pain, suffering, embarrassment, humiliation, or loss of reputation. Under this Act the media can act with intentional or reckless disregard toward the truth, immunizing itself from all but economic damages, as long as it prints a timely retraction. Nevertheless, plaintiffs are afforded public correction even when they are unable to prove actual malice, when case law requires such a showing.

Figure 14-3 summarizes the essential points of defamation law.

PRIVILEGES

A plaintiff may lose even if she proves defamation if the defendant can establish that he was privileged. Privileges can either be **absolute,** in which instance the privilege applies regardless of the defendant's motives, or **qualified,** in which case they apply only when the defendant acts on the basis of certain well-defined purposes (see Figure 14-4).

FIGURE 14-3 Summary of Defamation Law

1. Plaintiffs who are public figures or public officials must prove actual malice.
2. Plaintiffs who are private figures need not prove actual malice, but must prove falsity and establish fault when suing a media defendant over speech involving matters of public concern.
3. If the statement involves a public matter, plaintiffs must prove at least negligence and cannot recover presumed or punitive damages unless they can show actual malice.
4. If the challenged statement involves a private matter, private plaintiffs need not prove actual malice to recover presumed or punitive damages.

Absolute Privileges

Absolute privileges emanate largely from the nature of the defendant's job or function. Judges, lawyers, parties, and witnesses enjoy an absolute privilege for the statements they make during judicial proceedings, regardless of the motives for their statements. Such statements must, however, bear some relation to the matter at issue (Restatement (Second) of Torts §§ 585–589). Similarly, legislators acting in furtherance of their legislative function during a legislative hearing enjoy an absolute privilege. Witnesses testifying before

---

◼ PUTTING IT INTO PRACTICE 14.6 ☐

The November 1983 issue of *Hustler* Magazine features an "ad" in which Jerry Falwell (a well-known minister) says that his "first time" was with his mother in an outhouse. The ad is a "parody" of a liquor advertisement that featured interviews with celebrities about their "first times." Small print at the bottom of the page contains the disclaimer, "ad parody—not to be taken seriously." The magazine's table of contents lists the ad as "Fiction; Ad and Personality Parody."

1. Is this a potential slander or libel claim?
2. Is Falwell a public figure for purposes of this case?
3. Is the parody defamatory?

FIGURE 14-4 Privileges

ABSOLUTE PRIVILEGES

- Judges, lawyers, parties, and witnesses during judicial proceedings.
- Legislators acting in furtherance of legislative function.
- Witnesses testifying before legislature.
- Federal officials, governors, and high-ranking state officials acting in official capacity.
- Husband-wife communications.

QUALIFIED PRIVILEGES

- Reports of public proceedings (e.g., judicial and legislative hearings).
- Statement made to someone with capacity to act in the public interest.
- Statement made to protect one's own interests as long as not for the purpose of obtaining a competitive advantage.

the legislature are also absolutely privileged. All federal officials, governors, and high-ranking state officials have absolute immunity while acting in their official capacities. The states are in disagreement, however, as to whether absolute immunity extends to lower-ranking officials, such as police officers. Note that no privilege applies to statements issued outside the course and furtherance of the defendant's job.

Absolute immunity can also evolve out of a relationship. Husband-wife communications, for example, are absolutely privileged. If, however, the defamation originates with a third person and is relayed from one spouse to another, the repetition will still be considered a publication and the third person will be liable for the privileged repetition of his or her defamatory statement. Any publication to which a plaintiff consents is considered absolutely privileged.

Qualified Privileges

Reports pertaining to public proceedings, such as court cases and legislative hearings, enjoy a qualified privilege of immunity. Because of *Sullivan* and *Gerst* the privilege is no longer necessary in those cases involving public officials or public figures unless the plaintiff can prove the defendant acted with actual malice. If the report involves a private figure, the actual malice

requirement is not applicable and the press is limited to a right to comment accurately on a public proceeding.

A statement made to one who has the capacity to act in the public interest, such as a public official, is subject to a qualified privilege. An accusation to a prosecutor about purported criminal activity, for example, is privileged unless the person making the accusation makes it recklessly. A defendant is also privileged in protecting his or her own interests as long as those interests are sufficiently important and the defamation is directly related to those interests. A defendant who protects his property, for example, by telling the police about his suspicions that the plaintiff stole his property is privileged.

Making a defamatory statement for the purpose of gaining a competitive advantage is not privileged, such as telling potential customers about the poor workmanship of the competition. A defendant may be qualifiedly privileged to act for the protection of the recipient of his or her statement if the recipient is someone to whom making such a statement would be considered "within the generally accepted standards of decent conduct" (Restatement (Second) of Torts § 595 (1)(b)). Statements made within the parameters of "decent conduct" must be made in response to a request and within the context of a close personal or business relationship. Credit-reporting agencies, for example, enjoy a qualified privilege in many states in giving their subscribers creditworthiness reports on potential customers (Restatement (Second) of Torts § 595, cmt. h).

A qualified privilege can be lost if it is abused. For example, a defendant who makes a statement knowing it to be false or who acts in reckless disregard as to the truth or falsity of the statement will lose the privilege. If the primary purpose behind the defendant's statement is something other than protecting the interest for which the privilege was originally granted, the privilege will be lost. Suppose an employee's former employer informs his new employer about the employee's alleged dishonesty. These allegations will not be privileged if the primary motivation is preventing the employee from leaving his employment rather than warning the new employer. A privilege is also considered abused if a statement is made to more people than is reasonably necessary to protect the interest in question. In the same vein, the privilege is abused if more damaging information is added than is reasonably necessary. A defendant who reports her suspicions to the police that the plaintiff has stolen her property will probably lose the privilege if she adds her belief that the plaintiff is promiscuous (Restatement (Second) of Torts § 605).

PUTTING IT INTO PRACTICE 14.7

1. The state attorney general issues a press release explaining why his office has been delayed in prosecuting certain cases. In the release he accuses Geraldine of suppressing evidence. Can the attorney general be found liable for defamation? Would your answer change if a local district attorney has made the announcement?
2. In his opening remarks to the jury, a prosecuting attorney makes statements about the defendant that he knows are false. Can the defendant sue him for defamation?
3. Pam overhears a conversation in which she thinks a plot is being conceived to kill Connie. She calls the police and tells them Mary Sue is planning to kill Connie. The police arrest Mary Sue. Is Pam liable for defamation if it turns out there was no plot to kill Connie?

INVASION OF PRIVACY

The right to privacy, sometimes referred to as "the right to be let alone," has a unique origin. Prior to 1890 such a tort had never been recognized by the English or American courts. But in that year Samuel Warren and Lewis Brandeis, fueled by their perception that individuals needed protection from what they viewed as an increasingly invasive press, authored a *Harvard Law Review* article proposing the creation of a new tort. Their proposal was the subject of extensive academic debate and was accepted as a basis of recovery in some lower courts. The New York Court of Appeals generated a storm of public disapproval when it denied recovery to a plaintiff whose picture had been used to advertise flour without her consent. The New York legislature went on to pass a statute allowing recovery in such cases. Today every state except Rhode Island has recognized the right to privacy in some form or another.

Invasion of privacy actually comprises four distinct torts, dissimilar in every respect except that they all protect the plaintiff from unreasonable interference with his or her privacy. These four torts are appropriation, unreasonable intrusion, public disclosure of private facts, and false light (see Figure 14-5).

FIGURE 14-5 Invasion of Privacy

APPROPRIATION	UNREASONABLE INTRUSION
Value of plaintiff's name or picture is used by defendant for financial gain.	Defendant intentionally intrudes upon seclusion of plaintiff and the intrusion would be highly offensive to a reasonable person.

PUBLIC DISCLOSURE OF PRIVATE ACTS	FALSE LIGHT
Defendant publicizes details of plaintiff's private life and matter publicized would be highly offensive to a reasonable person.	Defendant puts plaintiff before public in false light that would be highly offensive to a reasonable person.

Appropriation

If the value of a plaintiff's name or picture is used by a defendant for his or her own financial gain, the plaintiff can sue for this **appropriation.** Note that the value of the plaintiff's name must be appropriated and not the name itself. In other words, the mere use of a name the same as that of the plaintiff's does not impose liability. The purpose for the appropriation, however, typically may be for either commercial or noncommercial purposes, although some state statutes limit recovery to commercial appropriations. The unauthorized use of an actress's photograph for the purposes of advertising could give rise to a cause of action for appropriation. Notice that appropriation was one of the allegations made by Robyn Douglass in *Douglass v. Hustler Magazine, Inc.*

CASE

Douglass v. Hustler Magazine, Inc.
769 F.2d 1128 (7th Cir. 1985).

POSNER, Circuit Judge.

Robyn Douglass, the actress and model, obtained $600,000 in damages in this diversity suit against the corporation that publishes *Hustler* magazine, for invasion of her right of privacy. . . . *Hustler* (as we shall call the magazine and its publisher interchangeably) has appealed, raising questions of tort law, freedom of the press, and trial procedure; Douglass has cross-appealed, complaining about the judge's action in reducing the punitive damages awarded by the jury.

Robyn Douglass moved to Chicago in 1974 and began a career as an actress and model. That year she posed nude together with another woman for the free-lance photographer Augustin Gregory, a codefendant with *Hustler* in the district court. The photographs were intended for a forthcoming feature in *Playboy* magazine, the "Ripped-Off" pictorial. Gregory testified that he required all his photographic models to sign releases allowing him to do with the photographs whatever he wanted. Robyn Douglass testified (and the jury was entitled to believe) that all she signed was a release authorizing *Playboy* to publish or otherwise use the pho-

tographs "for any lawful purpose whatsoever, without restrictions." The release does not refer to sale as such; but in granting rights not only to *Playboy* but to its "assigns and licensees," Douglass in effect gave *Playboy* carte blanche to dispose of the photos in any lawful way it wanted. Some of the photographs were published in *Playboy* in March 1975 as planned. Gregory had in 1974 also taken nude photographs of Douglass for a "Water and Sex" pictorial, also intended for *Playboy*; and there is a similar conflict over the release.

Douglass's career throve in the following years. She appeared eight times nude in *Playboy* but also made television commercials for Chicago advertising agencies and appeared in television dramas and in movies—notably "Breaking Away," where she had a starring role. Meanwhile in 1980 Gregory had become the photography editor of *Hustler*. This move was not unconnected with his earlier photographing of Douglass. The magazine wanted to publish nude photos of celebrities and in negotiations over becoming *Hustler*'s photography editor Gregory had shown management some of his photographs of Douglass. After he was hired, management asked Gregory for releases authorizing publication of these photographs. He testified that he couldn't find the releases at first but that eventually he submitted to *Hustler* two releases signed by Douglass, one for the photo session for the "Ripped-Off" pictorial, the other for the "Water and Sex" pictorial. At trial *Hustler* was able to produce only photostats of the releases allegedly signed by Douglass. The parties stipulated that, if called as a witness, a handwriting expert would testify that Douglass's signature had been forged on one of the releases and that the photostat of the other was too poor to allow the authenticity of the signature to be determined.

Douglass heard that there was to be a photo feature on her in the January 1981 issue of *Hustler* (an acquaintance had seen an announcement of it in a previous issue). She complained to the magazine that it had no authority to publish any photos of her. It responded with photostatic copies of the alleged releases, which within two or three days she denounced to *Hustler* as forgeries. The issue containing the feature had already been printed and distributed to retailers; and though it had not yet appeared on newsstands or been mailed to subscribers, *Hustler* made no effort to recall the issue, and it was widely sold. The feature, entitled "Robyn Douglass Nude," contained nude photographs from the two photo sessions for *Playboy* and stills (not nude) from two of her movies. The magazine paid Gregory a fee, over and above his regular salary, for the photographs he had supplied.

This suit charges that Gregory and *Hustler* invaded Douglass's right to privacy under the common law of Illinois by publishing "Robyn Douglass Nude." The feature, she charged, invaded her right of privacy in two ways: it cast her in a "false light," and it appropriated valuable commercial rights that belong to her. At trial she presented evidence that the publication of the feature had caused her emotional distress, and had killed her career of making commercials in Chicago because advertisers thought she has voluntarily appeared in what they considered an extremely vulgar magazine. An economist testified that the present value of her lost earnings was $716,565 at the time of trial (1983).

The judge gave the jury a verdict form with a blank beside each defendant's name for the amount of compensatory damages if the jury found either defendant liable, and a separate blank beside each name for punitive damages. The jury found both defendants liable and awarded the plaintiff $500,000 in compensatory damages against each defendant and $1,500,000 in punitive dam-

ages against *Hustler*. The judge remitted all but $100,000 of the punitive damages and Douglass accepted the remittitur. The award of compensatory damages against Gregory was not executed because on the eve of the trial he had made an agreement with Douglass that if he testified truthfully, and consistently with his deposition, she would not execute any judgment against him. Hence the real judgment was only $600,000. Gregory has not filed an appearance in this court.

Hustler argues that the facts, even when viewed favorably to the plaintiff, do not make out a cause of action under the Illinois common law of privacy, so that the judgment should be reversed with directions to dismiss the complaint; or that if they do, still the complaint must be dismissed because the plaintiff failed to prove "actual malice" by clear and convincing evidence, as required by the Constitution. Alternatively it argues that a new trial should be ordered because of errors in the instructions to the jury, and other trial errors.

First of all, *Hustler* denies that Illinois even recognizes the "false light" tort. Illinois' substantive law governs this suit, apart from the defendants' First Amendment defense; and no Illinois court has ever found liability for such a tort, . . . In cases in which that tort has been charged, albeit unsuccessfully, the Illinois courts have proceeded as if it existed in Illinois. In *Leopold v. Levin,* the only false-light case decided by the Illinois Supreme Court, Leopold, the surviving defendant in the Leopold and Loeb murder case, brought suit against the author of a book about the case, charging that the book *(Compulsion)* placed Leopold in a false light. The Illinois Supreme Court held that Leopold had no cause of action. He had forfeited any right of privacy by the notoriety of his crime; the book was represented to the public as a fictionalized rather than literal account; Leopold was a public figure; and to award tort damages would have unduly limited freedom of expression. These points would have been unnecessary to make if the court had thought that the false-light tort was not part of the common law of Illinois. . . . Incidentally, we do not read *Leopold v. Levin* to deny the protection of the tort to any and all public figures (Robyn Douglass, as we shall see, is a public figure). Leopold's status as a public figure was relevant to but not, as we read the opinion, conclusive on whether his rights had been violated.

Like every other division of the tort law of privacy, the "false light" tort . . . can be criticized, especially for overlapping with the tort of defamation. . . . Why should a plaintiff be able to circumvent the technical limitations with which the tort of defamation is hedged about by calling his suit one for placing him in a false light? Several answers are possible, however:

1. Some of those limitations seem not to reflect considered policy, but instead to be fossil remnants of the tort's prehistory in the discredited practices of Star Chamber and the discredited concept of seditious libel. . . . If they are gotten around by allowing a plaintiff to plead invasion of privacy, there is no great loss.

2. The principal limitations concern the requirement of proving special damages in some cases. . . . Since Robyn Douglass proved special damages (i.e., a pecuniary loss), these limitations would not have impeded her even if she had brought this suit as one for defamation. As for the other limitations in the law of defamation, *Hustler* has not shown how any of them, either, would have posed an embarrassment for Douglass on the facts of this case. And if she had sued for defamation she would not have had to prove (though it was not difficult to prove) that the offending materials had been widely publicized, an element of invasion of privacy that has no counterpart in the law of defamation.

3. Part of Douglass's claim is that *Hustler* insinuated that she is a lesbian; and such a claim could of course be the basis for an action for defamation. But the rest of her claim fits more comfortably into the category of offensive rather than defamatory publicity. The difference is illustrated by *Time, Inc. v. Hill,* 385 U.S. 374, 87 S.Ct. 534, 17 L.E.2d 456 (1967). *Life* magazine had presented as true a fictionalized account of the ordeal of a family held hostage by escaped convicts. The members of the family were shown being subjected to various indignities that had not actually occurred. The article did not defame the family members in the sense of accusing them of immoral, improper, or other bad conduct, and yet many people would be upset to think that the whole world thought them victims of such mistreatment. The false-light tort, to the extent distinct from the tort of defamation (but there is indeed considerable overlap), rests on an awareness that people who are made to seem pathetic or ridiculous may be shunned, and not just people who are thought to be dishonest or incompetent or immoral. We grant, though, that the distinction is blurred by the fact that a false statement that a woman was raped is actionable as defamation, . . . though in such a case the plaintiff is represented to be a victim of wrongdoing rather than a wrongdoer herself.

At all events, the criticisms of the false-light tort have to our knowledge persuaded the courts of only one state that recognizes a tort of invasion of privacy to withhold recognition of this subtype of the tort—North Carolina. . . . Almost all signs point to Illinois' recognizing it when a suitable case arises. A more difficult question is whether the facts of this case make out a false-light tort. We must decide in what light *Hustler* may be said to have cast Robyn Douglass, and (by comparison with her activities as a *Playboy* model) in what if any sense the light could have been found to be a false one. To answer these questions we shall have to enter imaginatively into a world that is not the natural habitat of judges—the world of nude modeling and (as they are called in the trade) "provocative" magazines.

The feature "Robyn Douglass Nude" in the January 1981 issue of *Hustler* occupies three full pages about a third of the way from the end of the magazine. The first page is dominated by a picture of Douglass, shown from the front, rain-splattered, wearing only an open raincoat. This is one of the photos that had been taken for the "Water and Sex" pictorial. Her mouth is open and her eyes closed. The text on the page reads:

> She played Katherine, the Midwestern coed in the film *Breaking Away,* and Jamie, the shapely newspaper reporter in the TV series *Galactica 1980* (below). But in HUSTLER seductive young actress Robyn Douglass plays herself. In these never-before-published photos this hot new star strips away her screen image to reveal the flesh of a real woman. An accomplished stage performer and TV-commercial model (Orbit gum, Gatorade and United Airlines), Robyn has been trained to use her body as a tool of her trade. These photos show just how well she's learned to use that tool.

The "below" reference is to an innocuous still photo from the television series.

The second page of the feature is given over to four more photographs of Douglass, two from "Water and Sex," and two from the "Ripped-Off" pictorial. (To be precise, these and the other nude photos in "Robyn Douglass Nude" were photos that had been taken for the two *Playboy* pictorials but, apparently, had not actually been published.) The photographs from "Water and Sex" again show Douglass from the front with the raincoat playing out behind her. In one picture her mouth is open while in the other she seems to be looking abstractedly at herself. In the two photos from "Ripped-Off," Douglass, now wearing a slip rather than a raincoat, appears to be engaged in erotic play with the other woman in the pictorial.

The last page of the feature has the following text beneath a picture of Douglass, fully clothed, on a motorcycle:

> When asked to audition for the role of Katherine in *Breaking Away* (above), Robyn sought out the character's most emotional scene to read for director Peter Yates. "You only have a short time to prepare; so I went through the script to try to find the climactic moments for Katherine." From the looks of Robyn (who's blond in the photos of her and a female friend), she's never had difficulty finding climactic moments.

The rest of the page is given over to two photographs from the "Ripped-Off" pictorial. The underwear visible in the other two photographs from this session has indeed been ripped off; the two women are naked. Douglass is straddling the other woman and the two appear to be engaged in sexual activity.

Douglass argues that the *Hustler* feature casts her in a false light in two respects. First, it insinuates that she is a lesbian, which (all agree) she is not. Second, it insinuates that she is the kind of person willing to be shown naked in *Hustler*. Nothing in the feature itself suggests that the nude photographs of her are appearing without her permission and against her will, and readers might well assume that she had cooperated in the preparation of the feature in order to stimulate interest in her films. Moreover, she had been described in a previous issue of *Hustler* as a forthcoming "Hustler celebrity-exclusive," and in another issue *Hustler*'s chairman, Larry Flynt, had announced in an editorial column that he does not publish photographs of women without their consent. It is (or so a jury could find) as if *Hustler* had said, "Robyn Douglass is proud to pose nude for *Hustler* magazine." To complete this part of her argument Douglass asserts that voluntary association with *Hustler* as a nude model is degrading.

We would not ourselves think that *Hustler* was seriously insinuating—or that its readership would think—that Robyn Douglass is a lesbian. *Hustler* is a magazine for men. Few men are interested in lesbians. The purpose of showing two women in apparent sexual embrace is to display the charms of two women. Moreover, the photos obviously are posed rather than candid shots; they show what the photographer wanted the women to do, not necessarily what the women wanted to do. Nevertheless we cannot say that a reasonable jury seeing the pictures and reading the accompanying text with its references to "climactic moments" and "female friend"

could not infer that Douglass was being represented to be a lesbian.

The question whether she was also being depicted in a degrading association with *Hustler* invites attention to the difference between libel and false light. It would have been difficult for Douglass to state this claim as one for libel. For what exactly is the imputation of saying (or here, implying) of a person that she agreed to have pictures of herself appear in a vulgar and offensive magazine? That she is immoral? This would be too strong a characterization in today's moral climate. That she lacks good taste? This would not be defamatory. . . . The point is, rather, that to be shown nude in such a setting before millions of people—the readers of the magazine—is degrading in much the same way that to be shown beaten up by criminals is degrading (although not libelous, despite the analogy to being reported to have been raped), though of course if Douglass consented to appear nude in this setting she is responsible for her own debasement and can get no judicial redress.

That the setting is indeed a degrading one requires only a glance through the issue of *Hustler* in which "Robyn Douglass Nude" was published to confirm. The cover shows a naked woman straddling and embracing a giant peppermint stick. The titles of several articles in the issue are printed on the cover, next to the picture, including along with some titles that are not related to sex "New Discovery: How to Give Women Vaginal Orgasms." This is directly below "Nude Celebrity: Robyn Douglass, Star of Galactica and Breaking Away." The inside cover is a full page of advertisements for pornographic video cassettes. On page 5 there is the "publisher's [Larry Flynt's] statement"—a call to tax the churches. This sounds another theme of Hustler: "irreverence," which has the practical meaning in *Hustler* of hostility to or contempt for racial, ethnic, and religious minorities. Then there is a "World News Roundup"—the news is all concerned with sex—and a page of coarse advice to readers who have sexual problems. Between these two features is a full-page advertisement entitled "Get Any Girl *Within 5 Minutes* or YOU PAY NOTHING!" with subtitles such as "Turn Women Into Putty." The issue contains many similar sexual advertisements, some with obscene pictures and text. . . .

We shall leave off here, . . . having sufficiently indicated the character of the magazine. To be depicted as *voluntarily* associated with such a sheet . . . is unquestionably degrading to a normal person, especially if the depiction is erotic . . . for although the magazine is offensive on several planes, the sexual is the one most emphasized. These features of the case help to distinguish *Ann-Margret v. High Society Magazine, Inc.,* 498 F.Supp. 401, 404–06 (S.D.N.Y. 1980), where a semi-nude still of an actress was published without her authorization in a magazine *(High Society Celebrity Skin)* described by the judge merely as "tacky," *McCabe v. Village Voice, Inc.,* 550 F.Supp. 525, 529 (E.D.Pa. 1982), a case like *Ann-Margret* except that the magazine was completely inoffensive; and *Brewer v. Hustler Magazine, Inc.,* 749 F.2d 527, 530 (9th Cir. 1984), where a previously published photograph was republished in a "sexually explicit" magazine—none other than *Hustler* itself—but apparently the plaintiff did not argue that the magazine was degrading, as distinct from merely explicit. And the photograph was of Brewer pretending to shoot himself in the head (for unexplained reasons, he had this photograph printed on his business cards); he was not associated with the magazine's view of sex. More important, in none of these cases was it argued that the subject was being represented as appearing voluntarily in the magazine, and (except in *McCabe*) the photographs had previously been published elsewhere. These points are related. If a photograph has been published previously the implied representation that its present publication is with the consent of the subject is weakened; the first publication may have put the photograph in the public domain. But the nude photographs of Robyn Douglass that *Hustler* published had not been published before.

Hustler argues that publication of "Robyn Douglass Nude" could not be degrading to one who had posed nude for *Playboy.* This fact distinguishes the case from the two cases that give the most support to Douglass's false-light claim: *Wood v. Hustler Magazine, Inc.,* 736 F.2d 1084 (5th Cir. 1984), where the plaintiff was not a model or actress and her nude photo (taken by her husband) had not been published previously and had not been intended to be published; and *Braun v. Flynt,* 726 F.2d 245 (5th Cir. 1984), where the photo of the plaintiff that was published on the same page with offensive matter in another "provocative" magazine published by Flynt *(Chic)* was not a nude photo; the plaintiff was wearing a bathing suit. . . . (It should be apparent by now that this little niche of the law of privacy is dominated by Larry Flynt's publications.)

To evaluate *Hustler*'s contention required the jury to compare the two magazines. We shall use for comparison the issue of *Playboy* in which the "Ripped-Off" pictorial appeared, though the jury had other issues of *Playboy* to peruse as well. The cover shows a young woman with partially naked buttocks and thighs but otherwise clothed. The only (other) suggestion of sex on the cover is the words "Ripped Off! A Torrid Nine-Page Pictorial," which by its position on the cover appears to be a reference to the cover girl. The inside cover is a conventional advertisement for Scotch whisky. Besides advertisements (none sexual), the issue contains fiction, a column of sexual advice (more refined than its *Hustler* counterpart), book reviews (only one of a book on sex), and articles. None of the stories or articles is obscene, though one story is erotic (a "Ribald Classic") and there are many bawdy cartoons and jokes (but not vicious ones, like many of those in *Hustler*) and four nude pictorials. In one of the pictorials a woman is doing exercises and being massaged; some of the frames contain an erotic suggestion of a mild sort. Two of the other pictorials show nude women in various poses but there is no suggestion that they are engaged in erotic activity. The last nude pictorial is "Ripped-Off," which turns out to consist of photographs of nude women (some in erotic poses) by different photographers. Two of the photographs are by Gregory, and one of them is of Robyn Douglass, though she is not identified by name. Although she is shown removing the slip of the other woman, as in the *Hustler* pictures, the text beneath the picture weakens any inference of lesbianism: "How long since you've seen a girl—let alone two—in lingerie like this? 'I pick very feminine, almost outdated slips for the girls to wear in this scene,' says photographer Gregory. 'To me, that made it more of a fantasy, more of a turn-on.' " Among other pictures in "Ripped-Off," one could be taken to be an (obviously simulated) photograph of sexual intercourse.

Although many people find *Playboy,* with its emphasis on sex and nudity, offensive, the differences between it and *Hustler* are palpable. *Playboy,* like *Hustler,* contains nude pictorials, but the erotic theme is generally muted, though there are occasional photographs that an earlier generation would have considered definitely obscene. And unlike *Hustler, Playboy* does not carry sexual advertisements, does not ridicule racial or religious groups, and avoids repulsive photographs—though most of the jokes and cartoons have sex as their theme, and not all are in good taste. We cannot say that it would be irrational for a jury to find that in the highly permissive moral and cultural climate prevailing in late twentieth-century America, posing nude for *Playboy* is consistent with respectability for a model and actress but that posing nude in *Hustler* is not (not yet, anyway), so that to portray

Robyn Douglass as voluntarily posing nude for *Hustler* could be thought to place her in a false light even though she had voluntarily posed nude for *Playboy.* Apart from the evidence of the magazines themselves, Douglass presented evidence that advertising agencies in Chicago were afraid of their clients' reactions if she appeared in commercials after her appearance in *Hustler,* but cared nothing about her appearing nude in *Playboy.* And of course the issue for us is not whether the jury was right but whether a reasonable jury could have found a false-light tort on the facts of this case.

However, since Douglass gave a general release to *Playboy,* it can be argued that she consented to have her photographs appear in any lawful setting; and there is no contention that "Robyn Douglass Nude," or the issue of *Hustler* in which it appeared, could lawfully have been suppressed on obscenity or other grounds. The jury could find, however, that only Douglass or *Playboy* could give consent to the publication of the photographs and that neither had done so. True, by giving *Playboy* a general release Douglass took a risk that her nude photographs would end up in an offensive setting that would damage her career as a model for television commercials, and it might seem that someone who takes such a risk cannot have a high regard for her privacy. But the risk she took and the risk that materialized were not the same. She took what may have seemed a trivial risk that *Playboy* would resell her photographs to a competitor, not the risk that the competitor would steal them. *Playboy* has an interest, on which Douglass could reasonably rely in executing a release to *Playboy,* is not degrading its models and in maintaining exclusive rights to its photos of them. The woman in the *Wood* case assumed the risk that her husband would sell *Hustler* the nude photograph that he took of her, but this did not deprive her of the right to sue for invasion of privacy when *Hustler* published the photograph having gotten it from someone who had broken into her house and stolen it.

We conclude that Robyn Douglass has a cause of action against *Hustler* for portraying her in a false light. Further, we think the jury did not exceed the bounds of reason in finding that *Hustler* also violated her rights under the commercial-appropriation branch of the right of privacy—what is sometimes called the "right of publicity," which *Hustler* concedes is a part of the common law of Illinois. This is the right to prevent others from using one's name or picture for commercial purposes without consent. Although originally the forbidden use was putting one's name or picture into an advertisement, it is

apparent from *Zacchini v. Scripps-Howard Broadcasting Co.,* 433 U.S. 562 (1977), that the right can extend to publication in the nonadvertising portions of a magazine or broadcast. This extension is closely related to copyright. . . . Zacchini had perfected a "human cannonball" act that lasted about 15 seconds. A television station broadcast the whole act as part of a news program. The station argued that the act was newsworthy; in copyright terms this would make the broadcasting of it a "fair use." *Hustler* makes a similar argument here—Robyn Douglass is newsworthy and "Robyn Douglass Nude" was fair comment on her career. But the station could have done a story on Zacchini without showing his entire act; and showing the whole act was likely to shrink the paying audience for it—people could see it on television for nothing. Thus there was an invasion of Zacchini's rights, analogous to copyright, under state tort law. Similarly, Robyn Douglass or her agents must have control over the dissemination of her nude photographs if their values is to be maximized. *Hustler* can run a story on her and use any photographs that are in the public domain or that it can buy but it cannot use photographs made by others for commercial purposes and (temporarily) withheld from public distribution. . . .

The unauthorized publication did impair the commercial exploitation of Douglass's talents, though probably not as much as she asserts and mainly because of where they were published. But an important aspect of the "right of publicity" is being able to control the places as well as time and number of one's public appearances; for example, no celebrity sells his name or likeness for advertising purposes to all comers. In any event, Douglass was not paid by *Hustler* for the right to publish nude photos of her.

Of course the issue in *Zacchini* was not whether the common law created a right of action against the television station—let alone the common law of Illinois (the case came from Ohio)—but whether the Constitution barred such a right of action if it existed in state law. There are not Illinois cases like *Zacchini.* But forced to guess, we guess that Illinois would recognize a "right of publicity" on the facts of *Zacchini* and the analogous facts of the present case. Indeed, this may be an easier case than *Zacchini,* where the performance had been in public, though in a different medium. This case approaches very closely to a violation of common law copyright, as in the theft and unauthorized publication of an author's manuscript. Of course Douglass would have no claim if Gregory had gotten a general release from her. But by executing only a limited release, she retained a right in the photos he took of her that, if not quite a property right, is nevertheless given legal protection under the (misleading) rubric of privacy.

But it was error to allow the jury to find an invasion of Douglass's right of publicity in the fact that *Hustler* published stills from her movie and television shows—whether reversible error we need not decide (for reasons to appear). Apparently these stills were in the public domain, for they had been published and *Hustler* is not accused of copyright infringement in republishing them. Republishing previously published, uncopyrighted photographs of a celebrity is a fair use justified by the newsworthiness of celebrities, and it therefore does not violate the right of publicity. . . . To forbid *Hustler* to publish any photographs of people without their consent, merely because it is an offensive, though apparently a lawful, magazine, would pretty much put *Hustler* out of the news business, would probably violate the First Amendment, and would in any event cross outside the accepted boundaries of the right of publicity. But as noted earlier the nude photographs of Douglass that *Hustler* published had not been published before. They were, in a sense that tort law recognizes, part of her portfolio. She had a legally protected interest in deciding at least their first place of publication, provided *Playboy* did not exercise its rights to publish them or to license their publication to others, a right for which Douglass had been compensated in executing the release to *Playboy*.

Although we reject *Hustler*'s argument that Douglass failed to prove an invasion of her right of privacy, we must also consider among other issues whether a reasonable jury could have found "actual malice" by *Hustler*. For failure to show actual malice would (possibly subject to qualification, as we shall see) be a defense, based on the First Amendment, to her tort suit. As the term is used in relation to the limitations that the First Amendment has been held to place on suits for defamation and "false light" invasion of privacy, it means knowledge of falsity or reckless disregard for truth. . . .

As *Hustler* does not so much as argue that it ever believed that Douglass was a lesbian, it was at the very least reckless in representing her as one, which we said a reasonable jury could have found it had done in "Robyn Douglass Nude." With regard to "actual malice" in representing her as voluntarily associating with the magazine, the only question is whether *Hustler* knew it was acting without authorization—knew, in other words, that Douglass was not voluntarily associating herself with the magazine—or didn't care. *Hustler* argues that it relied on

Gregory to supply authentic releases and cannot be found to have acted with actual malice if he submitted forged ones. The absence of any release from the other woman in the "Ripped-Off" pictorial undermines this claim; but a more important point is that Gregory was *Hustler*'s photography editor, acting within the scope of his employment, so that his knowledge of the falsity of the releases was the corporation's knowledge. It makes no difference whether in submitting the photographs he was acting as an independent contractor, as *Hustler* argues, or as an employee. As photography editor, which is to say in his capacity as an employee, he had some—it does not matter precisely how much—responsibility for the provenance of the photographs that were published. If someone had submitted nude photographs of Robyn Douglass to him without a release and he had told his superiors there was a release, he would have been acting within the scope of his employment. It makes no difference that in fact he was the seller as well as the buying agent. The doctrine of respondeat superior is fully applicable to suits for defamation and invasion of privacy, notwithstanding the limitations that the First Amendment has been held to place on these torts. . . .

Although there is no basis for ordering the complaint dismissed, there were a number of trial errors which together persuade us that there must be a new trial. The first relates to the judge's failure to instruct the jury that it must find actual malice by "clear and convincing" evidence. This is one of the requirements that the Supreme Court has imposed in the name of freedom of the press on suits for defamation . . . and we can think of no reason why it might be inapplicable to suits against the press for invasions of privacy, at least when the invasion takes the form of casting the plaintiff in a false light—a form of invasion of privacy that, as we have seen, overlaps the tort of defamation. Courts have assumed as a matter of course that the requirement of proving actual malice by clear and convincing evidence indeed applies to the false-light tort. . . .

The judge here said that his error did not matter because the evidence of actual malice *was* clear and convincing. It may have been, but that did not make the error harmless. Douglass was not entitled to a directed verdict. Therefore the error in the instruction on burden of proof was not harmless. . . .

All of this assumes of course that actual malice must be proved regarding even so mundane a question as whether consent was obtained to publish some photographs, which is the only question on which *Hustler*'s knowledge is a matter of fair debate. As an original matter we would have our doubts. The purpose of requiring proof of knowledge of falsity, or reckless disregard for the truth, is to lighten the investigative burdens on the press of determining the truth of what it writes. It is no great burden to determine whether a release has been executed; it is not like ascertaining the truth about allegations that a government official took a bribe or engaged in insider trading or fudged casualty statistics. A requirement that the plaintiff prove that the defendant was negligent in mistaking the existence of the release might be quite enough to protect the press from having to make costly investigations. The contrary argument is that the law under the First Amendment is complicated enough without attempting to make distinctions among the types of fact as to which actual malice is required in torts so closely related as defamation and false light. The qualification, however, and the analogy to copyright which supports Douglass's right-of-publicity claim, suggest that knowledge or even care is irrelevant at least to that claim; for it is no defense to copyright infringement that the infringer reasonably but mistakenly thought he had a license. . . .

Fortunately we need not try to unravel this tangled skein. The plaintiff does not argue that she was excused from having to prove actual malice because of the nature of her claim or the nature of *Hustler*'s falsity in regard to her. She does argue that she was excused from having to prove actual malice because she is not a public figure. But a successful actress and model who has appeared nude many times in *Playboy* magazine cannot be called a "private person"; she is a public figure in a literal sense. The lifting of the burden of proving actual malice in defamation cases from the shoulders of plaintiffs who are not public figures reflects two things: the fact that people who do not thrust themselves into the public eye have on average a greater sense of privacy than those who do; and the difficulty that obscure people have, compared to celebrities, in commanding the media's attention to efforts to rebut innuendoes about them (whether defamatory, or merely offensive in a false-light sense). . . . But

not only is Robyn Douglass no shrinking violet; she is a budding celebrity eager to be seen in the nude by millions of people—she *had* been seen in the nude by millions of people, the readers of *Playboy,* before *Hustler* got hold of her photographs. She is not like the plaintiff in *Braun v. Flynt, supra,* who did not become a public figure merely because her job in a local amusement park included feeding "Ralph, the Diving Pig" from a bottle of milk while treading water.

As an original matter one might want to confine the class of public figures to government officials and other politicians; freedom of political speech, and in particular freedom to criticize government officials and aspirants to public office, was the original concern of the First Amendment. But it is too late in the day to make such a distinction, at least at this judicial level. Art, even of the questionable sort represented by erotic photographs in "provocative" magazines—even of the artless sort represented by "topless" dancing—today enjoys extensive protection in the name of the First Amendment. . . . And so with news about art and entertainment. Entertainers can therefore be public figures for purposes of a publisher's or a broadcaster's First Amendment defense to a charge of false-light invasion of privacy. . . . Robyn Douglass clearly is one.

There is, incidentally, some question whether a plaintiff in a false-light case, merely because he (or she) is not a public figure, is relieved from having to prove actual malice, as would be true in a defamation case. The question was left open in *Cantrell v. Forest City Publishing Co.,* 419 U.S. at 250–51, 95 S.Ct. at 469. An argument can be made that the injury that being cast in a false light creates is less serious than that created by being defamed, and therefore the plaintiff should have a tougher row to hoe. We need not resolve the question here, but mention it lest our discussion of whether Robyn Douglass is a public figure be taken to have resolved it implicitly. . . .

The judgment is reversed and the case remanded for a new trial. No costs in this court.

Reversed and remanded.

PUTTING IT INTO PRACTICE 14.8

1. In what two ways does Robyn Douglass claim her right to privacy has been invaded?
2. Why does the court think the plaintiff should be able to "circumvent the technical limitations" of defamation by claiming invasion of privacy?
3. On what grounds does Douglass claim that *Hustler* placed her in a false light?
4. Could a reasonable jury have concluded that Douglass was being represented as a lesbian?
5. Could voluntary association with *Hustler* by allowing one's nude photographs to be published therein be considered degrading?
6. Could a portrayal of Douglass as voluntarily agreeing to pose nude for *Hustler* place her in a false light even though she had voluntarily posed nude for *Playboy*?
7. Why did the court conclude that Douglass had a false light claim even though she had consented to being photographed nude by *Playboy*?
8. On what basis did Douglass have a commercial appropriation (or "right of publicity") claim against *Hustler*?
9. Why was publication of stills from Douglass's movies and TV shows not an invasion of privacy?

Unreasonable Intrusion

A defendant who intentionally intrudes upon the seclusion of another is liable for invasion of privacy if his intrusion would be considered "highly offensive to a reasonable person" (Restatement (Second) of Torts § 652B). Physical intrusion includes the use of mechanical devices, such as binoculars or wiretaps. A private detective, for example, who in the process of seeking evidence for a lawsuit rents a room in a house adjoining the plaintiff's residence and monitors the plaintiff's activities for a period of time using a telescope will be considered to have invaded the plaintiff's privacy. Unreasonable intrusion may also be committed by opening the plaintiff's private mail, searching her purse, or examining her private bank account.

When consumer advocate Ralph Nader planned to publish a book attacking the safety of automobiles manufactured by General Motors, the company attempted to harass Nader by making threatening telephone calls, interviewing his acquaintances, tapping his phone, eavesdropping on him using electronic equipment, using women to make illicit proposals to him, and conducting surveillance on him in public places. The court held that Nader had a cause of action for invasion of privacy because of the wiretapping and electronic eavesdropping. The other activities, however, did not constitute invasion of privacy because the court did not consider them unreasonably intrusive (*Nader v. General Motors Corp*, 255 N.E.2d 765 (N.Y. 1970)).

Public Disclosure of Private Facts

By the same token, publicizing the details of the plaintiff's private life may also constitute invasion of privacy. The matter publicized must be of the type that would be "highly offensive to a reasonable person" and must "not be of legitimate concern to the public" (Restatement (Second) of Torts § 652D). For example, a disgruntled creditor who posts a notice in the window of his store saying that the plaintiff owes him money invades the plaintiff's privacy (Restatement (Second) of Torts § 652D, illus. 2).

No invasion of privacy exists if the details publicized are contained in a public record. If the name of a deceased rape victim is broadcast on television, the victim's parents have no claim for invasion of privacy because the victim's name would be available in an indictment, which would be available for public inspection at the suspect's trial (*Cox Broadcasting Corp. v. Cohn,* 420 U.S. 469 (1975)). Similarly, a murder suspect whose past history and daily life are recorded in the newspaper cannot claim invasion of privacy, because his activities would be considered matters of legitimate concern to the public (Restatement (Second) of Torts § 652D, illus. 13).

False Light

A plaintiff put before the public eye in a **false light** that would be highly offensive to a reasonable person can also sue for invasion of privacy (Restatement (Second) of Torts § 652E). Suppose that a newspaper publishes an article about local taxi drivers cheating on their fares and uses the plaintiff's photograph to illustrate the article. If the photograph clearly implies that the plaintiff resorts to such practices (and in fact he does not), the plaintiff may recover for invasion of privacy. Such "false light" actions can be brought only if the plaintiff can show that the defendant deliberately portrayed the plaintiff in a false light or acted in reckless disregard of the issue (*Time, Inc. v. Hill,* 385 U.S. 374 (1967)).

A "false light" case may or may not be considered grounds for defamation. The *Douglass* court considers the similarities and dissimilarities between false light and defamation and discusses why a plaintiff may opt for a false light claim rather than a defamation claim. In addition to being easier to prove in some respects than defamation, the court points out, the tort of false light allows recovery for offensive publicity (depicting a plaintiff as pathetic or ridiculous) and not just defamatory publicity (depicting the plaintiff as immoral or dishonest).

Suppose a movie is made about a war hero's life and the movie contains details regarding the fictitious private life of the war hero, including a nonexistent romance. Even if the moviemaker were aware of the falsity of some of the portrayal, the plaintiff could not sue for defamation as long as the movie did not tend to harm the plaintiff's reputation. He could, however, sue for invasion of privacy if the presentation would be considered "highly offensive to a reasonable person" (Restatement (Second) of Torts § 652E, illus. 5).

■   PUTTING IT INTO PRACTICE 14.9   ☐

1. A 1982 edition of the *National Enquirer* details Clint Eastwood's romantic involvement with singer Tanya Tucker and actress Sondra Locke. Eastwood alleges in part:

(a) The offending article falsely states that Eastwood "loves" Tucker and that Tucker means a lot to him.
(b) The offending article falsely states that Eastwood was, in late February, 1982, swept off his feet and immediately smitten by Tucker; that Tucker makes his head spin; that Tucker used her charms to get what she wanted from Eastwood; and that Eastwood now daydreams about their supposedly enchanted evenings together.
(c) The offending article falsely states that Eastwood and Tucker, in late February, 1982, shared 10 fun-filled romantic evenings together; were constantly, during that period, in each other's arms; publicly

Continued on next page

"cuddled" and publicly gazed romantically at one another; and publicly kissed and hugged.

(d) The offending article falsely states that Eastwood is locked in a romantic triangle involving Tucker and Sondra Locke ("Locke"); is torn between Locke and Tucker; can't decide between Locke and Tucker; is involved in a romantic tug-of-war involving Locke and Tucker; that Locke and Tucker are dueling over him; that Tucker is battling Locke for his affections; and that when he is with Locke, Tucker is constantly on his mind.

(e) The offending article falsely states that, in or about late February of 1982, there were serious problems in Eastwood's relationship with Locke; that he and Locke at that time had a huge argument over marriage; that he and Locke had a nasty fight; and that Locke stormed out of his presence.

(f) The offending article falsely states that after his supposed romantic interlude with Tucker, Locke camped at his doorstep and, while on hands and knees, begged Eastwood to "keep her," vowing that she wouldn't pressure him into marriage; but that Eastwood acted oblivious to her pleas.

Does Eastwood have a viable false light claim? If the *Enquirer* featured Eastwood's name and photograph along with the subject of the article in a telecast advertisement, would he have a claim for appropriation?

2. June, who is hospitalized with a rare disease, is approached by a reporter who requests an interview over the phone, which June refuses. The reporter then comes to the hospital and photographs June, over her objection. What, if any, tort has the reporter committed?

3. Marie is told she will have to have a cesarean operation. A doctor asks if he can videotape the operation to show to medical students for educational purposes. Marie agrees. Later the doctor shows the video to the public in a commercial theater. What tort, if any, has the doctor committed?

4. Jean Valjean, who had served time for robbery, has changed his name, concealed his identity, and led an exemplary life in another city for twenty years. A reporter discovers Valjean's criminal history and publishes an article in which Valjean's true identity is revealed. Valjean's life and career are ruined. What, if any, tort has been committed?

5. A young child is photographed after being hit by a car. A few years later her photo is included in an article on the negligence of children with the caption "They Ask to Be Killed." What, if any, tort has been committed?

Injurious Falsehood

Injurious falsehood protects plaintiffs against false statements made against their business, product, or property rights. If the plaintiff's goods or business are falsely disparaged, the tort committed is typically referred to as **trade libel** but if the disparagement refers to property rights of the plaintiff, the tort is usually referred to as **slander of title.**

Trade Libel

To recover for trade libel, the plaintiff must show that the defendant made a false statement clearly referring to the plaintiff's goods or business that disparaged those goods or business. A defendant who falsely claims during an interview on national television that his company is the only one of its kind may be liable for disparaging a plaintiff's business that is identical to his.

Note that trade libel differs from defamation in that the false statement need not ridicule or disgrace the plaintiff. As with defamation, however, the plaintiff must show the statement was published and that he suffered some kind of pecuniary harm. The defendant must also either know his statement is false, act with reckless disregard for the truth or falsity of his statement, or (according to some courts) act out of spite toward the plaintiff.

The same defenses that are applicable to defamation are applicable to trade libel. A defendant is also privileged to fairly compete with a plaintiff by making general comparisons between his product and the plaintiff's. A competitor is in fact permitted to "puff" even if he is aware that his statements are false and are made for the purpose of taking business away from the plaintiff. The defendant is not privileged, however, if he makes specific false allegations about the plaintiff's product.

Slander of Title

If a defendant falsely disparages the property right of another, he commits slander of title. For example, if he interferes with the plaintiff's right to hold or dispose of property by filing a false document, such as a mortgage or levy of execution, he commits slander of title. Leases, mineral rights, trademarks, copyrights, and patents may all be subjected to slander of title. The same intent, defenses, and privileges applicable to trade libel apply to slander of title. Additionally, a defendant has a qualified privilege to protect his own interest by asserting a bona fide claim to property. An assertion of infringement on a patent right is privileged as long as the assertion is made in good faith and in the absence of any motive of a desire to do harm.

■   PUTTING IT INTO PRACTICE 14.10   □

The CBS news program "60 Minutes" airs a program based on a report published by the Natural Resources Defense Council discussing the detrimental effects of pesticide use by farmers. The program highlighted the effects of the herbicide Alar, which is used by apple growers to stimulate growth and enhance apple appearance. As a result of the program some consumers boycotted apples and apple products. Do apple growers have a viable cause of action against CBS and the Natural Resources Defense Council?

SUMMARY

Defamation consists of the related torts of libel and slander. A statement is defamatory if it tends to harm the reputation of another so as to lower him in the estimation of the community or deter others from associating with him. In addition to proving that a statement is defamatory a plaintiff must also prove publication and, at the very least, negligence.

Slander requires proof of suffering of some kind of special harm except in cases of slander per se. Under the common law special harm did not have to be proved because damages were presumed. Under Supreme Court decisions in cases involving matters of public concern, however, a plaintiff cannot be awarded presumed damages unless she can prove actual malice.

A defamatory statement must have a tendency to harm the reputation of the plaintiff even though the plaintiff's reputation is not in fact injured. If the statement involves a matter of public interest and the defendant is a media defendant, the plaintiff must prove that the statement was false. At least one person must reasonably interpret the statement as being defamatory even if the statement could be interpreted in several different ways. If the defamatory content of the statement is not recognizable unless certain extrinsic facts are known, the plaintiff must specifically show the innuendo in his or her pleadings. Expressions of opinion generally are not considered defamatory.

Defamation requires publication. Mere repetition of a defamatory statement is considered publication even if the person repeating the statement does not believe it. An entire edition of a book or periodical is treated as one publication under the single publication rule.

Under *New York Times Co. v. Sullivan,* public officials and public figures are required to prove actual malice. A public figure is one who has achieved "pervasive fame or notoriety" or who "voluntarily injects himself or is drawn into a particular public controversy."

A successful plaintiff can recover for compensatory damages, including such nonpecuniary losses as loss of friendship, illness, and humiliation. Punitive damages can be recovered in matters of public interest if the plaintiff is able to prove the defendant acted with actual malice and in matters of private concern when only negligence is shown.

In certain circumstances defendants may be able to claim an absolute or qualified privilege of immunity. Judges, lawyers, parties, and witnesses, for example, have absolute immunity for the statements they make during judicial proceedings. Reports pertaining to public proceedings, as well as statements made to those having the capacity to act in the public interest, are subject to a qualified privilege. Qualified privileges can be lost if they are abused.

The right to privacy consists of four separate torts: appropriation, unreasonable intrusion, public disclosure of private facts, and false light. Appropriation consists of the use of the value of the plaintiff's name or picture for the defendant's financial gain. Unreasonable intrusion occurs when the defendant intentionally intrudes upon the seclusion of another and his intrusion would be considered highly offensive to a reasonable person. Publicizing details of the plaintiff's private life that would be highly offensive to a reasonable person and would not be of legitimate concern to the public constitutes public disclosure of private facts. If the details publicized are contained in a public record, no tort is committed. The so-called "false light" cases occur when the plaintiff is put in the public eye in a false light that would be highly offensive to a reasonable person.

A false statement made against a plaintiff's business, product, or property opens one to a claim of injurious falsehood. A false statement made in reference to the plaintiff's goods or business is usually referred to as trade libel, but a false statement in reference to the property rights of the plaintiff is referred to as slander of title.

PRACTICE POINTERS

Suppose your attorney asked you to find out what happened when the Gerry Spence case was remanded to the trial court. Was Spence awarded damages against *Hustler*? If so, in what amount? How would you go about getting this information given that the lower court decision was never published?

You could contact Gerry Spence's law office and talk to his staff about the case. But how would you get the telephone number? What if you did not know the name of the city or state in which Spence was practicing law? The appellate decision gives the name of the city and state in which Spence's attorney is practicing. Knowing the probable location of Spence's practice, you could look in the *Martindale-Hubbell Law Directory,* a compilation of the names of attorneys, their areas of practice, and personal data, including phone number, fax number, address, e-mail, and Web site.

Continued on next page

PRACTICE POINTERS—Continued ☐

Alternatively, you could go to the trial court to which the case was remanded and, using the court's indexing system, pull the court file. If you went to the court clerk's office, you could ask for the plaintiff or defendant's index and look under Spence or *Hustler*. In this file you might find, in addition to information about the disposition of the *Spence* matter, a gold mine of information, including copies of interrogatories, requests for production, and various motions that may be well researched and even well written. If the case is recent enough, you might use the jury instructions to assist in drafting jury instructions for similar cases. Once the file is reviewed, copies of exemplary documents should be copied. If the case is particularly instructive, don't be afraid to ask the attorneys or their staff questions or to see their files. Remember that imitation is the sincerest form of flattery.

On remand, the *Spence* case might have been assigned to another judge. If that were so, you could contact the original judge, whose name would be included in the appellate decision. The judge or his or her staff would probably be glad to find out who the assigned judge was.

Most appellate decisions are not published and memorandum decisions are often not readily available. In these cases you may have to contact the appellate court and find out how to get a copy of a memorandum decision. You have to go to the clerk of the appellate court and look in an index that is similar to that used by the trial courts. Once again, you might want to look in these files at briefs to take advantage of the research done in preparing them. You might also look for transcripts of the oral arguments, which may upon request of the clerk's office be available on audiotape.

TORT TEASERS ☐

1. Review the hypothetical scenario at the beginning of this chapter. What will the "heartthrob" have to prove if he sues for defamation? Are there any elements you anticipate he will have difficulty proving? Do you think he would be considered a public figure? Would it be easier for him to prove libel or slander? Why?

What must the plaintiff prove in cases 2–4?

2. *Time Magazine* publishes a report that Plaintiff and her husband, both of whom are wealthy socialites, were granted a divorce based on adultery, when in fact the divorce was granted on other grounds. The court's final judgment reads (in part):

According to certain testimony in behalf of the defendant, extramarital escapades of the plaintiff were bizarre and of an amatory nature which would have made Dr. Freud's hair curl. Other testimony, in plaintiff's behalf, would indicate that defendant was guilty of bounding from one bedpartner to another with the erotic zest of a satyr. The court is inclined to discount much of this testimony as unreliable. Nevertheless, it is the conclusion and finding of the court that neither party is domesticated, within the meaning of that term as used the Supreme Court of Florida. . . . In the present case, it is abundantly clear from the evidence of marital discord that neither of the parties has shown the least susceptibility to domestication, and that the marriage should be dissolved.

Time's article reads as follows:

Divorced. By Russell A. Firestone Jr., 41, heir to the tire fortune: Mary Alice Sullivan Firestone, 32, his third wife; a onetime Palm Beach schoolteacher, on grounds of extreme cruelty and adultery; after six years of marriage, one son; in West Palm Beach, Fla. The 17-month intermittent trial produced enough testimony of extramarital adventures on both sides, said the judge, "to make Dr. Freud's hair curl." *Time, Inc. v. Firestone*, 424 U.S. 448 (1976).

3. The manager of Defendant's motel sends a certified letter to Plaintiff, who had been a guest at the motel. In the letter he alleges that Plaintiff left without making payment and "accidentally packed" several items of motel property. The letter is received by Plaintiff's maid and read by Plaintiff's wife. Defendant is unaware that the Plaintiff is married. *Barnes v. Clayton House Motel*, 435 S.W.2d 616 (Tex. 1968).

4. Defendants author a book in which they claim that the models at Neiman-Marcus are "call girls" and that most of the salesmen are "fairies." Fifteen of the total of twenty-five salesmen sue on their own behalf and on behalf of the others, and all nine models sue for defamation. *Neiman-Marcus v. Lait*, 13 F.R.D. 311 (S.D.N.Y. 1952).

5. What might the defendants want to argue in the following case? Defendants file a letter with the grievance committee of the Association of the Bar of the City of New York alleging that Plaintiff has been fraudulent and dishonest in his practice as an attorney. Plaintiff claims that such allegations are defamatory. *Wiener v. Weintraub*, 239 N.E.2d 540 (N.Y. 1968).

6. A high school wrestling coach testifies at an investigatory hearing of the Ohio High School Athletic Association after his team is involved in an altercation at a wrestling match. He testifies again during a suit filed by several parents; the county court overturns a ruling in favor of the Athletic Association. The day after the court's decision a local reporter writes a column implying that the coach committed perjury. The column's heading was "Maple beat the law with the 'big lie'" and contained the following relevant passages:

[A] lesson was learned (or relearned) yesterday by the student body of Maple Heights High School, and by anyone who attended the Maple-Mentor wrestling meet of last Feb. 8.

A lesson which, sadly, in view of the events of the past year, is well they learned early.

It is simply this: If you get in a jam, lie your way out.

If you're successful enough, and powerful enough, and can sound sincere enough, you stand an excellent chance of making the lie stand up, regardless of what really happened.

The teachers responsible were mainly head Maple wrestling coach, Mike Milkovich, and former superintendent of schools H. Donald Scott.

* * *

Anyone who attended the meet, whether he be from Maple Heights, Mentor, or impartial observer, knows in his heart that Milkovich and Scott lied at the hearing after each having given his solemn oath to tell the truth.

But they got away with it.

Is that the kind of lesson we want our young people learning from their high school administrators and coaches?

I think not.

Is the wrestling coach a public figure? Does the article constitute opinion that is protected, or does the coach have an actionable claim for defamation? *Milkovich v. Lorain Journal Co.*, 497 U.S. 1 (1990).

7. A man sues his ex-wife for defamation because of her claims that he is homosexual and that Plaintiff is his lover. The ex-wife asks Defendant, a deputy sheriff, to secure a hair sample from Plaintiff while he is hospitalized. Defendant pays an orderly, who obtains combings from Plaintiff's hair brush and a discarded

adhesive bandage. Plaintiff does not learn of this intrusion until after it occurs. *Froelich v. Werbin,* 548 P.2d 482 (Kan. 1976). What tort should Plaintiff allege?

8. Plaintiff, a manufacturer of loudspeaker systems and other audio equipment, claims that Defendant consumer product-testing organization published false statements in its review of Plaintiff's loudspeakers. What claim might Plaintiff file in addition to a defamation claim? *Bose Corp. v. Consumers Union,* 508 F. Supp. 1249 (C.D. Mass. 1981).

KEY TERMS

Absolute privilege
Absolute defense to defamation, regardless of defendant's motives.

Actual malice
Acting with knowledge of the falsity of one's statement or with reckless disregard as to the truth or falsity of one's statement.

Appropriation
Use of the value of plaintiff's name or picture for defendant's financial gain.

Defamation
Statement that tends to harm the reputation of another, encompassing both libel and slander.

False light
Representing the plaintiff to the public in a way that would be highly offensive to a reasonable person.

Injurious falsehood
False disparagement of a plaintiff's business, product, or property rights.

Innuendo
Use of extrinsic facts to convey the defamatory meaning of a statement.

Libel
Written defamatory statements.

Pecuniary
Monetary; that which can be valued in terms of money.

Presumed damages
Damages that ordinarily stem from a defamatory statement and that do not require the showing of actual harm.

Publication
Hearing or seeing of a defamatory statement by someone other than the plaintiff.

Public figure
One who has achieved persuasive fame or notoriety or who becomes involved in a public controversy.

Qualified privilege
Privilege that applies only when a defendant acts on the basis of certain well-defined purposes.

Slander
Oral defamatory statements.

Slander of title
False disparagement of the plaintiff's property rights.

Slander per se
Slander in which pecuniary harm can be assumed.

Special harm
Harm of a pecuniary nature.

Trade libel
False disparagement of the plaintiff's goods or business.

Part Three

WHOM TO SUE

CHAPTER

15

Vicarious Liability

CHAPTER OBJECTIVES

In this chapter you will learn to:
- Identify the circumstances in which an employer is vicariously liable for the acts of an employee or an independent contractor
- Distinguish between an employer-employee relationship and an employer-independent contractor relationship
- Identify the exceptions to the bailor nonliability rule as applied to the owners of automobiles
- Recognize situations in which contributory negligence is imputed
- Identify the circumstances in which parents are vicariously liable for the acts of their children

Let us take a brief excursion into the not-too-distant future when you have completed your program of study and have assumed a position as a legal assistant. Suppose you are asked by your supervising attorney to draft a contract and the attorney, who is called out of town on a personal emergency, never reviews the contract. As he dashes out of the office he yells back at you to be sure that the contract is signed by the parties within the week. Before you can utter a word of protest he is gone. Can he be held liable for any provisions in the contract that eventually inure to the detriment of the client?

Suppose that your attorney asks you to do a research project in the library. While enroute to the library you happen to pass a very elite clothing store, which you are aware is having an outrageous one-day-only sale. Knowing that this is your only chance to take advantage of these bargains, you stop by the store for a few minutes. You put your briefcase on the floor so your hands are free to do some serious shopping. Another customer fails to notice your briefcase, catches her heel on its handles, and falls to the ground. The tumble she takes is a bad one and paramedics have to be called. Will this woman be able to sue your employer, as you were engaged in your shopping diversion during your work time?

Now suppose that, unnerved by the incident at the clothing store, you rush off to the library. Once there you immerse yourself in the task at hand. Suddenly whose face appears among the book stacks but your ex-spouse's? Because you have only recently escaped the chains of matrimony, within thirty seconds the two of

you are engaged in a full-scale verbal war. Without warning, some demonic urge possesses you and you find yourself using your briefcase (the same one that just wreaked havoc on the customer) as a weapon. Will your ex be able to recover from your employer for the injuries sustained as a result of your pugilistic activities? These and other related questions are explored in this chapter.

OVERVIEW OF VICARIOUS LIABILITY

Under the doctrine of **vicarious liability,** an individual is held liable for the tortious acts of another. These acts are imputed to him because of the special relationship he holds to the tortfeasor. The most common relationship is the one between employer and employee, in which the employer is held vicariously liable for the tortious acts of his or her employee. Vicarious liability may also arise in relationships between employers and independent contractors and in activities involving joint enterprises. Furthermore, automobile consent statutes and the family purpose doctrine contain elements of vicarious liability (see Figure 15-1).

EMPLOYER-EMPLOYEE RELATIONSHIP

An employer is vicariously liable for the acts of an employee under the doctrine of **respondeat superior,** which translates as "let the person higher up answer." This doctrine applies to negligent torts, intentional torts, and strict liability actions (see Figure 15-2). The rationale most commonly used to justify this doctrine is that employers should consider the expense of reimbursing those injured by their employees as part of the cost of doing business. As a practical matter, keep in mind that typically the employee is judgment-proof, whereas the employer is the proverbial "deep pocket."

For the doctrine to be applicable the employee must be acting "within the scope and furtherance of his employment" (Restatement (Second) of Agency § 229). An employee will be considered to be doing this as long as he is intending to further his employer's business purpose. Even if the means he chooses are

---

FIGURE 15-1 Examples of Vicarious Liability

Employers-Employees
Employers-Independent Contractors
Members of Joint Enterprise
Automotive Consent Statutes
Family Purpose Doctrine

FIGURE 15-2   Employer-Employee Liability (Respondeat Superior)

EMPLOYER IS LIABLE	EMPLOYER IS NOT LIABLE
• Employee is acting within the scope and furtherance of employment. • Employee commits intentional tort reasonably connected to job. • Employee's deviation from business purpose is reasonably foreseeable. • Employee commits acts expressly forbidden by employer but within scope of employment. • Employee negligently delegates his or her rights and authority to another without the employer's authorization.	• Employee goes on "frolic" or "detour." • Employee is traveling to or from work.

indirect or foolish or if his intent is a combination of serving his employer and meeting his personal needs, he will be viewed as acting "within the scope and furtherance of his employment." Travel to and from work, however, is generally not included as falling within the scope of employment.

Intentional Torts

What if an employee intentionally injures another? The employer will still be liable as long as the tort is reasonably connected to the employee's job. A company may be liable, for example, for false imprisonment committed by an overzealous security guard who unreasonably detains a customer she suspects of shoplifting or for assault and battery committed by an employee who resorts to Rambo-style techniques in trying to collect a debt for the company. The employer will not be liable if the employee's acts are driven by some purely personal motive, such as vengeance.

Frolics and Detours

An employer is not vicariously liable when an employee goes on a "frolic" or "detour" of his own. Suppose an employee of a pizza parlor, having completed his deliveries, drives twenty miles out of his way for a lit-

tle rendezvous with his girlfriend. His twenty-mile side trip would likely be considered a "frolic" or "detour" and, under the traditional view, his employer would not be vicariously liable for any acts of negligence he might commit. However, if the employee became involved in an accident while enroute back to the pizza parlor, the employer would once again become vicariously liable because once he got back on track, the employee would be acting within the scope of his employment.

Under the more modern view the employee would be seen as acting within the scope of his employment if his deviation from his business purpose was "reasonably foreseeable." Under this approach an employee whose deviation is slight in terms of time and distance is considered acting within the scope of his employment even when he is on a personal errand. The reasoning underlying this approach is that employers should be liable for those things that can generally be anticipated as one of the risks of doing business.

Forbidden Acts

Is the employer liable even if he or she explicitly forbids the employee to engage in certain acts and the employee does so anyway? Yes, as long as the acts are done within the scope and furtherance of employment.

Suppose a store expressly forbids its employees from using physical force to detain someone suspected of shoplifting. The store will nevertheless be vicariously liable for the negligence of its employees who countermand those orders, and wrestle to the ground and hogtie an uncooperative customer whom they suspect of shoplifting.

Delegation of Authority or Rights

Vicarious liability may or may not exist when an employee delegates his or her authority or rights to another without the employer's authorization. What if an employee hires someone without the employer's permission? Or what if he allows an unauthorized person to use the employer's property, such as the company car, and that person commits a tort? In both cases vicarious liability will exist if the employee acted negligently. If the employee knew or should have known that the individual lacked skills and would be unable to safely complete the job, the employer will be vicariously liable. Notice that the issue of vicarious liability hinges on the employee's negligence and not the third party's negligence, because vicarious liability is based on the link existing between the employer and the employee.

■ PUTTING IT INTO PRACTICE 15.1 ☐

1. Mr. Stone, a car salesman, is involved in a fatal accident on the way to pick up Mr. Urban, a customer. Is the car dealership liable for the injuries Stone caused, considering that no one at the dealership authorized or even knew about his trip? What factors would you consider in answering this question?
2. Richard, an employee of Staggs-Bilt Homes, is hired to patrol several subdivisions that are under construction. He is instructed to observe and report suspicious behavior but not to get involved. While filling up a Staggs truck at a service station, Richard pulls his gun from his holster, either in horseplay or to show Rex, the service station attendant. The gun accidentally discharges, injuring Rex. Is Staggs-Bilt Homes vicariously liable for Richard's negligence?
3. A janitor negligently starts a trash fire when he burns the refuse. He was specifically ordered not to dispose of trash by burning it. Is his employer vicariously liable?
4. Contrary to his employer's instructions not to let anyone drive the truck or even ride in it, a truck driver allows a thirteen-year-old to drive the truck. If they are involved in an accident while the teenager is driving, under what conditions will the employer be liable to the injured party?
5. Tena, a cocktail waitress, is involved in an accident while she is enroute to the assistant manager's house immediately following her shift. At the request of a band member, she is picking up a microphone part, which the band needs to complete its performance. The band has been hired by the restaurant to draw people into the restaurant. Members of the band are staying at the assistant manager's house. Should the restaurant be held liable for the accident Tena caused?
6. In accordance with directions by his employer, a clerk takes home papers to work on. He is involved in an accident on his way back to work. Should his employer be held vicariously liable?

EMPLOYERS–INDEPENDENT CONTRACTORS

Generally, one who hires an independent contractor will not be held vicariously liable for the tortious acts of that person. Several exceptions, however, can be found to that basic rule.

Before dealing with those exceptions we must first distinguish between an employee and an independent contractor. An employee is typically viewed as someone under the control of the person who hired him; an **independent contractor,** although hired to produce certain results, is considered her own boss. An inde-

pendent contractor works at her own pace, in her own way, under her own supervision.

Under this definition, would a newspaper carrier be considered an employee or an independent contractor? *Santiago v. Phoenix Newspapers, Inc.* raised this question. The court considers a number of factors, including the amount of control exercised by the employer over the carrier's work, the nature of the carrier's work, the length of employment, the method of payment, and so on. Notice that the language in the parties' contract does not determine the nature of their relationship.

CASE

Santiago v. Phoenix Newspapers, Inc.
794 P.2d 138 (Ariz. 1990)

GRANT, Chief Judge.

The appellant, William Santiago (Santiago), asks this court to review the court of appeals' decision affirming the trial court's entry of summary judgment in favor of Phoenix Newspapers, Inc. (PNI). We granted review to consider whether the trial court correctly found as a matter of law that PNI was not vicariously liable for the injuries Santiago sustained in a collision with a PNI delivery agent. . . .

PROCEDURAL HISTORY

On April 20, 1986, a car driven by Frank Frausto (Frausto) collided with a motorcycle driven by Santiago. At the time Frausto was delivering the Sunday edition of the Arizona Republic on his route for PNI. Santiago filed a negligence action against Frausto and PNI, alleging that Frausto was PNI's agent. Both parties moved for summary judgment. The court, finding no genuine issues of material fact, concluded that Frausto was an independent contractor. The court of appeals agreed, stating that "[p]arties have a perfect right, in their dealings with each other, to establish the independent contractor status in order to avoid the relationship of employer-employee,

and it is clear from the undisputed facts that there was no employer-employee relationship created between PNI and Frausto." . . .

FACTS

Frausto began delivering papers for PNI in August 1984 under a "Delivery Agent Agreement," prepared by PNI. The agreement provided that Frausto was an "independent contractor," retained to provide prompt delivery of its newspapers by the times specified in the contract. Although Frausto had the right to operate the business as he chose, he could engage others to deliver papers on his route for no more than 25% of the delivery days. He was free to pursue any other business activities, including delivering other publications, so long as those activities did not interfere with his performance of the PNI contract. Frausto was also required to provide PNI with satisfactory proof of liability insurance, a valid driver's license, and a favorable report from the Arizona Motor Vehicle Division.

The contract was for a period of six months, renewable at PNI's option. Either party could terminate the agreement prior to six months without cause with 28 days notice and for cause with no notice. Under the contract, cause for termination by PNI existed if complaints from home delivery subscribers exceeded an undefined "acceptable" level, or if Frausto failed to maintain "acceptable" subscriber relations or provide "satisfactory service," defined as banding and bagging newspapers to insure they were received in a dry and readable condition. PNI was also free to breach the agreement if it ceased publishing the paper, defined in the contract as "excusable non-compliance." There is no correlative definition of cause for termination by Frausto. Customers paid PNI directly and any complaints about delivery were funneled through PNI to Frausto. Additionally, the contract required Frausto to allow a PNI employee to accompany him on his route "for the purposes of verifying distribution, subscriber service, or regular newspaper business."

Early each morning, Frausto drove to a PNI-specified distribution point to load the papers into his car. He then delivered the papers before a PNI-specified time to addresses on a delivery list provided and owned by PNI. He could deliver the papers to listed addresses only. When customers were added to and taken from this list by PNI, Frausto was required to incorporate these changes into his route. According to Frausto, the number of papers delivered fluctuated by as much as thirty papers. For these services, PNI paid Frausto a set amount each week. That amount did not vary when addresses within or beyond the contracted delivery area were added to or taken away by PNI from the delivery list. PNI provided Frausto with health and disability insurance, but did not withhold any taxes.

In ruling on the summary judgment motion, the court considered the affidavits of Frausto and David L. Miller, a delivery agent and former employee driver. Frausto stated in his affidavit that, despite the contractual nomenclature, he considered himself an employee and delivered the papers any way his supervisor directed him to. This included placing the paper in a particular spot if requested by the customer. If he did not comply with these requests, his supervisor would speak to him and he could be fired. Miller stated in his affidavit that he had been a service driver, later switched to being a delivery agent, and that, in his view, there was no significant difference between the level of supervision provided to those holding the two positions.

DISCUSSION

If the inference in this case is clear that no master-servant relationship exists, the trial court was correct in granting summary judgment; if it is not clear, the case should have been presented to the jury to decide. . . . We apply the rule in this case by asking whether the courts below correctly decided that no inferences could be drawn from the material facts suggesting Frausto was acting as PNI's employee when the accident occurred.

Section 220 of the *Restatement (Second) of Agency*, adopted by Arizona, . . . defines a servant as "a person employed to perform services in the affairs of another and who with respect to the physical conduct in the performance of the services is subject to the other's control or right to control." The *Restatement* lists several additional factors, none of which is dispositive, in determining whether one acting for another is a servant or an independent contractor. We now review those factors, along with the cases considering them, for evidence of an employer-employee relationship which could preclude the entry of summary judgment.

As a prefatory note, we reject PNI's argument that the language of the employment contract is determinative. Contract language does not determine the relationship of the parties, rather the "objective nature of the relationship, [is] determined upon an analysis of the totality of the facts and circumstances of each case." . . .

In determining whether an employer-employee relationship exists, the fact finder must evaluate a number of criteria. They include:
1. The extent of control exercised by the master over details of the work and the degree of supervision;
2. The distinct nature of the worker's business;
3. Specialization or skilled occupation;
4. Materials and place of work;
5. Duration of employment;
6. Method of payment;
7. Relationship of work done to the regular business of the employer;
8. Belief of the parties.

ANALYSIS OF RELATIONSHIP BETWEEN FRAUSTO AND PNI

1. The extent of control exercised by the master over the details of the work

Such control may be manifested in a variety of ways. A worker who must comply with another's instructions about when, where, and how to work is an employee. *See Restatement* § 220 comment h. In *Throop,* the plaintiff's husband was killed in a collision with a car driven by Hennen, a salesman for the defendant company. Plaintiff sought recovery against the company on a theory of vicarious liability. At the close of evidence, the trial court granted a directed verdict in favor of the company. On appeal, we examined the record for evidence of the company's control. Hennen was required to call on accounts in person and to present all inventory items, to submit written reports on these visits and to make collections. Although Hennen had these responsibilities for a seven-year period, he could sell anywhere in the country, visit prospects whenever he chose, use his own vehicle exclusively, and select all prospects himself, visiting the office only a few times a year. Based on these facts, we agreed the trial court properly directed the verdict in the company's favor because no reasonable juror could find it had exercised sufficient control over Hennen to make him an employee.

Missing in *Throop* was the right to control the details of how Hennen made his sales. Where this right of control exists, the inference of the employer-employee relationship is strengthened. For example, an appellate court overturned the trial court's finding of no employer-employee relationship in *Gallaher v. Ricketts*. . . . The newspaper carrier in *Gallaher* provided his own transportation and was paid a commission for every dollar worth of papers delivered on his assigned route. The company conducted training programs, including tips on how to distribute the paper and stimulate sales, reimbursed him for some transportation expenses, and retained the right to terminate him at any time. The court concluded that these indices of control demonstrated that the carrier "was merely a cog in the wheel of the defendant's enterprise," and held that Ricketts was an employee. . . .

A strong indication of control is an employer's power to give specific instructions with the expectation that they will be followed. . . .

In this case, PNI designated the time for pick-up and delivery, the area covered, the manner in which the papers were delivered, *i.e.,* bagged and banded, and the persons to whom delivery was made. Although PNI did little actual supervising, it had the authority under the contract to send a supervisor with Frausto on his route. Frausto claimed he did the job as he was told, without renegotiating the contract terms, adding customers and following specific customer requests relayed by PNI.

2. The distinct nature of the worker's business

Whether the worker's tasks are efforts to promote his own independent enterprise or to further his employer's business will aid the fact finder in ascertaining the existence of an employer-employee relationship. *Tanner v. USA Today* . . . . The agent in *Tanner* contracted with

USA Today to distribute papers. The agent in turn hired carriers to deliver the papers using his trucks. USA Today had no control over the choice of drivers, the trucks used, or the route taken. Under these circumstances, and despite USA Today's imposition of time parameters for delivery, the court found insufficient evidence to raise the issue of an employer-employee relationship.

A concomitant inquiry to this factor also considers whether the worker's job performance results in a profit or loss for the worker. Thus, where the worker purchases the product and then sells it at a profit or loss, the worker is more likely to be found an independent contractor. . . .

As far as the nature of the worker's business, Frausto had no delivery business distinct from that of his responsibilities to PNI. Unlike the drivers in *Tanner,* Frausto had an individual relationship and contract with the newspaper company. Furthermore, he did not purchase the papers and then sell them at a profit or loss. Payments were made directly to PNI and any complaints or requests for delivery changes went through PNI. If Frausto missed a customer, a PNI employee would deliver a paper.

3. Specialization or skilled occupation

The jury is more likely to find a master-servant relationship where the work does not require the services of one highly educated or skilled. *See Restatement* § 220 comment h. PNI argues that its agents must drive, follow directions, and be diligent in order to perform the job for which they are paid. However, these skills are required in differing degrees for virtually any job. Frausto's services were not specialized and required no particular training. In addition, an agreement that work cannot be delegated indicates a master-servant relationship. *Restatement* § 220 comment j. In this case, Frausto could delegate work but only up to twenty-five percent of the days.

4. Materials and place of work

If an employer supplies tools, and employment is over a specific area or over a fixed route, a master-servant relationship is indicated. *Restatement* § 220 comment h. In this case, PNI supplied the product but did not supply the bags, rubber bands, or transportation necessary to complete the deliveries satisfactorily. However, PNI did designate the route to be covered.

5. Duration of employment

Whether the employer seeks a worker's services as a one-time, discrete job or as part of a continuous working relationship may indicate that the employer-employee relationship exists. The shorter in time the relationship, the less likely the worker will subject himself to control over job details. *See Restatement* § 220 comment j. In addition, the employer's right to terminate may indicate control and therefore an employer-employee relationship. The "right to fire" is considered one of the most effective methods of control. . . . In this case, the contract provided for a six-month term, renewable as long as the carrier performed satisfactorily. Frausto could be terminated without cause in 28 days and with cause immediately. The definition of cause in the contract was defined only as a failure to provide "satisfactory" service. A jury could reasonably infer that an employer-employee relationship existed since PNI retained significant latitude to fire Frausto inasmuch as the "satisfactory service" provision provides no effective standards. In addition, the jury could also infer that PNI provided health insurance to encourage a long-term relationship and disability insurance to protect itself in case of injury to the carrier, both of which support the existence of an employer-employee relationship.

6. Method of payment

PNI paid Frausto each week, but argues that because Frausto was not paid by the hour, he was an independent contractor. Santiago responds that payment was not made by the "job" because Frausto's responsibilities changed without any adjustment to his pay or contract.
. . .

7. Relation of work done to the employer's regular business

A court is more likely to find a worker an employee if the work is part of the employer's regular business. *Restatement* § 220 comment h. The court of appeals addressed this factor in *Anton* . . . The contractor in that case, Perkins, entered into an agreement to harvest certain trees and deliver the lumber to Southwest. Southwest gave Perkins detailed specifications for the wood which Perkins passed on verbatim to his woodcutters. Perkins hired Anton as one of these woodcutters under a written contract. That contract required Anton to fell trees, cut them into logs, stack the logs into cords, and clean up the forest afterwards, all in accordance with the Southwest specifications. Perkins reserved to himself only the task of picking up and delivering the wood to Southwest. During the process, Perkins checked Anton's work, making sure he cut the logs correctly, selected the correct quality of wood, stacked the timber as directed, cleaned the forest sufficiently, and worked quickly.

The court noted that in reality the woodcutters conducted virtually every facet of Perkins' enterprise related to the Southwest contract. In deciding whether Anton was an employee for purposes of workers' compensation, the court considered whether the work performed was an *integral* part of the employer's *regular* business. . . . It found Anton was an employee because Perkins had not limited his attempt to contract to a particularly "well-defined incidental activity . . . ancillary to the central concerns of his business . . . but rather the ongoing basic employee activity" itself. . . .

We find the *Anton* . . . [analysis] particularly apt here. Home delivery is critical to the survival of a local daily paper; it may be its essential core. As one court explained:

> The delivery of newspapers within a reasonable time after publication is essential to the success of the newspaper business. For the greater portion of its income the paper depends on advertising, and the rates for advertising are governed by the paper's circulation. Circulation is a necessity for success. The delivery boys are just as much an integral part of the newspaper industry as are the typesetters and pressmen or the editorial staff.

PNI is hard-pressed to detach the business of delivering news from that of reporting and printing it, especially when it retains an individual relationship with each carrier. . . .

8. Belief of the parties

As stated above, Frausto believed that he was an employee, despite contract language to the contrary. Even if he believed he was an independent contractor, that would not preclude a finding of vicarious liability. As the *Restatement* explains: "It is not determinative that the parties believe or disbelieve that the relation of master and servant exists, except insofar as such belief indicates an assumption of control by the one and submission of control by the other." *Restatement* § 220 comment m. . . . In addition to the parties' belief, the finder of fact should look to the community's belief. "Community custom in thinking that a kind of service is rendered by servants . . . is of importance." *Restatement* § 220 comment h. The fact that the community regards those doing such work as servants indicates the relation of master and servant. The newspaper's customers did not have individual contact or contracts with Frausto. All payments, complaints, and changes were made directly to PNI. From these facts, a jury could infer that the community regarded Frausto as PNI's employee.

Again, analyzing these factors in relation to the facts of this case a jury could determine that an employer-employee relationship existed between PNI and Frausto.

CONCLUSION AND DISPOSITION

Whether an employer-employee relationship exists may not be determined as a matter of law in either side's favor, because reasonable minds may disagree on the nature of the employment relationship. A jury could infer from these facts that Frausto was an employee because PNI involved itself with the details of delivery, received directly all customer complaints and changes so as to remove much of Frausto's independence, retained broad discretion to terminate, and relied heavily on Frausto's services for the survival of its business. The jury could also infer that Frausto was an independent contractor because he used his own car, was subject to little supervision, provided some of his own supplies, and could have someone else deliver for him within limits. Therefore, the trial court erred in finding as a matter of law that Frausto was an independent contractor. Summary judgment on the vicarious liability claim was inappropriate. The opinion of the court of appeals is vacated and the case is remanded to the superior court for proceedings consistent with this opinion.

PUTTING IT INTO PRACTICE 15.2

1. Why does Santiago want to sue PNI?
2. What is the question before the court?
3. Is the language of the employment contract determinative of the nature of the relationship between Frausto and PNI?
4. What factors does the court consider in determining whether an employer-employee relationship exists?
5. What factor is a strong indication of control, according to the court? What facts indicate that PNI had control over Frausto?
6. Does the court find Frausto's business to be distinct from his responsibilities to PNI? What facts support this conclusion?
7. Does the court find Frausto's job to be specialized?
8. Did PNI supply the "tools" of the trade to Frausto? Was the route he was to take fixed?
9. Which is more likely an indication of an employer-employee relationship, a one-time discrete job or a continuous working relationship? What effect does the right to terminate have on this classification? What factors does the court consider in reference to duration of employment in the context of the PNI-Frausto relationship?
10. Is a court more likely to find a worker to be an employee if his work is part of the employer's regular business? Is the delivery of newspapers part of PNI's regular business?
11. Did Frausto believe he was an employee? If he had believed that he was an independent contractor, would that have precluded a finding of vicarious liability?

The mere fact that an employer refers to someone as an independent contractor is not dispositive in classifying the relationship. The nature of the relationship and not the label that is attached to the relationship determines its classification. Therefore, an employer cannot evade liability by simply casting the label of independent contractor on an employee.

Exceptions to Nonliability Rule for Independent Contractors

Several exceptions to the nonliability rule for independent contractors exist. First, if the employer himself is negligent in dealing with an independent contractor, he can be found liable. For example, if the employer hires someone that he knows will not perform the work safely (such as an individual who has a poor safety record), or if he fails to inspect work after it is done, the employer can be liable even if the injuries stem from the contractor's negligence (see Figure 15-3).

Nondelegable Duties

Some duties of care are so important that they are nondelegable. A city that hires a private contractor to work on its streets cannot delegate to the company its duty to keep its streets in good repair. For this same reason the owner of a shopping mall can be held vicariously liable for damages resulting from an independent contractor's negligent repair of its roof. The courts have not clearly defined what is and is not a "delegable" duty, but their decisions are generally moti-

FIGURE 15-3 Employer-Independent Contractors

GENERAL RULE:
• Employers are not vicariously liable for torts of independent contractors.

EXCEPTIONS TO NONLIABILITY RULE:
• Employer is negligent in dealing with independent contractor.
• Employer delegates nondelegable duty to independent contractor.
• Employer hires independent contractor to conduct an activity involving unusual risks that are recognizable in advance.
• Employer contracts for performance of an illegal act.
• Doctors are liable for negligent acts of those under their control (this doctrine has been abolished in some jurisdictions and limited in others).

vated by a desire to prevent employers from avoiding liability by hiring independent contractors to carry out their responsibilities.

One of the most litigated exceptions to the independent contractor nonliability rule is the "retained control" exception, adopted from the Restatement (Second) of Torts § 414, which provides:

One who entrusts work to an independent contractor, but who retains control of any part of the work, is subject to liability for physical harm to others whose safety the employer owes a duty to exercise reasonable care, which is caused by his failure to exercise his control with reasonable care.

For this section to apply to a situation, the control exercised by the employer must go beyond retaining control over the premises; the control must instead relate to the actual manner in which the work performed by the contractor is done. Supervising the sequence of the work is not enough; the employer must have actual control over the details of how the work is done.

In one case, for example, a woman was injured when she fell over a chalk line erected by an employee of a contractor hired to remodel a department store. The court found that the store had insufficient control over the contractor to come within the retained control exception (*Koepke v. Carter Hawley Stores,* 682 P.2d 425 (Ariz. Ct. App. 1984)). Although the department store retained control over the general process of remodeling (to ensure that the contractor complied with contractual specifications), the store had no control over scheduling or operational procedures. In reaching its decision the court relied on comment c to § 414:

It is not enough that [the employer] has merely a general right to order the work stopped or resumed, to inspect its progress or receive reports, to make suggestions or recommendations which need not necessarily be followed, or to prescribe alterations and deviations. Such a general right is usually reserved to employers, but it does not mean that the contractor is controlled as to his methods of work, or as to operative detail. There must be such a retention of a right of supervision that the contractor is not entirely free to do the work in his own way.

The court did find liability under § 422 of the Restatement, which provides:

A possessor of land who entrusts to an independent contractor construction, repair, or other work on the land, or on a building, or other structure on it, is subject to the same liability as though he had retained the work in his own hands to others on or outside of the land for physical harm caused them by the unsafe conditions on the structure
(a) while the possessor has retained possession of the land during the progress or work, or
(b) after he has resumed possession of the land upon its completion.

This section sets forth a nondelegable duty of employers to business invitees. In justifying its application of § 422(a) to the facts before it, the court reasoned that the store elected to benefit economically from staying open during remodeling rather than taking the precaution of shutting down temporarily. The court also pointed out that the store was in a position to prevent or minimize risks by carefully hiring the contractor and making sure that safety procedures were followed.

Extraordinary Risks

Employers continue to be vicariously liable if they hire independent contractors to carry out activities involving risks that require more than ordinary precautions. If an employer hires an independent contractor to relocate date palm trees, for example, special precautions obviously would have to be taken in securing the trees to ensure that transportation along public highways was done without endangering others. In the case of an accident the employer would be vicariously liable. This special rule of liability applies only to unusual risks and not to risks arising out of ordinary forms of negligence. Suppose the contractor were asked to transport common shrubs in an enclosed truck rather than freestanding palm trees. In that case the employer would not be liable if the contractor drove negligently, because the risk involved in hauling shrubs is not an unusual one.

Employers will not be liable if the risks involved are not recognizable in advance. If a family hires a lawn care service to tend their lawn while they are on vacation and one of the caretakers decides to add water to the pool and forgets to shut it off, the family will not be vicariously liable for the flood damage to their adjoining neighbor's property. The risk of overfilling the pool would not be considered an inherent or foreseeable risk of lawn care.

Illegal Acts

Another exception to the nonliability of employers for the acts of independent contractors is in the area of illegal acts. If an employer contracts for the performance of an illegal activity, he or she will be vicariously liable for any damage caused by the contractor.

Physicians

Historically, physicians were exceptions to the nonliability rule. A physician was vicariously liable for the negligence of nurses, other physicians, paramedical personnel, and hospital administrators who, although not under her employ, were for legal purposes considered to be under the physician's control. The courts reasoned that a physician acting in a supervisory role over other medical personnel was the "captain of the ship" and thus should be held vicariously liable for their negligent acts. The impetus behind this doctrine probably lay in the court's attempt to circumvent charitable immunity and find a solvent defendant. With the demise of charitable immunity, this doctrine has been abolished in many places and in other jurisdictions has been strictly limited to acts committed during surgery. This same rationale has been used, however, by plaintiffs to reach hospitals that hire private franchises to carry out special functions in the hospital, such as radiology and serology.

PUTTING IT INTO PRACTICE 15.3

1. After being cited for speeding, Faustino appears before Justice of the Peace Phares and pays a fine. Due to a clerical or administrative error, the receipt of Faustino's payment is not noted; during a subsequent review of his file, Phares determines that the fine has not been paid and issues a bench warrant for Faustino. Later Faustino is stopped for a minor traffic violation and is arrested and incarcerated overnight because of the outstanding bench warrant. Faustino appears before Phares and the clerical error is discovered and corrected. Apologies are made and Faustino is released. Later Faustino sues Phares and the county that employs Phares. Is the county vicariously liable for Phares's actions?

2. A motion picture company employs an independent contractor to provide a circus act using performing lions. While the picture is being made, one of the lions escapes and injures an actor. Is the motion picture company vicariously liable for the injuries sustained by the actor?

3. The van that a hotel uses to convey passengers to the airport is damaged in a collision. The hotel contracts with a rental company to use one of its vans to take hotel guests to the airport. The only driver available is inexperienced, and while driving the passengers from the hotel he is involved in an accident because he inadvertently hits the accelerator instead of the brake. Is the hotel liable to the driver of the other vehicle involved in the accident? Would your answer change if the driver had been experienced but had been talking to one of the passengers and not watching where he was going when he ran into the other vehicle?

4. Fisher is a member of a chicken-catching crew that was assembled by Reid, a weighmaster who was working for Townsends, a chicken-processing business. Fisher is injured while he is riding in a vehicle driven by Reid. At the time Reid is driving he is working for Townsends.

   Reid has worked for Townsends for five years exclusively. Their relationship began with oral understandings; shortly before the accident Townsends presented Reid with a written Catching Crew Agreement. This agreement, which indicates that Reid is an independent contractor, was not intended to change their oral agreement. The parties disagree about whether the Catching Crew Agreement was executed prior to Reid's accident.

   Townsends supplies Reid with Daily Movement Sheets that identify the farm where the day's work is to be done, the birds that are to be removed, which crew is to be assigned to a job, and the time the crew is to report. Townsends owns and supplies the trucks, forklifts, cages, and stools that are used to catch chickens, as well as the paper masks and disposable gloves worn by the catchers. Townsends' manager visits the farms periodically to see if the weighmasters, truck drivers, or forklift operators are experiencing problems. Townsends requires its weighmasters to keep two-way radios in the vehicles they use to transport their crews. Townsends supplies Reid with these radios, which allows Townsends to keep Reid advised of changes in work sites and work orders and enables him to communicate with Townsends' processing plant, truck drivers, and forklift operators regarding work-related problems.

   Apply the criteria set forth in *Santiago v. PNI* and decide how you would characterize the relationship between Townsends and Reid.

Continued on next page

---

5. In celebration of Japan Week, Jetro and Chamber contract with Marutamaya to provide a fireworks display. Marutamaya then contracts with R. Borgman Sales Co. to conduct the display. During the display two of the shells explode prematurely, injuring two of the operators, both of whom are employees of Borgman and experienced, licensed pyrotechnic operators. Should Jetro and Chamber be held liable for the operators' injuries, or did they delegate their responsibility to Marutamaya by hiring the company as an independent contractor?

6. A workman is killed in a dirt slide while performing an excavation on a site owned by a mining company, Kennecott Copper Company. The company was in the process of expanding its facilities and had contracted with the employer of the deceased workman to do the job. Under its contract with the contractor, Kennecott maintained control over employee selection and over salaries to be paid to key employees. Kennecott could discharge any employee on the job and had to approve drawings detailing how work was to be performed. Should Kennecott be held liable for the death of the employee of its contractor?

BAILMENTS

If a party temporarily entrusts goods to the care of another, the party who hands over the goods is referred to as a **bailor;** the person who receives custody of the goods is a **bailee.** When you take your car in for repair, you are the bailor and the service station is the bailee. The question in terms of vicarious liability is whether a bailor should be liable for the negligence of a bailee.

Under the common law majority rule, a bailor is not vicariously liable for the acts of a bailee (see Figure 15-4). Thus, if someone rents a car from a rental agency and negligently injures a plaintiff while driving such a car, the rental agency (bailor) is not vicariously liable for the acts of the individual who rented the car (bailee). The bailor may be liable for his own negligence if he entrusts control of his property to a person that he knows or reasonably should know is likely to endanger others. Therefore, if the rental agency in this example was aware that the driver was intoxicated or otherwise unable to control the vehicle, it could be held vicariously liable for the driver's negligent acts.

Exceptions to Bailor Nonliability

The courts, for the most part, have been dissatisfied with the nonliability rule regarding bailors when that rule is applied to owners of automobiles who allow others to drive. They have adopted a number of strategies by which vicarious liability can be placed on the owners of vehicles. The implicit reasoning behind the notion of owner liability is that owners are more likely to be able to pay for damages than those to whom they loan their vehicles and that owners, not drivers, are expected to carry insurance.

In some courts the mere presence of the owner in the car creates the presumption that the owner had control over the driving. As a result the owner is considered vicariously liable for the acts of the driver. Some courts have retreated from this position by making the presumption a rebuttable one. Others have negated the presumption altogether and treat the nondriving owner as if she were a guest in her own car. The courts will not, however, impute the driver's negligence to the owner if the owner is not present.

FIGURE 15-4   Bailments

GENERAL RULE:
• Bailors are not vicariously liable for the acts
of a bailee.

EXCEPTIONS TO NONLIABILITY RULE
• Bailor negligently entrusts property to one he knows
or should know will endanger others.
• In some states, mere presence of owner in vehicle
makes owner vicariously liable for acts of driver.
• Family Purpose Doctrine—driver (nonowner) is
presumed to be carrying out family purpose, making
owner vicariously liable.
• Automobile Consent Statutes—owner is vicariously
liable for negligent acts committed by anyone using
the vehicle with the owner's permission.
• Joint Enterprise Doctrine—owner is vicariously
liable for negligent acts committed by joint venture.

Family Purpose Doctrine

In their struggle to circumvent the nonliability rule for absent owners, some courts created a legal fiction called the *family purpose doctrine*. Under this doctrine the assumption is made that the driver is carrying out a "family purpose," making the family head, typically the most financially responsible person in the family, vicariously liable. This doctrine is maintained even though, typically, the driver is using the vehicle on his or her own behalf. So long as the driver is a member of the family's household and has permission to use the car, the head of the family is vicariously liable for the driver's negligent acts.

The family purpose doctrine is in effect in less than half the states today and is complicated by a host of exceptions. It arises most often in cases in which a minor is relegated to driving a particular vehicle. Typically the parents provide only as much insurance on a vehicle driven by a minor as mandated by law, but provide more extensive coverage on the vehicles they themselves drive. Anyone injured by the minor will find little compensation in the minor's coverage and will often be motivated to turn to the parents for relief.

If the plaintiff can meet the requirements of the family purpose doctrine, she can recover from the parents instead of the minor.

Automobile Consent Statutes

Dissatisfaction with the rule of nonliability of bailors led several state legislatures to adopt *automobile consent statutes*. These statutes make the owner vicariously liable for negligent acts committed by anyone using the car with the owner's permission. If the borrower (bailee) of the car exceeds the scope of the owner's consent, the owner (bailor) is generally not vi-cariously liable unless the deviation is a relatively minor one. If the bailee in turn lends the car to a third person, the courts are divided in terms of the owner's liability. In one case a rental agency explicitly forbade customers from allowing anyone else to drive the car. The court found that the agency was deemed to have impliedly given consent and held the agency liable when its customer allowed a third person to drive who subsequently caused a collision (*Shuck v. Means,* 226 N.W.2d 285 (Minn. 1974)). Not all courts agree with this case, however, and such courts are less likely to find liability when the bailee is not in the vehicle at the time of the accident.

The *omnibus clause* in most automobile liability insurance policies has substantially reduced the need for automobile consent statutes. Such clauses extend insurance coverage to members of the insured's household and to any person using the automobile with the insured's permission as long as the use falls within the scope of the permission given. Consequently, plaintiffs have no incentive to find liability on the part of the owner, at least up to the policy limits.

Joint Enterprises

Another court-created doctrine designed to make the owner of an automobile vicariously liable is the joint enterprise doctrine (see Figure 15-5). A **joint enterprise** consists of four elements:
1. An express or implied agreement among members of a group.

FIGURE 15-5 Joint Enterprise

GENERAL RULE:
• All joint venturers are vicariously liable for the negligent acts of other joint venturers.

ELEMENTS OF JOINT ENTERPRISE
• Express or implied agreement.
• Common purpose or goal.
• Common pecuniary interest.
• Equal right to control direction of enterprise.

---

2. A common purpose or goal to be carried out by the group.

3. A common pecuniary interest in the purpose or goal.

4. An equal right of each member to control the direction of the enterprise.

Restatement (Second) of Torts § 491, cmt. c.

A social trip is not a joint enterprise because it involves no sharing of a pecuniary interest. The mere sharing of expenses is not enough by itself to establish a pecuniary interest. Furthermore, the courts frequently find that a passenger on a social trip has no right of control over the driver. For this doctrine to be applicable, each of the joint venturers must have some say in how the car is to be driven. Each person need not have a right to arbitrarily steer the car at any time, but each must have an equal say in what route will be followed, how fast the car will travel, and so on. Two partners in a law firm, for example, who carpool together would be considered members of a joint enterprise.

Once the joint enterprise requirements are met, each of the joint venturers is vicariously liable for the negligence of the others. This doctrine almost always arises in the context of automobile cases. Typically the plaintiff is a passenger in another car and wishes to recover against a passenger (usually the "deep pocket") in the joint venturer's vehicle. By imputing the negligence of the driver to the passenger, the plaintiff is then allowed to recover.

IMPUTED CONTRIBUTORY NEGLIGENCE

Suppose the driver of an automobile and a truck driver for Company X negligently collide with each other. Should the truck driver's negligence be imputed to—that is, charged against or attributed to—Company X, making Company X contributorily negligent and thus barring it from suing the automobile driver, who was also negligent? Under traditional common law, the answer to that question was yes. The negligence of a driver was imputed to the passengers. Because of the contributory negligence imputed to him, an injured passenger could not sue the other driver. Similarly, a few courts have actually used the **imputation of negligence** to preclude a passenger from suing the driver of the vehicle in which he was riding when the driver and passenger are joint venturers. The driver's negligence is imputed to the passenger, who is then considered contributorily negligent and thus barred from recovering from the driver.

Under the modern rule, however, contributory negligence is imputed only if the relationship is such that the plaintiff would be vicariously liable if he or she were a defendant (Restatement (Second) of Torts § 485). In the earlier example of the passenger wanting to sue the driver of the vehicle with which he collided, the passenger would not be vicariously liable for the negligence of the driver of the vehicle in which he was a passenger. Therefore, no negligence would be imputed to the passenger and he could recover for his injuries (see Figure 15-6).

The rationale for not imputing a driver's negligence to a passenger is that a passenger basically has no control over the acts of the driver of the vehicle in which he or she is riding. The passenger should not, therefore, be saddled with responsibility for the driver's negligence. In other words, contributory negligence should not be imputed unless negligence can also be imputed.

In the case of the truck driver, because the employer (Company X) would be vicariously liable for the truck driver's acts, the truck driver's negligence would be

FIGURE 15-6 Imputation of Negligence

The rule regarding the imputation of negligence is in general disfavor today. In most states the negligence of one spouse is not imputed to the other (except in some community property states where recovered damages are treated as community property), nor are parents or children barred from recovery because of the negligence of the other. Under the modern rule the contributory negligence of a bailee is generally not imputed to the bailor, even when the bailor would be liable as a defendant pursuant to an automobile consent statute.

In derivative claims, such as wrongful death actions and loss of consortium claims, the contributory negligence of the injured party is imputed to the plaintiff. Because the plaintiff's claim is derived from and dependent on another person's injury, the imputed negligence doctrine is applicable. Therefore, if a driver is killed in a collision and her family sues the other driver in a wrongful death action, any negligence on the part of the decedent will be imputed to the family.

PARENTAL LIABILITY

Some states, in an effort to curb juvenile delinquency, have enacted statutes that hold parents liable for the tortious acts of their children. These torts can involve either personal injury or property damage, but they must be intentional torts. Most such statutes have damage ceilings, which can be as high as several thousand dollars. A Georgia statute that provided no such ceiling was held void under the due process clause (*Corley v. Lewless,* 182 S.E.2d 766 (Ga. 1971)).

A parent may also be vicariously liable if he or she encourages the commission of a tortious act or accepts benefits from it. Similarly, a parent who negligently entrusts a dangerous object to a child or who fails to protect others from dangerous tendencies of the child will be held liable. In one case the parents of a fifteen-year-old boy were held liable for the injuries suffered by a five-year-old girl he molested while babysitting. The boy's parents were aware of his history of molestation of young girls (*Schurk v. Christensen,* 497 P.2d 937 (Wash. 1972)).

imputed to the employer and the employer would be prevented from suing the other driver. Because the employer bears responsibility for the acts of his employees, imputing the negligence of employees to their employer seems neither illogical nor unfair, according to the prevailing reasoning of the courts. The negligence of the employee is not imputed to the employer, however, if the employer is suing the employee rather than a third party.

PUTTING IT INTO PRACTICE 15.4

1. Steven, who is twenty years old, is involved in a motor vehicle accident. The driver of the other vehicle seeks grounds upon which he can sue Steven's father, because Steven is financially insolvent. The driver discovers the following: Steven paid for the car and liability insurance himself; his father co-signed for the car so that the financing agency would loan Steven the money; the car was registered in the father's name; Steven exercised exclusive control of the car, and his father had driven the car only a couple of times. Do you think the injured driver will be able to recover from Steven's father under the family purpose doctrine?

2. The owner of a vehicle specifically instructs her teenage daughter not to let anyone else drive her vehicle. One day she allows her daughter to drive to a friend's house on an errand but insists that the daughter return immediately after performing the errand. Instead of returning directly home, the daughter picks up some teenage friends and drives to the outskirts of town. One of the girls takes over the wheel and, while driving at high speed, runs into two boys on a bicycle. Is the owner of the vehicle liable for the injuries to the boys if an automobile consent statute is in effect?

3. A group of hikers is crossing a rock slide area when one of the hikers accidentally knocks rocks down to the road below. A driver coming down the roadway is unable to avoid all of the rocks and is forced to drive over one of them, causing damage to his vehicle. The insurer of the company brings suit against the leader of the hikers under a theory of joint enterprise. Do you think the insurer is likely to be successful?

4. Is the negligence of one spouse imputed to the other spouse under the laws of your jurisdiction?

5. Are parents liable for the tortious acts of their children under the laws of your jurisdiction?

SUMMARY

The doctrine of vicarious liability provides that an individual is liable for the tortious acts of another if he or she shares a special relationship with the tortfeasor. Examples of such special relationships are those between employers and employees, employers and independent contractors, parents and children, and parties involved in a joint enterprise. Both the family purpose doctrine and automobile consent statutes involve elements of vicarious liability.

The doctrine of respondeat superior is applicable if an employee is acting "within the scope and furtherance of his employment" but not if an employee goes on a "frolic" or "detour" of his or her own. Even if an employee engages in conduct specifically prohibited by the employer, the employer remains liable as long as the acts are done within the scope and furtherance of the employment. An employer also retains liability if an employee negligently delegates his or her authority or rights to a third party without the employer's authorization and the third party commits a tort.

In general, one who hires an independent contractor is not vicariously liable for the tortious acts of that individual. Exceptions to the nonliability rule for independent contractors exist. An employer who is negligent in dealing with an independent contractor can be found liable, as can an employer who contracts for the performance of an illegal activity. Some duties of care cannot be delegated; thus, in some cases at least, employers will be prevented from evading liability by hiring an independent contractor. Employers will be vicariously liable if they hire independent contractors to carry out activities that involve risks requiring more than ordinary precautions, but they will not be liable if those risks are not recognizable in advance.

Under the majority rule, bailors are not vicariously liable for the acts of bailees unless they negligently entrust control of their property to a person they know or reasonably should know is likely to endanger others. Dissatisfaction with this rule as applied to owners of automobiles led some courts to create the presumption that an owner's mere presence in the car establishes his control over the driving, making him vicariously liable.

In accordance with the court-created family purpose doctrine, a driver is assumed to be carrying out a "family purpose" as long as he or she is a member of the owner's household and has permission to use the car.

Along similar lines, many state legislatures have adopted automobile consent statutes, which make an owner vicariously liable for the negligent acts committed by anyone using the car with the owner's permission unless the bailee exceeds the scope of the owner's consent. The joint enterprise doctrine, also created by the courts, renders the owner of an automobile vicariously liable for the negligence of the driver if the two are involved in a joint enterprise.

Modern courts generally impute contributory negligence only if the relationship is such that the plaintiff would be vicariously liable if he were a defendant. Under this rule an employee's negligence is imputed to the employer, which prevents the employer from suing any other third party who is negligent as well.

PRACTICE POINTERS

One of the easiest ways to gain information about an employer's relationship to a worker is through the use of interrogatories. In comparison to depositions, interrogatories are relatively inexpensive to prepare. They do not, however, provide the same type of information that depositions do.

Depositions give attorneys an opportunity to see how an individual reacts to pressure and allows them, in general, to assess the individual's probable performance on the witness stand. Additionally, depositions allow attorneys to follow up immediately on questions and to pursue a line of questioning aggressively without giving the individual an opportunity to collect his or her thoughts. Although depositions are typically a more helpful discovery device, their expense precludes extensive use. Therefore, law firms spend considerable time preparing and answering interrogatories.

Interrogatories give more insight into the attorney's thoughts than to the client's. This is because attorneys assist clients in responding to interrogatories and, in some cases, actually prepare the answers for the client's signature. Generally, attorneys strive to avoid answering any questions they do not absolutely have to and they try to reveal no more information than is ethically required.

Because attorneys often delegate the task of drafting interrogatories to their legal assistants, you should become familiar with this process. Interrogatories should be as specific and narrow as possible. General questions promote general answers. If you want to know how the plaintiff was injured, do not ask broad questions such as "How did the accident occur?" Design questions that call for specific information. Divide the accident into relatively short time sequences and ask questions pertaining to each sequence. Ask, for

Continued on next page

■   PRACTICE POINTERS—Continued   □

example, what the defendant was doing immediately preceding the accident, which direction he was headed in, what time of day it was, what the lighting conditions were, what intersection the accident occurred at, when the defendant first observed the plaintiff, and so on.

Avoid asking questions that can be truthfully answered with "yes" or "no" unless you intend to follow up with detail-seeking questions. Include specific requests for names, addresses, and titles of witnesses. Ask who the other side intends to call as witnesses and what their anticipated testimony will be. Also ask about the documentation and exhibits opposing counsel intends to use at trial.

Phrase questions carefully to prevent opposing counsel from having an excuse for evading any question. Questions that violate any privileges (such as the privilege against self-incrimination, the attorney-client privilege, or the attorney work-product rule) should be avoided, as should questions that are irrelevant or overly burdensome for opposing counsel to respond to.

When formulating questions it is often helpful to mentally walk through the chain of events that led up to the plaintiff's injury and that ultimately culminated in the plaintiff's seeking legal assistance. The sequence of your questions should follow that same chronological order. Imagine that you are photographing the scene as it unfolds and that now, as you ask your questions, you have slowed down the camera speed so that you can see one frame at a time. Try to ask at least one question for each frame of action. Even when this proves impractical, this frame-by-frame approach will encourage you to ask extremely narrow questions.

When you review your questions, check to see that they are straightforward and concise. Confusing or convoluted questions often beget confusing, convoluted answers. Simplicity and precision are the key to effective interrogatories.

SAMPLE INTERROGATORIES

1. How long has Laura Huxley been associated with your company?
2. What was the original purpose of the association?
   (a) Has that purpose changed? If yes, what is the current purpose of her association?
3. Has Laura Huxley ever signed a contract or agreement with your company?
   (a) If so, please attach a copy of any such documents if you will do so without a subpoena.
4. List the specific duties Laura Huxley was assigned when she was first associated with your company.
   (a) Have those duties changed? If yes, specify the duties she is currently assigned.
5. What was Laura Huxley's title when she was first associated with your company?
   (a) What titles has she held since that time?
   (b) What is her current title?
6. How did you first learn that Laura Huxley was or might be available to provide services for your company?
7. Did Laura Huxley in the past, or does she currently, have her own office outside of your company?
8. Did Laura Huxley in the past, or does she currently, advertise her services to others?
9. Did Laura Huxley in the past, or does she currently, have her own equipment?

Continued on next page

---

10. Do you exercise any control over who Laura Huxley can hire or work with on projects for your company?

11. Is Laura Huxley covered by any insurance policies owned or paid for by your company?

    (a) If so, list each such policy.

■   TORT TEASERS   ☐

1. Review the three hypothetical questions posed at the beginning of this chapter and determine if the attorney in each case would be liable for the acts of his employee (you).

2. At a Christmas office party Defendant (an employee) becomes drunk and while driving home negligently causes the Plaintiff injury. What would you need to know to determine if Defendant was acting within the scope of his employment? *Harris v. Trojan Fireworks Co.,* 120 Cal. App. 3d 157, 174 Cal. Rptr. 452 (1981).

3. Defendant collides with a car driven by Plaintiff as a result of brake failure. Defendant had her brakes overhauled by a mechanic three months prior to the accident. Defendant claims that the mechanic's negligent repair was the cause of the accident. Should Defendant be held liable? *Maloney v. Rath,* 445 P.2d 513 (Cal. 1968).

4. Employee, entrusted with a vehicle by Employer, suffers an epileptic seizure and causes an accident that results in the death of one person. Employer hired Employee six weeks before the accident. Three weeks before the accident Employee suffered dizzy spells and had minor accidents on three separate occasions, two of which were brought to the attention of Employer. Employer arranged to have Employee examined by a physician, who found nothing wrong with Employee. Should Employer be held vicariously liable in a wrongful death action? *Syah v. Johnson,* 55 Cal. Rptr. 741 (Ct. App. 1966).

5. The owner of a vehicle brings his car to a car wash. It is attached to a tow line and towed without its operator through the car wash. When it emerges from the wash it rolls down an incline and strikes Plaintiff's automobile. Is the car wash liable for the damages to Plaintiff's car?

Assume that the motor vehicle code of that state provides that the negligence of one who uses or operates a vehicle with the owner's express or implied permission is imputed to the owner of the vehicle. In accordance with this statute, should the vehicle owner be held liable for the property damage to Plaintiff's vehicle? *Allcity Insurance Co. v. Old Greenwich Delicatessen,* 349 N.Y.S.2d 240 (Civ. Ct. 1973).

6. Defendant driver collides with a school bus while acting as a chauffeur for the owner of the vehicle he is driving. Defendant is driving with the owner's permission for the purpose of keeping the car running in good shape. If Defendant was contributorily negligent, can the owner sue the driver and owner of the school bus for the damages sustained by his vehicle? Can the two passengers in the vehicle at the time of the accident recover for their injuries? Can the driver's wife recover for her injuries (assume this is a community property state)? *Muhammad v. United States,* 366 F.2d 298 (9th Cir.), *cert. denied,* 386 U.S. 959 (1966).

KEY TERMS

Bailee
One who is temporarily entrusted with the custody of goods.

Bailor
One who entrusts his or her goods to the temporary custody of another.

Imputed negligence
Negligence that is charged or attributed to another.

Independent contractor
Someone hired to do a job who works at his own pace, in his own way, under his own supervision.

Joint enterprise
Two or more persons who agree to a common goal or purpose, who share a common pecuniary interest, and who have an equal right to control the direction of the enterprise.

Respondeat superior
Doctrine establishing the vicarious liability of employers for the acts of their employees.

Vicarious liability
Liability for the tortious acts of another.

CHAPTER

16

Joint Liability

CHAPTER TOPICS

Joint and Several Liability
Satisfaction
Contribution
Release
"Mary Carter" or "Gallagher" Agreements
Indemnification

CHAPTER OBJECTIVES

In this chapter you will learn to:
- Identify situations in which tortfeasors are jointly and severally liable for their acts
- Apply the concepts of contribution, satisfaction, and indemnification
- Distinguish between releases and covenants not to sue
- Recognize the problems associated with releases in light of contribution

You and a friend go out West for a week's vacation. While there you decide to take in the local scene by going on a trail ride through the desert. The ostentatious resort where you are staying sponsors these rides, which are designed for "dudes" such as yourself. It is advertised as a peaceful, scenic ride that allows you to enjoy the panoramic vistas of the desert. When you arrive at the stable, you tell the trail hands, Tex and Rex, of your ignorance about horses. Tex and Rex, engaging in a little cowboy humor, put you on Molly, a mare noted for her impulsive urges to return to her stablemates without giving any notice to her rider. Unfortunately, Molly succumbs to this urge while you are a passenger. She dumps you unceremoniously on the rocky ground, never demonstrating the least bit of remorse as she gallops back to the stable.

You suffer several broken bones and a concussion as a result of this little adventure and decide to sue Tex and Rex, the stable that employed them, and the resort that promoted the trail ride. Assuming you are able to prove liability on behalf of all the defendants, can you elect to recover your damages only from the resort, even though Tex and Rex were primarily responsible for your injuries? Can the resort then turn around and seek reimbursement from the stable for its portion of the damages? If the stable is held liable only because the negligence of Tex and Rex is imputed to it, can the stable seek reimbursement from Tex and Rex? If Tex comes to you and says that the whole scheme was Rex's idea, can you agree to absolve Tex from all liability in exchange for securing his testimony against Rex? See if you can answer these questions after reading this chapter.

JOINT AND SEVERAL LIABILITY

Two or more persons who act in concert to produce a negligent or intentional tort are called **joint tortfeasors.** A joint tortfeasor is *jointly and severally liable,* in that he or she is totally liable for the entire loss suffered by the plaintiff if that loss is indivisible. A loss that cannot be apportioned among the defendants is considered indivisible. The rule of joint liability also applies to **concurrent tortfeasors,** those whose independent acts concur (combine) to cause the plaintiff's injury. Notice that joint tortfeasors act together whereas concurrent tortfeasors act independently, but their combined acts cause the plaintiff's injuries.

Under the rule of **joint and several liability,** if a harm is indivisible and no rational apportionment is possible, each defendant can be held responsible for the entire harm or any designated portion of the harm (see Figure 16-1). Although a plaintiff may recover from one or all of the joint tortfeasors, he or she may recover only once for the total damages. As a result of this rule, one defendant can be held responsible for payment of all damages even though his or her contribution to the plaintiff's injuries was relatively minor. Therefore, if the plaintiff suffered damages in the amount of $10,000 and five defendants acted together to cause the injuries, the plaintiff could recover $2,000 from each defendant, $10,000 from one defendant, or $1,000 from four of the defendants and $6,000 from one of the defendants, and so on.

If the plaintiff dies as a result of the independent or concerted acts of the defendants, each defendant will be held liable for the plaintiff's death because death is not apportionable. Similarly, if the plaintiff's property is destroyed, the harm is considered indivisible and nonapportionable.

Even if one of the defendants directly causes the plaintiff's injuries, all the defendants will be held liable if a court concludes that they acted in concert. Suppose two young men are drag-racing down a public street and one of them collides with the plaintiff's car. Both will be held liable even though only one of them actually came in contact with the car. The reasoning is that the tortious conduct of one encouraged the tortious behavior of the other and the combination led to the harm caused. *See, e.g., Bierczynski v. Rogers,* 234 A.2d 218 (Del. 1968).

Harm That Cannot Be Apportioned

The rule of joint and several liability does not apply if the harm can be apportioned. In other words, if 60

FIGURE 16-1 Joint and Several Liability

JOINT LIABILITY	SATISFACTION	CONTRIBUTION
Each torfeasor is liable for entire loss if loss is indivisible.	Plaintiff is entitled to only one satisfaction (payment) of judgment.	A defendant who pays more than his or her pro rata share of damages is entitled to contribution (partial reimbursement) from other defendants.

	RELEASE	INDEMNIFICATION	
	A plaintiff who agrees to release a defendant absolves that defendant of all liability.	A tortfeasor who agrees to indemnify another tortfeasor accepts all financial responsibility on behalf of that tortfeasor.	

percent of the harm was caused by defendant A and the remainder by defendants B and C, defendant A will be responsible for 60 percent of the damages and defendants B and C will be responsible for the other 40 percent. As discussed in Chapter 8 on damages, if the harm can be apportioned but can be done so only with great difficulty, the burden of allocating harm will shift to the defendants. If the defendants are unable to satisfactorily prove who was responsible for each percentage of the damages, all the defendants will be held jointly and severally liable.

Status of Joint and Several Liability

Joint and several liability has been abolished in some states, primarily because of the concern that the doctrine is used to go after the "deep pocket" defendant, who may actually be responsible for only a minimal portion of the harm. A corporation, for example, whose negligence contributed to only 10 percent of the plaintiff's harm may be held totally responsible for the plaintiff's damages under the rule of joint and several liability simply because the more blameworthy defendant is penniless.

Pared to its essentials, the question of whether to retain joint and several liability is a matter of social policy—where society wants to assign the burden when a liable party cannot pay damages. Without joint and several liability, the injured plaintiff bears the loss. Although society pays less, some plaintiffs will not be fully compensated. If joint and several liability is in effect, the loss is assigned to other liable defendants, who routinely pass on their added costs to society as a whole.

Many criticisms of joint and several liability center on the risks and costs it forces on defendants. Critics maintain that defendants should not be required to shoulder the burden for harm caused by others. Others argue that joint and several liability hurts industry because even if a business can pass on its tort-related costs to society as a whole through higher prices, those higher prices hurt the business. Using business to provide "insurance" only encourages plaintiffs to find wealthy business defendants to sue, resulting in a tort system that is no longer grounded in moral obligation and that serves up defendants as scapegoats.

One well-publicized case that illustrates the policy questions posed by the doctrine of joint and several liability involves a sympathetic plaintiff and a nominally negligent defendant. In this case a husband and wife, Gene and Cynthia Ellwood, and Cynthia's four children from a previous marriage were crowded inside a van Gene was driving. Gene failed to notice a stop sign as he headed into a busy intersection at forty miles per hour, and went directly into the path of a school bus loaded with a soccer team. The officer at the scene said there was nothing the bus driver could have done to avoid the accident. The impact killed Cynthia's ten-year-old son and left Cynthia in a coma from which the doctors said she would never recover. She will require constant care in a nursing home as long as she lives, at a total cost of $1 million or more.

Gene was insured for $100,000; beyond that he had few if any assets. His insurance company paid immediately, but the $100,000 barely covered the medical bills for the first month after the crash.

The bus driver admitted during a deposition that she never saw the Ellwood car approaching the intersection. The side road on which the Ellwoods were traveling joined the highway at a slant from the bus driver's left. Nothing blocked vision in the area between the roads. Based on this testimony the attorney representing the bus company estimated the bus driver's negligence at under 10 percent. The attorney representing Cynthia estimated the worth of the case as somewhere between $4 and $5 million.

Fifteen months after the accident, and just days before trial was to begin, the insurance carrier paid $1.9 million on its $2 million policy and the case was dismissed. The attorney for the insurance carrier says he settled out of court because "we just couldn't risk going to trial" and facing responsibility under joint and several liability for a verdict greater than $2 million.

The ultimate question in this case was "Who should pay?" If the bus company's insurance had not provided $2 million for Cynthia's expenses, she would have had no one to take care of her except Social Security. Joint and several liability thus tapped a minimally negligent defendant to provide a safety net for Cynthia. However, because of this doctrine a nominally responsible defendant was forced to pay large damages.

This case was the topic of heated debate and during legislative hearings was used to illustrate the abuses countenanced by a doctrine that most jurisdictions have since abolished or modified. Some states, for example, limit the liability of tortfeasors whose contribution to the plaintiff's damages falls below a certain percentage; such tortfeasors are liable only for their equitable share of the damages. For a more in-depth discussion of joint and several liability as it relates to the broader topic of tort reform, see Chapter 17.

CASE

Hall v. E.I. DuPont de Nemours & Co.
345 F. Supp. 353 (E.D.N.Y. 1971)

MEMORANDUM AND ORDER
WEINSTEIN, District Judge.

These two cases arise out of eighteen separate accidents scattered across the nation in which children were injured by blasting caps. Damages are sought from manufacturers and their trade association, the Institute of Makers of Explosives (I.M.E.). The basic allegation is that the practice of the explosives industry during the 1950's—continuing until 1965—of not placing any warning upon individual blasting caps and of failing to take other safety measures created an unreasonable risk of harm resulting in plaintiffs' injuries.

In most instances the manufacturer of the cap is unknown. The question posed is whether a group of manufacturers and their trade association, comprising virtually the entire blasting cap industry of the United States, can be held jointly liable for injuries caused by their product. Our answer is that there are circumstances, illustrated by this litigation, in which an entire industry may be liable for harm caused by its operations.

While the cases are closely linked in their litigation history and underlying legal theory, they differ in several crucial respects. *See Hall v. E.I. DuPont de Nemours & Co.,* 312 F. Supp. 358 (E.D.N.Y. 1970) for an earlier phase of the litigation. In *Chance,* the name of the manufacturer who actually produced the cap causing a particular injury is apparently unknown. In *Hall* it is, plaintiffs allege, known. We turn to *Chance* first since it presents the more difficult legal problems.

I. THE *CHANCE* CASE
A. Facts and Proceedings

Thirteen children were allegedly injured by blasting caps in twelve unrelated accidents between 1955 and 1959. The injuries occurred in the states of Alabama, California, Maryland, Montana, Nevada, North Carolina, Tennessee, Texas, Washington and West Virginia. Plaintiffs are citizens of the states in which their injuries occurred. They are now claiming damages against six manufacturers of blasting caps and the I.M.E. on the grounds of negligence, common law conspiracy, assault, and strict liability in tort. In addition, two parents sue for medical expenses. Federal jurisdiction is based on diversity of citizenship. 28 U.S.C. § 1332.

While the plaintiffs' injuries occurred at widely varied times and places, the complaint alleges certain features common to them all. Each plaintiff, according to the complaint, "came into possession" of a dynamite blasting cap which was not labeled or marked with a warning of danger, and which could be easily detonated by a child. In each instance an injurious explosion occurred.

The complaint does not identify a particular manufacturer of the cap which caused a particular injury. It alleges that each cap in question was designed and manufactured jointly or severally by the six corporate defendants or by other unnamed manufacturers, and by their trade association, the I.M.E.

Plaintiffs' central contention is that injuries were caused by the defendants' failure to place a warning on the blasting caps, and to manufacture caps which would have been less easily detonated. This failure, according to the plaintiffs, was not the result of defendants' ignorance of the dangerousness of their product to children. The complaint states that the defendants had actual knowledge that children were frequently injured by blasting caps, and, through the trade association, kept statistics and other information regarding these accidents. Recognizing the dangerousness of their product to children, the defendants, through the trade association, used various means—such as placards and printed notices—to warn users of the caps and the general public. These measures were allegedly inadequate in light of the known risks of injury. Moreover, defendants are said to have jointly explicitly considered the possibility of labeling the caps, to have rejected this possibility, and to have engaged in lobbying activities against legislation which would have required such labeling. The long-standing industry practice of not placing a warning message on individual blasting caps was, it is urged, the result of a conscious agreement among the defendants, in the light of known dangers, with regard to this aspect of their product.

* * *

B. Issues Presented
* * *
(1) The Elements of Joint Liability

Joint liability has historically been imposed in four distinguishable kinds of situations:

(1) the actors knowingly join in the performance of the tortious act or acts; (2) the actors fail to perform a common duty owed to the plaintiff; (3) there is a special relationship between the parties (e.g., master and servant or joint entrepreneurs); (4) although there is no concerted action nevertheless the independent acts of several actors concur to produce indivisible harmful consequences . . .

These categories reflect three overlapping but distinguishable problems with which the law of joint liability has been concerned. The first is the problem of joint or group control of risk: the need to deter hazardous behavior by groups or multiple defendants as well as by individuals. The second is the problem of enterprise liability: the policy of assigning the foreseeable costs of an activity to those in the most strategic position to reduce them. The third is the problem of fairness with respect to burden of proof: the desire to avoid denying recovery to an innocent injured plaintiff because proof of causation may be within defendants' control or entirely unavailable. The complaint and defendants' motion to dismiss raise all three problems for consideration. [The discussion of causation has been omitted here.]

(2) Joint Control of Risk

The problem of joint control of risk was early posed in a case of group assault. In imposing joint liability, [one] court reasoned that "[with] all coming to do an unlawful act, and of one party, the act of one is the act of all" . . . . Even in its earliest form the doctrine of joint liability for concerted action contained all the elements necessary for its future development: (1) causing harm (2) by cooperative or concerted activities (3) which violated a legal standard of care.

American courts have imposed joint liability for concerted action in cases involving a complex interaction of the three elements of the doctrine. "Cooperation" or "concert" has been found in various business and property relationships, group activities such as automobile racing, cooperative efforts in medical care or railroad work, and concurrent water pollution. "Express agreement is not necessary; all that is required is that there shall be a common design or understanding." . . .

The standard of care to which defendants have been jointly held has ranged from assault and reckless driving to negligence in building maintenance, brush burning, water pollution, and manufacture of explosives . . . .

These diverse cases impose joint liability on groups whose actions create unreasonable hazards of risks of harm, even though only one member of the group may have been the "direct" or physical cause of the injury. Where courts perceive a clear joint control of risk—typically the racing and assault cases, as well as those involving common duties or joint enterprise—the issue of who "caused" the injury is distinctly secondary to the fact that the group engaged in joint hazardous conduct.

This rationale was recognized in the nineteenth century. In a case involving a horse race in a crowded street, a New York court noted that the collision was "not willful or intentional on the part of the defendants," but it upheld a jury determination that the negligent racing of the defendants was the joint cause of injury. Imposing liability on the defendant not involved in the actual collision, the court stated that "these defendants were acting together and in concert in this race. It was the race that created the condition that resulted in the accident." . . . By participating in a joint creation of negligent risk, both defendants were held liable for the consequences . . . . Analogous language focusing on the joint creation of risk can be found in the "common duty" cases, as when several defendants neglect to maintain a party wall . . . .

Joint control of risk can also arise through business relations or joint enterprise. . . . The opinions frequently refer to the defendants' violations of a common duty of care not only in terms of joint control of risk, but also as concurrent causes which combine to produce injury . . . .

Defendants argue that their participation in the I.M.E. safety program, and their cooperative or parallel activities regarding the safety features of blasting caps do not give them joint control over the risks of injury for pur-

poses of tort liability. Joint control of risk and consequent joint responsibility arises, in their view, only when manufacturers enter into a conspiracy to commit intentional harm, or into a partnership or joint venture. The key to a joint venture, they assert, is an agreement to share profits and to pursue a limited number of business objectives over a short period of time. Since the defendants' membership in their trade association involves neither profit-sharing nor a limited time-span, they contend that no joint responsibility arises from the association and its members' activities.

The problem with this argument is that the elements of joint control of risk do not coincide with those in the formal doctrine of joint venture.

* * *

[A] joint venture exists when there is "an agreement between the parties under which they have . . . a joint interest, in a common business undertaking, and understanding as to the sharing of profits and losses, and a right of joint control."

* * *

The lesson is clear that joint control of risk can exist among actors who are not bound in a profit-sharing joint venture. This point is thoroughly confirmed by cases imposing joint liability on "joint enterprises," which are distinguished from "joint ventures" as being "non profit undertaking[s] for the mutual benefit or pleasure of the parties" . . . and on which joint liability is imposed because of the parties' effective joint control of the risk.

Joint control may be shown in one of three ways. First, plaintiffs can prove the existence of an explicit agreement and joint action among the defendants with regard to warnings and other safety features—the classic "concert of action." Second, plaintiffs can submit evidence of defendants' parallel behavior sufficient to support an inference of tacit agreement or cooperation. Such cooperation has the same effects as overt joint action, and is subject to joint liability for the same reasons . . . .

Third, plaintiffs can submit evidence that defendants, acting independently, adhered to an industry-wide standard or custom with regard to the safety features of blasting caps. Regardless of whether such evidence is sufficient to support an inference of tacit agreement, it is still relevant to the question of joint control of risk. The dynamics of market competition frequently result in explicit or implicit safety standards, codes, and practices which are widely adhered to in an entire industry . . . . Where such standards or practices exist, the industry operates as a collective unit in the double sense of stabilizing the production costs of safety features and in establishing an industry-wide custom which influences, but does not conclusively determine, the applicable standard of care . . . . As our decision in *Hall* below indicates, the existence of industry-wide standards or practices alone will not support, in all circumstances, the imposition of joint liability. But where, as here . . ., individual defendant-manufacturers cannot be identified, the existence of industry-wide standards or practices could support a finding of joint control of risk and a shift of the burden of proving causation to the defendants . . . .

In view of the allegations of explicit cooperation among members of the industry, it is apparent that plaintiffs have chosen the fist of the above three alternative theories. We have set forth the other two lines of possible proof only to suggest the a fortiori position presented in the instant case.

There is thus no support for defendants' argument that to establish joint control of risk, plaintiffs must demonstrate that the explosives industry was "rigidly controlled" through the trade association with regard to blasting cap design, manufacture, and labeling, and that the object of such control was some particularly reprehensible breach of duty. The variety of business and property relationships in which joint control of risk has been found demonstrates the flexibility of the doctrine. Liability is not limited to particular formal modes of cooperation, nor to illegal or grossly negligent activities.

Two recent cases provide examples under both strict liability and negligence standards. In *Vandermark v. Ford Motor Co.*, 61 Cal.2d 256, 37 Cal.Rptr. 896, 391 P.2d 168 (1964), . . . [h]olding the retailer strictly liable was . . . justified on the grounds that "in some cases the retailer may be the only member of [the] enterprise reasonably available to the injured plaintiff." . . . . Joint liability "affords maximum protection to the injured plaintiff and works no injustice to the defendants, for they can adjust the costs of such protection between them in the course of their continuing business relationship." . . .

In the *Vandermark* case, the factors considered relevant to the issue of joint liability were (1) the standard of care—itself a function of the foreseeability and gravity of risk and the capacity of avoiding it; (2) the participants' capabilities of promoting the requisite safety in the risk-creating process; (3) the need to protect the consumer, both in terms of ascertaining responsible parties and providing compensation; and (4) the participants' ability to adjust the costs of liability among themselves in a continuing business relationship.

The Fifth Circuit looked to similar considerations in a case involving the question of joint control of risk in the context of res ipsa loquitur. The plaintiff in *Dement v. Olin-Mathieson Chemical Corp.*, 282 F.2d 76 (5th Cir. 1960), had been injured while working with an explosive charge containing three component parts. Evidence indicated that two of the components—the blasting cap and the dynamite—might have caused the accident. One of the defendant-manufacturers argued that the plaintiff was not entitled to the aid of res ipsa, since only one of the components had been under its exclusive control.

This "musical chairs argument" was rejected on the grounds it was not necessary that

> in order for res ipsa to apply one particular force must be severed out, identified and held as a matter of law to be the cause of the premature explosion. The various components were manufactured to be a part of one combination. . . . Even in cases in which there is no combination as there obviously is here, the Texas courts recognize joint liability against actors completely independent and unrelated to each other in circumstances where their conduct has caused indivisible injury which cannot be accurately apportioned and identified by the plaintiff.

Like the Supreme Court of California in *Vandermark,* the Fifth Circuit emphasized the defendant-manufacturers' high duty of care to guard against defects in explosives, the defendants' control over the products at the critical stage when care was needed, the necessity of not imposing impenetrable procedural and burden of proof requirements on injured plaintiffs, and the possibility of cost adjustment among the defendants . . . .

Plaintiffs' allegations in this case raise genuine issues under these criteria. As discussed in detail above, the allegation that defendants had actual knowledge of risks to children and of feasible safety measures provides a basis for finding an applicable duty of care under negligence and strict liability principles. Plaintiffs further allege that the defendant manufacturers obtained this knowledge through a jointly-sponsored trade association; the manufacturers delegated, in effect, at least some functions of safety investigation and design (such as labeling) to an industry-wide entity. Whether defendants collected and shared this knowledge as a group, and made joint or cooperative decisions on the basis of the known risks, are critical issues which require full factual development.

Factors which must be explored to determine both the existence of joint control of risk and appropriate remedies (if any) include the size and composition of the trade association's membership, its announced and actual objectives in the field of safety, its internal procedures of decision-making on this issue, the nature of its information-gathering system with regard to accidents, the safety program and its implementation by the association and member manufacturers, and any other activities by the association and its members (such as legislative lobbying) with regard to safety during the time period in question . . . .

(3) Enterprise Liability

Joint liability has been traditionally imposed on multiple defendants who exercise actual collective control over a particular risk-creating product or activity. In a related but distinguishable fashion, joint or vicarious liability has been imposed on the most strategically placed participants in a risk-creating process, even though injuries are caused "directly" or partially by other participants under their general supervision . . . .

A similar principle of enterprise liability is embedded in the doctrine of respondeat superior—an employer's vicarious liability to third parties for employees' wrongs committed "in the scope of their employment." In the pure vicarious liability case, an employer is not charged himself with violating a standard of care—such as failing to properly supervise the inspection or labeling of a product. Rather, the employer is held liable because, despite reasonable precautions, his employee has violated the applicable standard of care . . . . The employer may be held liable even though the employee's acts (or failure to act) were forbidden or intentionally wrongful . . . .

The rationale for an employer's vicarious liability to third parties has been analyzed as being very close to the enterprise liability basis of workmen's compensation. In both types of cases

[w]e are not . . . looking for the master's fault but rather for risks that may fairly be regarded as typical of or broadly incidental to the enterprise he has undertaken. . . . [O]ne of the purposes for such a quest is to mark out in a broad way the extent of tort liability (as a cost item) that it is fair and expedient to require people to expect when they engage in such an enterprise, so there can be some reasonable basis for calculating this cost. . . . What is reasonably foreseeable in this context, however, is quite a different thing from the foreseeably unreasonable risk of harm that spells negligence. In the first place, we are no longer dealing with specific conduct but with the broad scope of a whole enterprise. Further, we are not looking for that which can and should reasonably be avoided, but with the more or less inevitable toll of a lawful enterprise. The foresight that should impel the prudent man to take precautions is not the same measure as that by which he should perceive the harm likely to flow from his long-run activity in spite of all reasonable precautions on his own part. The proper test here bears far more resemblance to that which limits liability for workmen's compensation than to the test for negligence. The employer should be held to expect risks, to the public also, which arise "out of and in the course of" his employment of labor . . . .

Enterprise liability is also apparent in the long line of cases imposing joint and vicarious liability on owners, employers and manufacturers for breach of "nondelegable duties", or for miscarriage of "inherently dangerous activities" by their contractors, employees, and distributors . . . .

A review of the cases demonstrates that the range of non-delegable duties is very broad; Dean Prosser suggests that the only unifying criterion is "the conclusion of the courts that the responsibility is so important to the community that the employer [—in the broad sense of one who utilizes the services of another—] should not be permitted to transfer it to another." The list of "inherently dangerous activities" is also long, running from classic categories such as the keeping of vicious animals or blasting to any activity "in which there is a high degree of risk in relation to the particular surroundings" and which thus requires definite or special precautions . . . .

This body of precedent, whether couched in the language of non-delegable duty or inherently dangerous activity or both, is addressed essentially to the problem of when it is justifiable for an owner, employer, or manufacturer to rely on the services of another to guard against known or foreseeable risks . . . The factors which must be considered in deciding whether such reliance is justifiable include

the competence and reliability of the person upon whom reliance is placed, his understanding of the situation, the seriousness of the danger and the number of persons likely to be affected, the length of time elapsed, and above all the likelihood that proper care will not be used, and the ease with which the actor himself may take precautions.

In many instances the most strategic point of foresight, precaution and risk distribution may be the individual manufacturer, supplier, or employer. In other situations—typically water or air pollution by multiple emitters—the only feasible method of ascertaining risks, imposing safeguards and spreading costs is through joint liability or other methods of joint risk control . . . . The point is not only that the damage is caused by multiple actors, but that the sole feasible way of anticipating costs or damages and devising practical remedies is to consider the activities of a group. We do not, of course, suggest that private actions are the best way to meet these problems but only that in the absence of preemptive legislation, tort principles will support a remedy. . . .

The allegations in this case suggest that the entire blasting cap industry and its trade association provide the logical locus at which precautions should be taken and liability imposed. It is unlikely that individual manufacturers would collect information about the nation-wide incidence and circumstances of blasting-cap accidents involving children, and it is entirely reasonable that the manufacturers should delegate this function to a jointly-sponsored and jointly-financed association.

In the event that the evidence warrants it, the imposition of joint liability on the trade association and its members should in no way be interpreted as "punishment" for the establishment of industry-wide institutions. Such liability would represent rather the law's traditional function of reviewing the risk and cost decisions inherent in industry-wide safety practices, whether organized or unorganized. . . .

To establish that the explosives industry should be held jointly liable on enterprise liability grounds, plaintiffs, pursuant to their pleading, will have to demonstrate defendants' joint awareness of the risks at issue in this case and their joint capacity to reduce or affect those risks. By noting these requirements we wish to emphasize their special applicability to industries composed of a small number of units. What would be fair and feasible with regard to an industry of five or ten producers might be manifestly unreasonable if applied to a decentralized industry composed of thousands of small producers. . . .

PUTTING IT INTO PRACTICE 16.1

1. How many separate accidents are represented in this case?
2. Who are the defendants? What is the basic allegation against them?
3. How does the case involving Hall differ from that involving Chance?
4. What kinds of joint activities are the defendants alleged to have engaged in?
5. What is the question before the court in relationship to joint liability?
6. What three problems with respect to joint liability does the court examine?
7. What is the defendants' argument regarding joint control? What problem does the court find with this argument?
8. In what three ways does the court indicate that joint control can be shown? Which of these theories did the plaintiffs rely on?
9. Must the plaintiffs prove that the explosives industry was "rigidly controlled" or that the object of the control was some illegal or grossly negligent activity?
10. What factors does the court indicate must be explored to determine if the defendants exerted joint control?

Continued on next page

---

11. What is enterprise liability?
12. What must the plaintiffs show if they are to hold the manufacturers jointly liable on the grounds of enterprise liability? Would these requirements be the same if thousands of producers were involved rather than five or ten?

■   PUTTING IT INTO PRACTICE 16.2   □

1. A psychiatric patient goes to a general practitioner, complaining of certain pains; the patient is hospitalized and rehospitalized. The first physician calls in a psychiatrist, who diagnoses the patient as suffering from chronic anxiety reaction and continues to treat her. After her discharge from the hospital, the psychiatrist prescribes drugs that the patient believes caused her to have an automobile accident. The first physician never sees the patient after she is discharged from the hospital and the psychiatrist treats her until she is involved in the accident.

   The patient alleges that the two physicians are jointly liable, on the grounds that (1) one prescribed an excessive quantity of dangerous drugs and failed to inform her of the risks of driving while taking the drugs and (2) the other failed to inform her that the physician to whom he had referred her was a psychiatrist and gave her insufficient information to enable her to decide whether to accept the recommended treatment. Are the physicians jointly liable if they independently diagnosed and treated the patient?

2. Two pediatricians negligently fail to diagnose phenylketonuria (a rare childhood disease that begins at birth and results in progressive mental retardation) in a timely manner. A jury returns a verdict in favor of the plaintiff for $80,000. Should both of the physicians be jointly and severally liable for the $80,000 if the second physician began treating the plaintiff after the first physician had already initiated treatment?

3. A young woman is injured when the bumper car she is driving on a ride at Disney World is struck by a bumper car driven by her fiancé. At trial the jury apportions 14 percent of the fault to the young woman, 85 percent to her fiancé, and 1 percent to Disney World. The plaintiff does not join the fiancé as a defendant to the action. Can Disney World be held liable for 86 percent of the damages?

4. A university sues a manufacturer, a contractor, an engineer, and a subcontractor for negligently failing to complete a project for football practice fields. Is each of the parties individually and collectively responsible for the damages suffered by the university?

SATISFACTION

If tortfeasors A, B, and C are jointly and severally liable for a $10,000 judgment and the plaintiff recovers the full amount from A, he or she cannot collect anything from B and C. Additional recovery is not allowed because the plaintiff is entitled to only one **satisfaction** (payment) of the claim. Although she can collect from all the tortfeasors, she can collect on her judgment only once.

CONTRIBUTION

Tortfeasor A may, however, be entitled to **contribution** from B and C. In other words, A may turn to B and C for partial reimbursement because he paid more than his pro rata share of the damages. Early American courts denied contribution to intentional tortfeasors and eventually denied it to all joint tortfeasors. That common law rule was severely criticized and has today been changed by statute or judicial decision. Under the majority rule, today contribution is permitted to some extent. Although typically allowed for negligent tortfeasors, contribution is often denied for intentional tortfeasors. The justification underlying contribution is that one tortfeasor should not be saddled with all the damages while others are allowed to escape without any responsibility.

The courts disagree about the division of damages in the context of contribution. In some jurisdictions each defendant is required to pay an equal share of the damages. In those states that have adopted comparative negligence, the damages are generally divided in proportion to each defendant's contribution to the plaintiff's harm. A defendant to whom a jury assigns 25 percent fault but who pays the entire judgment can collect 75 percent of that amount from the other defendants in a comparative negligence state.

Contribution hinges on joint liability. If a defendant can raise a defense, such as immunity, that would bar recovery by the plaintiff, then the other defendants cannot seek contribution from him or her. Similarly, contribution cannot be sought against an employer if a workers' compensation statute prevents the plaintiff employee from suing the employer. (Under workers' compensation statutes, employees can recover from insurance carried by their employers for any work-related injury, regardless of who was at fault. Employees who recover under these statutes are then barred from suing their employers in tort.)

RELEASE

Contribution becomes particularly problematic when a **release,** a document absolving a defendant of all liability, is given to one defendant. Under the common law, a plaintiff had a single, indivisible cause of action against all joint tortfeasors. Therefore, a release of one tortfeasor released all tortfeasors. To avoid the restrictive results of a release, a plaintiff who settled with one defendant would enter into a **covenant not to sue,** in which he or she promised not to sue that particular defendant but continued to hold all other defendants liable.

According to Restatement (Second) of Torts § 885, which reflects the majority rule, all tortfeasors are released if the release is silent regarding their continuing liability. To illustrate this point, suppose the plaintiff is injured by defendant A and seeks medical treatment from defendant B, who aggravates the injury through negligent treatment. If the plaintiff receives payment from defendant A and signs a release that does not mention defendant B, defendant B can later point to the common law rule regarding releases and escape all liability.

A plaintiff may preserve his or her rights against other tortfeasors by specifically including a provision to that effect in the release. A desire to reserve one's right to sue may be proved by external evidence, such as verbal statements. This evidentiary rule was promulgated out of a desire to protect those who enter into such releases without legal advice but who clearly intend to reserve their rights to sue the nonsettling defendants (Restatement (Second) of Torts § 885, cmt. d).

Differences Between a Release and a Covenant Not to Sue

Note the distinction between a release and a covenant not to sue. A plaintiff who enters into a release surrenders her claim; a plaintiff who enters into a covenant not to sue does not surrender her claim but agrees that she will not sue on it. If the plaintiff later reneges on a covenant not to sue and decides to sue, the defendant with whom she entered into the covenant will have a counterclaim for breach of contract.

Plaintiffs should be cautioned against entering into releases prematurely. If a plaintiff's injuries turn out to be more extensive than originally realized, the release may have to be set aside on the grounds of fraud or mistake. Litigation regarding the validity of releases can be avoided by simply refraining from entering into releases until the full extent of the plaintiff's injuries is known.

Problems with Releases in Light of Contribution

Problems arise in the context of contribution when one defendant is granted a release and the other defendants are not (see Figure 16-2). Suppose the plaintiff accepts $2,000 from defendant A and releases him and then sues defendant B and obtains a judgment for $20,000. Can B obtain contribution from A? Under the traditional majority rule the answer was yes. Unfortunately, however, this rule discourages defendants from settling because they know they may be subject to contribution at a later time.

To prevent this problem some courts disallow contribution but reduce the plaintiff's claim against the nonreleased defendant on a pro rata basis. Suppose that, as in the previous example, the plaintiff releases defendant A and is later awarded damages in a jury trial against defendant B for $20,000. The plaintiff will be allowed to recover only $10,000 from defendant B because, by settling with defendant A, she liquidated half of her total right to recovery. Defendant B, however, would not be allowed to obtain contribution from defendant A. This rule is also problematic in that it discourages plaintiffs from settling as much as the previous rule discouraged defendants from settling.

To encourage settlement, therefore, some courts relieve the settling defendant from contribution liability altogether. Both the plaintiff and the settling defendant must reach settlement in "good faith." They must also show they did not act in collusion with each other. The issue of good faith often ends up being litigated under this approach.

FIGURE 16-2 Three Approaches to the Problem of Releases in the Context of Contribution

SOLUTION A	SOLUTION B	SOLUTION C
Nonreleased defendant can seek contribution from released defendant.	Nonreleased defendant <u>cannot</u> seek contribution, but plaintiff's claim against nonreleased defendant is reduced.	Nonreleased defendant <u>cannot</u> seek contribution and plaintiff's claim is unaffected by release, as long as parties negotiate in good faith.
Problem Associated with Solution A: Discourages defendants from settling.	**Problem Associated with Solution B:** Discourages plaintiffs from settling.	**Problem Associated with Solution C:** Leads to litigation regarding issue of good faith.

CASE

Panasuk v. Seaton
277 F. Supp. 979 (D. Mont. 1968)

JAMESON, Chief Judge.

Plaintiff, Paul Panasuk, brought this action for personal injuries sustained while riding as a passenger in an automobile driven by his brother George when it collided with a truck-trailer driven by the defendant Arlynn Seaton and owned by the defendant Arden Leas. Defendants have filed an answer and also a third-party complaint against George Panasuk as third-party defendant and Leas has filed a cross-claim for damages to his truck and cargo.[2] Seaton and Leas, as third-party plaintiffs, pray, in the event a verdict is recovered against them by plaintiff, that the third-party defendant, George Panasuk, "be held primarily liable" and that they have "judgment over and against the third-party defendant, George Panasuk, for the amount recovered by plaintiff."

The third-party defendant, George Panasuk, has filed a motion to strike and dismiss the amended third-party complaint of Seaton and Leas and to dismiss the cross-claim of Leas. . . .

Third-party defendant first contends that the claim of third-party plaintiffs in effect seeks contribution between joint tortfeasors, and that this may not be done under the law of Montana. Third-party plaintiffs contend (1) that the law of Montana does not prohibit application of the doctrine of "contribution;" and (2) if the amended complaint does not state a claim for relief for "contribution," it does state a claim for relief in "indemnity."

The rule is well settled in Montana that, "if the concurrent negligence of two or more persons causes an injury to a third person, they are jointly and severally liable, and the injured person may sue them jointly or severally, and recover against one or all."[3] . . . The Montana court also recognized the general rule that "one of the several wrongdoers cannot recover against another wrongdoer although he may have been compelled to pay all the damages for the wrong done."

The "conflicting views" regarding the right of contribution as between joint tortfeasors were well-summarized in an annotation in 60 A.L.R.2d 1368, as follows:

> "A relatively large majority of jurisdictions in which the contribution rights of negligent joint tortfeasors are not controlled by statute hold that the fact that joint tortfeasors' injury-causing conduct was negligent, rather than wilful or intentional, furnishes no basis for freeing them of the burden of the general rule that there can be no contribution among joint tortfeasors." . . .
>
> "The minority—and, it seems, growing—view on the question presently under consideration is this: the rule which bars contribution among joint tortfeasors is not appropriately applied to joint tortfeasors guilty of nothing more than negligence; hence, there is a common-law right of contribution as between such joint tortfeasors." . . .

Third-party plaintiffs rely upon cases from jurisdictions permitting contribution among joint tortfeasors, . . . which clearly represent the minority view.

It may be, as third-party plaintiffs contend, that Montana has not expressly adopted the majority rule barring contribution among joint tortfeasors, but as noted

---

2. It is alleged in the amended third-party complaint that the third-party defendant operated his car in a grossly negligent and reckless manner, that the accident was caused solely by his negligence, and that if third-party plaintiffs were negligent, their negligence was secondary or passive, whereas the negligence of the third-party defendant was primary and active. In the Leas cross-claim it is alleged that the Panasuk vehicle was operated in a negligent and careless manner. Leas would of course be entitled to recover from third-party defendant upon proof of ordinary negligence proximately causing the accident, in the absence of contributory negligence.

3. It is recognized that plaintiff might recover from the defendants and not from the third-party defendant. As pointed out in brief of third-party plaintiffs, under the Montana Guest Statute (R.C.M.1947 § 32-1113), a guest passenger may not recover unless the damage is caused "directly and proximately by the grossly negligent and reckless operation" of the motor vehicle. We are not concerned here, however, with the question of whether plaintiff may recover from third-party defendant for the latter's gross negligence, but whether third-party plaintiffs may do so under the principles of "contribution" or "indemnity." This question could arise in any action by a third party (whether a guest passenger or not) where one or both of the motorists claimed the other was more culpable by reason of gross negligence and recklessness.

supra, it clearly recognized the rule in *Variety, Inc. v. Hustad Corporation.* There is no reason for this court to assume that the Montana court will now adopt the minority view. It is my conclusion that the amended third-party complaint fails to state a claim for relief on the theory of contribution.

The question then arises as to whether the complaint states a claim for relief under applicable principles of indemnity.

In *Great Northern Railway Company v. United States,* . . . this court recognized the general rule that joint tortfeasors are not entitled to contribution from each other, but permitted recovery on the theory of indemnity since the act was not caused by any act of the plaintiff. The exception to the general rule was stated as follows:

> "Where the parties are not in pari delicto, and an injury results from the act of one party whose negligence is the primary, active and proximate cause of the injury, and another party, who is not negligent or whose negligence is remote, passive and secondary, is nevertheless exposed to liability by the acts of the first party, the first party may be liable to the second party for the full amount of damages incurred by such acts. . . .

Counsel have not cited nor have I found, any case in which indemnity, as distinguished from contribution, has been held applicable in a case involving a collision between two motor vehicles. This situation was considered in an annotation in 88 A.L.R.2d 1356. The annotation first summarizes the general situations in which indemnity may be granted:

> "(1) Where the indemnitee has only an imputed or vicarious liability for damage caused by the indemnitor.
> "(2) Where the indemnitee has incurred tort liability by performing at the direction of and in reliance upon the indemnitor an act not manifestly wrong.
> "(3) Where the indemnitee has incurred liability by reason of his reliance, even though negligent, upon the duty of care which the indemnitor owed as a supplier of goods.
> "(4) Where the indemnitee has incurred liability for failure to correct a hazardous condition which, as between indemnitor and indemnitee, it was the duty of the indemnitor to make safe.
> "The ratio decidendi of cases granting indemnity has frequently been expressed in such general terms as that the indemnitee was not personally at fault (see

(1) above); the parties were not in pari delicto (see (2) above); the negligence of the indemnitee was merely passive as compared to the negligence of the indemnitor which was active (see (3) above); and the liability of the indemnitee was only secondary as compared to the liability of the indemnitor, which was primary (see (4) above)."

With specific reference to whether a tortfeasor guilty of ordinary negligence may recover indemnity from a joint tortfeasor guilty of gross negligence, the annotation continues:

> "* * * Hence, it would seem that such general propositions as have been adduced in support of particular results in cases allowing indemnity as an exception to the general rule will not serve as adequate standards to determine whether or not a tortfeasor guilty of ordinary negligence may recover indemnity against a tortfeasor guilty of gross negligence, wilful or wanton misconduct, or intentional wrongdoing.
> "* * *
> "The one case found which deals directly with the problem under consideration holds that indemnity is not available as respects the persons and situations postulated." . . .
> "There are a number of cases which, without expressly referring to the distinction between ordinary negligence, on the one hand, and the wilful or wanton misconduct or gross negligence, on the other, use language indicating the court's belief that the mere fact that one of two or more persons whose misconduct contributed to the injury of a third person was guilty of more morally reprehensible conduct or of greater negligence than another is insufficient to warrant the granting of indemnity in favor of the latter." . . .

Jacobs v. General Acc. F. & L. Assur. Corp., . . . suggests several cogent reasons why the rule of indemnity should not be applied in such cases, including (1) "it seems undesirable * * * in automobile accident situations, to extend the effect of the distinction between gross and simple negligence beyond those effects already recognized;" and (2) any "rule allowing indemnity in this situation would tend to increase or prolong automobile personal injury litigation because of the advantage one defendant would hope to gain by showing that another defendant was guilty of gross negligence."

In *Builders Supply Co. v. McCabe,* a third party obtained a judgment against Builders Supply Co.

Builders sought contribution or indemnity from McCabe. In reversing a judgment in favor of Builders, the Pennsylvania Supreme Court said in part:

> The right of indemnity rests upon a difference between the primary and the secondary liability of two persons each of whom is made responsible by the law to an injured party.
>
> "It is right which enures to a person who, without active fault on his own part, has been compelled, by reason of some legal obligation, to pay damages occasioned by the initial negligence of another, and for which he himself is only secondarily liable.
>
> "The difference between primary and secondary liability is not based on a difference in degrees of negligence or on any doctrine of comparative negligence,—a doctrine which, indeed, is not recognized by the common law.
>
> It depends on a difference in the character or kind of the wrongs which cause the injury and in the nature of the legal obligation owed by each of the wrongdoers to the injured person. * * * *"

After citing examples, the court continued:

> "Without multiplying instances, it is clear that the right of a person vicariously or secondarily liable for a tort to recover from one primarily liable has been universally recognized. But the important point to be noted in all the cases is that secondary as distinguished from primary liability rests upon a fault that is imputed or constructive only, being based on some legal relation between the parties, or arising from some positive rule of common or statutory law or because of a failure to discover or correct a defect or remedy a dangerous condition caused by the act of the one primarily responsible."

Third party plaintiffs rely strongly on *United Airlines, Inc. v. Wiener, . . .* involving 31 cases arising out of a midair collision between a commercial airliner owned by United and an Air Force jet fighter. All of the actions were brought under the Nevada Wrongful Death Statute. Nevada has no statutes relating to contribution or indemnity. In considering whether United was entitled to indemnity, the court recognized that the "common law principles of non-contractual indemnity and contribution among persons jointly liable in tort to a third party are not susceptible of definite and precise articulation." The court analyzed the various bases of liability for indem-

nity, citing the annotation in 88 A.L.R.2d quoted supra. In concluding that United was entitled to indemnity in the nongovernment employee cases, the court said in pertinent part:

> "United's duty to appellees' decedents was to exercise the highest degree of care; the government's duty was to exercise ordinary care. The government's negligent acts occurred literally from the start to the finish of this tragic incident. The cumulative effect of these negligent acts was to dispatch United's flight 736 and the government's high-speed jet training mission, conducted by a student pilot who was virtually blindfolded and an instructor whose cockpit preoccupations were greater than ordinarily demanded of pilots flying under VFR conditions and responsibilities, into the same area without warning to those in control of either craft. If we accept the government's assertions, the government's pilots discovered United's peril in time to effectively respond but engaged in a maneuver destined to encounter rather than to evade. Contrasted with all of this is the finding that United's pilots, to some disputed degree of probability, could have seen the jet and, in discharge of the obligation to exercise the highest degree of care for their passengers, should have seen and avoided the jet.[10] In view of the disparity of duties, the clear disparity of culpability, the likely operation of the last clear chance doctrine and all the surrounding circumstances, the findings that United and the government were *in pari delicto* are clearly erroneous and we hold that there is such difference in the contrasted character of fault as to warrant indemnity in favor of United in the nongovernment employee cases."[11]

As noted supra, no case has been found where this rule has been extended to a collision between two motor vehicles. If indemnity were permitted in a case of this nature, it could arise in any action where a third person had a possible cause of action against two motorists.

---

10. In a footnote the court pointed out that it is "generally agreed * * * that the failure to discover unsafe conditions created by a joint tortfeasor constitutes 'passive' negligence and does not bar indemnity."

11. United is distinguishable from the instant case. The United States owed a duty to warn the pilot in charge of the United craft, and its negligence in sending its training mission into the same area without warning to those in control of either craft created the unsafe condition which resulted in a midair collision.

Each motorist could claim indemnity by alleging gross negligence of the other. This would result in the undesirable situation suggested by the Wisconsin court in *Jacobs*. The plaintiff in this action in order to recover from the defendants must of course prove that the defendants were negligent and that their negligence was a proximate cause of plaintiff's injury. If this is not established, there is no liability, and no question of possible indemnity could arise. It is my conclusion that this is not a case where the principles of indemnity are applicable.

In view of my conclusion that the third-party complaint should be dismissed, it is unnecessary to consider the remaining questions raised by third-party defendant.

It is ordered that the third-party complaint is dismissed for failure to state a claim, and that the cross-claim of the defendant Arden Leas is dismissed without prejudice.

PUTTING IT INTO PRACTICE 16.3

1. Who is the third-party defendant and why he is involved in this case?
2. Who are the third-party plaintiffs and why are they involved in this case?
3. What is the first point of contention between the parties?
4. What is the majority view regarding contribution amongst joint tortfeasors? What is the minority view?
5. How does the court dispense with the contribution question in this case?
6. What is the next question the court entertains?
7. Does the court find any cases supporting the application of indemnity to a collision between two motor vehicles?
8. On what basis was United Airlines entitled to indemnification?
9. On what basis does the court distinguish the case involving United Airlines from the instant case?
10. What does the court decide in reference to indemnification in the context of collisions between two motor vehicles? Why?

"MARY CARTER" OR "GALLAGHER" AGREEMENTS

Plaintiffs and defendants sometimes enter into agreements known as "Mary Carter" or "Gallagher" agreements. ("Mary Carter" agreements have been so designated because of the case of *Booth v. Mary Carter Paint Co.,* 202 So. 2d 8 (Fla. Dist. Ct. App. 1967) in which such an agreement was first reviewed by the appellate courts.) Under these agreements the defendant (or some of the defendants) agrees to guarantee the plaintiff a certain amount of money if the plaintiff loses or recovers less than a stated amount. The plaintiff agrees to refund part of the defendant's payment in the event of a verdict against the defendants in excess of a stated amount. Funds may actually change hands prior to trial or may be transferred on paper alone. Numerous variations on this theme exist, but the important feature is that the contracting defendant, although still a party in the case and usually a participant at the trial, benefits by the size of the judgments against the other defendants.

A typical agreement may also prohibit the plaintiff from settling with nonagreeing defendants for an amount less than the guaranteed amount without the agreeing defendant's consent, and might require that the parties conceal the agreement not only from the jury but also from the court and other parties. The terms of "Gallagher" agreements are fully disclosed, thereby distinguishing them from "Mary Carter" agreements, which are cloaked in secrecy.

Plaintiffs benefit from such arrangements because they pressure settling defendants, who have a substantial interest in a sizeable plaintiff's recovery, to cooperate with the plaintiff in discovery, peremptory challenges, trial tactics, witness examination, and influencing the jury. By having the settling defendants remain at trial, the plaintiff is relieved of dealing with the "empty chair" defense. Besides obtaining security by being guaranteed payment, the plaintiff is able to present a more streamlined, simplified case merely by reducing the number of defendants. She may also profit from disputes that break out during trial between the settling and nonsettling defendants as they maneuver to establish the other's liability.

Likewise, settling defendants benefit by eliminating the risk of paying more than the amount agreed on. The cost of litigation is reduced because the need for an aggressive defense is no longer warranted. Most importantly, the settling defendant has in effect purchased part of the plaintiff's claim, giving him a chance to recover all or part of what it has paid or agreed to pay. If the parties to a Mary Carter or Gallagher agreement succeed in their attack on the remaining defendants, the settling defendants may end up paying nothing— even if the jury finds substantial fault on their part.

The vast majority of courts tolerate these agreements even though the secrecy of their terms is subject to great controversy. A few states, however, have found that such agreements violate public policy. In a case that illustrates the structure and potential abuses of these agreements, the Texas court struck down Mary Carter agreements as being contrary to public policy. *Elbaor v. Smith*, 845 S.W.2d 240 (Tex. 1992). In *Elbaor* the plaintiff, Carole, received emergency treatment for her ankle at the Dallas/Fort Worth Medical Center-Grand Prairie by Dr. Syrquin after being severely injured in a motor vehicle accident. Subsequent to this treatment she was transferred to Arlington Community Hospital, where she received treatment from a team of physicians including Dr. Elbaor, an orthopedic surgeon, as well as a plastic surgeon and an infectious disease specialist. Later she was operated on twice as a result of complications from her ankle injury. Ultimately Carole brought a medical malpractice suit against Dallas/Fort Worth Medical Center-Grand Prairie, Arlington Community Hospital, Drs. Elbaor and Syrquin, and other doctors. Prior to trial, Carole entered into Mary Carter agreements with Dr. Syrquin, Arlington Community Hospital, and another doctor. She then settled with Dallas/Fort Worth Medical Center-Grand Prairie, releasing them from the suit. Dr. Elbaor, who filed cross-claims against the other doctors and Arlington Community Hospital for contribution in the event he was found liable, remained as the sole nonsettling defendant.

Under the terms of her Mary Carter agreement with Dr. Syrquin, Carole accepted $350,000 and under the terms of her agreement with Arlington Community Hospital she accepted $75,000. Both defendants retained a financial stake in the lawsuit and were required to participate at trial. The jury found that Carole's damages totaled $2,253,237.07, of which Dr. Elbaor was responsible for 88 percent, and Dr. Syrquin for 12 percent. After deducting all credits for Dr. Syrquin's percentage of causation, and Carole's settlements with other defendants, the trial court rendered judgment against Dr. Elbaor for $1,872,848.62.

In finding Mary Carter agreements contrary to public policy, the court characterized Mary Carter agreements as agreements that skew the trial process, mislead the jury, promote collusion among adversaries, and create the likelihood that a less culpable defendant will be held liable for the full judgment. The court balanced the public policy of judicial integrity against judicial economy and found that the need for fair trials outweighed the desirability of Mary Carter agreements as partial settlement tools.

The court pointed to specific evidence of abuses that occurred during this trial. For example, even though Carole's own experts testified that Dr. Syrquin committed malpractice, her attorney stated during both voir dire and opening statements that Dr. Syrquin's conduct was "heroic" and that it was Dr. Elbaor's negligence that caused Carole's damages. The attorneys for the settling defendants characterized Carole's damages as "devastating," "astoundingly high," and "astronomical." On cross-examination, they elicited testimony from Carole that was favorable to her case and requested recovery for pain and mental anguish.

As the facts of *Elbaor* demonstrate, these agreements may promote settlement, but they can also be abusive to nonsettling defendants, who may be faced with a lower chance of resolving the dispute as well as an increased exposure for damages. Although most courts now require the disclosure of such agreements, at least to the court and the nonsettling parties, these agreements continue to affect trials covertly. They skew the litigation process by hiding from the jury the full extent of the allegiance between the plaintiff and the settling defendant and by distracting the parties and the court from the merits of the case. As can be seen by the events in *Elbaor,* these agreements may force attorneys into questionable ethical situations and can encourage settling defendants to share with the plaintiff information obtained from other defendants during joint defense efforts.

In effect these agreements allow parties relief from any no-contribution rule. If the no-contribution rule is in effect and a plaintiff executes a judgment against a "deep pocket" defendant, that defendant will be unable to limit his or her liability by seeking relief from the other joint tortfeasors. Mary Carter and Gallagher agreements, however, allow defendants to limit their liability, in essence circumventing rules prohibiting contribution.

INDEMNIFICATION

When one tortfeasor accepts total financial responsibility for another tortfeasor, he or she is said to have **indemnified** that other tortfeasor. The party against whom indemnification is sought is referred to as an *indemnitor* and the party seeking to be indemnified is an *indemnitee.* Indemnification can be distinguished from contribution in that contribution involves a sharing of liability, whereas indemnification involves a shift of liability from one tortfeasor to another. A discussion of the rules of both contribution and indemnity is found in *Panasuk v. Seaton,* excerpted earlier in this chapter. (Carefully read the procedural history, which is found in the first two paragraphs.) The most frequent way indemnification arises is by virtue of a contractual agreement in which one party promises to indemnify another, as is often the case in contracts between general contractors and their subcontractors.

The right to indemnity also arises out of the law's attempt to avoid unjust enrichment of tortfeasors, as in cases involving vicarious liability. The unjust enrichment occurs when a tortfeasor is not required to reimburse a tortfeasor who pays the claim, resulting in the discharge of them both. An employer, for example, pays a judgment incurred by one of its employees only because it is vicariously liable for the torts of its employees. The courts reason that if the employer was not then indemnified by its employee so that it could recover the full amount of what it paid in damages, the employee would be unjustly enriched by being allowed to shirk his responsibility to pay for damages he caused. Because employers and employees are generally covered under a single insurance policy, however, liability of both parties is satisfied by the insurance company's payment of the claim, and so indemnification is rarely sought.

In addition to situations involving vicarious liability, indemnity also applies to defendants who are liable only because they failed to discover or prevent another's misconduct. A retailer, for example, who innocently fails to discover a defect in goods that he sells will be indemnified by the manufacturer of the defective goods. If, however, the retailer knows of the defect, the manufacturer will not be obligated to indemnify him. Some courts also deny indemnity if the retailer acts negligently.

The issue of indemnification sometimes arises when an individual follows the directions of another and reasonably believes the directions to be lawful. Typically this occurs in the context of a principal-agent relationship in which the agent acts under the direction of the principal. But it can also take place when a sheriff is instructed to seize someone's property and no lawful basis for such seizure exists. As long as the sheriff reasonably believes that the orders are lawful and engages in no deliberate wrongdoing, he will be indemnified by the governmental agency for which he works.

Indemnity is sometimes allowed in cases in which the plaintiff's injuries were aggravated by negligent treatment. If a driver, for example, pays for the total damages incurred by the plaintiff whom she injured, she can be indemnified by the doctor who aggravates the plaintiff's injuries by negligent medical care. The driver would be entitled to indemnification for that portion of the plaintiff's damages that were attributed to the negligent treatment.

Traditionally indemnity was an all-or-nothing situation, requiring that the indemnitor pay the indemnitee the full amount that the indemnitee paid the plaintiff. Under the doctrine of equitable indemnity, the amount of indemnity is dependent on the relative fault of the tortfeasors. Therefore, a tortfeasor may conceivably be indemnified for only part of the total damages she paid. Suppose a judgment is paid in full by an individual because the other defendants are penniless. In accordance with the doctrine of equitable indemnity, if that individual were to be indemnified by her principal, she would be indemnified only to the extent that she was actually responsible for the plaintiff's damages. The doctrine of equitable indemnity is inapplicable in cases in which the indemnitee's liability is purely vicarious.

PUTTING IT INTO PRACTICE 16.4

1. A subcontractor's employee is injured when he falls from a ladder at a construction site. He obtains a judgment against the owner and the general contractor for his injuries. On what basis might the owner and general contractor recover from the subcontractor?

2. Ms. Hall sues Stich, a psychologist, claiming that he engaged in sexual improprieties while treating her. She also sues Dr. Schulte, from whom Stich is renting office space, and the Schulte Institute for Psychotherapy and Human Sexuality. During the trial Stich agrees to pay Ms. Hall $500,000 in exchange for the following agreement:

   Hall covenants not to enforce or execute on any judgment entered against Stich, expressly reserving the right to proceed against James and Marjorie Schulte and the Schulte Institute on all of Hall's claims against Schulte including, but not limited to, the respondeat superior, implied agency, ostensible agency and apparent authority claims based upon the acts of Stich.

   Is this agreement a release or a covenant not to sue?

3. Students, parents, and teachers bring a product liability action against the manufacturer of chlordane after alleging injury from exposure to this termiticide. The plaintiffs and manufacturer reach a settlement. If the board of education and other companies in the chain of distribution are sued by the plaintiffs, what

Continued on next page

---

is their recourse? What effect will the settlement between the plaintiff and the manufacturer have on their options?

4. One of the defendants in a case in which a jury verdict for $1.5 million is rendered agrees to settle with the plaintiff for $5,000, in the hope that the defendant who had to pay the remainder of the judgment would be barred from obtaining contribution against the settling defendant. The settling defendant is a relative of the plaintiff. Will the nonsettling defendant be barred from contribution?

5. Jill and Jose are involved in a motor vehicle accident with a tractor-trailer driven by Richard. The cause of the accident is in dispute. Jill, who was seriously injured, sues Jose and Richard as well as Richard's employer and the employer's insurance carrier. Prior to trial Jose's insurance company and Jill enter into a compromise settlement of her claim against Richard. On the morning of trial, the defendants and the trial court are advised of the settlement, but not of its terms. Richard remains in the suit as a named defendant at trial. The other defendants demand that the settlement agreement be produced at trial and admitted into evidence. Do you think they will be successful?

SUMMARY

Joint tortfeasors are those who act together to produce a negligent or intentional tort. If the harm created is indivisible, each tortfeasor is jointly and severally liable for the harm suffered by the plaintiff. If all the defendants acted in concert, all will be held liable even though only one of the defendants directly caused the plaintiff's injuries. If the harm can be apportioned (divided), the rule of joint and several liability is inapplicable. Joint and several liability has been abolished in some states and limited in others.

A plaintiff is entitled to only one satisfaction of his or her claim. A defendant who has paid more than his or her pro rata share may, however, turn to the other defendants for contribution. Although contribution was denied under the common law, it is allowed in most states for negligent torts. The courts are not in agreement as to how damages should be divided in the context of contribution.

Contribution becomes particularly problematic when a release is given to one defendant. The rules created by the courts to deal with contribution when a release has been granted have discouraged either plain-tiffs or defendants from settling. Under the common law, a release of one tortfeasor was a release of all tortfeasors. Under the Restatement, however, those defendants not parties to a release are absolved of liability only if the release is silent regarding their continuing liability.

Plaintiffs and defendants sometimes enter into Mary Carter or Gallagher agreements. In such agreements, one (or more) of the defendants agrees to guarantee the plaintiff a certain amount of money regardless of the outcome of the case and the plaintiff agrees to reimburse the defendant if the verdict exceeds a stated amount.

Indemnification involves one tortfeasor's acceptance of total financial responsibility for another. An employer that is vicariously liable for the torts of its employee may be indemnified by that employee, in that it can recover the full amount of what it paid in damages. Defendants who are liable only because they failed to discover or prevent another's misconduct may also be indemnified. The doctrine of equitable indemnity, which has been adopted by some courts, allows indemnity to be based on the relative fault of the tortfeasors.

■   PRACTICE POINTERS   ☐

Legal assistants are sometimes asked to draft releases, which are typically prepared by defense counsel or the defendant's insurance carrier. They are accompanied either by a draft of the agreed-to settlement terms or a letter stating that such draft will be provided upon return of the executed release agreement by the plaintiff.

Some of the things you may want to consider when preparing a release are:
- Designate the capacities and authorities of the releasors and the released parties
- Include reference to all officers, directors, agents, and employees
- Identify the consideration for the release and the time and manner of making payment as consideration
- Disclose all legal rights and obligations of parties without a release
- Identify the common law, statutory, constitutional, administrative, and contractual rights of action and recovery affected
- Identify the effect of the release on heirs, successors, or assigns of parties
- Describe the claim or liability released
- Describe the scope of the release and exceptions to or limitations on the release
- Identify the rights and obligations not affected by the release
- Explain how the release is affected by matters unknown and unknowable by parties at the time of execution
- Explain how the release is affected by criminal acts; intentional torts; illegal acts; malicious, reckless, or wanton misconduct; or grossly negligent acts or omissions
- Explain how the release is affected by the conduct of agents, officers, or employees acting beyond the scope of duty, authority, agency, or employment
- Explain how the release is affected by damage or injury to the releasor
- Identify the duration of the release
- Identify the grounds for and manner of terminating or invalidating the release
- Include the releasor's acknowledgment of understanding the terms, conditions, and effect of the release; a statement of the releasor's capacity to understand and execute; and the releasor's acknowledgment of delivery and acceptance of consideration and release
- Identify the date and place of execution and the signatures of the parties
- Designate representative capacities and authority
- Notarize signatures

The following is a sample release, which contains some, but not all, of the provisions previously listed.

MUTUAL RELEASE AGREEMENT (Sample)

THIS AGREEMENT is entered into by and between James T. Smith, a single man (hereinafter referred to as "Smith"), and ABC Insurance Corporation, a Delaware corporation (hereinafter referred to as "ABC").

Smith/ABC
Mutual Release
Page 1 of 2

Continued on next page

FOR AND IN CONSIDERATION of the entering into of this Agreement, and other good and valuable consideration, the receipt of which is hereby acknowledged, Smith does hereby remise, release, and forever discharge ABC, its subsidiaries and the other affiliates, and their respective officers, directors, employees, and agents, and ABC does hereby remise, release, and forever discharge Smith from any and all actions, claims, liabilities, promises, and demands whatsoever which they now have or may hereafter have on account of or arising out of or otherwise associated with, or assertable in, that certain litigation instituted by Smith against ABC entitled "James T. Smith, plaintiff, vs. ABC Insurance Corporation, a Delaware corporation, Defendant," bearing Cause No. CV 99-12345 in the Alpha County Superior Court (the "Lawsuit").

As additional consideration for this Release, Smith shall cause the Litigation to be dismissed forthwith with prejudice. Upon receipt of the fully executed Notice of Dismissal with Prejudice, and this fully executed release, ABC shall pay to Smith the sum of Thirty-three Thousand Dollars ($33,000.00).

It is expressly understood that this Release includes any consequences which may hereinafter develop as well as those that have already developed and are not apparent as the result of the dealings between the parties relating to the issues or facts involved in the Lawsuit. This Release includes all claims, known and unknown.

As further consideration for the execution of this Agreement, the parties hereto warrant that (1) no promises or agreements not herein expressed have been made to or by them; (2) in executing this Release they are not relying upon any statements or representations made by any party, their agents, servants, or attorneys concerning the nature, extent, or duration of the damages, if any, or other thing or matter, but they are relying solely upon their own judgment; (3) the above-referenced consideration is received by each party in full settlement and satisfaction of all the claims that were or could have been asserted in the Lawsuit, known or unknown, or that otherwise arise out of the facts relating to the issues in the Lawsuit; (4) they are over the age of eighteen (18) years and legally competent to execute this Release; and (5) before signing this Release they have fully informed themselves of its contents and of the meanings thereof and have executed the same with full knowledge and advice of their attorneys.

It is further agreed and understood by the parties that this is a compromise settlement and is not in any way to be considered as an admission of liability on the part of either party hereto.

IN WITNESS WHEREOF, the parties hereto have executed this Mutual Release on this _____ day of August, 1999.

Smith:

_____

James T. Smith, a single man

ABC:

ABC INSURANCE CORPORATION, a Delaware corporation,

By _____

_____

Its Duly Authorized Representative

Smith/ABC
Mutual Release
Page 2 of 2

TORT TEASERS

1. Discuss the questions raised at the beginning of this chapter. What additional information would you need to fully answer these questions?

2. A is injured as a result of the combined negligence of B and C. A settles with B for $2,000 and releases him. A then sues C and obtains a judgment for $30,000. If C pays $30,000, can he obtain contribution from B?

3. An automobile passenger injured in a one-vehicle accident enters into an agreement with his host driver to limit the amount of liability the driver will be exposed to, regardless of the verdict in the passenger's action against the city. Assuming there is no evidence of unethical conduct or collusion, is such an agreement in violation of public policy? *City of Glendale v. Bradshaw,* 493 P.2d 515 (Ariz. 1972).

4. Defendant encourages an assailant to attack Plaintiff and stops others from coming to Plaintiff's aid. Is Defendant liable even though he takes no part in the attack? *Thompson v. Johnson,* 180 F.2d 431 (5th Cir. 1950).

5. Plaintiffs are injured when the car in which they are passengers collides with a taxicab. Plaintiffs sue the owner of the taxicab but not the owner of the car in which they were riding. What are the options of the taxicab owner? *Knell v. Feltman,* 174 F.2d 662 (D.C. Cir. 1949).

KEY TERMS

Concurrent tortfeasors
Tortfeasors who independently cause the plaintiff injury.

Contribution
Partial reimbursement of a tortfeasor who has paid more than his or her pro rata share of the damages.

Covenant not to sue
Promise by a plaintiff not to sue a particular defendant.

Indemnification
Total acceptance of financial responsibility by one tortfeasor for another.

Joint and several liability
Liability for an entire loss if the loss is indivisible.

Joint tortfeasors
Those who act together to cause the plaintiff's injury.

Release
Agreement to absolve a defendant of all liability.

Satisfaction
Payment of a judgment.

Part Four

TORTS IN PRACTICE

CHAPTER

17

Tort Reform

CHAPTER OBJECTIVES

In this chapter you will learn to:
- Identify the goals of the tort system
- Identify the historical roots of tort reform
- Describe the primary issues that drive the tort reform movement today
- Critique the measures being proposed to reform the tort system in reference to punitive damages, joint and several liability, collateral source payments, and frivolous lawsuits

A burglar falls through a skylight during a robbery. A jury grants him a lifetime award of $206,000 with a monthly award of $1500 a month.

These are the "facts" as represented by an American Tort Reform Association publicity pamphlet. But is this what really happened? Actually, there was no jury award, because the case was settled. The plaintiff was a teenager who had climbed up on the school roof to take a floodlight. The skylight was painted over and the boy was rendered paraplegic as a result of his fall. A similar accident had resulted in a death at another school eight months earlier and school officials had contracted to board over the skylights to resolve maintenance and safety problems.

USA Today laments:

Everybody in the USA suddenly seems to want to sue anybody with liability insurance coverage. The explosion of litigation has choked court dockets. And too-few lawyers tell potential clients that some cases are a waste of time.

. . . The greed has turned the temple of justice, long a hallowed place, into a pigsty. The time has come to clean it up.

"Hold Down Awards to Ease the Crisis," *USA Today,* June 6, 1986, at 12A, col. 1. Copyright 1986, USA Today. Reprinted with permission.

Former Vice President Dan Quayle blasted lawyers and the tort system:

We have become a crazily litigious country. Today a baseball comes crashing through a window, and instead of picking it up and returning it to the neighbor whose kid knocked it through—and who pays the glazier's bill in a reasonable, neighborly way—the "victim" hangs on to the baseball as evidence and sues the neighbor. (Or the baseball's manufacturer. Or the glassmaker. Or usually all three.) Several lawyers are soon billing hours, and the civil docket has been further crowded by one more pointless case that's probably going to be part of the 92 percent of cases that get settled before they come to trial—but not before a huge amount of time and money has been wasted on everything from "discovery" to picking a jury that will be discharged before it ever deliberates this case that shouldn't have gotten started in the first place. In America we now sue first and ask questions later. The system—and the mind set—are inefficient and anticompetitive. By not paying the huge legal costs their U.S. counterparts are bearing year after year, foreign companies have a tremendous advantage. American businesses and individuals spend more than $80 billion annually on the direct costs of litigation and higher insurance premiums. Include the extra costs and the figure can top $300 billion.

Dan Quayle, *Standing Firm* 312 (HarperCollins 1994). (The origins of the $80 billion and $300 billion figures are examined in M. Galanter, "News from Nowhere: The Debased Debate About Civil Justice," 71 *Denver U.L. Rev.* 77 (1993).)

Journalism and publicity of this nature inflame the public, but do little to bring any real understanding of the problems facing the tort system. Reformation of the tort system has become a highly charged public debate and too frequently sides are chosen based on rhetoric and partisan politics rather than on insightful analysis. True comprehension of the nature of the problems besetting the tort system today requires a review of the goals of the tort system and a thoughtful evaluation of those goals.

GOALS OF THE TORT SYSTEM

What are these goals? First, the tort system is designed to compensate victims. Not only are victims served by this compensation, but society also benefits because tort victims who are compensated are less likely to become public charges, thereby alleviating some of the stress on an overburdened social welfare system. Second, tort law serves a deterrent function, providing individuals with an incentive to act in socially responsible ways. Over time, both individuals and businesses learn to consider the social consequences of their actions. Third, tort law spreads the risk of injury amongst members of society. By incorporating the costs of this social "insurance" into the costs of goods and services, all are protected from the expenses of catastrophic loss. Fourth, justice is served when victims are made whole. Restoring victims to the positions in which they would have been but for the defendant's wrong serves the collective conscience. Fifth, tort law exposes corruption, incompetence, and a variety of other forms of misconduct. Behaviors that might otherwise have escaped public attention are brought into the limelight of public scrutiny and rectified. (See Figure 17-1.)

Two key questions that should be uppermost in the minds of tort reformers are: (1) Are these viable goals? and (2) If they are, is the tort system as it is presently structured effectively meeting these goals? For example, *should* the tort system serve a deterrent function, or is that function better left within the purview of the criminal justice system? If it is a viable goal, do punitive damages, for example, effectively deter would-be tortfeasors? Broad policy questions such as these must be addressed before a meaningful discussion about specific issues is possible.

HISTORICAL ROOTS OF TORT REFORM

A brief review of the historical roots of tort reform illustrates the consequences of changes in goals. After World War I, in the Progressive Era of tort reform, legal commentators were primarily concerned with plaintiffs being adequately compensated. Because at the time the tort system tended to protect defendants' interests, reformers opted for changes in the law that were plaintiff-oriented, such as workers' compensation

FIGURE 17-1   Goals of the Tort System

- Compensation
- Deterrence
- Cost-spreading
- Restoration
- Exposure

and strict liability. Seeing the role of the tort system as something of a "karmic adjustor," through which the wrongs of society could be righted by means of a type of social engineering, they advocated no-fault approaches that made the plaintiff whole at the defendant's expense.

From the 1960s through the 1980s, a series of social phenomena influenced the evolution of tort law. In the late 1960s, medical costs rose sharply, according to health care providers, because more patients filed negligence claims. In the late 1970s, manufacturers experienced rising liability insurance premiums. In the late 1980s, insurance companies, which complained of continuing financial losses, cancelled or refused to reissue policies held by high-risk policyholders. The public assigned the tort system primary blame for these perceived crises and began to associate lawsuits with shackling business.

The legal community also became disenchanted with the focus on plaintiff compensation and sought to correct what it saw as the excesses of the Progressive Era. Focusing on the goal of deterrence, the classical tort reformers sought the repeal of any rules that were not aimed at deterring potential tortfeasors from engaging in risky behavior. In particular, they sought to eliminate any rules they viewed as being particularly harsh toward defendants.

What specific changes occurred as a result of the classical reform movement? In the 1970s, responding to the medical crisis of the 1960s, at least forty-three states passed legislation that limited the potential malpractice liability of health care providers. The second wave of classical reforms resulted in many states eliminating joint and several liability and imposing caps on noneconomic damages, particularly punitive damages. Several states reestablished sovereign immunity doctrines; others allowed defendants to pay awards periodically rather than in lump sums; some penalized plaintiffs who brought frivolous lawsuits; still others mandated some form of alternative dispute resolution. By 1991 nearly all states had enacted some form of tort reform. (See Figure 17-2.)

FIGURE 17-2 Pendulum Swing of Tort Reform

PROGRESSIVE REFORM	CLASSICAL REFORM
Plaintiff-oriented	*Defense-oriented*

FOCUS OF TODAY'S REFORMERS

What is the rallying cry of today's reformers? Most have focused on the law's plaintiff orientation, the litigiousness of society, the excessiveness of jury verdicts, and the inhibition of medical and business practices. (See Figure 17-3). The insurance industry in particular has accused the plaintiff orientation of the tort system of making it nearly impossible to predict risks and set prices.

Plaintiff Orientation

Specific examples of plaintiff orientation singled out for blame are the expansion of liability to include no-fault liability, the relaxation of causation requirements, the adoption of comparative negligence, and the abolition of privity.

No-Fault

No-fault (strict liability) for defective design, manufacture, and warnings is the primary example raised to illustrate the unbridled expansion of tort liability. One of the most noteworthy examples of no-fault involves Restatement (Second) of Torts § 402A. To review, this section shifts the costs of injuries resulting from unreasonably dangerous products to manufacturers, who, the drafters of the Restatement reasoned, are better able to absorb the costs of injuries into their overall business expense. Expansive interpretations of this Restatement section (which was widely adopted by state legislatures) have allowed escalated claims against manufacturers and prompted calls for reform.

Causation Requirements

Relaxed causation requirements have also fueled the debate about the permissiveness of contemporary tort law. The case most often pointed to in this regard is *Sindell v. Abbott Laboratories,* 607 P.2d 924 (Cal. 1980) (see Chapter 7). Recall that in this class action, a group of women, whose mothers had received DES during pregnancy to prevent miscarriage, sued when the drug was later linked to the daughters' cancer. In what some perceive as a radical liberalization of the rules concerning proof of causation, the California Supreme Court found each defendant manufacturer of DES liable for its market share of the damages to the plaintiff class, even though the plaintiffs were unable to prove which companies had actually supplied DES to their mothers. This waiver of proof as to who actually caused the plaintiffs' injuries dramatically altered causation principles, despite this doctrine's limitation to certain factual situations.

Comparative Negligence

Comparative negligence also enhanced plaintiffs' ability to recover by loosening up the harsh recovery-barring effects of contributory negligence. (See Chapter 9.) Comparative negligence opened the door to plaintiffs who might have been excluded by the restrictive parameters of contributory negligence.

Privity

By the same token, abolition of privity allowed a plaintiff who did not buy directly from the manufacturer to sue the manufacturer as well as the retailer. Recall that privity requires a plaintiff suing in negligence

FIGURE 17-3 Focus of Today's Reformers

- Plaintiff orientation
  - —No-fault
  - —Causation requirements
  - —Comparative negligence
  - —Privity
- Litigiousness
- Runaway verdicts
- Inhibition of medical practice and business

to have direct contact with the defendant. This liberalization of the scope of suit further expanded the realm of tort liability and opened up the universe of potential defendants.

Litigiousness

Today's reformers diagnose society as suffering from the pangs of overlitigiousness. One book, *The Litigation Explosion: What Happened When America Unleashed the Lawsuit* by Walter Olson (1991), suggested that Americans bring too many lawsuits and spend too much money on litigation. The author accused lawyers of inciting business people to sue rather than negotiate and of encouraging individuals to pursue claims and defend rights they might otherwise ignore. Although the book certainly fueled the debate on tort reform, the author provided little in the way of empirical evidence to support his claims. To the contrary, a Rand Institute for Civil Justice study revealed that in 1989, only one in ten Americans who were injured sought compensation from someone involved in the accident. Most of these were auto accidents. In nonauto, nonwork accidents, the attempted claim rate was only three out of one hundred (Hensler et al., *Compensation for Accidental Injuries in the United States* (1990)). American Bar Association statistics show that personal injury claims represent only 9 percent of all civil cases, and that since 1986 there has been little or no increase—whereas domestic relations claims have risen 43 percent. (*State Court Caseload Statistics Annual Report 1992,* published February 1994. The report was a joint project of the Conference of State Court Administrators, the State Justice Institute, and the National Center for State Courts Court Statistics Project.)

State Courts

Much of the emphasis by those urging reform is on data from the federal courts; however, 98 percent of all civil litigation takes place in state courts (Galanter, "The Day After the Litigation Explosion," 46 *Md. L. Rev.* 3, 5 (1986)). At the state level, tort filings increased only 1 percent more than population growth from 1978 to 1984. The National Center for State Courts provided this analysis of state caseload trends, based on data provided by the courts for 1978, 1981, and 1984. Filings of civil cases exceeded population growth from 1978 to 1981, but from 1981 to 1984, per capita rates of filings actually declined. From 1981 to 1984, only five of seventeen courts for which tort data was available showed increases in filings that were significantly more than the population growth; in eight of these courts, tort filings actually decreased (National Center for State Courts, *State Court Caseload Statistics: Annual Report 1984,* pt. 2 (Ct. Statistics & Information Management Project 1986)).

Federal Courts

At the federal level, the number of tort filings increased from 25,691 in 1975 to 37,522 in 1984 (17 percent increase). Almost two-thirds of this increase was due to product liability cases (272 percent increase). (Director of the Administrative Office of the United States Courts, *1975 Annual Report* 346; *1984 Annual Report* 253.) Overall, the federal courts have experienced a 123 percent increase in overall filings in the past decade (Galanter, *supra,* at 10). Interestingly, the federal government itself accounts for the largest fraction of the increase in litigation, with a 6,683 percent increase in filings (*id.* at 16, 23, Tables 2 and 3).

What Do the Statistics Mean?

When assessing claims of litigiousness, several questions should be raised. Is the increase in the number of lawsuits filed commensurate with increases in population? Although more lawsuits are being filed today, the question is whether any increase in litigation *per capita* has occurred. Are Americans more litigious than citizens of other countries? Some studies show that American litigation rates are not significantly higher than those in other industrial countries. Although many countries have much lower rates of litigation, per capita use of courts in Canada, Australia, New Zealand, England, Denmark, and Israel appears to be within the same range as the United States (Galanter, "Reading the Landscape of Disputes: What We Know and Don't Know (and Think We Know) About Our Allegedly Contentious and Litigious Society," 31 *UCLA L. Rev.* 4, 53 (1983)). How do litigation rates today compare with those of 100 years ago? Several studies document higher per capita rates of civil litigation in nineteenth- and early twentieth-century America, as well as in colonial times (McIntosh, "150 Years of Litigation and Dispute Settlement: A Court Tale," 15 *Law & Soc'y Rev.* 823 (1980–81)). Furthermore, the 1930s and 1940s, which form the baseline for many comparisons, were a historic low point for litigation (Seacat, "The Problem of Decreasing Litigation," 8 *U. Kan. City L. Rev.* 135 (1940)).

Even a finding that filings have increased, however, does not necessarily mean that society has become more litigious. An increase might not mean that plaintiffs are more litigious but that defendants are more resistant to resolving disputes outside of litigation, or that the number of transactions between parties has increased. If doctors, for example, are having more doctor-patient contacts, and thereby providing more medical care, more injuries and consequently more complaints could be anticipated.

To summarize, empirical evidence is needed to substantiate claims of overly litigious behavior. Once the evidence is amassed, it must be carefully analyzed before any relevant conclusions can be drawn regarding American attitudes toward litigation.

Runaway Verdicts

The issue of runaway jury verdicts is also subject to dispute. According to the Jury Verdict Research organization in Horsham, Pennsylvania, the national median for jury awards in personal injury cases rose 17 percent in 1995 to $62,000. Jury Verdict Research maintains a nationwide database of verdicts and settlements for personal injury claims, receiving verdicts from every state. This is the second year in a row the verdict median has increased. The rise reverses a down-

FIGURE 17-4 Jury Awards

YEAR	MEDIAN JURY AWARD
1995	$62,000
1993	$50,000
1990	$66,698

ward trend, however (see Figure 17-4). Furthermore, the median jury award in the product liability area is declining ($500,000 in 1993, $379,685 in 1994, and $260,000 in 1995).

Some data indicates that both smaller and larger awards are more frequent than they were twenty years ago. Data from Cook County, Illinois, for example, shows that for some types of litigation, the distribution in awards increased during the 1970s, increasing the frequency of both larger and smaller awards (M. Peterson & G. Priest, *The Civil Jury: Trends in Trials and Verdicts, Cook County, Illinois, 1960–1979*, viii (Institute for Civil Justice 1982)). To explain this phenomenon some have pointed to states' use of smaller juries. Smaller juries are more likely to produce variable results than larger juries. Therefore, although the alleged unpredictability of jurors may be attributed to policy changes, it may simply be a result of the natural variability that occurs when a small sample is used.

Interpreting the Statistics

Interpreting these results is another matter, say those at Jury Verdict Research. Because the tracking organization does not poll jurors, it does not know jurors' rationales. Furthermore, the statistics may simply reflect a random fluctuation rather than a statistical trend. Some argue that statistical trends are unimportant anyway and that individual excessive awards are the primary indicia of a dysfunctional system. The American Tort Reform Association often uses specific cases to illustrate its premise that jury awards are sometimes irrational. Caution must be used, however, in evaluating these claims, because sometimes not all of the facts are included in the case summaries (as illustrated in the opening of this chapter).

When evaluating statistics for median jury awards, researchers are likely to make adjustments for inflation of health care costs—but what about the costs of rehabilitation? Because medicine is better able to prolong life and to rescue people who just a few years ago would have died, jurors are more likely now to factor the cost of round-the-clock medical care and rehabilitation into their awards. If plaintiffs live longer and receive more treatment, jury awards should be expected to reflect those increases in longevity. Alternatively, increases in jury awards may reflect the types of cases attorneys are bringing into the courts. If more people are bringing their claims to attorneys and attorneys consequently have a higher quality pool of cases from which to select, they are likely to choose those cases with large potential recoveries.

Consequently, even if jury awards are on the increase, the reasons behind this increase must be explored before one can conclude that the system is out of control. Given that one of the goals of the tort system is restoring the victim to wholeness, does an increase in awards reflect a cultural value that should be nurtured, or misguided philanthropy that should be brought into balance? If jurors today tend to place a higher value on human life and health, should that trend be discouraged or encouraged?

Along the same line, another criticism of the tort system is that all of society bears the brunt of an increase in jury awards ("we all pay"). In light of the cost-spreading goal of the tort system, should we accept any increased costs as part of the social price of security, or should we reevaluate the wisdom of this goal? After all, if the system is designed to remove some of the burden of accidents from the individual and shift it to the larger society, redesigning the system so that individuals bear the brunt of their misfortune is a fundamental social change. This change has widespread implications, apart from the monetary ramifications, that should be examined.

Inhibition of Medical and Business Communities

Finally, supporters of tort reform claim that increased tort liability has obstructed product development and created the practice of "defensive medicine" (the conservative practice of medicine aimed at the avoidance of potential lawsuits rather than the furtherance of patient needs). Essentially, tort reformers maintain that excessive tort liability has deterred business, resulting in higher prices and fewer new products. In medicine, the tort system has allegedly thwarted the practice of good medicine by increasing prices, encouraging unnecessary tests, and inhibiting doctors from the performance of high-risk procedures.

As evidence to the contrary, the American Medical Association reported that by 1994, the number of claims against doctors and hospitals had dropped at an average rate of 1.9 percent per year since the large increases of the 1980s (Martin Gonzalez, *Socioeconomic Characteristics of Medical Practice* 41–45 (AMA 1994)). Nevertheless, the 1992 claims rate of 8.9 percent (claims per 100 physicians) was the highest since 1985, when the claims rate was 10.2 percent (*id.*). Some attribute the decrease in claims to the high procedural cost of filing a malpractice claim (costs for medical reports, expert witnesses, second opinions, etc.) (Physician Payment Review Commission, *Annual Report to Congress* 291 (1994)).

In fact, some believe that the crisis in the medical arena and business community is not that so many needless and capricious claims are being filed but that so many wrongs are going unredressed. A review of patient records in California hospitals, for example, revealed that 1 in every 126 patients suffered from iatrogenic (induced by medical error) injuries, and yet fewer than 1 in 10 of those patients sought any compensation (Danzon, "An Economic Analysis of the Medical Malpractice System," 1 *Behavioral Sci. & L.* 39, 42 (1983)). If this study is representative of what is transpiring in the larger health care system, then consideration might be given to enhancing incentives to bringing suit rather than reducing them.

Interestingly, plaintiffs prevail in a smaller fraction of malpractice cases that go to trial than in any other category of litigation (M. Peterson & G. Priest, *The Civil Jury: Trends in Trials and Verdicts, Cook County, Illinois, 1960–1979,* table 3, p. 19 (Institute for Civil Justice 1982). This relatively small rate of recovery may reveal that most claims are meritless or that juries tend to give health care practitioners the benefit of the doubt. If, as some data indicates, the fraction of plaintiff verdicts is increasing (*id.* at 17), perhaps the increase can be attributed to a change in jury attitudes or a change in the quality of cases being brought to trial.

One scholar has suggested that the tort system is now so unwieldy and costly that only a select few can maneuver through its obstacles. Those few may receive awards that exceed their just compensation. Although those recoveries may represent only a tiny fraction of the real costs of injury, they may serve as an effective deterrent that is out of proportion to their actual costs to defendants and insurers. Such a system would create an image of unfairness to the public because of the few plaintiffs who received large awards, while the unfairness to the many plaintiffs who were uncompensated remained invisible (Michael Saks, "If There Be a Crisis, How Shall We Know It?," 46 *Md. L. Rev.* 63, 67 (1986)).

Judicious Use of Statistics

Discerning trends and making comparisons is important in gaining an understanding of litigation in relationship to the business and medical world, but statistics must be used and evaluated with care. A case in point involves an oft-cited statistic that the average verdict in product liability cases is over $1 million. This claim can be traced to a report by Jury Verdict Research, Inc. in 1984, which indicated that the average award in product liability cases was $1,021,956 (*Injury Valuation: Current Award Trends IV,* No. 304, at 19 (1986)).

Several points should be made regarding this statistical claim. First, this average was computed on the basis of plaintiffs' verdicts alone—and yet less than half of product liability cases tried by a jury result in a plaintiff verdict (*id.* at 20). Second, this average is based on a small sample of product liability verdicts (the 1984 average was derived from only 337 plaintiff verdicts), which represents only a small portion of the universe of product liability verdicts (*id.* at 19). Third, the sampling of Jury Verdict Research includes only "significant" or "important" verdicts, not typical ones (*id.* at 12). Therefore, the averages of Jury Verdict Research appear to be weighted toward the high end of the range.

Can Tort Reform Benefit the Business Community?

Is there any evidence that tort reform could actually benefit the business world? Tort reformers can now point to a study released by the National Bureau of Economic Research in Cambridge, Massachusetts, which suggests a possible link between the adoption of tort reform and increases in employment and productivity. The study uses economic data from 1969 to 1990 and looks at eight legal reforms: punitive damage reform, limits on damage awards, elimination of joint and several liability, caps on contingency fees, elimination of the collateral source rule, adoption of comparative negligence, institution of periodic rather than lump-sum payments, and required payment of prejudgment interest. The study showed that the adoption of plaintiff-friendly doctrines, such as comparative negligence, led to declines in employment and productivity, whereas adoption of defendant-oriented reforms led to increased employment and productivity.

The authors of the study are quick to point out that these gains may have been due to other state policies, such as lower taxation. Also, they argue, capital may flow from high-liability to low-liability states. Or companies in low-liability states may have lower costs simply because they are not bearing the true costs of production (as reflected in states where companies are more likely to be sued). Although the results do not support any definitive conclusions, they certainly provide fodder for additional research and support tort reformers' claims that expansive tort liability is bad for business.

IS THERE REALLY A PROBLEM?

Many of the allegations about the "system gone berserk" are unsubstantiated by empirical evidence, or the evidence is subject to contention (see Figure 17-5). Nevertheless, some very real problems do exist. Insurance premiums keep going up, insurance coverage is getting more difficult to obtain, and the insurance industry appears to be losing money. The caseload of the courts is growing, even if that growth is simply proportional to population growth. Some plaintiffs are overcompensated for their injuries and others are either undercompensated or receive nothing at all.

How do we set about constructively remodeling the system? Do we search for empirical evidence, or is the controversy more ideological in nature? Consider a $150 million verdict against General Motors in *Hardy v. General Motors Corp.*, CV-93-56 (Ala. Cir. Ct., Lowndes County, verdict June 3, 1996). To some the verdict ($50 million in compensatory damages and $100 million in punitive damages) for a thirty-eight-year-old driver who was rendered paraplegic illustrates the chaos and lack of control in the tort system. For others, the verdict exemplifies the need for deterrence of indifferent corporate behavior and the role that punitive damages should play. In this case the driver argued that he was injured when he was ejected through a driver-side door that opened because of a defective door latch. GM had allegedly been informed of the defective latch by its engineers but had made no efforts to remedy it. GM claimed that the driver, who had admitted to not wearing a seat belt, and who GM claimed had been drinking, was ejected through the windshield and that the driver-side door had never opened.

What can we glean from this case? Does it serve as evidence of a tort system run amuck, or it is an aberration? Or was the award reasonable in the context of all the evidence presented? Should we use individual cases like this one as the impetus to remodel the system, or do these cases simply further polarize opponents? If individual cases are insufficient, what data should we be collecting? Once we have data, how do we deter-

FIGURE 17-5 Questioning the Criticisms of the Tort System

Criticism: Americans have become too litigious.
- Is increase in lawsuits commensurate with population growth?
- Do most Americans sue when injured?
- Are increases in litigation at the state or federal level?
- Have plaintiffs become more litigious, or are defendants more resistant to suit?
- In areas of law that have experienced increases in litigation, has there been a concomitant increase in the number of transactions?
- Are Americans more litigious than citizens of other nations?
- Are Americans more litigious today than they were 100 years ago?

Criticism: Jury awards are out of control.
- Has there been a substantial increase in median jury awards?
- Are increases in jury awards due to random fluctuation, or do they represent a change in jurors' thinking?
- When analyzing this issue, should we focus on statistical trends or individual cases?
- Do increases in some types of awards reflect increases in longevity and the resulting costs of long-term care?
- Are attorneys bringing better cases to trial today?
- Are jurors today placing a higher value on health and life?
- Should we reexamine the cost-spreading goal of the tort system?
- If the frequency in both small and large awards has increased (as some data would indicate), is this increase due to the use of smaller juries?

Criticism: The increase in tort liability has hampered the business and medical communities.
- Are more claims being filed against doctors and hospitals today?
- Are there significant numbers of patients who are injured but never compensated?
- Do medical malpractice claims so often fail because they are meritless, or because jurors tend to give health care practitioners the benefit of the doubt?
- If the percentage of plaintiff verdicts is increasing, is this increase due to a change in juror attitudes or to the better quality of cases being brought to trial?

mine its relevance before assigning cause-and-effect relationships? As you can see, revamping the tort system is a bit more complex than it might appear at first glance.

PUTTING IT INTO PRACTICE 17.1

Evaluate the allegations about the tort system made by former Vice President Quayle in the quotation at the beginning of this chapter.

TORT REFORM IN PRACTICE

Operating from the assumption that society is overly litigious and that jury awards are excessive, the primary objectives of today's tort reformers are to curb what are perceived as unduly high damage awards and to reduce the number of claims filed. Several avenues have been pursued to fulfill these objectives (see Figure 17-6). Caps have been proposed on damage awards, particularly punitive damages; joint and several liability and the collateral source rules have been modified; efforts have been made to discourage frivolous lawsuits. (Other reform measures being considered that are not discussed in this chapter relate to statutes of repose, rules of discovery, alternative dispute resolution, workers' compensation immunity, auto insurance, periodic payments, sovereign immunity, and limits on attorney fees.)

FIGURE 17-6 Objectives of Today's Tort Reform

- Damage award caps
- Modification of joint and several liability
- Modification of collateral source rule
- Discouragement of frivolous lawsuits
- Statutes of repose
- Rules of discovery
- Alternative dispute resolution
- Workers' compensation immunity
- Automobile insurance
- Periodic payments
- Sovereign immunity
- Attorney fee limitations

The Common Sense Reform bills illustrate these proposals. When the Republican Party gained control of Congress in 1994, the momentum of tort reform shifted from the state to the federal level. Tenet 9 of their Contract with America called for a variety of tort reforms, including punitive damage limitations, reformation of product liability rules, and institution of the British rule of fee-shifting (see section later in this chapter on frivolous lawsuits). In the first 100 days of office, the party introduced four Common Sense Reform bills. Several of the bills precluded a plaintiff from recovering punitive damages unless she could show by clear and convincing evidence that the defendant had acted with conscious indifference to the plaintiff's safety (actual malice). Most of the bills limited punitive damages to the greater of $250,000 or three times the plaintiff's economic injury. They also eliminated joint and several liability and reduced the liability of a manufacturer for a plaintiff who misused a defective product to a proportion equal to the percentage of harm caused by the misuse. All of the bills sought to deter frivolous lawsuits.

Damage Caps

Let us examine each of these measures individually, beginning with a topic that most state legislatures have tackled: damage caps. Why is the limitation of damages such a concern? Assigning a precise numerical value to a physical injury is virtually impossible. For this reason, jury verdicts for compensation for bodily harm are always unpredictable. Responding to this unpredictability, the majority of states has passed some kind of legislation aimed at regulating damage awards. The American Bar Association, in contrast, has criticized these reforms as depriving those who are most seriously injured of their due compensation.

The courts' responses to these caps have varied depending on whether the damage award involved economic damages, noneconomic damages, or punitive damages. Restrictions on economic damages have not generally been favored by the courts. For example, an Ohio statute restricting general damages to $200,000 was found to violate the Equal Protection Clause because it unfairly burdened those plaintiffs least able to pay their medical and legal expenses. The court observed that "the legislative scheme of shifting responsibility for loss from one of the most affluent segments of society to those who are most unable to sustain that burden, i.e., horribly injured or maimed individuals, is not only inconceivable, but shocking to this court's conscience." *Duren v. Suburban Community Hospital,* 495 N.E.2d 51, 58 (Ohio 1985).

When noneconomic rather than economic damages are restricted, the courts have been more willing to uphold the regulating statute. In so doing, courts either defer to rational legislative objectives or they uphold across-the-board limitations that they see as fair, consistent, and promoting settlement. Some courts have pointed out that excessive awards can be prevented by trial courts' use of remittur.

Punitive Damages

Purpose of Punitive Damages.   In the debate over the capping of damages, the lion's share of attention has gone to punitive damages. The primary purpose of punitive damages is to deter undesirable behavior and to punish those who engage in such behavior. In one decision, the Alabama Supreme Court opined that often the only recourse for victims of fraud is litigation and that punitive damages have historically served as part of the remedy for those victims. *Life Insurance Co. v. Johnson,* 1996 WL 202543 (Ala.). The court quoted an author who explained that punitive damages have been used "to help equalize the playing field between the powerful and the powerless—whether between king and subject, railroad and passenger, or corporation and consumer" (Jonathon Massey, "Why Tradition Supports Punitive Damages: And How the Defense Bar Misreads History," *Trial,* Sept. 1995, at 19). The court reviewed the historical use of punitive damages in England against the crown and the aristocracy and in nineteenth-century America against the railroads and robber barons. It then concluded that the consumer plaintiff suing the corporate defendant falls within the historical legacy of using punitive damages to redress imbalances in relationships.

When caps on punitive damages are proposed, some question whether some companies will knowingly produce defective products if they no longer feel constrained by the deterrent value of large punitive damages. Will they see it as cost-effective to bypass safety measures? (See *Grimshaw v. Ford Motor Company,* 174 Cal. Rptr. 348 (Ct. App. 1981) in which the company deliberately decided against including safety measures it knew would save human lives because those measures were not considered cost-effective.) Punitive damages put such manufacturers on notice that indifference to human life is not acceptable and will be subject to severe sanctions. A cap on punitive damages, in contrast, arguably allows companies to more accurately predict punitive damages, enhancing the probability that they will cut costs without thought to the possible consequences to consumers.

Criticisms of Punitive Damages.   Critics have warned that punitive damages either do not deter at all or lead to overdeterrence, as in the case of manufacturers who act overly cautiously to avoid liability. The development of new and useful products, they argue, is particularly jeopardized by nervous manufacturers who fear stepping into the minefield of potential litigation. Critics have also charged that punitive damages lead to excessive litigation by plaintiffs, who pursue litigation in the hope that defendants wishing to avoid the expense and risk of litigation will settle. Some further argue that plaintiffs unfairly benefit from a windfall of monies intended to punish tortfeasors. This windfall further encourages litigious behavior. Finally, punitive damages have been criticized for hampering business by increasing the cost of insurance. Specifically, in the medical arena, critics claim that punitive damages victimize doctors serving socially useful functions (particularly in such high-risk areas as obstetrics) and inhibit doctors as a group from taking risks. (See Figure 17-7.)

A great deal of ink has been spilled critiquing the problem of punitive damages. Do punitive damages actually wreak havoc on the system? A study by the RAND Institute for Civil Justice indicated that the frequency and magnitude of punitive damage awards changed little from 1962 to 1987 (William Landes & Richard Posner, *The Economic Structure of Tort Law* 15 (1987)). Furthermore, the General Accounting Office examined data from five states from 1983 to 1985 and concluded that punitive damage awards were neither excessive nor frequent (General Accounting Office, *Report to the Chairman, Subcommittee on Commerce, Consumer Protection, and Competitiveness,* GAO/HRD-88-89, at 2 (Sept. 1989)). Another study conducted by legal scholars, which analyzed 25,627 jury verdicts from 11 states, found that plaintiffs received punitive damages in only 4.9 percent of these cases and that in most cases "the amount was generally modest" (Stephen Daniels & Joanne Martin, "Myth and Reality in Punitive Damages," 75 *Minn. L. Rev.* 1, 28–31 (1990)).

In contrast, a RAND study of two counties in California found a 1,500 percent increase in the average punitive damage awards from 1980 to 1984 in one of the counties (American Tort Reform Association, "Punitive Damage Update, Relevant Studies on Tort Reform/Punitive Damages" (Apr. 12, 1989)).

FIGURE 17-7 Criticisms of Punitive Damages

- Inhibits product development
- Fosters excessive litigation
- Gives windfalls to plaintiffs
- Inhibits medical practice

However, the author of a *Harvard Law Review* note concludes that a study with such a small sample size cannot displace larger studies that show contradictory results, and that the "lion's share of empirical evidence" points away from allegations that runaway punitive damage awards are widespread (Note, "Common Sense Legislation: The Birth of Neoclassical Tort Reform," 109 *Harv. L. Rev.* 1765 (1996)). Although some studies have shown slightly greater use of punitive damages, most evidence points away from the claim that runaway punitive damage awards are widespread. A study of cases from state courts in the nation's 75 largest counties from July 1, 1991, to June 30, 1992, for example, found that punitive damages were awarded in only 4 percent of tort cases in which plaintiffs won jury verdicts (Bureau of Justice Statistics, *Special Report No. NCJ 154346, Civil Jury Cases and Verdicts in Large Counties* 8 (1995)).

Reforms Being Implemented. Despite the lack of data supporting the notion of a punitive damage crisis, reform in this area is now burgeoning. In 1995 alone, nine state legislatures enacted reform measures addressing punitive damages (Illinois, Indiana, New Jersey, North Carolina, North Dakota, Oklahoma, Oregon, Texas, and Wisconsin). To illustrate, under Indiana's new laws, punitive damages are capped at the greater of $50,000 or three times the compensatory damages. New Jersey's cap is the greater of $350,000 or five times the compensatory damages, except for particularly abhorrent offenses such as drunk driving or child molestation. The American College of Trial Lawyers itself has recommended that the recovery of punitive damage awards be limited to the greater of twice the amount of compensatory damages or $250,000.

Oklahoma's new Tort Reform Law provides an interesting example of punitive damage reform. Under this law, punitive damage awards are divided into three categories. In Category I, the plaintiff must prove by clear and convincing evidence that the defendant acted with reckless disregard for the rights of others (the prior statute required a preponderance of the evidence).

Having done that, the plaintiff may recover punitive damages in the amount of the actual damages or $100,000, whichever is greater. In Category II, if the plaintiff proves that the defendant acted intentionally and with malice toward others, she may recover the greater of $500,000, twice the amount of actual damages, or the increased financial benefit that the defendant derived as a direct result of its misconduct. This last measure is subject to reduction by the amount that the defendant has already paid in punitive damages in Oklahoma state court actions to other plaintiffs based on the same conduct. In Category III, no limits are placed on punitive damages, but the plaintiff must prove that the defendant acted intentionally and with malice toward others and also engaged in life-threatening conduct toward humans.

The decision of how to classify an action (Category I, II, or III) now falls to the jury rather than the judge, and the jury must make these findings under a clear-and-convincing-evidence standard. (Both the jury and judge must decide if a case comes under Category III.) The determination of the appropriate category is made separately from the determination of the amount of the award. Because the defendant's financial condition is not relevant to determining the defendant's liability, evidence of the defendant's net worth is not admissible until after actual damages have been awarded and the jury has selected the appropriate category for the defendant's conduct.

Some states have created specific defenses to punitive damages. In North Dakota, for example, punitive damages may not be awarded against a manufacturer when the product complied with federal or administrative regulations or was certified by a federal agency.

A few states have responded to those who feel that punitive damages represent an undeserved windfall to plaintiffs. They have followed the lead of Chief Justice Rehnquist, who recommended that punitive damages be awarded "to the State, not to the plaintiff—who by hypothesis is fully compensated." *Smith v. Wade,* 461 U.S. 30, 59 (1983). The Alabama Supreme Court, for example, implemented a new procedure for trying punitive damage claims. In *Life Insurance Co. v. Johnson,* 1996 WL 202543 (Ala.), the court required half of any punitive damage award to be distributed to the state after attorney fees were paid. Although Alabama was the first state to impose an award-sharing requirement by court order, other states, such as Illinois and Iowa, have adopted this requirement by statute.

The bifurcated procedure for determining punitive damages established by the Alabama court is interesting. After determining liability and compensatory damages, the jury must decide by special verdict whether the evidence supports the imposition of punitive damages. If the jury answers in the affirmative, a second trial is held in which the jury determines the amount of punitive damages it finds appropriate.

Can Punitive Damage Awards Violate the Constitution?

The United States Supreme Court considered the issue of whether exorbitant punitive damages could violate the Constitution in *Browning-Ferris Industries v. Kelco Disposal Inc.,* 492 U.S. 257 (1989). In that case the jury awarded $6 million for a violation of antitrust laws. The Court held that the excessive fines clause of the Eighth Amendment applies only to fines imposed by the government. Justice O'Connor, in her dissent, argued that neither history nor precedent suggest that the Eighth Amendment does not apply to damages awarded between private parties. Justice Brennan, in a concurring opinion, suggested that the due process clause could limit the award of punitive damages in civil cases involving private parties.

Read a more recent Supreme Court decision, *BMW of North America, Inc. v. Gore,* 116 S. Ct. 1589 (1996), to see how the Court applied the due process clause to conclude that a $2 million punitive damage award was excessive. The plaintiff, who had purchased a BMW and later discovered that it had been repainted (thereby lowering its value), sued for compensatory and punitive damages, alleging that the failure to disclose the repainting constituted fraud. BMW admitted that it had a nationwide policy of not disclosing predelivery damage that did not exceed 3 percent of the vehicle's suggested retail price. The jury returned a verdict of $4,000 in compensatory damages and $4 million in punitive damages. The Alabama Supreme Court reduced the punitive damage award to $2 million on the basis that the jury had erred in its computation by improperly multiplying the plaintiff's compensatory damages by the number of similar sales throughout the United States rather than in Alabama alone.

CASE

BMW of North America, Inc. v. Gore, Jr.
116 S. Ct. 1589 (1996)

Justice STEVENS delivered the opinion of the Court.

The Due Process Clause of the Fourteenth Amendment prohibits a State from imposing a "'grossly excessive'" punishment on a tortfeasor. *TXO Production Corp. v. Alliance Resources Corp.,* 509 U.S. 443, 454, 113 S.Ct. 2711, 2718, 125 L.Ed.2d 366 (1993) (and cases cited). The wrongdoing involved in this case was the decision by a national distributor of automobiles not to advise its dealers, and hence their customers, of predelivery damage to new cars when the cost of repair amounted to less than 3 percent of the car's suggested retail price. The question presented is whether a $2 million punitive damages award to the purchaser of one of these cars exceeds the constitutional limit.

I

In January 1990, Dr. Ira Gore, Jr. (respondent), purchased a black BMW sports sedan for $40,750.88 from an authorized BMW dealer in Birmingham, Alabama. After driving the car for approximately nine months, and without noticing any flaws in its appearance, Dr. Gore took the car to "Slick Finish," an independent detailer, to make it look "'snazzier than it normally would appear.'" Mr. Slick, the proprietor, detected evidence that the car had been repainted. Convinced that he had been cheated, Dr. Gore brought suit against petitioner BMW of North America (BMW), the American distributor of BMW automobiles. Dr. Gore alleged, inter alia, that the failure to disclose that the car had been repainted constituted suppression of a material fact. The complaint prayed for $500,000 in compensatory and punitive damages, and costs.

At trial, BMW acknowledged that it had adopted a nationwide policy in 1983 concerning cars that were damaged in the course of manufacture or transportation. If the cost of repairing the damage exceeded 3 percent of the car's suggested retail price, the car was placed in company service for a period of time and then sold as used. If the repair cost did not exceed 3 percent of the suggested retail price, however, the car was sold as new without advising the dealer that any repairs had been made. Because the $601.37 cost of repainting Dr. Gore's car was only about 1.5 percent of its suggested retail price, BMW did not disclose the damage or repair to the Birmingham dealer.

Dr. Gore asserted that his repainted car was worth less than a car that had not been refinished. To prove his actual damages of $4,000, he relied on the testimony of a former BMW dealer, who estimated that the value of a repainted BMW was approximately 10 percent less than the value of a new car that had not been damaged and repaired. To support his claim for punitive damages, Dr. Gore introduced evidence that since 1983 BMW had sold 983 refinished cars as new, including 14 in Alabama, without disclosing that the cars had been repainted before sale at a cost of more than $300 per vehicle. Using the actual damage estimate of $4,000 per vehicle, Dr. Gore argued that a punitive award of $4 million would provide an appropriate penalty for selling approximately 1,000 cars for more than they were worth.

In defense of its disclosure policy, BMW argued that it was under no obligation to disclose repairs of minor damage to new cars and that Dr. Gore's car was as good as a car with the original factory finish. It disputed Dr. Gore's assertion that the value of the car was impaired by the repainting and argued that this good-faith belief made a punitive award inappropriate. BMW also maintained that transactions in jurisdictions other than Alabama had no relevance to Dr. Gore's claim.

The jury returned a verdict finding BMW liable for compensatory damages of $4,000. In addition, the jury assessed $4 million in punitive damages, based on a determination that the nondisclosure policy constituted "gross, oppressive or malicious" fraud.

BMW filed a post-trial motion to set aside the punitive damages award. The company introduced evidence to establish that its nondisclosure policy was consistent with the laws of roughly 25 States defining the disclosure obligations of automobile manufacturers, distributors, and dealers. The most stringent of these statutes required disclosure of repairs costing more than 3 percent of the suggested retail price; none mandated disclosure of less costly repairs. Relying on these statutes, BMW contended that its conduct was lawful in these States and therefore could not provide the basis for an award of punitive damages.

BMW also drew the court's attention to the fact that its nondisclosure policy had never been adjudged unlawful before this action was filed. Just months before Dr. Gore's case sent to trial, the jury in a similar lawsuit filed by another Alabama BMW purchaser found that BMW's failure to disclose paint repair constituted fraud. *Yates v. BMW of North America, Inc.* 642 So.2d 937 (Ala. 1993).[8] Before the judgment in this case, BMW changed its policy by taking steps to avoid the sale of any refinished vehicles in Alabama and two other States. When the $4 million verdict was returned in this case, BMW promptly instituted a nationwide policy of full disclosure of all repairs, no matter how minor.

In response to BMW's arguments, Dr. Gore asserted that the policy change demonstrated the efficacy of the punitive damages award. He noted that while no jury had held the policy unlawful, BMW had received a number of customer complaints relating to undisclosed repairs and had settled some lawsuits. Finally, he maintained that the disclosure statutes of other States were irrelevant because BMW had failed to offer any evidence that the disclosure statutes supplanted, rather than supplemented, existing causes of action for common-law fraud.

The trial judge denied BMW's post-trial motion, holding, inter alia, that the award was not excessive. On appeal, the Alabama Supreme Court also rejected BMW's claim that the award exceeded the constitutionally permissible amount. 646 So.2d 619 (1994). . . . Based on its analysis, the court concluded that BMW's

conduct was "reprehensible"; the nondisclosure was profitable for the company; the judgment "would not have a substantial impact upon [BMW's] financial position"; the litigation had been expensive; no criminal sanctions had been imposed on BMW for the same conduct; the award of no punitive damages in *Yates* reflected "the inherent uncertainty of the trial process"; and the punitive award bore a "reasonable relationship" to "the harm that was likely to occur from [BMW's] conduct as well as . . . the harm that actually occurred." *Id.,* at 625–627.

The Alabama Supreme Court did, however, rule in BMW's favor on one critical point: The court found that the jury improperly computed the amount of punitive damages by multiplying Dr. Gore's compensatory damages by the number of similar sales in other jurisdictions. Having found the verdict tainted, the court held that "a constitutionally reasonable punitive damages award in this case is $2,000,000," and therefore ordered a remittitur in that amount.[10] The court's discussion of the amount of its remitted award expressly disclaimed any reliance on "acts that occurred in other jurisdictions"; instead, the court explained that it had used a "comparative analysis" that considered Alabama cases, "along with cases from other jurisdictions, involving the sale of an automobile where the seller misrepresented the condition of the vehicle and the jury awarded punitive damages to the purchaser."

Because we believed that a review of this case would help to illuminate "the character of the standard that will identify constitutionally excessive awards" of punitive damages . . . we granted certiorari.

II

Punitive damages may properly be imposed to further a State's legitimate interests in punishing unlawful conduct and deterring its repetition. *Gertz v. Robert Welch, Inc.,* 418 U.S. 323, 350 (1974). In our federal system, States necessarily have considerable flexibility in determining the level of punitive damages that they will allow in different classes of cases and in any particular case. Most States that authorize exemplary damages afford the jury similar latitude, requiring only that the damages awarded be reasonably necessary to vindicate the

---

8. While awarding a comparable amount of compensatory damages, the *Yates* jury awarded no punitive damages at all. . . .

10. The Alabama Supreme Court did not indicate whether the $2 million figure represented the court's independent assessment of the appropriate level of punitive damages, or its determination of the maximum amount that the jury could have awarded consistent with the Due Process Clause.

State's legitimate interests in punishment and deterrence. Only when an award can fairly be categorized as "grossly excessive" in relation to these interests does it enter the zone of arbitrariness that violates the Due Process Clause of the Fourteenth Amendment. For that reason, the federal excessiveness inquiry appropriately begins with an identification of the state interests that a punitive award is designed to serve. We therefore focus our attention first on the scope of Alabama's legitimate interests in punishing BMW and deterring it from future misconduct.

No one doubts that a State may protect its citizens by prohibiting deceptive trade practices and by requiring automobile distributors to disclose presale repairs that affect the value of a new car. But the States need not, and in fact do not, provide such protection in a uniform manner. Some States rely on the judicial process to formulate and enforce an appropriate disclosure requirement by applying principles of contract and tort law. Other States have enacted various forms of legislation that define the disclosure obligations of automobile manufacturers, distributors, and dealers. The result is a patchwork of rules representing the diverse policy judgments of lawmakers in 50 States.

That diversity demonstrates that reasonable people may disagree about the value of a full disclosure requirement. Some legislatures may conclude that affirmative disclosure requirements are unnecessary because the self-interest of those involved in the automobile trade in developing and maintaining the goodwill of their customers will motivate them to make voluntary disclosures or to refrain from selling cars that do not comply with self-imposed standards. Those legislatures that do adopt affirmative disclosure obligations may take into account the cost of government regulation, choosing to draw a line exempting minor repairs from such a requirement. In formulating a disclosure standard, States may also consider other goals, such as providing a "safe harbor" for automobile manufacturers, distributors, and dealers against lawsuits over minor repairs.[14]

We may assume, arguendo, that it would be wise for every State to adopt Dr. Gore's preferred rule, requiring full disclosure of every presale repair to a car, no matter how trivial and regardless of its actual impact on the value of the car. But while we do not doubt that Congress

has ample authority to enact such a policy for the entire Nation, it is clear that no single State could do so, or even impose its own policy choice on neighboring States. Similarly, one State's power to impose burdens on the interstate market for automobiles is not only subordinate to the federal power over interstate commerce, but is also constrained by the need to respect the interests of other States.

We think it follows from these principles of state sovereignty and comity that a State may not impose economic sanctions on violators of its laws with the intent of changing the tortfeasors' lawful conduct in other States. Before this Court Dr. Gore argued that the large punitive damages award was necessary to induce BMW to change the nationwide policy that it adopted in 1983.[18] But by attempting to alter BMW's nationwide policy, Alabama would be infringing on the policy choices of other States. To avoid such encroachment, the economic penalties that a State such as Alabama inflicts on those who transgress its laws, whether the penalties take the form of legislatively authorized fines or judicially imposed punitive damages, must be supported by the State's interest in protecting its own consumers and its own economy. Alabama may insist that BMW adhere to a particular disclosure policy in that State. Alabama does not have the power, however, to punish BMW for conduct that was lawful where it occurred and that had no impact on Alabama or its residents. Nor may Alabama impose sanctions on BMW in order to deter conduct that is lawful in other jurisdictions.

In this case, we accept the Alabama Supreme Court's interpretation of the jury verdict as reflecting a computation of the amount of punitive damages "based in large part on conduct that happened in other jurisdictions." . . . The Alabama Supreme Court therefore properly eschewed reliance on BMW's out-of-state conduct, and based its remitted award solely on conduct that occurred within Alabama. The award must be analyzed in the light

14. Also, a state legislature might plausibly conclude that the administrative costs associated with full disclosure would have the effect of raising car prices to the State's residents.

18. Dr. Gore's interest in altering the nationwide policy stems from his concern that BMW would not (or could not) discontinue the policy in Alabama alone. "If Alabama were limited to imposing punitive damages based only on BMW's gain from fraudulent sales in Alabama, the resulting award would have no prospect of protecting Alabama consumers from fraud, as it would provide no incentive for BMW to alter the unitary, national policy of nondisclosure which yielded BMW millions of dollars in profits." The record discloses no basis for Dr. Gore's contention that BMW could not comply with Alabama's law without changing its nationwide policy.

of the same conduct, with consideration given only to the interests of Alabama consumers, rather than those of the entire Nation. When the scope of the interest in punishment and deterrence that an Alabama court may appropriately consider is properly limited, it is apparent—for reasons that we shall now address—that this award is grossly excessive.

Elementary notions of fairness enshrined in our constitutional jurisprudence dictate that a person receive fair notice not only of the conduct that will subject him to punishment but also of the severity of the penalty that a State may impose. Three guideposts, each of which indicates that BMW did not receive adequate notice of the magnitude of the sanction that Alabama might impose for adhering to the nondisclosure policy adopted in 1983, lead us to the conclusion that the $2 million award against BMW is grossly excessive: the degree of reprehensibility of the nondisclosure; the disparity between the harm or potential harm suffered by Dr. Gore and his punitive damages award; and the difference between this remedy and the civil penalties authorized or imposed in comparable cases. We discuss these considerations in turn.

Degree of Reprehensibility

Perhaps the most important indicium of the reasonableness of a punitive damages award is the degree of reprehensibility of the defendant's conduct. As the Court stated nearly 150 years ago, exemplary damages imposed on a defendant should reflect "the enormity of his offense." *Day v. Woodworth,* 13 How. 363, 371, 14 L.Ed. 181 (1852). This principle reflects the accepted view that some wrongs are more blameworthy than others. . . . [P]unitive damages may not be "grossly out of proportion to the severity of the offense."

In this case, none of the aggravating factors associated with particularly reprehensible conduct is present. The harm BMW inflicted on Dr. Gore was purely economic in nature. The presale refinishing of the car had no effect on its performance or safety features, or even its appearance for at least nine months after his purchase. BMW's conduct evinced no indifference to or reckless disregard for the health and safety of others. To be sure, infliction of economic injury, especially when done intentionally through affirmative acts of misconduct, or when the target is financially vulnerable, can warrant a substantial penalty. But this observation does not convert all acts that cause economic harm into torts that are sufficiently reprehensible to justify a significant sanction in addition to compensatory damages.

Dr. Gore contends that BMW's conduct was particularly reprehensible because nondisclosure of the repairs to his car formed part of a nationwide pattern of tortious conduct. Certainly, evidence that a defendant has repeatedly engaged in prohibited conduct while knowing or suspecting that it was unlawful would provide relevant support for an argument that strong medicine is required to cure the defendant's disrespect for the law. Our holdings that a recidivist may be punished more severely than a first offender recognize that repeated misconduct is more reprehensible than an individual instance of malfeasance.

In support of his thesis, Dr. Gore advances two arguments. First, he asserts that the state disclosure statutes supplement, rather than supplant, existing remedies for breach of contract and common-law fraud. Thus, according to Dr. Gore, the statutes may not properly be viewed as immunizing from liability the nondisclosure of repairs costing less than the applicable statutory threshold. Second, Dr. Gore maintains that BMW should have anticipated that its failure to disclose similar repair work could expose it to liability for fraud.

We recognize, of course, that only state courts may authoritatively construe state statutes. As far as we are aware, at the time this action was commenced no state court had explicitly addressed whether its State's disclosure statute provides a safe harbor for nondisclosure of presumptively minor repairs or should be construed instead as supplementing common-law duties. A review of the text of the statutes, however, persuades us that in the absence of a state-court determination to the contrary, a corporate executive could reasonably interpret the disclosure requirements as establishing safe harbors. . . . Perhaps the statutes may also be interpreted in another way. We simply emphasize that the record contains no evidence that BMW's decision to follow a disclosure policy that coincided with the strictest extant state statute was sufficiently reprehensible to justify a $2 million award of punitive damages.

Dr. Gore's second argument for treating BMW as a recidivist is that the company should have anticipated that its actions would be considered fraudulent in some, if not all, jurisdictions. This contention overlooks the fact that actionable fraud requires a material misrepresentation or omission. This qualifier invites line drawing of just the sort engaged in by States with disclosure statutes and by BMW. We do not think it can be disputed that there may exist minor imperfections in the finish of a new car that can be repaired (or indeed, left unrepaired) without materially affecting the car's value. There is no evidence that BMW acted in bad faith when it sought to establish the appropriate line between presumptively minor damage and damage requiring disclosure to purchasers. For this purpose, BMW could reasonably rely on state disclosure statutes for guidance. In this regard, it is also significant that there is no evidence that BMW persisted in a course of conduct after it had been adjudged unlawful on even one occasion, let alone repeated occasions.

Finally, the record in this case discloses no deliberate false statements, acts of affirmative misconduct, or concealment of evidence of improper motive . . . . We accept, of course, the jury's finding that BMW suppressed a material fact which Alabama law obligated it to communicate to prospective purchasers of repainted cars in that State. But the omission of a material fact may be less reprehensible than a deliberate false statement, particularly when there is a good-faith basis for believing that no duty to disclose exists.

That conduct is sufficiently reprehensible to give rise to tort liability, and even a modest award of exemplary damages, does not establish the high degree of culpability that warrants a substantial punitive damages award. Because this case exhibits none of the circumstances ordinarily associated with egregiously improper conduct, we are persuaded that BMW's conduct was not sufficiently reprehensible to warrant imposition of a $2 million exemplary damages award.

Ratio

The second and perhaps most commonly cited indicium of an unreasonable or excessive punitive damages award is its ratio to the actual harm inflicted on the plaintiff. The principle that exemplary damages must bear a "reasonable relationship" to compensatory damages has a long pedigree. . . . Our decisions in both *Haslip* and *TXO* endorsed the proposition that a comparison between the compensatory award and the punitive award is significant.

In *Haslip* we concluded that even though a punitive damages award of "more than 4 times the amount of compensatory damages," might be "close to the line," it did not "cross the line into the area of constitutional impropriety." *TXO,* following dicta in *Haslip,* refined this analysis by confirming that the proper inquiry is " 'whether there is a reasonable relationship between the punitive damages award and the harm likely to result from the defendant's conduct as well as the harm that actually has occurred.' " Thus, in upholding the $10 mil-

lion award in *TXO,* we relied on the difference between that figure and the harm to the victim that would have ensued if the tortious plan had succeeded. That difference suggested that the relevant ratio was not more than 10 to 1.

The $2 million in punitive damages awarded to Dr. Gore by the Alabama Supreme Court is 500 times the amount of his actual harm as determined by the jury.[35] Moreover, there is no suggestion that Dr. Gore or any other BMW purchaser was threatened with any additional potential harm by BMW's nondisclosure policy. The disparity in this case is thus dramatically greater than those considered in *Haslip* and *TXO.*

Of course, we have consistently rejected the notion that the constitutional line is marked by a simple mathematical formula, even one that compares actual and potential damages to the punitive award. Indeed, low awards of compensatory damages may properly support a higher ratio than high compensatory awards, if, for example, a particularly egregious act has resulted in only a small amount of economic damages. A higher ratio may also be justified in cases in which the injury is hard to detect or the monetary value of noneconomic harm might have been difficult to determine. It is appropriate, therefore, to reiterate our rejection of a categorical approach. Once again, "we return to what we said . . . in *Haslip:* 'We need not, and indeed we cannot, draw a mathematical bright line between the constitutionally acceptable and the constitutionally unacceptable that would fit every case. We can say, however, that [a] general concer[n] of reasonableness . . . properly enter[s] into the constitutional calculus.' " In most cases, the ratio will be within a constitutionally acceptable range, and remittitur will not be justified on this basis. When the ratio is a breathtaking 500 to 1, however, the award must surely "raise a suspicious judicial eyebrow."

Sanctions for Comparable Misconduct

Comparing the punitive damages award and the civil or criminal penalties that could be imposed for comparable misconduct provides a third indicium of excessiveness. As Justice O'CONNOR has correctly observed, a reviewing court engaged in determining whether an

---

35. Even assuming each repainted BMW suffers a diminution in value of approximately $4,000, the award is 35 times greater than the total damages of all 14 Alabama consumers who purchased repainted BMW's.

award of punitive damages is excessive should "accord 'substantial deference' to legislative judgments concerning appropriate sanctions for the conduct at issue." In *Haslip,* the Court noted that although the exemplary award was "much in excess of the fine that could be imposed," imprisonment was also authorized in the criminal context. In this case the $2 million economic sanction imposed on BMW is substantially greater than the statutory fines available in Alabama and elsewhere for similar malfeasance.

* * *

The sanction imposed in this case cannot be justified on the ground that it was necessary to deter future misconduct without considering whether less drastic remedies could be expected to achieve that goal. The fact that a multimillion dollar penalty prompted a change in policy sheds no light on the question whether a lesser deterrent would have adequately protected the interests of Alabama consumers. In the absence of a history of noncompliance with known statutory requirements, there is no basis for assuming that a more modest sanction would not have been sufficient to motivate full compliance with the disclosure requirement imposed by the Alabama Supreme Court in this case.

We assume, as the juries in this case and in the *Yates* case found, that the undisclosed damage to the new BMW's affected their actual value. Notwithstanding the evidence adduced by BMW in an effort to prove that the repainted cars conformed to the same quality standards as its other cars, we also assume that it knew, or should have known, that as time passed the repainted cars would lose their attractive appearance more rapidly than other BMW's. Moreover, we of course accept the Alabama courts' view that the state interest in protecting its citizens from deceptive trade practices justifies a sanction in addition to the recovery of compensatory damages. We cannot, however, accept the conclusion of the Alabama Supreme Court that BMW's conduct was sufficiently egregious to justify a punitive sanction that is tantamount to a severe criminal penalty.

The fact that BMW is a large corporation rather than an impecunious individual does not diminish its entitlement to fair notice of the demands that the several States impose on the conduct of its business. Indeed, its status as an active participant in the national economy implicates the federal interest in preventing individual States from imposing undue burdens on interstate commerce. While each State has ample power to protect its own consumers, none may use the punitive damages deterrent as a means of imposing its regulatory policies on the entire Nation.

As in *Haslip,* we are not prepared to draw a bright line marking the limits of a constitutionally acceptable punitive damages award. Unlike that case, however, we are fully convinced that the grossly excessive award imposed in this case transcends the constitutional limit. Whether the appropriate remedy requires a new trial or merely an independent determination by the Alabama Supreme Court of the award necessary to vindicate the economic interests of Alabama consumers is a matter that should be addressed by the state court in the first instance.

The judgment is reversed, and the case is remanded for further proceedings not inconsistent with this opinion.

It is so ordered.

Justice SCALIA, with whom Justice THOMAS joins, dissenting.

Today we see the latest manifestation of this Court's recent and increasingly insistent "concern about punitive damages that 'run wild.'" Since the Constitution does not make that concern any of our business, the Court's activities in this area are an unjustified incursion into the province of state governments.

In earlier cases that were the prelude to this decision, I set forth my view that a state trial procedure that commits the decision whether to impose punitive damages, and the amount, to the discretion of the jury, subject to some judicial review for "reasonableness," furnishes a defendant with all the process that is "due." I do not regard the Fourteenth Amendment's Due Process Clause as a secret repository of substantive guarantees against "unfairness"—neither the unfairness of an excessive civil compensatory award, nor the unfairness of an "unreasonable" punitive award. What the Fourteenth Amendment's procedural guarantee assures is an opportunity to contest the reasonableness of a damages judgment in state court; but there is no federal guarantee a damages award actually be reasonable.

. . . The Constitution provides no warrant for federalizing yet another aspect of our Nation's legal culture (no matter how much in need of correction it may be), and the application of the Court's new rule of constitutional law is constrained by no principle other than the Justices' subjective assessment of the "reasonableness" of the award in relation to the conduct for which it was assessed.

* * *

One might understand the Court's eagerness to enter this field, rather than leave it with the state legislatures, if it had something useful to say. In fact, however, its opinion provides virtually no guidance to legislatures, and to state and federal courts, as to what a "constitutionally proper" level of punitive damages might be.

Justice GINSBURG, with whom THE CHIEF JUSTICE joins, dissenting.

The Court, I am convinced, unnecessarily and unwisely ventures into territory traditionally within the States' domain, and does so in the face of reform measures recently adopted or currently under consideration in legislative arenas. The Alabama Supreme Court, in this case, endeavored to follow this Court's prior instructions; and, more recently, Alabama's highest court has installed further controls on awards of punitive damages. I would therefore leave the state court's judgment undisturbed, and resist unnecessary intrusion into an area dominantly of state concern.

* * *

The Court finds Alabama's $2 million award not simply excessive, but grossly so, and therefore unconstitutional. The decision leads us further into territory traditionally within the States' domain, and commits the Court, now and again, to correct "misapplication of a properly stated rule of law." The Court is not well equipped for this mission. Tellingly, the Court repeats that it brings to the task no "mathematical formula," no "categorical approach," ante, at 1602, no "bright line." It has only a vague concept of substantive due process, a "raised eyebrow" test, as its ultimate guide.[5]

_____

5. Justice BREYER'S concurring opinion offers nothing more solid. Under _Haslip,_ he acknowledges, Alabama's standards for punitive damages, standing alone, do not violate due process. But they "invit[e] the kind of scrutiny the Court has given the particular verdict before us." Pursuing that invitation, Justice BREYER concludes that, matching the particular facts of this case to Alabama's "legitimate punitive damages objectives," the award was "grossly excessive." The exercise is engaging, but ultimately tells us only this: too big will be judged unfair. What is the Court's measure of too big? Not a cap of the kind a legislature could order, or a mathematical test this Court can divine and impose. Too big is, in the end, the amount at which five Members of the Court bridle.

In contrast to habeas corpus review under 28 U.S.C. § 2254, the Court will work at this business alone. It will not be aided by the federal district courts and courts of appeals. It will be the only federal court policing the area. The Court's readiness to superintend state court punitive damages awards is all the more puzzling in view of the Court's longstanding reluctance to countenance review, even by courts of appeals, of the size of verdicts returned by juries in federal district court proceedings. And the reexamination prominent in state courts and in legislative arenas serves to underscore why the Court's enterprise is undue.

The United States Supreme Court found the award "grossly excessive" in relationship to the state's legitimate interests in punishment and deterrence. The plaintiff argued that the large punitive damage award was necessary to induce BMW to change its nationwide policy regarding disclosure, but the Court explained that allowing Alabama to do this would infringe on the policy choices of other states. Although a state has a right to protect its own consumers and economic interests, it cannot impose its will on other states. The Court concluded that BMW's conduct was not egregious enough to warrant a $2 million award: its actions were not sufficiently reprehensible; the ratio between the plaintiff's compensatory damages and his punitive damages was 500:1 (a ratio outside the bounds of reasonableness); and the award exceeded the sanctions for comparable misconduct in Alabama and elsewhere.

The Courts' analysis offers little guidance to the lower courts, as Justice Ginsburg pointed out in her dissent. "What is the Court's measure of too big? Not a cap of the kind a legislature could order, or a mathematical test this Court can divine and impose. Too big is, in the end, the amount at which five Members of the Court bridle." 116 S. Ct. at 1618. Justice Scalia reiterated this criticism in his dissent, lamenting that he could not understand why the Court entered the fray if it was not going to provide any guidance to legislatures in reference to the "constitutionally proper" level of punitive damages. _Id._ at 1610. Justice Ginsburg further suggested that tort reform at the federal level is a moot point now that so many states have taken on the reform issue themselves: "The Court, I am convinced, unnecessarily and unwisely ventures into territory traditionally within the States' domain, and does so in the face of reform measures recently adopted or currently under consideration in legislative arenas." *Id.* at 1614.

Are Punitive Damage Caps Effective?

Do the caps being proposed by such bills as the Common Sense Reform bills protect businesses? The Common Sense Product Liability Legal Reform Act of 1996 (which was vetoed by President Clinton on the ground that it would harm consumers more than it would correct the injustices of the legal system) was designed to establish a nationwide ceiling for punitive damage awards in product liability cases. The Act would have limited punitive damage awards to the greater of $250,000 or twice the plaintiff's total economic and noneconomic damages (pain and suffering, emotional distress, and loss of companionship). This Act would not protect small businesses, which would be devastated by a $250,000 verdict. Even large companies would face insolvency if the plaintiff's damages were high, as they are in a typical toxic tort case.

One way to assess the viability of proposed damage caps in preventing runaway awards is to apply the legislation to an actual jury award. Applying the provisions of the Product Liability Legal Reform Act to the $150 million verdict against General Motors in *Hardy* would have had no effect on that verdict. The jury in that case awarded $40 million in compensatory damages to the plaintiff, $10 million to the plaintiff's wife, and $100 million in punitive damages. Therefore, the $100 million punitive damage award was within the acceptable range of twice the compensatory damage award of $50 million.

Alternatives to Punitive Damage Caps

Some scholars suggest (as some states, such as Alabama, are already doing) that plaintiffs should be required to relinquish punitive damage awards to a third party, such as the state. Medical malpractice awards, for example, may be allocated toward improving the quality of medical care, thereby deterring physician misconduct. Doing so would discourage plaintiffs from bringing meritless suits. Also, because plaintiffs would not be the beneficiaries of such awards, relinquishment would address the criticism that punitive damages are a windfall to plaintiffs. Such claims would presumably be pressed by state-appointed attorneys who would pursue defendants with an eye for deterrence.

Others have suggested that structured guidelines be established for punitive damages. These guidelines could be structured around such factors as the actual harm the plaintiff suffered, the harm not covered by compensatory damages, the likelihood that plaintiffs will sue, and the chances that the defendant will escape detection. Having uniform guidelines would protect against excessive awards when deep-pocket defendants are involved and would still deter defendants whose actions resulted in social harm.

Punitive Damages: A Summary

Although punitive damages may serve a socially useful service of punishing tortfeasors, their deterrence value, their effects on plaintiffs' decisions to sue, and their potential inhibition of the medical and business communities are questionable. The Supreme Court concluded that punitive awards can violate the Due Process Clause if they are "grossly excessive," but the *BMW* decision will probably have little effect on the majority of cases involving punitive damages. Many states have imposed punitive damage caps, but these caps would not affect many cases, even those involving very large punitive damage awards.

Alternatives to damage caps have also been proposed, but two questions remain despite the efforts to curb punitive damages. First, are excessive punitive damages really a primary problem facing the tort system? Second, will any of the legislative reform being proposed or currently enacted actually change litigant behavior and jury outcomes? Or will it open the doorway for potential misconduct, particularly in the business and medical world?

■ PUTTING IT INTO PRACTICE 17.2 □

Assume you represent General Motors in *Hardy v. General Motors Corp.* What arguments would you make on appeal to support your contention that the punitive damage award was excessive? What arguments do you think the plaintiff would make in rebuttal?

Joint and Several Liability

Historically, the Progressive Era reformers heralded joint and several liability because it dispersed losses amongst defendants rather than plaintiffs and provided plaintiffs with full compensation for their injuries. They believed it was more important to compensate a victim of negligence than to protect a negligent tortfeasor from disproportionate liability.

Classical reformers, in contrast, labelled joint and several liability the "deep-pocket" theory, because it allowed plaintiffs to go after defendants with maximum financial resources even if they had minimal culpability. Besides perceiving that holding nominally culpable defendants wholly responsible was patently unfair, they also pointed out that plaintiffs must bear the risk of insolvent defendants in multiple-defendant actions just as they bore the risk of an insolvent defendant in a single-defendant action. (See Figure 17-8.) As one court noted, "Between one plaintiff and one defendant, the plaintiff bears the risk of the defendant being insolvent; on what basis does the risk shift if there are two defendants, and one is insolvent?" *Bartlett v. New Mexico Welding Supply, Inc.,* 646 P.2d 579, 585 (N.M. Ct. App. 1982). Further, they argued that this practice increased insurance costs because it precluded insurance companies from being able to accurately predict potential liability. Their reasoning was that anything that interfered with the insurer's predictive capacities led to increased costs. Some advocates of joint and several liability argue that elimination of this doctrine could lead to increased insurance rates because nonjoint liability would require more proceedings and longer court delays as more plaintiffs sued defendants individually (for strategic reasons).

The doctrine of joint and several liability was originally warmly embraced; by 1973, it was found in every state. Some studies, however, show that in actual practice joint and several liability is seldom relied upon. One Wisconsin study, for example, showed that joint and several liability played a role in only 1.6 percent of 834 personal injury jury verdicts (Paul Bargen, "Comment, Joint and Several Liability: Protection for Plaintiffs," 1994 *Wis. L. Rev.* 453).

Two conflicting objectives thus dominate the discussion of joint and several liability. The first objective is to hold defendants liable only for their proportionate share of fault. The second objective is to compensate plaintiffs fully for their injuries. When joint and several liability was originally instituted, the doctrine of contributory negligence prevailed. Under that doctrine, usually only wholly innocent plaintiffs could recover. Therefore, when the innocent plaintiff was compared to the tortfeasor, fairness dictated that the

FIGURE 17-8 Criticisms of Joint and Several Liability

- Unfair to defendants
- Plaintiff, not defendant, should bear risk of insolvency
- Increases insurance costs
- Under comparative negligence, joint and several liability is no longer necessary
- Causes increased taxes and reduced services by municipalities

guilty party bear the damages for other insolvent, unreachable, or unknown defendants.

Comparative negligence, however, changed this equation. Most states that adopted comparative negligence modified joint liability so that only defendants whose fault was relatively large in comparison to the plaintiff were jointly liable. In the words of one court:

> Previously when the plaintiff had to be totally without negligence to recover and the defendants had to be merely negligent to incur an obligation to pay, an argument could be made that justified putting the burden of seeking contribution on the defendants. Such an argument is no longer compelling because of the purpose and intent behind the adoption of the comparative negligence statute. It appears more reasonable for the legislature to have intended to relate duty to pay to the degree of fault. Any other interpretation [of the statute] destroys the fundamental conceptual basis for the abandonment of contributory negligence.

Brown v. Keill, 580 P.2d 867, 874 (Kan. 1978).

To see the inequities that can still result when joint and several liability coexists with comparative negligence, consider the case of a husband and wife who, while riding on a motorcycle, ran into an automobile. A jury determined that the husband was 99 percent negligent and that the driver of the automobile was 1 percent negligent. Although the husband was precluded from recovering, the defendant driver had to compensate the wife for the entire amount of her injuries because her husband was immune from suit.

Dunham v. Kampman, 547 P.2d 263 (Colo. Ct. App.), *aff'd en banc,* 560 P.2d 291 (Colo. 1977).

The drive to modify joint and several liability has stemmed from injustices such as this. Local governments also complained of being deep pockets even when their comparative fault was relatively low, and argued that such liability resulted in increased taxes and reduced services. At least thirty-five states responded by either abolishing or modifying the joint and several liability rule. Some states have abolished or modified joint and several liability except for certain types of torts (for example, those involving hazardous wastes) or when the plaintiff is fault-free (in which case joint and several liability applies). In other states, the doctrine applies only to certain types of damages (as in California, where joint and several liability was retained for economic damages but abolished for noneconomic damages), or its application depends on the percentage of the defendant's fault (as in Iowa, where joint and several liability applies unless a tortfeasor's fault is less than 50 percent of the total fault assigned to all parties).

To resolve the inequities of this doctrine, some have suggested that if a plaintiff is unable to collect from a defendant, the remaining parties, whether defendant or plaintiff, should be held accountable for that uncollected share, based on their individual fault percentage (assigned by the jury). This suggestion resolves the issue of unfairly burdening defendants who have committed minimal wrongs and, at the same time, ensures that joint tortfeasors are made to internalize costs created by an insolvent tortfeasor.

PUTTING IT INTO PRACTICE 17.3

Do you think joint and several liability should be maintained in a comparative negligence jurisdiction? Why or why not?

Collateral Source Payments

Under the collateral source rule, admission of evidence of payments already received by the plaintiff is precluded. The rationale for this rule is that the tortfeasor should not benefit from payments made by others for damages he has caused nor from insurance protection the plaintiff obtained on her own initiative. Furthermore, the reasoning underlying this rule holds that if the plaintiff's recovery were offset by collateral benefits, the deterrent effect of tort law would be diminished. Under this rule, the plaintiff is assured full compensation for all medical, physical, and emotional injuries.

Today, however, legal sentiment no longer favors double recovery for the same injury. At least nineteen states have passed statutes forbidding or limiting duplication in awards from multiple sources. The reasoning is that plaintiffs should be allowed to recover only an amount that provides compensation for actual injuries. The ability to admit evidence of supplemental benefits at trial ensures that liability is divided among all tortfeasors in accordance with their respective degrees of culpability.

Frivolous Lawsuits

In the Progressive Era, the notion of frivolous lawsuits was foreign to legal scholars, because the common law rules tended to be pro-defendant. Pretrial screening mechanisms made it unlikely that nonmeritorious claims would survive. As reforms led to the liberalization of tort rules, classical reformers observed that some plaintiffs were filing claims with the primary intent of inducing defendants to settle, in order to avoid the costs of litigation or the possibility of a large award. Because of this, insurance claims—and hence insurance premiums—escalated.

Reformers looked first to Rule 11 of the Federal Rules of Civil Procedure, which allows sanctions to be issued against parties who file frivolous lawsuits. Although this Rule was at first used infrequently by the courts, amendments to the Rule have eroded courts' reluctance to impose sanctions and encouraged them to use it as a tool to discourage frivolous lawsuits. More recently, however, the Common Sense Reform bills propose adoption of the British rule, which requires that losers in a lawsuit pay all or part of the winner's attorney fees. This rule is clearly intended to discourage plaintiffs from bringing claims they are likely to lose and to discourage defendants from settling frivolous claims to avoid the costs of trial, as those costs will be borne by the losing party.

Some argue that the British rule may actually increase administrative costs of the judicial system. When both parties believe they are going to win, they are less likely to settle under this rule, because the amount they estimate they will save by settling is unimportant if they believe their litigation costs will be covered. If fewer cases settle under this rule, administrative costs will rise.

A one-way fee-shifting rule has also been proposed by some scholars. This rule rewards plaintiffs who are successful, by reducing their litigation costs, but does not penalize plaintiffs who lose. Although such a rule encourages potential tortfeasors' compliance with the law, it does not discourage plaintiffs from suing. Therefore, such a rule does nothing to curb frivolous lawsuits and is unlikely to be given serious consideration in today's political climate.

An Alternative View

John Hasnas, Ph.D., J.D. (assistant professor at Georgetown University and Senior Research Fellow at the Kennedy Institute of Ethics) believes that the litigation explosion should come as no surprise. John Hasnas, "What's Wrong with a Little Tort Reform?" 32 *Idaho L. Rev.* 557 (1996). Dr. Hasnas sees this increase as a predictable consequence of Prosser's premise that the "business of the courts is to make precedent where a wrong calls for redress even if lawsuits must be multiplied" (Prosser, *Handbook of the Law of Torts* 202 (1941)). He claims that if the purpose of the tort system is to vindicate the wrongs suffered by members of society, then as the demands of social justice increase, new causes of action must be created to keep pace with newly recognized wrongs. Furthermore, the system's procedures must be changed to assist plaintiffs in getting before the courts, and the system must contain a punitive element to deter misconduct by potential tortfeasors.

Given these parameters, the litigation explosion is a natural consequence, not an aberration. The reforms in the past were intended to discourage unsafe practices by providing plaintiffs with the opportunity to recover from wealthy defendants. Certainly these reforms provided the incentive for defendants to avoid lawsuits by adopting safer procedures—but what was not considered was that they would also provide the incentive for plaintiffs to bring lawsuits, by making it easier and more profitable for them to sue.

Hasnas proposes that the real question about tort reform is not how to perfect the system but whether we are better off with an imperfect, self-correcting system than with a centrally planned, inherently static system. The common law, he argues, is a continually self-correcting (albeit never perfectly correct) system that is constantly evolving in response to problems as they arise. The rules of the system change as technology, economic conditions, and belief systems change. This system is a dynamic one that relies on trial and error to adapt to changing conditions. Ineffective decisions are abandoned while effective ones are assimilated into the body of the law.

Centrally planned legal reforms are spearheaded by legislators, judges, lawyers, and scholars. These reforms often create new problems, unanticipated by the reformers, that then have to be corrected by the next generation of reformers. Hasnas says that we have only to look at the history of tort reform to confirm this proposition. Tinkering with the system rarely effects "cures," he notes, because such manipulations fail to account for the dynamics of the social system.

Hasnas cites the recent decline in jury verdicts as evidence of how the common law works. After being deluged for the last few years by news articles and programs highlighting outrageous jury awards, the public has become acutely aware of the limitations of a policy of compensating those who have been wronged. It no longer perceives corporate America as a bottomless pit of financial wealth that can be mined indiscriminately. As a result, the *National Law Journal* has reported a decline in the overall number of "massive verdicts," as well in the level of ordinary awards in personal injury cases involving neither products liability nor medical malpractice ("Verdict Trends in 1995 Disregard the Clamor," *National Law Journal,* Feb. 5, 1996, at C2). Furthermore, Hasnas believes that lack of inflated awards in automobile accident cases may be due to jurors' understanding of the effects large awards have on their insurance premiums. He appeals to the common sense of jurors to allow tort reform to occur naturally, as part of the evolutionary development of the law, and counsels avoidance of the structured approach now being followed.

PUTTING IT INTO PRACTICE 17.4

What do you think Hasnas's assessment of the Common Sense Reform bills would be and why?

SUMMARY

Before a comprehensive reform of the tort system is attempted, a careful review of the goals of the system should be undertaken to determine if the goals are still viable and if they are being achieved by the current system. A historical review of the Progressive Era and classical reform movements illustrates how changes in goals have resulted in changes in tort law.

The deficiencies that today's reformers perceive in the tort system are that it is too plaintiff-oriented, that it encourages overly litigious behavior, that it promotes excessive jury awards, and that it inhibits the business and medical communities. Examples of plaintiff-oriented changes that reformers point to are the development of no-fault doctrines, the relaxation of causation requirements, the evolution of comparative negligence, and the abolition of privity. Claims of over-litigiousness, excessive jury awards, and inhibition of business and medical practices lack the support of unequivocal empirical evidence. Before these claims can be intelligently addressed, their validity must be verified and claims of cause-and-effect relationships must be carefully studied.

The primary objectives of tort reformers today are curbing damage awards and reducing the number of claims filed. Toward those ends, legislation has been proposed at the federal level and enacted at the state level that implements damage caps, that abolishes or modifies joint and several liability and the collateral source rule, and that discourages frivolous lawsuits. Although little evidence supports the contention that punitive damage awards are out of control, the bulk of reform measures has been directed at punitive damages. Whether the reforms that have been implemented actually solve the problems they are intended to address remains in question. In reviewing large punitive damage awards, the United States Supreme Court refused to apply the fines clause of the Eighth Amendment, but used the Due Process Clause to overturn an award that it found to be grossly excessive.

Since the introduction of comparative negligence, most states have abolished or modified the doctrine of joint and several liability, to avoid unfairness to wealthy defendants. By the same token, many states have modified the collateral source rule to limit some of the duplication that arises when the plaintiff is compensated by multiple sources. Federal Rule of Civil Procedure 11 has been amended, and some have recommended adoption of the British rule of fee-shifting as a means of discouraging frivolous lawsuits.

One scholar, Dr. John Hasnas, suggests that the litigation explosion should come as no surprise if the purpose of the tort system is to vindicate wrongs suffered by victims of torts. He suggests that we allow the system to self-correct through a natural evolutionary process rather than trying to change the system artificially.

TORT TEASERS

1. What reform measures have been instituted in your state in regard to damage caps, joint and several liability, the collateral source rule, and frivolous lawsuits? How effective have they been? What reform measures are currently proposed?

2. How would you answer this question: "Are the benefits that parties and attorneys reap by fighting in the courts worth the cost to the rest of society?" Explain your answer.

3. What is the essence of the debate surrounding joint and several liability? Summarize the arguments made for its retention and for its abolition. Do you think joint and several liability should be retained, abolished, or modified? Why?

4. Critique the Punitive Damages Act of New Jersey, which provides a cap on punitive damages of the greater of $350,000 or five times the defendant's liability for compensatory damages. The cap does not apply to certain "abhorrent offenses." The plaintiff must prove that the defendant acted with "actual malice" or "wanton or willful disregard" of injury to possible plaintiffs by clear and convincing evidence (the old law required a preponderance of the evidence). Punitive damages cannot be awarded for negligent or

grossly negligent conduct. In what ways does this statute satisfy the criticisms levied against punitive damages? What problems does it not resolve?

5. In the *National Law Journal,* on October 24, 1994, the lawyer who represented Stella Liebeck in the McDonald's "hot coffee" case had this to say:

Stella Liebeck, 79, purchased a cup of McDonald's coffee while a passenger in her grandson's automobile. Ms. Liebeck attempted to hold the cup securely between her knees while she removed the plastic lid. It tipped over, causing third-degree burns that necessitated hospitalization for eight days, whirlpool treatment for debridement of her wounds and skin grafting, and led to permanent scarring and disability for more than two years. The jury awarded her $200,000 in compensatory damages, reduced by 20 percent for her negligence, and $2.7 million in punitive damages.

The jury found that the product was unreasonably dangerous and was sold in breach of the implied warranty of fitness imposed by the Uniform Commercial Code.

McDonald's Corp. sold its coffee at 180–190 degrees Fahrenheit by corporate specification. McDonald's coffee, if spilled, could cause full-thickness burns (third degree to the muscle/fatty tissue layer) in two to seven seconds.

McDonald's knew about this unacceptable risk for more than 10 years; it was brought to the company's attention by other lawsuits (more than 700 reported claims from 1982 to 1992). The company's witnesses testified that it did not intend to turn down the heat. McDonald's generates revenues in excess of $1.3 million daily from the sale of coffee alone.

Ms. Liebeck's treating physician testified that this was one of the worst scald burns he had ever seen. Other expert witnesses termed the risk of harm from McDonald's coffee to be unacceptable. Most consumers don't know that coffee this hot causes such injuries. Nor do they know McDonald's made a practice of serving its coffee this hot.

The jury applied the law of punitive damages to deter McDonald's and other similarly situated corporations from exposing consumers to this risk. It imposed a penalty of two days' revenue from coffee sales, or $2.7 million, for willfully ignoring the safety of customers who feed the McDonald's money tree . . . .

The news media, the day after the verdict, established that coffee at the McDonald's in Albuquerque is now sold at 158 degrees. At that temperature, it would take about 60 seconds to cause third-degree burns.

Do you think the punitive damage award was a reasonable one in light of the facts given here? Why or why not? Does this award satisfy the purpose of punitive damages? Does it illustrate any of the criticisms levied against punitive damages? If you think the award was unreasonable, propose a workable alternative.

CHAPTER

18

Automobile Insurance

CHAPTER TOPICS

CHAPTER OBJECTIVES

In this chapter you will learn to:
- Identify the characteristics of medical payment, collision, comprehensive, UM, UIM, and umbrella coverage
- Recognize an insurer's subrogation and termination rights
- Recognize when reformation of policies is appropriate
- Describe the arbitration process used to resolve disputes
- Identify the characteristics of no-fault automobile insurance

As Pauline and Perry are leaving their local fast-food restaurant, Perry prepares to make a left turn across traffic on a four-lane street immediately in front of the restaurant. Upon pulling out into traffic, Pauline and Perry's 1990 Chevrolet, a one-half-ton pickup, is broadsided in the second lane of traffic by Denise, who is driving a 1963 Chrysler. Her fourteen-year-old brother, David, is a passenger. Perry, who is not wearing a seat belt, is critically injured in the accident and dies ten days later. Pauline, who is wearing her seat belt, is also seriously injured. She suffers a broken shoulder, a concussion, extensive scarring to the side of her face, and severe soft tissue injuries, including cervical strain and sprain.

Neither Denise, a sixteen-year-old unlicensed driver, nor David is wearing a seat belt. Denise's injuries require only minor medical treatment. David, however, is catapulted from the front seat through the windshield of the Chrysler and suffers severe facial injuries as well as nerve damage that renders him a paraplegic.

Pauline and Perry's automobile insurance policy for the pickup, set forth in Appendix D, provides $100,000/$300,000 liability coverage, $10,000 medical payments coverage, $50,000 property damage coverage, and $15,000/$30,000 in both UM (uninsured motorist) coverage and UIM (underinsured motorist) coverage. They also have a $500 deductible collision coverage and a zero deductible comprehensive provision. The Chrysler that Denise is driving, which she took without her parent's permission, has no applicable insurance. Her father had purchased the car five months earlier and was in the process of restoring it.

At the time of the accident Denise was driving with her headlights off. Pauline tells the investigating officers that she was looking to the left when her husband was making his turn and did not see the Chrysler coming. Wilma, a registered nurse who was immediately behind Pauline and Perry at the restaurant exit, tells the investigating officer that she saw the Chrysler approaching even without seeing its headlights. Warren, a construction worker driving a van, tells the investigating officers that he was approximately fifty yards behind Denise at the time of the accident and that Denise was driving at the speed limit but never applied her brakes prior to impact with Perry's pickup. Warren also states that the Chrysler did not have illuminated taillights. In fact, he says, he almost ran into Denise's car earlier because the car, being dark green and unilluminated, was difficult to see at night.

Denise's father is an assembler at a local electronics plant, where he works the night shift from 4 to 12 P.M. Her mother has been hospitalized for two weeks with a serious illness, which has severely strapped the family's financial resources. Because her mother was hospitalized and her father was working, Denise had the responsibility of watching out for David. For this reason she had access to the keys to the Chrysler. Prior to this joy riding incident Denise had always been a very responsible teenager and was an honor student at her high school. We will use this scenario in the Tort Teasers section at the end of the chapter to apply the concepts presented throughout this chapter.

OVERVIEW OF AUTOMOBILE INSURANCE

As mentioned in Chapter 17, more litigation arises out of the automobile insurance contract than any other type of insurance. The horrendous number of automobile accidents, coupled with the mandatory insurance legislation in most states, has created this proliferation of lawsuits. Failure to obtain and maintain the minimal insurance coverage required by state law can prevent an automobile owner from either registering or driving a vehicle. Additionally, in most states either civil or criminal sanctions await those who unlawfully drive without mandatory insurance coverage.

The types of automobile insurance coverage available vary, depending on whether the state is *fault* or *no-fault*. No-fault insurance is based on the concept that the insured's carrier should pay for the insured's damages regardless of who is at fault.

AUTOMOBILE LIABILITY COVERAGE

The primary purpose of automobile insurance is to provide liability coverage to the insured for the bodily injury or property damage he or she causes while operating an automobile. (See Figure 18-1.) An example of the terms and conditions of liability and property damage coverage is set forth in coverage N (Section III) of the insurance policy in Appendix D. This coverage provides either split limits or single-limit coverage. With split limits coverage, each individual may recover a set amount of damages, with an aggregate amount available for damages independent of the total number of individuals injured. A single-limit coverage amount for property damage resulting from the insured's negligence is usually provided.

An example of split-limits coverage is the minimum limits set by many states, in which $15,000 must be available for each person injured and $30,000 must be available as an aggregate amount for all individuals injured. If a minimum of $10,000 were required to cover property damage, the liability limits of such a policy would be described as $15,000/$30,000/$10,000.

Figure 18-2 lists types of automobile insurance coverage.

Umbrella Policy

The total limits of liability available for bodily injury and property damage are as high as the maximum amount provided by the carrier issuing the policy. As a practical matter, however, bodily injury limits

---

FIGURE 18-1   Characteristics of Automobile Policies

- Single limit versus split limits
- Coordination of benefits provisions
- Primary versus secondary coverage
- Subrogation rights
- Arbitration rights

---

in excess of $250,000 to $500,000 and property damage in excess of $100,000 generally are not covered by the automobile policy itself but by a separate policy called an **umbrella policy.** The umbrella policy may be written by the same carrier issuing the automobile insurance policy or by a different carrier. Such a policy is usually subject to a large deductible.

The umbrella carrier is liable only after the first insurer pays the full limits of its coverage. If, for example, a primary insurer pays $500,000 to the person injured by the insured for bodily injuries but the individual actually sustains $750,000 in damages for bodily injuries, the umbrella carrier would pay the additional $250,000 (or the amount up to the limits of the insured's umbrella policy).

Reformation of Policy

If an insurance carrier attempts to issue a policy with limits less than those required by the statute, the courts will **reform the policy** by construing it to provide the minimum statutory coverage. In some instances the insurance policy itself provides terms and conditions to conform the policy to state law in the event the cancellation or nonrenewal provisions are contrary to the laws of the state. An example of this type of provision is shown in the policy in Appendix D in Section V, part VIII, paragraph 15.

Subrogation

If an insurer pays its insured, the insurer is then subrogated to the rights of the insured and can sue the responsible party. **Subrogation** allows an insurer to institute suit against the responsible person, in the name of the insured, to collect the amounts paid by the insurer to the insured. Subrogation is universally allowed with respect to uninsured motorist, collision, and comprehensive payments made by the insurer. If subrogation is allowed, the insured has an obligation to cooperate with his or her insurer in the subrogation claim. Cooperation could include assisting the insurer at trial and in the discovery process.

FIGURE 18-2   Types of Coverage

LIABILITY COVERAGE	Coverage for losses caused by the insured while operating a motor vehicle.
MEDICAL PAYMENT	Reimbursement of medical expenses incurred when injured in vehicle covered by policy.
COMPREHENSIVE	Coverage for losses resulting from something other than collision.
COLLISION	Reimbursement for repair or replacement of damaged vehicle.
ACCESSORY COVERAGE	Emergency road service. Car rental. Death and disability.
UNINSURED MOTORIST COVERAGE	Coverage for losses caused by uninsured motorist.
UNDERINSURED MOTORIST COVERAGE	Coverage for losses caused by motorist whose liability insurance is insufficient to cover the insured's losses.

An example of a subrogation provision is shown in the policy in Appendix D in coverage P (Section III), paragraph 6, and endorsement 303 (Section III), paragraph 6. A subrogation provision called a trust agreement provides that the insured will take no action that would cause the insurer to lose any of its rights of recovery against either the uninsured or underinsured motorist. In many states there is no right of subrogation for underinsured motorist claims.

PUTTING IT INTO PRACTICE 18.1

1. A single-limit policy provides for $300,000 in bodily injury coverage and $50,000 in property damage coverage. How would you shorthand the coverage available?
2. An umbrella policy can also provide extended protection for uninsured (UM) and underinsured motorist (UIM) coverage. Check with your insurance agent and determine the additional cost to put UM and UIM coverage under an umbrella policy.

MEDICAL PAYMENT COVERAGE

Medical payment coverage provides for reimbursement of all reasonable medical expenses incurred by an insured while occupying a covered vehicle or when the insured, as a pedestrian, is struck by a different vehicle. In some states medical payment coverage is referred to as *personal injury protection* (PIP). If the insured is injured in a motor vehicle owned by someone other than the insured, the owner's medical payment coverage will be **primary.** In other words, the automobile owner's medical payment coverage will be primarily responsible for payment of the insured's medical expenses up to the limits of the owner's medical payment coverage.

If the insured's medical expenses exceed the owner's limits, the coverage available to the insured under his or her own medical payment coverage will come into effect. Suppose an automobile owner's medical payment coverage is $5,000 and the individual injured has medical payment coverage of his own for $10,000. If the individual incurs reasonable medical expenses of $20,000, the first $5,000 will be paid by the owner's policy, the next $10,000 by the injured person's medical payments carrier, and the balance of $5,000 by the injured party or his own health insurance policy, assuming no third party is liable for the injuries.

Most medical payment policies provide that benefits are payable only for those medical expenses incurred within a fixed time period after the date of the accident. Typically, these time periods range from one to three years after the accident. If medical expenses are incurred after this time has elapsed, the insurer is not responsible for payment.

In most instances, an injured party may receive benefits under medical payment coverage in addition to any benefits received under any of his or her other medical policies. Some policies have a **coordination of benefits provision,** which precludes payment if other insurance is available. If neither the medical payments nor the health insurance coverage has a coordination of benefits provision, the injured party can lawfully recover twice for medical expenses. Such recovery is, of course, subject to any deductible or co-insurance limit in the health insurance policy. This double recovery, allowed under the so-called collateral source rule (see Chapter 8 on damages), is premised on the idea that the insured, who is paying a separate premium for each type of coverage, may reap the benefits of his or her investment.

Many medical payment plans also provide for benefits in the event of the insured's death. Death benefits are usually fixed at a certain dollar amount and are intended, in part at least, to cover burial expenses. Medical expenses incurred by the deceased up to the date of death are also covered.

The terms and conditions of a typical medical payment provision are listed in coverage Q (Section III) of the insurance policy in Appendix D. Be aware that the exclusions are applicable to all coverage in Section III of the policy.

COMPREHENSIVE COVERAGE

Comprehensive automobile insurance provides coverage for loss to the insured vehicle and, in some cases, to a nonowned automobile for losses other than those resulting from collision. Coverage for property damage and loss caused by fire, theft, windstorm, and hail is included. Losses typically recovered under comprehensive coverage are from a shattered windshield, from the theft of valuables from a vehicle, and from the loss of a vehicle and its contents due to fire or theft. Reimbursement for a lost or damaged item is determined by its *actual cash value* (purchase price less depreciation) or its *replacement cost.* Many policies require physical signs of forced entry before the insured can be reimbursed for stolen property. Some policies are subject to a deductible, which is the responsibility of the insured to pay.

State insurance departments do not require comprehensive coverage to be part of the standard automobile insurance contract. However, if a vehicle is being financed through some kind of financing institution, the insured may be required to maintain comprehensive as well as collision coverage. Typical provisions providing comprehensive coverage are shown in Appendix D under coverages R and S (Section III).

COLLISION INSURANCE

Collision insurance reimburses the insured if he or she must repair or replace a damaged vehicle. Like medical payment insurance, collision insurance provides coverage irrespective of who is to blame for the damages. In the case of a negligent motorist, the carrier is subrogated to the rights of the insured and can seek reimbursement from the motorist for any expenses it incurs in repairing the insured vehicle. If the damage is caused by the insured's own negligence, the insurer has no right to seek payment from the insured. Most collision policies are issued subject to a deductible. Typical examples of the protection provided by having collision coverage are also set forth in the policy in Appendix D under coverage T (Section III).

MISCELLANEOUS COVERAGE

The automobile insurance contract can also include coverage for emergency road service, which pays for towing and any other emergency services occurring on the road, up to a maximum amount (often $25). Its primary purpose is to pay for towing a disabled vehicle to the nearest service station. Other available coverages include death and disability insurance and car rental insurance. Most provisions of this type establish the absolute maximum amount for which the insurer is liable as well as the maximum per diem expense that will be paid.

Care should be taken in selecting these accessory coverages. Make sure the premium for the risk to be covered is in proportion to the premiums and risk covered in a regular disability or accidental death policy. The latter may provide coverage whether or not the incident triggering coverage resulted from the use of an automobile.

These types of "miscellaneous" coverage provisions are shown in Appendix D as endorsements 323, 334, 335, and 368 (Section III).

UNINSURED MOTORIST COVERAGE

Next to liability insurance, the most important coverage available under the standard automobile insurance contract is uninsured motorist coverage (UM), which provides coverage only for injuries caused by an uninsured motorist. The percentage of uninsured motorists on the road is alarmingly high, especially in those states requiring automobile insurance coverage but not requiring written proof of such insurance when one registers a motor vehicle. Because many uninsured motorists are financially incapable of paying any substantial award for damages they inflict, UM coverage ensures that funds are available to compensate the injured insured. This coverage guarantees that the insured will be compensated, up to the limits of his policy, by his own insurer to the extent that a third party (the uninsured motorist) is responsible for his injuries.

An *uninsured motorist* is typically defined as a motorist having no applicable automobile insurance policy for the vehicle being driven or having an applicable policy with an insolvent insurance carrier. In some policies a hit-and-run driver may be considered an uninsured motorist.

Most states require that UM coverage be provided with the issuance of a liability policy. The minimum limits of this coverage are generally set by statute and are often the same as the minimum coverage limits required for liability insurance coverage. Uninsured motorist coverage typically does not provide for any deductible to be paid by the insured. In most states the insured's carrier can reduce the amount of damages paid to its insured in proportion to the insured's own negligence.

If payment is made to the insured, the UM carrier is subrogated to the rights of its insured and can bring an action in the name of its insured against the responsible party. Subrogation relieves the insured of having to chase the uninsured motorist to either obtain or collect a judgment.

An insurance company cannot, for the most part, attempt to offset monies paid under a medical payment policy against the amount otherwise due the insured under a UM policy, especially if the policy is the minimal amount allowed by law. Suppose an insured has $10,000 in medical payment coverage and $15,000 in UM coverage (the statutory minimum). The carrier cannot credit monies paid under medical payments to the amount otherwise due the insured under her UM coverage. That credit might, however, be allowed if the insured has UM coverage in excess of the statutory minimum.

Primary versus Secondary Coverage

Most UM policies provide coverage regardless of whether the insured was driving the automobile specifically referred to in the policy or a different vehicle. If the insured was driving a different vehicle, the uninsured motorist coverage will be coordinated with the coverage that would otherwise be available on the vehicle being driven. Most policies designate the coverage provided with the vehicle being driven as **primary** and the policy covering the driver (the insured in this case) as **secondary.** The primary carrier is liable for all damages up to the limits of its policy. At that point the secondary carrier is liable for any damages sustained by the insured above the limits of the primary policy up to the amount of the insured's loss or the limits of the excess policy, whichever is less.

Coordination of Benefits

If an insured has applicable insurance in addition to that provided by his or her automobile policy, the **coordination of benefits provision** of most policies will require the insurance carrier to be responsible for its pro rata share of the damages, as long as the insured is driving his or her own vehicle. A carrier's pro rata share is determined by the proportion of its coverage to the total amount of available insurance. Suppose the insured has UM coverage of $50,000 per person and an additional $100,000 of coverage under a different but applicable policy. The UM insurance carrier would be responsible for no more than one-third of the damages ($50,000/$150,000), up to a total maximum liability of $50,000. Because the other carrier that provided $100,000 of coverage probably has a comparable coordination of benefits provision, litigation between the two carriers would likely be necessary to determine their respective obligations. Coordination of benefits provisions also apply to underinsured coverage.

Typical provisions contained in a policy providing uninsured motorist coverage are set forth in coverage P (Section III) of Appendix D.

UNDERINSURED MOTORIST COVERAGE

Underinsured motorist (UIM) coverage protects the insured who is injured by a motorist whose liability coverage is insufficient to fully compensate the insured for his or her injuries. UIM coverage is applicable, for example, when the insured sustains $50,000 in damages but the responsible party has only $15,000 worth of liability coverage. In that case the responsible party's insurance carrier will pay $15,000 and the insured's UIM policy will compensate the insured for the remaining $35,000, assuming the UIM coverage limit is $35,000 or greater. Underinsured motorist coverage typically does not provide for any deductible to be paid by the insured.

Most states prohibit **stacking** of UM and UIM coverage. In other words, UM and UIM are not available to the insured for the same accident. Therefore, an uninsured motorist who is the responsible party cannot be alleged by the insured to be both uninsured for the purposes of UM coverage and underinsured for purposes of UIM coverage. In multivehicle accidents, however, UM coverage may be applicable to one joint tortfeasor and UIM coverage may be applicable to another.

Typical provisions contained in a policy providing underinsured motorist coverage are set forth in endorsement 303 (Section III) of Appendix D.

---

1. To reduce premiums, some companies are now providing medical payment coverages that have deductible and co-insurance provisions. What would be the advantage of having medical payments insurance if you had your own nonautomotive medical insurance?
2. Refer to the scenario at the beginning of this chapter. Assuming that Denise's vehicle had an applicable liability policy for property damage, why might Pauline have her vehicle repaired under her own collision coverage, even with its $500 deductible?
3. A comprehensive coverage loss is usually evaluated on the basis of actual cash value. Why might it be worth the additional premium expense to purchase replacement cost coverage?
4. Some states have begun to make uninsured motorist coverage optional rather than required. Is UM coverage still required in your state? Does it have to be *offered* to you even if you are not required to have it?
5. Does your state allow the insurer subrogation for the amount it pays to the insured under underinsured motorist coverage?

ARBITRATION

Most policies require arbitration for disputes arising out of medical payment, UM, and UIM coverage with respect to the amount of damages sustained by the insured. As most states favor the use of arbitration to resolve contractual disputes, these policy provisions are generally enforceable. Both the insured and the carrier are usually required to select and pay for an arbiter of their choosing. The two arbiters then select a third arbiter, whose compensation is split evenly by the insured and the insurer.

In a hearing before the three arbiters, local evidentiary rules are often applied; a decision rendered by two of the arbiters is binding on both parties. Often, however, the arbitration clause provides that if an award is entered in excess of the statutory minimal limits for bodily injury, the arbitration award will not be binding. If either party contests an award, a trial de novo, in which the issue of damages is relitigated without regard to the arbiters' findings, is held. An arbiter's findings with respect to the insured's damages are not admissible at trial.

A typical arbitration requirement is shown in Appendix D in paragraph 5 of coverage P (Section III). These arbitration provisions relate only to uninsured and underinsured motorist coverage claims. However, many policies also require that disputes with respect to medical payments be arbitrated.

TERMINATION

An automobile insurance contract can be terminated at the request of the insured or due to the acts of the insured. If the insured chooses to terminate his or her policy, the termination is effective on the date notice is given, usually to the insured's agent. The insured is then entitled to a return, usually pro rata, of any advance premiums paid.

Voluntary termination has been complicated in some states by mandatory insurance requirements. In certain circumstances termination can result in the insured forfeiting his or her registration rights to the vehicle unless another policy that meets state requirements is taken out. Statutes and case law should be carefully researched to determine the implications of voluntary termination.

If the insurer initiates termination, it must comply with the policy's notification requirements as well as the terms and conditions upon which termination is permitted in that state. Termination is always an option for an insurer if an insured fails to pay the premiums. In most instances the insured must be given written notice. Termination for nonpayment may become effective only after a designated time period following the giving of written notice. The insurer may also terminate a policy if an insured or driver who lives with the insured has his or her license suspended or revoked. In accord with current societal attitudes about intoxication, most policies allow termination if an insured is convicted of driving while intoxicated.

PUTTING IT INTO PRACTICE 18.3

1. A policy clause regarding arbitration provides that local rules of law regarding arbitration apply. Does your jurisdiction have applicable arbitration statutes? Does your court have rules of mandatory arbitration for lawsuits?
2. If you had a small claim that was subject to arbitration, would the prospect of having to pay for 1.5 arbitrators to have it evaluated affect your position on settlement?
3. How many days' notice does your state require for an automobile insurance policy to be terminated for nonpayment of the premium? For too many tickets? For conviction of DUI?

NO-FAULT INSURANCE

No-fault automobile insurance was created in response to what was perceived as a crisis in the automobile insurance industry—a crisis caused by the increasing volume of tort claims for automobile accidents. In concept, no-fault insurance was to result in prompt payment to injured insureds for economic damages and in reduced automobile insurance premiums. Neither goal has been attained.

In a pure no-fault jurisdiction the insured gives up her right to sue in tort for damages sustained as a result of a third party's negligence. The injured insured's own carrier pays for the damages she sustains, up to the limits of her own policy. The ability to recover for pain and suffering is relinquished in exchange for a promised reward of lower premiums and prompt payment for economic loss. Of the more than twenty states that have adopted no-fault statutes, none is "pure" no-fault.

In all no-fault states, the right to sue for tort damages is retained for intentional injuries inflicted with an automobile and for injuries caused by intoxicated drivers. Many no-fault states have set limits above which the injured party may sue the responsible party for tort damages. In Colorado, for example, the injured insured cannot sue in tort until her medical expenses exceed $2,500. (Legislators are constantly tinkering with the no-fault figures, so this number may have already changed by the time you read this.)

These thresholds are generally tied to an injured person's medical expenses. They begin as low as $200 (New Jersey) and go as high as $5,600 (Hawaii). Some states, such as New York ($50,000), have higher thresholds but are not tied to medical expenses alone. Some no-fault states allow tort damage claims if the injured person suffers a permanent disability or disfigurement.

States also vary greatly in the minimum amount of benefits they require insureds to purchase. These benefits, often called *personal injury protection,* vary from a few thousand dollars to an unlimited amount. Separate limits may be set for various types of damages; for example, medical expenses, lost wages, and rehabilitation may all have different limits. Alternatively, an aggregate limit, such as $50,000, may be set for all economic damages sustained in an accident.

The no-fault experiment has not been particularly successful. In many states, such as New Jersey, the threshold for suing in tort is so low that the no-fault benefits are merely add-on costs for the typical tort suit that follows. The existence of a threshold amount also appears to have increased treatment expenses in no-fault states. To illustrate, when one no-fault state raised its threshold amount, the average cost of treatment expenses went up by an equal amount. In that same state the average number of chiropractic visits per automobile accident went from 10 to 30 and the total payout for chiropractic services increased 320 percent.

In many ways the no-fault system closely parallels the workers' compensation acts discussed in Chapter 20. In a no-fault system the right to sue is relinquished; medical expenses are paid; and, after a prescribed waiting period, lost wages are paid for a preset percentage of the insured's average monthly wage. Unlike workers' compensation, no-fault medical and rehabilitation expenses are limited by the amount of coverage purchased, as is the amount of lost wages.

Ideas currently under discussion include prohibiting uninsured motorists from suing for damages they sustain, because they have not contributed to the insurance pool. A less punitive approach is to prohibit uninsureds from suing for pain and suffering but to allow them to claim economic losses.

No-fault is a relatively new concept, and one that has been implemented fairly recently in many states. Changes occur with great frequency in almost every no-fault jurisdiction. The applicable limits for the various required coverages and the threshold levels for suit are constantly being adjusted. No jurisdiction has yet allowed no-fault and traditional tort remedies to co-exist. The possibility of that occurring now appears more likely, however, as neither system has lived up to the expectations of its proponents. One stumbling block to greater experimentation with no-fault is the states' constitutions, many of which have provisions prohibiting interference with citizens' right to sue.

SUMMARY

The primary purpose of automobile insurance is to protect the insured for expenses incurred as a result of bodily injury or property damage caused while the insured is operating his or her automobile. Both single-limit and split-limits coverage are available. Umbrella policies are available as a secondary source of coverage when the full limits of the primary coverage are exceeded. Courts will reform policies in which the policy limits are less than those required by statute.

The insurer is subrogated to the rights of the insured, which allows the insurer to institute suit against the responsible person in the name of the insured. Many states prohibit subrogation with respect to UIM claims. An insured has an obligation to cooperate with his or her insurer in subrogation claims.

Medical payment coverage reimburses the insured for all reasonable medical expenses incurred while occupying a covered vehicle or when, as a pedestrian, he or she is struck by a different vehicle. If an insured is injured in a motor vehicle owned by someone other than the insured, the automobile owner's medical payment coverage is primarily responsible for payment of the insured's medical expenses up to the limits of the owner's medical payment coverage. Once that limit is exceeded, the insured's own medical payment coverage takes effect. If the medical payment coverage has a coordination of benefits provision, the injured may not be allowed to recover twice for his or her medical expenses.

Other types of available automobile insurance coverages include comprehensive, collision, and "accessory" coverages such as towing, car rental, and death and disability insurance. Comprehensive coverage applies to property damage and losses caused by fire, theft, windstorm, and hail. Collision insurance provides coverage regardless of who is to blame for the damages.

Most states require uninsured motorist (UM) coverage. A carrier cannot credit monies paid under a medical payment policy to the amount due the insured under his or her UM coverage unless the insured has UM coverage in excess of the statutory minimum. Most UM policies provide coverage regardless of whether the insured was driving the automobile referred to in the policy or a different vehicle. Underinsured motorist (UIM) coverage protects an insured who is injured by a motorist whose liability coverage is insufficient to fully compensate the insured for the injuries sustained. Most states prohibit stacking of UM and UIM coverage.

Arbitration is usually required as a means of resolving disputes that arise with respect to coverage. An arbitration award is often not binding if it exceeds the statutory minimum limits for bodily injury.

An insured can voluntarily terminate his or her automobile insurance contract by giving notice to the agent. Likewise, an insurer can terminate the contract for nonpayment of premiums, or because the insured's license is suspended or revoked, or if the insured is convicted of driving while intoxicated.

No-fault insurance is an alternative to the tort system for dealing with automobile accident cases. In no-fault the insured gives up the right to sue for pain and suffering (in varying degrees) for promised prompt payment of economic losses and reductions in automobile insurance premiums. This relatively new concept is in the experimental stage, but the results to date have not met its proponents' expectations.

■ PRACTICE POINTERS □

Once your law firm has been retained (and sometimes before), you will want to review the client's automobile insurance policy. In many cases the client has been with the same insurer for some time and may not be able to find his policy; or he may not be able to find all the various endorsements and amendments that have been made a part of the original policy. Make sure that you are aware of all insurance policies that might provide coverage for the accident. An injured passenger, for example, might have his own medical payments coverage, which might be available to him if the medical payments coverage on the vehicle in which he is injured is insufficient to pay for all his medical expenses.

If your client cannot find a current policy, or if you think that the documents provided are not complete, have the client contact his insurance agent and request a copy of the policy that was in effect on the date of the accident. Most of the relevant facts regarding the policy can be found on the declarations page of the policy. Many companies make the declarations page a part of their annual or semiannual billing. On policies that are paid monthly, the declarations page is generally not included with the monthly invoice.

In Appendix D, at the end of part VIII, is the declaration page for Pauline's policy. It provides bodily injury coverage of $100,000 per person, $300,000 per accident and $50,000 for property damage (a $100,000/$300,000/$50,000 liability policy). Medical payments coverage is $10,000 per person and $30,000 per accident. Uninsured and underinsured motorist coverage are the same: $15,000 per person,

Continued on next page

$30,000 per accident. There is no provision showing either collision or comprehensive coverage. The bells and whistles for towing, car rental, etc. are not shown and should not be a part of the policy.

After reviewing the policy for the types of coverage and their dollar limits, discuss the results with the client. It is not unusual for a client to think he had coverage not shown on the declarations page (and/or not to know of coverage he *does* have). Any questions raised should be thoroughly investigated.

In many policies, accessory coverages like towing, car rental, additional living expenses, etc., are not detailed on the declarations page. Often they are shown only by a notation such as "additional coverage (or additional endorsements)—323, 324, 368." Some companies use letters rather than numbers to designate additional coverage. What is important, as shown in endorsements 323, 324, and 368 above, and which are set forth in detail in the Appendix D, Endorsements Applicable to Section III, are the details and amount of coverage specified in the policy. With the new insurance coverages and provisions (such as having a deductible and co-insurance with medical payments coverage) being offered, each policy must be thoroughly examined.

Your supervising attorney should direct you on how to proceed after coverage is decided. Some firms assist in filing related claims for towing, car rental, and so on. Others bring such matters to the client's attention so that he can institute the procedures and paperwork for reimbursement with the insurer.

While you are identifying and reviewing all applicable automobile insurance policies, also examine the client's medical insurance policies. It may be that the client can legally submit his medical expenses to both the automobile insurer and the medical insurer. It is also possible that his medical insurer is an ERISA plan, which is governed by the federal law. ERISA plans provide for reimbursement from the insured for any medical expenses incurred as a result of the acts of third parties if the insured is paid damages by the third party. The client's medical policy may also have provisions that the client should be reminded of, such as the deductible (if any), co-insurance, dollar limits on chiropractic or other treatment, exclusion of certain types of treatment from coverage, and so forth. Make sure that you and the client know about any insurer that may make a claim on any portion of the proceeds from settlement or trial, as well as the amount of the claim.

TORT TEASERS

Reread the introductory scenario at the beginning of this chapter and use the insurance policy in Appendix D when necessary to answer the following questions.

1. Pauline seeks legal advice to determine her rights in reference to the medical expenses incurred by her and her late husband, the damages she sustained, and Perry's wrongful death. Denise and David also see an attorney, who says that she cannot represent both Denise and David because David may have a claim against Denise. She then refers Denise to another attorney.

If the parties sustain the following damages, the questions before us are who has a claim against whom and what portions of Pauline and Perry's insurance policy are applicable.

• Perry—medical expenses of $6,000, funeral expenses of $4,000.

• Pauline—medical expenses of $15,000, personal damages of $90,000, wrongful death claim with respect to Perry of $250,000, property damage claim of $16,000.

• Denise—medical expenses of $500, personal damages of $3,500.

• David—medical expenses of $24,000, future medical expenses of $76,000, personal damages of $2.5 million.

• Denise's father—property damage claim of $840.

Use this scenario to review the concepts you have learned. To resolve issues of damages you will first need to assess the liability of the parties and determine any defenses they can raise. To assist in doing this you might want to review Chapters 5–9, 15–16.

2. How much, if any, would Perry and Pauline's insurance carrier have to pay of Pauline's medical expenses of $15,000, the $6,000 in medical expenses incurred by Perry prior to his death, and Perry's funeral expenses of $4,000?

3. Does Pauline have a claim against Denise that should be compensated by the uninsured motorist coverage of Perry's policy?

4. If Pauline pursues a wrongful death claim, who will be the appropriate party to sue? Can Pauline look to any coverage under her own policy for payment of all or a portion of the claim?

5. How much will Pauline's insurer have to pay of her property damage claim of $16,000?

6. Does Denise have a potential recovery claim for her medical expenses and personal damages? If so, against whom should the claim be made? What defenses to her claim could be alleged?

7. Against whom does David have a claim?

8. Can Denise's negligence be imputed to David? Did David assume the risk by voluntarily going with Denise?

9. Do you think Pauline's insurance carrier will offer to settle David's claim for the policy limits of $100,000? Why or why not?

10. Does Denise's father have a claim against Perry? If so, how would you evaluate Denise's father's claim?

11. In terms of potential recovery, which of the following claims would you rather be representing? Explain why. What defenses might be raised in each case?

    a. Pauline's wrongful death claim

    b. Pauline's personal injury claim

    c. Perry's damages claim

    d. Denise's damages claim

    e. David's damages claim

    f. Denise's father's claim

12. Is the interspousal immunity doctrine in effect in your state? If so, does that change any of your answers to the previous question? Why or why not?

13. Is any claim by Denise barred because of her wrongful use of the family vehicle and lack of a driver's license?

14. Will Pauline's wrongful death claim be affected by the fact that Perry was not wearing his seat belt at the time of the accident? Assume that an accident reconstructionist will testify that although Perry would have suffered serious injuries, he would not have been killed had he been wearing a seat belt.

KEY TERMS

Coordination of benefits provision
Policy provision that precludes payment to the insured if the insured has other insurance available.

Primary coverage
Insurance providing initial coverage for all damages up to the limits of the policy.

Reformation of a policy
Construing a policy to provide the minimum coverage required by statute.

Secondary coverage
Insurance that provides coverage for damages incurred but that does not do so until the limits of the primary policy have been exhausted.

Stacking of policies
Using one or more policies to provide coverage for the same incident.

Subrogation
The right of an insurer to institute suit in the name of the insured against the responsible party to collect for monies paid by the insurer to the insured.

Umbrella policy
Policy that provides a secondary source of coverage after the deductible has been paid, usually coordinated with the limits of the underlying policy.

CHAPTER

19

Bad Faith

CHAPTER TOPICS

How Bad Faith Is Committed
Historical Development of Bad Faith
Overview of Bad Faith
First-Party versus Third-Party Claims
Declaratory Judgment Actions
Uninsured and Underinsured Motorist Coverage

CHAPTER OBJECTIVES

In this chapter you will learn to:
• Identify the elements of a bad faith claim
• Recognize the rationale behind the development of bad faith actions
• Distinguish between first-party and third-party claims for purposes of bad faith and recognize the importance of that distinction

On a Labor Day weekend Jerry and a number of his fraternity brothers and sorority sisters decide to spend their three-day holiday near a place called Rocky Point on the Gulf of California in Mexico. The entire group has to wait in line to enter the gate that allows vehicles to enter Sandy Beach. Jerry steps up on the back bumper of a Jeep driven by Dick when Dick suddenly accelerates his Jeep to move up in line. The sudden movement catches Jerry unaware and he is thrown backward, striking his head on the hard-packed sand. He is knocked unconscious for a few minutes and when he comes to his fraternity brothers put him in the back of a van to recuperate. After a few hours it becomes apparent that Jerry has suffered a serious injury and he is taken to a hospital. He is hospitalized for two weeks and is ultimately forced to withdraw from the first semester of his sophomore year at the university. He suffers short-term memory loss with respect to the accident and has some longer term problems with his speech, reading abilities, and memory retention.

Both Dick and Jerry are insured by the same automobile insurance carrier and each of their policies provides liability coverage for any accident that occurs in Mexico as long as the accident takes place within fifty miles of the United States border. Dick's policy was issued in Colorado, a no-fault state. It does not provide medical payments coverage (called personal injury protection in Colorado) on Dick's Jeep when it is outside the United States. Jerry's policy does provide medical payments coverage in Mexico if the accident occurs within fifty miles of the United States border.

Your attorney, who represents Jerry, submits Jerry's medical expenses to his insurance carrier but the carrier neither accepts nor rejects the claim. After eight months of insurer inaction, your attorney files suit against the carrier for breach of contract and bad faith. After the suit is filed the carrier hires a professor who analyzes information obtained from various witnesses (whom the carrier had not interviewed prior to the filing of the bad faith action). The professor concludes that the accident occurred somewhere between 51 and 51.5 miles outside the United States border. Your

attorney hires an expert who determines that the accident occurred between 49.63 and 51 statute miles from the United States border.

The key issue is whether the accident occurred outside the fifty-mile geographical limitation of Jerry's policy. The policy does not define a mile as being a statute mile (5,280 feet) or a nautical mile (6,080.1 feet). Unquestionably, if nautical miles are used the accident occurred within the fifty-mile limit. The insurance carrier provides many of its insureds with maps indicating that the area of the accident is not more than 48 statute miles from the United States border. Keep this fact pattern in mind as you read about bad faith as a cause of action.

HOW BAD FAITH IS COMMITTED

Bad faith is considered an intentional tort; mere negligence on the part of the insurance carrier is not actionable. Bad faith can occur if: (1) the insurance carrier unreasonably delays payment on a policy; (2) the carrier acts unconscionably toward its insured; or (3) the carrier engages in unfair claims practices (see Figure 19-1).

HISTORICAL DEVELOPMENT OF BAD FAITH

Historically courts held that insurance carriers have an implied covenant of good faith and fair dealing in reference to their insureds. Later, courts classified some insurance contracts as adhesion contracts. **Adhesion contracts** are standardized contracts commonly used in business (an example of which is the contract signed by consumers when financing a car). They are characterized

FIGURE 19-1 What Constitutes Bad Faith

- Insurer unreasonably delays payment.
- Insurer acts unconscionably toward insured.
- Insurer engages in unfair claims practices.

by the courts as those contracts in which the party drafting the contract has superior bargaining power and the other party is typically unfamiliar with the terms of the contract and also has no real opportunity to negotiate what those terms will be. Focusing on the unequal bargaining power between insureds and insurers, as well as the public interest in insurance contracts, the courts scrutinized insurance contracts more carefully than many other contracts in which the parties were assumed to know and understand the terms of the contracts they signed. The courts also realized that insureds rely heavily on their insurance carriers to protect their interests. Therefore, the courts created various mechanisms to protect insureds' contract rights as well as their "reasonable expectations" regarding policy provisions.

In accordance with their vision of insurance contracts as adhesion contracts, courts held that certain policy provisions could not necessarily be utilized against an insured and that the insured was not presumed to understand all the terms of the insurance contract. Courts later developed a rule of law requiring contracts to be interpreted in favor of the nondrafter (the insured) so that any "ambiguities" in a contract would be construed against the carrier and in favor of the insured. This rule was propagated in the hope that insureds would be protected from complex insurance contracts and that the insurance industry would be pressured into drafting contracts comprehensible to those who read them.

Interpreting contracts in favor of the nondrafter eventually evolved into the modern-day rule generally referred to as the *reasonable expectations doctrine*. This doctrine protects the insured's reasonable expectation that coverage will be provided and not defeated by provisions that would be unanticipated by the ordinary insured and that were never negotiated between the insured and the carrier. The court will reform the contract to the reasonable expectations of the insured even though a detailed review of the contract itself does not support those expectations.

In their efforts to curb the sometimes misused discretion of insurance carriers, courts have looked for remedies outside of those found in contract law, because such remedies impose a relatively small penalty on overreaching carriers. A carrier found in breach of contract is liable only for the amount owed to the insured plus attorney fees and court costs. Because insurance companies know that, at the worst, they will have to pay only a minor penalty for their indiscretions, they can afford to be rather cavalier in their actions toward their insureds. Accordingly, insurers have little incentive to be concerned about the majority of their insureds, who can ill afford the tremendous expense involved in litigating with a major company.

Some courts have found a fiduciary duty between the insurance carrier and the insured. Objectionable acts of a carrier as well as objectionable terms of an insurance contract are then found to be a breach of the fiduciary duty owed the insured. As a result, objectionable terms can be eliminated from the contract.

Some states have restricted the strict interpretation of contracts by providing the insured with standard tort remedies. For example, recovery for intentional infliction of mental distress has been allowed when an insurance company has committed especially egregious acts. In many cases, however, the physical complications required for this cause of action cannot be shown in the context of an insurer-insured relationship.

OVERVIEW OF BAD FAITH

As can be seen from this brief historical review, bad faith evolved as a means of providing relief to the insured. Bad faith is a question of fact for the jury. Only when the court determines that no reasonable person could conclude that bad faith has occurred can the court take the case from the jury.

Initially, bad faith applied only to *third-party claims* (claims in which the insured paid damages to a third party). Most jurisdictions now recognize the tort of bad faith in cases of *first-party claims* (claims in which an insured demands payment from his insurer in his own right).

Bad faith cases also involve a breach of contract claim as well. Some jurisdictions, however, recognize that bad faith can occur even when the contract is not breached. A bad faith claim can occur without a breach of the insurance contract when the insurer unreasonably denies a claim. The unreasonable denial of the claim can support a cause of action for bad faith even when a court subsequently determines that the insurer had no contractual obligation to provide coverage for the claim. An insurance carrier might, for example, deny coverage without a proper investigation of the claim and later, after being sued, discover evidence that supported its original denial of coverage. Such a discovery would not, however, diminish the carrier's initial failure to act in good faith.

Suing the Insured

Although theoretically possible, an insurance carrier rarely sues an insured for bad faith. The duty of good faith is an unconditional and independent contractual obligation of the insurer and most states provide relief even when the insured has not fulfilled all of his or her contractual duties. Those courts that have recognized bad faith claims against insureds have allowed the insurers to recover contractual damages only. Tort damages as well as punitive damages have been denied. Conceivably, however, comparative negligence could be used to reduce an insured's award of damages if an insured acted in bad faith.

FIRST-PARTY VERSUS THIRD-PARTY CLAIMS

In first-party cases the plaintiff (insured) and defendant (insurer) are easily defined. The insured, pursuant to a contractual right emanating from his or her insurance contract, sues the insurer. As previously mentioned, most bad faith claims include a breach of contract claim and, if supported by the insurer's acts, a claim for punitive damages. Although the requisite conduct for punitive damages varies, the trend is to award punitive damages only when an "evil mind guides the evil hand."

Third-party suits follow a more circuitous route to the courthouse. Most states do not allow those who have been injured by the insured and then damaged by the insurer's actions toward its insured to file suit directly against the insurance company, because injured parties are not considered third-party beneficiaries under the insured-insurer contract. A third-party case usually reaches trial in the name of the insured only after the insured "cuts a deal" with the injured party.

Resolution of Third-Party Claims

A third-party action often arises after the insurer fails to settle the injured party's claim against the insured for an amount less than or equal to the policy limits. After trial and the entry of an **excess judgment** (a judgment for more than the policy limits), the insured will often assign to the injured party all of her rights under the contract, including any claims she might have for bad faith. Although many states prohibit the assignment of "pure" personal injury claims, most allow the assignment of contract rights. Because a bad faith claim arises out of a contract and is not considered a pure tort, most courts allow its assignment. Some states also allow the assignment of any right the insured might have to punitive damages.

Once the assignment is made, the injured party then pursues the insurer in the name of the insured. Because the lawsuit is filed in the insured's name, as part of the assignment the insured must assure her cooperation in the action against the insurer. The lawsuit will in fact be orchestrated by the injured party.

The insured may also assign her rights to the injured party when the insurer denies coverage for the injured party's claim and/or agrees to defend the insured only under a *reservation of rights*. An insurance carrier that defends its insured under a reservation of rights initially tells its insured it will provide a defense to the claim. At the same time, however, the carrier reserves its rights to later deny that coverage exists, in which

448, Tort Law for Legal Assistants

case it can withdraw the defense previously offered. In most cases the insurance carrier's reservation of rights letter will advise the insured to consider employing his or her own counsel.

Insured's Option When Denied Coverage

An insured's remedies upon being denied coverage are often based on whether coverage was denied outright or whether his position was compromised as a result of a reservation of rights. If coverage is flatly denied, the insured has no chance of indemnity for any judgment rendered against him, and no opportunity to mount a defense except from his own pocket.

Because of the vulnerability of an insured that has been denied coverage, some courts allow the insured to enter into an agreement with the injured party, stipulating to the amount of the judgment to be entered in favor of the injured party. The injured party must still present evidence to substantiate the damages claimed, but with no adversary attempting to exclude evidence the injured party usually has little difficulty obtaining a large judgment. Once the judgment is entered, the insured assigns all rights under the insurance policy to the injured party. Then, once again in the name of the insured, the injured party sues the insurance carrier, seeking indemnity for the amount of the judgment entered, or garnishes the insurer.

When this procedure is allowed, an insurance carrier's liability usually does not exceed the policy limits unless the carrier has denied coverage in bad faith. In that case the injured party can recover the amount of the judgment obtained (up to the policy limits) for breach of contract and can also pursue an independent bad faith claim against the insurance carrier.

Insured's Option When Insurer Defends Under a Reservation of Rights

If an insurer defends under a reservation of rights, the insured is not left completely naked. The insurer, in essence, loans him a "coat" but at the same time advises the insured that the "coat" may be recalled at any time.

Under these circumstances some courts have allowed the insured to enter into an agreement with the injured party that basically protects the insured if the insurer subsequently denies coverage. Entering into such an agreement is not considered a violation of the cooperation clause, found in most insurance contracts, that mandates the insured's cooperation with the insurer.

In a typical reservation of rights case the insured enters into negotiations with the injured party to protect the insured from being exposed to an uninsured judgment. Any agreement normally provides for a judgment to be entered based on evidence presented to the court, usually without objection from the insured. Care must be taken to ensure that no fraud is perpetrated on the court when such an agreement is entered into. After judgment is entered the insured assigns all rights under her insurance contract to the injured party.

In a reservation of rights case an insured must usually advise the insurer of the terms and conditions of the agreement prior to entering into any agreement. The insurer then has one last opportunity to withdraw its reservation of rights and provide an unconditional defense to the insured.

The reservation of rights case is resolved when the injured party files suit against the insurer in the name of the insured. Alternatively, the injured party can garnish the insurer. Suit is considerably different from the trial of a denial of coverage case. The injured party must prove that the insurance policy issued to the insured covers the claim and that the agreement between the insured and the injured party was not a fraud on the court. He or she must also show that the judgment entered by the court was not fraudulent and was fair and reasonable considering the issue of liability, the facts relating to actual damages, the advantages and risks of going to trial, and the risks of the insurer not being liable under the policy. Under this scenario the jury must be told the terms and conditions of the agreement and the fact that the insured was released from liability. The jury would also be advised, however, that the insurer had reserved the right to deny coverage and that it was the concern of noncoverage that motivated the insured to enter into its agreement with the injured party.

This "trial within a trial" allows the insurer to introduce all relevant evidence that counters any of the positions taken by the plaintiff (the injured party, who is acting in the name of the insured). If the jury determines that no coverage exists, it will enter a judgment for the defendant (insurer). If the jury determines that the judgment obtained in accordance with the agreement between the insured and the injured party was excessive, it can award damages in a lesser amount.

Failure to Settle Claim

The insurer can be subjected to bad faith even when it acknowledges coverage and provides a complete defense. This type of bad faith occurs when the insurance carrier has a reasonable opportunity to settle the injured party's claim within the policy limits. If the insurer refuses to settle, the insured can be liable for the amount of the judgment in excess of the policy limits.

Of particular concern to the insured are areas of liability in which the potential damages are extremely large. In those instances the insurer might be tempted to "roll the dice" by going to the jury in the hope of getting a defense verdict. Because the insurer's liability does not exceed the insured's policy limits, the insurer has nothing to lose by going to trial. The insurer, after entry of an excess judgment, can pay the amount of its policy limits and leave the insured to deal with the injured party. The insured would then have a potential bad faith claim against the insurance carrier for its failure to settle the claim within the policy limits. As the insured would probably be very happy to be relieved from having to pay the injured party, she would likely assign to that party any rights she might have against the insurer. The injured party would then proceed, in the name of the insured, in a bad faith claim against the insurer.

Some have questioned whether an insured who knows the insurer has refused to settle within the pol-

icy limits is in a position to strike a deal with the injured party before an excess judgment has actually been entered. Most courts have held that an insured in this situation is bound to cooperate with the insurer and may not enter into an agreement with the injured party until after judgment is entered. The courts reason that the insured, having selected the limits of coverage, cannot shift her responsibility to adequately insure herself to her insurer when those limits turn out to be too low to cover the risk that actually occurred.

Damages—Third-Party Claims

The amount of damages to be awarded in third-party cases is based on four factors: (1) the amount of judgment entered against the insured in excess of the policy limits (i.e., the amount the insured must pay out of his own pocket); (2) the legal fees the insured has incurred in pursuing the claim against the insurer; (3) the emotional distress, if any, suffered by the insured; and (4) any other monetary loss or damage to the insured's credit or reputation. (See Figure 19-2.)

If the insurer's actions have been sufficiently egregious, punitive damages might also be available. Punitive damages are intended to prevent similar misconduct in the future rather than to compensate the plaintiff. Therefore, the amount of punitive damages to be awarded is based on the financial condition of the insurer and the degree of its misconduct rather than the impact of its misconduct on the insured. Because the insurance business is often very lucrative, a plaintiff asking for relatively small actual damages may seek punitive damages in the millions of dollars range.

FIGURE 19-2 Damage Factors—Third Party Claim

• Amount of judgment entered against insured in excess of insured's policy limits.
• Legal fees incurred by insured.
• Emotional distress suffered by insured.
• Monetary loss or damaged credit reputation of insured.

Resolution of First-Party Claims

A first-party bad faith case is more straightforward than a third-party case because only two parties are involved. In a first-party bad faith case the insured is denied the benefits of her contract with her insurer due to the insurer's failure to deal with her fairly and in good faith. An insurer acts in bad faith by either failing to investigate a claim made by the insured or by inadequately investigating a claim. If coverage is denied as a result, or if an unreasonably low evaluation of the damages is made, a claim for bad faith will lie.

An insurance carrier's delay tactics in investigating and evaluating a claim can also lead to bad faith. A carrier obviously benefits financially by delaying payment of a claim as long as possible. Such a delay allows the carrier to obtain the maximum benefits of its investment of the insured's premium.

Because an insurer is obligated to properly investigate its insured's claim, many courts refuse to allow information obtained after the filing of a bad faith lawsuit to be used by the insurer to justify its prior actions. Suppose an insurer denies coverage but never investigates the claim. That insurer usually cannot later submit evidence supporting its denial of coverage if it finds this evidence by virtue of an investigation conducted after the insured files a bad faith suit.

An additional basis for bad faith in first-party cases involves fraudulent or harassing practices by the carrier. In some states violation of state statutes governing unfair claim settlement procedures can result in claims for bad faith.

Damages—First-Party Claims

Determining the amount to be paid in first-party cases entails consideration of elements similar to those used in third-party claims (see Figure 19-3). The major difference is that first-party claims involve the loss of unpaid benefits, whereas third-party claims involve an excess judgment. Unpaid benefits include the insured's loss of the benefit of the bargain, any resulting consequential damages, and lost interest on the unpaid amount due the insured.

In many cases, such as those involving health or disability insurance claims, wrongful denial results in not only the insured's inability to pay bills but also the loss of his and his family's credit rating. If such losses can be proved to stem from the wrongful acts of the insurer they can also be recovered. Care must be taken, however, in evaluating losses alleged to have occurred as a result of the insurer's bad faith. Asking a jury to stretch its concept of proximate cause may result in a backlash against the insured, who may be perceived as overreaching.

Standards Used to Determine Bad Faith

An insured is often exposed to lesser risk in first-party bad faith cases than in third-party matters. In first-party cases the insurer does not have sole control of litigation relating to the insured's potential liability, which it has in third-party cases. Additionally, in first-party cases the insured makes her claim directly in her own name and does not face losses in excess of her policy limits.

Because of these differences, many courts use a different standard in a first-party case than in a third-party case to determine whether bad faith has been committed. In first-party situations the standard is based on the reasonableness of the insurer's position. Some courts consider denial of a claim reasonable (and therefore not in bad faith) if the claim is "fairly debatable." Some courts require a showing of more than mere negligent conduct before they will find that an insurer acted in bad faith. For those courts an unintentional mistake, oversight, or carelessness of an insurer's employee does not constitute bad faith even

---

FIGURE 19-3   Damage Factors—First-Party Claim

- Unpaid benefits of policy.
- Legal fees incurred by insured.
- Lost interest on unpaid amount due insured.
- Emotional distress suffered by insured.
- Any other financial losses of insured caused as a result of insurer's bad faith.

PUTTING IT INTO PRACTICE 19.1

Refer to the hypothetical scenario at the beginning of this chapter.

1. Does Jerry have a third-party claim? Against whom?
2. Does Jerry have a first-party claim? What portions of his automobile insurance policy would it be covered under?
3. Why might Dick's carrier initially defend him from any claim by Jerry under a reservation of rights? Could a bad faith claim be made if an insurer sent out a reservation of rights letter to an insured without first investigating the claim?
4. Assume the insurer alleges that it investigated the accident but was unable to determine its exact location, because all of the witnesses had been drinking and the accident occurred in the evening. Would that change your opinion about the viability of a breach of contract claim? Bad faith?
5. Does the existence of a map, distributed by the insurer, affect your analysis?
6. How reasonable would it be for Dick's attorney to argue that nautical rather than statute miles should be used to determine the extent of coverage?

---

though a jury, with hindsight, could objectively determine that the carrier's actions were unreasonable.

Because in third-party situations the insured has almost no control over the processing of the claim against him or her, most courts have held the insurer to a higher standard of care. The courts go beyond asking whether an insurer's position was fairly debatable. Many inquire whether the insurer gave as much consideration to its insured's interests as it did to its own (the "equal consideration" test).

CASE

General Accident Fire & Life Assurance Corp., Ltd. v. Little
443 P.2d 690 (Ariz. 1968)

UDALL, Vice Chief Justice:

The appellee, Irene Bernice Little, brought this action as the assignee of Elza A. Allen and Claudie Beatrice Allen, who were the named insureds under an automobile public liability policy carried with the appellant, hereinafter referred to as General.

On October 11, 1959 Mrs. Allen was involved in an accident which resulted in the death of Mrs. Little's seventeen-year-old son. Appellee thereafter brought suit against the Allens, during the pendency of which General was offered an opportunity to settle for $4,000.00. This

offer was rejected and a jury ultimately returned a verdict in favor of Mrs. Little, administratrix, in amount of $17,500.00. Thereafter General paid its policy limits, $5,000, and accrued costs on the judgment. With no execution being levied or any other steps being taken to collect the balance of the judgment, Mrs. Little accepted from the Allens the following assignment:

"WE, ELZA A. ALLEN and CLAUDIE BEATRICE ALLEN, for value received, hereby assign to IRENE BERNICE LITTLE, Administratrix of the estate of

JIMMY ANDREW HAVNER, deceased, her executors, administrators and assigns, all our right, title and interest in our claims, rights of action and causes of action against The General Accident Fire and Life Assurance Corporation, Ltd., and Potomac Insurance Group doing business as The General Accident Group, based on the negligence, breach of contract and bad faith of said Company in failing to settle cause No. 111201, Superior Court of Maricopa County, State of Arizona, within the policy limits of our liability policy with said company and we authorize IRENE BERNICE LITTLE, Administratrix of JIMMY ANDREW HAVNER, deceased, her executors, administrators and assigns, to commence action on, prosecute and collect thereon, and take all legal or other measures deemed proper or necessary, with the same force and effect as we could do.

"This assignment is made *to secure the payment of a judgment rendered against us in cause No. 111201, Superior Court of Maricopa County, Arizona, the payment of which obligation will render this assignment void; otherwise, to be of full force and effect.*" [emphasis added]

Armed with this assignment Mrs. Little instituted the present action. The complaint herein alleged the death of Jimmy Havner, Mrs. Little's son; the prior suit and judgment, the issuance of a liability policy by General, the defense of the prior action by General, the offer and refusal of settlement within policy limits and further alleged that such refusal was based on the bad faith and negligence of General resulting in damage to the Allens in amount of $12,500 (amended complaint); and, finally, the assignment to Mrs. Little was alleged.

General defended on the basis that the complaint failed to state a claim on which relief could be granted. General admitted the accident, the issuance of the policy and the defense of the claim under the terms of the policy; but denied that the accident and death were caused by any negligence of Claudie, or that General had been negligent or had acted in bad faith in refusing to accept the offers of settlement and further denied that the Allens had sustained any damage or that any claim of the Allens had been assigned to Mrs. Little. As to the latter denial the trial court entered a pre-trial order "that the cause of action asserted by plaintiff is properly in the plaintiff by virtue of the assignment in question and the trial of said cause shall proceed on the merits."

Trial resulted in a jury verdict of $12,500. General's motions objecting to the form of judgment entered thereon (which provided for interest), for a new trial, and for judgment notwithstanding the verdict were all denied. This appeal follows.

This is only the second opportunity this court has had to review an "excess liability" case. As we noted in the earlier case the "law in this regard is of comparatively recent development and the cases are not entirely harmonious," *Farmers Insurance Exchange v. Henderson* . . . . *Farmers* is authority for the proposition that an insurer must give equal consideration to the interests of an insured in determining whether to settle or defend a claim, and that a failure to do so does not constitute good faith. . . .

The appellant contends that looking at all the evidence in the light most favorable to Mrs. Little, she failed to sustain her burden of proving bad faith and hence the trial court erred in overruling the motions for directed verdict and for judgment notwithstanding the verdict.

What constitutes a breach of duty to exercise good faith? In *Farmers Insurance Exchange v. Henderson,* we said:

"* * * It occurs to us that when the insurer is defending litigation against the insured, employs attorneys to represent the interests of both and has sole power and opportunity to make a settlement which would result in the protection of the insured against excess liability, common honesty demands that it not be moved by partiality to itself nor be required to give the interests of the insured preferential consideration. A violator of this rule of equality of consideration cannot be said to have acted in good faith. (citations omitted) The enunciation of the rule is not difficult but its application is troublesome. *It is a matter of consideration of comparative hazards.*" . . . (Emphasis added)

California also follows the "equality of consideration" doctrine and in looking to the elements of its "troublesome" application in *Brown v. Guarantee Insurance Co.,* the California court set out the following factors:

"* * * the strength of the injured claimant's case on the issues of liability and damages; attempts by the insurer to induce the insured to contribute to a settlement; failure of the insurer to properly investigate the circumstances so as to ascertain the evidence against the insured; the insurer's rejection of advice of its own attorney or agent; failure of the insurer to inform the insured of a compromise offer; *the amount of financial risk to which each party is exposed in the event of a* *refusal to settle;* the fault of the insured in inducing the insurer's rejection of the compromise offer by misleading it as to the facts; and any other factors tending to establish or negate bad faith on the part of the insurer." [emphasis added] . . .

Several of the factors mentioned by the California court are not in issue in the present case. For instance there was never any discussion of contributions toward a settlement on the part of the Allens; there is nothing in the record to show General was misled by the Allens as to the facts of the original accident; it is not claimed that insured rejected the advice of its own attorney. (In fact at the time of trial the attorney for the company evaluated the settlement value of the case at $2,000 and felt the prospects of a verdict were 60–40% in favor of the defendant); there is no contention that the insurer failed to keep the insured informed as to settlement offers.

As to the adequacy of the investigation itself the record is undisputed that the company had an investigator on the job commencing with the day of the accident. On that date he obtained the statement of Claudie Allen, the statement of a witness to the accident, the police reports and photographs of the Havner motorcycle and the Allen automobile. Subsequently, and within a week of the accident a lengthy statement was taken from another eye witness, the Havner home was contacted, the accident was discussed with the Allens on numerous occasions and the results of the investigation were all submitted to the Phoenix Claims Office of the company. The file was subsequently submitted to the company attorney who, in his own further investigation, obtained knowledge about the working condition of the Havner motorcycle from a friend of the deceased Havner lad, and information from plaintiff's attorney relative to the earnings of Jimmy Havner (who had been a carry-out boy at a market, $25 to $30 a week), damages to his motorcycle, and funeral expenses. The adequacy of the investigation has not been challenged by the appellee on appeal—nor do we see how a jury could have found any bad faith in this regard.

The claim was evaluated by the company claims manager and defense counsel. No effort was made by appellee to impeach their qualifications or their competency.

Now, let us look to the strength of claimant's case on the issue of liability and damages, as it would have appeared prior to the trial. Clearly, all can now see through hindsight that it would have been better for both the insureds and the insurer to have accepted the offer of settlement, but as was said in *Ferris v. Employers Mutual Casualty Company,*

"* * * Again there is the implication that we should judge the fairness of the decision not to settle by the result. We suggest that if we are to venture into the area of what counsel 'should have known' in advance of the trial of a lawsuit as shown by the final outcome, by a jury's decision, we are requiring of him the gift of foretelling the future not often given to mankind. We know of no mortal who has been vouchsafed this power since the days of the Bible prophets; and as we understand it, these ancient seers had access to some inside information not presently available to counsel in damage cases. The court placed an unfair burden on the defendant here . . . .

"* * * We may not measure the reasonableness of the offer by the ultimate result of the litigation; it must be considered in the light of the case as it fairly appeared to the insurer and its authorized agents and attorneys at the time the offer was made. Whether Mr. Mitchell was mistaken in his judgment that he could successfully defend may be argued; but a mere mistake in judgment is not enough to show bad faith" . . .

This accident occurred at 8:30 in the morning. Mrs. Allen was proceeding south on 17th Avenue, came to a stop at Buckeye Road where traffic was jammed or stacked up. A Mr. Ruth, traveling west on Buckeye moved his truck a little so Mrs. Allen could traverse the intersection. She thereafter proceeded through the opening Ruth had provided. Ruth then observed the Havner boy coming east on Buckeye at a distance of some 200 to 300 feet. According to Ruth the boy was lying down on the motorcycle, bent forward from the waist; his speed was estimated at 55 to 60 miles per hour and remained constant from the first time Ruth observed the motorcycle right up to the impact. Further, according to Ruth, no attempt to apply the brakes was ever made.

The physical evidence revealed no skid marks. Both the attorney for the insured and the attorney for the claimant recognized contributory negligence as an issue in the case. In evaluating liability prospects the claims manager felt that the chances of a defense verdict were 75% and, as stated previously, the insurer's attorney felt that the odds in favor of defendant were at least 60-40.

As to the potential damage should a verdict be rendered against the insured the company saw that he was 17 years old at the time of the accident, unmarried, without dependents, and earning from 25 to 30 dollars a week. In determining what a possible verdict might be the attorney for the company felt that under our death statute the jury might well mitigate its verdict because of the fact that the boy was riding the motorcycle at the time.

With all these factors in mind the insurance attorney determined that if a jury returned a plaintiff's verdict it would range between a low of $3,000 and tops of $7,500 and the claims manager felt that it could not exceed $10,000. Within the judgment of General, then, first, that they had a fighting chance of winning the case hands down, and secondly, that if they did lose the verdict would range from $3,000 to $10,000 does it appear that they exercised equal consideration in measuring the comparative hazards of the insured and the insurer . . . ?

The appellee argues that the insured had only one interest and that was the financial loss they would incur if the verdict exceeded the policy limits; and that the company in refusing to accept settlement when offered within those limits gave no consideration to that interest. Mrs. Little contends that, under the well-established rule that the evidence must be viewed in the most favorable light to appellee, she established her prima facie case through the testimony of the company claims manager and the company attorney. This testimony in substance had the effect of showing that neither the claims manager nor the attorney took into consideration the policy limits in evaluating the claim . . . .

We cannot agree with appellee's argument. It is obvious that they have rested their case on a gross misconstruance of the meaning of "equal consideration." Clearly the value of an unlitigated claim is determined on its own apparent merits or lack of them, or the possibility of liability being established, and on injuries and their extent being proven, and on such other factors as the breadwinning capacities of the injured party.

Surely all would agree that an insurance company would not breach its duty of good faith to the insured if it refused to settle a claim for $4,999.99 on a $5,000 policy when the question of liability was highly debatable, the apparent injury was extremely minor, and the injured was an unemployed adolescent. We state it in the ridiculous to point up the fallacy of appellee's argument.

Thus it should be clear that the evaluation of a case should not be determined by looking to the policy limits. When an insurance company evaluates a claim without looking to the policy limits and as though it alone would be responsible for the payment of any judgment rendered on that claim it views that claim objectively, and in doing so renders "equal consideration" to the interests of itself and the insured. . . .

Where an insurance company acts honestly and in good faith upon adequate information it should not be held liable because it failed to prophecy the result. If the insurer in good faith believed that it could successfully defend, it was not bound to relieve the Allens of all possible harm that might come from their election to purchase only $5,000 coverage in the light of present day dollar values and verdicts.

The record, however, also shows and clearly that General recognized the plaintiff, Mrs. Little, would most probably be able to establish a prima facie case against Mrs. Allen and thus that the question of liability would be for jury determination. As has been previously pointed out the liability carrier also recognized and told their insureds that in the event a verdict were returned for plaintiff, Mrs. Little, it could "be greatly in excess of $5,000." Mr. Allen, who by virtue of the marital relationship was a co-defendant and jointly subject to such excess liability insisted or strongly urged that the lawsuit be settled.

This was a wrongful death claim and the complaint prayed for relief in amount of $100,000. A seventeen year old boy had been taken from his mother. It appears to this court that General and its attorney were being less than realistic when they estimated a potential verdict at a low of $3,000 and a high of $10,000. In Arizona there is no statutory ceiling on wrongful death verdicts and the jury "shall give such damages as it deems fair and just with reference to the injury resulting from the death to the surviving parties * * * having regard to the mitigating or aggravating circumstances attending the wrongful act, neglect or default * * *" A.R.S. § 12-613. As opposed to General's estimate it is to be noted that the attorney for the plaintiff, who testified he had handled hundreds of personal injury cases, estimated a potential plaintiff's verdict in this case of from $10,000 to $30,000.

We agree with the courts and legal writers who have noted that even with the expertise and experience afforded liability carriers and competent trial lawyers they yet are not endowed with the gift of being able to accurately prophecy a jury verdict. However, under the terms of the policy the company is contractually given the exclusive right to determine whether a settlement offer should be accepted.

When we apply the test of *Farmers Insurance Exchange* to the facts of this case; when we note by General's own conservative and self-serving evidence that there were four chances in ten of losing this case and the possibility of suffering a verdict "greatly in excess of the policy limits"; and we note further that in accepting the settlement offer of $4,000 General would be paying only $1,500 more than its $2,500 offer of settlement, part of which would be and was spent in legal fees and court costs, we do not find it difficult to sustain the jury's finding that General did not exercise its duty of good faith. It did not give equal consideration to its own and the insured's comparative hazards.

Where policy limits should have no place in an objective evaluation of a claim, once that claim has been evaluated and there is determined, as here, at least a 40% possibility of liability being established and an obvious recognition that an adverse verdict can reasonably be expected to "greatly exceed" policy limits, equal consideration of the comparative hazards demands that the insurer give attention to the policy limits. . . .

Finally, General contends that the lower court erred in refusing to give its tendered instructions on the meaning of "bad faith" and on the proper burden of proof. We believe under the facts of this case the instructions were properly denied. It is true that actions based on fraud must be proven by "clear and convincing" evidence, . . .; and it is equally true that one obvious species of "bad faith" is fraud. But, as we have shown above, the species of "bad faith" relied upon in this case was not actual fraud but a failure on the part of General to exercise its duty of giving "equal consideration" to the comparative hazards to its own interest and the interests of the policyholder. Under the rule of *Farmers Insurance Exchange v. Henderson,* the instruction given by the trial court adequately covered the issue of good faith.

There being no contention of fraud in this case the proper burden of proof test was the usual "preponderance of the evidence."

Judgment affirmed.

Although the equal consideration test varies somewhat from jurisdiction to jurisdiction, the concept is illustrated in *General Accident Fire & Life Assurance Corp. v. Little,* 443 P.2d 690 (Ariz. 1968). Eight factors deemed important to the *Little* court in determining whether the insurer had given equal consideration to its insured were (also see Figure 19-4):
1. The relative strength of the injured party's claim in reference to the issues of liability and damages against the insured.
2. The insurer's failure to properly investigate the claim so as to determine the availability of relevant evidence.
3. The insurer's failure to advise its insured of an offer to settle within policy limits.
4. The insurer's failure to follow the advice of its own attorney or agent.
5. The extent of the financial risk to its insured if the insurer refused to settle.
6. Any attempt by the insurer to get the insured to contribute to the settlement.
7. Any action by the insured that might have influenced the insurer to reject any compromise settlement offers.
8. Any other factors that might support or disprove bad faith on the part of the insurer.

A third-party bad faith claim does not have to have elements of each of these considerations.

FIGURE 19-4   Equal Consideration Factors for Third-Party Claims

- Relative strength of injured party's claims in references to issues of liability and damages against insured.
- Insurer's failure to properly investigate claim so as to determine availability of relevant evidence.
- Insurer's failure to advise insured of offer to settle within policy limits.
- Insurer's failure to follow advice of its attorney or agent.
- Extent of financial risk to insured if insurer refused to settle.
- Attempt by insurer to get insured to contribute to settlement.
- Action by insured that might have influenced insurer to reject any compromise settlement offers.
- Any other factors that might support or disprove bad faith on the party of insurer.

PUTTING IT INTO PRACTICE 19.2

1. Does the *Little* court appear, at first, to favor the position of the insurer?
2. At the time *Little* was decided, contributory negligence was a complete defense; comparative negligence was not in existence. Do you believe that the insurer really thought that there was only a 40 percent chance for a plaintiff's verdict? (The insurer admitted that the plaintiff could make out a prima facie case.)
3. What was the court really saying when it stated "General and its attorney were being less than realistic when they estimated a potential verdict at a low of $3,000 and a high of $10,000"?
4. Does the outcome of *Little* turn on the court's perception of the credibility of the insurer and its attorney in evaluating the case? If so, is mere negligence, in this case, grounds for a finding of bad faith?

DECLARATORY JUDGMENT ACTIONS

Insurance carriers will often institute a declaratory judgment action to determine if coverage exists. In a **declaratory judgment action** the court renders an opinion with respect to a matter of law or with regard to the rights of the parties, but orders no action to be taken. Such an action can serve both defensive as well as offensive purposes. Offensively, a declaratory judgment action can serve to determine that no coverage exists and that the insurer need not defend or compensate its insured. Defensively, such an action allows a carrier to dispute coverage, as well as to go before a

court hoping that the potential for a bad faith claim will be minimized by its efforts to obtain a judicial determination of its position.

UNINSURED AND UNDERINSURED MOTORIST COVERAGE

Uninsured (UM) and underinsured (UIM) motorist coverage has characteristics of both first-party and third-party claims. One first-party characteristic is that the insured is obligated to make payment directly to the insurer. A third-party characteristic is that the insurer stands in the shoes of the allegedly responsible

---

PUTTING IT INTO PRACTICE 19.3

1. Why might Dick's and Jerry's insurer want to file a declaratory judgment action and seek a court ruling finding no coverage for the accident?
2. Would the value of the declaratory judgment action be the same if the insurer waited until after Jerry filed suit against it or Dick?
3. The insurer has the burden of proof in a declaratory judgment action. Does that burden affect your analysis of whether the insurer should file such an action? On its timing?

---

party. As such the insurer can assert any defense that the responsible party might have, including comparative or contributory negligence, assumption of risk, and denial of liability.

Most UM and UIM policies prohibit the insured from suing his or her carrier over the issue of damages. If an insurer and its insured cannot reach agreement with respect to damages, the matter is submitted to arbitration. The issue of coverage, however, is not subject to arbitration in most UM and UIM policies. Coverage is determined in a separate lawsuit.

Because many states require automobile policies to provide UM and UIM coverage, some argue that carriers should have to meet the standard appropriate for third-party claims. Most courts, however, view UM and UIM claims as first-party claims. As first-party claims, the maximum benefit due an insured as a result of an insurer's breach of its contractual obligations is the policy limits. If a UM or UIM claim is fairly debatable, most courts hold that the insurer is not liable to its insured on the basis of bad faith.

UM and UIM carriers have tried to convince the courts that because they stand in the shoes of the allegedly responsible party, an adversarial relationship exists between them and their insureds. This argument, for the most part, has been rejected. The courts have, however, reasoned that bad faith has not occurred if the liability of the allegedly responsible party is reasonably in question and the amount of damages that must be paid the insured is reasonably disputed.

PUTTING IT INTO PRACTICE 19.4

1. Does Jerry have a first-party claim? More than one?
2. If Dick is denied coverage, most states (and insurance policies) would deem him an uninsured motorist. Does that fact influence how the insurer would react to a claim by Jerry (i.e., denial of coverage, defend under a reservation of rights, or tender an unconditional defense)?
3. If Jerry eventually went to trial and it was determined that Dick's policy provided coverage for the accident, could Jerry then make an underinsured motorist claim?

SUMMARY

Bad faith is an intentional tort that occurs when a party to an insurance contract breaches its implied covenant of good faith and fair dealing. Most cases of bad faith involve allegations against the insurance carrier. Bad faith arises when (1) the insurer wrongly refuses to provide coverage for a client, (2) fails to adequately investigate a claim before making its decision to deny coverage or pay only a portion of the insured's claim, or (3) unreasonably refuses to settle a third-party claim within the limits of the insured's policy.

In most jurisdictions the standard of care owed to an insured by the insurer depends on whether the case is a first- or third-party claim. In first-party claims, some jurisdictions use the "fairly debatable" standard. Under that standard, if a claim submitted by an insured is fairly debatable the insurer's actions in refusing to pay the claim will not constitute bad faith. For third-party claims, most courts impose a higher duty on the insurer. This higher duty, sometimes referred to as an "equality of consideration" standard, requires the insurer to give the same consideration to the insured's interests as it does to its own. In most jurisdictions something more than mere negligence is required before the courts will find that the insurer has violated its implied covenant of good faith and fair dealing.

The position of an insured varies depending on whether the insurer denies coverage or defends the insured under a reservation of rights. The insured is able to negotiate an agreement more freely with an injured party when coverage of the claim is denied. He or she may still be able to work out an agreement with the injured party when the insurer is defending him or her under a reservation of rights. The insured does, however, have greater obligations to the insurer, including a duty to advise the insurer of the agreement so that the insurer can withdraw its reservation of rights before the agreement becomes effective.

UM and UIM coverage has aspects of both first- and third-party claims. Most jurisdictions treat UM and UIM claims as first-party claims. UM and UIM policies generally prohibit suit over the issue of damages, but the issue of coverage is often resolved in a declaratory judgment action.

■ PRACTICE POINTERS ☐

Bad faith cases are very fact-intensive. What the insurer did, and when it did it, is as important as what the insurer knew at the time it took action. Most insurers maintain what is known as a *claims file*. The claims file should contain all notes and memoranda prepared by the adjuster, along with copies of all correspondence and attachments. Care must be taken when documents are requested from an insurer. Because each company has its own way of handling claims, merely requesting the claims file may not result in the production of all of the documents you want. If, for example, an adjuster's case evaluation and the amount of reserve set aside for a claim were maintained in a special file, a request for the claims file, and its subsequent production, would not contain all relevant information.

Another fertile area of dispute is trial preparation materials. Because an insurance carrier is often involved in litigation, it can and often does argue that everything it does in handling a claim is in preparation for trial. That argument has not been completely successful. Because the insurance business deals, to a great

Continued on next page

PRACTICE POINTERS—Continued

extent, with handling claims, the courts have rejected the position that all acts in adjusting a claim are in preparation for trial. Once it becomes clear that litigation will result, subsequent documents may not be subject to discovery. If your jurisdiction follows the Federal Rules of Civil Procedure, review Rule 26.

Review some of the reported bad faith cases for the past few years in your jurisdiction. Try to find a case that refers to a discovery dispute relating to trial preparation or attorney-client materials. Go to the trial court file and review the arguments submitted by each side. There will probably be a motion for a protective order or a motion to compel discovery. The documents that were requested, and that created the dispute, should be set out in the pleadings.

TORT TEASERS

Review the hypothetical scenario at the beginning of this chapter and answer the following questions.

1. What is the significance of the insurer providing its insureds with maps showing that the Rocky Point area is within forty-eight statute miles of the United States border?

2. Can Jerry use these maps to prevent the insurer from alleging that the accident occurred more than fifty statute miles from the United States border?

3. Would your answer to the preceding question be different if Jerry testified that not only was he unaware of the maps issued by his insurer, but he was also unaware at the time of the accident that he had coverage for medical payment expenses and UM in Mexico?

4. How does the insurer's actions in obtaining an expert to determine the location of the accident affect your analysis of whether bad faith has been committed?

5. If the insurer hires experts and denies coverage prior to a bad faith suit being instituted, does that change your evaluation of Jerry's claim?

6. If the insurer institutes a declaratory judgment action before Jerry files his bad faith action, does that affect your opinion as to whether the insurer acted in bad faith?

7. The insurer argues that because it neither accepted nor denied Jerry's claim, it cannot be found to have acted in bad faith. How would you respond?

8. The insurer has determined that the accident occurred more than fifty statute miles from the United States border, so it has denied liability coverage to Dick and UM coverage to Jerry. Suppose Dick loses his coverage argument in the suit he institutes in the Colorado courts against his insurer. Is it possible that at the same time Jerry could win his case in the Arizona courts regarding his UM benefits?

9. What type of agreement could Dick enter into with Jerry upon denial by Dick's insurer that he had liability coverage for the accident?

10. With respect to each of the possible claims that Jerry and Dick may have, determine what type of coverage the claim would be made under and whether it would be a first- or third-party claim.

KEY TERMS

Adhesion contract
Standardized contract characterized by the unequal bargaining power of the parties and the lack of negotiation regarding the terms of the contract.

Declaratory judgment action
Action in which the court renders an opinion as to a matter of law or in reference to the rights of the parties but does not order any action to be taken.

Excess judgment
Judgment for more than the insured's policy limits.

CHAPTER

20

Workers' Compensation

CHAPTER TOPICS

What Is Workers' Compensation?
Historical Background
The Statutory Framework
Today's Systems
Filing a Workers' Compensation Claim
Current Issues in Workers' Compensation

CHAPTER OBJECTIVES

In this chapter you will learn to:
- Explain the historical basis for the workers' compensation system
- Explain the statutory and administrative procedures followed in workers' compensation cases
- Identify the requirements for filing a workers' compensation claim
- Identify current workers' compensation issues

Juan Lopez was a farm worker. While he was operating a small farm tractor in a cotton field near Phoenix, Arizona, a rock became lodged in a piece of equipment he was towing. Juan got off the tractor and attempted to dislodge the rock. He was unsuccessful in doing so manually and asked a co-worker to back the tractor a few inches. The co-worker, who was not familiar with the tractor, pulled forward, causing Juan's right foot to be run over by a tire on the equipment being pulled.

Juan was a sixty-five-year-old diabetic who had returned to work only five weeks prior to the accident. He had been out of work for seven months while recovering from a vascular bypass in his right leg, necessitated by his diabetes. The accident occurred at the height of the harvest season when Juan was working eighty to ninety hours per week (at $5.00 per hour).

The accident occurred late Sunday evening; on Monday Juan went to a doctor recommended by his employer and was treated for a swollen foot and minor abrasions. On Tuesday the foot became very painful and Juan went to the emergency room. On Friday Juan had the toenail removed from the big toe on his right foot. Four weeks later his big toe was amputated. Two months after that, his right leg was amputated just below the knee.

Juan's medical expenses totaled $84,000. His postoperative care, including prosthesis, came to $28,000. The initial physician charged $45 for the office visit and billed Juan's employer's workers' compensation carrier. Because Juan did not know what workers' compensation was, or that he had sustained an employment-related injury, his hospital and related expenses were charged to, and paid by, his personal medical insurer.

Juan was denied workers' compensation benefits for the loss of his leg. The carrier took the position that it was his diabetes, not the accident, that caused the loss of his leg. Juan's unfortunate experience affords us an opportunity to explore the intricate functioning of the workers' compensation system.

WHAT IS WORKERS' COMPENSATION?

Workers' compensation is a relatively new concept conceived to circumvent certain problems of the tort system and to protect workers who are injured, whether or not due to their own negligence. It also relieved employers from tort responsibility for on-the-job injuries to their employees. Workers' compensation systems were intended to provide fast and efficient relief to injured workers without regard to fault. In theory, an injured worker gave up her right to sue her employer (and the right to a jury) in return for the implied promise that her reasonable medical expenses would be taken care of and that she would be compensated for the wages she lost as a result of the injury.

What has actually evolved is a system that rivals the entire tort system in cost and has become so complicated that many states recognize workers' compensation as a legal specialty. Just as tort reform preoccupies legislative bodies on a regular (if not continuous) basis, rarely does a year go by that legislators do not tinker with workers' compensation statutes.

HISTORICAL BACKGROUND

Workers' compensation systems arose out of the industrial revolution of the nineteenth century. Hard physical labor with machines and equipment designed to perform tasks without regard for the protection of operators resulted in numerous injuries. The tort system of the time was ill-equipped, from the employee's standpoint at least, to handle the medical expenses and lost wages of injured workers. Several common law defenses were available to the employer, such as contributory negligence, assumption of risk, and the **fellow servant rule** (which rendered an employer nonliable for an injury inflicted upon an employee through the negligence of a fellow employee, but made every employee liable to his fellow workers for his own negligence). Because of these defenses and the employer's superior financial position, injured workers had little chance to obtain compensation through the courts.

Even when the courts began to relax enforcement of the common law defenses, the injured worker, with no income and mounting medical expenses (if he were able to get treatment), stood in such an inferior financial position to his employer as to preclude an effective legal remedy. Employees (including those injured) were not eager to testify against their employers and face potential unemployment.

Beginning in Germany in the mid-1800s, in response to a growing public outcry about the way workers were treated, a system began to develop to take the issue of fault out of the workplace and provide benefits for injured workers. England adopted a "faultless" system in the late 1800s and the United States, beginning in the early 1900s, followed suit. Although the new concept initially faced, and lost, constitutional challenges, the issue was resolved in favor of a new, noncompulsory system by the United States Supreme Court in *New York Central Railroad v. White,* 243 U.S.

219 (1917). An earlier, compulsory version had been held to violate due process. Shortly thereafter, the vast majority of states adopted their own doctrines of workers' compensation. Today all states have a workers' compensation system.

The two major types of workers' compensation are mandatory coverage and voluntary coverage. In mandatory-coverage jurisdictions, the employee has no alternative other than to accept the benefits and restrictions imposed by the statutory framework adopted in her state. In voluntary-coverage jurisdictions, the employee may opt out of the system and retain her right to sue the employer in state court. Because most workers are unaware of what the system does or how it actually works, voluntary opting out is more illusory than real. Additionally, in most states if one accepts *any* benefits (medical expenses or lost wages), one is conclusively deemed to have opted in.

PUTTING IT INTO PRACTICE 20.1

1. Would Juan be deemed to have opted in to the workers' compensation system in your state?
2. Does your state have voluntary or compulsory coverage?

THE STATUTORY FRAMEWORK

What appears to be a straightforward goal—compensation of injured workers without regard to fault—has not been easily implemented. To process disputed or questioned claims outside of the court system, an entire administrative hierarchy had to be created. Judges and juries were replaced with administrative law judges or hearing officers. The rules of civil procedure were replaced and/or supplemented by administrative rules and regulations.

Exceptions to coverage for intentional or self-inflicted injuries and those caused by intoxication were

grafted onto the framework. For example, in *Coleman v. Wyoming Workers' Compensation Division,* 915 P.2d 595 (Wyo. 1996), the deceased worker's family was denied benefits based on the finding that his intoxication *contributed* to the accident, even though the decedent's inexperience in driving the vehicle actually caused the accident. Wyoming has a statute, similar to those of many other states, that prohibits recovery if intoxication of the worker is involved.

Different types of injuries were **scheduled** and a fixed method of determining the amount of compensation to the worker was devised. In many states injuries such as loss of an eye, total blindness, or loss of an appendage are scheduled, that is, a fixed benefit (usually a set number of months' compensation) is paid for the injury without regard to lost wages or medical expenses. Some injuries, such as back injuries, produce varying types of symptoms and could not be scheduled as easily as, for example, the loss of an eye or a limb. New rules for these unscheduled injuries had to be created. Notice requirements and specialized forms were devised, and failure to use them (or to use them correctly) had potentially drastic implications for both the employer and the employee.

A new insurance industry was created to allow the employer to spread the risk of the new system. Employers who chose not to be insured (rules and regulations determined who could and could not self-insure) risked the loss of their businesses, as they became personally liable for the costs to which injured workers would become entitled. To cover that situation, most jurisdictions developed a fund that stepped in to cover the worker when his employer lacked insurance or the funds (or willingness) to pay the statutory sums due or when the employer's insurance carrier became insolvent.

PUTTING IT INTO PRACTICE 20.2

How would your state treat Juan's injuries? Would the loss of his leg be scheduled?

TODAY'S SYSTEMS

A typical constitutional and statutory scheme for workers' compensation is found in Arizona. The state constitutional provision enabling the workers' compensation statutes is article XVIII, § 8, which states:

The Legislature shall enact a Workers' Compensation Law applicable to workmen engaged in manual or mechanical labor in all public employment whether of the State, or any political subdivision or municipality thereof as may be defined by law and in such private employments as the Legislature may prescribe by which compensation shall be required to be paid to any such workman, in case of his injury and to his dependents, as defined by law, in case of his death, by his employer, if in the course of such employment personal injury to or death of any such workman from any accident arising out of and in the course of, such employment, is caused in whole, or in part, or is contributed to, by a necessary risk or danger of such employment, or a necessary risk or danger inherent in the nature thereof, or by failure of such employer, or any of his or its agents or employee or employees to exercise due care, or to comply with any law affecting such employment; provided that it shall be optional with any employee engaged in any such private employment to settle for such compensation, or to retain the right to sue said employer or any person employed by said employer, acting in the scope of his employment, as provided by this Constitution; and, provided further, in order to assure and make certain a just and humane compensation law in the State of Arizona, for the relief and protection of such workmen, their widows, children or dependents, as defined by law, from the burdensome, expensive and litigious remedies for injuries to or death of such workmen, now existing in the State of Arizona, and producing uncertain and unequal compensation therefor, such employee, engaged in such private employment, may exercise the option to settle for compensation by failing to reject the provisions of such Workmen's Compensation Law prior to the injury, except that if the injury is the result of an act done by the employer or a person employed by the employer knowingly and purposely with the direct object of injuring another, and the act indicates a wilful disregard of the life, limb or bodily safety of employees, then such employee may, after the injury, exercise the option to accept compensation or to retain the right to sue the person who injured him.

The percentages and amounts of compensation provided in House Bill No. 227 enacted by the Seventh Legislature of the State of Arizona, shall never be reduced nor any industry included within the provision of said House Bill No. 227 eliminated except by initiated or referred measure as provided by this Constitution.

The United States Supreme Court has held that workers' compensation statutes do not violate the United States Constitution's Due Process Clause. Nevertheless, each state has had to look to its own constitution to determine if a constitutional amendment was necessary to allow implementation. In Arizona an original constitutional provision prohibited abrogation of the right to sue. If the workers' compensation provision had not been a part of the original state constitution, a constitutional amendment to legalize the workers' compensation statutes would have been required. A partial statutory index for the legislatively mandated program of Arizona is shown in Figure 20-1 to give you an idea of the complexity of the statutory framework and the areas the statutes specifically address.

In most jurisdictions, a governmental entity was created to administer the new laws. The Arizona Industrial Commission, for example, administers the workers' compensation system in Arizona. To date it has enacted sixty-four rules of procedure for workers' compensation hearings (Ariz. Admin. Code §§ R20-5-101 through R20-5-164). These rules, which supplement the statutory framework, must be followed by employee and employer alike. Failure to follow the rules often results in the loss of benefits or the right to contest the award. Some of the rules modify the normal procedure for obtaining witnesses (R20-5-141), the use of interrogatories (R20-5-144), and independent medical examinations (R20-5-144).

Is Workers' Compensation a Fair Deal?

The theoretical benefits anticipated by advocates of workers' compensation have not always been realized. Many of the roadblocks that existed in the early 1900s are no longer part of the American legal system. Unsafe working conditions, machinery without safety devices, and an employer-friendly tort system are not prevalent problems in today's workplace.

The bureaucracy that was birthed to solve the problems of the injured worker has created many new problems. To illustrate, state legislatures control the benefits to be paid and how they are to be calculated. Therefore today's employers may have as much control over their employees as they did before the onset of workers' compensation. Although outdated wage scales and artificial maximum benefits may spur injured employees to return to work as soon as possible, they do not necessarily provide adequate compensation for injured employees with valid claims. Furthermore, fraud is rampant amongst employees and insurance carriers have resorted to "hardball" tactics to counteract this deception. Such responses to workers' compensation have created a climate of fear and distrust between employees and employers.

The system does not always fairly compensate injured employees. An injured worker is generally not entitled, for example, to continued employer contributions for retirement benefits while she is off work because of an injury. Furthermore, she may lose her job, seniority, and/or job advancement opportunities. The compensation she is paid is almost always less than her earnings prior to the accident even though the employer remains liable for her medical expenses.

Most states limit employees' compensation by putting a cap on the monthly wage they can be paid.

FIGURE 20-1   Partial Statutory Index for the Arizona Workers' Compensation Statutes and Rules

A PARTIAL INDEX FOR ARIZONA WORKERS' COMPENSATION STATUTES:

23-901.	Definitions.
23-901.01.	Occupational disease; proximate causation.
23-901.02.	Liability of last employer; exception.
23-901.03.	Appointment of committee of medical consultants . . . .
23-901.04.	Compensation precluded by misconduct, self-exposure or disobedience of orders of commission; self-exposure defined.
23-901.05.	Occupational disease . . . .
23-901.06.	Volunteer workers.
23-901.07.	Handicapped persons . . . .
23-902.	Employers subject to chapter; exceptions.
23-903.	Application of chapter . . . .
23-904.	Effect of injury without the state . . . .
23-905.	Minor employees . . . .
23-906.	[R]ight of employee to make election; procedure . . . .
23-907.	Liability of employer . . . .
23-908.	Injury reports by employer and physician . . . .
23-909.	Motion picture exemption.
23-910.	Exemption for licensees.
23.921.	Administration of chapter.
23-926.	Inspection of employer records . . . .
23-927.	Power to enter places of employment.
23-928.	Investigation by agents.
23-929.	Enforcement of chapter.
23-930.	Unfair claim processing practices; bad faith . . . .
23-932.	Violations; classification.
23-933.	Priority of judgment against assets of employer.
23-941.	Hearing rights and procedure.
23-942.	Awards of administrative law judge . . . .
23-943.	Decision upon review.
23-944.	Effective date of orders . . . .
23-945.	Petition for hearing on validity of order . . . .
23-946.	Action asserting invalidity of order . . . .
23-946.01.	Stay of court proceedings . . . .
23-947.	Time within which hearing must be requested . . . .
23-948.	Jurisdiction of actions; . . . right of appeal.
23-949.	Effect of action concerning order . . . .
23-950.	Priority of actions.
23-951.	Writ of certiorari to review lawfulness of award . . . .
23-952.	Continuation of order or award pending . . . appeal.
23-961.	Methods of securing compensation by employers . . . .
23-962.	Insurance by governmental units . . . .

FIGURE 20-1   Partial Statutory Index for the Arizona Workers' Compensation Statutes and Rules—Continued

FIGURE 20-1   Partial Statutory Index for the Arizona Workers' Compensation Statutes and Rules—Continued

23-1066.	Minor or incompetent claimant . . . .
23-1067.	Commutation of compensation to lump sum payment.
23-1068.	Assignment of compensation . . . .
23-1069.	Attorney's fees; payment; time limitation.
23-1070.	Medical, surgical and hospital benefits . . . .
23-1070.01.	Request for early hearing; stipulation . . . .
23-1071.	Notice of disabled employee . . . .
23-1072.	Autopsy in death claims . . . .
23-1073.	Processing of prior claims.
23-1081.	Administrative fund; purposes and administration.
23-1091.	Assigned risk plan.

A PARTIAL INDEX FOR THE RULES OF PROCEDURE FOR WORKERS' COMPENSATION HEARINGS BEFORE THE INDUSTRIAL COMMISSION OF ARIZONA:

R20-5-101.	Notice of Rules; Part of Record; Effective Date
R20-5-102.	Location of Office and Office Hours
R20-5-103.	Time for Filing; Computation; Responses to Motions
R20-5-104.	Address of Claimant
R20-5-105.	Definitions
R20-5-106.	Forms Prescribed by Commission
R20-5-107.	Manner of Completion of Forms and Documents
R20-5-108.	Commission Claims Files
R20-5-109.	Microfilmed Files
R20-5-110.	Employer's Report; Report of Fatality
R20-5-111.	Request for Autopsy
R20-5-112.	Physician's Initial Report of Injury
R20-5-113.	Subsequent Medical Reports . . .
R20-5-114.	Examination at Request of Commission, Carrier or Employer
R20-5-115.	Requests for Out-of-State Medical Treatment
R20-5-116.	Transportation and Living Expenses of Employee
R20-5-117.	Medical, Hospital and Burial Expense
R20-5-118.	Notice of Claim Status
R20-5-119.	Notice of Third Party Settlement
R20-5-120.	Settlement Agreements, Compromises and Releases
R20-5-121.	Present Value; Basis of Calculation
R20-5-122.	Lump Sum Commutation
R20-5-123.	Rejection of Workers' Compensation Law
R20-5-124.	Rejection Not Applicable to New Employment
R20-5-125.	Rejection Prior to Employers Securing Insurance
R20-5-126.	Revocation of Rejection
R20-5-127.	Insurance Carrier's Notification to Commission . . .
R20-5-128.	Employer's Notification to Commission of Coverage

FIGURE 20-1   Partial Statutory Index for the Arizona Workers' Compensation Statutes and Rules—Continued

The injured employee is paid only a percentage of what his average monthly wage was before the accident. In Arizona, for example, the injured worker who cannot return to work is paid 66.7 percent of his average monthly wage at the time of the accident. Because no state or federal taxes (including Social Security and

Medicare) are withheld from payments made to the injured worker, a reduction of one-third of the employee's gross wage appears reasonable on the surface. For wage earners with a family, however, whose state and federal tax rate is very low or nonexistent, the reduction results in a real loss of disposable income of as much as 25 percent.

Many major injuries are scheduled. Loss of an arm or leg is worth so many months' compensation, in addition to payments received for being unable to return to work due to an accident. In Arizona, loss of the dominant arm is worth an additional 60 months' compensation; loss of a leg is worth 50 months' compensation (compensation is at 55 percent of the injured worker's average monthly wage).

For example, a secretary making $7.50 per hour would earn $1,300 per month, calculated as follows:

$7.50 per hour
× 40 hours
× 4.33 weeks
――――――――――
$1,300 per month

If she lost her leg due to a work-related accident, she would receive an additional benefit of 55 percent of her average monthly wage ($715) for 50 months. That monthly benefit would be paid for the prescribed period (50 months) in addition to any other benefits to which she might be entitled (which would be a maximum of $866.67 per month, 66.7 percent of $1,300). For an executive secretary earning $3,000 per month,

the respective benefits would be $1,155 (loss of leg at 55 percent) for 50 months and $1,400 (66.7 percent of maximum monthly wage of $2,100) while she was temporarily permanently disabled. The $866.67 monthly payment, but not the $715 for the loss of her leg, will cease when she can return to work.

If the loss of her leg resulted in her being unable to earn the same amount of income after recovering from the injury, she would be entitled (in Arizona) to payments equal to 66.7 percent of the difference between her postinjury earning capacity and her preinjury average monthly income. She would also be entitled to postinjury training and rehabilitation.

In most jurisdictions, the statutory monthly wage is not tied to the cost of living index or the state's actual average monthly wage. It is changed, if at all, only by legislative action. In Arizona the maximum average wage has not been changed from the current $2,100-per-month level since June of 1991. The previous maximum was $1,800.

The elaborate statutory framework and rules associated with workers' compensation have not gone unchallenged. In Arizona, over 1,700 reported cases (not including memorandum decisions) have made it to the appellate courts. Note that a workers' compensation case can be appealed, in Arizona, only after a final decision by an administrative law judge. To appeal to an appellate court, a petition to review the decision must be made to the Industrial Commission.

■   PUTTING IT INTO PRACTICE 20.3   □

1. How would you calculate Juan's average wage for benefit purposes? If Juan worked only eight months a year, would that make a difference?
2. What is the average monthly wage for a legal assistant who is paid $12 per hour for a 40-hour work week? In your state, what is the dollar value for the loss of her dominant arm?

The Adversarial Part of "No Fault"

All workers' compensation systems provide for resolution of disputed claims. The employer's premium is based on its claims history. It is, therefore, in the employer's best interest to minimize the number of claims and get the injured worker stabilized and back to work (or able to get back to work) as soon a possible. The employer's insurance carrier acts as a watchdog, monitoring the claims it processes to check for and weed out malingerers and frauds.

This adversarial aspect of the system causes the greatest delays in claims resolution. The employer, usually acting through its insurance carrier, can require the injured employee to submit to an independent medical examination (IME) by a doctor of the employer's choosing. (An IME is sometimes not allowed in states where the employer can require the employee to be treated by an approved workers' compensation physician.) When disputes occur they are heard by administrative law judges. The hearings are often bifurcated to allow the physicians to testify at times convenient for them. These procedural requirements slow down the resolution process.

If the employee wants to get a second opinion regarding his condition, he must usually pay for it. The procedures for getting a new treating physician vary but usually require the acquiescence of the employer or an order from the agency overseeing the workers' compensation system.

Employees have caused many of the problems with a system designed to ensure fast and efficient resolution of claims. Outright fraud and attempts to continue receiving benefits after recovery are widespread. In California, for example, it is estimated that 10 percent of all claims and 25 percent of all payments are the result of fraud (G.T. Schwartz, "Waste, Fraud, and Abuse in Workers' Compensation: The Recent California Experience," 52 *Md. L. Rev.* 983, 988 (1993)). Surveillance of claimants, to catch them performing physical acts of which they are supposedly incapable, is commonplace. The results appear to justify the money spent on such surveillance.

Employees' attempts to circumvent the system rarely result in criminal prosecution. The most the employee stands to lose is benefits to which he is not entitled. Hardball insurance carriers also have little fear of predatory practices. Bad faith claims in workers' compensation cases are difficult to prove. Many states have statutes protecting insurers from liability for their actions in workers' compensation cases. Many of those activities, if they occurred in other contexts such as with homeowners or automobile insurance claims, could subject the carrier to general tort damages, including punitive damages.

FILING A WORKERS' COMPENSATION CLAIM

The first requirement for filing a workers' compensation claim is that the employee be injured "on the job." Whether an employee was on the job is the subject of many of the reported cases. The answer is not as easy as it might first appear. For example, is an employee on the job when she is on her way to work? When she is parking her car in the employee parking lot? Leaving the parking lot to go home? On a personal errand but on company time? Dropping off a package for her boss on her way to lunch?

Once an on-the-job accident has occurred, the employer and employee have independent obligations to report it. The employee must report to the employer and the employer must notify the agency overseeing the workers' compensation system (and the employer's insurance carrier). Depending on the nature of the accident and the amount of time lost by the injured employee, the system reacts in different ways. A minor injury might result in no medical expenses and little or no lost time for the employee. The amount of lost time is important because compensation is usually not paid for the first few days (generally five to seven days) that the employee misses work. Medical expenses are paid from the time of the accident. The treating physician is usually required to give notice if the physician believes the injury to be job-related.

If the injury results in lost work time greater than the minimum time period prescribed, the employer will normally submit information to the agency to establish the employee's average monthly wage. The rules and procedures (and case law) in this area are quite complicated. Rules vary, for example, depending on whether the claimant is a new hire who has just received a raise. To illustrate, imagine the difficulty in computing the average monthly wage for a felon, just recently released from prison after three years, who had been on the job for only a week before the accident.

In most cases the average monthly wage is determined by the prior year's income. Separation from employment for illness or family emergency confuses the issue. A recent increase in pay may be averaged in with the prior year's income. Such a computation effectively reduces the average monthly income to less than that actually being earned by the employee at the time of the accident.

Once the monthly wage for benefit purposes has been established, the payments to the employee are generally made on a monthly basis. When the injury has stabilized, a decision is made regarding the permanency of the injury and whether the employee has suffered a loss of earning capacity. The rules for payment of permanent partial disability vary but are usually based on a percentage of the difference between an employee's preinjury earning capacity and his postinjury earning capacity (which requires a whole category of expert testimony). Compensation is not allowed for permanent impairment. For example, an employee with a permanent limp will not be compensated if the limp does not affect earning capacity. The same is true for scarring.

If an injury is caused by a co-employee, no claim can be made by the injured worker. If a third party caused the injury on the job, the employee can assert any tort claims she may have against the third party. The laws of most jurisdictions, however, provide that the employer (or its insurance carrier) has subrogation rights to the extent of any medical or wage payments made to the employee. In many states the claim is actually assigned by operation of law to the employer or its carrier if the employee does not assert her rights against the responsible party.

The subrogation claim that might have to be paid from the settlement or litigation of any lawsuit against a third party could be an impediment to the employee asserting his rights. In the third-party context, the employee would be subject to all tort defenses, including contributory negligence, comparative negligence, assumption of risk, etc. Most attorneys would not take an employee's tort claim if, due to the amount of the carrier's lien, only the attorney and the insurer would get paid. In states where the employee's third-party rights are transferred to the employer, the employer could pursue the employee's claim against the responsible third party in the name of the employee.

PUTTING IT INTO PRACTICE 20.4

1. What ethical problems might arise for those representing the employer in pursuing an employee's third-party claim?
2. If Juan did not know he had a claim, would the system get notice of his accident without his input?
3. How long do benefits get paid in your state? Is there an offset for Social Security benefits? What if the worker lives to be ninety-five? If he retires and draws a pension and Social Security?

CURRENT ISSUES IN WORKERS' COMPENSATION

Just as society has grappled with workplace issues such as sexual harassment, creation of a hostile environment, AIDS, and employee rage, so too has the workers' compensation system. Many systems are still groping for the appropriate ways to handle issues supposedly addressed by federal and state legislation.

For example, is potential exposure to AIDS a compensable injury if the worker does not become infected? Do the psychological stresses caused by the fear of possibly contracting AIDS, which could result in a person's being unable to work, constitute a work-related injury? Psychological incapacity due to sexual harassment and/or hostile work environments must also be addressed. Many systems are also having problems dealing with pure psychological injuries that have no physical cause.

In one case, the New York Court of Appeals held that the psychological injury caused to a secretary by the psychic trauma of finding her boss's body right after he had committed suicide was compensable to the same extent as any physical injury. *Wolfe v. Sibley, Lindsay & Curr Co.,* 330 N.E.2d 603 (N.Y. 1975). The dissent in *Wolfe* expressed concern about allowing compensation for "pure" psychological injuries arising out of an occurrence in which the claimant was not a participant. Would you, for example, approve of a Social Security system that provided benefits when an individual experienced everyday mental trauma, such as the loss of a family member?

Furthermore, the Americans with Disabilities Act of 1990, 42 U.S.C. § 12101 *et seq.* (ADA), has created some potential problems. In the past most states did not require an employer to keep an injured worker on as an employee when she recovered from her injury. The ADA may affect what an employer can do if an employee suffers a recognized disability as a result of an industrial accident.

PUTTING IT INTO PRACTICE 20.5

1. Does your state's workers' compensation law allow recovery for pure psychological injuries, such as those in *Wolfe?*
2. How does your state deal with AIDS? Does it have a statute addressing the issue?
3. Etta worked in a munitions factory. She was constantly harassed by fellow employees, who would throw things at her and make noises like a bomb exploding. She had a son who had been injured in training during the Persian Gulf War. Her co-employees would put depictions of dead and mutilated soldiers on her workstation. She twice attempted suicide as a result of the harassment and insults she faced at work. Shortly after her second discharge from a hospital's psychiatric unit, she filed a claim for benefits for psychiatric impairment. Should her claim be allowed?

SUMMARY

Workers' compensation is a system that was statutorily implemented in the early 1900s to protect injured workers from poverty. The employer agreed to be responsible for all work-related injuries and the employee gave up his right to sue and to a jury trial. Today's systems are either mandatory or voluntary.

Many of the reasons underlying establishment of workers' compensation no longer exist.

With artificially low payments and aggressive claims handling, the injured worker can easily fall below today's poverty level if she becomes unable to return to work due to a job-related injury. Increases in benefits can be obtained only through legislative action. Worker fraud is prevalent and provides support for both aggressive claims-handling processes and pay-ment of benefits that do not return the injured worker to her preinjury financial condition.

AIDS, psychological impairment, and the ADA have generated difficult questions for the workers' compensation system. The adversarial nature of the system, the delay in processing claims, and the current disputes regarding compensable and noncompensable injuries, as well as the continued viability of workers' compensation, remain issues that must be addressed.

PRACTICE POINTERS

In many workers' compensation cases it will be the legal assistant's duty to review the file. Most states have an administrative body (such as Arizona's Industrial Commission) that maintains the file. The administrative body where the transcript of proceedings and all filings must be made is the official repository.

As in the court system, documents filed at the central repository can usually be reviewed without court order. The administrative body often contracts with court reporters, so it may not be possible to make copies of all of the documents in the file. If you want a copy of the transcript for review, you may have to contact the reporter who was present at that proceeding and pay for the copy.

All medical records, billings, doctors' reports, and notices that were sent to the employer, employee, or treating physician are in the file. Many states require the treating physician to file regular progress reports. Notices of any change in status are in the file, such as termination of benefits notices, return to work notices, and the like. The calculation of the monthly wage is also in the file.

Due to the volume of workers' compensation cases, many states maintain a paper file for only a short period of time. The documents are often transferred to microfiche or electronic storage. It is important to understand and be able to search the storage media, to ensure that all important documents you need to review can be found and that any relevant documents that you may not know about will not be overlooked.

Review some of the reported workers' compensation cases from the past five years in your jurisdiction. You want to find a case that refers to documents that should be in the file and, preferably, a case that refers to a transcript, perhaps the testimony of a doctor. Once you have reviewed and briefed the case, go to the depository of the file. Your task will be to locate all documents referred to in the reported case.

If the case you choose is in paper form and your jurisdiction uses other storage media for older cases, review one of those case files to see how the documents are handled. In some jurisdictions the filings are copied chronologically, some with and some without an index. If electronic media are used, check to see the type, if any, of indexing that is used. What kind of searches can be made? If the electronic storage is graphic rather than text-based, you need to be sure that you do not miss an important document during your review of the file. Without an index or the ability to search the database, you will have to physically review each document in the file, much like the procedure with court files.

TORT TEASERS

1. If Juan came to your office for advice, what additional, factual information would you need to give your supervising attorney in order for her to make a decision regarding representation of Juan?

2. Review the statutory framework for your state's workers' compensation system. How does it compare with Arizona's?

3. How would you argue that Juan's seven-month break in employment should not be considered in determining his average monthly wage?

4. Calculate Juan's average monthly wage according to the laws of your state, assuming that Juan usually works forty-five hours per week (six months of the year) and overtime (eighty to ninety hours per week) for two months of the year. Juan does not, and had not for some years, work more than eight months a year.

KEY TERMS

Fellow servant rule
Doctrine that shields employers from liability for damages incurred for injuries to an employee due to the negligence of a co-worker.

Scheduled injuries
Injuries, such as loss of sight or of an appendage, for which stated benefits are paid.

APPENDIX

A

Suggested Responses to "Putting It into Practice" Exercises

CHAPTER 3

3.1 Assault/Battery

If Tyson believes the fan's intent is to contact Tyson's body with his fists and the fan has an apparent ability to carry out the threatened contact, an assault has been committed even if Tyson is unafraid of being injured.

3.2 False Imprisonment

These facts are based on an actual case, *May Department Stores Co., Inc. v. Devercelli*, 314 A.2d 767 (D.C. 1974). The jury concluded that the officer lacked probable cause to apprehend the plaintiff and the majority found that the evidence supported their conclusion. The dissent, in contrast, believed that probable cause existed as a matter of law and that despite the conflicting testimony no disagreement existed regarding the material facts.

3.3 Intentional Infliction of Emotional Distress

These are the facts of *Tandy Corp. v. Bone*, 678 S.W.2d 312 (Ark. 1984). The court held that the manager's reaction to stress and his request for Valium put his employer on notice that he was not someone of "ordinary temperament" and that he would probably not be able to endure the stressful situation to which he had been subjected. This notice to the employer provided the basis for a jury question of extreme outrage.

3.4 Trespass

In *Copeland v. Hubbard Broadcasting, Inc.,* 526 N.W.2d 402 (Minn. 1995), from which these facts were taken, the court found that a claim for trespass could exist. The district court concluded that the television station was entitled to summary judgment because the student did not exceed the boundaries of the Copelands' consent—they did not expressly limit their consent to her educational goals. The appellate court, however, recognized trespass as a remedy when secret cameras are used for gathering news and held that newsgathering does not create a license to trespass into a private home. The court remanded the case to the jury to determine the nature of the Copelands' consent to the student.

3.5 Trespass to Chattels/Conversion

These hypotheticals are taken from the Restatement (Second) of Torts § 222A, illus. 5, 6, 12, 25, and 26. No conversion is committed when Matthew puts the furniture in storage and changes the locks, but Matthew does convert John's property when he moves it to a distant warehouse that greatly inconveniences John. John does not convert Matthew's car when he drives the extra ten miles, but he does convert it when he gets into an accident.

3.6 Consent

In *Berthiaume v. Pratt*, 365 A.2d 792 (Me. 1976), the court found no grounds for consent. The surgeon argued that the medical importance of the photographs overrode any apparent objections of the patient, but the court refused to create any medical exception to the rules surrounding consent.

3.7 Self-Defense

Some facts are lacking, such as the man's distance from George and Sandy, but as long as a reasonable person in George's situation would have believed deadly force was immediately necessary to protect himself and another, George would be justified in defending himself and Sandy. Because the man is threatening with deadly force (a knife), George would be justified in responding with deadly force. The fact that the man is mentally ill does not change the answer unless his mental illness and the harmlessness of the knife would have been apparent to a reasonable person in that situation.

3.8 *Katko v. Briney*

1. Frustrated by a series of trespassings and burglaries to an abandoned house on their property, the Brineys installed a spring gun that was aimed at an intruder's legs. The plaintiff broke into the house, which he believed to be abandoned, to take some bottles and fruit jars. When he entered the bedroom, the spring gun went off, shooting him in the leg, causing serious physical injury.
2. The value of human life outweighs property rights. If there is a threat to personal safety.
3. If the law prohibits the use of deadly force when one is present, that same degree of force is prohibited in one's absence.
4. The infliction of serious bodily injury cannot be used to prevent trespassing.
5. Yes.

3.9 Regaining Possession of Chattel

The officers did appear to exceed their authority in detaining the man for more than an hour, in their attempts at intimidation (refusing his request to make phone calls and slapping the gun), and in their use of duress to induce him to sign a release. The court found that the officers lacked probable cause to arrest the man and should have kept him under surveillance longer before detaining him for questioning.

3.10 Private/Public Necessity

These hypotheticals are taken from the Restatement (Second) of Torts § 262, illus. 1, and § 263, illus. 1. Both the fireman and Liz are privileged. The fireman is not liable for damages to Maryann's car, but Liz is liable for damages to the scarf.

CHAPTER 5

5.1 Attractive Nuisance Doctrine

1. A subjective standard is used with this doctrine, because the age, intelligence, and experience of the plaintiff are taken into consideration.
2. According to the Restatement (Second) of Torts § 339(i), illus. 5, the company is not liable because the attractive nuisance doctrine does not apply when the defendant is maintaining "normal, necessary and usual implements" that are essential to a business and that "reckless children can use to their harm in a spirit of bravado or to gratify some other childish desire" with full perception of the risks involved. The fact that Jed accepted the dare indicates that he was aware of the risk.
3. The second hypothetical is taken from illustrations 6 and 7 in § 339(i) of the Restatement. The pond owner owes a duty to Marie if she is three but not if she is ten, because the ten-year-old is expected to be aware of the dangers of the pond whereas the three-year-old is not. If Marie were not able to appreciate the dangers of drowning because of some unique mental or physical disability, the owner could owe her a duty even if she were ten.
4. The third hypothetical is taken from illustration 9 of § 339(i) of the Restatement. The railroad company could be liable if it could have easily installed a locking device, but would not be liable if the locking device would have seriously interfered with its business. The

difference in answers arises out of a balancing test—balancing the risk to the children against the utility of the dangerous condition (the turntable). The company would probably not be liable, however, if Micki had been forewarned about the dangers of the turntable (illustration 8), because he was aware of the risks involved and chose to ignore those risks out of recklessness or bravado.

5.2 Invitees/Licensees/Trespassers

1. According to the Restatement (Second) of Torts § 332, from which these examples were taken, the appropriate classifications are:
   a. Licensee (comment b)
   b. Licensee (comment d)
   c. Invitee (commend d)
   d. Invitee (comment e)
   e. Loses invitee status when she goes behind counter where she does not have permission to go; becomes a trespasser (comment l)

2. Because the child is a licensee (a social guest), the homeowners owe her a duty to warn her of hidden danger. The court in this case grappled with whether a pool was a hidden peril to a nineteen-month-old child and decided that it was a matter of fact for the jury to determine. The court noted that even if the homeowners made the parents aware of the pool, they did not necessarily fulfill their duty to the child. *Shaw v. Peterson,* 821 P.2d 220 (Ariz. Ct. App. 1991).

3. The store has a duty to inspect the premises for hidden dangers. The store owner might reasonably expect that customers' attention will be diverted by the displays and that they will not discover what is obvious, the owner has a duty to take reasonable steps to protect customers from what is otherwise an obvious condition. Restatement (Second) of Torts § 343A, illus. 2.

5.3 *Kline*

1. The plaintiff was criminally assaulted in the hallway of her apartment complex. Violent crimes had been occurring at the apartment complex with increasing frequency in the months preceding this assault.

The security protection provided to the plaintiff when she first moved into her apartment was no longer available even though the plaintiff and others had appealed to the landlord to better secure the building.

2. Does a landlord have a duty to protect tenants from foreseeable criminal attacks committed by third parties?

3. Private persons have no duty but innkeepers do. The difference in duty is due to the nature of the innkeeper-guest relationship. Guests' entrustment of their safety to the innkeeper entitles guests to expect innkeepers to use reasonable care to protect them from attack.

4. The court found the attack foreseeable because the landlord had notice of the previous crimes committed against the persons and property of the tenants in recent months.

5. The court reasons that the landlord, not the tenant nor even the police, is in the best position to protect tenants from foreseeable criminal activity in the hallways, entryways, and other commonways in an apartment complex. The court further argues that an implied contract between landlord and tenant obligates landlords to provide reasonable protective measures. The court also analogizes to the innkeeper-guest relationship and applies the same duty to the landlord-tenant relationship in reference to third-party criminal attacks.

6. The court holds the landlord to the standard of care that the landlord employed when the plaintiff first became a resident. The court also looks to the standard of protection provided by apartments of the same character and type in that community.

7. These facts come from *Turner v. United States,* 473 F. Supp. 317 (D.D.C. 1979). The court concluded that no duty was owed the plaintiff to protect her from criminal assault. The facts that distinguish this case from *Kline* are the relationship between the plaintiff and the defendant (unlike the landlord-tenant relationship, the court found that the employer-employee relationship created no "implied contract" that implicitly guaranteed the plaintiff's safety from violent acts); the lack of knowledge of previous criminal assaults

within the building in recent times; and the agency's adherence to community standards of care.

5.4 *New York v. Riss*

1. "Because we owe a duty to everybody, we owe it to nobody."

2. Holding the state liable will result in a financial disaster for New York City, because every time a crime is committed inadequate police protection will be claimed and the city will be sued.

3. No municipality has gone bankrupt because it was held liable for negligent police actions. The burden on the city's budget for tort claims in other areas has not been burdensome. Under a negligence standard the police are held to a standard of reasonableness, not perfection. In the instant case the plaintiff would not have been able to recover under a negligence standard if she had been attacked after her first visits to the police station. The police were negligent only after failing to provide her protection after verifying her claims that her life was in danger.

4. This case had nothing to do with a decision regarding the allocation of resources or manpower. Furthermore, courts frequently review administrative practices in other types of tort claims involving municipalities and in so doing they routinely apply the principles of vicarious liability. If an injury is a result of failure to allocate sufficient funds, agencies can opt either to improve their administrative practices or to accept the cost of compensating those who have been injured.

5. The real costs of negligent police protection have been hidden by charging those costs to those who have been injured rather than to the community, which had the power to prevent those injuries.

6. It establishes the standard of conduct that should be followed and the penalties for failing to follow those standards.

5.5 Duty to Protect

The court in this case (*Figueroa v. North Park College*, 879 F.2d 1427 (Ill. 1998)) concluded that the plaintiff was not an invitee. The court used a three-part test:

1. Did she enter the premises by express or implied invitation?
2. Was her entry connected with an activity the owner conducted or permitted to be conducted on the land?
3. Was there a mutuality of benefit or a benefit to the owner? The court determined that the first two parts of the test could be subject to reasonable dispute but concluded that as a matter of law the plaintiff failed to meet the third part of the test, finding that any "public relations benefit" to the defendant was "too remote to confer invitee status."

The court also used a voluntary undertaking analysis and found that North Park had voluntarily undertaken to provide security measures and that it had an obligation to provide reasonable protection to the plaintiff. The court further found that North Park had not been negligent in preventing the crime against the plaintiff, as the plaintiff had failed to prove that the assault against her had been foreseeable.

CHAPTER 6

6.1 *Eimann v. Soldier of Fortune Magazine*

1. 9. Extortion; jailbreaks.

2. No.

3. The average subscriber would understand that certain phrases were solicitations for illegal activities based on the context of those ads (e.g., the presence of other classified ads as well as display ads). No, he could not distinguish ads.

4. SOF did not have a duty to refrain from publishing a facially innocuous classified ad whose context made its message ambiguous.

5. They have used it to determine whether a defendant has an obligation to act as a reasonable person would under the circumstances at issue and what standard of conduct would satisfy that obligation. Under this test a risk becomes unreasonable when its magnitude outweighs the social utility of the act or omission that creates it.

6. Yes.

7. Yes. As many as nine ads had served as links in criminal plots, ranging from extortion to jailbreaks. SOF staff had participated in at least two police investigations in which these ads had played a role.

8. To recognize and refrain from publishing ads that " 'reasonably could be interpreted as an offer to engage in illegal activity' based on their words or 'context.' " This burden was too heavy based on the ambiguity of the Hearn ad and the pervasiveness of advertising in our culture.

9. The serious harm created by these ads combined with the gravity of that harm does not outweigh the onerous burden of requiring publishers to reject all ads for products or services that might pose a threat of harm.

6.2 Using the Restatement to Determine Reasonableness of Conduct

The utility of the state's inaction must be weighed against the risk to those who might be harmed by diving into shallow waters. Although the state's failure to warn could certainly result in harm to those unaware of the dangers of shallow water, the question is "the extent of harm likely to be caused," the chance that such harm would occur, and "the number of persons whose interests are likely to be invaded if the risk takes effect in harm." The utility to the state pertains to the feasibility of the state inspecting the terrain of the park for hidden dangers, considering the size and nature of the park. In balancing the risk against the utility of the state's conduct one would have to consider: (1) the size of the park, (2) the extent of use of the lake and of the cove in question, (3) the accessibility of the cove, (4) the extent to which the park was and could reasonably be patrolled, (5) the time and resources that would have to be expended in taking the requisite precautions, and (6) the obviousness of the danger the cove presented. After weighing the magnitude of the risk of the cove against the utility of the state's conduct, one might expect the state to inspect locations such as the cove for hidden dangers and either remove them or post warnings regarding their existence, or one might find such an inspection impracticable; or, alternatively, that inspections were unreasonable but that reasonable care required posting signs prohibiting diving. To see the court's analysis of this case, see *Markowitz v. Arizona Parks Board,* 706 P.2d 364 (Ariz. 1985).

6.3 What the Reasonable Person Is Expected to Know

1. Yes. The dangerous nature of icy roads is common knowledge in the community. Restatement (Second) of Torts § 290, illus. 4.

2. Yes. The danger of explosion is common knowledge in the community. Restatement (Second) of Torts § 290, illus. 3.

3. Yes. Susan is charged with knowledge of the ordinance and should expect the trolley to stop. Restatement (Second) of Torts § 290, illus. 7.

4. The court in *Dolezal v. Carbrey,* 778 P.2d 1261 (Ariz. 1989) concluded that reasonable minds could differ as to whether it was "foreseeable that an otherwise gentle horse might bolt in reaction to out-of-the-ordinary cues" from an inexperienced rider. The questions the court believes should be considered in assessing the reasonableness of Frank's conduct are whether Frank should have let an inexperienced rider ride an animal accustomed to proper and subtle cues, whether he sufficiently instructed Carole before she rode, and whether he adequately supervised her riding and dismount.

6.4 Standard of Care in Special Circumstances

1. In *Breunig v. American Family Insurance Co.,* 713 N.W.2d 619 (Wis. 1970), the court did not allow the defendant to claim insanity as a defense. The court noted, however, that if the defendant had not experienced similar delusions previously, it would have allowed the insanity defense, because if insanity strikes suddenly with no forewarning individuals cannot do anything to avoid liability.

2. The minor could be held to an adult standard of

care if a court concluded that hunting is a dangerous activity engaged in by adults and not children. But if a court concluded that minors commonly hunt, the minor would be held to the standard of care of a child of the defendant's age, intelligence, and experience.

3. If the driver had never experienced a seizure previously, he would not, as a reasonable person, be expected to take any precautions to prevent an accident. But having been treated for epilepsy, he would be held to the standard of a reasonable epileptic. According to the Restatement (Second) of Torts § 283C, cmt. c, it might be negligence for such a person to drive at all, although the fact that the driver had been seizure-free for more than ten years makes that unlikely.

6.5 Negligent Per Se

1. According to the Restatement (Second) of Torts § 286 illus. 5, the statute establishes the standard of conduct for the cow hit by the train but not for the poisoned cow.

2. The purpose of the statute is to protect the public from incompetent physicians. The defendant's violation of the statute does not by itself establish negligence; the plaintiff must prove that the defendant was incompetent (that he fell below the standard of care of a reasonable physician). *Brown v. Shyne,* 151 N.E. 197 (N.Y. 1926).

3. Marjorie can but Helena cannot because the statute was designed to protect employees, not visitors. Restatement (Second) of Torts § 286, illus. 1.

4. The court says the statutory "standard established was to prevent the police from being injured but not to prevent the plaintiff from being injured." *Good v. City of Glendale,* 722 P.2d 386 (Ariz. 1986).

CHAPTER 7

7.1 Actual Causation

1. No. Although the plaintiff may argue that but for the misrepresentation, she would not have bought the condo (and she can certainly claim damages for that misrepresentation), she cannot apply the but-for test to the broken pipes because the representation by the broker made no reference to the plumbing. Therefore, there is no causal link between the broken pipes and the misrepresentation.

2. No, the court found no causal connection between the Association's sponsorship and the plaintiff's loss. According to the court, "The only connection between the conduct of [Ford] and plaintiff's injury was an aura of legitimacy given to the race by the participation of a nationally-known sponsor." *McCulloch v. Ford Dealers Advertising Ass'n,* 234 Cal. App. 3d 1385 (1991).

3. Because most diseases can be tied to a number of causal factors, they will have difficulty proving with a reasonable degree of medical certainty that Agent Orange was in fact the precipitating cause of the plaintiffs' injuries. The defendant will scrutinize the medical histories of the plaintiffs, looking for signs of cigarette smoking, alcohol abuse, drug use (prescription and nonprescription), family history, exposure to other toxic chemicals and to pathogens (such as bacteria and parasites), and any other factors connected with the diseases in question. The plaintiffs will have to present strong expert testimony and epidemiological evidence (and to a lesser degree animal studies) to establish causation.

7.2 *Palsgraf*

1. Yes. No.

2. A duty.

3. She must show a "wrong to herself, i.e., a violation of her own right." It is defined in "terms of the natural or probable."

4. When "it results in the commission of a wrong, and the commission of a wrong imports the violation of a right."

5. No, the negligence must be in relation to the plaintiff.

6. A duty to "protect society from unnecessary danger, not to protect A, B, or C alone."

7. To "refrain from those acts that may unreasonably threaten the safety of others." No.

8. "Because of convenience, of public policy, of a

rough sense of justice, the law arbitrarily declines to trace a series of events beyond a certain point." Practical politics. It is a matter of expediency.

9. Because the chauffeur's negligence was not the proximate cause of their injuries, because a prudent person would not have foreseen these consequences. Because he should be responsible for what might reasonably be expected to follow from an explosion.

10. No. A question of judgment.

11. Yes.

7.3 Actual Cause versus Proximate Cause

The *Markowitz* court found that reasonable people could find the state's failure to post warning signs to be the cause of David's injuries because they could have concluded that David would have avoided diving if an adequate warning had been given. The question of actual causation revolves around whether the state's inaction in fact caused David's injury, i.e., can it be argued that but for the state's failure to warn, David would not have been injured, or that the state's inactivity was a substantial factor leading up to David's injury? The question of proximate cause is a question of foreseeability: was David's injury a reasonably foreseeable consequence of the failure to post warning signs, or was the connection too remote to find proximate cause?

7.4 Exceptions to Cardozo Rule

1. Yes, according to the court in *In re Kinsman Transit Co.,* 338 F.2d 708 (2d Cir. 1964). All of the river-bank landowners were members of the general class as to which there was a general foreseeability of harm, because loose ships and failure to raise a drawbridge pose a danger to river-bank property owners in general. Even though the precise way the accident occurred was not foreseeable, a general, foreseeable risk existed that a loose ship and an unraised drawbridge would damage adjoining property. The harm suffered by the landowners was of the same general type that made the defendants' conduct negligent.

2. Yes. Under the "eggshell skull" rule, even if a nor-mal person in Helen's position would have recovered after leaving the plant, Helen's psychological vulnerability would not break the chain of causation. In fact, the court (in what the appellate court refers to as the case of the "dynamite heart") found that Helen failed to prove actual causation and denied her recovery for her hypochondriacal injuries on that basis. *Stoleson v. United States,* 708 F.2d 1227 (7th Cir. 1983).

7.5 Intervening versus Superseding Causes

1. Yes, as long as Lucinda was being reasonably careful in learning to use her crutches. Her behavior in walking across the narrow walkway was probably unreasonable and would be considered an abnormal consequence of the original broken leg, making her actions a superseding cause. Restatement (Second) of Torts § 460, illus. 1 and 2.

2. The court found that the driver was an intervening cause and that the defendants' negligence exposed Charles to the type of harm that might foreseeably have occurred even though the intervening act occurred in an unforeseeable manner. *Bigbee v. Western Electric,* 93 Cal. App. 3d 451 (1979).

3. No, because the extraordinary and gross negligence of the ship's captain would be considered a superseding cause. The trial court found that the "captain's failure to plot fixes . . . was entirely independent of the fact of breakout." *Exxon Co. v. Sofec, Inc.,* 116 S. Ct. 1813 (1996).

CHAPTER 8

8.1 Damages in Case of VA Patient

These facts are taken from *Christopher v. United States,* 237 F. Supp. 787 (E.D. Pa. 1965). The plaintiff was awarded damages for lost wages, future lost earnings (reduced to present value), future medical expenses, and pain and suffering. He received no compensation for past medical expenses because those had been paid for by the government. The court deducted past disability payments from his award because the government had already paid these sums to the plaintiff and under the servicemen's benefit laws he could not recover twice for the same injury.

The court looked at the plaintiff's past salary, the wages he had lost since his operation, the projected salaries he would have earned had he been able to work until he was sixty-five (his proven earning ability along with his prospects for future employment), the operations he would probably need, and the rehabilitation and counseling he would need. In assessing his pain and suffering award the court considered the daily humiliation he endured, his physical pain, his depression, his loss of sexual powers, and his disfigurement and anxiety, as well as the ongoing mental and physical distress he would continue to suffer. A "day in the life" video would be helpful in such a case and, in fact, in considering pain and suffering damages, the court alluded to one incident that required the plaintiff to be "washed down with a hose" after having an involuntary bowel movement while on an outing with friends.

8.2 Punitive Damages

1. Punitive damages are not justified according to this court in this case. *Woolstrum v. Maillioux*, 141 Cal. App. 3d Supp. 1 (1983). The defendants were negligent, not wilful and wanton. The evidence did not show that the "defendant knew his fence was dangerously weak . . . and that he consciously disregarded the probability (not possibility) that a cow would lean against it and that, if it did, the cows would escape and probably (not possibly) cause a serious accident."

2. The court held that as a "matter of law the evidence of the plaintiff fell far short of showing a wanton disregard by defendant of a probable" injury.

8.3 Wrongful Death/Survival Claims

These facts are taken from *Bendalin v. Valley National Bank*, 540 P.2d 194 (Ariz. 1975).

8.4 Damages for Mental Suffering

1. In *Sinn v. Burd*, 404 A.2d 672 (Pa. 1979), the court allowed a claim of infliction of emotional distress because the plaintiff was "located near the scene of the accident, the shock resulted from a direct emotional impact upon the plaintiff from the sensory and contemporaneous observance of the accident, and the plaintiff and victim were closely related."

2. In *Mazzagatti v. Everingham*, 516 A.2d 672 (Pa. 1986), the court reasoned that "where the close relative is not present at the scene of the accident, but instead learns of the accident from a third party, the close relative's prior knowledge of the injury to the victim serves as a buffer against the full impact of observing the accident scene. By contrast the relative who contemporaneously observes the tortious conduct has no time in which to brace his or her emotional system."

3. In allowing the emotional distress claim, the court in *Chizmar v. Mackie*, 896 P.2d 196 (Alaska 1995), held "that the emotional distress resulting from a misdiagnosis of AIDS is foreseeable and that such distress is serious or severe . . . . The significance of a false imputation of AIDS is unquestionable."

CHAPTER 9

9.1 Contributory Negligence

1. Jeff can recover for the initial damages to his car because his negligence in speeding did not cause the accident, but because his negligence did result in his losing control of his car, he cannot recover for his personal injuries or the damages resulting from going into the ditch. Restatement (Second) of Torts § 465, illus. 1.

2. Yes, under the last clear chance doctrine.

a. The last clear chance doctrine still applies.

b. The last clear chance doctrine does not apply because Corinne's negligence preceded her encounter with Geraldine. Therefore, she did not have the "last clear chance" to avoid the accident. Restatement (Second) of Torts § 479, illus. 1–3.

3. No, because the last clear chance doctrine does not apply. Christy's prior negligence prevented her from

discovering Margaret's car. Restatement (Second) of Torts § 479, illus. 4.

9.2 Contributory Negligence, State Law

[Answers depend on the laws of your state.]

9.3 Assumption of Risk

1. The ticketholder may not read the waiver and thus may claim lack of notice; because the printing is so small, notice of the waiver is unlikely. No signature is required, so any agreement on the part of the ticketholder is hard to prove.

2. Yes, according to the court in *Wertheim v. United States Tennis Ass'n,* 150 A.D.2d 157 (N.Y. 1989), which held as a matter of law that being hit by a tennis ball is a risk normally associated with the sport.

3. For an interesting review of this question, read K. Cahill, "Should There Be an Assumption of Risk Defense to Some Hostile Work Environment Sexual Harassment Claims?," 49 *Vand. L. Rev.* 1107 (1995), in which the author concludes that assumption of risk should be allowed in some form.

9.4 Immunity

1. No, according to the court in *Lovitt v. Concord School District,* 228 N.W.2d 479 (Mich. 1975), because the program was a governmental rather than proprietary function. The fact that the school charged admission to football games did not influence the court's analysis. However, in reference to the claims against the coaches the court found that the "liability of the teachers is not based upon negligence imputed to them as public functionaries, but rather it arises from their individual conduct. . . . [E]ven if it is assumed that the teachers . . . could be considered 'public officers' otherwise sharing in the protection of governmental immunity, they would still be subject to liability because they invaded the rights of specific persons."

2. The United States Supreme Court has prohibited § 1983 claims against public defenders by ruling that they do not act "under color of state law." Most courts have refused to grant immunity to public defenders in malpractice claims, arguing that the public defender is not like a judge or prosecuting attorney, but rather like a private attorney whose only duty is to the client, and that it would be unfair to deprive indigent defendants of this remedy. Others have granted immunity relying on policy arguments regarding the limited funds and heavy caseloads that face public defenders, the possible "chilling effect" that liability would have on the public defender's defense strategies, and the problems that liability would have on recruiting attorneys to work as public defenders. They distinguish public defenders and private attorneys on the basis that public defenders cannot decline clients, even those with meritless cases.

3. In *Schultz v. Roman Catholic Archdiocese,* 472 A.2d 531 (N.J. 1984), the court held that the Charitable Immunity Act prevented a charity from being found liable for negligence. The dissent, however, argued that statutory charitable immunity does not apply to intentional torts and that the "negligent hiring, supervision and retention of potentially harmful employees by the entity constitutes an exception to the rule of charitable immunity."

4. Not if the state in which he resides has adopted, by statute or judicial decision, parent-child immunity. For an exemplary case, *see Richards v. Richards,* 604 So. 2d 487 (Fla. 1992).

9.5 Statutes of Limitations

[Consult the applicable statutes in your state.]

CHAPTER 10

10.1 *Togstad*

1. Because Miller (the attorney she consulted) told her she did not have a case and did not contact her after their initial meeting, which she believed he said he would if his partner thought she had a case.

2. Because she relied on Miller's legal opinion.

3. That he had told Mrs. Togstad that his firm had no expertise in medical malpractice, that she should get

another opinion, and that his firm would not be interested in taking her case.

4. An attorney-client relationship existed; the defendant acted negligently or in breach of contract; such acts were the proximate cause of the plaintiff's damages; but for the defendant's acts the plaintiffs would have been successful in pursuing their medical malpractice claim.

5. Yes.

6. Because Miller failed to do the research that a reasonably prudent attorney would do before giving an opinion.

7. Yes.

8. The defendants did not litigate the issue at trial and it was reasonably inferable that Mrs. Togstad did not consult another attorney until after the statute had run.

9. Yes.

10.2 Malpractice Claim

1. The court found that the estate had failed to establish a prima facie case of malpractice because the medical expert's testimony failed to express the requisite degree of medical certainty. "An expert fails this standard of certainty if he testifies 'that the alleged cause "possibly," or "could have" led to the result, that it "could very probably account" for the result, or even that it was "very highly probable" that it caused the result.' " *Hoffman v. Brandywine Hospital,* 661 A.2d 397 (Pa. 1995).

2. The appellate court concluded that the expert testimony failed to establish a causal link between the anesthesiologist's actions and Herman's myoclonus. The court characterized the expert's conclusion regarding proximate cause as "mere speculation." Because Herman was unable to prove the underlying medical malpractice claim, his legal malpractice claim must fail. *Stanski v. Ezersky,* 644 N.Y.S.3d 220 (N.Y. 1996).

10.3 Informed Consent

1. The court found a lack of informed consent, in that the hospital's silence as to the risks "amounted to an assurance that there were none whereas its own questions to patients regarding reactions to this specific procedure demonstrate[d] that [it] . . . recognized the substantial possibility of complications." *Keel v. St. Elizabeth Medical Center,* 842 S.W.2d 860 (Ky. 1992).

2. The court found a lack of informed consent because the doctors failed to describe the advantages and disadvantages of the various replacement valves and to disclose the recognized risks of the Beall valve. The court explained that doctors must discuss alternative valves when they "represent medically recognized alternatives." *Stover v. Association of Thoracic & Cardiovascular Surgeons,* 635 A.2d 1047 (Pa. 1993).

10.4 Battery versus Negligence

Because Patricia is claiming that she was harmed by the drug, not by the insertion of the needle, the court refused to find a battery. The fact that the doctor or nurse had to touch Patricia in order to insert the needle was not sufficient to invoke the battery doctrine. The court agreed with the plaintiff, however, that it was time to adopt a negligence standard, because "[a] patient's decision to undergo drug therapy should be no less informed than a decision to undergo surgery." *Wu v. Spence,* 605 A.2d 395 (Pa. 1992).

CHAPTER 11

11.1 Intentional Misrepresentation

1. The doctor's representations regarding the results of the operation are not fraudulent. Lucille's scar was in fact lowered and the surgery, except for the blistering, accomplished the results she expected. His promises to fix the problem were not misrepresentations in that he did continue to treat her and never refused to see her. Lucille opted to consult other doctors, so she did not rely on the doctor's representations and suffered no damages as a result of these postsurgical promises. *Stone v. Foster,* 164 Cal. Rptr. 901 (Ct. App. 1980).

2. The court allowed the claim of misrepresentation in *Barbara A. v. John G.,* 193 Cal. Rptr. 422 (Ct. App. 1983). The court refused to allow recovery in a

"wrongful birth" case, however, for social policy reasons (invasions of privacy and concern for the welfare of the child). The court distinguished the cases based on the damages: damage to a woman's body caused by an ectopic pregnancy versus the "damage" of an unexpected child accompanied by support obligations.

3. An annulment was granted. Although the trial court opined that "if there were false representations, the plaintiff condoned them," the appellate court concluded that Maria's actions had to be considered in light of her background and the atmosphere in which she was living and that she "was no more capable of 'condoning' defendant's false representations than would be an infant or one of unsound mind." *Zmyslinski v. Zmyslinski,* 151 N.Y.S.2d 774 (App. Div. 1956).

4. The court refused to allow Peter to recover because he failed to prove the element of reliance, noting that the plaintiff had "elected to stand upon [the complaint] without exercising his leave to amend." *Peter W. v. San Francisco Unified School District,* 131 Cal. Rptr. 854 (Ct. App. 1976).

5. The court found no misrepresentation. The court saw no more in Kaiser's literature than a "generalized puffing" to the effect that the Foundation's doctors would exercise good judgment in their care. The court also concluded that the "incentive" plan used by Kaiser was recommended by professional organizations as a means of reducing unnecessary medical costs and that it was not evidence that any doctors had acted negligently or that they had refrained from recommending necessary diagnostic procedures or treatments. *Pulvers v. Kaiser Foundation Health Plan,* 160 Cal. Rptr. 392 (Ct. App. 1980).

11.2 Negligent Misrepresentation

The court concluded that William had a claim for negligent misrepresentation because he relied (to his detriment) on the doctor's misrepresentations regarding his experience as well as the lack of risk of amputation. The court suggested that William had a viable claim for lack of informed consent as well. *Bloskas v. Murray,* 646 P.2d 907 (Colo. 1982).

11.3 *Gibbs v. Ernst*

1. Whether common law fraud can be applied in the adoption context.

2. The need for prospective parents to be given as much information as possible to ensure a successful placement with parents who are emotionally and financially able to care for the children they adopt versus the concern that an undue burden placed on adoption agencies would diminish the number of children being successfully placed in homes.

3. Yes.

4. Yes. No.

5. The Act is silent. The legislature would need to take affirmative steps to indicate it did not want tort law to be applicable.

6. Intentional non-disclosure involves an intentional concealment of a material fact rather than the making of an affirmative misrepresentation.

7. They have all allowed intentional misrepresentation and several have recognized negligent misrepresentation.

8. The court allows them to proceed on both claims.

9. Because the agencies are not required to guarantee that the information they provide is accurate; they are required only to use reasonable care in their investigations.

11.4 Innocent Misrepresentation

The court affirmed a judgment for the Ballards against the broker on the grounds that brokers have a duty to know about the property they are selling and that as professionals possessing superior knowledge buyers should be expected to rely on their representations. Brokers, the court suggested, could protect themselves "by investigating the owner's statements, or by disclaiming knowledge, by requiring the seller to sign at the time of listing a statement setting forth representations which will be made, certifying that they are true and providing for indemnification if they are not." The facts supported a misrepresentation claim, in that the listing, which mentioned a 100-foot well, would reasonably lead buyers to assume the well was good; the listing misrepresented the well; and the Ballards relied on that misrepresentation. *Bevins v. Ballard*, 655 P.2d 757 (Alaska 1982).

11.5 *Wood v. Picillo*

1. The odors of chemicals were obvious, as was visual evidence of chemicals in a trench and chemicals flowing from barrels. Trucks from chemical companies were seen entering the property. Soil samples were tested and found to contain a number of toxic chemicals. Testimony showed that the chemicals were traveling from the dump site to waters inhabited by fish and used by humans.

2. Nuisance requires a showing of unreasonable injury rather than unreasonable conduct.

3. The neighbors showed signs of exposure to toxic chemicals and testimony showed that the chemicals found on the defendants' property threatened wildlife and human life with possible death, cancer, and liver disease.

4. The science of hydrology has grown since 1934 when *Rose* was decided and societal concern for environmental protection has grown considerably since that time, so that the scientific and societal considerations that governed *Rose* no longer apply.

5. No.

11.6 Nuisance

1. Yes; the court found that the landlords had not acted reasonably in dealing with the problem. *Lew v. Superior Court,* 25 Cal. Rptr. 2d 42 (Ct. App. 1993).

2. Yes. The court observed that public nuisance is not confined to physical injury to the senses and that a public nuisance can be a condition or use of property that offends public morals or decency. *Bensenville v. Botu, Inc.,* 350 N.E.2d 239 (Ill. 1976).

3. No. The court refused to find a private nuisance on the basis that publicity concerning the contamination of groundwater in the area (not the plaintiffs' groundwater) had caused a diminution in property value. The court observed that "negative publicity resulting in unfounded fear about dangers in the vicinity of the property does not constitute a significant interference with the use and enjoyment of land." Although property depreciation is an element of damages in a nuisance action, such an allegation by itself does not establish a claim of private nuisance. *Adkins v. Thomas Solvent Co.,* 487 N.W.2d 715 (Mich. 1992).

4. Damages for injuries resulting from the noise, according to the court in *Griggs v. Allegheny County,* 369 U.S. 84 (1962).

11.7 Interference with Business Relations

1. The court granted summary judgment to Pro-Image on the interference with existing contractual relations claim because the evidence showed that Pro-Image was acting to protect its own legitimate business interests rather than to harm University Graphics. The court also granted summary judgment on the prospective contractual relations claims, noting that when a "defendant acts at least in part for the purpose of protecting some legitimate interest which conflicts with that of the plaintiff, a line must be drawn and the interests evaluated" and that interferences that "are sanctioned by the 'rules of the game' which society has adopted" are regarded as privileged. Pro-Image's expression of its concerns regarding University Graphics "falls within the 'rules of the game' permitted by society" and was justified as a means of protecting its own interests. *University Graphics, Inc. v. Pro-Image Corp.,* 913 F. Supp. 338 (C.D. Pa. 1996).

2. The court granted summary judgment to the attorney, because as a legal adviser to the students, he was privileged to advise them to breach their contracts with the school. As an attorney, he "was required to make a full and complete investigation of his clients' allegations"; he was also justified in contacting witnesses and in giving legal advice regarding the enforceability of contracts. The court noted that "an attorney who in good faith counsels a client to breach a contract with a

third party must not be hindered or impeded by fear of retaliatory lawsuits." *Brown Mackie College v. Graham,* 768 F. Supp. 1457 (D. Kan. 1991).

11.8 Misuse of Process

1. A jury found the defendant firefighter liable and awarded Robert $500,000 in damages, but the appellate court reversed because it found the defendants, who were public employees acting within the scope of their employment, to be immune. *Tur v. City of Los Angeles,* 59 Cal. Rptr. 2d 470 (Ct. App. 1997).

2. The court found that Nursefinders had probable cause for requesting a restraining order and injunction on the ground that the facts showed evidence of a threatened breach of contract by Rosemary. Numerous efforts by Nursefinders' attorney to contact Rosemary were unsuccessful, thereby precluding any possibility of resolution of their conflict. The court affirmed summary judgment in favor of Nursefinders on both the malicious prosecution and abuse of process claims. *McLain v. Nursefinders of Mobile, Inc.,* 598 So. 2d 853 (Ala. 1992).

CHAPTER 12

12.1 Animals

1. The court refused to instruct the jury that Smokey had unmistakable vicious propensities based on Smokey's having bitten the man who kicked him. The jury found for the defendant. *Deardorff v. Burger,* 606 A.2d 489 (Pa. 1992).

2. The jury concluded that Bandit did not have a dangerous or vicious propensity. *Drake v. Dean,* 19 Cal. Rptr. 2d 325 (Ct. App. 1993).

12.2 Abnormally Dangerous Activities

1. The court found fire-eating acts to be "foolhardy" but not abnormally dangerous, noting that fire-eating acts are performed throughout the world without incident. *Thomalen v. Marriott Corp.,* 880 F. Supp. 74 (C.D. Mass. 1995).

2. Based on the Restatement of Torts, Virginia case law, and case law from other jurisdictions, the court

found that the operation of a railway is not an abnormally dangerous activity. *Warner v. Norfolk & Western Railway Co.,* 758 F. Supp. 370 (Va. 1991).

3. The court found that the contamination of the Fletchers' property created a high degree of risk of great harm, that disposal of PCB-laden waste by dumping it onto land or into a drainage system was not a matter of common usage, that it was inappropriate in any location, and that is was not essential to Tenneco's gas transmission and thus was of no value to the community. The Fletchers also sued on the basis of nuisance and trespass. *Fletcher v. Tenneco, Inc.,* 1993 WL 86561 (E.D. Ky. 1993).

4. The court held that setting off public fireworks is an abnormally dangerous activity that is not of common usage and that presents an "ineliminably high risk of serious bodily injury or property damage." *Klein v. Pyrodyne Corp.,* 810 P.2d 917 (Wash. 1991).

5. The court found strict liability inapplicable because it considered the storing and removing of gasoline from commercial underground gasoline storage tanks to be widespread and routine and noted that having service stations in residential areas was appropriate because they provide a necessary resource for residents. In this case the tanks were dangerous only because they were in a defective condition and not because they were dangerous in their "normal or nondefective state." If the risk of harm can be avoided by reasonable care, the court observed that negligence is the appropriate remedy. *Arlington Forest Ass'n. v. Exxon Corp.,* 774 F. Supp. 387 (C.D. Va. 1991).

12.3 Defenses

1. The trial judge accepted the defense expert's opinion that the damage to the transformer was incurred as an act of nature (lightning), precluding the plaintiff from recovering. *Boyd v. Washington-St. Tammany Electric Cooperative,* 618 So. 2d 982 (La. 1993).

2. The manufacturer could (and did) raise the defense of assumption of risk and argued that the plaintiff's conduct was the proximate cause of his injuries. In refusing to admit evidence of Kramer's conduct, the

court noted that although his conduct was a but-for cause of his injuries, such evidence had little probative value; "the fact that Kramer's conduct was a 'but for' cause [did] not give the jury reason to conclude that the forklift defect—also a 'but for' cause—was not a proximate cause of Kramer's injuries." Such evidence did, however, have a "significant potential to mislead the jury into thinking that Kramer should not recover if he was negligent." Because the manufacturer failed to show that Kramer was aware of the forklift defect, the court ruled as a matter of law that Kramer had not assumed the risk. *Kramer v. Raymond Corp.,* 840 F. Supp. 333 (C.D. Pa. 1993).

3. No; because Martin was obviously aware of the danger, he assumed the risk. Restatement (Second) of Torts § 523, cmt. d.

4. No, Lynn's negligence does not bar her estate from recovering under strict liability. Restatement (Second) of Torts § 524A, illus. 1.

CHAPTER 13

13.1 Warranty

1. a. Express warranty.

b. The court remanded the case to the trial court to determine whether "the time and place availability to Elite of normal working hours services at a Carrier facility" provisions of the warranty were met. If a jury found that Carrier were unavailable to Elite in a meaningful way prior to Elite's arrival in California, the essential purpose of the remedy accorded by the warranty would have failed. *Elite Professional, Inc. v. Carrier Corp.,* 827 P.2d 1195 (Kan. 1992).

2. They might argue breach of implied warranty on the ground that the drug was not "fit for the ordinary purposes" for which it was intended. If the manufacturer made any claims about the medication, the plaintiffs might argue breach of express warranty and submit proof that the drug did not conform to those promises.

3. No. The court said statements made by the companies could not be "considered warranties against

adverse health effects since the dangers of cigarette smoking ha[d] long been known to the community." No, although the court never reached this question because of its finding that the statements were not express warranties. *Marks v. R.J. Reynolds Tobacco Co.,* 1997 WL 242126 (W.D. La.).

13.2 Strict Liability

1. No, as long as the vaccine is properly prepared and is accompanied by proper directions and warning. It is considered an unavoidably unsafe product.

2. The court held that selling tickets to the public for go-cart usage constituted providing access to a product, not a service. The court suggested several public policy reasons to support a strict liability claim: the owner of the go-cart was in a better position to bear the cost of the injury; because the go-cart owner profited from the public's use of the go-cart, the cost of injury should be imposed on him; placing liability on the owner would ensure that he would use care in selecting responsible go-cart manufacturers to minimize his risks of operation. *Golt v. Sports Complex, Inc.,* 644 A.2d 989 (Del. 1994).

3. The court agreed with the manufacturer and found that "foreseeability . . . plays no part in the initial determination of defect in strict liability." In analyzing the negligence issue, the court observed that even though "foreseeability is an integral part of the duty analysis in negligence," it is not in strict liability; thus, "holding 'no duty' in strict liability does not per se eliminate consideration of the duty factor in negligence law." In applying a risk-utility analysis to the facts presented, the court concluded that failure to childproof the lighter was unreasonable if "the high social value placed on the safety of people and property threatened by childplay fires, the high gravity of risk, the considerable probability of risk, and the likelihood of a reasonably available alternative . . . outweigh[ed] BIC's interest in producing its lighters without childproofing features." *Griggs v. BIC Corp.,* 981 F.2d 1429 (3d Cir. 1993).

4. The court contrasted the facts of *Griggs* with this

case and concluded that it was not clear from the record whether the intended user recommendation on the box pertained to children who were chronologically 1-1/2 to 5 years old or to those who were developmentally within that age range. Noting that "although foreseeability is not a term that should be associated with strict liability, the concept, to the extent it implies an objective test, is not entirely foreign to a strict liability analysis, although it is applied in a more narrow sense than in negligence law." The court explained that "unless the use giving rise to a strict liability cause of action is a reasonably obvious misuse, or the user a reasonably obvious unintended user, as was the case in *Griggs,* or unless the particular use or user is clearly warned against, the manufacturer is not obviously exonerated." The court concluded that the "intended user" should be determined in the "context of the knowledge and assumptions of the ordinary consumer in the relevant community." *Metzgar v. Playskool, Inc.,* 30 F.3d 459 (3d Cir. 1994).

5. Under the consumer expectation standard, the question is whether the reasonable consumer would consider DES defective. The defendants in this case argued that the "consumer" was the physician, not the person who purchased the drug, because the manufacturer's warnings were directed to physicians.

The risk-utility test balances the risks and benefits of having such a drug. The defendants argued that this test could not be applied to prescription drugs, because they could not be "redesigned" but instead are created in accordance with a scientific formula. The court disagreed because it believed that the plaintiff might be able to demonstrate that the drug could be reformulated to be safer or that other, less harmful drugs were available to prevent miscarriages, and the benefit of such alternate drugs could be weighed against the advantages of DES.

The court declined to apply a strict liability standard to prescription drugs because "public policy favors the development and marketing of beneficial new drugs, even though some risks, perhaps serious ones, might accompany their introduction, because

drugs can save lives and reduce pain and suffering." Being subject to strict liability, the court explained, could intimidate drug manufacturers and deter them from developing new drugs or distributing existing drugs, and could elevate prices to the point that drugs were no longer affordable to some consumers. In support of this argument, the court cited drugs and vaccines that manufacturers refused to market because of fear of anticipated lawsuits, pointing out that only two vaccine manufacturers remain in the market. To illustrate, the court cited the cost of one vaccine as having risen from 11 cents in 1982 to $11.40 in 1986, $8 of which was for an insurance reserve, with the price increase paralleling the increase in lawsuits from one in 1978 to 219 in 1985. *Brown v. Abbott Laboratories,* 751 P.2d 470 (Cal. 1988).

6. Consider (a) who you can sue, (b) what damages you can recover, and (c) whether you are in a position to sue. Strict liability is generally the easiest to prove and includes the broadest range of plaintiffs (extending to bystanders in some cases). Warranty has the broadest range of damages and is the theory of choice when economic losses are unaccompanied by personal injury or property damage. Negligence is harder to prove than strict liability and is less liberal than the UCC as far as damages, but should still be pleaded whenever possible, especially when the court for policy reasons is likely to deny a claim for strict liability. Of course, plead all three theories if possible.

13.3 Losses

1. Because Elite did not seek to recover for the refrigeration unit itself, the court characterized the loss of meat as property damage. It defined "pure economic losses" as those "including loss of use of the defective product, cost of replacing the product, loss of profits to plaintiff's business, or damage to plaintiff's business reputation from use of the product." *Elite Professionals, Inc. v. Carrier Corp.,* 827 P.2d 1195 (Kan. 1992).

2. No, they are a property loss.

3. No, because the firm's losses are solely economic. The court was unimpressed with the firm's argument

that the economic loss rule is an "anachronism" and concluded that without being able to show injury to persons or property, the firm could not recover. *Bamberger & Feibleman v. Indianapolis Power & Light Co.,* 665 N.E.2d 933 (Ind. 1996).

13.4 *Turner v. GMC*

1. Can a manufacturer and retailer be held strictly liable for a defectively designed vehicle that enhances injuries but does not cause accidents?

2. A roof structure that provides inadequate protection to occupants in the event of a rollover.

3. The issue of crashworthiness.

4. Yes.

5. No. No.

6. No. Unreasonable risk of injury in the event of a collision.

7. Intended use.

8. Yes.

9. Yes.

10. Courts lack the expertise to deal with such complex matters; sporadic court decisions will result in wrong and contradictory standards; Congress has already begun to set safety standards.

11. No. The industry custom was unreasonably dangerous.

13.5 Defects

1. a. Negligence, warranty, and strict liability (being in a defective condition unreasonably dangerous).

   b. Defective design, failure to warn.

   c. The court relies on the doctor's expectations rather than the consumer's.

   d. The court, in opposition to the *Brown* court (discussed in "Putting It into Practice" 13.2), finds "it consistent with the purposes underlying strict products liability that manufacturers should be deterred from marketing certain products and that the cost of the defense of strict products liability litigation and any resulting judgments should be borne by the manufacturer who is able to spread the cost through insurance and by charging more for its products." In applying a "risk/benefit" analysis to the facts at hand, the court

explained that the factfinder should consider "the seriousness of the side effects or reactions posed by the drug, the likelihood that such side effects or reactions would occur, the feasibility of an alternative design which would eliminate or reduce the side effects or reactions without affecting the efficacy of the drug, and the harm to the consumer in terms of reduced efficacy and any new side effects or reactions that would result from an alternative design" and balance those factors against "the seriousness of the condition for which the drug is indicated." *Shanks v. Upjohn Co.,* 835 P.2d 1189 (Alaska 1992).

2. Obviousness of danger. The district court reasoned that the risk of a small child choking on one of Playskool's smaller blocks was so objectively obvious as to preclude the necessity of a warning, but the appellate court remanded the issue for jury deliberation. *Metzgar v. Playskool, Inc.,* 30 F.3d 459 (3d Cir. 1994).

3. The court allows Wilma's claim to stand; it finds the reasoning in *Brown* to be inapplicable because "unlike strict liability for design defects, strict liability for failure to warn does not potentially subject drug manufacturers to liability for flaws in their products that they have not, and could not have, discovered. Drug manufacturers need only warn of risks that are actually known or reasonably scientifically knowable." *Carlin v. Upjohn Co.,* 920 P.2d 1347 (Cal. 1996).

4. State-of-the-art defense. *Sternhagen v. Dow Co.,* 935 P.2d 1139 (Mont. 1997).

5. Argue foreseeable misuse. The court found that injuries to children were a foreseeable risk and that this risk was known or should have been known to the manufacturers. *Hall v. E.I. DuPont de Nemours & Co.,* 345 F. Supp. 353 (E.D.N.Y. 1972).

6. The court granted the defense motion because the plaintiff failed to introduce expert testimony to show that a feasible alternative cigarette design existed at the time the plaintiff's wife was smoking, that she would have availed herself of this design, that this design would have prevented her illness, and that such a design would have been reasonable under a risk-benefit test. *Marks v. R.J. Reynolds Tobacco Co.,* 1997 WL 242126 (W.D. La.)

13.6 Defenses

1. Causation (failure to prove who the manufacturers of the blasting caps that caused injury were and failure to prove that the lack of warnings caused the children's injuries); no duty to children (unforeseeable users; unreasonable cost of taking precautions (cost/benefit analysis)); misuse of product. Check statute of limitations also.

2. Assumption of risk; contributory negligence; comparative negligence.

3. Disclaimer; limited remedy.

4. The court held that the action accrued when Joseph knew or reasonably should have known of his illness and a possible causal connection between his illness and his use of cigarettes, in this case no later than 1988 when he was diagnosed with COPD. The court was not persuaded by his argument, because the discovery about the research came in November 1995, four months after the complaint was filed (July 1995), and because Joseph knew in 1988 that he was addicted to and had been injured by cigarettes and was thereby in possession of sufficient information to commence an action. *Arnold v. R.J. Reynolds Tobacco Co.,* 956 F. Supp. 110 (D.R.I. 1997).

5. Express preemption.

CHAPTER 14

14.1 Libel or Slander

1. Libel (*see* Restatement (Second) of Torts § 568A).

2. Libel (*see* Restatement (Second) of Torts § 568, illus. 3).

3. Slander (*see* Restatement (Second) of Torts § 568, illus. 4).

14.2 Defamatory Statements

In *Robins v. National Enquirer,* 1995 WL 776708 (D.S.C. 1995), the court noted that Lorinda did not allege that the statements made in the article were false and that although "the article, in hindsight, may have made her seem insensitive . . . [the] quotes have no bearing upon Plaintiff's integrity or reputation."

14.3 Opinion

In *Huggins v. Povitch,* 1996 WL 515498 (N.Y. Sup. Ct. 1996), the court considered the context in which the statements were made (on a talk show organized around controversial topics and designed to encourage public debate) and concluded that reasonable listeners would know they were listening to the "subjective opinion of Ms. Moore upon the emotionally charged topic of her divorce and its financial consequences." The court pointed out that "both the host and other guests repeatedly pointed out, and Moore confirmed, that her statements were her own personal views and that her ex-husband denies her 'charges' or 'allegations.' "

In examining the quoted excerpts the court found that the statements were "vague and contain[ed] loose figurative language that [did] not refer to verifiable acts of criminal conduct." The court explained that her belief that she "should share in" property does not mean her husband committed a crime but "merely expresses her dissatisfaction with the distribution approved by the court." Moore used the fact that her ex-husband failed to share partnership assets to support her opinion about him and "[o]pinions, false or not, are constitutionally protected if the facts supporting them are set forth."

14.4 *Street v. National Broadcasting Co.*

1. Did a historical drama defame the plaintiff or place her in a false light by depicting her as one who falsely accused others of raping her?

2. Because the historical events portrayed were considered public events, requiring the plaintiff to prove malice, which the evidence did not support.

3. As a perjurer, a woman of bad character, and a woman who falsely accused the Scottsboro boys of raping her.

4. a. Was there a public controversy?

b. What was the "nature and extent" of the plaintiff's participation in the public controversy?

5. Yes.

6. As the only prosecutrix, she played a prominent role in the controversy; she had ample access to the

media; she thrust herself voluntarily into the controversy by granting interviews and aggressively promoting her version of the events outside of the courtroom.

7. The question raised by the trial was whether the justice system could provide fair trials to blacks in the South, and that remains a "living controversy."

8. Because no evidence was presented to show bad faith or extreme disregard of the truth.

14.5 Public Figure

1. She will have to prove actual malice, because she is considered a public figure.

2. The court in *White v. Manchester Enterprise, Inc.,* 871 F. Supp. 934 (E.D. Ky. 1994) refused to classify White as a public figure, explaining that "public concern about wasteful public expenditures is not sufficient unless the individual is surrounded by a specific controversy." The court cited *Hutchinson v. Proxmire,* 443 U.S. 111, 99 S. Ct. 2675, 61 L. Ed. 2d 411 (1979), (in which a federal research grant recipient who reported on Senator Proxmire's Golden Fleece Award for wasteful public spending was not given public figure status even though the recipient had sufficient access to the media to rebut attacks on the value of his research): "Clearly, those charged with defamation cannot, by their own conduct, create their own defense by making a claimant a public figure."

3. In *Spence v. Flynt,* 816 P.2d 771 (Wyo. 1991), *Hustler* argues that in taking on the fight against pornography, Spence thrust himself into a public controversy, thereby casting himself as a public figure. Alternatively, *Hustler* argues that by virtue of writing about his case against *Hustler* he became a public figure. The court points out that Spence's book was published after his litigation involving *Hustler* and so he was not a public figure on that basis for purposes of this litigation. The court also notes that a "professional person, who may be a 'public figure' for some purposes, should be free to offer his services to a client as a private professional without being subjected to public figure defamation. To hold otherwise would have a chilling effect upon attorneys who undertake to represent clients in difficult, unpopular, high profile, or sensational types of cases. . . . Free speech cannot equate with the freedom to intimidate, destroy and defame an advocate seeking to represent a client."

14.6 Review of Defamation

1. Libel.

2. Yes.

3. In this case, *Hustler Magazine v. Falwell,* 485 U.S. 46 (1988), the jury found against Falwell, deciding that the parody could not "reasonably be understood as describing actual facts about [Falwell] or actual events in which [he] participated."

14.7 Privileges

1. The attorney general enjoys an absolute privilege; the privilege of the district attorney is qualified even if the press release is within the scope of his official duties. *See* Restatement (Second) of Torts § 591, illus. 3–4.

2. No (*see* Restatement (Second) of Torts § 586).

3. Not as long as she did not make the allegation recklessly.

14.8 *Douglass v. Hustler*

1. By placing her in a false light and appropriating a commercial right.

2. The tort allows plaintiffs to get around some of the outdated historical limitations of defamation; in this case the limitations of defamation would not have impeded the plaintiff's case; her claim is better classified as "offensive" than defamatory.

3. By insinuating that she was a lesbian and that she was the type of person willing to appear nude in *Hustler.*

4. Yes.

5. Yes.

6. Yes.

7. Because the jury could reasonably conclude that only Douglass or Playboy could have consented to the publication of those photos.

8. Because *Hustler* used photos that were made by others for commercial purposes.

9. Because they were in the public domain.

14.9 Invasion of Privacy

1. The *Enquirer* did not contest the false light claim. In finding that the *Enquirer* had commercially exploited Eastwood's name, the court observed that the magazine had used Eastwood's fame and personality to its commercial advantage and "to generate maximum curiosity and the necessary motivation to purchase the newspaper." *Eastwood v. National Enquirer,* 198 Cal. Rptr. 342 (Ct. App. 1983).

2. Unreasonable intrusion (*see* Restatement (Second) of Torts § 652B, illus. 1).

3. Public disclosure of private facts (*see* Restatement (Second) of Torts § 652D, illus. 11).

4. Although disclosure of a crime is generally not a tort, when the disclosure is made several years later and the revelation destroys the life of a reformed criminal, the tort of public disclosure of private facts may have been committed. *See* Restatement (Second) of Torts § 652D, illus. 26.

5. False light (*see* Restatement (Second) of Torts § 652E, illus. 8).

14.10 Injurious Falsehood

The court dismissed the case (and the appellate court affirmed the dismissal) on the ground that the growers failed to prove that the claims were "verifiably false." In response the growers in several states introduced the so-called "veggie libel laws," which authorize damages for "the disparagement of any perishable agricultural product." *Auvil v. CBS "60 Minutes,"* 800 F. Supp. 941 (E.D. Wash. 1992), *aff'd,* 67 F.3d 816 (9th Cir. 1995).

CHAPTER 15

15.1 Scope of Liability of Employer

1. Yes. The court observed that picking up customers to try to sell them cars, even on off-hours, was consid-ered commonplace for salesmen; Mr. Stone had done business with Mr. Urban on previous occasions; the route Mr. Stone had taken was the route to Mr. Urban's house. *Ray Korte Chevrolet v. Simmons,* 571 P.2d 699 (Ariz. Ct. App. 1977).

2. No. Although the accident occurred during Richard's hours of employment and at a place where he was authorized to be, his display of his gun was not related in any way to his employment. *Olson v. Staggs-Bilt Homes,* 534 P.2d 1073 (Ariz. Ct. App. 1975).

3. Yes, because the employer had an obligation to control the janitor's behavior. Restatement (Second) of Agency § 230, illus. 2.

4. If the truck driver was negligent in entrusting the driving to the thirteen-year-old or was negligent in supervising the teenager's driving.

5. Yes. An employer is vicariously liable "for the conduct of an employee engaged in a special errand for the employer, even though the errand may be different from the type of work usually performed for the employer." *Love v. Liberty Mutual Insurance Co.,* 760 P.2d 1085 (Ariz. Ct. App. 1988).

6. No. The court explained that his possession of his employer's papers was merely incidental and did not, in itself, convert his travel to work into a part of his employment. *S.&W. Construction Co. v. Bugge,* 13 So. 2d 645 (Miss. 1943).

15.2 *Santiago v. PNI*

1. Because he was injured in a collision with Frausto, one of PNI's newspaper carriers, and wants to hold PNI liable.

2. Is the relationship between PNI and Frausto that of employer-employee or employer-independent contractor?

3. No.

4. Extent of control exercised by the employer and the degree of supervision; distinct nature of the worker's business; degree of specialization of worker's occupation; materials provided by employer; duration of employment; method of payment; relationship of

worker's work done to the regular business of the employer; belief of the parties.

5. Employer's power to give specific instructions with the expectation that they will be followed. PNI selected the time and place for delivery, the area to be covered, and the manner in which papers were to be delivered. PNI also added customers and relayed customer requests to Frausto.

6. No. He had no delivery business distinct from his work with PNI; he did not purchase papers and resell them; payments were made and complaints were directed to PNI; PNI delivered if he missed a customer.

7. No.

8. They provided the papers but not the bags, rubber bands, or transportation. Yes.

9. A continuous working relationship. A right to terminate indicates control and thus an employer-employee relationship. Frausto could be terminated with cause at any time and without cause after twenty-eight days; his contract was for six months; PNI provided health and disability insurance.

10. Yes. Yes.

11. Yes. No.

15.3 Independent Contractors

1. No. A justice of the peace is not an employee or agent of the county; the independence of judges is "based on the constitutional doctrine of the separation of powers and the lack of a principal-agent relationship between elected officials and other governmental bodies." *Hernandez v. Maricopa County,* 673 P.2d 341 (Ariz. 1983).

2. Yes, because the lions are inherently dangerous. Restatement (Second) of Torts § 427A, illus. 1.

3. Yes, because the hotel was aware of the driver's lack of experience. Yes; the hotel would not be liable if the accident was due to unforeseen negligence on the part of the driver. Restatement (Second) of Torts § 411, illus. 3 and 4.

4. The court said that the determination is a factual one and remanded the case to the trial court for a jury's

deliberation. *Fisher v. Townsends,* 695 A.2d 53 (Del. 1997).

5. Yes. Jetro and Chamber were not entitled to delegate their responsibility to exercise care when dealing with a product that created a grave risk of serious bodily harm. They were the ones that primarily benefited from the fireworks display and they could protect themselves from liability by selecting a qualified independent contractor. *Ramsey v. Marutamaya Ogatsu Fireworks Co.,* 140 Cal. Rptr. 247 (Ct. App. 1977).

6. Yes. The court found Kennecott liable under the retained control exception of § 414 of the Restatement. *Welker v. Kennecott Copper Co.,* 403 P.2d 330 (Ariz. Ct. App. 1965).

15.4 Bailments

1. No. The family purpose doctrine is inapplicable because the father had not furnished the vehicle for general family use and did not exercise control over the car. "Mere ownership demonstrated by record title-holder status is not conclusive on the issue of liability under the family purpose doctrine." *Madrid v. Shyrock,* 745 P.2d 375 (N.M. 1987).

2. Yes. The court reasoned that "parents cannot blind themselves to the realities of youthful behavior, the universal proclivity of young people for joyriding, and the inclination of young people to permit friends to drive their automobiles." *Granley v. Crandall,* 180 N.W.2d 190 (Minn. 1970).

3. No, because no pecuniary interest existed on the part of the hikers. *Farmers Insurance Exchange v. Parker,* 936 P.2d 1088 (Utah 1997).

4. [Consult the applicable law in your state.]

5. [Consult the applicable law in your state.]

CHAPTER 16

16.1 *Hall v. DuPont*

1. Eighteen.

2. Explosives manufacturers and their trade association (I.M.E.). The practice of not placing warnings on individual blasting caps and of failing to follow other

safety measures created an unreasonable risk of harm that resulted in the plaintiffs' injuries.

3. In *Hall* the plaintiffs know the name of the manufacturer that produced the cap causing the plaintiff's injury; in *Chance* the identity is unknown.

4. They designed and manufactured blasting caps, they considered and rejected the possibility of labeling caps, and they lobbied to prevent such labeling.

5. Do the parallel safety practices of the defendants form a basis for joint liability?

6. Joint control of risk; enterprise liability; proof of causation.

7. They did not have joint control over the risks of injury because they did not enter into a conspiracy to commit intentional harm or into a partnership or joint venture. The elements of joint control of risks differ from those of joint venture.

8. By showing an explicit agreement or joint action; by presenting evidence that supports an inference of a tacit agreement or cooperation; by showing evidence of an industry-wide standard or custom. The first one.

9. No.

10. The size and composition of the trade association, its announced and actual objectives in reference to safety, its internal procedures and decision-making process in relationship to safety, the nature of its information-gathering system regarding accidents, the design and implementation of a safety program, and the nature of any other activities (such as lobbying) relating to safety.

11. Assigning of foreseeable costs of an activity to those in the best position to reduce those costs.

12. Joint awareness of the risks involved and joint capacity to reduce or affect those risks. No.

16.2 Joint and Several Liability

1. No, because a physician who calls in another physician is not liable for the other's malpractice if there are no concerted actions by the two physicians. *Stovall v. Harms,* 522 P.2d 353 (Kan. 1974).

2. No. The first physician should be liable for the full amount of the plaintiff's damages and the second physician should be liable for only that portion of damages that occurred after his treatment of the plaintiff began. In this case the jury held both physicians jointly and severally liable for $20,000 and the first physician individually liable for the remaining $60,000. *Naccarato v. Grob,* 180 N.W.2d 788 (Mich. 1970).

3. Yes, if this jurisdiction has adopted the doctrine of joint and several liability. *Walt Disney World v. Wood,* 515 So. 2d 198 (Fla. 1987).

4. Yes, because the parties performed separate acts that combined to produce a single, indivisible economic injury. *University of Miami v. All-Pro Athletic Surfaces, Inc.,* 619 So. 2d 1034 (Fla. Dist. Ct. App. 1993).

16.3 *Panasuk v. Seaton*

1. George Panasuk. He was driving the automobile that collided with the truck-trailer driven by Seaton.

2. Seaton was driving the truck-trailer that collided with George Panasuk and Leas is the owner of the vehicle. Both were sued by Paul Panasuk, who was a passenger in the car driven by his brother, George, and have filed third-party complaints against George for the damages to the truck-trailer.

3. Does Montana law prohibit contribution among joint tortfeasors?

4. Majority view bars contribution amongst joint tortfeasors, whereas the minority view allows it.

5. It finds that the third-party complaint fails to state a claim for relief based on contribution (prohibited by Montana law).

6. Does the third party's complaint state a claim for relief under the principles of indemnity?

7. No.

8. Because of the extreme difference in negligence between United Airlines' pilots and the government's pilots (i.e., they were not *in pari delicto*).

9. The government owed a duty to warn the pilots of United that it was sending a training mission into the area in which United was flying.

10. Indemnification does not apply, because application of this doctrine would increase or prolong

litigation as a result of motorists seeking to prove the driver of the other vehicle was grossly negligent.

16.4 Contribution, Releases, and Indemnification

1. They could seek contribution and indemnification (both contractual and based on the employer-employee relationship).

2. A covenant not to sue. *Hall v. Schulte,* 836 P.2d 989 (Ariz. 1992).

3. They can seek contribution and indemnification. The court concluded that as long as the settlement was in "good faith," the nonsettling defendants were barred from contribution but not from indemnification. *Dunn v. Kanawha County Board of Education,* 459 S.E.2d 151 (W. Va. 1995).

4. No, because the agreement is collusive and therefore not in "good faith." *International Action Sports, Inc. v. Sabellico,* 573 So. 2d 928 (Fla. 1991).

5. The court adopted this rule in reference to Mary Carter agreements:

> When a settlement agreement is entered into between the plaintiff and one or more, but not all, alleged defendant tortfeasors, the parties entering into such agreement shall promptly inform the court in which the action is pending and the other parties to the action of the existence of the agreement and its terms. If the action is tried to a jury and a defendant who is a party to the agreement is a witness, the court shall, upon motion of a party, disclose the existence and content of the agreement to the jury unless the court finds in its discretion such disclosure to the jury will create substantial danger of undue prejudice, of confusing the issues, or of misleading the jury.

Ratterree v. Bartlett, 717 P.2d 1063 (Kan. 1985).

CHAPTER 17

17.1 Quayle on Tort Reform

Consider the arguments made throughout this section. Are Americans overly litigious?

17.2 *Hardy v. General Motors Corp.*

Argument: Defendant's conduct did not justify punitive damages; award was windfall to plaintiff; award will encourage others to sue.

Rebuttal: Defendant's callous indifference to dangers created by design warranted punitive damages; award will offset costs of litigation for plaintiff; awards like these deter businesses from ignoring safety issues.

17.3 Joint and Several Liability

Consider reasons for adopting joint and several liability and whether those needs still exist when comparative negligence is operative.

17.4 Hasnas on Tort Reform

He would most likely see them as artificial manipulations that were doomed to failure because they attempt to thwart the natural evolution of law.

CHAPTER 18

18.1 Subrogation

1. $300,000/$50,000.
2. [Answer will vary; fact-specific.]

18.2 Underinsured Motorist Coverage

1. It could pay your deductible and co-insurance costs.

2. If there is a question of liability, Denise's carrier may refuse to pay to repair the vehicle until after judgment. It is often easier to deal with your own insurer and pay the deductible than to deal with the other party's carrier. Because there is a right of subrogation, if your insurer pays and it is determined the other party was responsible, your insurer will pay you back the deductible when it collects from the other insurance company. If you do not prevail on liability, your insurer may treat the accident as your fault.

3. Replacement cost coverage means that there will be sufficient proceeds to buy a new item rather than a used item. Many items depreciate very quickly (cars, computers, clothes, etc.). If there is a deductible, the

money received from an actual cash value policy may be insufficient.

4. [Answer will vary by state.]

5. [Answer will vary by state.]

18.3 Termination

1. The policy provision in Appendix D regarding arbitration provides that local rules of law regarding arbitration apply. Does your jurisdiction have applicable arbitration statutes? Does your court have rules of mandatory arbitration for lawsuits?

2. It should. Most arbitrators are attorneys. The hourly charges for 1.5 arbitrators can quickly exceed the total value of a small claim. You may also have your own attorney's costs in addition to those for the arbitrators.

3. [Answer will vary by state.]

CHAPTER 19

19.1 First-Party versus Third-Party Claims

1. Yes, he has a liability claim against Dick.

2. Yes, he can make a claim under his medical payments coverage.

3. When a carrier defends under a reservation of rights while it investigates the claim, the insured is not left without a defense. Because the insurer is providing a defense (but might refuse to indemnify), even though the defense may be withdrawn, the chances of the insurer's being subjected to a bad faith claim are substantially lessened. An insurer that denies coverage and refuses to provide a defense faces tremendous exposure if it is later determined that there is coverage.

Insurers are in the business of investigating and settling claims. The failure of an insurer to investigate a claim before sending a reservation of rights letter is almost per se bad faith.

4. It is the insured's duty to prove that the policy was in effect at the time of the accident. It is the insurer's obligation to prove lack of coverage. If it does not have sufficient evidence to deny coverage, it must either provide coverage or do an investigation that is thorough enough to show where the accident occurred.

5. The map may be important to show that the insurer had no reasonable basis to deny coverage or defend under a reservation of right. The fact that the company sent out the map does not necessarily bind it to any errors in the map.

6. Although the argument has some initial appeal, it is unlikely that nautical miles would win out. If we look at the reasonable expectations of the parties, it is hard to argue that nautical miles (that most people do not even know exist) were expected. If it is alleged that the lack of specificity creates an ambiguity that must be resolved in favor of the insured, it will still be difficult to argue that a term that is foreign to most insureds (and insurers) should be used rather than the commonly used statute mile.

19.2 Resolution of First-Party Claims

1. Yes. Not until late in the opinion does the court state that the insurer's evaluation of the case was "less than realistic."

2. Contributory negligence was a complete defense that, if found by the jury, would bar any recovery by the plaintiff. The defense of contributory negligence was seldom the basis of a jury verdict.

3. The court did not believe that the attorney or his client could legitimately value the life of a seventeen-year-old boy so low.

4. It appears that it does. It also appears that the court did not look at the unrealistically low evaluation of the case as mere negligence. Rather, it appears that the court did not believe that the values stated were the true values as determined by the attorney or the insurer.

19.3 Declaratory Judgment Actions

1. If the insurer truly believes that there is no coverage for the accident, a declaratory judgment action would confirm the lack of coverage. Seeking prompt declaratory judgment relief would also save the insurer the majority of the cost of defending the claims, even if a defense was tendered under a reservation of rights. A court ruling that there was no coverage would also

greatly reduce the possibility of a bad faith action being filed.

2. Possibly. Until suit is filed, technically there is no duty to defend. However, most claims are settled before suit is filed. The insurer could be in a very poor position if it handled the claim as though there were coverage (i.e., negotiated with Jerry or his attorney) and then later claimed there was no coverage.

3. Yes. If the insurer cannot prove that the accident is excluded from coverage, a declaratory judgment action would result in a finding for the insured. Although there may not be a finding of coverage, the judgment would show that the insurer does not have sufficient evidence to deny coverage.

Timing would be very important. Until the claim had been investigated and evidence found that there is a basis for a filing of no coverage, any court action would be to the insurer's detriment.

19.4 Uninsured and Underinsured Motorist Coverage

1. Jerry has his claim for medical payments under his automobile insurance policy. If his insurer denied coverage for Dick, Jerry could also put in a claim under his uninsured motorist coverage. If his insurer did not deny coverage for Dick, Jerry may have a claim under his underinsured motorist coverage.

2. Yes. Because denial of coverage to Dick would almost have to result in coverage for Jerry, it would be prudent for the insurer to file a declaratory judgment action. The insurer would have to have completed its investigation before filing suit.

3. Yes, if his damages were greater than Dick's liability coverage.

CHAPTER 20

20.1 Historical Background

1. [Use your state's statutes and rules to determine if Juan is deemed to have opted in.]

2. [Use your state's statutes and rules to determine if your state has voluntary or compulsory coverage.]

20.2 The Statutory Framework

[Answer will vary by state.]

In Arizona the employer takes the employee as he is (i.e., the eggshell plaintiff). If the industrial injury contributed to Juan's hospitalization and subsequent treatment, the injuries would be compensable. Juan's loss of his leg would be compensable under Ariz. Rev. Stat. § 23-1044(B)(15) for 50 months compensation at 55 percent of his average monthly wage.

20.3 Is Workers' Compensation a Fair Deal?

1. [Use your state's statutes and rules in determining Juan's average wage.] In Arizona, Ariz. Rev. Stat. § 23-1041 provides that the monthly wage is the average wage paid during and over the month in which the injury occurs. If the injured worker has not been employed for a month, different methods of determining the average wage are used. Because Juan had been working for 5 weeks, his average wage would be: $5.00 per hour × 85 hours per week × 4.33 weeks per month = $1,840.25 per month. Seasonal employment may be taken into account, as well as unusual, non-repetitive wages (such as overtime).

[Use your state's statutes and rules in determining Juan's average wage if he works only 8 months per year.] In Arizona his average wage, excluding the overtime issue, would be 8/12 of $1,840.25 or $1,226.83.

2. $12.00 per hour × 40 hours per week × 4.33 weeks per month = $2,078.40 per month. [Use your state's statutes and rules to calculate this answer.] In Arizona, loss of a dominant arm is scheduled at 55 percent for 60 months for a total of $68,587.20 (.55 × $2,078.40 per month × 60 months).

20.4 Filing a Workers' Compensation Claim

1. Who would the real client be? What obligations would there be to maximize recovery if your "true"

client wanted to get only the benefits they paid back? How would you deal with the injured employee? Would there be a conflict of interest between what the employer wants and what the employee would want? In the standard case, the attorney would attempt to negotiate a lower payment to the employer (if representing the employee). Would you have to advise the employee that it would be in her best interest to retain an attorney to pursue her claim? What would happen if the claim had already been assigned to the employer by operation of law?

2. [Use your state's statutes and rules to determine who is required to give notice of an industrial injury.] In Arizona, Ariz. Rev. Stat. § 23-908(A) requires that the employer (if it learns of the accident) and the treating physician must file a report with the Arizona Industrial commission. Paragraph D of that statute requires the injured employee report the accident to the employer.

3. [Use your state's statutes and rules in determining how long benefits are paid.] In Arizona, Ariz. Rev. Stat. § 23-1045 provides that permanent total disability payments shall continue for the life of the injured person. Ariz. Rev. Stat. § 23-1044 provides that temporary partial disability payments shall continue so long as there is a reduction in earning capacity of the worker due to the accident. In Arizona there is no offset for Social Security benefits nor any age limitation. Arizona also allows an injured worker to draw retirement benefits without penalty.

20.5 Current Issues in Workers' Compensation

1. [Use your state's statutes and rules in determining if pure psychological injuries are compensable.] In Arizona, Ariz. Rev. Stat. § 23-1043.01 provides that some unexpected, unusual, or extraordinary stress related to employment must be a substantial contributing factor for benefits to be paid.

2. [Use your state's statutes and rules in determining how AIDS is dealt with.] Ariz. Rev. Stat. § 23-1043.02 provides specific steps for testing employees who may have been exposed during the course of employment.

3. Etta's claim was allowed in *Conley v. Workers' Compensation Division,* 483 S.E.2d 542 (W. Va. 1997). The law was changed after she filed her claim (in 1991) to preclude any claims based on injuries that were caused by nonphysical means and did not involve any physical injury.

APPENDIX
B
Interviewing

Johnny and Susie are lovers. Johnny has just bought a new red Corvette and, of course, he wants to impress Susie with his acquisition, so he picks her up at her house to take her to a very expensive French restaurant. While enroute he enters the intersection at Seventh Avenue and Primrose Lane at the same time that Harriet, driving to the weekly meeting of the local Library Preservation Society in her fourteen-year-old Chrysler, turns in front of him. Neither sees the other vehicle until a few split seconds before impact. No one is permanently injured but the Corvette suffers extensive damage and Harriet's car, although relatively unscathed, needs minor repairs. Within a month of the accident Johnny comes into your office with Susie in tow. Your supervising attorney asks you to interview them. What do you do?

POTENTIAL CONFLICT OF INTEREST

Suppose that as you escort Johnny and Susie into your office Johnny impulsively blurts out that the investigating officer and two of the witnesses are liars and are out to get him. In this spontaneous diatribe he further alleges that Harriet was drunk and that three witnesses will testify that the other two witnesses are lying when they said Johnny ran a red light. Without taking a breath he assures you that the witnesses are also prepared to testify that the officer was incorrect when he concluded that Johnny was speeding at the time of the accident.

Having heard this capsulized version of Johnny's defense, you are now alerted to the potential conflict that may exist between Johnny and Susie. Susie, if she were injured, may have to name Johnny in her suit, as he may have been wholly or partially to blame for her injuries. Caution and conservatism are now your best attributes. You should either get assistance from your supervising attorney to guide you according to your firm's policy or take the risk that further investigation of this potential conflict may preclude the firm from representing either Johnny or Susie.

Be forewarned that Susie is likely to protest that she could never consider suing Johnny because it was all Harriet's fault. Also, Susie herself saw that the light was green and that Johnny was not speeding. Do not be pacified by this assertion. Before getting any information from Susie or even discussing the case further with the two of them together, you must determine whether Susie's claim is so inconsistent with Johnny's that they need separate representation.

If you conclude that Susie's and Johnny's claims are so at odds that they cannot be represented by the same attorney, you must advise Susie accordingly and then ask her to wait in the reception area. Note that Susie and not Johnny is asked to leave because it is Johnny who made statements to you with respect to the case. Because Susie has said nothing at this point, your firm can still represent Johnny. Susie, however, needs to seek alternate counsel.

FIGURE B-1   Diagram of Accident

Seventh Ave.

A = Harriet's vehicle

B = Johnny's vehicle

Primrose Lane

SETTING THE STAGE

Typically your first contact with Johnny will be after he has spoken with the attorney who will handle the case. Interviewing Johnny will be far easier if he has already met with the attorney, because the basic cause(s) of action already will have been determined by the attorney and you can narrow your questions to those particular claims. Your role as a legal assistant in this case will have been explained by your attorney prior to your meeting with Johnny. Nevertheless, it is imperative that Johnny understand from the outset what your duties and limitations are.

If you are the first person to talk with Johnny, remember that in the opening moments of your conversation you will establish the tenor of his relationship with your firm. His decision on whether to use the firm may be determined by this initial contact. Furthermore, you must not only obtain essential bio-graphical and background information but also ascertain the potential claims he may have. You need to glean sufficient information so that the attorney can decide whether Johnny has a cause of action, whether the claim is the type your firm would pursue, and, if not, to whom Johnny might be referred. You may also be expected to field some of Johnny's questions regarding his case.

Before you start asking questions, you should try to establish a rapport with Johnny so that he will feel free to speak openly and frankly to you about his case. Remember that you may need to ask very personal questions about, for example, injuries sustained, emotional damage, sexual dysfunction, and scarring. Such information is not easily revealed to friends, let alone complete strangers, so you must put Johnny at ease if you are going to elicit such sensitive disclosures.

At the outset, you should impress upon Johnny that anything he says to you is privileged and that this privilege is just as applicable to conversations he has with you as it is to conversations he has with the attorney. Also advise him that the privilege is applicable even if he and the firm do not enter into a contractual relationship. Try to interview him in the privacy of an office or relatively small room. Your assurances regarding the confidentiality of the information he gives you will have little meaning if strangers pass through while you are interviewing him.

You can help create a relaxed environment by the way in which you arrange the furniture. Relegating Johnny to a low-backed reception chair while you stare at him from behind a palatial desk, seated in an imposing high-backed chair, will not promote trusting, uninhibited communication. You can appear more approachable if you position your chair alongside his. Be careful, however, that you do not get so close that you make him feel uncomfortable by "invading his space."

You can also offer him a cup of coffee, glass of water, or some soda to help break the ice. Devoting a few minutes to small talk will give him an opportunity to get used to you and his surroundings. Taking time to create a comfortable setting will be time well spent and will certainly reap more benefits than immediately bombarding him with questions.

HOW TO ASK AND HOW TO LISTEN

Once you have succeeded in relaxing Johnny, you should try to determine as soon as possible why he came to the office. Although he may be unable to articulate the precise legal basis of his concern, he can probably convey the general nature of his claim, i.e., personal injury, trespass, nuisance, slander, and so on. Of course, regardless of what he believes the claim to be, the facts as they unfold may not support his claim as he perceives it, or may support additional claims that will become apparent when subject to appropriate legal analysis.

Rather than asking for directed responses at the beginning of an interview, allowing a client to give a free-flowing narrative of his or her version of what happened is often better. Therefore, you might start by letting Johnny tell his side of the story. Then you can follow up with more directed questions to fill in the gaps and clarify any points of confusion you might have. You might consider structuring these follow-up questions using the five W's demanded of a good journalist—who, what, where, when, and why. Who are the key actors involved? What did they do? Where and when did they do it? Why did they do it? Making sure you can answer these key questions will minimize your chances of forgetting to ask relevant questions.

Using notes and prepared questions to organize your thinking will be helpful if you know in general what you will be discussing with Johnny. You can use your notes to refresh your memory about key points you want to explore. Do not, however, become so dependent on your notes that you are unable to deviate in any way. Be flexible; adapt your questions to Johnny's statements. Do not fail to hear what Johnny is telling you. Free yourself of any preconceived notions and be willing to explore avenues that you had not previously considered.

Most importantly, *listen* carefully to Johnny. Pay attention to the details. Note any omissions in his story. Be aware of his body language and the pace, volume, and pitch of his speech. These subtle clues may reveal more than his verbal communication. When you think you have gathered all the pertinent information, summarize what you think he has said to you. You may be surprised at how many discrepancies exist between what you think you heard and what he thinks he said.

An awareness of basic human nature comes in handy when conducting interviews. Some people will provide you with only the sketchiest of details. They will treat each piece of information you extract from them as if it were some kind of valuable ore. Others will inundate you with details, digressing into so many subplots of their story that you will begin to lose sight of their central theme. Some will reexperience the emotional trauma of the events and become so distraught that they will be unable to recount what happened to them.

Although you must distance yourself emotionally enough to be objective regarding the legal claims, you must remain sensitive to the emotional needs and psychological defenses of those you interview. A certain amount of detachment is necessary to do your job, but divorcing yourself from your own humanity is neither necessary nor desirable. You must develop your own means of cajoling information from the reclusive, channeling the storytellers, and reassuring the distressed. And you must do this as you are clinically evaluating their potential causes of action—a formidable task!

Remember that interviewing is a two-way street. Just as you are assessing Johnny, so he is assessing you. Be conscious of the messages you are sending. Are you acting bored? Incredulous? Impatient? Condescending? You must communicate a sense of receptivity and warmth if you want him to trust you and cooperate with you fully.

GATHERING BACKGROUND INFORMATION

In almost all cases you need to obtain relatively detailed background information. For example, suppose a minor is involved in the case. The nonclient parent may be the primary custodial parent and the one who has actual authority to institute litigation on behalf of the minor. If a shared custody agreement exists providing that the parents are jointly responsible for decisions made on behalf of the child, one parent alone may be unable to select the child's attorney. You may find yourself in an embarrassing situation if you involve your employer in litigation only to find out that your client is not authorized to institute the suit. Consequently, obtain relatively detailed background information, including residential address, marriages, children, employment history, medical history, and the like. In any tort case, but especially in a personal injury case such as Johnny's, this information is essential.

Any tort case also requires that a complete insurance profile be constructed. First, determine if Johnny has automobile insurance for the vehicle and, if so, whether it provides medical payments and collision coverage. If he has such coverage, assure Johnny that, except for the deductible, the collision coverage will repair his new Corvette. The medical payments coverage, as you should point out, will help pay for his medical expenses as well as Susie's, even if she subsequently submits a claim against him. Note that if Johnny were a pedestrian or a bicyclist who had been injured in an accident involving a motor vehicle, some coverage would be available from his homeowner's policy.

Review any applicable insurance policies *very, very* thoroughly in the context of state statutes and court decisions. Be particularly concerned with the enforceability of clauses in the policies. The mere fact that an insurance policy appears to deny coverage does not mean that that provision is necessarily enforceable. (We discuss this problem in Chapter 18.)

Obtain basic information from Johnny, such as his date of birth, Social Security number, the addresses of his residence and place of employment, the identity of his insurance carrier and, to the extent known, his coverage and its limits. Then ask for detailed information regarding the nature and extent of his injuries. If his injuries could potentially interfere with his relationships with third parties, such as parents, children, and perhaps even brothers and sisters, consider the possibility of filing a separate loss of consortium claim against Harriet.

Inquire about Johnny's prior medical history. Who is his family physician? What injuries or diseases has he had? What physical examinations has he had, including those for obtaining employment, for school attendance, or for other activities? This information is important because Johnny's medical history prior to the accident may have a significant impact on the amount of damages he will be entitled to receive.

Find out if Johnny was taken to an emergency room and, if so, whether he was taken by ambulance or if he drove himself. Identify Johnny's treating physicians, if any, since the accident and find out how many times he has seen them and for what reasons. Note whether Johnny has been unable to work or has been able to do only those jobs characterized as "light duty." In many instances, an injury does not prevent the client from working but may preclude him or her from working in certain activities or force the client to forgo certain benefits, such as overtime.

You also need to determine the nature and extent of the damages to Johnny's vehicle. Depending on your firm's policy, you may become involved in assisting Johnny with his property damage claim.

SCENE OF THE ACCIDENT

When you first ask Johnny to describe the accident he may want to relate what happened in a conclusory fashion. He may say, for example, "I was obeying the law and this drunk turned in front of me on a green light." Let him ventilate. Once he has done that, you need to piece together the chain of events leading up to the accident and to verify the validity of what he has given you. Suppose, for example, that Johnny tells you that the accident occurred at 8:00 P.M. on Saturday evening, April 9, one month ago. You need to confirm that April 9 was a Saturday. Later, if your firm accepts this case, you will need to ascertain the weather and road conditions at the time of the accident. For example, was there any construction? Was the road made of dirt, granite, asphalt, or concrete? How many lanes of traffic were there in each direction?

In piecing together the events that preceded the accident you will need to take Johnny back to the time he woke up that morning. What time did he get up? Where had he been the night before? Did he have breakfast? What did he do prior to the accident? Did he have lunch? Did he have anything to drink during the afternoon? Was he with friends who could confirm his whereabouts and activities? Did he have a good night's sleep or was he overtired? Did he have dinner Saturday evening? Did he go to Susie's to pick her up or was she with him to begin with? Do they live together? Did he have anything to drink prior to the accident?

You will also want to question Johnny regarding his new Corvette. Had he had it for a long time? Was he accustomed to driving it? Had he had prior traffic violations? Were his headlights on? Was the car functioning properly? What was he doing prior to the accident? Was he talking to Susie? Was he looking forward or to the left or right? Did he see Harriet before she made the turn? Did he see Harriet making the turn? What evasive actions did either Johnny or Harriet make prior to the collision? You will want to find out how much traffic was on Primrose Lane and on Seventh Avenue that night at 8:00 P.M. How well lit was the intersection? Were Harriet's headlights on? Had Harriet turned on her turn signal? Did Harriet appear to hesitate and then speed up or did she make the left-hand turn as though there were no oncoming traffic? Were

Johnny and Susie wearing seat belts? Was Harriet wearing a seat belt?

Then you need to zero in on what happened at the scene of the accident. Does Johnny recall slamming on the brakes and hearing any sounds associated with skidding tires? Did the brakes of the Corvette lock up? Where exactly was the point of impact? Could Johnny or Susie get out of the vehicle immediately after the accident? Were they coherent? Was anyone cut? Was blood evident anywhere? Did the vehicle itself remain secure, i.e., did the seats break their mountings or did the backs collapse? How much damage was done to Harriet's old Chrysler? Who was the first person on the scene? Did Johnny, Susie, or Harriet speak to that person? Did Johnny or Susie speak to Harriet? Did they speak to any of the other witnesses? Where were the other witnesses at the time of the accident? Did any of them almost collide with Harriet or Johnny? Did any of them actually collide with either? Did any other accidents occur as a result of the collision between Harriet and Johnny?

Johnny indicated that an officer eventually came to the scene, so you should determine what law enforcement agency the officer worked for. Did Johnny speak to the officer? What was the nature of their conversation? What was Johnny's attitude at the time, i.e., was he angry, subdued, crying, in pain? Did the officer speak with Susie or Harriet? Does Johnny know whether the officer spoke with any of the other witnesses and, if so, which ones? Did the officer make any measurements at the scene of the accident that Johnny is aware of?

Johnny made several allegations during his earlier soliloquy. Now you need to follow up on those. Johnny indicated to you that Harriet was drunk. How does he know that? Did he speak with Harriet or smell her breath? Did the officer indicate that he was citing Harriet for driving under the influence? Johnny said that the officer cited him for speeding. Did the officer tell him the basis for making that determination? Johnny also stated that other witnesses said he ran a red light. Was he cited for running a red light? Where were those alleged witnesses when they saw Johnny run the red light? In which direction were they facing?

DISCOVERING THE WEAKNESSES

As you conduct the interview do not become so wrapped up in the tale that is being told that you fail to notice any time gaps or apparent inconsistent statements. The appropriate time to discover any problems with your case is when you first become involved, not after a great deal of time, money, and effort have been expended in pursuit of the claim. Remember that not everyone who is involved in an automobile accident is entitled to compensation, and even if a victim is entitled to compensation it may well be that problems with respect to liability (i.e., who was at fault and to what extent), will discourage the firm from representing that person. Someone with $100,000 worth of injuries, for example, who is 99 percent responsible for those injuries has a $1,000 case, not a $100,000 case (in a comparative negligence state). The recoverable damages would not justify a firm's investment in such a case.

STATUTE OF LIMITATIONS PROBLEMS

Clients often "sit" on their claims for some time before acting on them, and when they do finally get around to pursuing their claims they may be barred because the statute of limitations has expired. Be aware of the appropriate statute and act in a timely fashion, both to protect the client's claim and to protect your firm from being sued for malpractice for inadequate representation. If the expiration of the statutory time period were imminent in Johnny's case, the attorney might opt to draft a bare-bones complaint naming Johnny as his own attorney. This would prevent the attorney from having to evaluate the case too hastily and would still protect the interests of all involved. If the client serves as his or her own attorney, no paperwork will have to be filled out for substitution of attorney if your firm decides to decline representation.

INVESTIGATING OFFICER INTERVIEW

Having determined Johnny's side of the story, you must now interview the third parties involved to find out their recollections of the events. The first person to start with is the investigating officer. Although in most cases the officer has no personal firsthand information other than the measurements taken, he or she may have talked to some of the witnesses. In some states the actual investigation with respect to skid marks, point of impact, estimated speed of travel, and so forth is left to civilian employees of the police department. Therefore, you must determine which individuals actually investigated the accident scene and what their training, job classification, and responsibilities were.

Should your jurisdiction be one of those in which the police officer does the actual investigation, including making measurements and interviewing witnesses, interview the officer as soon as possible. The notion that police officers can recall specific details of every investigation they conduct by simply reviewing their notes is erroneous. Remember, they are involved in numerous incidents on a daily basis and substantial time has usually passed between the accident in question and your interview. Nothing is as important as fresh, firsthand information.

Any attempt to interview the investigating officer should begin with the Police Liaison Unit. This unit, which exists in one form or another in most jurisdictions, is primarily involved in ensuring that the officers involved in a criminal case are aware of the events that are occurring and the times when they must appear in court. You can also use this unit to make arrangements to interview the officer about the strictly civil portions of an incident. It is often possible for the officers to be paid for the time involved in meeting and discussing the case with you, so it is imperative, at the outset at least, to work with the Police Liaison's office. Certainly officers will be far happier talking with you if they know they are getting paid or being given release time for the time spent with you, rather than receiving only the standard jurisdictional witness fee.

Additionally, because police officers frequently encounter attorneys in an adversarial context, they are often prepared to do battle. Therefore, make sure you are well prepared for the interview. Do not create the impression of wasting the officer's time with irrelevant or nonsensical questions. When you interview a police officer you should have a detailed outline of your questions.

Prior to interviewing the officer, mentally retrace the events leading up to, during, and after the accident in as much detail as possible, noting the names of any witnesses that you are aware of. Using precise questions will not only enhance your credibility with the officer but will also greatly reduce the amount of time necessary to complete the interview.

If departmental procedures allow it and the officer has no objections, tape-record the interview. Transcribe the interview as soon as possible and send it to the officer, asking him or her to make appropriate corrections. Let the officer know about this procedure at the beginning of the interview if you intend to tape it.

Never "talk down" to an officer or try to contradict him or her. Establishing a good rapport will serve you well later in the case, whereas being patronizing will result in an adversarial rather than a cooperative relationship. You should maintain control of the interview and strive to earn the officer's respect but you must do so without sacrificing his or her ego. You will undoubtedly encounter the arrogant officer who will test your capacity to control your tongue. Before you succumb to the temptation to engage in verbal repartee, remember that an officer who dislikes your style of questioning could become a liability rather than an asset to your case. Prudence is often the wisest course of action.

All basic background information, such as time on the force, experience in accident investigation, and training, is important. Focus, however, on the information contained in the report the officer prepared. Determine what information in the report came from the officer's firsthand observations at the accident scene, which information came from witnesses the officer deemed credible, and which information the

officer rejected because he or she thought the witnesses were not credible.

The officer writing the report may not have interviewed some of the witnesses, so you need to ascertain which officers spoke to which witnesses and, if necessary, interview each of those officers. You need to find out, for example, if there was a backup unit that assisted the investigating officer and if those officers talked to witnesses, if statements were taken by any other officers, and if measurements were made by a different officer or by a civilian accident investigator. You need to get the names of these individuals and establish the relevance of the information they may have to offer to determine if you should also interview them.

At this juncture you must determine whether the officer has any independent recollection of the accident. Then you must distinguish what the officer knows by virtue of independent recollection versus what he or she remembers by reviewing the police report and other documents that you brought to the interview. Knowing when and where to give information to the officer comes from experience and intuition. What you should do will vary on a case-by-case and officer-by-officer basis.

LAY WITNESS INTERVIEWS

As soon as possible after the incident and, with luck, before they are spoken to by the adverse party, contact all lay witnesses. Many people are very concerned about the perceived hazards of having to testify in court and you should do everything possible to allay their fears. It is not unusual for someone to "not recall" an event to ensure that her testimony will not be required. Meeting the person at his or her home after work or for lunch can make a reluctant witness feel more comfortable and less "put out" than requesting that the person come to your office.

Once you know whether the witness will either support or negate your client's position, you will need to decide whether to tape-record the interview, assuming the witness will allow it. If the witness's recollections are supportive of your client's position, you might want to provide a copy of the tape to opposing counsel in the hope of speeding up settlement. Note, however, that the presence of a tape recorder makes many people very uncomfortable and may therefore be counterproductive. If you opt to record the interview, be sure the witness feels comfortable and at ease before starting. Be forewarned that several evidentiary obstacles must be overcome before tape-recorded statements can be used in court, even for impeachment purposes.

Once again, you must explain at the beginning of an interview who you are, why you want to talk to the witness, and what the potential ramifications of talking with you could be. You should also advise witnesses that the opposing parties' attorney or legal assistant may also want to interview them. Any attempts to influence the testimony of witnesses or to discourage them from speaking with opposing counsel could, and should, result in your being fired. Such overt attempts to influence witnesses could also, in many jurisdictions, result in criminal charges being filed against you.

Typically one begins questioning by allowing the witness to give a free-flowing narrative of the events he or she observed. Note that the ability to make these observations depends on conditions at the time of the incident. For example, the witness may be wearing glasses at the time of the interview, but that does not mean that she had her glasses on as she observed the events. Her observations may therefore be suspect.

Try to pinpoint the exact location of the witness at the time the events occurred to determine whether the observation was possible. It is not uncommon for witnesses to make materially false statements and be honestly unaware of their falsity. For example, a driver who was behind a vehicle that was involved in an accident may state that he saw the driver of the other vehicle lose physical control of the automobile. In reality, all he could see was the back of the other driver's head. If later he saw paramedics remove somebody from the driver's seat of the vehicle, he would assume, quite logically, that the person he observed being removed from the driver's side of the car was the person he had observed driving the car, which is not necessarily true. Consequently, his statement regarding the driver's identity could be honest but false.

What if the witness is hostile and alleges, for example, that the accident was all your client's fault and that he should be punished for what he did? In such a case you will have to summon all of your interpersonal skills to get an in-depth and accurate interview. Pin down a hostile witness with as many specific facts and details as possible. You need to find out exactly where the witness was standing, what she was doing, who was at the scene, what they were wearing, who was doing what to whom, and so on. If nothing else, by restricting the witness to exacting factual details, she may be more easily impeached at a later date should other witnesses or physical evidence conflict with her statements.

Witnesses may ask to review the transcription of the tape recording, obtain a copy of the tape, or review your notes. Be aware of your firm's policy in this regard. In most instances there would be no problem in allowing a witness to review the transcribed interview or taking a copy of the actual tape recording itself. Problems arise, however, if the tape recording or its transcription is discoverable when in the hands of the witness but not discoverable when in the possession of one of the party's attorneys. It may be prudent to advise witnesses that the tape recording or its transcription is available for review at the attorney's office but legal procedural rules prohibit a copy being given to them.

Do not assume that only personal, firsthand information is of any value. A witness may be able to provide you with useful information that leads to legally admissible evidence. She may, for example, advise you that a photographer from one of the local newspapers took photographs of the scene, that other individuals in the vicinity observed the accident, or that she was accompanied by friends whose names are not on the police report. This information might allow you to obtain additional collaborative evidence to support your client's story or to impeach the recollections of a hostile witness.

Finally, and most importantly, always be gracious. An interview is not the place for aggressive, hard-hitting questions. Witnesses do not have to talk to you. If you irritate them, they may terminate the interview. You cannot afford to burn bridges at the initial stages of an investigation only to find out later that the witness you alienated is the one you most need.

APPENDIX
C
Overview of Insurance

TYPES OF INSURANCE COVERAGE AVAILABLE

Learning about all the different types of insurance coverage would be of value but too time-consuming. However, to give you some appreciation for the vast number of coverages, the table of contents of W. Freedmans, *Richards on the Law of Insurance* (6th ed., Lawyers Coop, 1991) is duplicated below (and see Figure C-1):

- accident insurance
- airplane insurance
- annuities and endowment insurance
- asbestos insurance
- automobile insurance
- boiler insurance
- burglary, robbery, theft, and larceny insurance
- burial insurance
- business interruption insurance
- casualty insurance
- condominium insurance
- confiscation insurance
- contractor's insurance
- credit insurance
- crop insurance
- directors and officer liability insurance
- disability and impairment insurance
- earthquake insurance
- elevator insurance
- employers' liability insurance
- errors and omissions insurance
- fidelity and guaranty insurance
- fire insurance
- flood insurance
- fraternal or mutual benefit insurance
- group life insurance
- hazardous waste and environmental liability insurance
- health or sickness insurance
- homeowners' insurance
- inland marine insurance
- jewelers' block insurance
- liability insurance
- life insurance
- lightning insurance
- marine insurance
- medical and dental malpractice insurance
- plate glass insurance
- product liability insurance
- property insurance
- reciprocal or interindemnity insurance
- reinsurance
- strike insurance
- title insurance
- unemployment insurance
- use and occupancy insurance
- worker's compensation insurance

FIGURE C-1   Overview of Types of Insurance Coverage Available

FIRE INSURANCE	Covers rebuilding, repair, and replacement of property damaged by fire.
ACCIDENT INSURANCE	Provides fixed benefits in event of accidental injury.
HEALTH INSURANCE	Reimbursement for expenses resulting from sickness or accidental injury.
HOMEOWNERS' INSURANCE	Reimbursement for losses related to damage to one's residence (excludes losses stemming from use of automobile).
LIABILITY INSURANCE	Reimbursement for losses for which insured is liable (usually excluding intentional and criminal acts).
LIFE INSURANCE	Payments to insured's estate or beneficiaries in event of insured's death.
MARINE INSURANCE	Reimbursement for losses incurred in shipping of goods.
MALPRACTICE INSURANCE	Reimbursement for losses stemming from professional negligence.
PRODUCT LIABILITY INSURANCE	Reimbursement for losses stemming from defective products.
PROPERTY INSURANCE	Reimbursement for losses sustained to property.
TITLE INSURANCE	Coverage for losses resulting from defective title to property.
UNEMPLOYMENT INSURANCE	Provision of compensation for losses caused to an employee due to termination of employment.

SPECIFIC TYPES OF INSURANCE

Fire Insurance

As you have seen, the types of insurance available are many and varied. For the right premium an insurer can be found to insure against almost any contingency. One of the most prevalent types of insurance, however, is fire insurance. Fire insurance may be found in different types of policies but is most often encountered in the standard homeowners' policy. The 1943 New York Standard Policy provides the pattern for the standard coverage in today's homeowners' policies. This insurance prototype has been extensively reviewed by the courts and its contents are familiar to insurance regulators in all states.

One of the important provisions of the 1943 policy is the right given to the insurer to rebuild the damaged structure, repair it, or if necessary replace it. An insurer will obviously select the most economical option available. These options, which are similar to those available to the insurer under automobile collision coverage, often result in disputes between the insured and the insurer as to whether the option selected by the insurer was appropriate. Quite possibly, for example, a residence that is rebuilt because of severe fire damage may have a stigma attached to it that results in a substantial reduction of its fair market value. One vital prerequisite to recovery under any fire insurance policy is that the insured must not have intentionally caused the damage or conspired with another to intentionally cause the damage.

Irrespective of the amount of fire insurance obtained by an insured on a particular piece of property, the amount to be paid by the insurer will not be greater than the property's fair market value or replacement cost, depending on the type of insurance purchased. The mere fact that an insured purchases fire insurance for $100,000 on a building worth only $50,000 does not allow him or her to collect $100,000 in the event of the total loss of the structure.

Accident Insurance

Accident insurance is designed to provide the insured with specified coverage in the event of an accidental injury. A policy might provide a fixed amount for the loss of one eye, a greater amount for the loss of both eyes, a fixed sum for the loss of a leg, and so on. Often the accident insurance policy provides a fixed benefit in the case of an accidental death. Accident insurance, unlike health insurance, does not reimburse the insured for expenses incurred as the result of an accident. Rather, it provides an agreed-upon payment if an accidental injury covered by the policy should occur.

Health Insurance

Health insurance is designed to provide reimbursement for medical expenses incurred by the insured as a result of sickness or accidental injury. Most health insurance policies provide for a deductible that must be paid by the insured before benefits become payable.

In addition, most health insurance policies require the insured to be responsible for a percentage of the medical expenses incurred above the deductible, up to what is called the co-insurance limit. Above the co-insurance limit the insurer is totally responsible for payment of expenses. Suppose the insurer is responsible for 80 percent of the medical expenses incurred above the deductible of $1,000, to a total of $5,000 above the deductible (the co-insurance limit). If $10,000 in medical expenses were sustained, the insured would have to pay the deductible of $1,000 plus 20 percent of $5,000 ($1,000). The insurer would then be totally responsible for the remainder of the expenses ($4,000) and would have to pay 80 percent of the $5,000 above the deductible, for a total of $8,000.

Most health insurance policies have a maximum figure for which the insurer will be responsible for medical expenses as the result of any one claim. Once the policy limits are met by the insurer, the insured is responsible for the payment of any shortfall. Depending on the policy, that maximum might be reinstated if the insured were to sustain medical expenses as a result of a different cause. Some policies also have lifetime maximums that will be paid irrespective of the number of claims.

The standard health insurance policy provision requires that the insured remain treatment-free as a result of any preexisting conditions for a fixed period of time after the policy is issued. A *preexisting condition* is any medical condition suffered by the insured prior to securing a policy from the insurer. The time period required varies from policy to policy but can be as short as ninety days or as long as two years. Any medical expenses incurred or treatment begun prior to expiration of the period set forth in the policy will not be covered. The insurer may also provide specific exclusions for preexisting conditions. For example, a policy could contain an exclusion precluding payment for expenses relating to any injury to the insured's knee. Such an exclusion would be required by the insurance carrier because of prior problems with or treatment of the insured's knee.

One problem that often arises in health insurance policies is an allegation by the insurer that the insured failed to give a full and complete disclosure of a prior medical condition on the health insurance application. How the courts deal with such nondisclosure varies but most policies allow for cancellation if the insurer refunds the premiums paid. If an insured can show that the insurer would have issued a policy with only an exclusion for the type of injury that was not disclosed and that the injury that he or she sustained was not related to any misrepresentation on the application, some courts will require the insurer to pay the expenses despite the misrepresentation. Other courts look to the material misrepresentation and allow the insurer to avoid its contractual obligations, even though the misrepresentation was unrelated to the injury or sickness actually sustained by the insured.

Homeowners' Insurance

Homeowners' insurance policies have been designed for the owner-occupant of a single-family residence. Homeowners' insurance may provide either basic or extended coverage. *Basic coverage* provides for protection against loss due to fire, lightning, windstorm, or hail. *Extended coverage* provides personal liability protection as well as "all risk" coverage, which is coverage for all risk of physical loss to insured property except for exclusions specifically listed in the policy. Most lenders require, at the minimum, that a homeowner/insured maintain coverage for fire, windstorm, hail, vandalism, and malicious mischief. The purpose of this requirement is to ensure that any losses sustained that may affect the security of the lender will be reimbursed by the homeowner's insurance carrier.

The standard homeowners' policy specifically excludes any liability that might be imposed on the insured arising out of the operation of a motor vehicle. It may, however, provide liability coverage for the insured and the insured's family for acts that occur at locations other than the residence insured under the policy. One fertile field of litigation with respect to the standard homeowners' policy is the issue of liability for the death of minor children in a homeowner's swimming pool. Injuries caused to others by the insured or members of his or her family are also hotly litigated. If, for example, the insured's son injures his friend while engaging in unreasonably rough horseplay while on the premises, or if the insured's dog bites a guest, the insured's homeowners' policy should provide coverage.

Many homeowners' insurance policies provide for medical payments insurance. They also frequently require that the insured specifically list (and pay an extra premium for) items of unusual value such as works of art, musical instruments, jewelry, excessive cash, and weapons.

Liability Insurance

Liability insurance is one of the more comprehensive types of insurance available. Under this policy the insurer must reimburse (indemnify) the insured for any loss covered by the policy for which the insured may be responsible. Liability insurance covers damages the insured may be required to pay as a result of bodily injury or property damage caused by the insured's negligence.

Illegal or intentional acts of the insured are not covered in a standard liability policy. Most policies, either by their specific language or by court interpretation, do not provide coverage for punitive damages.

Liability insurance is written either in single-limit or split-limits coverage. Under the *single-limit* approach, a set amount is all that is available to injured third parties, irrespective of the total amount of the injuries they sustain. For example, a $300,000 single-limit policy provides coverage for damages up to a maximum of $300,000 no matter how many claimants apply and no matter how great their actual losses are. Potentially, one claimant could recover $300,000 and the other claimants could be left with nothing under this type of policy.

Under *split-limits* coverage a fixed amount is set for each individual claim, along with a different fixed amount for the total of all claims arising out of the same incident. The split limits coverage of a $100,000/$300,000 policy, for example, would allow a maximum recovery of $100,000 for each person injured and a maximum recovery of $300,000 for all persons injured. This type of coverage would prevent one claimant from usurping all of the $300,000 by putting a $100,000 cap on individual recovery.

As mentioned previously, liability insurance is a standard part of the homeowners' insurance policy. In most cases it is also a required part of the automobile insurance policy.

Life Insurance

Unlike the other types of insurance we have discussed, life insurance does not indemnify the insured for any losses sustained. In essence, a life insurance contract is an agreement by the insurance carrier to pay the insured's estate or the named beneficiary a fixed amount upon the insured's death. Unlike liability insurance or, for that matter, most other forms of insurance, the event insured against (death) is certain to happen.

Life insurance carriers have devised a variety of life insurance plans because of the perceived diverse needs of the American public (see Figure C-2). They have also attempted to capitalize on the tax benefits that have been granted to the life insurance industry. These tax benefits, which arguably stem from Congress's perception of life insurance as a type of savings, have provided life insurance carriers with sales pitches unavailable to other types of insurers. For example, insurers can offer policies that allow the insured to accumulate tax-free interest during the term of the policy and to pay taxes only upon actually receiving the funds. When the monies are received the insured is typically in a much lower tax bracket, according to the insurance carrier, usually as a result of retirement. Individual life insurance premiums are not tax deductible and the face amount of the policy paid to the beneficiary upon the insured's death is generally not taxable.

The most common types of life insurance now available are ordinary life, term life, joint life, and survivorship insurance.

Ordinary Life Insurance

An ordinary life insurance policy has a fixed monthly or yearly premium based on the age of the insured at the time the policy is taken out. This premium is paid during the life of the insured in consideration of the payment (based on the face amount of the policy) guaranteed to be paid his or her estate or beneficiary at the insured's death. Some ordinary life

FIGURE C-2   Types of Life Insurance

ORDINARY	TERM
Insured pays fixed premium with benefits paid to estate or beneficiaries in event of insured's death.	Insured pays fixed premiums with benefits paid to estate or beneficiaries in event of insured's death.

JOINT	SURVIVORSHIP
Benefits payable upon death of one or more insureds.	Benefits payable only to survivors of two or more insureds.

insurance policies are set up so that premiums are pro-rated through a certain age such as sixty, sixty-five, or seventy-five, at which time the policy is considered fully paid.

Typically the ordinary life insurance policy provides for the building of a cash value, which occurs after the first few years. Initially the payments provide the means for the agent to be paid a commission. As a result, the insurer pays the insured the cash value of the policy if the policy is canceled prior to his or her death. Alternatively, the insurer could loan the insured monies in an amount equal to the *loan value* of the policy, as determined by the insurance contract. The loan value of a policy varies depending on the number of years the policy has been in effect and the internal rate of return of the insured. If the insured takes a loan on the policy, the policy stays in effect as long as premiums and loan payments are paid on a timely basis.

Term Insurance

Term insurance has a fixed term, usually a year, and provides for payment only if the insured dies during that term. Unlike ordinary life insurance, the rates of term insurance vary on a periodic basis, depending on the age of the insured at the time the policy is taken out. Term insurance is more like other types of insurance in that the risk insured against (death during the term of the policy) is not certain to occur. Term insurance is often the insurance of choice for younger couples who want to provide for their dependents in the event of their own demise but who are unable to afford the higher premiums demanded by ordinary life insurance. Some term policies, while allowing the premium to vary with the age of the insured, guarantee insurability to the insured. Many waive the need for a physical examination as long as the insured renews the policy prior to the expiration of every term, so that no break in the coverage occurs.

Joint Life Insurance

With joint life insurance the benefits become payable upon the death of one of the insureds covered by the policy. Joint life insurance requires at least two insureds, although a limitless number of insureds could theoretically be covered.

Joint life insurance is particularly advantageous when a small group of individuals, each of whom is vital to the group, begins a joint enterprise. Because the death of any group member could adversely affect the success of the endeavor, a joint life policy provides a fund from which the survivors can be compensated for the loss of one of their members. Term insurance, taken in the name of each individual, can result in premiums that exceed the enterprise's ability to pay. Joint life insurance, in contrast, provides reimbursement to the enterprise at a minimal cost. Subsequent to the death of one of the group members, the survivors could obtain a second policy covering the survivors.

Survivorship Insurance

A survivorship policy is the mirror image of a joint life policy. Joint life insurance provides benefits when one of the insureds dies; survivorship insurance provides benefits when all but one of the insureds has died (i.e., it pays the last survivor). Survivorship insurance might be preferable to term insurance for a married couple in which one spouse is considerably older than the other. Although a survivorship policy would cost more than a term policy issued on the eldest spouse it would cost less than purchasing term policies for both of them. This type of policy might also be advantageous to a group in which the efforts of individual deceased members could be duplicated but a lone survivor would be unable to carry on the enterprise.

Marine Insurance

Marine insurance, the oldest form of insurance, protects against losses incurred in shipping goods. It covers the loss itself as well as lost profits. Modern-day marine insurance traces its beginning to the emergence of England as a maritime power in the sixteenth century. The preeminent insurer in this area, Lloyds of London, issues the industry standard, called the "English Lloyds policy."

Malpractice Insurance

Malpractice insurance is analogous to the *errors and omissions policy* used to protect officers and directors of major corporations. Malpractice insurance applies to professionals, who are held to the standard of care reasonably expected of similar professionals in the geographic area in which they practice. The major distinction between errors and omissions insurance and malpractice insurance lies in the standard of care. As previously noted, negligence is measured in terms of the standard of care of a "reasonable person." The standard of care for malpractice, however, is based on the expectations of a reasonable professional in a particular field and geographic area. Malpractice insurance is available for medical and dental practitioners, including pharmacists, hospitals, and nurses, as well as for lawyers, psychologists, veterinarians, and other professionals.

One of the factors that differentiates malpractice insurance from errors and omissions insurance is that malpractice insurance requires state licensure, whereas errors and omissions generally does not. Licensing is one of the first things to consider when determining what type of insurance might be available, although it is not a consistent requirement. Most real estate salespeople, for example, are required to be licensed and yet their coverages are still considered errors and omissions policies rather than malpractice policies.

One fairly recent change in malpractice policies lowers the amount of coverage available to a claimant by including the cost of his or her defense as part of the insurance coverage. Including defense costs is an illusory attempt to lower premiums while maintaining the same face value of coverage. In the past the cost of defending a lawsuit was not considered part of the policy. Under these terms, a claimant could avail herself of a sum equal to the face value of the policy minus the deductible. Under the new policy the amount available to the claimant is the face value of the policy minus the malpractice carrier's cost of defending the insured.

Product Liability Insurance

Product liability insurance is a creation of the twentieth century. Manufacturers and producers of goods obtain product liability insurance to protect themselves against claims by the ultimate users and/or handlers of their products. Because most product liability cases are based on strict liability, the potential for loss is very high. In some industries, such as the airline industry, a single incident can result in numerous multimillion-dollar claims.

Because of this exposure, product liability insurance is very expensive but, from a practical standpoint, necessary to any entity that either manufactures or produces products. Problems arise when the cost of product liability insurance results in the production or manufacture of the product no longer being economical. At that point the maker of the goods must decide whether to go uninsured and hope that no claims are made, or to discontinue manufacturing the product altogether.

Testing of new products and modification of old products is often required by providers of product liability insurance. Underwriters Laboratory's "seal of approval," for example, allows manufacturers promotional advantages by being able to prominently display the "UL" symbol. But, more importantly, testing may be a prerequisite to the obtaining of product liability insurance.

In the marketplace the cost of product liability insurance unquestionably inhibits the introduction of new products. Many hope this cost will spur manufacturers to exhibit greater concern for consumers, but the cost/benefit ratio is still difficult to determine. The question remains whether the high cost of admission to the marketplace has created artificial barriers to the introduction of new and innovative concepts.

Property Insurance

Property insurance is an agreement by the insurer to indemnify the insured for any losses sustained to his or her property. Property insurance is included in many different types of coverage, including homeowners' coverage. Fire insurance and flood insurance are both types of property insurance. Property insurance, however, covers far more perils than fire and flood and frequently includes windstorm, lightning, rain, hail, and similar natural catastrophes.

Property insurance generally comes in two forms—*actual cash value* (the initial cost minus accrued depreciation) or *replacement cost* (the cost of replacing the article at the date of loss rather than at its depreciated value.) Therefore, most replacement cost policies require higher premiums than actual cash value policies.

Title Insurance

The primary purpose behind title insurance is to provide coverage to the insured for any loss that may result due to a defect in the title to property (not losses due to defects in or damage to the property itself). An insured is obligated to prove the nature and amount of the loss incurred and the insurer then indemnifies the insured against only that loss. In many instances, a problem with a title results in no or only insubstantial damages.

Suppose a title insurer issues a policy of title insurance for a parcel of land but fails to disclose an easement over the south ten feet of the property. If the title policy insured ownership of the entire parcel to the policy holder, the policy holder would be entitled to indemnification for only the loss in value due to the existence of the unknown easement. Very likely an easement for five or ten feet would be relatively insignificant with respect to the total value of the property. In contrast, if such an undisclosed easement divided the property in half, the value of the remaining parcels might be dramatically affected.

Title insurance comes in a variety of forms, including the owner's policy, the lender's policy, and the American Land Title Association (ALTA) policy. The *owner's policy* tries to meet the needs of real estate buyers, the *lender's policy* protects the interest of the financing entity in a real estate transaction, and the *ALTA policy* provides the maximum protection to the insured. Because of its extensive coverage the ALTA policy is substantially greater in cost per dollar of coverage than other title policies.

Unemployment Insurance

Unemployment insurance is extensively regulated by state law. In most instances the benefits are fixed and mandated by statute, as are the procedures for the redress of aggrieved employers and employees. Unemployment insurance matters require a very detailed examination of state statutes and the case law interpreting them.

Workers' Compensation

Workers' compensation, like unemployment insurance, is highly regulated. All states have regulatory agencies whose purpose is to insure that employees have a source of compensation for work-related injuries. In most instances, the acceptance of workers' compensation benefits provided by statute precludes the employee from suing the employer for negligence. Workers' compensation, in general, provides benefits without regard to fault of the injured party. In other words, even though the employee was negligent in not abiding by the safety rules and regulations established by the employer, he or she is still entitled to workers' compensation benefits in the event of injury. As with unemployment insurance, the statutory framework in reference to workers' compensation claims must be extensively analyzed in light of relevant court decisions. Workers' compensation insurance is discussed in Chapter 20.

Automobile Insurance

Perhaps nowhere in our court system is more litigation threatened or initiated than in reference to liability arising out of motor vehicle accidents. Automobile insurance, with all its variations, possesses most of the attributes of the other types of insurance. Automobile insurance is discussed in some detail in Chapter 18.

DEFENSES AN INSURANCE COMPANY CAN RAISE AGAINST ITS INSURED

The issuance of an insurance policy begins when an insured or his or her agent fills out an application. The primary purpose of the application is to answer certain relevant questions surrounding the issuance of the policy. A health insurance application, for example, deals primarily with the applicant's previous medical history. The insurer needs this information to determine whether any preexisting conditions should be excluded from the policy as well as to assess the overall insurability of the applicant.

Misrepresentations

If an applicant makes any material misrepresentations relating to any risks that are insured, the insurer may be able to void the policy should the insured make any claim relating to those risks (see Figure C-3). If the applicant attempts to conceal material facts or deliberately misrepresent material issues in the application, he or she may be denied any coverage whatsoever and may be relegated to, at most, reimbursement of the premiums paid to date. Many policies provide that after two years have elapsed since issuance of the policy, the insurer cannot use any error or misrepresentation on the application to void the insurance contract.

Failure to Abide by Terms of Policy

A policy can also be voided by the insured's failure to abide by the terms of the policy. Insureds are most likely to be at odds with their insurance company in one of two ways. The first involves the insured's duty to cooperate with the insurer in dealing with the claim. The second involves the policy's provisions requiring the insured to give prompt notice of any potential claim.

Failure to Cooperate

An insured potentially violates the duty to cooperate if he or she refuses to give a statement to the insurance company, refuses to make books and records available (where applicable), or refuses to allow the insurance company to enter his or her premises for inspection purposes in the case of a fire or property damage claim. The insured also violates the duty to cooperate when he or she is sued and fails to participate in the discovery process by refusing to attend depositions, answer interrogatories, respond to requests for admissions, or assist in the production of documents.

Failure to Notify

Failure to notify an insurance company of a claim is a second potential point of contention between insureds and their insurance companies. Although most policies require reasonable notice, some attempt to set an outer time limit by which any claim must be reported. Before an insured can be said to have violated the duty to give notice, he or she must know or have reason to know that a claim is forthcoming. What might appear, for example, to be a minor motor vehicle collision with no property damage and no personal injury could result in a subsequent claim. If the insured reasonably believes that no damage occurred and no claim will be made, failure to advise the carrier about the accident will not give the insurance company grounds for denying coverage.

In a similar vein, the insured has a duty to advise the insurance company of any suit that is actually filed against him or her. If the carrier is unable to answer the complaint because of the insured's failure to notify it in a timely manner and a default judgment is entered, the insurer can attempt to deny coverage. Alternatively, the

FIGURE C-3   Defenses Insurer Can Raise

- Insured makes material misrepresentation in application.
- Insured fails to cooperate with insurer in dealing with claim.
- Insured fails to give timely notice to insurer of potential claim.
- Insured commits intentional act.

insurer might seek reimbursement for the damages it sustained as a result of the default judgment against the insured. Suppose an insured, through his own inaction, allows a default judgment to be entered against him. The carrier may then be relieved of the responsibility of paying the judgment, or may be allowed to attempt to set aside the judgment as far as it relates to its duty to indemnify the insured.

Intentional Acts

Most insurance policies exempt coverage for intentional acts of the insured. Such acts include intentionally setting fire to insured property, suicide (although many life insurance policies cover suicide if committed after a fixed period of time following the issuance of the policy), intentionally using a motor vehicle to cause damage, or intentionally assaulting a third party.

Reservation of Rights

An insurer may find it difficult to immediately determine whether it has a right to deny coverage under the policy. Therefore, most insurance carriers, until they are sure they have a right to deny coverage, will defend the insured under a reservation of rights. Under a reservation of rights the insurer advises the insured that coverage may not be available but that it will defend the insured until that determination is made. In many cases the insurer will institute a declaratory judgment action seeking a court determination regarding the issue of coverage. If an insurer proceeds under a reservation of rights, it may later withdraw from representation of the insured and seek reimbursement for its defense costs.

Insurer's Actions

An insurance carrier can by its own actions lose its right to assert a defense against an insured. In such cases the insurer will be deemed to have waived its rights to contest the policy and may, in some circumstances, be estopped (prevented) from asserting defenses because of its prior acts.

As with all areas of insurance, court rulings and statutory enactments affecting the policy in question must be carefully researched. In some instances the plain wording of the policy and the insurer's actions have been deemed wrongful and in violation of "public policy." Public policy attempts to reconcile legislative enactments, prior court decisions, and the public good in overriding provisions perceived as inequitable. Public policy requirements will be read into an insurance policy and terms and conditions conflicting with public policy will either be ignored or deemed unenforceable. Provisions in a policy that exclude members of an insured's family from coverage, for example, may be deemed in violation of public policy and therefore unenforceable by the insurer.

APPENDIX
D
The Country Squire

A Package of Protection for
Today's Farmer and Rancher
Farm Bureau
Family of Insurance Services
Western Agricultural Insurance Company
P.O. Box 20180, 2618 South 21st Street,
Phoenix, Arizona 85036-0180

A MESSAGE TO OUR POLICYHOLDERS

This is your Farm and Ranch Country Squire Insurance Policy. It is written in easy to read and understand language. We believe it provides you the best property and liability insurance coverage on the market today. Everything about this policy has been designed with today's farm and ranch family in mind.

We urge you to read this policy carefully, including the attached Declarations page. If you have any questions, your Farm Bureau agent welcomes your call.

WHERE TO LOOK—INDEX

Be sure to check your Declarations page, attached to this policy, to see which of the following apply to you.

Definitions Applicable to Sections I, II, IV

Conditions (General) Applicable to Sections I, II, III, IV

Section I—Property Insurance
Coverage A—Your Dwelling(s)
Coverage B—Additional Living Expense

Coverage C—Personal Property (Household Goods), Special Limits, Property Not Insured, Supplementary Coverages
Coverage D—Farm Personal Property
Livestock Coverage, Limited Crop Coverage, Coinsurance Clause, Inspection and Audit, Records and Electronic Data Processing, Property Coverage Limitation, Exclusions
Coverage E—Additional Buildings
Materials and Supplies, Buildings, Utility Poles, Fences, New Construction, Outdoor Radio and T.V. Antennas
Additional Coverages
Debris Removal, Repairs, Trees-Shrubs-Plants, Refrigerated Products, Fire Department Service Charges
Perils Insured Against (Causes of Loss)
Exclusions—Applicable to Section I
(What we specifically exclude from Coverage)
Conditions—Applicable to Section I
Endorsements—Applicable to Section I
(If purchased and listed on Declaration)

Section II—Your Liability Protection
Coverage F—Bodily Injury Liability and Property Damage Liability
Coverage G—Premises Medical
Coverage H—Employer's Liability
Coverage I—Medical Payments for Farm Employees
Coverage J—Medical Payments (Named Persons)
Coverage K—Death of Livestock by Collision

DEFINITIONS APPLICABLE TO SEC. I, II, IV

The following definitions apply to Sections I, II and IV; they do not apply to Sections III or V:

Throughout these sections we, us and our mean the Company named in the Declarations. You and your mean the person named in the Declarations and that person's spouse if a resident of the same household. You and your also refer to a partnership, corporation, estate or trust named in the Declarations.

Bodily Injury means physical injury or death to a person caused by an **occurrence.**

Business means a trade, profession or occupation, other than **farming** or **custom farming. Business** includes rental of all or any part of an **insured location** to others, or held for rental by you other than:
1. Your **residence premises** if rented occasionally;
2. Garages or stables, if not more than three (3) car spaces or stalls are rented or held for rental;
3. One-, two-, three-, or four-family **dwellings** described in the Declarations; or
4. Your farm.

Business does not include:
1. The operation of roadside stands principally for the sale of produce raised on the **insured location; or**
2. Newspaper delivery, baby-sitting, lawn care or similar activities normally performed by minors, when the activity is not the principal occupation of any **insured.**

Custom Farming means the use of any draft animal or **mobile agricultural machinery** in connection with **farming** operations for others for any charge.

Dwelling means a one-, two-, three-, or four-family **dwelling** listed in the Declarations, including its grounds and private garages.

Farm Employee means someone employed by you whose duties are in connection with the maintenance or use of the **insured location** as a farm, including the maintenance or use of your farm equipment. **Farm employee** does not include you, your spouse, or a minor child of either, but does include exchange labor.

Farm Personal Property means your personal property which is usual and incidental to the operation of a farm and is used on your farm. It includes live-stock, poultry, **mobile agricultural machinery,** tools, supplies, equipment, and harvested crops used in or resulting from your **farming** operation. It includes property being purchased under an installment plan whether or not you have title to the property.

Farming means the production of fruit, nut or field crops, or the raising or keeping of livestock, poultry, fish, fur-bearing animals or bees. It includes wholesale but not retail sales, except incidental retail sales of your unprocessed farm products with the resulting gross income being less than 25 percent of your combined **farming** gross income.

Insured means you and if residents of your household:

1. Your **relatives;** and
2. Minors in the care of those named above.

Under Section II of this policy, **insured** also means a person while operating machinery, watercraft, or, in charge of your domestic or farm animals with your permission in your operations covered by this policy.

Insured Location means

1. All locations listed in the Declarations where you maintain a farm or residence, including private approaches;
2. Locations acquired by you during the policy period where you maintain a farm or residence, including private approaches;
3. Individual or family cemetery plots or burial vaults;
4. A location in which you temporarily reside but do not own; and
5. Vacant land owned by you and listed in the Declarations or acquired by you during the policy period.

Insured Location does not include property on which a **business** is conducted.

Medical Expenses means reasonable charges for medical, surgical, x-ray, dental, ambulance, hospital, professional nursing and prosthetic devices.

Mobile Agricultural Machinery means a land vehicle, including any machinery or attached apparatus, whether or not self-propelled, usual to the operation of a farm and used exclusively for agricultural purposes, not subject to registration and designed for use principally off public roads.

Mobile agricultural machinery includes implements of husbandry which are defined as a vehicle or piece of equipment or machinery designed for agricultural purposes, used primarily in the conduct of agricultural operations and used principally off the highway.

Motor Vehicle means a motorized land vehicle, trailer, or semi-trailer (including any attached machinery or apparatus) designed principally for travel on public roads. The following are not considered **motor vehicles** unless they are being towed by or carried on a **motor vehicle:**

1. A utility, boat, camping or travel trailer;
2. **Mobile agricultural machinery;**
3. **Recreational motor vehicles;**
4. Any equipment which is designed for use principally off public roads and not subject to registration or licensing.

Occurrence means an unexpected and unintended event, including continuous or repeated exposure to conditions, which results in **bodily injury** or **property damage** during the policy period. All **bodily injury** and **property damage** resulting from a common cause shall be considered the result of one **occurrence.**

Personal Property means personal property usual and incidental to the use of the **dwelling premises** as a **dwelling.**

Property Damage means injury to or destruction of tangible property caused by an **occurrence.**

Recreational Motor Vehicle or Recreational Vehicle means any motorized vehicle designed for recreation, principally used off public roads, and not subject to licensing.

Relative means a person related to you by blood, marriage, or adoption who is a resident of your household, including a ward or foster child.

Residence Employee means someone employed by you who performs duties in connection with the maintenance or use of the **residence premises.** This includes a person who performs duties for you elsewhere of a similar nature not in connection with your **business** or **farming.**

Residence Premises means a one-, two-, three-, or four-family **dwelling** which is your principal residence, including its grounds, and private garages.

Residence premises also means that part of any other building which is your principal residence but does not include any portion used for **business.**

GENERAL CONDITIONS APPLICABLE TO SEC. I, II, III, & IV

Unless otherwise indicated, the following conditions are applicable to Sections I, II, III, and IV:

1. **Agreement.** We will provide the insurance described in this policy and Declarations if you have paid the premium and have complied with the policy provisions and conditions. This policy is divided into four sections, some with multiple coverages. You have only the coverages for which you have paid premium. These coverages are indicated in the Declarations and are subject to the indicated limits of insurance.

READ THE DECLARATIONS TO DETERMINE WHICH COVERAGES PERTAIN TO YOU.

2. **Abandonment of Property.** We need not pay for nor accept any property abandoned by an **insured.**

3. **Appraisal** (Not applicable to liability coverages). If you and we fail to agree on the amount of loss, either one can demand that the amount of loss be set by appraisal. If either makes a written demand for appraisal, each shall select a competent, independent appraiser and notify the other of the appraiser's identity within 20 days of receipt of the written demand. The two appraisers shall then select a competent, impartial umpire. If the two appraisers are unable to agree upon an umpire within 15 days, you or we can ask a judge of a court of record in the state where the **residence premises** is located to select an umpire. The appraisers shall then set the amount of the loss. If the appraisers submit a written report of an agreement to us, the amount agreed upon shall be the amount of the loss. If the appraisers fail to agree within a reasonable time, they shall submit their differences to the umpire. Written agreements signed by any two of these three shall set the amount of the loss. Each appraiser shall be paid by the party selecting that appraiser. Other expenses of the appraisal and the compensation of the umpire shall be shared equally.

4. **Assignment.** Assignment of this policy shall not be valid unless we give our written consent.

5. **Audit Premium.** The premium stated in the Declarations shall be computed according to our rules and rating plans. The premium is for insurance from the inception date in the Declarations (12:01 a.m.) to the expiration date in the Declarations (12:01 a.m.); date and time being at your **residence premises.** This premium, however, is an estimated premium only. We shall be permitted to examine and audit your books and records during the policy period and within three (3) years after the final termination of the policy, to obtain information about the premium basis of this insurance. The earned premium for the insurance shall be computed according to our rules and rating plans. If the earned premium exceeds the estimated premium you paid, you shall pay us the excess; if the earned premium is less, we shall return the overpayment to you.

6. **Bankruptcy of An Insured.** Bankruptcy or insolvency of an **insured** shall not relieve us of our obligations under this policy.

7. **Cancellation.** You may cancel this entire policy by mailing to us written notice stating when this cancellation shall be effective. Our cancellation rights appear on back pages of this policy labelled "Cancellation".

8. **Concealment or Fraud.** We will not provide coverage if any **insured** has intentionally concealed or misrepresented any material fact or circumstance relating to this insurance.

9. **Death.** Upon your death, we will continue through the current policy period to insure any member of your household who is an **insured** at the time of your death. We will also insure:
   a. With respect to your property, the person having proper temporary custody of the property until appointment and qualification of a legal representative; or
   b. The legal representative of the deceased, but only with respect to the premises and property of the deceased covered under the policy at the time of death.

10. **Declarations.** By acceptance of this policy, you agree that the Declarations indicate the coverages you

purchased. This policy embodies the only agreements existing between you and us or any of our agents relating to this insurance.

11. **Deductible Clause.** Loss from each **occurrence** shall be adjusted separately. The deductible stated in the Declarations shall be subtracted from each adjusted loss or the limit of insurance, whichever is less. Under the special limits applicable to Coverage C, however, the deductible shall be subtracted from only the adjusted loss.

12. **Dividends or Credits.** Any obligation of ours for dividend or credit shall not in any way extend or change the policy period.

13. **Inspection and Audit.** We shall be permitted to inspect and audit your insured property and operation at any time. We are not obligated, however, to conduct inspections and any inspection or report shall not be considered a representation that the operation or property is safe.

14. **Liberalization Clause.** If we adopt any revision which would broaden the coverage under this policy without payment of additional premium within 60 days prior to or during the policy period, the broadened coverage will immediately apply to this policy.

15. **Loss Payment** (Not applicable to liability coverages). We will adjust all losses with you. Payment for loss will be made within 60 days after we receive your signed, sworn statement of loss and ascertainment of the loss is made either by agreement with you, entry of a final judgment, or the filing of an appraisal award with us. Actual cash value in this policy means replacement cost less depreciation.

16. **Mortgage Clause** (Limited to Sections I and IV). The word "mortgagee" includes a trustee of a deed of trust.

If a mortgagee is named in this policy, any loss payable under Sections I or IV shall be paid to the mortgagee and you, as interests appear. If more than one mortgagee is named, the order of payment shall be the same as the order or precedence of the mortgages.

If we deny your claim, that denial shall not apply to a valid claim of the mortgagee, if the mortgagee:

a. Notifies us of any change in ownership, occupancy or substantial change in risk of which the mortgagee is aware;

b. Pays any premium due under this policy on demand if you have neglected to pay the premium; and

c. Submits a signed, sworn statement of loss within 60 days after receiving notice from us of your failure to do so. Policy conditions relating to Appraisal, Suit Against Us and Loss Payment apply to the mortgagee.

If the policy is cancelled by us, notice shall be mailed to the mortgagee at least 10 days before the date cancellation takes effect.

If we pay the mortgagee for any loss and deny payment to you:

a. We are subrogated to all the rights of the mortgagee granted under the mortgage on the property; or

b. At our option, we may pay to the mortgagee the whole principal on the mortgage plus any accrued interest. In this event, we shall receive a full assignment and transfer.

Subrogation shall not impair the right of the mortgagee to recover the full amount of the mortgagee's claim.

17. **No Benefit to Bailee.** We will not recognize any assignment or grant any coverage for the benefit of any person or organization holding, storing or transporting property for a fee regardless of any other provision of this policy.

18. **Nonduplication of Insurance Benefits.** No person entitled to benefits under any coverage of this policy shall recover duplicate benefits for the same elements of loss under other coverages of this policy or other policies written by us.

19. **Our Option.** If we give you written notice within 30 days after we receive your signed, sworn statement of loss, we may:

a. Take all or any part of the property at the agreed or appraised value; or

b. Repair or replace any part of the property damaged with equivalent property. We will not be liable for any loss resulting from delay in repair or choice of repairmen.

20. **Policy Period.** This policy applies only to **occurrences** which take place during the policy period.

21. **Policy Renewals.** Subject to our consent, you may renew this policy for successive periods by payment to us of the premium we require to renew the policy. Premium payment for any renewal period shall be due on the expiration of the preceding policy period.

22. **Policy Termination.** If you fail to pay the premium when due, the policy shall terminate on the expiration date of the policy without any notice or action by us.

23. **Subrogation—Our Right to Recover Payment.**

   a. If we make payment under this policy and the person to or for whom payment was made has a right to recover damages, we will be subrogated to that right (have that right transferred to us). That person must do whatever is necessary to enable us to exercise our rights and must do nothing after the loss to prejudice our rights.

   b. If we make a payment under this policy, and the person to or for whom payment was made recovers damages from another, that person must hold the proceeds of the recovery in trust for us and must reimburse us to the extent of our payment.

24. **Suit Against Us.** No action shall be brought against us unless there has been compliance with the policy provisions. No one shall have any right to join us as a party to any action against an **insured.** Further, no action with respect to liability coverages shall be brought against us until the obligation of the **insured** has been determined by final judgment or agreement signed by us.

25. **Terms of Policy to Conform to Statute.** Terms of this policy which are in conflict with the statutes of the state where the policy is issued are hereby amended to conform to such statutes.

26. **Waiver or Change of Policy Provisions.** A waiver or change of any provision of this policy must be in writing by us to be valid. Our request for an appraisal or examination shall not waive any of our rights.

SECTION I—PROPERTY INSURANCE

We cover the property insured under Section I against direct physical loss only for specified perils. The perils and our limit of liability applicable to each coverage are indicated in the Declarations.

COVERAGE A

Your Dwelling(s)

We cover the following:

1. The **dwelling** on the **residence premises** shown in the Declarations used principally as your private residence, including structures attached to the dwelling and outdoor equipment pertaining to the **dwelling** and materials and supplies located on or adjacent to the **residence premises** for use in the construction, alteration or repair of the **dwelling** or private garage on the **residence premises.**

2. Your **dwelling(s)** other than the **dwelling** on the **residence premises,** shown in the Declarations and used principally as a private residence, including structures attached to and outdoor equipment pertaining to them and materials and supplies on these **dwelling premises** for the construction, alteration or repair of them or their private garages.

Coverage for outdoor radio and television antennas, aerials, and satellite receivers, including their lead-in wiring, masts, and towers, is subject to a maximum payment of $250, unless such equipment is specifically insured elsewhere for a greater amount. Fences within 250 feet of the **dwelling** on the **residence premises** are covered. Field and pasture fences are excluded.

We cover detached private garages and storage sheds pertaining to the above **dwelling(s).** Coverage for these structures shall not exceed ten percent (10%) of the amount of the insurance specified for the applicable **dwelling** as an additional amount of insurance. We do not cover these structures if used for **business,** professional or **farming** purposes. We also do not cover any garage or storage shed rented to someone other than a tenant of the **dwelling.**

COVERAGE B

Additional Living Expense

If a loss covered under Coverage A of this policy makes the **dwelling** uninhabitable, we pay the following not to exceed the applicable limit stated in the Declarations:

1. **Additional Living Expense.** Any necessary increase in living expenses incurred by you so that your family can maintain its normal standard of living. Payment shall be for the shortest time required to repair or replace the premises or, if you permanently relocate, the shortest time required for your household to settle elsewhere. This period of time is not limited by expiration of this policy.

2. **Fair Rental Value.** The fair rental value of the **dwelling premises.** Payment shall be for the shortest time required to repair or replace the part of the premises rented or held for rental. This period of time is not limited by expiration of this policy. Fair rental value shall not include any expenses that do not continue while part of the **dwelling premises** rented or held for rental is uninhabitable.

3. **Prohibited Use.** If a civil authority prohibits you from use of the **dwelling premises** as a result of direct damage to neighboring premises by a peril insured against in this policy, we cover any resulting additional living expenses or fair rental value loss incurred by you for a period not exceeding two weeks during which use is prohibited.

We do not cover loss or expense due to cancellation of a lease or agreement. No deductible applies to Coverage B.

COVERAGE C

Personal Property

We cover **personal property** owned or used by any **insured** while it is anywhere in the world. At your request, we will cover personal property owned by others while the property is in that part of the **residence premises** occupied exclusively by an **insured.** Your **personal property** in a newly acquired principal residence is covered only for thirty days immediately after you begin to move the property there. If your **personal property** is distributed between your **residence premises** and this newly acquired principal residence, the limit of liability shall apply at each location in the proportion that the value at each location bears to the total value of all property distributed between the two locations.

If you have more than one **dwelling** insured under Coverage A of this policy a different Coverage C limit of liability applies to each **dwelling.** These limits are stated in the Declarations. The limit applicable to one insured **dwelling** can not be applied to a loss at another insured **dwelling.**

Our limit of liability for your **personal property** usually situated at your **dwelling premises** insured under Coverage A, located at other than your principal **dwelling** on the **residence premises,** is five percent (5%) of the limit of liability for that **dwelling premises** insured under Coverage A, unless the Declarations indicate you have purchased additional coverage. Any additional coverage is limited to the amount indicated for that particular location.

1. **Special Limits of Liability.** These limits do not increase the Coverage C limit of liability.

The special limit for each following category is the total limit for each **occurrence** for all property in that category:

   a. $200 on money, bank notes, numismatic property, bullion, gold other than goldware, silver other than silverware, platinum, coins, medals, stamps, and other philatelic property;

   b. $1,000 on securities, accounts, deeds, evidences of debt, letters of credit, notes other than bank notes, manuscripts, passports and tickets;

   c. $1,000 on watercraft, including their trailers, furnishings, equipment, and outboard motors. We do not cover any loss by windstorm or hail to this property unless it is inside a fully enclosed building;

d. $1,000 on utility trailers not otherwise insured;

e. $1,000 on grave markers;

f. $1,000 for loss by theft of jewelry, watches, furs, precious and semi-precious stones;

g. $1,000 for loss by theft of firearms;

h. $2,500 for loss by theft of silverware, silver-plated ware, goldware, gold-plated ware and pewterware.

2. **Property Not Insured.** We do not insure under Coverage C:

a. **Farm personal property;**

b. Animals, birds, fish or pets;

c. Motorized land vehicles and parts, including **mobile agricultural machinery** except vehicles used to service your **dwellings** and not licensed for road use, such as power lawnmowers;

d. Aircraft and parts;

e. Property of roomers, tenants and boarders not related to an **insured;**

f. **Business** personal property, including, but not limited to office equipment, supplies, furnishings, merchandise, samples, tools, and **business** papers and records;

g. **Recreational vehicles,** trailer homes and campers;

h. Any **personal property** located at any **dwellings** which are owned by you and not insured under Section I;

i. Articles separately described and specifically insured by this or other insurance.

3. **Supplementary Coverages.** The following supplementary coverages do not increase the applicable limit of liability under this policy:

a. Consequential loss. We also cover loss to property insured under Coverage C while at the **insured location** due to change in temperature as a result of physical damage to the building or equipment therein caused by a peril insured against.

b. Credit Card, Bank Transfer Card, Counterfeit Currency and Forgery. We will pay up to $1,000 for:

(1) The legal obligation of an **insured** to pay because of the theft or unauthorized use of credit cards or bank transfer cards issued to or registered in any **insured's** name. We do not cover credit card or bank card use if any **insured** has not complied with all terms and conditions under which the card was issued;

(2) Loss suffered by an **insured** caused by forgery or alteration of any check or negotiable instrument;

(3) Loss suffered by an **insured** through acceptance in good faith of counterfeit United States or Canadian paper currency.

We do not cover losses resulting from **business** pursuits or dishonesty of any **insured.**

COVERAGE D

Farm Personal Property

We cover your unscheduled **farm personal property** on the **insured location.** This coverage is further extended for your **farm personal property** away from the **insured location** except while:

1. Stored in or being processed in manufacturing plants, public elevators, warehouses, seed houses, or drying plants;

2. In transit by common or contract carrier; or

3. In public sales barns or sales yards.

We will cover **farm personal property** leased, rented or borrowed by you to conduct your **farming** operation. This **farm personal property** may not be available for your regular use and may not be used on a co-operative exchange basis. This coverage is excess over insurance which the owner has on the property.

1. **Livestock Coverage.** We cover your **livestock** for the specified perils only if death occurs.

Livestock is defined as cattle, horses, mules, swine, poultry, donkeys, goats and sheep. Dogs, cats and fur-bearing animals are not covered. Our limit of liability shall in no case exceed the actual cash value of the livestock subject to the maximum per head limit stated in the Declarations. Death must result within fifteen (15) days from the date of **occurrence.**

2. **Limited Crop Coverage.** Hay, straw and fodder are covered for loss caused by peril 1 (fire) only not to exceed the amount stated in the Declarations in any one stack or building. If a stack or hay building is exposed within 125 feet by another stack or building, the applicable limit shall apply to the aggregate of all such exposed stacks or buildings. For example, if stack Y is 100 feet from stack X and stack Z is 100 feet from stack Y but 200 feet from stack X, the aggregate limit applicable to stacks X, Y and Z is the Coverage D stack limit stated in the Declarations.

3. **Coinsurance Clause.** You must maintain insurance on all your eligible unscheduled **farm personal property** to the extent of at least eighty percent (80%) of the actual cash value at the time of loss and no less than at the time of our auditing or taking inventory. For example, if at the time of loss your unscheduled **farm personal property** is worth $100,000, then the amount of insurance must be at least $80,000. If you fail to keep this agreed percentage of coverage, you will share in each loss in addition to the deductible. We will pay the proportion of each loss represented by the amount you did insure at the time of loss divided by the amount you should have insured.

If the aggregate claim for any loss under this coverage is less than two percent (2%) of the total amount of insurance under Coverage D, you will not be required to furnish an inventory of the undamaged property. This does not mean we waive any of our rights concerning the application of this coinsurance clause.

4. **Inspection and Audit.** We shall be permitted to inspect and audit your insured **farm personal property** at any reasonable time.

5. **Coverage Limitation to Records and Electronic Data Processing Property.** Our liability for loss to:

a. Books of account, manuscripts, abstracts, drawings, card index systems and other records except electronic data processing records shall not exceed the cost of blank books, cards or other blank material, plus the cost of labor incurred by you for transcribing or copying such records;

b. Film, tape, disc, drum, cell and other magnetic recording or storage media for electronic data processing shall not exceed the cost of such media in unexposed or blank form.

6. **Exclusions.** Coverage D does not cover:

a. **Personal property;**

b. Animals, other than **livestock;**

c. Accounts, bills, currency, deeds, evidences of debt, money and securities;

d. Vegetables (except threshed peas and beans), root crops, bulbs, fruits, cotton, tobacco and silage;

e. Permanently installed irrigation pumps, buried water lines; and permanently installed or portable sprinkler lines and sprinkler equipment (including any sprinkler's electrical equipment);

f. Fences, sawmill equipment, windmills, wind chargers and their towers, private power, light and telephone poles, radio and television towers and antennas, vehicles primarily designed and licensed for road use other than wagons and trailers designed for **farming** purposes and used principally on the insured premises;

g. Trucks, automobiles, housetrailers, motorcycles, watercraft, **recreational motor vehicles,** aircraft, or their parts or accessories;

h. Standing growing crops or stubble. However, 10% of the amount specified for Coverage D will cover standing corn, wheat, oats, barley, rye, flax, soybeans and other grains against loss by fire only;

i. Grain, seeds, peas, beans, hay, straw, and fodder unless loss is caused by peril 1 (fire);

j. Structures and buildings except portable buildings on skids in an amount not to exceed $300 per building;

k. Any damage arising from wear and tear, freezing, mechanical breakdown or failure;

l. Under collision or overturn coverage: damage to tires, unless damaged by the same cause as other loss covered under Coverage D;

m. Bee boards or their larvae and bees;

n. Loss to **livestock** caused by the direct or indirect result of fright, freezing, running into fences or other objects, running into streams or ditches, or smothering;

o. Livestock losses caused by collision with any **insured's** vehicle or with the roadbed; or

p. Property which is separately described and specifically insured in whole or in part by this or any other insurance.

COVERAGE E

Additional Buildings

We cover your **dwellings,** barns, buildings, fences and structures listed on the schedule of additional buildings.

1. **Materials and Supplies.** Coverage on a building or structure is extended to cover all materials and supplies on the premises or adjacent to them intended to be used in the construction, alteration or repair of such building or structure.

2. **Coverage on Buildings.** Coverage on buildings includes permanent fixtures and sheds attached to the described buildings, but excluding fences.

3. **Utility Poles.** Coverage on private utility poles includes attached switch boxes, fuse boxes, and other electrical equipment mounted on the poles.

4. **Fences and Similar Structures.** Our liability for loss to fences, corrals, pens, chutes and feed racks shall not be for a greater proportion of any loss than the amount of insurance bears to the total value of that particular property at the time of loss.

5. **New Construction.** We will pay up to $5,000 per **occurrence** for loss to newly constructed additional dwellings, barns, or buildings when erected on the **insured location.** This includes all materials and supplies on the premises to be used in the construction. This coverage shall cease sixty (60) days from the date construction was begun or the policy expiration date, whichever occurs first. For additional coverage, you must request it and pay the required premium. This extension does not cover additions, alterations or repairs to existing dwellings, barns or buildings. Perils 1–9 apply to New Construction Coverage.

Coverage to outdoor radio and television antennas, aerials, and satellite receivers including their lead-in wiring, masts and towers, is subject to a maximum payment of $250, unless such equipment is specifically insured for a greater amount.

ADDITIONAL COVERAGES—SECTION I

No deductible applies to these additional coverages.

1. **Debris Removal.** We will pay the reasonable expense incurred by you in the removal of debris of covered property provided coverage is afforded for the peril causing the loss. Debris removal expense is included in the limit of liability applying to the damaged property. When the amount payable for the actual damage to the property plus the expense for debris removal exceeds the limit of liability for the damaged property, an additional 5% of that limit of liability will be available to cover debris removal expense.

2. **Reasonable Repairs.** We will pay the reasonable costs incurred by you for necessary repairs made solely to protect covered property from further damage provided coverage is afforded for the peril causing the loss. This coverage does not increase the limit of liability applicable to the property being repaired.

3. **Trees, Shrubs and Other Plants** (Limited to Coverage A—Your Dwellings). We cover trees, shrubs, plants and lawns within 250 feet of the **dwelling premises** for loss caused by the following perils: fire or lightning, explosion, riot or civil commotion, aircraft, vehicles not owned or operated by a resident of the **dwelling premises,** vandalism or malicious mischief or theft. The limit of liability for this coverage shall not exceed five percent (5%) of the limit of liability specified for the Coverage A **dwelling** at the same **dwelling premises.** Our limit of liability for any one tree, shrub or plant is $500. We do not cover property grown for **business** or **farming** purposes under this paragraph.

This coverage shall not increase the applicable Coverage A limit under your policy.

4. **Refrigerated Products.** If Coverage C applies to your policy, we will pay an amount not to exceed $500 for loss or damage to contents of a freezer or refrigerator at the **residence premises.** This coverage does not apply to **farm personal property.** If a different amount is stated in the Declarations, that amount applies. The loss or damage must be caused by a change in temperature resulting from:

   a. Interruption of electrical service to refrigeration equipment caused by damage to the generating or transmission equipment which results in a breakdown in the system; or

   b. Mechanical or electrical breakdown of the refrigeration system.

You must exercise diligence in inspecting and maintaining refrigeration equipment in proper working condition. If interruption of electrical service, mechanical or electrical breakdown is known, you must exercise all reasonable means to protect the insured property from further damage.

5. **Fire Department Service Charge.** We will pay up to $300 for your liability assumed by contract or agreement for fire department charges incurred when the fire department is called to save or protect covered property from a peril insured against. No deductible applies to this coverage. Coverage afforded under this clause applies only if the covered property is not located within the limits of the city, municipality or protection district furnishing such fire department response. This coverage does not apply to property located in Arizona.

PERILS INSURED AGAINST—SECTION I

We cover for direct physical loss to property insured caused by the following perils:

1. **Fire** or **lightning.**
2. **Removal.**

   When property is removed because it is endangered by other insured perils, we pay for direct loss from any cause for accidental loss to that property while it is being removed and for thirty (30) days after removal to a proper place.

3. **Windstorm** or **hail.**

   a. This peril does **not** include loss to the interior or contents of a building caused by rain, snow, sleet, sand or dust unless the direct force of wind or hail damages the building causing an opening in a roof or wall through which the rain, snow, sleet, sand, or dust gets in;

   b. This peril does **not** include loss caused directly or indirectly by frost, cold weather, ice (other than hail), snowstorm or sleet, all whether driven by wind or not;

   c. This peril does **not** include loss to watercraft and their trailers, furnishings, equipment and outboard motors while outside a fully enclosed building.

4. **Explosion.**

  This peril does not include:

   a. Concussion unless caused by explosion;

   b. Electrical arcing;

   c. Water hammer;

   d. Rupture or bursting of steam boilers, steam pipes, steam turbines, steam engines, or water pipes, if owned by, leased or actually operated under the control of an **insured;** or

   e. Rupture or bursting due to expansion or swelling of the contents of any building or structure, caused by or resulting from water;

   f. Rupture or bursting of rotating parts of machinery caused by centrifugal force; or

   g. Shock waves caused by aircraft, including a sonic boom.

5. **Riot** or **civil commotion.**

6. **Aircraft,** including self-propelled missiles and spacecraft.

7. **Vehicles.**

  This peril does **not** cover loss:

   a. To a fence, driveway, walk, or structure insured under Coverage E, caused by a vehicle owned or operated by you, your employees or by a resident of the premises; or

b. To any **motor vehicle** or trailer.

NOTE: Loss by Perils 6 (Aircraft) and 7 (Vehicles) includes only direct loss by actual physical contact of an aircraft or vehicle with the covered property.

8. **Smoke,** meaning sudden and accidental damage from smoke.

This peril does **not** include loss caused by smoke from agricultural smudging or industrial operations.

9. **Vandalism or malicious mischief,** meaning only the willful and malicious damage to or destruction of the property covered.

This peril does **not** cover:

a. Loss if the **dwelling** has been vacant or unoccupied for more than thirty (30) consecutive days immediately before the loss. A **dwelling** being constructed is not considered vacant or unoccupied;

b. Wear and tear caused by tenants or members of their household.

10. **Theft,** including attempted theft and loss of property from a known location when it is likely that the property has been stolen.

Property of a student who is an **insured** is covered while at a residence away from home only if the student has been there at any time during the forty-five (45) days immediately before the loss.

The term "theft" shall **not** include escape, inventory shortage, wrongful conversion or embezzlement.

This peril does **not** include loss:

a. Committed by any **insured;**

b. In or to a building under construction;

c. Of materials, tools and supplies for use in the construction of a building until it is completed and occupied;

d. From any part of a **dwelling premises** rented by an **insured** to other than an **insured;**

e. Of property while in the custody of the postal service or similar government or private business;

f. Caused by tenants, their employees, or members of their households.

In the event of loss by theft, you shall give immediate notice to the nearest law enforcement officer. We will not pay any reward you offer for the return or recovery of any stolen property.

11. **Breakage of glass or safety glazing** material which is part of the covered building. This coverage extends to storm doors and storm windows in summer storage. This peril does **not** include loss if the building has been vacant more than thirty (30) consecutive days immediately before the loss. A building being constructed is not considered vacant.

12. **Weight of ice, snow,** or **sleet** which causes damage to a building or property contained in a building. This peril does **not** include loss to an awning, fence, patio, pavement, swimming pool, foundation, retaining wall, bulkhead, pier, wharf, or dock.

13. **Collapse** of a building or any part of a building.

This peril does **not** include loss to an awning, fence, patio, pavement, swimming pool, underground pipe, flue, drain, cesspool, septic tank, foundation, retaining wall, bulkhead, pier, wharf or dock unless the loss is a direct result of the collapse of a building. Collapse does **not** include: settling, cracking, shrinking, bulging or expansion.

14. **Accidental discharge or overflow** of water or steam from within a plumbing, heating or air conditioning system or from within a household appliance. We also pay for tearing out and replacing any part of the covered **dwelling** necessary to repair the system or appliance from which the water or steam escaped.

This peril does **not** include loss:

a. To a **dwelling** caused by continuous or repeated seepage or leakage for more than thirty (30) days;

b. On the **dwelling premises,** if the **dwelling** has been vacant for more than thirty (30) consecutive days immediately before the loss. A **dwelling** being constructed is not considered vacant;

c. To the system or appliance from which the water or steam escaped;

d. Caused by or resulting from freezing; or

e. On the **dwelling premises** caused by accidental discharge or overflow which occurs off the **dwelling premises.**

15. **Sudden or accidental tearing apart, cracking, burning** or **bulging** of a steam or hot water heating system, an air conditioning system, or an appliance for heating water.

We do **not** cover loss caused by or resulting from freezing under this peril.

16. **Falling objects.** This peril does **not** include loss to the interior of a building or property contained in the building unless the roof or an exterior wall of the building is first damaged by a falling object. This peril does not include loss to outdoor equipment, awnings, fences, and retaining walls. Damage to the falling object itself is not included.

17. **Freezing of a plumbing, heating or air conditioning** system or of a household appliance.

This peril does not include loss on the **dwelling premises** while the **dwelling** is vacant, unoccupied, or being constructed unless you have:

   a. Maintained heat in the building; or
   b. Shut off the water supply and drained the system and appliances of water.

18. **Sudden and accidental damage from artificially generated electrical current.**

This peril does **not** include loss to a tube, transistor or other electronic components.

19. **Collision with another object or overturn.** This peril does not apply to **livestock.** Impact with the ground or roadbed is not considered a collision.

20. **Electrocution.** This peril applies only to **livestock.**

21. **Attack by dogs or wild animals.** This peril applies only to **livestock.** It does **not** include attack by dogs owned by you or any person residing on the **insured location.**

22. **Accidental shooting.** This peril applies only to **livestock.** This peril does not include loss caused by any **insured,** employees of an **insured,** or persons residing on the **insured location.**

23. **Loading, unloading, collision or overturn while in transit.** This peril applies only to **livestock.** Impact with the ground or roadbed is not considered a collision.

24. **Drowning.** This peril applies only to **livestock** and excludes swine under thirty (30) days old and poultry.

25. **All risk.**

We insure for all risks of physical loss to the property insured **except:**

   a. Those losses excluded under **"Exclusions Applicable to Section I";**
   b. Freezing of a plumbing, heating or air conditioning system or of a household appliance, or by discharge, leakage or overflow from within the system or appliance caused by freezing, while the **dwelling** is vacant, unoccupied or being constructed unless you have used reasonable care to:
      (1) Maintain heat in the building; or
      (2) Shut off the water supply and drained the system and appliances of water.
   c. Freezing, thawing, pressure or weight of water or ice, whether driven by wind or not, to a fence, pavement, patio, swimming pool, foundation, retaining wall, bulkhead, pier, wharf or dock;
   d. Theft in or to a building under construction, or of materials, tools and supplies for use in the construction until the building is completed and occupied;
   e. Vandalism and malicious mischief or breakage of glass and safety glazing materials if the building has been vacant or unoccupied for more than thirty (30) consecutive days immediately before the loss. A building being constructed is not considered vacant or unoccupied;
   f. Continuous or repeated seepage or leakage of water or steam for more than thirty (30) days within a plumbing, heating or air conditioning system or from within a household appliance;
   g. Wear and tear; marring; deterioration; inherent vice; latent defect; mechanical breakdown; rust; mold; wet or dry rot; contamination; smog; smoke from agricultural smudging or industrial operations; settling, cracking, shrinking, bulging, or expansion of pavements,

patios, foundations, walls, floors, roofs or ceilings; loss caused by birds, vermin, rodents, insects or domestic animals. If any of these cause water to escape from a plumbing, heating or air conditioning system or household appliance, we cover loss caused by the water. We also cover the cost of tearing out and replacing any part of a building necessary to replace the system or appliance. We do **not** cover loss to the system or appliance from which this water escaped.

If Peril 25 applies to Coverage C, the following additional exclusions also apply:

h. Breakage of eye glasses, glassware, statuary, bric-a-brac, porcelains, and similar fragile articles, other than jewelry, watches, bronzes, cameras, and photographic lenses. These items are covered, however, if breakage results from Perils 1 through 10 or 13 through 16;

i. Dampness of atmosphere or extremes of temperature unless the direct cause of loss is rain, snow, sleet or hail;

j. Loss arising from refinishing, renovating or repairing property other than watches, jewelry and furs;

k. Collision other than collision with a land vehicle; sinking, swamping or stranding of watercraft, including their trailers, furnishings, equipment and outboard motors.

Under items g and a through d above any ensuing loss not excluded is covered.

EXCLUSIONS APPLICABLE TO SECTION I

We do not cover loss under Section I resulting directly or indirectly from:

1. **Ordinance or law,** meaning enforcement of any ordinance or law regulating the construction, repair, or demolition of a building or other structure, unless specifically provided under this policy.

2. **Earth movement,** including but not limited to earthquake, landslide, mudflow, earth sinking, rising or shifting. Direct loss by fire, explosion, theft, or breakage of glass or safety glazing materials resulting from earth movement is covered.

3. **Water damage,** meaning:

a. Flood, surface water, waves, tidal water, overflow of a body of water, or spray from any of these, whether or not driven by wind;

b. Water which backs up through sewers or drains;

c. Water below the surface of the ground, including water which exerts pressure on, or seeps or leaks through a building, sidewalk, driveway, foundation, swimming pool or other structure. Direct loss by fire, explosion or theft resulting from water damage is covered.

4. **Volcanic eruption.**

5. **Neglect,** meaning neglect of an **insured** to use all reasonable means to save and preserve property at and after the time of loss, or when property is endangered by a peril insured against.

6. **War,** including undeclared war, civil war, insurrection, rebellion, revolution, warlike act by military force or military personnel, destruction or seizure for use for any purpose by any governmental authority, and including any consequence of any of these. Discharge of a nuclear weapon shall be deemed a warlike act even if accidental.

7. **Power, heating or cooling failure** unless the failure results from physical damage to power, heating or cooling equipment situated on the **dwelling premises** where the loss occurs. This failure must be caused by a peril insured against.

8. **Depreciation, decay, deterioration, change in temperature or humidity, loss of market,** or from any other consequential or indirect loss of any kind.

9. **Any sound reproducing, receiving or transmitting equipment** designed for use as an eight-track player, cassette player, citizens band radio, two-way mobile radio or telephone, scanning monitor, radar detection or similar device, or any tape, wire, record, disc, or other medium for use with any such device while any of this property is in or upon any motorized vehicle, farm equipment, boat or aircraft, and capable of being operated by power supplied from these

vehicles. These devices are covered if factory installed in **mobile agricultural machinery** insured under Coverage D.

10. **Nuclear hazard,** meaning any nuclear reaction, radiation, or radioactive contamination, all whether controlled or uncontrolled or however caused, or any consequence of any of these. Loss caused by the nuclear hazard shall not be considered loss caused by fire, explosion, or smoke, whether these perils are specifically named or otherwise included within the perils insured against in Section I.

The above exclusions, 1 through 10, apply even if the following contribute to the loss: faulty, inadequate or defective planning; zoning; development; maintenance of property on or off the insured location by any person or organization.

11. **Any damage caused intentionally** by or at the direction of any **insured.**

CONDITIONS APPLICABLE TO SECTION I

1. **Insurable Interest and Limit of Liability.** Even if more than one person has an insurable interest in the property covered, we shall not be liable:
   a. To the **insured** for an amount greater than the **insured's** interest; nor
   b. For more than the applicable limit of liability.

2. **Your Duty after Loss.** In case of a loss to which this insurance may apply, you must see that the following duties are performed:
   a. Give written notice to us or our agent, as soon as practicable, and also give notice to the police if loss is suspected to be in violation of a law. In case of loss under the credit or bank card coverage, also notify the issuing card company;
   b. Protect the property from further damage, make reasonable and necessary repairs required to protect the property and keep an accurate record of repair expenditures;
   c. Prepare an inventory of damaged property showing in detail, the quantity, description, actual cash value and amount of loss. Attach to the inventory

all bills, receipts and related documents that substantiate the figures in the inventory;
   d. As often as we may reasonably require, exhibit the damaged property and submit to examination under oath and subscribe the same;
   e. Within sixty (60) days after our request, submit to us your signed, sworn statement of loss which sets forth the following information to the best of your knowledge and belief:
      (1) The time and cause of loss;
      (2) The interest of the **insured** and all others in the property involved and all encumbrances on the property;
      (3) Other insurance which may cover the loss;
      (4) Changes in title or occupancy of the property during the term of the policy;
      (5) Specifications of any damaged building and detailed estimates for repair of the damage;
      (6) An inventory of damaged property as described above;
      (7) Receipts for additional living expenses incurred and records supporting any fair rental value loss; and
      (8) Evidence or affidavit supporting a claim under the credit card or bank card coverage stating the amount and cause of loss.

3. **Loss Settlement.** Subject to the applicable limits stated in the Declarations, covered property losses are settled as follows:
   a. **Personal Property,** structures that are not buildings, **farm personal property,** and buildings insured under Coverage E, at actual cash value at the time of loss but not exceeding the amount necessary to repair or replace;
   b. Floor coverings, domestic appliances, awnings, outdoor antennas and outdoor equipment, whether or not attached to the buildings, at actual cash value at the time of loss but not exceeding the amount necessary to repair or replace;
   c. Buildings insured under Coverage A:
      (1) When the full cost of repair or replacement for loss to a building under Coverage A is

less than $1500, Coverage A is extended to include the full cost of repair or replacement without deduction for depreciation.

(2) If the limit of liability on the damaged building is less than 80% of its replacement cost at the time of the loss, we pay the larger of the following:

   (a) Actual cash value of the damaged part of the building; or

   (b) That proportion of the replacement cost of the damaged part which our limit of liability on the building bears to 80% of the full current cost of the building.

(3) If the limit of liability on the damaged building is at least 80% of its replacement cost at the time of loss we pay the full cost of repair or replacement of the damaged part without deduction for depreciation, but not more than the smallest of the following amounts:

   (a) The limit of liability applicable to the building;

   (b) The cost to repair or replace the damage on the same premises using materials of equivalent kind and quality to the extent practicable; or

   (c) The amount actually and necessarily spent to repair or replace the damage.

(4) When the cost to repair or replace exceeds 5% of the applicable limit of liability on the damaged building, we are not liable for more than the actual cash value of the loss until actual repair or replacement is completed. You may make a claim for the actual cash value amount of the loss before repairs are made. A claim for any additional amount payable under this provision must be made and construction started within one hundred and eighty (180) days after the loss.

4. **Increased Hazard.** We shall not be liable for any loss to property insured under this policy occurring while the hazard is increased by any means within the control or knowledge of any **insured.**

5. **Loss to a Pair or Set.** In case of a loss to a pair or set, we may elect to:

   a. Repair or replace any part or restore the pair or set to its value before the loss; or

   b. Pay the difference between the actual cash value of the property before and after the loss.

6. **Glass Replacement.** Covered loss for breakage of glass shall be settled on the basis of replacement with safety glazing materials when required by ordinance or law.

7. **Waiver of Subrogation.** You may waive in writing before a loss all right of recovery against any person. If not waived, we may require an assignment of rights for a loss to the extent that payment is made by us.

8. **Other Insurance.** If you are carrying other insurance on the property to which this policy applies, the coverage under this policy is null and void. We may permit other insurance, however, by endorsement to this policy. If other insurance is permitted, we will not be liable for a greater portion of any loss than our pro rata share in excess of any deductible.

9. **Vacancy.** When a building insured under this policy has been vacant, unoccupied or abandoned for a period of six (6) consecutive months at the initial inception date of this policy or any time after that, our liability is reduced fifty (50) percent. Outbuildings, which are in a seasonal state of vacancy or unoccupancy due to normal practices of **farming** operations, are not considered vacant or unoccupied as defined in the policy and therefore, our liability is not reduced under the provisions of this clause.

ENDORSEMENTS APPLICABLE TO SECTION I

Each of the following endorsements may be purchased by your payment of an additional premium. All policy provisions apply to these endorsements unless an endorsement specifically states otherwise. **An**

endorsement applies only when it is listed in the Declarations and you pay this premium.

No. 111 Replacement Cost—Personal Property.

Losses under Coverage C shall be settled at replacement cost without deduction for depreciation.

Property Not Eligible

Property listed below is not eligible for replacement cost settlement. Any loss shall be settled at actual cash value at the time of loss but not exceeding the amount necessary to repair or replace.

1. Antiques, fine arts, paintings, statues and other articles which by their inherent nature cannot be replaced with new articles.

2. Articles whose age or history contribute substantially to their value, including but not limited to memorabilia, souvenirs, and collectors items.

3. Personal property of others.

4. Articles not maintained in good or workable condition.

5. Articles that are outdated or obsolete and are stored or not being used.

Replacement Cost

1. We will pay not more than the smallest of the following amounts:

 a. Replacement cost at time of loss without deduction for depreciation;

 b. The full cost of repair at time of loss;

 c. 400% of the actual cash value at time of loss;

 d. Any special limit of liability applicable under Coverage C; or

 e. The total limit of liability applicable to Coverage C.

2. When the replacement cost for the entire loss under this endorsement exceeds $500, we will pay no more than the actual cash value for the loss or damage until the actual repair or replacement is completed.

3. You may make a claim for loss on an actual cash value basis and then make claim within 180 days after the loss for any additional liability in accordance with this endorsement.

4. This endorsement also covers domestic appliances, floor coverings, awnings, outdoor antennas, and outdoor equipment pertaining to a **dwelling** insured under Coverage A.

No. 114 Borrowed Equipment Endorsement.

We cover under Coverage D loss to **mobile agricultural machinery** in which you have no interest, provided such machinery has been borrowed by either you or **your employees** and is actually being used in the conduct of your own farm operation, is not available for your regular use, and is not used on a cooperative exchange basis. This coverage, however, shall apply as excess over any insurance which the owner has on this borrowed property. Our limit of liability per **occurrence** under this endorsement is stated in the Declarations.

No. 120 Inflation Guard Endorsement.

It is agreed that the Limit of Liability specified in the Declarations for Section I—Property under Coverage A (Dwelling), Coverage B (Additional Living Expense) and Coverage C (Personal Property), shall be increased at the same rate as the increase in the Company Index as developed monthly from available Governmental and Appraisal Company Indices and kept on file in the Home Office.

In no event will the limit of liability be less than the amount specified in the Declarations.

At each renewal date after this endorsement becomes effective, the amount of insurance on the above coverages will be corrected to the nearest $100 in accordance with the above factor and renewal premium will be adjusted accordingly.

No. 130 Elimination of Livestock under Coverage D.

There is no coverage for livestock under Coverage D.

No. 171 Glass Deductible Waived.

No deductible will apply to glass breakage to the building(s) insured under Coverage A of Section I.

No. 183 Guaranteed Replacement Cost Endorsement.

We agree that our limit of liability for buildings insured under Coverage A is not limited by the amount shown on the Declarations page provided:

1. You have insured your **dwelling** and other structures to 100% of their replacement costs as we determine based on the accuracy of information you furnish, and you pay the premium we require;

2. You accept the property insurance adjustment condition in paragraph 1 above, agree to accept any annual adjustment, and pay the additional premium charged;

3. You notify us within ninety (90) days of the start of any additions or other physical changes which increase the value of your **dwelling** or other structures on the dwelling premises by $5,000.00 or more, and pay the additional premium charged.

Losses under this endorsement are covered for the full cost of repair or replacement of the damaged part without deduction for depreciation, but not more than the amount actually and necessarily spent to repair or replace the damage on the same premises using materials of equivalent kind and quality to the extent practical.

Parts c(1), (2) and (3) of the loss settlement clause of "Conditions Applicable to Section I" are deleted. This endorsement is void if you fail to comply with its provisions.

SECTION II—YOUR LIABILITY PROTECTION

COVERAGE F

Liability

If a claim is made or a suit is brought against any **insured** for damages because of **bodily injury** or **property damage** caused by an **occurrence** to which this coverage applies, we will:

1. Pay up to our limit of liability for the damages for which the **insured** is legally liable;

2. Provide a defense at our expense by counsel of our choice. We may make any investigation and settlement of any claim or suit that we decide is appropriate. Our obligation to defend any claim or suit ends when the amount we pay for damages equals our limit of liability.

COVERAGE G

Premises Medical

We will pay the necessary medical and funeral expenses incurred within three years from the date of an **occurrence** causing **bodily injury.** This coverage does not apply to you or regular residents of your household other than **residence employees.** As to others, this coverage applies only:

1. To a person on the **insured location** with the permission of any **insured;** or

2. To a person off the **insured location,** if the **bodily injury:**

   a. Arises out of a condition in the **insured location** or the ways immediately adjoining;

   b. Is caused by the activities of any **insured;**

   c. Is caused by the activities of a **farm** or **residence employee** in the course of employment by an **insured;**

   d. Is caused by an animal owned by or in the care of any **insured;**

   e. Is sustained by any **residence employee** and arises out of and in the course of employment.

No payment shall be made under Coverage G unless the person to or for whom such payment is made shall have signed an agreement that the amount of such payment shall be applied toward the settlement of any claim, or the satisfaction of any judgment for damages entered in the person's favor against any **insured** because of **bodily injury** to which Coverage F of this policy applies. (This paragraph is not applicable if this policy is issued in Arizona.)

COVERAGE H

Employer's Liability

If a claim is made or suit brought against you or your **relatives** because of **bodily injury** caused by an **occurrence** sustained by any **farm employee** arising out of and in the course of employment by you, we will:

1. Pay up to our limit of liability for the damages for which you are legally liable;

2. Provide a defense at our expense by counsel of our choice. We may make any investigation and settle any claim or suit that we decide is appropriate. Our obligation to defend any claim or suit ends when the amount we pay for damages resulting from the **occurrence** equals our limit of liability.

COVERAGE I

Medical Payments for Farm Employees

We will pay the necessary **medical** and funeral expenses incurred within three years from the date of **occurrence** to or for each **farm employee** who sustains **bodily injury** caused by an **occurrence** arising out of and in the course of employment by you.

No payment shall be made under Coverage I unless the person to or for whom such payment is made shall have signed an agreement that the amount of such payment shall be applied toward the settlement of any claim, or the satisfaction of any judgment for damages entered in the person's favor because of **bodily injury** to which Coverage H of this policy applies.

COVERAGE J

Medical Payments (Named Persons)

We will pay the necessary **medical** and funeral expenses incurred within three years from the date of **occurrence** to or for each person named in Coverage J of the Declarations, who sustains **bodily injury** caused by an **occurrence.**

No payment shall be made under Coverage J unless the person to or for whom such payment is made shall have signed an agreement that the amount of such payment shall be applied toward the settlement of any claim, or the satisfaction of any judgment for damages entered in the person's favor against any **insured** because of **bodily injury** to which Coverage F or H of this policy applies.

COVERAGE K

Death of Livestock by Collision

We will pay, subject to the limits of liability stated in the Declarations, for loss by death of any cattle, horse, or hybrid thereof, hog, sheep or goat owned by you and not otherwise covered, caused by collision between such animal and a **motor vehicle,** provided:

1. The **motor vehicle** is not owned or operated by an **insured** or any **insured's** employee;

2. The animal is within a public highway and is not being transported;

3. Death to the animal occurs within fifteen days after the date of the collision.

We further extend this coverage to include the death of livestock when killed by any train, provided you first present a claim in your name to the railroad company involved.

COVERAGE L

Custom Farming

Coverage F also covers your **custom farming.**

Coverage L does **not** apply to:

1. Any damage or injury to the land or crops upon which the **custom farming** is performed or is to be performed, arising from:

    a. The mixing or application of fertilizers, herbicides, pesticides, fungicides, or other chemical treatment of real property, seeds or crops;

    b. Any goods, products, or their containers manufactured, sold, handled or distributed by or on behalf of any **insured.**

2. Injury or damage resulting from:

    a. A delay in or lack of performance by or on behalf of any **insured** of any contract or agreement, written or oral; or

    b. The failure of any **insured's** products or work performed by or on behalf of any **insured** to meet the level of performance, quality, fitness or result warranted or represented by any **insured.**

COVERAGE M

Damage to Property of Others

We will pay for **property damage** to property of others caused by an **insured.** We will not pay for **property damage:**

1. Caused intentionally by any **insured** who is thirteen (13) years of age or older;

2. To property owned by or rented to any **insured,** a tenant of any **insured,** or a resident of any **insured's** household; or

3. Arising out of:

   a. Any **business;**

   b. The ownership, maintenance, use, loading or unloading of a **motor vehicle,** watercraft, or aircraft;

   c. Theft, mysterious disappearance, or loss of use;

   d. Mechanical or electrical breakdown, wear and tear, latent defect or inherent vice;

4. To tires.

Coverage M is subject only to the above exclusions and not to the general exclusions applicable to Section II.

Limit of Liability. Our limit of liability under Coverage M for **property damage** arising out of any **occurrence** shall not exceed the lesser of:

1. The actual cash value of the damaged property at the time of the loss; or

2. What it would then cost to repair or replace the damaged property with other of like kind and quality; or

3. The limit of liability stated in the Declarations for Coverage M.

If Section I of this policy also applies to a loss under Coverage M, Section I is primary and Coverage M is excess. You must pay any applicable Section I deductible before Coverage M applies.

We may pay for the loss in money or may repair or replace the property and may settle the claim for loss to property either with the owner or with you. Any property paid for or replaced shall, at our option, become our property.

We have no obligation under Coverage M to provide a defense against any claim or suit brought against any insured.

SECTION II—ADDITIONAL COVERAGES

Section II includes the following:

1. **Fire Legal Liability.** Coverage F is extended to cover **property damage** to a lodging place and its furnishings rented to, occupied or used by or in the care of an **insured** if such **property damage** arises out of fire, smoke or explosion. For purposes of this fire legal coverage, **insured** shall include only you and those persons listed in Paragraphs (1) and (2) of the definition of **insured.** The care, custody and control exclusion does not apply to this extension of coverage.

2. **Newly Acquired Locations.** Section II is extended to cover locations you acquire by ownership or leasehold if similar to premises or **dwellings** described in the Declarations, if you notify us of these acquisitions on or prior to the next renewal date of this policy. The insurance afforded to these acquisitions is limited to the insurance applicable to the locations already described in the Declarations.

This extension of coverage does not apply to loss for which you have other valid and collectible insurance. You must pay any additional premium required because of the application of this insurance to such newly acquired locations.

SECTION II—ADDITIONAL PAYMENTS

Under Coverages F and H, we will pay the following expenses in addition to our limits of liability, but our obligation for these payments ceases when our obligation to defend ends:

1. Expenses for first aid to others incurred by any **insured** for **bodily injury** covered under this policy. We will not pay for first aid to you or any other **insured;**

2. Expenses incurred by us and costs taxed against any **insured** in any suit we defend;

3. Premiums on bonds required in a suit defended by us, but not for bond amounts greater than the limit of liability provided by this policy. We are not obligated

to apply for or furnish any bond;

4. Reasonable expenses incurred by any **insured** at our request, including actual loss of earnings (but not loss of other income) up to $50 per day for assisting us in the investigation or defense of any claim or suit;

5. Interest on the entire judgment which accrues after entry of that part of the judgment which does not exceed the limit of liability that applies and before we pay, tender or deposit in court that part of the judgment which does not exceed the limit of liability that applies.

EXCLUSIONS APPLICABLE TO SECTION II

The following exclusions apply to all coverages under Section II except Coverage M. Section II does not cover **bodily injury** or **property damage:**

1. Arising from any **insured's business** activities or any professional service;

2. Arising from any location which an **insured** owns, rents, leases, or controls, other than an **insured location.** This exclusion does not apply to **bodily injury** of **residence employees** arising out of and in the course of employment by an **insured;**

3. Which is intentionally caused by any **insured;**

4. Arising from the maintenance, operation, use, loading or unloading of any of the following which any **insured** owns, borrows, rents, leases or operates:

   a. Any aircraft, except model aircraft of the hobby variety not used or designed for the transportation of people or cargo;

   b. Any **motor vehicle,** coverage however, applies on the **insured location** if the **motor vehicle** is not licensed for road use because it is used exclusively on the **insured location;**

   c. Any watercraft:

      (1) If powered by an inboard or inboard-outboard motor of more than fifty (50) horsepower;

      (2) If a sailing vessel twenty-six (26) feet or more in overall length.

      Exclusion 4.c. does not apply while the watercraft is stored on the **insured location.**

   d. Any **recreational vehicle** if the **bodily injury** or **property damage** occurs away from the **insured location.** Exclusion 4.d. does not apply to golf carts while used for golfing purposes.

   Exclusions 4.c. and 4.d. do not apply to watercraft or **recreational vehicles** borrowed or rented by an **insured** for less than 10 days. Damage to the borrowed or rented **recreational vehicle** or watercraft, however, is not covered. Exclusion 4 does not apply to **bodily injury** sustained by a **residence employee** in the course of employment.

5. Arising out of the use of any aircraft, **motor vehicle, mobile agricultural machinery,** watercraft or **recreational vehicle,** while being used in or following any prearranged or organized racing, speed or stunting activity or in practice or preparation for any such contest or activity;

6. Which results from liability arising out of any contract or agreement;

7. Arising out of **custom farming** when total receipts exceed $10,000 in a calendar year. This exclusion does not apply if coverage is indicated under Coverage L in the Declarations;

8. Caused by or resulting from declared or undeclared war, civil war, insurrection, rebellion, revolution, warlike act by a military force or military personnel, destruction or seizure or use for any government purpose, and including any consequence of these. Discharge of a nuclear weapon shall be deemed a warlike act even if accidental;

9. Resulting from any act or omission of a **residence** or **farm employee** who is also an **insured** while away from the **insured location,** if the employee is under the control and direction of some person other than an **insured;**

10. Caused by a substance released or discharged from an aircraft owned or operated by an **insured** in connection with dusting or spraying operations;

11. Caused by any goods, products or containers manufactured, processed, sold, handled or distributed by an **insured,** except farm products raised on the **insured location.** Loss arising out of the failure of seed sold by

an **insured** to conform to the variety, purpose or quality specified by the insured, however, is not covered. The term "seed" means seeds, bulbs, plants, roots, tubers, cuttings or other similar means of plant propagation;

12. Arising out of the discharge, dispersal, release or escape of smoke, vapors, soot, fumes, acids, alkalis, toxic chemicals, liquids or gases, waste materials or other irritants, contaminants, or pollutants into or upon land, the atmosphere or any water course or body of water. This exclusion does not apply to:

  a. Crop damage resulting from the accidental above ground contact with herbicides, pesticides, fungicides and fertilizers caused by the application of the same to an insured site which results in actual damages within one growing season of said application.

  b. Bodily injury resulting from the accidental above ground contact with herbicides, pesticides, fungicides and fertilizers caused by the application of the same to an insured site which results in medical treatment within one year (365 days) of said application.

13. Sustained by you or any **insured** as defined in paragraphs (1) and (2) of the definition of **insured;**

14. Arising out of a violation of a criminal law, except traffic violations, if committed by any **insured;** or

15. With respect to which any **insured** under this policy is also an **insured** under a nuclear energy liability policy issued by a nuclear energy liability insurance association, mutual atomic energy liability underwriters, nuclear insurance association of Canada, or any similar organization, or would be an **insured** under any such policy but for its termination upon exhaustion of its limits of liability;

16. Arising out of the entrustment by the **insured** of a **motor vehicle** to any person; coverage, however, applies on the **insured location** if the **motor vehicle** is not licensed for road use because it is used exclusively on the **insured location.**

Exclusion 16 does not apply to bodily injury sustained by a residence employee in the course of employment.

Section II does not cover:

17. Property owned by, used by, rented to, or in the care, custody or control of any **insured** or his employees, or as to which any **insured** or his employees exercise physical control for any purpose (This exclusion is the care, custody and control exclusion referred to in **Section II Additional Coverages—Fire Legal Liability.**);

18. Any **property damage** to work completed by or for an **insured,** any damage arising out of such work, or out of the materials, parts, or equipment furnished in connection with such work;

19. Any **property damage** to goods or products, including containers, which an **insured** manufactures, sells, handles, raises or distributes;

20. Damages claimed for the withdrawal, inspection, repair, replacement, or loss of use of your products, or work completed by or for you or for any property of which such products or work form a part, if such products, work or property are withdrawn from the market or from use because of any known or suspected defect or deficiency;

21. Punitive or exemplary damages;

22. **Bodily injury** to any person eligible to receive any benefits required to be provided or voluntarily provided by any **insured** under any worker's compensation, non-occupational disease, disability or occupational disease law;

23. **Property damage** to an **insured location** arising out of the alienation (for example, selling, leasing, separating, etc.) of that location;

24. **Bodily injury** under Coverage G sustained by any person residing on the **insured location** except a **residence employee;**

25. Under Coverages G, I and J:

  a. **Bodily injury** involving hernia or back injury, unless it is of recent origin, it is accompanied by pain, it was immediately preceded by some accidental strain suffered in the course of employment, and it did not exist prior to the date of the alleged injury;

  b. Any person while conducting his **business** on the **insured location,** including the employees of that person;

   c. **Bodily injury** to the extent that any medical expenses are paid or payable under the provision of any:

     (1) Auto or premises insurance;

     (2) Accident, disability, or hospitalization insurance;

     (3) Medical or surgical reimbursement plan prepaid or otherwise;

     (4) National, state or other governmental plan; or

     (5) Worker's compensation or similar law.

26. Under Coverages F and G, **bodily injury** sustained by any **farm employee** arising out of employment;

27. Loss of use of property which has not been physically injured or destroyed, resulting from:

   a. A delay in or lack of performance by or on your behalf of any contract or agreement; or

   b. The failure of your products or work performed by or on your behalf to meet the level of performance, quality, fitness or durability warranted or represented by you;

28. **Bodily injury** or **property damage** which arises out of the transmission of:

   a. Acquired Immune Deficiency Syndrome (AIDs); or

   b. Genital herpes, syphilis, gonorrhea or other venereal disease caused wholly or in part by the acts of an **insured, farm employee,** or **residence employee;**

29. Any **bodily injury** sustained by any person arising out of or resulting from the molesting of minors by:

   1) any **insured,**

   2) any **farm employee** or **residence employee** of any **insured,** or

   3) any volunteer

We shall not have any duty to defend any suit against the **insured** seeking damages on account of such **bodily injury.**

CONDITIONS APPLICABLE TO SECTION II

1. **Duties after Loss.** In case of an accident or **occurrence,** the **insured** shall perform the following duties:

   a. Give written notice to us or our agent as soon as practicable, which sets forth:

     (1) The identity of the policy and **insured;**

     (2) Reasonable available information on the time, place and circumstances of the accident or **occurrence;**

     (3) Names and addresses of any claimants and witnesses.

   b. Immediately forward to us every notice, demand, summons or other process relating to the accident or **occurrence;**

   c. At our request, assist in:

     (1) Making settlement;

     (2) The enforcement of any right of contribution or indemnity against any person or organization who may be liable to any **insured;**

     (3) The conduct of suits and attend hearings and trials;

     (4) Securing and giving evidence and obtaining the attendance of witnesses.

   d. The **insured** shall not, except at the **insured's** own cost, voluntarily make any payment, assume any obligation or incur any expense other than for first aid to others at the time of the **bodily injury;**

   e. Under Coverage M—Damage to the Property of Others—submit to us within 60 days after the loss, a sworn statement of loss and exhibit the damaged property, if within the **insured's** control.

2. **Duties of an Injured Person**—Coverages G, I and J. The injured person or someone acting on behalf of the injured person shall:

   a. Give us a written proof of claim, under oath if required, as soon as practicable;

   b. Execute authorization to allow us to obtain copies of medical reports and records; and

   c. Submit to physical examination by a physician selected by us when and as often as we reasonably require.

3. **Cooperation of Insured**—If any **insured** fails to cooperate with us or send us legal papers as required,

we have the right to refuse any further coverage for the **occurrence** or loss.

4. **Payment of Claim.** Any payment under Section II is not an admission of liability by any **insured** or us.

5. **Limits of Liability**—Coverages F and H.

Regardless of the number of:

(a) **insureds** under this policy,

(b) persons or organizations sustaining **bodily injury** or **property damage,** or

(c) claims made,

our liability for each **occurrence** is subject to the following limitations:

a. Our total combined single limit of liability under Coverage F for all **bodily injury** and **property damage** resulting from one **occurrence** shall not exceed the applicable limit of liability stated in the Declarations.

b. Our total limit of liability under Coverage H for all **bodily injury** resulting from one **occurrence** shall not exceed the applicable limit stated in the Declarations.

c. **Products Liability Limits.** The per **occurrence** combined single limit of liability for **bodily injury** and **property damage** caused by farm products produced on the **insured location** is also the total limit of our liability for all such **occurrences** during the policy period.

6. **Limits of Liability**—Coverages G, I and J. The limit of liability for Coverages G, I and J as stated in the Declarations as applicable to each person is our limit of liability for all expenses incurred by or on behalf of each person who sustains **bodily injury** resulting from an **occurrence.** Subject to the limit of liability for each person, our total limit of liability for each occurrence for **bodily injury** sustained by two or more persons is the per **occurrence** limit of liability stated in the Declarations.

7. **Other Insurance**—The insurance under Section II is excess over any other valid and collectible insurance except insurance written specifically to cover as excess over the limits of liability that apply in this policy.

ENDORSEMENTS APPLICABLE TO SECTION II

Each of the following endorsements may be purchased by your payment of an additional premium. All policy provisions apply to these endorsements unless an endorsement specifically states otherwise. **An endorsement applies only when it is listed in the Declarations and you pay this premium.**

No. 204 Employer's Nonownership Liability Endorsement.

We agree that Coverage F of Section II covers the liability of you and any of your executive officers arising out of the use of any **nonowned motor vehicle** used in your farm or household **business** by any person other than you.

1. **Definitions.**

In this endorsement only, **nonowned motor vehicle** means a land motor vehicle, trailer or semitrailer not owned by, registered in the name of, hired or leased by, or loaned to you.

2. **Application of Insurance.**

a. This endorsement does not apply to any **motor vehicle** owned by any of your executive officers or their spouses.

b. This insurance does not apply to any **motor vehicle** owned by or registered in the name of a partner if your **business** is in the form of a partnership.

3. **Other Insurance.**

This insurance shall be excess insurance over any other valid and collectible insurance.

SECTION III—AUTOMOBILE

DEFINITIONS

The following definitions apply to Section III:

Throughout this section, we, us, and our mean the Company named in the Declarations. You and your mean the person named in the Declarations and that person's spouse if a resident of the same household. You and your also refer to a partnership, corporation, estate, or trust named in the Declarations.

Bodily Injury means physical injury or death to a person caused by an occurrence.

Insured means:

1. Under Coverages N, R, S and T with respect to an **insured vehicle:**

    a. You and any **relative;**

    b. Anyone using an **insured vehicle** within the scope of your permission or within the scope of permission of your adult **relative;**

    c. Any person or organization legally responsible for the **insured vehicle,** provided the use of the **insured vehicle** is by you or with your permission and within the scope of such permission.

2. Under Coverage N with respect to a **nonowned vehicle,** you or your **relatives** when operating a **nonowned vehicle,** or when that vehicle is operated by your agent and with your permission and within the scope of such permission.

Insured Vehicle means:

1. Any vehicle shown in the Declarations;

2. Under Coverages N, P and Q, any private passenger automobile, pickup, panel truck, farm truck, van, motorcycle or motorhome, ownership of which is acquired by you during the policy period;

3. If you have Coverages S and T, any private passenger automobile, pickup, panel truck, farm truck, **trailer,** camper, van or motorhome, ownership of which is acquired by you during the policy period provided the vehicle falls within the year model limitation indicated in the Declarations.

The vehicles in 2 and 3 above are not insured vehicles unless we insure all of your vehicles and you ask us to insure the newly acquired vehicle during the policy period or within 30 days of its acquisition, whichever is shorter. A newly acquired vehicle includes a vehicle which replaces one shown in the Declarations.

4. A **temporary substitute vehicle** which is a **motor vehicle** or **trailer** you do not own while temporarily used as a substitute for a vehicle described in the Declarations when that vehicle cannot be used because of breakdown or servicing;

5. Under Coverage N only, any **trailer** while attached to a vehicle described in the Declarations. Also included is a **trailer** while being used with a **temporary substitute vehicle.**

Medical Expenses means reasonable charges for medical, surgical, x-ray, dental, ambulance, hospital, professional nursing, and prosthetic devices.

Motor Vehicle means a motorized land vehicle designed principally for travel on public roads. The term **motor vehicle** does not include a **trailer.**

Nonowned Vehicle means a **trailer** or **motor vehicle** not exceeding two-tons in capacity operated by you or your **relatives** or in the custody of you or your **relatives** provided the actual use is with the permission of the owner. This vehicle must not be owned by you or your **relatives** or be available for regular use by you or your **relatives.**

Occupying means in, on or getting in or out of.

Occurrence means an accident arising out of the ownership, maintenance or use of a **motor vehicle,** including continuous or repeated exposure to conditions, which results in unexpected **bodily injury** or **property damage** during the policy period. All **bodily injury** and **property damage** resulting from a common cause shall be considered the result of one **occurrence.**

Property Damage means injury to or destruction of tangible property caused by an **occurrence.**

Relative means a person related to you by blood, marriage or adoption who is a resident of your household, including a ward or foster child.

Trailer means a vehicle designed for towing by a private passenger automobile or farm truck. It also includes a farm wagon, farm semi-trailer or farm implement while towed by an **insured vehicle. Trailer** does not include vehicles used:

1. To haul passengers;

2. As an office, store or for display purposes;

3. As a permanent residence.

SECTION III COVERAGES
COVERAGE N
Liability

If a claim is made or a suit is brought against any **insured** for damages because of **bodily injury** or **property damage** arising out of an **occurrence** involving an **insured vehicle** or a **nonowned vehicle,** we will:

1. Pay up to our limit of liability for the damages for which the **insured** is legally liable;
2. Provide a defense at our expense by counsel of our choice. We may make any investigation and settlement of any claim or suit that we decide is appropriate. Our obligation to defend any claim or suit ends when the amount we pay for damages equals our limit of liability.

Additional Payments

We will pay the following in addition to our limits of liability, but our obligation for these payments ceases when our obligation to defend ends:

1. Expenses for first aid to others incurred by any **insured** for **bodily injury** covered under this policy. We will not pay for first aid to you or any other **insured;**
2. Expenses incurred by us and costs taxed against any **insured** in any suit we defend;
3. Premiums on bonds required in a suit defended by us, but not for bond amounts greater than the limit of liability provided by this policy. We will also pay up to $250 for the premium of any bail bond required of an **insured** because of an arrest in connection with an accident resulting from the use of an **insured vehicle.** We are not obligated to apply for or furnish any bond;
4. Reasonable expenses incurred by any **insured** at our request, including actual loss of earnings (but not loss of other income) up to $50 per day for assisting us in the investigation or defense of any claim or suit;
5. Interest on the entire judgment which accrues after entry of that part of the judgment which does not exceed the limit of liability that applies and before we pay, tender or deposit in court that part of the judgment, which does not exceed the limit of liability that applies.

COVERAGE P
Uninsured Motorist

See the back pages of this Section III entitled "Uninsured Motorist Coverage".

COVERAGE Q
Medical Payments

We will pay the necessary **medical** and funeral expenses incurred within three (3) years from the date of **occurrence** to each **insured** who sustains **bodily injury** caused by an **occurrence.**

The following are **insureds** under Coverage Q:

1. You or any person **occupying** an **insured vehicle** with your permission or the permission of an adult **relative** and sustaining **bodily injury** caused by an **occurrence** resulting from the use of this **insured vehicle;**
2. You or your **relatives** sustaining **bodily injury** caused by an **occurrence** while **occupying** a **nonowned vehicle;**
3. Any person sustaining **bodily injury** while **occupying** a **nonowned vehicle,** if the **bodily injury** results from:
   a. Its operation by you or on your behalf by a private chauffeur or domestic servant;
   b. Its operation by a **relative.**
4. You and your **relatives** sustaining **bodily injury** while a pedestrian or a bicyclist when struck by a **motor vehicle** or **trailer.**

No payment shall be made under this coverage unless the person to or for whom such payment is made shall first execute a written agreement that the amount of the payment shall be applied toward the settlement of any claim, or the satisfaction of any judgment of damages entered in the person's favor against any **insured** because of **bodily injury** to which Coverage N or P of this policy applies. (This paragraph is not applicable if this policy is issued in Arizona.)

COVERAGE R

Fire and Theft Only

We will pay for any direct and accidental loss of, or damage to, your **insured vehicle** and its equipment caused by:

1. Fire, lightning or windstorm;
2. Smoke or smudge due to a sudden, unusual and faulty operation of any heating equipment serving the premises in which the vehicle is located;
3. The stranding, sinking, burning, collision or derailment of any conveyance in or upon which the vehicle is being transported; or
4. Theft.

If Coverage R applies to your **insured vehicle,** it will also extend to a **nonowned vehicle.**

COVERAGE S

Comprehensive

We will pay for any direct and accidental loss of, or damage to, your **insured vehicle** and its equipment not caused by collision or rollover. Loss or damage from missiles, falling objects, theft, collision with animals, or accidental glass breakage are comprehensive losses.

If Coverage S applies to your **insured vehicle,** it will also extend to a **nonowned vehicle.**

COVERAGE T

Collision and Roll Over

We will pay for direct and accidental loss to your **insured vehicle** and its equipment when it is hit by or hits another vehicle, or object, or rolls over. We will waive any applicable deductible if the collision involves **insured vehicles** of two or more of our policyholders. If Coverage T applies to your **insured vehicle,** it will also extend to a **nonowned vehicle.**

Additional Payments

1. **Loss to Luggage.**

If as a result of other loss covered under Coverages R, S or T, damage results to clothing or personal luggage, including contents of the luggage being transported by the insured vehicle, we will pay up to $200 for this loss. Exclusion 13 does not apply to this coverage.

2. **Loss of Use by Theft—Reimbursement.**

Following a theft of an **insured vehicle** covered under Coverage R or S, we will reimburse you for expenses up to $25 a day to a maximum of $500 incurred for the rental of a substitute automobile including taxi cabs. This reimbursement is limited to such expense incurred during the period commencing 48 hours after the theft has been reported to us and the police, and terminating, regardless of expiration of the policy period, on the date the automobile is returned to you and on such earlier date as we make or offer settlement for this theft.

EXCLUSIONS APPLICABLE TO SECTION III

Section III does not cover:

1. Any **insured** while using any vehicle to carry persons for a fee. This exclusion does not apply to a share-the-expense car pool;
2. Any **insured** for any vehicle rented or leased to others;
3. Any **insured** while using any vehicle in a prearranged race, speed contest, or other competition, or preparation for any of these activities;
4. Any damages which are intentionally caused by any **insured;**
5. Any **nonowned vehicle** while an **insured** is using it in the business of selling, repairing, servicing, storing or parking **motor vehicles,** including road testing and delivery;
6. Any damage caused by nuclear reaction, radiation, or radioactive contamination;
7. Any radar or similar detection device; any device or instrument designed for the recording, reproduction, amplification, receiving, or transmitting of sound, radio waves, microwaves, or television signals; or tapes, records, or other discs designed for use with this equipment. This exclusion does not apply to a

device or instrument if it is permanently installed in the dash or console opening;

8. Damages caused by declared or undeclared war, invasion, insurrection, civil war, other assumption of power, or confiscation by a duly constituted governmental or civil authority;

9. Exemplary or punitive damages;

10. **Bodily injury** to anyone eligible to receive benefits which an **insured** either provides or is required to provide under any worker's compensation or occupational disease law;

11. Any damages arising out of the ownership, maintenance or use of any type of emergency vehicle; gas, oil, or newspaper delivery truck; logging truck; or any non-farm commercial truck;

12. Under Coverage N, **bodily injury** sustained by:

   a. You;

   b. The operator of the **insured vehicle,** or the residents of the operator's household who are related to the operator by blood, marriage or adoption, including a ward or foster child.

13. Under Coverage N, damage to property owned or transported by any **insured;**

14. Under Coverage N, damage to property rented to, used by, or in the care, custody or control of an **insured.** This exclusion does not apply to **property damage** to a residence or private garage rented to an **insured;**

15. Under Coverages N, and P, liability arising out of any contract or agreement;

16. Under Coverage Q, **bodily injury** sustained while an **insured vehicle** is used as a residence or temporary living quarters;

17. Under Coverage Q, **bodily injury** sustained by a person engaged in the maintenance or repair of an **insured vehicle;**

18. Under Coverage Q, **bodily injury** to anyone eligible to receive benefits under any:

   a. Automobile or premises insurance affording benefits for medical expenses;

   b. Worker's compensation, disability benefits or similar law;

   c. National, state or other governmental plan.

19. Under Coverages R, S and T, any loss by collapse, explosion or implosion of any tank or container;

20. Under Coverages R, S and T, any equipment or accessories contained in a motorhome, camper unit or trailer unless the equipment or accessories are built in and form a permanent part of the vehicle;

21. Under Coverages, R, S and T, loss caused by recall of an **insured vehicle;**

22. Tires, unless damaged concurrent with other loss covered under Coverages R, S, or T;

23. Damages caused by wear and tear, freezing, mechanical or electrical breakdown or failure other than burning of wiring, unless the damage results from other loss covered under Coverages R, S, or T.

CONDITIONS APPLICABLE TO SECTION III

1. **Out of State Insurance.** If you have liability insurance under this policy and if you are traveling in a state or province which has a compulsory insurance, financial responsibility, or similar law affecting nonresidents, we will automatically provide the legally required minimum amounts and types of coverages if your policy does not already provide these coverages, or the limits stated in the Declarations whichever are greater, with respect to the operation or use of the insured vehicle in that state or province. The required coverage, however, will be excess over any other collectible insurance.

2. **Two or More Vehicles.** When two or more vehicles are covered by this policy, the policy terms will apply separately to each. A vehicle, however, and an attached **trailer** will be considered one vehicle under Coverages N, P and Q and separate vehicles under Coverages R, S and T; any deductible will be applied to each vehicle.

The maximum limits of liability set forth in Paragraphs 3 and 10 of these conditions shall not be increased in any way by this paragraph.

3. **Other Vehicle Insurance in the Company.** If this policy and any other vehicle insurance policy issued to

you by this company apply to the same **occurrence,** the maximum limit of our liability under all of the policies will not exceed the highest applicable limit of liability under any one policy. This is the most we will pay regardless of the number of **insureds,** claims made, **insured vehicles** or premiums.

4. **Duties after Loss.** In case of an accident or **occurrence,** the **insured** shall perform the following duties:

a. Give written notice to us or our agent as soon as practicable, which sets forth:

(1) The identity of the policy and **insured;**

(2) Reasonably available information on the time, place and circumstances of the accident or **occurrence;**

(3) Names and addresses of any claimants and witnesses;

b. Immediately forward to us every notice, demand, summons or other process relating to the accident or **occurrence;**

c. At our request, assist in:

(1) Making settlement;

(2) The enforcement of any right of contribution or indemnity against any person or organization who may be liable to any **insured;**

(3) The conduct of suits and attend hearings and trials;

(4) Securing and giving evidence and obtaining the attendance of witnesses.

d. The **insured** shall not, except at the **insured's** own cost, voluntarily make any payment, assume any obligation or incur any expense other than for first aid to others at the time of the **occurrence.**

5. **Duties after Loss—Coverages R, S, and T.** In the case of the loss to which this insurance applies, you shall perform the following duties:

a. Give written notice to us or our agent, as soon as practicable, and also give notice to the police if loss is suspected to be in violation of a law;

b. Protect the property from further damage, make reasonable and necessary repairs required to protect the property and keep an accurate record of repair expenditures. If you fail to do these things, further damage is not insured under this policy;

c. Prepare an inventory of damaged property showing in detail, the quantity, description, actual cash value and amount of loss. Attach to the inventory all bills, receipts, and related documents that substantiate the figures in the inventory;

d. As often as we may reasonably require, exhibit the damaged property and submit to examination under oath and subscribe the same;

e. Within sixty (60) days after our request, submit to us your signed, sworn statement of loss which sets forth the following information to the best of your knowledge and belief:

(1) The time and cause of loss;

(2) The interest of the **insured** and all others in the **insured vehicle** involved and all encumbrances on the **insured vehicle;**

(3) Other insurance which may cover the loss;

(4) Changes in title of the **insured vehicle** during the term of the policy.

6. **Duties of an Injured Person—Coverages P and Q.** The injured person or someone acting on behalf of the injured person shall:

a. Give us a written proof of claim, under oath if required, as soon as practicable;

b. Execute authorization to allow us to obtain copies of medical reports and records; and

c. The injured person shall submit to physical examination by a physician selected by us when and as often as we reasonably require.

7. **Cooperation of Insured.** If any **insured** fails to cooperate or send us legal papers as required, we have the right to refuse any further protection for the **occurrence** or loss.

8. **Territory.** This policy applies only to **occurrences** within the United States of America and Canada. Section III Coverages are extended for trips into that part of the Republic of Mexico lying not more than

100 miles from the nearest boundary line of the United States of America. If applicable to your insured vehicle, our liability for Coverages R, S and T will be determined on the basis of cost at the nearest United States point.

WARNING: Automobile accidents in the Republic of Mexico are considered a criminal offense, rather than a civil matter. The insurance provided by this policy will not meet the Mexican automobile insurance requirements. If you are in an automobile accident in Mexico and have not purchased insurance through a licensed Mexican insurance company you may be jailed and may have your automobile impounded.

9. **Payment of Claim.** Any payment under Section III is not an admission of liability by any **insured** or us.

10. **Limits of Liability.** Regardless of the number of:

   (a) **insureds** or vehicles insured under this policy,

   (b) persons or organizations sustaining **bodily injury** or **property damage,** or

   (c) claims made,

our liability for each **occurrence** is subject to the following limitations:

   a. Our total combined single limit of liability under Coverage N for all **bodily injury** and **property damage** resulting from any one **occurrence,** shall not exceed the applicable limit of liability stated in the Declarations.

   b. Under Coverage Q the **medical** limit for each person is our limit of liability for all expenses incurred by or on behalf of each person who sustains **bodily injury** resulting from an **occurrence.**

   c. Under Coverages R, S, and T, our limit of liability will be the actual cash value of the stolen or damaged property at the time of loss. If the loss is a part of that stolen or damaged property, we will pay the actual cash value of that part at the time of loss or what it would cost to repair or replace the part with like kind and quality.

11. We will apply the combined single limit of liability to provide any separate limits required by law for **bodily injury** or **property damage.** This provision,

however, will not increase our total limit of liability.

12. **Other Insurance.** The insurance under Section III is excess over any other valid and collectible insurance except insurance written specifically to cover as excess over the limits of liability that apply in this policy.

13. **Loss Payable Clause.** This clause is applicable only if a lienholder is named in the Declarations.

   a. We will pay you and the lienholder named in the policy for loss to an **insured vehicle,** as interest may appear.

   b. Section III covers the interest of the lienholder unless the loss results from fraudulent acts or omissions on your part.

   c. We may cancel the policy during the policy period. Notice of cancellation shall be mailed to the lienholder at least ten (10) days before the date the cancellation takes effect.

   d. If we make any payment to the lienholder, we will obtain his rights against any other party.

COVERAGE P

Uninsured Motorist Coverage

We will pay damages which an **insured** is legally entitled to recover from the owner or operator of an **uninsured motor vehicle** because of **bodily injury** sustained by an **insured** and caused by an **occurrence.** The owner's or operator's liability for these damages must arise from the ownership, maintenance or use of the **uninsured motor vehicle.**

The following additional definitions apply to Coverage P:

1. **Insured** means:

   a. You and any **relative;**

   b. Anyone occupying an **insured vehicle;** or

   c. Anyone **occupying** a **nonowned vehicle** while operated by you or any **relative.**

2. **Uninsured motor vehicle** means a **motor vehicle** or **trailer:**

   a. To which a **bodily injury** liability bond or policy does not apply at the time of the **occurrence;**

   b. For which an insuring or bonding company denies coverage or is or becomes insolvent; or

c. Which is a hit-and-run vehicle and neither the driver nor the owner can be identified. The hit-and-run vehicle must hit an **insured,** and **insured vehicle** or a vehicle which an **insured** is **occupying;**

d. Which is insured by a **bodily injury** liability bond or policy at the time of the **occurrence** but its limit of **bodily injury** liability is less than the minimum limit for **bodily injury** specified by the financial responsibility law of the state in which your **insured vehicle** is principally garaged.

3. An **uninsured motor vehicle** does not include any **motor vehicle** or **trailer:**

a. Owned by any governmental unit or agency; (Not applicable if this policy is issued in Arizona.)

b. Designed for use mainly off public roads while not on public roads;

c. Used as a residence;

d. Owned by or furnished for the regular use of you or any **relative;** or

e. Which is an **insured vehicle.**

Exclusions

In addition to the general exclusions of Section III, the following exclusions apply to Coverage P. Coverage P does not apply to:

1. **Bodily injury** sustained by any **insured** while **occupying** a **motor vehicle** or **trailer** without the permission of the owner.

2. The direct or indirect benefit of any insurer or self-insured under any worker's compensation, disability benefits or similar law.

Conditions

In addition to the general conditions applicable to Section III, the following conditions apply to Coverage P only.

1. **Limits of Liability.**
Our total limit of liability under Coverage P for all **bodily injury** resulting from one **occurrence** shall not exceed the applicable limit of liability stated in the Declarations.

2. **Non-stacking of Limits.**
Regardless of the number of **insured vehicles, insureds,** policies of insurance with us, claims made or vehicles involved in the **occurrence,** the most we will pay for all damages resulting from any **occurrence** is the limit of liability shown in the Declarations subject to reduction as outlined in the next paragraph.

3. **Reduction of Amounts Payable.** Amounts payable for damages under Coverage P will be reduced by:

a. All sums paid by or on behalf of persons or organizations who may be legally responsible for the **bodily injury** to which this coverage applies. This includes all amounts paid under the liability coverage of this or any other policy;

b. The sum of all amounts payable under any worker's compensation, disability, or similar law;

c. All sums paid under medical payments or death benefits coverages of any policy issued by us. Any payment under this coverage to or for an **insured** will reduce any amount that person is entitled to receive under this policy's liability coverages.

4. **Hit-and-run Accident.** At our request, the **insured** shall make available for inspection any **motor vehicle** or **trailer** which the **insured** occupied at the time of a hit-and-run accident. The **insured** must notify the police within twenty-four (24) hours of a hit-and-run accident.

5. **Arbitration.**

a. If we and an **insured** disagree whether the **insured** is legally entitled to recover damages from the owner or driver of an **insured motor vehicle** or do not agree as to the amount of damages, either party may make a written demand for arbitration. In the event, each party will select an arbitrator. The two arbitrators will select a third. If they cannot agree upon a third arbitrator within thirty (30) days, either may request that selection be made by a judge of a court having jurisdiction. Each party will pay the expenses it incurs and bear the expenses of the third arbitrator equally.

b. Unless both parties agree otherwise, arbitration will take place in the county in which the **insured** lives. Local rules of law as to arbitration procedure and evidence will apply. A decision agreed to by two of the arbitrators will be binding.

6. **Trust Agreement.** If a claim or payment is made under this coverage:

a. We will be entitled to reimbursement of payments we have made to an **insured** to be taken from the proceeds of any judgment or settlement;

b. An **insured** will hold in trust all rights or recovery for us against any person or organization. That person will also do whatever is proper to secure those rights and do nothing after the loss to prejudice any rights of recovery;

c. If we make the request in writing, the **insured** must take any necessary or appropriate action to recover damages from any other person or organization through any representative we designate. Any action may be taken in the **insured's** name and in the event of recovery, we will be reimbursed for any expenses, costs, and attorney fees we incur; and

d. The **insured** must execute and deliver any document to us that may be appropriate for the purpose of securing the rights and obligations for the **insured** and for us as established by this provision.

7. **Payment of loss.** We have the option to pay any amount due under this coverage as follows:

a. To the **insured;**

b. If the **insured** is deceased, to the **insured's** surviving spouse; or

c. To a person authorized by law to receive such payment, or to a person who is legally entitled to recover the damages which the payment represents.

8. **Nonbinding Judgments.** No judgment resulting from a suit brought without our written consent is binding on us, either in determining the liability of the **uninsured motor vehicle** operator or owner or the amount of damages to which the **insured** is entitled.

ENDORSEMENTS APPLICABLE TO SECTION III

Each of the following endorsements may be purchased by your payment of an additional premium. All policy provisions apply to these endorsements unless an endorsement specifically states otherwise. **An endorsement applies only when it is listed in the Declarations, and you pay this premium.**

No. 323 Drive Other Car.

Coverage N of Section III is amended to cover you while you are operating a **motor vehicle** that does not qualify as a **nonowned vehicle,** provided you have the permission of the owner of the vehicle. This endorsement does not cover a **motor vehicle:**

1. Owned in whole or in part by you or any **relative;**
2. Registered in your name or in the name of any **relative;**
3. Used in transporting persons or property for hire. This endorsement shall not cover the owner of the **motor vehicle** you are driving.

No. 334 Emergency Road Service.

We will pay for reasonable and necessary towing and labor expense, but not to exceed $40, caused by the disablement of your **insured vehicle,** provided the expense is incurred at the place of disablement. No deductible applies to this coverage.

No. 335 Additional Living Expense.

If loss exceeds the applicable deductible to your **insured vehicle** we will pay for your reasonable and necessary additional living expense incurred as a result of the disablement of your vehicle due to loss covered under Coverages S or T. The maximum we will pay for this additional living expense is $75 per day up to a maximum of $300 per disablement. The loss must occur more than 100 miles from the place of principal garaging for this additional living expense coverage to apply. No deductible applies to this coverage.

No. 368 Car Rental Reimbursement.

If a loss exceeds the applicable deductible to the **insured vehicle** under Coverages S or T, we agree to reimburse you for:

1. The expense incurred by you for the rental fee (excluding all other charges) of a substitute automobile from a car rental agency or garage; or
2. The expense incurred by you for taxicabs during a period starting at 12:01 a.m. on the date following:
   a. The date of loss if as a direct result of this loss the **insured vehicle** cannot be operated under its own power; or
   b. If the **insured vehicle** is operable, the date you authorize repairs and deliver the vehicle to the repair shop.

In no event, however, shall we be liable for more than $25 per day to a maximum of $500 for taxicab or for rental fees.

Regardless of the policy period, our liability for taxicab or rental fees shall end on the earliest of the following:

1. Upon completion of repair or replacement of property lost or damaged;
2. Upon such date as we make or tender settlement for the loss or damage.

This coverage shall not apply in the event of a theft of the **insured vehicle** for which reimbursement of transportation expense is provided elsewhere in this policy.

No. 303 Underinsured Motorist Coverage.

Coverage P is changed to include Underinsured Motorist Coverage.

We will pay damages which an **insured** is legally entitled to recover from the owner or operator of an **underinsured motor vehicle** because of **bodily injury** sustained by an **insured** and caused by an **occurrence.** The owner's or operator's liability for these damages must arise from the ownership, maintenance or use of the **underinsured motor vehicle.**

The following additional definitions apply to Coverage P:

1. **Insured** means:
   a. You and any **relative;**
   b. Anyone **occupying** an **insured vehicle;** or
   c. Anyone **occupying** a **nonowned vehicle** while operated by you or any **relative.**
2. **Underinsured motor vehicle** means a **motor vehicle** or **trailer** for which the sum of all liability bonds or policies applicable to an **occurrence** is less than the amount of damages an **insured sustains** because of **bodily injury** caused by that **occurrence.**
3. An **underinsured motor vehicle** does not include any **motor vehicle** or **trailer:**
   a. Owned or operated by a self-insured as defined by any applicable **motor vehicle** law; (Not applicable if this policy is issued in Arizona).
   b. Owned by any governmental unit or agency;
   c. Designed for use mainly off public roads while not on public roads;
   d. Used as a residence;
   e. Owned by you or any **relative,** or furnished or available for regular use by you or any **relative;**
   f. Which is an **insured vehicle;**
   g. Which is insured by a **bodily injury** liability bond or policy at the time of the **occurrence** but its limit of **bodily injury** liability is less than the minimum limit for **bodily injury** specified by the financial responsibility law of the state in which your **insured vehicle** is principally garaged.

Exclusions:

In addition to the general exclusions of Section III, the following exclusions apply to Coverage P. Coverage P does not apply to:

1. **Bodily injury** sustained by any **insured** while **occupying** a **motor vehicle** or **trailer** without the permission of the owner.
2. The direct or indirect benefit of any insurer or self-insured under any worker's compensation, disability benefits or similar law.

Conditions:

In addition to the general conditions applicable to Section III, the following conditions apply to Coverage P only.

1. **Limits of Liability.**

Our total limit of liability Coverage P for all **bodily injury** resulting from one **occurrence** shall not exceed the applicable limit of liability stated in the Declarations.

2. **Non-stacking of Limits.**

Regardless of the number of **insured vehicles, insureds,** policies of insurance with us, claims made or vehicles involved in the **occurrence,** the most we will pay for all damages resulting from any **occurrence** is the limit of liability shown in the Declarations subject to reduction as outlined in the next paragraph.

3. **Reduction of Amounts Payable.** Amounts payable for damages under Coverage P will be reduced by:

   a. The sum of all amounts payable under any worker's compensation, disability, or similar law;

   b. All sums paid under medical payments or death benefits coverages of any policy issued by us.

Any payment under this coverage to or for an **insured** will reduce any amount that person is entitled to receive under this policy's liability coverages.

4. **Hit-and-run Accident.** At our request, the **insured** shall make available for inspection any **motor vehicle** or **trailer** which the **insured** occupied at the time of a hit-and-run accident. The **insured** must notify the police within twenty-four (24) hours of a hit-and-run accident.

5. **Arbitration.**

   a. If we and an **insured** disagree whether the **insured** is legally entitled to recover damages from the owner or driver of an **underinsured motor vehicle** or do not agree as to the amount of damages, either party may make a written demand for arbitration. In this event, each party will select an arbitrator. The two arbitrators will select a third. If they cannot agree upon a third arbitrator within thirty (30) days, either may request that selection be made by a judge of a court having jurisdiction. Each party will pay the expenses it incurs and bear the expenses of the third arbitrator equally;

   b. Unless both parties agree otherwise, arbitration will take place in the county in which the **insured** lives. Local rules of law as to arbitration procedure and evidence will apply. A decision agreed to by two of the arbitrators will be binding.

6. **Trust Agreement.** If a claim or payment is made under this coverage:

   a. We will be entitled to reimbursement of payments we have made to an **insured** to be taken from the proceeds of any judgment or settlement;

   b. An **insured** will hold in trust all rights of recovery for us against any person or organization. That person will also do whatever is proper to secure those rights and do nothing after the loss to prejudice any rights of recovery;

   c. If we make the request in writing, the **insured** must take any necessary or appropriate action to recover damages from any other person or organization through any representative we designate. Any action may be taken in the **insured's** name and in the event of recovery, we will be reimbursed for any expenses, costs, and attorney fees we incur; and

   d. The **insured** must execute and deliver any document to us that may be appropriate for the purpose of securing the rights and obligations for the **insured** and for us as established by this provision.

7. **Payment of Loss.** We will pay only after all liability bonds or policies applicable to the **occurrence** have been exhausted by judgments or payments. We have the option to pay any amount due under this coverage as follows:

   a. To the **insured;**

   b. If the **insured** is deceased, to the **insured's** surviving spouse;

   c. To a person authorized by law to receive such payment, or to a person who is legally entitled to recover the damages which the payment represents.

8. **Nonbinding Judgments.** No judgment resulting from a suit brought without our written consent is binding on us, either in determining the liability of the **underinsured motor vehicle** operator or owner or the amount of damages to which the **insured** is entitled.

SECTION IV—INLAND MARINE

The coverage under this section applies as indicated by endorsements attached to and listed in the Declarations. All policy provisions apply to these endorsements unless an endorsement specifically states otherwise.

CONDITIONS APPLICABLE TO SECTION IV

1. **Your Duty after Loss.** In case of a loss to which this insurance may apply, you must see that the following duties are performed:
   a. Give written notice to us or our agent, as soon as practicable, and also give notice to the police if loss is suspected to be in violation of a law;
   b. Protect the property from further damage, make reasonable and necessary repairs required to protect the property and keep an accurate record of repair expenditures;
   c. Prepare an inventory of damaged property showing in detail the quantity, description, actual cash value and amount of loss. Attach to the inventory all bills, receipts, and related documents that substantiate the figures in the inventory;
   d. As often as we may reasonably require, exhibit the damaged property and submit to examination under oath and subscribe the same;
   e. Within sixty (60) days after our request, submit to us your signed, sworn statement of loss which sets forth the following information to the best of your knowledge and belief:
      (1) The time and cause of loss;
      (2) The interest of the **insured** and all others in the property involved and all encumbrances on the property;
      (3) Other insurance which may cover the loss;
      (4) Changes in title during the term of the policy;
      (5) Specifications of any damaged property and detailed estimates for repair of the damage;
      (6) An inventory of damaged property as described above.

2. **Loss to a Pair or Set.** In case of a loss to a pair or set, we may elect to:
   a. Repair or replace any part of or restore the pair or set to its value before the loss; or
   b. Pay the difference between the actual cash value of the property before and after the loss.

3. **Valuation.** We shall not be liable beyond the actual cash value of the property at the time of any loss or the applicable endorsement limit, whichever is less. In no event shall we be liable for more than what it would cost to repair or replace the property with material of like kind and quality.

4. **Other Insurance.** The insurance under Section IV is excess over any other valid and collectible insurance except insurance written specifically to cover as excess over the limits of liability that apply in this policy.

Special State Provision

Our state of location as stated in the Declarations will determine which of the following special provisions apply to your policy. Read the provisions following the applicable state heading to determine which paragraphs apply to you.

1. **Arizona**
   A. **Cancellation Sections I, II and IV**

You may cancel Sections I, II and IV of this policy at any time by returning it to us or by notifying us in writing of the date cancellation takes effect. The date of cancellation must not be earlier than the date you mail or deliver notice to us. If you cancel, the refund premium, if any, will be computed in accordance with the customary short rate tables and procedures.

We may cancel this policy only for the reasons stated in this condition by notifying you in writing of the date cancellation takes effect. This cancellation must be mailed to you at your last mailing address known by us. Proof of mailing will be sufficient proof of notice.

(1) When you have not paid the premium, whether payable to us or to our agent, we may cancel at any time by notifying you at least ten (10) days before the date cancellation takes effect.

(2) When this policy has been in effect for less than sixty (60) days and is not a renewal with us, we may cancel for any reason by notifying you at least ten (10) days before the date cancellation takes effect.

(3) When this policy has been in effect for sixty (60) days or more, or at any time if it is a renewal with us, we may cancel:

   (a) If there has been a material misrepresentation of fact which if known to us would have caused us not to issue the policy, or

   (b) If the risk has changed substantially since the policy was issued. This can be done by notifying you at least ten (10) days before the date cancellation takes effect.

   (c) **Non-renewal.** We may elect not to renew Sections I, II and IV of this policy. We must do so by mailing written notice to you at least thirty (30) days before the expiration date of this policy. This notice will be sent to your last mailing address known by us. Proof of mailing will be sufficient proof of notice.

(4) When this policy is cancelled, the premium for the period from the date of cancellation to the expiration date will be refunded to you.

If the return premium is not refunded with the notice of cancellation of when this policy is returned to us, we will refund it within a reasonable time after the cancellation takes effect.

If we cancel, the refund premium, if any, will be computed on a pro-rata basis.

B. Cancellation Section III

You may cancel Section III of this policy by returning it to us or by written notice mailed or delivered to us. The notice must give us the date to cancel which must not be earlier than the date you mail or deliver it to us.

We may cancel by mailing a notice of cancellation or termination to you at the address shown in the Declarations or by delivery of the notice. The notice will give the date the cancellation is effective. It will be mailed to you at least ten (10) days before the cancellation effective date.

Proof of mailing a notice is proof of notice.

If you cancel, the refund of premium, if any, will be computed in accordance with customary short rate tables and procedures. If we cancel, the refund, if any, will be computed on a pro rata basis. Any unearned premium may be returned at the time of cancellation or within a reasonable time thereafter. Delay in the return of unearned premium does not effect the cancellation.

The policy will automatically terminate at the end of the policy period if you or your representative do not accept our offer to renew or continue it. Your failure to pay the required renewal or continuation premium by the renewal or continuation date means that you have declined our offer.

If you obtain other insurance on your covered auto, any similar insurance provided by this policy will terminate as to that auto on the effective date of other insurance.

After this policy has been in effect for sixty (60) days, or if it is a renewal, we will not cancel or decline renewal unless:

   a. You fail to pay the premium when it is due;

   b. The policy was obtained through fraudulent misrepresentation;

   c. You or any other person who regularly drives the auto have:

      (1) Had his or her driver's license suspended or revoked during the policy period;

      (2) Become permanently disabled either mentally or physically, and do not submit a doctor's certificate testifying to his or her ability to drive;

      (3) Been convicted during the three years just before the effective date of the policy or during the policy period of:

(a) Criminal negligence resulting in death, homicide or assault in connection with the use of a motor vehicle.

(b) Driving while under the influence of alcohol or drugs.

(c) Leaving the scene of an accident.

(d) Reckless driving, or

(e) Lying to obtain a driver's license.

Even if this policy has been in effect for sixty (60) days or if it is a renewal, we retain unlimited right to cancel if:

a. This policy insures four or more autos;

b. The auto is used in the auto business.

c. The auto is available to the public for hire or is rented to others; or

d. The auto insured has a load capacity of 1,500 pounds or more.

Grace Period. A grace period of seven (7) days is allowed for the payment of premium due except the first. An initial payment on the renewal of a policy is not a first payment of premium.

If the premium due is not received by the end of the grace period, a cancellation notice will be mailed to you at the address shown in the Declarations. The cancellation will be effective on the date the notice is mailed to you.

2. **New Mexico**

Cancellation. You may cancel this entire policy by mailing to us written notice stating when this cancellation shall be effective. We may change or cancel this entire policy or any portion of it, by mailing it to you at the address shown in the Declarations, written notice stating when not less than ten (10) days thereafter the change or cancellation shall be effective. Payment or tender of unearned premium is not a condition of cancellation. The mailing of notice shall be sufficient proof of notice and the effective date and hour of cancellation stated in the notice shall become the end of the policy period. Delivery of this written notice, either by you or by us shall be equivalent to mailing.

If you cancel, earned premiums shall be computed according to our customary short rate table and procedure. If we cancel, earned premiums shall be computed pro rata. Premium adjustment may be made at this time or as soon after as is practical. Our check mailed or delivered shall be sufficient tender of any refund of premium.

SECTION V

YOUR PERSONAL AND/OR FARM AND RANCH UMBRELLA

[This portion of the policy has been omitted.]

SCHEDULE OF VEHICLES

AUTOMOBILE - ADDITIONAL POLICY DECLARATIONS

POLICY NO.   2SAMPLE   DOE, PERRY AND PAULINE   5/30/91

BILLING TERM 5/30/98 TO 5/30/99

LIABILITY LIMITS   MEDICAL LIMITS

B.I.   100,000 EA PER   10,000 EA PER
       300,000 EA OCC   50,000 EA OCC
P.D.   50,000 EA OCC

UNINSURED MOTORIST   UNDERINSURED MOTORIST

B.I.   15,000 EA PER   B.I.   15,000 EA PER
       30,000 EA OCC   30,000 EA OCC

I
T   *MATERIAL DAMAGE*
E   LIAB   MAT DAM
M   YR   MAKE   TYPE   COMP   COLL   PREM   PREM   LIEN

01   91   CHEV   S-102X   ACV*   500 DED   710.40   533.70   00000

       SERIAL NUMBER 1GC#S19Z0M123456

           * ACTUAL CASH VALUE

TOTAL ANNUAL PREMIUM = 1244.10 TOTAL

   * MATERIAL DAMAGE COVERAGE APPLIES ONLY TO VEHICLES SHOWN ON THE SCHEDULE OF
     VEHICLES INSURED FOR MATERIAL DAMAGE. NEWLY ACQUIRED VEHICLE(S) MUST BE
     REPORTED TO THE COMPANY OR AGENT WITHIN 30 DAYS OF ACQUISITION OR THE POLICY
     PERIOD, WHICHEVER IS SHORTER, IF MATERIAL DAMAGE COVERAGE IS DESIRED.

   * NEWLY ACQUIRED VEHICLES COVERAGE FOR COMP. OR COLL. APPLICABLE ONLY TO
     VEHICLES WITH MODEL YEAR 8 YEARS OLD OR LESS FROM CURRENT CALENDAR YEAR.

COUNTRY SQUIRE DECLARATION SHEET

WESTERN AGRICULTURAL INSURANCE CO.
PO BOX 20180 PHOENIX, ARIZONA 85036

ISSUE DATE 2/01/98

DOE, PERRY & P.   POLICY NUMBER 14311501
10505 N. 89TH ST.   COUNTY 07   AGENT 468
SUITE 600   TERM 1 YR   ONG, BRIAN
SCOTTSDALE, AZ 85253
POLICY TERM 1/09/98 12:01 A.M. TO 1/09/99 12:01 A.M.

INSURANCE IS PROVIDED ONLY WITH RESPECT TO THOSE COVERAGES DESIGNATED BELOW BY
EITHER PREMIUM OR THE WORD INCLUDED, BUT ONLY TO THE EXTENT SET FORTH IN THE SPECIFIC
FORMS AND ENDORSEMENTS MADE A PART OF THE POLICY. COVERAGE IS AS SPECIFIED ON
ATTACHED ADDITIONAL POLICY DECLARATION SHEETS.

SECTION I - PROPERTY COVERAGE EFF 1/09/98. . . . . 1,271.40

SECTION II - LIABILITY COVERAGE EFF 1/09/98. . . . . 180.80

SECTION III - AUTOMOBILE COVERAGE 00

SECTION IV - INLAND MARINE COVERAGE EFF 1/09/98 . . . . 36.60

SECTION V - UMBRELLA COVERAGE EFF 1/09/98 . . . . 353.00

                                        TOTAL ANNUAL PREMIUM   1,841.80

        ENDORSEMENTS-
391 (06-90) 111 120 114 F02A
438-BFU (5-42) EM-L (10-80) 401
30 (5-42) 408 L93 L95(11/89) L9
L97(11/89) L99(11/89) L30

        LEGAL LOCATION-
            REFER TO SCHEDULE OF LOCATIONS   LO
        MORTGAGE CLAUSE- IF A MORTGAGE AND/OR LOSS PAYABLE CLAUSE(S) SHALL BE APPLICABLE.

36822 SEC I
DEER VALLEY CR UN
P.O. BOX 8000
PHOENIX, AZ 85066

    THE INSURANCE AFFORDED BY THIS POLICY AS INDICATED WITHIN THIS DECLARATION
    SUPERSEDES AND REPLACES ALL INSURANCE PREVIOUSLY AFFORDED BY THIS POLICY.
    ASSIGNMENT OF THIS POLICY SHALL NOT BE VALID UNLESS WE GIVE OUR WRITTEN CONSENT.

_____

    COUNTERSIGNATURE   *SEE ATTACHED SCHEDULE(S)*

SCHEDULE OF ADDITIONAL DWELLINGS, PERSONAL PROPERTY, AND OUTBUILDINGS

AS144   COUNTRY SQUIRE - ADDITIONAL POLICY DECLARATION

POLICY NO. 14311501   DOE, PERRY & P.   2/01/98

BILLING TERM 1/09/98 TO 1/09/99

ITEM NO.	TYPE	DESCRIPTION	DED	PERIL	INSURANCE AMOUNT	PREMIUM	MORT. AMOUNT NO.
01	F.P.P.	FARM PERSONAL PROP.	100	1-24	16,275	109.00	
01	DWELLING	GUEST HOUSE	100	25	40,000	180.00	
04	DWELLING	EMPLOYEE MOBILE	100	1-9	3,000	13.00	
02	OUTBUILDING	HAY SHED	100	1-9	3,000	17.90	
03	OUTBUILDING	PIPE BARN	100	1-9	5,000	29.90	
04	OUTBUILDING	TENNIS CRT WNDSCRN	100	1-9	1,000	6.00	
05	OUTBUILDING	TENNIS COURT FENCNG	100	1-9	4,000	23.90	
06	OUTBUILDING	TENNIS COURT LGHTNG	100	1-9	5,000	29.90	
07	OUTBUILDING	STORAGE SHED	100	1-9	8,000	58.40	
01	ELEC. MOTOR	400AMP ELEC PANEL	100	25	3,000	64.70	
02	ELEC. MOTOR	WELL PMP MTRS#M729	100	25	2,000	43.10	
TOTALS					90,275	575.80	

80 PERCENT COINSURANCE ON ALL ELEC. MOTOR ITEMS.

REFERENCE ADDITIONAL INSUREDS, ADDRESSES OR DESCRIPTIONS

(ITEM 02)   '71 NATIONAL M/H, S#3856, 12' X 60'

(ITEM 03)   '74 PARK MANOR M/H, S#FPA-4173-E, 14' X 70'

(ITEM 04)   '72 STREAMLINE TRAVEL TRAILER, S# D25S2984, 8' X 26'

SPECIAL LIMITS OF LIABILITY ARE AS FOLLOWS—

COV D HAY, STRAW, AND FODDER, PER STACK OR BUILDING $10,000

COV D HORSE, CATTLE, MULE OR DONKEY, PER HEAD $ 500

COV D SWINE, SHEEP, OR GOAT, PER HEAD $ 100

END 114 BORROWED EQUIPMENT - SAME AS THE FARM P.P. LIMIT

SCHEDULE OF SECTION II

COUNTRY SQUIRE - ADDITIONAL POLICY DECLARATION

POLICY NO. 14311501   DOE, PERRY & P.   2/01/98

BILLING TERM 1/09/98 TO 1/09/99

   LIABILITY TERMS $300,000   BI-PD MEDICAL LIMITS   5,000 EA. PER.
                                    EA. OCC.   25,000 EA. OCC.

		AMT. OF INS. OR OTHER	ANNUAL PREMIUM
	LEGAL DESCRIPTION		
01	REFER TO SCHEDULE OF LOCATIONS	10 ACRES CROP	180.80
	-FOR ADDITIONAL LOCATIONS SEE SCHEDULE OF LOCATIONS		
	COV. F,G,M		INCL
	TOTAL PREMIUM		180.80

SPECIAL LIMITS OF LIABILITY ARE AS FOLLOWS

   COV M DAMAGE TO PROPERTY OF OTHERS, PER OCC. $500

SCHEDULE OF SECTION IV

COUNTRY SQUIRE - ADDITIONAL POLICY DECLARATION   AS145

POLICY NO. 14311501   DOE, PERRY & P.   2/01/98

BILLING TERM 1/09/98 TO 1/09/99

OTHER SCHEDULED PERSONAL PROPERTY.

ITEM	DESC & SERIAL NO	FORMS	DED. AMOUNT	AMOUNT OF INSURANCE	TOTAL PREMIUM
02	FEATHERED VASE	K	NIL	185	1.00
03	FISHING BOY	K	NIL	165	1.00
04	MORNING AIR	K	NIL	2,800	5.50
05	MOTHER AND COLT	K	NIL	2,500	5.00
06	FRIENDS	K	NIL	475	1.00
07	ECLIPSE	K	NIL	1,800	3.60
08	XEROX COPIER	K	NIL	750	1.50
09	TRS80 II MICRO CMPT 025717	X	NIL	1,000	9.00
10	TRS80 II DISK SYSTM 123601	X	NIL	700	6.30
11	TRS80 MDL 4 DM PRTR	X	NIL	300	2.70

*** TOTAL   36.60 ***
   FORMS TABLE

   K = 401
   X = 408

SCHEDULE OF SECTION V—UMBRELLA

AS1455   COUNTRY SQUIRE -   2/01/98
ADDITIONAL POLICY DECLARATION

POLICY 14311501   NAMED INSURED PERRY & PAULINE DOE
BILLING TERM 1/09/98 TO 1/09/99

LIABILITY LIMIT - $2,000,000 EACH OCCURRENCE
                $2,000,000 EACH AGGREGATE

SELF-INSURED RETENTION - $1,000

SCHEDULE OF UNDERLYING INSURANCE

PREMISES AND OPERATIONS LIABILITY -

(X) SECTION II
( ) OTHER POLICIES -

AUTOMOBILE LIABILITY -

( ) SECTION III
(X) OTHER POLICIES -

TYPE OF
POLICY

UM / UIM LIAB

ANNUAL PREMIUM - $353.00

ENDORSEMENTS - L9 L21

SCHEDULE OF LOCATIONS

COUNTRY SQUIRE - ADDITIONAL POLICY DECLARATION

AS141

POLICY NO. 14311501   DOE, PERRY & P.   2/01/98

ITEM NO.	LOCATION	ACRES	TYPE	DWELLING NO.
01	S29 T6N R3E			02
02	X-REF WITH ALL BUILDINGS			01
03	S29 T6N R3E	10	ACRES	01

GLOSSARY

abnormally dangerous activity   Activity for which a defendant is strictly liable if someone is injured; characterized as an activity having a high degree of risk of serious harm that cannot be eliminated with due care and whose value is outweighed by its dangerous attributes.

absolute privilege   Absolute defense to defamation, regardless of defendant's motives.

abuse of process   Use of litigation devices for improper purposes.

accrual   Time at which a statute of limitations begins to run, usually at the time the plaintiff is injured.

action in trespass (vi et armis)   Early cause of action involving serious, forcible breaches of peace that evolved to encompass even minor physical contact; no showing of fault was required.

actual cause   Cause in fact of the plaintiff's injuries.

actual malice   Acting with knowledge of the falsity of one's statement or with reckless disregard as to the truth or falsity of one's statement.

adhesion contract   Standardized contract characterized by the unequal bargaining power of the parties and the lack of negotiation regarding the terms of the contract.

affirmative defense   Any defense that a party asserts for which it bears the burden of proof.

answer   A pleading in which the defendant responds to the plaintiff's complaint.

appropriation   Use of the value of plaintiff's name or picture for defendant's financial gain.

assault   Intentional causing of an apprehension of harmful or offensive contact.

assumption of risk   Defense that the plaintiff voluntarily consented to take the chance that harm would occur if he or she engaged in certain conduct.

attractive nuisance   Dangerous condition on the defendant's property that is likely to induce children to trespass.

at-will employee   Employee who, because of the nature of his or her employment contract, can be discharged at any time for any reason.

avoidable consequences rule   Obligation of a plaintiff to minimize (mitigate) her damages.

bailee   One who is temporarily entrusted with the custody of goods.

bailor   One who entrusts his or her goods to the temporary custody of another.

battery   Intentional infliction of a harmful or offensive contact upon a person.

bench trial   Trial before a judge.

breach of duty   Failure to conform to the required standard of care.

burden of persuasion   Burden of proving the elements of a case by a preponderance of the evidence.

burden of production   Burden of producing sufficient evidence to avoid a directed verdict.

challenge for cause   Request to remove a potential juror because of his or her alleged inability to decide the case impartially.

charging the jury   Process in which the judge instructs the jurors in rules of law they are to apply.

chattels   Personal property.

collateral source rule   Right of a plaintiff to recover twice for damages.

comparative negligence   Defense that the plaintiff's recovery should be reduced in direct proportion to the plaintiff's percentage of contribution to his or her own injuries.

compensatory damages   Damages designed to compensate the plaintiff; consist of both general and special damages.

complaint   An initial pleading filed on behalf of the plaintiff the purpose of which is to provide the defendant with the material elements of the plaintiff's demand.

concurrent tortfeasors   Tortfeasors who independently cause the plaintiff injury.

contribution   Partial reimbursement of a tortfeasor who has paid more than his or her pro rata share of the damages.

contributory negligence   Defense that the plaintiff contributed to his or her own injuries and should therefore be barred from recovery.

conversion   Substantial interference with another's property to the extent that justice demands payment for the full value of the property.

coordination of benefits provision   Policy provision that precludes payment to the insured if the insured has other insurance available.

counterclaim   A claim presented by a defendant in opposition to the plaintiff's claim.

covenant not to sue   Promise by a plaintiff not to sue a particular defendant.

crossclaim   A claim brought by a defendant against a co-defendant in the same action.

deceit   Common law cause of action equated with intentional misrepresentation; also referred to as fraud.

declaratory judgment action   Action in which the court renders an opinion as to a matter of law or in reference to the rights of the parties but does not order any action to be taken.

defamation   Statement that tends to harm the reputation of another, encompassing both libel and slander.

default judgment   Judgment entered due to lack of opposition on behalf of the opposing party.

defective warning   Defect arising out of a manufacturer's failure to give adequate warnings or directions for use.

demand letter   A letter detailing a client's damages and setting forth the reasons for her demand.

demurrer   Motion for dismissal based on a defect in the form or content of a complaint.

deposition   Oral examination of a witness under oath.

derivative claim   Claim derived from underlying claim (e.g., loss of consortium).

design defect   Defect arising out of a manufacturer's use of an unreasonably dangerous design.

directed verdict   Dismissal of a case because of the opposing party's failure to meet the requisite burden of proof.

discounting an award   Reducing an award to its present value.

discovery   Process through which parties try find out as much as possible about the other side's case.

discretionary function   Act of a government employee requiring the use of judgment.

economic loss   Diminution in the value of a product.

excess judgment   Judgment for more than the insured's policy limits.

express warranty   Express representation by a seller that a product possesses certain qualities.

fair market value   Amount property could be sold for on the open market.

false imprisonment   Intentional confinement of another.

false light   Representing the plaintiff to the public in a way that would be highly offensive to a reasonable person.

family purpose doctrine   Doctrine that makes the owner of a car liable for the tortious acts of family members committed while driving.

fellow servant rule   Doctrine that shields employers from liability for damages incurred for injuries to an employee due to the negligence of a co-worker.

fiduciary relationship   Relationship based on trust and confidence that imposes an obligation to act in good faith; an example is the attorney-client relationship.

general damages   Compensatory damages that can generally be anticipated to result from the type of conduct the defendant engaged in.

general verdict   Verdict in which a jury decides issues of liability and damages.

governmental function   Task typically performed by a governmental entity.

immunity   Absolute defense derived from the defendant's status (e.g., a government official) or relationship to the plaintiff (e.g., spouse of the plaintiff).

implied warranty   Representations as to a product's qualities that are implied by virtue of the product being offered for sale.

imputed negligence   Negligence that is charged or attributed to another.

indemnification   Total acceptance of financial responsibility by one tortfeasor for another.

independent contractor   Someone hired to do a job who works at his own pace, in his own way, under his own supervision.

informed consent   Knowledgeable consent based on disclosure of all relevant facts that allows one to make an informed decision.

injurious falsehood   False disparagement of a plaintiff's business, product, or property rights.

innuendo   Use of extrinsic facts to convey the defamatory meaning of a statement.

intentional tort   Tort in which the tortfeasor intends to bring about a particular consequence or knows with substantial certainty that a result will occur.

interrogatories   Written questions submitted to the opposing party which that party must answer in writing and under oath.

intervening cause   Act that contributes to the plaintiff's injuries but does not relieve the defendant of liability.

invitee   Person invited by possessor of land onto her property for the purpose of conducting business.

JNOV (judgment notwithstanding the verdict)   A decision that the verdict reached was contrary to the evidence and the law.

joint and several liability   Liability for an entire loss if the loss is indivisible.

joint enterprise   Two or more persons who agree to a common goal or purpose, who share a common pecuniary interest, and who have an equal right to control the direction of the enterprise.

joint tortfeasors   Those who act together to cause the plaintiff's injury.

last clear chance doctrine   Doctrine that allows the plaintiff to recover in a contributory negligence system despite the plaintiff's negligence.

latent defect   Defect that is invisible or not readily discoverable.

libel   Written defamatory statements.

licensee   Person who has possessor's consent to be present on land.

loss of consortium   Loss of services, including companionship, sex, and earnings outside of the home.

manufacturing defect   Defect arising out of a deviation in the manufacturing process.

motion for protective order   Motion that protects a party from having to disclose privileged information.

motion for summary judgment   Motion requesting that the court enter a judgment on the party's behalf because there is no material fact at issue.

motion in limine   Motion to prevent evidence from being presented to the jury.

motion to compel   Motion to force the opposing party to comply with a request for discovery.

necessity Privilege that justifies the defendant's harming of the plaintiff's property in an effort to prevent great harm to the defendant or others.

negligence per se Presumed negligence that arises from the unexcused violation of a statute.

nominal damages Damages awarded when liability is shown but no actual damages are proved.

nuisance Substantial and unreasonable interference with a plaintiff's intent; includes public and private nuisance.

objective standard Comparison of a defendant's conduct to that of a reasonable person.

parasitic damages Damages attached to physical injury, e.g., mental suffering.

patent defect Defect that is visible or readily discoverable.

pecuniary Monetary; that which can be valued in terms of money.

peremptory challenge Request to remove a potential juror for no articulated reason.

preemption Prohibition of a state tort law claim due to a federal enactment.

present value Current value of money that is to be paid in the future, based on the assumption that money received today is worth more than money received in the future because of the investment potential of money.

presumed damages Damages that ordinarily stem from a defamatory statement and that do not require the showing of actual harm.

pretrial conference Conference involving the judge and parties at which issues and procedures for the trial are clarified and efforts are made at settlement.

primary coverage Insurance providing initial coverage for all damages up to the limits of the policy.

privity Requirement that the plaintiff must contract directly with the defendant in order to recover for losses.

proprietary function Function performed by the government that could just as easily be performed by a private entity.

proximate cause Legal cause of the plaintiff's injuries, emphasis is on the concept of foreseeability.

public figure One who has achieved persuasive fame or notoriety or who becomes involved in a public controversy.

public policy Consideration by judges of the effects of a proposed legal principle on society as a whole.

publication Hearing or seeing of a defamatory statement by someone other than the plaintiff.

punitive damages Damages designed to punish the defendant (also referred to as *exemplary damages*).

qualified privilege Privilege that applies only when a defendant acts on the basis of certain well-defined purposes.

reformation of a policy Construing a policy to provide the minimum coverage required by statute.

release Agreement to absolve a defendant of all liability.

request for admissions Request by one party asking the other party to admit certain facts.

request for medical examination Request that the opposing party be examined by a physician chosen by the party making the request.

request for production of documents Request for document in possession of the opposing party.

res ipsa loquitur Doctrine the plaintiff can turn to in proving negligence when it is difficult to obtain information about the defendant's conduct.

res judicata Legal principle stating that issues litigated cannot be relitigated at a later time.

respondeat superior doctrine Doctrine that makes employer liable for the tortious acts of employees committed in the scope and furtherance of their employment (vicarious liability).

satisfaction Payment of a judgment.

scheduled injuries Injuries, such as loss of sight or of an appendage, for which stated benefits are paid.

secondary coverage Insurance that provides coverage for damages incurred but that does not do so until the limits of the primary policy have been exhausted.

slander   Oral defamatory statements.

slander of title   False disparagement of the plaintiff's property rights.

slander per se   Slander in which pecuniary harm can be assumed.

slippery slope argument   Argument that once you take a first step in allowing something in one instance, you are in danger of sliding the "slippery slope" into a bottomless pit of circumstances requiring comparable treatment.

special damages   Compensatory damages specifically linked to (unique to) the plaintiff.

special harm   Harm of a pecuniary nature.

special verdict   Verdict in which the jury is required to answer special interrogatories, which the judge must review to determine who the prevailing party is.

stacking of policies   Using one or more policies to provide coverage for the same incident.

statute of limitations   Statute that limits the time period in which a claim can be filed.

statute of repose   Statute of limitations in product liability cases that limits the time period during which suit can be filed; statute of limitations in reference to sale of products.

strict liability   Liability imposed without a showing of intent or negligence.

structured settlement   Agreement to pay damages in installments rather than a lump sum.

subjective standard   Use of the defendant's own subjective perceptions to determine whether the defendant behaved reasonably.

subrogation   The right of an insurer to institute suit in the name of the insured against the responsible party to collect for monies paid by the insurer to the insured.

superseding cause   Act that contributes to the plaintiff's injuries to the extent that the defendant is relieved of liability.

survival action   Action that remains available after the decedent's death.

trade libel   False disparagement of the plaintiff's goods or business.

transferred intent doctrine   Intent with respect to one person (or tort) is transferred to another person (or tort).

trespass on the case   Early cause of action involving injuries inflicted indirectly and requiring some showing of fault.

trespass to chattels   Intentional interference with another's use or possession of chattels.

trespass to land   Intentionally entering or wrongfully remaining on another's land.

umbrella policy   Policy that provides a secondary source of coverage after the deductible has been paid, usually coordinated with the limits of the underlying policy.

unavoidably unsafe products   Products incapable of being made safe for their ordinary and intended use.

verification   Affidavit indicating that the plaintiff has read the complaint and to the best of his or her knowledge believes it to be true.

vicarious liability   Liability for the tortious acts of another.

voir dire   Process of jury selection involving the use of challenges for cause and peremptory challenges.

warranty of fitness for a particular purpose   Implied warranty that goods are suitable to be used for a particular (noncustomary) purpose.

warranty of merchantability   Implied warranty that goods are fit for the ordinary purpose for which they are used.

wrongful death action   Action brought by third parties to recover for losses they suffered as a result of the decedent's death.

INDEX